Lords of the Sunset Strip

Published by

The Spencer Company
PO Box 1862
Beverly Hills, CA 90213-1862

Many thanks to Portland State University for recommending student-intern, Cree Dueker, who scanned the
images for this book. Our heartfelt thanks to Cree for her time, flexibility and expeditious nature. It was
Cree's dream to meet Anthony and she did

Lords of the Sunset Strip

An Autobiography
By
BLACKIE DAMMETT

The Spencer Company

ON SALE NOW

RED HOT CHILI PEPPERS
DICKIES
WITH
GUNS N' ROSES
AND
THELONIOUS MONSTER

8:00PM OCTOBER 31st HALLOWEEN NIGHT
Ackerman Hall at UCLA

TICKETS AVAILABLE AT TICKETMASTER OUTLETS, INCLUDING UCLA.

DON'T FORGET AFTER HOURS PARTY AT THE SCREAM CLUB. SAVE $2.00 ON ADMISSION WITH TICKET STUB.

ANOTHER PACIFICONCERTS PRESENTATION   1986

Dedication

Daredevil prodigy, mischievous legend, covert philanthropy, fervent family father and best friend. This book, like my life, is dedicated to my son Anthony. Along the journey we'll find our way to the good surf.

I also salute the late journalist David Nicolette who put me in the Grand Rapids Press and kept me there with style.

Our trusty Austin-Healey.

Acknowledgements

Blackie 'Spider' Dammett expresses gratitude to all those who contributed to this party-crashing adventure. Too many to name, it's a Cecil B. De Mille cast. I acquiesce to the most notorious characters: Anthony Kiedis and the Red Hot Chili Peppers, Peggy, Johnny Reaser, Marty Lipp, my sister Judy, Tom Gravengood, Barb Folkersma, Thomas Creed Smith, Margie Dormier, both Katies, Deborah Lee, Fay Hart, Connie Foreman, Sonny and Cher, David Weaver, Alan Bashara, Anita Russell, Scott McClintock, Alice Cooper, Shep Gordon, Ashley Pandel, Rogers & Cowan, Jennifer Mayo, Violet, Audrey Maxwell, Alison Ridgway, Brendan Mullen, John Lennon, Keith Moon, Penny Lane, Shock, Candy, Tracii, Guns N' Roses, Dave Grohl, Mel Gibson, Drew Barrymore, James, Jandt, Paul Erickson, Brett Anderson, Scott Miller, Brenda and Jim, five wolves, Heidi Klum, Chanda, Alicia, my girl Stevie, and the ghost of Schuyler Ace St. John.

On the job: Chris Stein, Markus Cuff, Jackie Butler, Christopher Matthew Spencer, Craig Weeden, Janet Doomette Freeby, Erin Kaiser, Rebecca Billingham, Anthony O'Connor, Andjelka Stankovic, Rich Plenge, Sami Swan Thompson, Lisa Lizardi and Michigan media John Gonzalez, John Serba and John Sinkevics. On the wild West Coast, my agent John La Rocca kept me working at Universal, MGM, Fox, Warners, Paramount, Sony/Columbia and Disney. He ferreted out the best casting directors and put my mug in the spotlight.

I have a sentimental appreciation for the late great director Jack Starrett who gave me my first acting roles, and the fifty or more subsequent gigs directed or produced by the likes of Francis Ford Coppola, Richard Donnor, John Frankenheimer, Roger Corman, Anthony Quinn, Keenen Ivory Wayans, Howard Koch, Penelope Spheeris and many more. Damaged and dazzled, I found myself tutored by the genius of Lee Strasberg, Sam Peckinpah, Michael Gazzo, Harvey Lembeck, George Carlin, James Caan and the esteemed dean of music critics, Robert Hilburn at *The Los Angeles Times*. Their kindness will always stay with me.

Thank you home towns Grand Rapids, Los Angeles and Portlandia.

NATIONAL ENQUIRER

40¢

July 7, 1981   30586-2   LARGEST CIRCULATION OF ANY PAPER IN AMERICA

BLACKIE DAMMETT'S
Career Hits the Skids
Misses Katie

Hollywood insiders reveal that his rapid downhill slide has been accelerated even more by his booze problem.

Table of Contents

Chapter 1: Caught in the Cross Heirs

Home for Christmas in 1996, my son surprised me with startling news: the Miramax Brothers, Bob and Harvey Weinstein, wanted me to write a screenplay of my "Lord of the Sunset Strip" antics back in the 1970s when I was raising Cain and my 11-year-old son, Anthony Kiedis. After a few fits and starts and a bad hangover, I blew the project off. Twelve years later and my interest finally piqued, HBO wanted the story. Now a nominated 2011 Rock and Roll Hall of Fame Red Hot Chili Pepper, Anthony and his business associates set a tentative deal and hired John Sayles to write the pilot for a weekly series in the spirit of *Entourage* or *The Sopranos*. Anthony suggested I write my long-delayed memoirs with an emphasis on that period to augment the show. I had experienced an explosive 70 years; impenetrable as a Brazilian rainforest, provocative as sin, and adventurous as the 1940 film noir I was born into. I decided to tell the whole truth, so help me Aphrodite.

Anton Kiedis was a pugnacious Lithuanian who set out across the Atlantic Ocean for America at the dawn of the 20th century with his pregnant wife, Julia, and their children: George, Anton Jr. and Irene. Victoria was born at sea in a crowded steamship that would deposit them all at Ellis Island in the shadow of liberty. From New York, the family migrated to a small Lithuanian enclave in West Michigan. And at last, in 1914, the youngest child and pick of the litter was born on the 4th of July, a real All-American boy, my father, John Alden Kiedis.

In time, the family moved to the nearest metropolis and a date with fate: Mollie Rose Vander Veen born in 1920. She was a Duchess in the Dutch city of Grand Rapids; a symphony of French Canadian, English, Irish, Algonquian Native American and her Netherlandic origins that traced all the way back to 1066. In the 17th century, some of our more radical Vander Veens risked the whole kit and caboodle when they embarked on a treacherous voyage to find their own new land of opportunity. After first settling in New Amsterdam, my direct descendents migrated to upstate New York and intermarried with Mohican Indians. We were inexorably bred with volatile blood.

A local Rudy Vallee, my dark dad cut a cool groove of thirties jive, and his hepcat vocals had the girls swooning in the old vaudeville theaters. Slender, fair and a fan, my future mother would ultimately capture the heart of this gathering storm, my father. His wanderlust had a penchant for open roads, and the golden ring was California. Elder brothers George and Tony had already moved west to Los Angeles, and, as it turned out, that magnetic city of angels would ultimately tie five generations together with a love of the city that spanned a century. My vagabond father and his best friend, Pete St. John, had been hopping freight trains across the country for years; they motored west on Route 66 in a rakish convertible when the gals went too. Eventually Mom and Dad moved to Southern California and in early 1939, Mr. and Mrs. Kiedis conceived a child. The embryo soaked up a few sunny trimesters, but ultimately the parents decided to raise the tyke in our home town on the Grand River. In a typical Michigan blizzard on December 7, 1939, the much-anticipated child arrived and was proclaimed John Michael Kiedis. Soon after, the St. John's produced a natural partner for this new kid and named him Schuyler Ace St. John—Scott for short. The dynamic friendship would shape not only our lives, but an imperfect and imperative messiah not yet born. From my grandfather to my grandson is the journey.

Chapter 2: Aunts in My Pants

Jeez. The first two years went by so fast. Before you knew it, I was walking around and saying stuff like "Mommy" and "Daddy" and listening to *Fibber McGee and Molly* on the radio when I was supposed to be sleeping. Don't get me wrong, I slept plenty in that portable crib by the couch. At the beginning of every episode, Fibber McGee would be scavenging about for something in the overstuffed closet, and Molly would say, "Fibber, now don't go into…" and the whole mess would come tumbling down and the sound-effects guy would have a field day. I always thought that closet was the one by the front door at my house on Emerald Street NE. Info trickled into my consciousness. Somehow I had become Jackie and a cold-blooded villain who nearly scratched Scott St. John's eyes out when I broke into his crib. After that our families sort of disassociated.

It was at my second birthday party that President Franklin Delano Roosevelt declared my birthday "a day that will live in infamy!" Thanks a lot, FDR. December 7, 1941, the Japanese bombed Hawaii *and* my party, so we declared war on Germany, Italy and Japan. Everybody went home early and geared up for war. By now we had moved to Fulton Street NE, and I had a baby sister, Judy. There were miniature patriotic flags displayed in almost everybody's front window, indicating they had a soldier or sailor out there fighting in strange places like Anzio, New Guinea and El Alamein. None at our house though; Pops worked long hours at the American Seating Company doing his part for the war effort. Grand Rapids was the "Furniture Capitol of the World" back then. Michigan had endless forests and rapid rivers to deliver the lumber. Factories on the west side of town crafted the finest of furniture for kings and queens and the White House and G.I. Joe's house. American Seating had been converted from manufacturing church pews and auditorium seats to army tank and fighter plane cockpits. The giant complex was covered with camouflage nets to fool potential enemy bombers. Pop took me to the annual family open house, and I kept an eye out for those Jap bombers. He was a deadly serious father now. The happy-go-lucky guy who used to hop freights with hobos and croon to screaming bobby-soxers was trying to save the world and a marriage.

While Dad worked double shifts, Mom was double-dating sailors. She was seldom around anymore, and I learned to do my own thinking. A lot of things didn't add up. I was suspicious of adult rules, and I was only three. I decided to run away. The city bus stopped in front of our house, and I snuck up those three steps under the cover of ladies' legs in seamed hosiery. I rode the bus to the end of the line on the far west side of town before the driver got wise and called the police.

George Orwell wrote, "Autobiography is only to be trusted when it reveals something disgraceful. A man who gives a good account of himself is probably lying, since any life when viewed from the inside is simply a series of defeats." In fact I was often disgraced. I peed in my pants once and hid the evidence behind the washing machine. I tried to eat the Sweetheart soap in our bathtub, but found it tastier to snatch cookies from metal bins at the grocer's down the street.

Although it was forbidden, I had a secret hideout across the street in a woodsy area with a dangerous creek that had mint growing on the banks. Now it's Saint Thomas Aquinas College. There was a church next door that made a lot of racket on Sundays, but we never went.

A little libertine, my favorite indiscretion was unabashed depravity with five-year-old dainty Brenda. I was only four, and it was the summer before kindergarten. Our puppy love blossomed and gave us a naughty nudge. We snuck up into my attic and carefully made our way through the dusty potpourri that basked in the sunlight from a singular window that overlooked my neighborhood. As if playing a game of strip Old Maid, we alternately shed our clothing until we were stark naked. Giddy with childish delirium, we examined each other's secret nuances. Satiated, we finally dressed and went down stairs, blushing with enlightenment. Brenda was my first girlfriend, but like so many to come she wouldn't last long. The first day of school she traded me in for a kid named Mickey. He was my hated rival until we moved, and that would be soon.

Our parents divorced. I wasn't privy to the legal details, although I was curious. Dad got custody, but he had to work, so Jack and Judy got shuffled off to relatives and strangers for hire. The next three years were a meander in the Sinai. I never impugned my slightly-sainted missing-mother, but Pop became a tyrant. He punished us severely for even the slightest infraction. He was an old-fashioned by-the-book father with zero tolerance, and he was always yelling! Like a virtuoso, Pop made me chose which weapon he'd spanked me with--a belt, a tree branch, a whip, an umbrella, a broken table leg, or something novel that might be lying around. Once when Judy and I lived with the Swift family in Godwin Heights, my dad came to visit us and discovered Judy had written with crayons on their bedroom wall. Pop was so angry he held my baby sister upside down by her feet out the bedroom window and shook her violently from the second story. I cultivated a youthful toughness but was devastated I couldn't please him.

Bobby Swift was my first real buddy. The adults took photos of us in our army and navy military outfits that most kids had in the early 1940s. We went to Saturday afternoon movie matinees at the 4-Star Theater for cartoons and exciting serials of Flash Gordon or some other hero, who was on the precipice of disaster at the end of each episode so we'd be sure to come back next week. And that was fine with me. I loved the movies.

By now my dad was living in a small room at the YMCA, and occasionally I'd stay overnight with him in the same tiny bed. We also swam, exercised and ran around the elevated track. When I was a bit older, I became a YMCA member and went every Saturday for sports and swimming lessons. Everybody swam nude in the pool; no swim suits allowed. I wasn't too keen on that. The highlight of every summer was going to YMCA Camp Manitou-Lin on Barlow Lake. One year the entire camp listened to the heavyweight championship fight between Joe Louis and Jersey Joe Walcott over their intercom system.

After the "Y" on Saturdays, I could prowl around downtown for a couple hours before I caught my bus home. Monroe Avenue was a dynamic circus of fedoras and bonnets and well turned ankles and rosy cheeks and step-down Hudson Hornet sedans. There was a special block they called "dime store row" with wondrous emporiums like Woolworth's, W. T. Grant, Green's, J.J. Newberry, The Boston Store and Kresge's (that later evolved into K-Mart). I joyfully squandered my meager allowance on trinkets, painted turtles and phonograph records.

There were at least a dozen downtown movie theaters, opulent palaces of pleasure like the Majestic, the RKO Keith and RKO Regent, the Midtown and Savoy. Over on lower Monroe, were the B-movies and art movie houses. The Center Theater played scandalous film noir, and the Art Theater next door had a dirt floor and an admission of only a dime. Did I mention I loved the movies? When we moved to the west side, I went to Saturday matinees at the Royal Theater and saw the blazing cowboy adventures of Hopalong Cassidy, Roy Rogers, Gene Autry, Wild Bill Elliott, Lash La Rue, and my favorite, The Durango Kid. Later on, Dad took us to the North Park Theater on Friday nights. He'd bring a big brown grocery bag of his homemade popcorn, but I'm getting ahead of myself. Back to those Saturday afternoons after the YMCA, my most exciting adventure was climbing the fire escapes to the top of all the tallest downtown buildings. Without a Sherpa, I scaled the treacherous heights of the McKay Tower, Pantlind Hotel, Michigan National Bank Building, Morton Hotel, People's Bank and the Earle Hotel, where its gritty fire escape brushed against a tipsy, art deco *Tip Top Lounge* neon sign. I would pass this high-flying information onto Anthony and Flea one day. Tragically, it would lead to terrifying results.

My Aunt Irene lived in Lansing Michigan, and I spent much of my childhood with her when I was homeless. She had a congenital humped back and a grouchy traveling-salesman husband, named Leo Barnes, who sold Diversey Cleaning Products. Aunt Irene drank a case of Coca-Cola every day. Her classic 6 oz. bottles were delivered by a real Coke truck, as though we were a retail store. There was a perpetual haystack of wooden cases near the back door. Irene gladly accepted the challenge of surrogate mother and never relinquished it. She had been monitoring me from the day I was born. She loved me unconditionally, probably more than anyone ever did. I was the child she never had. She scrubbed me in her big cast iron bathtub, sang me lullabies and maintained all-night vigils when I had the measles or chicken pox. She rubbed my chest with Vicks when I had a cold and nursed my bloody noses. She gave me oriental massages and flossed my teeth. Once a week she'd give me an enema whether I needed it or not, and I always needed it not. She cooked my favorite delicacies and helped me with my school work during my multi-school tour of first grades. She was my heart and soul mate for many years.

I had another great aunt--literally. She was my dad's Aunt Marie Kyauskas, who had also emigrated from Lithuania. Her Polish husband, Charlie, was jolly as Santa Claus. Like my dad, he worked at a furniture factory and was a master craftsman at John Widdicomb. I lived with them for a while as a Harrison Park second grader, on the west side where the majority of East European immigrants had settled. Their home was full of old-country furnishings, Catholic paraphernalia, aged photos of patriarchs, and the taste and smell of foods like potato-pancake blynai and kugelis that were always simmering on the stove. Their intrinsic kindness was a pleasant respite from my father's temper. In the evening I'd lie on the living-room floor and listen to the big console radio before bed. Programs like *The Shadow, Gangbusters, The Lone Ranger; Boston Blackie; Little Orphan Annie; Captain Midnight; Yours Truly, Johnny Dollar; The Amos 'n' Andy Show* and *Sam Spade* took me to another world. A world I dreamed of inhabiting.

Aunt Marie and Uncle Charlie also had a cottage on Green Lake, north of Grand Rapids, where the lake itself and all the property belonged to Lithuanians. Everybody spoke the mother tongue at their refuge lake. There was a pavilion with card games, dancing and conspicuous consumption of alcoholic concoctions. Most of the men had bulbous red noses that gave them away. I took my first sip of Budweiser there. Fishing was the big attraction at Green Lake, but I preferred the colorful turtles and made them my pets. My turtle Hector went on an excursion and was run over by a Model T Ford. Uncle Charlie died while I was at camp one year, and I had to leave early for the funeral. I came to hate funerals, but at least the Lithuanians threw one heck of a wild drunken party.

Chapter 3: North Park

Michigan had 10,000 lakes, but darn it, Minnesota went and had 11,000. Competitive for a kid, I was a chauvinist long before I knew anything about Napoleon, Nicholas Chauvin or the revolutionary women who hijacked the word for their own feminine cause célèbre. I liked books more than toys and spent much of my childhood reading. Language was suitable for worship, even when it was profane. Conversely, I was suspicious of this mysterious God. I put my money on Superman. Captain Marvel and even Mighty Mouse were more believable. I was leap years from getting a grip on existentialism, but I was already disconcerted with the hostile-and-abandoned playground of life. It was me against an unfathomable universe, and I was frequently besieged with nightmares.

Always in some degree of jeopardy, I kept dodging Davy Jones' locker, which beckoned me in for sinister swims. I had my first brush at Big Star Lake when I was only a baby. I rolled off a dock and sank like a loaded diaper. Fully clothed and in high heels to boot, Mom jumped in and swam around underwater until she extracted me from the tangled seaweed. Our three-piece family used to rent a Big Star cabin back then. Our dog Fooey slipped out of the sedan at a Texaco gas station, and we inadvertently drove off without him, a harbinger of Fooey II and III and a bumpy road ahead.

The Michigan mitten's Great Lakes are Superior, Michigan, Huron, and Erie. Match those, Minnesota. When I was a notch older, we would bivouac at Grand Haven State Park on Lake Michigan. We'd spend the week swimming and climbing sand dunes. There were picturesque lighthouses and piers all along the 3,288 mile coast line, but occasionally violent storms would sweep unsuspecting tourists out to sea. Briefly reunited, Scott St. John and I took on an angry hurricane. The pier was closed and barricaded, but we were reckless with adrenaline and ventured out onto the long concrete-and-steel structure with not one but two lighthouses. We clung to the catwalk steel lattice as breakers strove to cast us overboard. Like an angry orca, a towering killer wave crashed over the pier, and we were sliced and diced into the black-water channel that was deep enough to accommodate international freighters. The Coast Guard rushed to battle stations while I tried to keep my head above the not-so-swell swells. Now at the approach to the Grand Haven pier there is a warning and a monument to the dead.

Drowning in asphyxia, I finally closed the casket on that damp trifecta when I was seven years old at our new home on Four Mile Road, in the woodsy suburb of North Park. Once again I tantalized the grim-but-incompetent reaper. In spring fever, my dad had up and suddenly married Eileen Van Bree, a deeply-religious and kind-hearted woman who consolidated our family again. She was a pretty blonde with a gracious smile. We were whole again: Jack and Judy, a new mom, a new home and the same old grumpy Daddy. I was so excited I even enrolled for the final two weeks of second grade where I managed to win the collective hearts of the four cutest girls in class. Legitimate again, I was the Norman Rockwell boy with his puppy on the cover of my favorite periodical, *The Saturday Evening Post*. It arrived in the mail every week, and I had dibs as soon as Pops was finished reading it in the bathroom. Personally, I preferred the enchanted stories in my very first private bedroom. Judy and I had the two upstairs rooms. I was still sleepwalking almost every night, and Eileen would find me crying and tangled up with the clothes hanging in the closet. In that freaky netherworld, I'd also pee in my poor sister's bunny slippers. Better off were my female conquests: Linda Prefontaine, Janice Gunnett, Janet Hulbert and Peggy Vroman. After three miserable years, I was suddenly viable with the girls again. Girls were special and indispensible.

Summer vacation began with great expectations. Judy and I had taken afternoon naps, and Eileen was cleaning the house. Dad was at work; the war was over, and American Seating was back to making stadium seats for the new economy. I woke up first and went outside to play. Our new house had a big yard, a chicken coup and rabbit hutches, a vegetable garden and a huge stand-alone garage, full of fun things to play with. Most interesting was a discarded ice box, a wood-and-porcelain cabinet that once used ice to keep food cold. We had one like it on the west side. Now we had ourselves a real electric refrigerator in the kitchen. I decided to hide in the empty ice box so I could jump out and surprise Judy when she came looking for me. (We were still investigating all the secret treasures.) I climbed in to the vault of death and pulled the door shut. Oh, oh. I had locked myself into a tomb, with no way of opening the door from the inside. It was a small chamber and I barely fit; that didn't leave much air to breath. The stifling atmosphere was bleak, an airtight case. I yelled and beat on the door, but I was far from help, deep in the bowels of hell.

My exertion had exhausted the remaining air supply. Sweat rolled down my face. Air, I needed air. I was going to die, and I was only a second grader. If I had a crayon I would have left a goodbye note. I decided to give it one more shot; one last grand stand bloody-murder scream. Eileen was vacuuming but thought she heard something ominous. Maybe it was momma intuition. She checked our beds and saw I was missing. Frantically, she sought the origin of that noise, which by now had stopped because I had already turned purple and was unconscious. She finally worked her way to the garage and discovered my limp body in the ice box. If not for Eileen, my memoirs would have been a simple memorandum, a brief eulogy. I had been seconds from becoming the late-and-dearly-departed Jack Kiedis, and just when I had finally found happiness.

Well, relative happiness. My dad still came home every night, yelling about whatever I had done wrong that day. I hid under the basement stairs, but he'd always find me. The spankings kept piling up, but I was resilient. Life in general was splendid; we were in the modern Oleomargarine postwar era. Although nifty new stuff was available, we still got our glass milk bottles delivered to our door by a horse-drawn wagon, and we shared one telephone party line with six other neighbors. We could listen into each other's calls if we wanted to. Summertime was delightful when you were seven. There were tall bottles of NEHI orange pop for a nickel at the corner grocer, a swing under the willow tree and, for dessert, those four new girlfriends.

Bright and early next year in the 3rd grade, a newer new kid arrived. Jim Swanlund was in the spotlight. And there was a new prize to fight over, Linda White, another new student. Jim and I had epic clashes over this cutie, and my adversary was undoubtedly redoubtable. We'd both show up at Linda's house and battle for her attention: valentines in autumn, tightrope walking on her porch railing, standup comedy and showing her our muscles. He challenged me to climb head first into a big wooden barrel and then put a vise-grip on my legs to keep me from crawling out so he could woo the queen unabated, while I blurted boyish expletives. Naturally, Jim and I became best friends. In those early days of television, long before my family ever had one, we spent hours at his house watching comedies and then writing our own TV sketches that we'd perform for our class and then the banquet circuits.

I learned to box at North Park; every year the school carnival had pint-size boxing matches. I befriended a chubby girl named Joan who nobody seemed to like; I thought she deserved a guy too. Time slipped silently into the optimistic happy days of the late forties. In *Collier's Weekly,* we saw our first glimpse into the future of space travel that scientists were already preparing for. The sky wasn't the limit anymore; it was to the moon and the stars. The sun was shining on America, or at least that was the propaganda. I was living in the good old days. My real Mollie Mom was now remarried and allowed to see us once a week. She politicized me at age nine, during the 1948 presidential campaign. A staunch Republican, my dad was for Thomas E. Dewey, but Mollie convinced me to support Democrat Harry S. Truman, who had been Roosevelt's vice president. We won. That Christmas, my Aunt Catherine on the Vander Veen side gave me some gift ideas for Mom and one was a brassiere. I rode the bus downtown to Gantos Fine Ladies Ware and gave the shopping list to a saleslady. She smiled when she read the bra size was 38C and complimented her figure. I was proud to learn this; it was an early lesson on a subject I would become enjoyably knowledgeable about.

While our life was dominated by my father, Judy and I did have a lively maternal side of our family. There were a multitude of aunts and uncles and cousins and my imposing retired-policeman grandfather, Richard Vander Veen, who lived in a formidable house on Hollister Street with my witty and intelligent grandmother. Their ancient, gothic house had a dank dungeon of a basement and an equally daunting attic, both of which were stuffed to the spider-web-covered ceilings with seventy years of their lives. There were boxes by the hundreds and newspaper clippings of everything from the Wright Bros. and Teddy Roosevelt to this afternoon's *Grand Rapids Press.* They had a circular wooden table in the dining room that seated twenty people. Holidays were always celebrated there. The kitchen still had an ice box and a wood cooking stove. In the bountiful back yard, there was rhubarb destined for my Grandma's pies and big purple concord grapes on vines that covered the high stone wall that separated their place from Mary Free Bed Hospital for children. The sequestered garage was filled to the top with obsolescence and an old Packard automobile. My Aunt Catherine's son Chip was my best friend cousin. I often stayed at his house on the rough and tumble south side of town.

Years later in 1974, my cousin Richard Vander Veen II was elected to the U.S. Congress for Michigan's 5th Congressional District when our representative, Jerry Ford, was promoted to Vice President, after Spiro Agnew was forced to resign. When Nixon also resigned, our hometown Gerald R. Ford became the 38th President of the United States. His presidential museum is downtown, and he's buried on the grounds overlooking the Grand River. West Michigan's district had always been solid Republican and still is today, but my cousin was the first Democratic congressman voted in since 1911.

Mom and Dad had never made us go to church; however, Eileen was on a mission to convert us. Her family was Calvinist Christian Reformed, and that meant no. No TV. No dancing. No swearing. And no fun. Church was four times on Sunday, with some other holy event every night of the week. We trekked downtown to the ornate mother ship, the Eastern Avenue Christian Reformed Church, at 8 for the main attraction on Sunday morning, followed by a consecutive church service at a satellite missionary chapel on Plainfield, within walking distance of our house. The second service was at 10, and then we had Sunday school at 11 and, later, an evening service at 7 p.m. This blue-collar chapel became my crucible.

The Elmer Gantry preacher in charge was a fire-and-brimstone evangelical missionary named Reverend Bykema, who had dogma coming out of his ears. My tortured weekly schedule went unabated with Youth for Christ, Catechism, Bible Class, Holy Spirit Jamboree and Revelations 101. I despised them all. Everything finally exploded for me one Sunday sermon when Bykema incontrovertibly espoused that the Holy Spirit was top dog of the trinity. God and Jesus might be forgiving, but the Holy Spirit was intractable. Blaspheme the Holy Spirit and you'd go *directly* to hell. That curious adventure was at my fingertips. I took the challenge and conjured up the most disrespectful things I could come up with. I wasn't afraid of this Holy Ghost story and I called his bluff. I poked him in the eye, and he wimped out. No more prestigious capitalization, just as I had earlier downsized god. Mythological superhero deities were whimsical, but this sci-fi god was merely a naive fairy tale. I was a self-taught atheist at the age of ten.

And then there was the alternative: Sex. Well, sort of. I discovered Vargas and Petty, the artists who created erotic girl calendars. Titillating, leggy girls were depicted with their skirt or blouse caught in a washing machine ringer or an elevator door, inadvertently revealing a glimpse of their secret mysteries. Fortunately, they were in reach of a crafty ten–year-old. Eileen would always find them though. Memo to kids: don't hide your pin-up girls in the sock drawer. Sex was exciting, powerful and mysterious, but I didn't have a clue about how to unlock the magic. I was delirious for the payoff that teetered on the anxious edge of my hormone happy Yosemite Falls.

There was one thing I did like about church, and she was an older, high-school girl named Linda de Young. She *was* divine. I'd always angle for a pew with a good vantage of her. At the church picnic I made my move, and her positive reaction had me off to Kresge's dime store to buy a cheap necklace in a fancy box. Our respective mothers put a stop to the May-September affair; love hurt. During a subsequent church service, I excused myself to the restroom and noticed a pile of oak partitions leaning against the wall. The preacher was pontificating and getting all the attention. Jealous and love sick, I yanked the lumber over on top of myself, making a commotion I knew Linda would notice. It turned out to weigh a ton, knocked me out cold and broke off my front tooth.

Grand Rapids had a swell amusement park on Reeds Lake where I often escaped for fun. Ramona Park had a bloodcurdling roller coaster called the Derby Racer, the usual rides and attractions, and an arcade of primitive peep shows, right between the skeet ball and a mechanical fortune teller. For only a nickel, I could squint at the flickering images of seductive semi-nude girls draped on a sunny plot of nature. I was only in the 6th grade, but nobody ever kicked me out. Subsequently, I nurtured a crush on Bettie Page, who dominated the stag films of the era. I usually required cooling off on the cruise ship that sailed around Reeds Lake. It had two levels with a long staircase between them. An unrepentant show off, I was entertaining the accumulated young girls with a daredevil attempt to jump from the top of the stairs to the bottom. I broke my arm in three places.

And then I had a new game to play. War. North Korea invaded South Korea and we rushed into the conflict. I joined my own army and patriotically began running around in the fields and hills surrounding Four Mile Road, with my authentic, toy steel-helmet and a machine gun I fashioned from a plumbing device for flushing toilets.

Jackie me in California.   John Michael Kiedis, Class of 1957.

Chapter 4: A Sentimental Education

When I was at the end of the 6th grade, Grandma Kiedis died of cancer. Julia had been a quiet woman, cut from the cloth of the old country. Her English was flawed, but her heart was sublime. Grandpa Tony was in poor health too. They owned a two-pump Mobil gas station way out in the country on a two-lane highway. From my young vantage point, the red-white-and-blue Mobil sign with its flying winged-horse soared to the sky, or at least to the top of the 30-foot steel pole. Gasoline was practically free, but you had to turn a crank to draw the fuel up into the pump. The stucco cubbyhole had a sign above the door that said KIEDIS SERVICE STATION. Inside, was a small counter with a cash drawer and a candy case. Cigarettes were 18 cents. We had a contract with Sky High Beverages for soda pop in every imaginable color.

When Grandpa died too, we sold our North Park house and moved into their tiny bungalow about ten steps from the gas station. It had outdoor plumbing, an outhouse and a hand pump for cooking, drinking and bathing. Eventually, my dad and I built two more bedrooms, a utility room and a real bathroom with running water.

The property had four overnight tourist cabins, set along a deep gully that divided the wooded dominion all the way to the banks of the mighty Grand River. Our competitive price was $2 a night. We also inherited their chickens, a cow and hundreds of young evergreen trees Grandpa had planted on a couple acres. Tom Sawyer and Huckleberry Finn were my imaginary friends. We built a raft and sailed to a large Treasure Island, a hundred yards down river. Grandpa left us a 1938 Ford coupe that I learned to drive at age 11. Starter and shift on the floor with jump seats in back. Our private gravel road had a circular turnaround at the river that catapulted me right back up to the gas station in a cloud of dust like the Speedrome stock car races in Comstock Park.

Next door I discovered a new best friend in Dan Van Dyke, a towhead Hollander with freckles and pink skin. In no time at all, we had our bedrooms connected by a string-and-tin-can communication system. We investigated the wonder of girls and this unfathomable miracle called sex. When Dad was at work we pumped gas, checked the oil and tires, washed windshields and handled the cabin transactions. When young couples suspiciously rented a cabin in the middle of the day we would charge through the gully and sneak up to the ephemeral den of iniquity. We peeked in their windows and smoked cigarettes after the denouement. It was X-rated.

Dad took us to a Tigers game in Detroit, and we stayed in a big hotel on the 25th floor. In the window of another hotel directly across the street was a beautiful woman, walking around in the nude. Nothing compared to this carnal magnetism; we just weren't quite sure what to do about it.

D.W. Richardson was my new school for the 7th and 8th grade. I took it by storm, but it was more like invading Monaco. The country school had only two rooms, two teachers and eight or nine kids in each grade. There was sweet camaraderie and just enough scuffles and cat fights to keep it interesting.

The 8th grade may have been the best year of my entire life. A sophisticated city girl named Gerri DeVos transferred into our lap and set my life on fire. She was tall and elegant, a girl with grown-up curves. All the guys were smitten. We were nibbling on puberty and here she was, a bona fide sex symbol, sitting at the next desk and cheerleading at our cow-pasture football games and smiling at me from across the lunch table. I dug deep and found the sweet spot; she capitulated and I was miraculously victorious. The delicious dream became an embracing reality as she held my trembling heart, and we slow danced to the *Tennessee Waltz*. I was delirious with love that final year of innocence. On our class trip to Detroit, she snuggled in my arms, and we made out on the long bus ride home.

Miss DeVos wasn't the only thing I was consumed with. The Lions won three NFL championships in the 1950s. I followed the Detroit Tigers across the radio dial and in person at Briggs Stadium. The Brooklyn Dodgers were my National League team. On the school grounds, I scored my own touchdowns and hit my own home runs, inspired by these heroes. I read comic books and couldn't avoid the Charles Atlas bodybuilder advertisements. I *was* a skinny 97-pound-weakling, and there were big bullies kicking sand in faces out there. I ordered the book and bought the barbells; I was determined to build myself into a tough guy.

Frankly, I was better at sensitive. One Saturday, I was cleaning a storage area and came across a packet of my father's poetry and short stories; it was a side of him I'd never seen. I started writing my own stories, and our teacher Mr. Lally read them to the whole school. I created a school newspaper, wrote all the copy and drew a comic strip. I wrote the 8th grade play. At home, we finally had television, and I'd make sick excuses to avoid Sunday evening church so I could stay home and watch the *Colgate Comedy Hour*, especially when the rotating comics were Dean Martin and Jerry Lewis. My dad despised their goofy humor, but at least he also refused to go to church. The golden age of television inspired me with dramatic programming like *Playhouse 90*. On the lighter side, *Your Hit Parade* rolled out the top seven songs of the week. Joni James' plaintive ballads kept me in perpetual chills.

My father was a competitive golfer and expected me to follow in his FootJoy spikes. He'd been teaching me since I was a wee lad of four. Frugal as Jack Benny, he still managed to join Green Ridge Country Club, one of the few pricey privileges he ever afforded himself. I didn't really like golf but did like the amenities. There was a swimming pool, and after a round of golf, I'd hang out in the men's lounge, playing cards. The men's locker room was intimidating with wrinkled, old naked-tale-swappers shuffling between the shower and their lockers. The Negro shoeshine fellows were always humming a tune. I made a decent living as a caddy but had to walk nine miles from our house to Green Ridge, lug heavy golf bags all day and then walk back home. Of course I'd caddy for my dad when he played in the State Amateur or the local tournaments. Golf was Pa's passion, but I wanted to play big time City League Football. My country-bumpkin-grade-school students all went to small town Rockford High. Ironically, today they're a dynamo in Michigan sports. I petitioned to enroll at Creston High, which was the closest Grand Rapids school and was given approval. Creston was a classic school with strong bloodlines. Proud beneath that hard-boiled façade of his, my sentimental father saved everything of mine, including all my 8th grade report cards from good old Mr. Lally.

1. Johnny does very well in his subjects but his antics are disturbing. He and Dan Van Dyke are quite a pair in a school room--believe me! Both, however, are excellent students.

2. Johnny's school work is good but his conduct is getting progressively worse--he is a constant "show-off" to the girls and is invariably doing something that he knows full well he shouldn't.

3. Johnny's behavior has vastly improved this time and I'm sure he will be a fine student in high school. I wish him the best of luck.

As the 8th grade came to an end my dad retired from American Seating and bought a drive-in restaurant called the *Homburg* in Grand Rapids. It was a comfortable landmark in the north end and had an arty, neon sign of a big brown derby homburg. I spent the summer working my butt off as chief, cook and bottle washer, plus soda jerk and car hop. I was the titular assistant manager, but my Aunt Victoria brandished more clout and a bigger spatula. The highly anticipated fall season finally arrived, and I got a special dispensation drivers license for my Grandpa's old '38 Ford to drive the eight miles back and forth to Creston. The year was 1953. I was a passionate, young teenager ready to completely unravel.

What do we do now!?

Chapter 5: Hey, Daddy-O

A *Rebel Without a Clue*, I was entering a new high school with few friends and plenty of anxiety. Traumatic teen angst was all but guaranteed. Snobby cliques trounced my ego. The freshman football players were giants, and I was a relative midget. The only person in school smaller than me was a kid named Mouse. The girls paid no attention. I wasn't any teacher's pet. I was confused and disconsolate. The bullish on Johnny Kiedis bravado bottomed out. If there was a silver lining, it was the astonishing pulchritude of higher learning. It was no coincidence there was a proliferation of freshmen boys hanging out in the senior and junior wings, where so many pointy-bra angora sweaters were tantalizingly exposed to accidental excuse-me bumps. But alas, the senior boys with their five o'clock shadows would give us a bump of our own and bring us back to an unfortunate reality.

I had been a straight A student at D.W. Richardson, but now I was struggling with doctorate courses. Only my English, history and art classes kept me afloat. Freshman football Coach Kaye was afraid for my life, but three weeks into practices they finally thrust me into a scrimmage as a running back. On my first play, all eleven beefy behemoths piled on top of me and broke my ankle. That was it for my first year, but I did come back in my junior year.

Of course I was on the golf team, but was never the star athlete Pop had hoped for, although we won the regional title in my junior year. Last player on the course, I sunk a putt on the final hole of the tourney that won the championship. Our four man lineup: Thom Rosely went professional, Denny Simmons mastered the art of golf-ball deception, Jack Van Bloyce was calm and steady, and I was the fourth man--the weak link but always with the loudest-screaming father in the gallery.

I was also on the swim team and ran cross country, even though I had asthma. I'd have to say high-school sports were not exactly my finest hour, but I did perform well in the junior and senior plays. I got the nerdy-element respect but never ran for class president or student council. Nobody ever voted me for home-coming king. I had been big man on campus all through elementary school, and now I was insignificant. My only real friends were old pals from North Park Elementary School, like Jim Swanlund.

I found solace in music. I had been grooving on tunes since I was a kid, with artists like Kay Starr and Tony Bennett--even the opera star turned pop singer Mario Lanza. In the 7th grade, my parents had given me a clock radio for Christmas, and I listened under the covers while everybody was asleep. One night I stumbled onto 50,000-watt radio station WLAC in Nashville that played rhythm and blues by performers like Jimmy Reed, The Speedos, Clovers, Flamingos, Little Willie John, Big Joe Turner, Jimmy Witherspoon, Little Walter, Ruth Brown, Faye Adams, Etta James and Muddy Waters. It was a revelation. With my allowance, I ordered a steady stream of 78 RPM packaged combos from the sponsor: Randy's Record Shop. They'd arrive in a cardboard box from Gallatin, Tennessee, via the mail. My new-found secret music was decidedly different than mainstream

America's musical taste. Although it was referred to as "race music," I was oblivious to the difference; my heroes Jackie Robinson and Joe Louis were the same sturdy color.

Dan Van Dyke was excelling at friendly Rockford High, getting all the triumphs I wasn't at Creston. Pops liked to head south so he could play golf in the winter, and we brought Dan on two notable trips. One year, we went to New Orleans for Mardi Gras. The next Christmas vacation, Dad and his friend Frank, and Dan and I hit the open road, Route 66, to Los Angeles. It was my first trip out west since I was a little boy. We knocked up Las Vegas, Hoover Dam, Palm Springs, the LA Open golf tourney at Rancho Park and finally the Rose Bowl game between Michigan State and UCLA. The Spartans won on a last-second field goal; Dan and I ran onto the field to help pull down the wooden goal post. We went to the Pike Amusement Park in Long Beach, and split off from my dad and Frank so we could check out the big league peep-show booths. We were busy getting an eyeful when my dad caught us red-handed. In San Francisco, Pop was tired so he let us go out on the town without supervision, and we saw the controversial foreign film *The Bed*. I was ready to explode.

Back in mundane Grand Rapids, I would often skip out of school and drive downtown to see movies like Mickey Spillane's *I the Jury* and James Dean's venerated *Rebel Without a Cause*. My pal Jim Swanlund bought a '49 Mercury like Dean's and wore the same red windbreaker. He did everything but date Natalie Wood. Even more auspicious was the gritty inner-city film *Blackboard Jungle* that opened and closed the credits with Bill Haley and His Comets' "Rock Around the Clock." Three years earlier and before my time, he had unleashed a slippery-slope version of an obscure rhythm, country-and-blues song called "Rocket 88" that heralded the future. Now "Rock Around the Clock" had mainstream's attention. That electric-guitar shiver down your spine changed history and sparked the rock and roll revolution. Hearing that unique sound for the first time was the most exhilarating moment ever. It was my moon landing and Bobby Thompson's "The Giants Win the Pennant!" home run. Life would never be the same after that afternoon in the darkness of the RKO Regent.

Rock and roll gave me hope, but I still had to deal with a furious father and frustrating mediocrity at school and work. I was on a path to certain doom until one day in my junior year when a velvet voice tapped me on the back with a counterfeit compliment. I turned to face the ghost of Schuyler Ace St. John, the golden Scott. My dad and his old best friend Pete St. John had long since gone their separate ways and raised divorced families. But now there he was, the long-lost playboy, at Joppe's lunch spot. Scott seemed to be extending a hand in friendship, and I certainly needed one. Sure his flattery was manipulative, but right now I was confronted by a force of nature and his snake-oil salvation. Scott was handsome, haunting, and as it turned out, a gifted troublemaker and notorious ladies' man. He was a prototype of The Fonz, except Arthur Herbert Fonzarelli would have a good heart behind the audacity. Scott had ulterior motives for everything.

In this case, it was my '54 Ford Crown Victoria with bubble skirts and dual exhausts that was the second-coolest car at Creston, after Don Siegel's customized hot rod. Yes, that Don Siegel, the class president and star quarterback and coolest guy in school. Not as cool as Scott maybe, but then Scott didn't go to Creston...very often. Although technically enrolled, he spent his idle time at home on the phone with chicks, smoking Luckies, drinking beer, listening to the Dells' "Oh, What a Night" and scheming up misdemeanors at Mary St. John's house on Dale Street, a block from the school he never went to.

Good for both us, he needed a cool car and a gullible buddy to drive it to his nefarious shenanigans. Six hours later I was standing at his mom's doorstep ready to rumble. From that day on, I was enrolled in a different curriculum: the school of pirating beer trucks, stealing hubcaps and impressionable hearts, scamming cigarettes at Peck's Drug Store and talking pretty young waitresses out of their paychecks. Basically, we gave society the boot. It was a reform school of hedonism, deception and bloodshed, all dramatically played out by Scott's cunning sweetness and intoxicating intelligence. I was to learn my own dark side and test my limits. I would create a new unique character for myself and rediscover pride.

My disingenuous friend was a repository of hep music and a diviner of hot parties and naughty girls. We made ourselves conspicuous at the Friday night dances, but nothing got us hyped up like the Alan Freed extravaganzas at the Civic Auditorium. Every rock and roll star in the business performed on these mega-cavalcades. Little Richard, Chuck Berry, LaVerne Baker, Fats Domino, The Everly Brothers, Carl Perkins, Buddy Holly, Gene Vincent, Frankie Lymon and the Teenagers, Jerry Lee Lewis, Screamin' Jay Hawkins, Bo Diddley, Bill Haley and His Comets, and all in my town. It was hostile rebellion heaven. Scott, however, was usually sidetracked, sneaking into the girls' restrooms and jimmying money from the Kotex machines.

Scott was a flatten-a-guy-a-day, legitimate street fighter in a time before guitar heroes or boy bands, back when the coolest guys where the toughest guys, successors of Wild West gunfighters and Japanese samurai. There was a colorful cast of young Damon Runyon back-alley pugilists in town, and soon enough I was getting bloody with the best of them. We were a combative city with a bloody chip on our shoulder, and the knucklehead nonpareil included the likes of Denny Simmons, Jim Van Loo, the Flynn brothers, Wycocki brothers, Fat Bomba, matinee idol Terry Haga (who was stabbed to death forty-three times in Dallas), old-school Stanley Ketchel and eight-time world champion Floyd Mayweather Jr.

To hang with Scott I'd have to raise it a notch. Nothing fancy, he just threw me into the battle. Tagged the "Dynamic Duo," I had to uphold my end of the reputation. We boxed at Wes Ramey's gym and worked out for the Golden Gloves, but we thrived best in unsanctioned rumbles-- north end versus the west side and the south end. The eastside hardly ever bothered to RSVP. We promoted epic fight clubs in alleys and vacant lots. I started drinking and twisting Luckies in my T-shirt sleeves. Dad hated these new bad influences, especially when the law started to catch up with us. Petty crimes, fights, speeding and vandalism; I had my own rap sheet. Hey, Mark Twain's "Youth is wasted on the young;" we'd have to dispute it. Consequences reared their retribution, though, and I was suspended from school. Pop grounded me indefinitely, except to work at the Homburg, and I wasn't allowed to associate with Schuyler Ace.

That summer, I ran away from home again, but this time it wasn't to the end-of-the-city bus run. I was working endless shifts and occasionally had to strap on a car-hop apron to hit the asphalt. No roller skates, but I sure felt like a dork. My sister Judy *was* a car hop; some joker ordered burgers, fries and oral sex. Bad move, joker. I yanked him out of the car by his hair and punched his ticket. Anarchy was no stranger to the Homburg. There was a diabolical pinball machine in one corner and a malevolent jukebox in the other. The

Jehovah Witnesses would drop by to scold us. Rowdy hoodlums would congregate, intimi-date and end up rumbling in the A&P parking lot next door. Hefty Aunt Victoria would emerge from the kitchen with a big meat cleaver and those thunderous tits of hers to scat-ter the hoodlums. Everybody feared my Pop. When John Kiedis Sr. pulled up in his new super sharp Ford Fairlane convertible, even the toughest hooligans would duck out, leaving coffee in their cup, dimes in the jukebox and quarters on the pinball machine.

Every night at closing, Dad would arrive to check out the register and drive me home to the miserable sound track of my life. You forgot to stack the dishes. The steam table wasn't spotless. There were pickles on the tarmac. I'd cringe and duck, but he'd still slap me silly. Home at last, I'd dash to my bedroom, close the door, pull the covers over my head and turn on my music. The Coasters would sing "Yakety yak. (Don't talk back)." Every night I would pray to the holy smoke screen that my father would be transformed into a regular dad like everybody else had; like Paul was transformed on his way to Damascus. I made a blood pact that my kids would have fun and enjoy their childhood.

Pop had put my car up on blocks so when I had to be somewhere, I borrowed Eileen's old coupe. Reckless as usual I rear-ended some poor lady. Naturally, Dad was seething. While Mom's hand-me-down was in the body shop, I did the unthinkable; the irrespon-sible son banged up Dad's beloved flashy red vehicle while evading the police at 100 mph. So angry, he was working on something beyond conventional punishment--something spectacular. Preemptively, I decided to leave town while I still had a chance. The next day I packed a small bag, collected my savings and went to work as usual. The city bus parked next to the Homburg so when the driver was ready to go I slipped out the back door and hopped on. Free as a bird and choking on adrenaline, I arrived at the downtown Union Train Station. Our cavernous depot had a cyclopean clock and the hustle and bustle of an Alfred Hitchcock set piece. Yellow cabs were fighting for leverage, and Red Caps were chucking leather suitcases. Competing newsboys bayed, and retorts recoiled across the tiled lobby. Like thoroughbreds in the gate, half a dozen locomotives chomped at their bits in the sweet steamy atmosphere next to the platforms. The loudspeaker rang the starting bell, "Chesapeake & Ohio departing for Chicago on platform three."

Six hours later, I exited my third Union Station of the day to peruse my arbitrary destination. Conveniently, there was a quaint park and the original Milwaukee YMCA. I marched in like an adult and signed up for a room. The desk manager gave me a furrowed brow and the key. Nobody questioned my legitimacy, even this waif on his own in a time long before runaway teens flooded California in the late sixties. Maybe I started something. I couldn't help but smile, so I settled in and then went exploring. The baseball Boston Braves had moved to Milwaukee in 1953, and the city was nuts for baseball. The new Braves broke attendance records, which motivated the defection of the Philadelphia Ath-letics to Kansas City and subsequently Oakland, the St. Louis Browns to Baltimore where they renamed themselves the Orioles, and the Brooklyn Dodgers and New York Giants to California. The new Milwaukee Braves had a Cooperstown lineup with superstars Hank Aaron, Eddie Mathews and Warren Spahn. I spent precious sunny afternoon memories at their ball park. Eventually the Braves moved again--to Atlanta.

I worked up the nerve to try out the brewery tours, Schlitz, Blatz, Pabst Blue Ribbon and Miller High Life. No problem: free beer. In the YMCA lobby, I watched the televised political conventions of Adlai Stevenson and Eisenhower in a rematch of their 1952 contest. Not surprisingly, I went to movies. The ground breaking Otto Preminger film, *The Moon Is Blue,* was condemned by the Catholic Legion of Decency but given four stars and thumbs up by me. I was transfixed by *Somebody Up There Likes Me,* the story of boxer Rocky Graziano, played with dazzling charm by a young Paul Newman. I paid my admission and watched it over and over. Already feeling my oats, I dared to dream about being an actor one day. When I started my first movie twenty years later, I reflected on that frightened kid at a matinee on Wisconsin Avenue. Paul Newman's sarcasm and dogged fortitude gave me the courage to persevere on this peculiar journey. It was lonely and got treacherous. I was mugged and had to go on a diet.

Life on the road was no picnic, and I was definitely homesick but still determined to show Pa I wasn't his punching bag anymore. I continued to wander the lonely streets until one day a man approached and struck up a conversation. He took me to lunch and then suggested a tried-and-true Milwaukee experience, parking at the end of the Billy Mitchell Airport runway to watch the planes take off and land. We set a time that evening, and he picked me up with a smorgasbord of refreshments. We parked and were watching the planes when he suddenly put his arm around me and attempted a kiss. Instead he got a solid right jab, but that only turned him on. I was confused by his behavior, but he was nice enough to drive me back to town. It was time to leave Milwaukee.

I packed my meager belongings, checked out of the YMCA and headed into the nearby railroad yards. With my Dad and Pete St. John's hobo exploits in mind, I crawled into the first freight car that had an open sliding door and waited. It was dark and creepy. I fell asleep after a while and didn't wake up until I realized we were slowly pulling out of the yards. Now I was at the mercy of an engineer and the corporate schedule. It would have been nice if the train had gone to Chicago and curved around the tip of Lake Michigan and back up to Grand Rapids, but no, it kept going past Chicago and headed south. Not that I knew that exactly. I was rumbling blind. My final destination was like the surprise in a box of Cracker Jack. It was September by now and getting cold. I was shivering, hungry and thirsty. When the train finally stopped, I was shocked to find myself in Birmingham, Alabama.

An inhospitable freight yard and smoke-stack steel factories were the unwelcoming party. I started hitchhiking north toward home. Shell-shocked, my mind was numbing. I took on any Kerouac two-lane road no matter what direction it was headed. I was booked on a circuitous route and ended up in Atlanta. Somewhere later in the rural South, I was accosted again, but now I knew the routine. Hit first and explain later. Nose to the grindstone, I kept going. Over the long haul, I felt I walked as many miles as I rode. Chattanooga. Nashville. Louisville. Indianapolis. Fort Wayne. Grand Rapids. Plainfield Avenue. Right here, sir, let me out at the Mobil gas station. I walked into the house; my family was eating dinner. They didn't say a thing. Pop barely looked up. Eileen made a place for me at the table like nothing had ever happened. I saw the tears in her eyes. I wanted to tell them my adventures, but Dad wouldn't allow me the pleasure. Better late than never I started my senior year. I was still only sixteen years old.

When Blackie was
Spider, San Francisco
1972.

Chapter 6: To Be or Not to Belligerent

As a senior I was legitimate again: popular, virile and confident. I was even team captain of the golf team. I was dating top-notch co-eds like sexy Bonnie Buss and varsity cheerleader Mary Jo Wooten. I had new friends like Marty Lipp from Catholic Central who transferred to Creston and moved to the north end. Mr. Lipp owned a liquor store across town on Chicago Drive where Marty worked for his dad. He had access to all the beer we could steal. He'd carry cases out to the alley behind the store, and Scott and I would be waiting in my getaway car.

A new character actor on the scene was a virulent oddball named Rich Klimavich, who even Scott was wary of. Rich was a lone mercenary gun–for–hire with no allegiance, and he was pissed at me for some wise-guy remark I'd made. Usually my quick vocabulary kept me out of harm's way; it was better than bruising my knuckles. Rich wanted a smack down and I was doing my best to avoid him. Half a block from the Homburg was a Tastee-Freez franchise, and the owner had added burgers and dogs to compete with our place. Overnight it became the cool hang out, and you didn't have to deal with John Kiedis Sr. I drove into their parking lot on a Friday night with Scott riding shotgun, and there was Rich with his snarl and piercing eyes and raw madness. Scott insisted I face the music and encouraged me with, "He'll probably kill you, but we'll know you weren't a coward." I took a deep breath and started to climb out. Klimavich blocked my exit, pinned me with the door and slugged me to kingdom come. In violation of the honor code, Rich was severely admonished, and I was elevated to a hero of sorts. Even Klimavich was disgusted with himself. He had hit me so hard my left eye lid was dangling on my cheek bone. We all went to the hospital and they sewed me up. From that day on Rich and I became pals, and I couldn't have had a better guy to watch my back. One momentous night, Scott and Rich did square off and basically fought to a draw on a grassy hill north of Saint Isadore Cathedral. The fight went on interminably like one of those old John L. Sullivan versus James J. Corbett bare-knuckle fights. In the end, they both collapsed in exhaustion. The curdled cream of the north end consolidated and formed our own copywronged gang, *The Saint Hoods.*

New wise guys from the west side joined us too. Craig Betteridge showed up at The Plantation, an old hulk of a nightclub from the past out on a desolate stretch of nowhere. It had a big, gravel parking lot that backed up to a rugged drop off, high on a bluff. Scottless, I was in the club with some new recruits. A fight started inside and the boss told us to take it outside. We faced off like the Sharks and the Jets and circled our way into the parking area adjacent to the cliff. The opposition's behemoth looked unassailable, and nobody on our team seemed up to the challenge. I looked around and realized it would have to be me, in a modern-day David-and-Goliath battle royal. This new guy Craig had followed us outside to watch. He was stocky but cuddly as a child's teddy bear. He assured me he could handle the monster and told me to step aside. Craig nonchalantly walked up to the big dude and hit him with such force he flew about ten feet and rolled over the steep bluff. The vanquished retreated sheepishly, and from that time on Craig was a lieutenant in the Saint Hoods. We tagged him "Cheeseburger."

Johnny Reaser was a friend of Craig's and lived with his grandma in Lincoln Park. We called him the Kid because his father was already infamous as a bon-vivant industrialist. Johnny was scholarly and sensitive, but shifty street wise guy Jim Beard wasn't. John was a connoisseur of unique personalities and tolerated him; I found him a nuisance. There was also a well-known party girl named Barb Folkersma, who kept us in raucous controversy. On my first trip to her west side apartment, the Arrendondo Brothers dismantled a gang of ill-fated thugs from out of town while Barb and her girlfriends sipped daiquiris and mopped up the gore. A week later and chaotically closer to the bone, local bullies Tom Gravengood and Norm Bellis walloped Scott and Craig so savagely that Reaser and I both dove out of Barb's second-floor kitchen window and ran all the way to his grandma's.

After that bloody night, we laid low and spent more time with higher society. We broke away for periods of astute enlightenment at libraries, seminars, colloquiums, and pool halls. We were both show-business aficionados, and he subscribed to *Photoplay* and *Movie Mirror*, the celebrity magazines of the day. They were full of movie-star revelations and the juicy gossip of Walter Winchell and Hedda Hopper. One Saturday afternoon downtown, we met the black beauty McGee sisters. They were cute as a couple of buttons and knocked us out with their big smiles and friendly dispositions; we both fell instantly in love. There was only one Negro at Creston and very few at Reaser's Union High. This was uncharted territory for both of us. Interracial affairs were rare then, and we were oblivious to the repercussions. About ten minutes later we were apprised. Their big brothers and their big friends saw us walking hand in hand on Monroe Ave. and came straight at us. They inflicted a scatter-fire of punches and fled. Johnny got the brunt of it. Still in double-date mode we went back to Grandma Reaser's and put a steak on his black eye. The McGee family lived on Buckley St. off South Division, an area I always called south central after the Chicago and Los Angeles ghettos. Johnny backed off from this romance, but I kept going to the girls' home until one day the brothers showed up again and chased me away with a baseball bat.

The Saint Hoods spent most of our time in souped-up hot rods on the way to a party or taking it on the lam from the cops. Terry Lucas drove a customized 1951 Ford in which he had installed a fake gas gage he could manipulate with a toggle switch so it could show empty, and we'd have to chip in for gas. We finally got wise to him. Eric Carpenter was his mad-scientist partner. The Greek was exuberant and kept a smile on our collective countenance. Local character Dennis Shookman shook it up by marrying Barb, thus changing her name to complicate matters. Our clubhouse was the Pines, an infamous desolate forest of pine trees off the East Beltline, where we'd party around a campfire and make out with the slutty girls. It was such a labyrinth we could easily escape into the maze when the sheriffs showed up. Scott was knocking up girls on a regular basis. I was still a virgin. Not that I wasn't trying. The sexual revolution was still only a glimmer in Hugh Hefner's eye. His early *Playboys* were still pretty tame. Despite anomalies like Scott St. John, the rest of society was relatively sexless.

With all due respect to the Bible Belt, there wasn't a more orthodox city in America than Grand Rapids. Strangely though, there was a tiny whore house district on Commerce

Street in an old neighborhood of dilapidated Victorian homes on the edge of downtown, where the police seemed to look the other way. In a concerted effort to equalize the disparity with Scott, I ventured into that mysterious world one night. I picked out one of the houses and walked up the winding stairway to the door and knocked. Maybe that was my knees. A madam finally answered and escorted me in. It was a proper civil establishment, and the colored prostitutes were all well-mannered. The madam took me to a room and told me to wait. Soon a pleasant but elderly lady arrived. She asked if I wanted to put money in a jukebox next to the bed. I said OK and deposited the coins. She asked me to undress and I started to, but then I chickened out and apologized to her for the inconvenience. I quickly departed and never did make any selections on that jukebox. I hope somebody else enjoyed the music and the sex.

My dad still took the family to Florida every winter, and my sister Judy had met a girl in Sarasota, who eventually came up north to visit. My Mother Mollie was on her third and final marriage to Ted Walker, a very cool artist who also worked at AMI, the jukebox maker. They lived in Lowell and had a Silver Stream Trailer parked in the yard. Scott was dating Judy, who had blossomed into the hottest girl at Creston, abetted by our Mom's hand-me-down figure. Judy's nickname at school was JJ—"Judy Jugs." A double date, Scott and Judy were fooling around in the back of the trailer. My date, like me, was a virgin, and it was time for both of us to finally do it. Miss Florida and I crawled into the bed in front. In the end there was blood and spermatozoa and a big sigh of relief. The monkey was off my back. I wouldn't have sexual intercourse again until I was a sophomore at college.

High school wound down as we wrapped up our four years and applied for colleges. The acclaimed went Ivy League, the next tier to Michigan, the average settled for Michigan State and the rest slunk furtively off to smaller state and junior colleges. I fell into the Michigan State group, but that was fine with me. It was only 60 miles from home and my favorite Aunt Irene lived there. Some of my best friends joined the military, and for a while I considered the Marines. I needed my dad to sign off because I was only 17, but in the end he said no. Instead, I chose a different adventure: one last summer of naiveté to enjoy.

The Ionia Free Fair was a major summer tradition. Forty miles from GR, it rivaled the State Fair in Detroit. There were musical acts, amusement rides, stock-car races, live-stock competitions and even burlesque shows—two white and a segregated, colored one. The burlesque-show tents were vulnerable to crafty teenage boys sneaking under the flaps. Scott and I had learned that the year before. This summer we decided to join the carnival and play *Toby Tyler, Ten Weeks with a Circus* like the well worn adventure book. All you had to do is sign up and they'd take you, like joining the army. The carnivals traveled across country, and we recruited Creston sad-sack Gil Ickes because he had an expendable car. On the last day of the two week run in Ionia, we drove out and hitched on. We were assigned to one of the food emporiums, but we'd also get to fill in on rides and booths. We helped break down the tents, packed everything up in trucks and rolled out of town in a cavalcade of misfits.

Our first stops were Huntington and Charleston in West Virginia. Gil Ickes flaked out after one day and drove home. Scott and I hung tough. We got to fill in as barkers for the World's Oldest Man exhibit. "Step right up and see the world's oldest man; only a dollar!" He was just another carnie, wrapped in a bunch of gauze. Scott even filled in as the world's oldest man. At the food booth, my job first thing every morning was to cut away the green mold on the hot dog wieners. Our favorite job was working the colored burlesque show. We helped put up their tent and tear it down. During the week, we helped inside and got to know the girls. There was a towering black man they called Big John who befriended us and watched out for us. Carnies, after all, are dirty, notorious criminal types who brandish their trademark rotten teeth, or so they say. John taught us how to survive in the tricky environment, and we started riding from town to town in a company truck with him.

Next stop was Spartanburg, South Carolina. We were old hands by now and had a certain pride in our work. Big John knew of a Negro nightclub out in the woods, and after we closed up shop on this Saturday night, we headed for the afterhours place. It was quite late when we finally got there and everybody was drunk and rowdy. The humidity was scorching and the music was just as hot. Dark-skinned women glistened under the bare light bulbs and danced with the storm. Scott and I were intentionally jostled in the frenzy and the specter grew ominous.

The scene was steamy with passionate tension and mocha shades of Dorothy Dandridge in *Carmen Jones*. This was Carolina in the segregated South. I definitely wasn't getting a warm reception. Trouble exploded, and an angry buck pulled out a Bowie knife. I never had a chance to react. Big John swept the guy up into the air like a rag doll and threw him down in a heap. John backed the crowd up with intimidating shouts, and a management type came running over to ask us to leave. We did, thank you. A couple days later, Scott decided to hitchhike home. I don't remember what I was trying to prove, but I stuck it out. From South Carolina, the carnival went up north to Scranton and then Reading, Pennsylvania. Halfway through Reading, I bailed and hitchhiked back to Grand Rapids. College would be a snap after this.

Chapter 7: Dangerous Curves

The transition to Michigan State University. Ah, I knew the drill: elementary to high school and now college. MSU has had its own transitions, starting out as Michigan Agricultural College and then Michigan State College and finally to its present moniker. Sixty miles to the east in Ann Arbor was the prestigious University of Michigan, established in 1817. Their student body still referred to MSU as a cow college, and at football games they would moo at us. Too bad, high-brows, we had the better sports teams and more students.

MSU is in East Lansing and has a beautiful campus, with the Red Cedar River running through it. It was the glorious autumn of 1957 with scarlet and gold leaves falling from grand old trees, and the red-brick buildings were covered with ivy and tradition. An eclectic student body from around the world strolled along winding walkways. There were dashing young men, high on haberdashery, and sporty guys in varsity letter jackets mingling with poodle skirted co-eds and bookish intellectual dames in horn rim glasses and tailored tweeds. There was a carillon bell tower, the Beaumont, and a statue of Sparty, which had to be protected from our rival Wolverines in Ann Arbor. We were the Spartans.

My Aunt Irene was thrilled to have me home again and thoroughly involved herself in all aspects of my orientation. I was assigned to Butterfield Hall, and we were introduced to my dormitory roommate, who was a quiet and unassuming 6 foot 9 freshman, athletic-scholarship basketball player from Chicago. Because he was the wrong color for her, my Aunt made the housing administration switch me to a white color. The replacement turned out to be Jewish, but they refused her second attempt to switch again, and I spent the year with a Judaic roommate known as "Big Deal" Dick Irwin. The basketball player never panned out as an accomplished hoopster but won marks as a gentleman and a scholar. Everything was cool. Aunt Irene delivered homemade cooking and treats to my dorm from her house in Lansing. She gave the doctors a good finger-wagging when accompanying me to the campus dispensary about my asthma and allergies. A long-time MSU booster, Irene and Uncle Leo had season seats for football games at Spartan Stadium, and soon I'd be joining them in the sporting arena. She was a steadfast champion of her pet nephew, and hell knows I needed a little help and support because I hardly knew a soul until I met the acerbic intellectual and soulful Thomas Creed Smith.

Tom Smith and his pal Carl Stellan were both from well-heeled East Grand Rapids, although their parents lived in one of the more middle-class neighborhoods. They were freshmen too and resided in Rather Hall next door. Tom was conservative; Carl was a ladies' man. Tom was an unabashed egghead; Carl was a spoiled party-boy. You'd expect I would have gravitated toward the Scott St. John type, but fortuitously I chose Tom. He was an ardent admirer of up-and-coming Republican politician Barry Goldwater and a wickedly witty political commentator and founder of the National Review, William F. Buckley.

Discovering cerebral friends was fine, but finding the girl of my dream was far more crucial. The campus abounded with thousands of attractive girls to choose from, but there was one in particular who was no less than a Vargas pin-up girl in my North Park sock drawer. I saw her near the Beaumont Tower at about the same time every day. Not that I was a stalker; I was way too shy. I was mesmerized. She was so grown up and self-confident I felt like a whelp. My mojo was way low. I could have no more approached her than run for class president or thrown my helmet into the football-captain competition. She was an aphrodisiac and a wet-dream fantasy. She wore soft, pastel sweaters that accentuated her painfully gorgeous breasts. She strode with such intriguing fluidity I kept bumping into obstacles while diligently tracking her groove. The bruises were proud battle scars.

As the frazzled freshmen shook the kinks out of their class schedules, mine eventually finalized. The news couldn't be worse. I was horrified to discover I had been dropped from basic gym and assigned to a dance class. A dance class!

I had always been a bashful wall flower at high school dances so I was a nervous mess, especially because the rest of the class had already been together for a week. I walked through the door and there she was: the Vargas dream girl, not an upperclassman as I had surmised but a freshman just like me. Her name was Margie Dormier, from Royal Oak, a suburb of Detroit, and her father worked for General Electric. Over the course of that class, I was only paired with her a couple times, but they were tantalizing slow dances. I furrowed into her golden hair, and my heart pounded out of control. She commented on my moves and smiled in a sweet way that sustained me for all those coming months I wouldn't dare to ask anybody else out on a date. Occasionally over the next term, I saw her on campus, but eventually I gave up on my dream girl. She was out of my league. I found consolation in a downtown Lansing movie theater with lines around the block to see Brigitte Bardot in Roger Vadim's *And God Created Woman*.

Tom Smith, Carl Stellan and I decided to join a fraternity. What-the-hell week. Why not? There were dozens of them. Joining a fraternity meant rushing, Hell Week and a life-time of servitude to snobby, sanctimonious golden boys with blue bloodlines and a green MSU letter sweater. The frat houses were oversized and under-supervised. Fraternity row ran the gamut from Alpha to Zeta, with popular houses like Phi Beta Kappa, Sigma Chi, and Sigma Alpha Epsilon in well-manicured neighborhoods with expensive cars parked in the driveways and "Big Men On Campus" hot shots lording it over the average blokes.

We did the tour. Carl Stellan landed Phi Delta right off the bat, but they weren't interested in us Philistines. Tom and I continued to knock on doors and finally on our third attempt, nerdy Psi Upsilon asked us to pledge. Next came the brutal Hell Week hazing. They force-fed us beer and bugs and animal guts. I threw up my own guts. We had to clean and scrub their toilets, do the dishes and dust and vacuum their twenty-room house. We had to wear humiliating signs to classes. My mind shut down, but somehow I survived. After Hell Week came the secret vote to determine which pledges would be anointed into the secret Greek society. Of the thirteen Psi U. pledges, only six had gotten this far. Frat brothers assembled and made the final choices. I was accepted; Tom Smith was not. Black-balled. Branded like a catastrophic plague. After additional secret rights mumbo jumbo that I was sworn never to reveal, I finally became official, a notable accomplishment or a culpable accomplice? Psi Upsilon was a snooty, distinguished fraternity established in 1833 with chapters in only the best schools: Princeton, Harvard, McGill, Yale and a few other Ivy-poisoned top-notch colleges. Nevertheless, it was all diminished by Tom's kick in the gut. Smitty had been a wrestler in high school and was pit-bull tough. He handled the rejection with dignity. We still had a lot of adventure in us.

I never really fit in with the Bloomfield Hills and Grosse Pointe crowd that dominated the Psi U. house, but I enjoyed the parties and got a kick out of the understated civility we exuded. We wore bowler hats, proper British black three-piece suits and carried black umbrellas. At Homecoming Week, all the other fraternities and sororities put up large ornate pageant tableaus on their front yards. It was a serious competition and the elaborate displays were junior versions of the Rose Bowl Parade. While the other Greeks vied for the prestigious Grand Trophy, charmingly Psi Upsilon traditionally hauled their little foot long sign out of the closet and stuck it into our front yard. Understated to a fault, it simply said, "Rah."

I never moved into the Psi U. house. By tradition, freshmen waited until their sophomore years. I remained at Butterfield as Tom Smith did at Rather. We ate together in the common dining area and studied together. There was piped in music, endless renditions of "Chances Are" from Johnny Mathis and Sam Cooke's "You Send Me." The school work was difficult and there wasn't that much time for play. Dorms were much stricter about rules and regulations back then. Boys and girls together in dorms were definitely prohibited. So was alcohol. There were no drugs to be concerned about. Toward the end of the second term in March of 1958, I came in possession of a GIQ 42-ounce bottle of Pfeiffer Famous Beer, probably left over from a frat party. I tied it to a bramble on the edge of the Red Cedar River and submerged it for safe keeping. A week later I retrieved the bottle to celebrate a successful exam and smuggled it up to my room. I hid it under my bed still uncapped, and of all things, the tyrannical upper classman Resident Assistant in charge of our floor did a random room check and found my Pfeiffer Famous Beer. The following morning I stood before the Dean of Students who laid down the law and informed me I was expelled from the university.

Now there was atonement to grapple with. I was the first Kiedis to ever go to college, so you can imagine how upset my father, family, friends and Aunt Irene were. I skulked home and went into hiding at 5009 Plainfield, a place I hadn't spent much time for the last couple years. My father was surprisingly subdued in his reprehension. He had finally released me to the difficult challenges of adulthood, and it was strangely bittersweet. For the first time, I realized that my ruffled childhood had in fact been a wonderful experience, and that what my dad had gone through for me was something I should have respected and appreciated more. Pop was building a new house in a new subdivision; the Kiedis family needed more room. I pitched in and helped. I used to always get the tools confused when I was little, and my Pa would blow his top. Now I was a man. He asked me to get a screwdriver, and I intentionally came back with pliers. He fell for it and started yelling. I handed him the screwdriver I was hiding behind my back. Now he felt like an idiot, and we both laughed.

That bucolic rural area I'd grown up in was now bustling with development. My old stretch of Plainfield had a shopping center, supermarkets, a drive-in movie and auto dealerships. Eileen and John Sr. had been busy from day one of their marriage raising kids. First was Cathleen, who was pretty sweet and lived a somewhat troubled life. She was sultry and dark like my dad. Cathy and I used to play in the big snow piles after we'd shoveled the gas station driveway when we were kids. The next child was Jeannie, who fell out of my dad's 1946 Dodge on the way to Uncle Jim's dentist office. She died when the suicide doors opened up on U.S. Route 16. She was only two years old and it traumatized me for life. I was too young for death and a funeral. Mary was born next. She was the new Jeannie in a way, blonde and fair. Mary turned out to be the perfect reincarnation of our lost girl. And then there was Robert, who was intense and brooding. Troubled and an alcoholic, he would die from liver cancer. Another boy followed, Thomas. Like Eileen, Tommy was Dutch fair and born religious. He would become a minister and the patriarch. I was the oldest and heir apparent but gladly abdicated. The last of the brood was Lizzy, a talented writer and photographer.

The college expelling had brought about the first bad vibe ever with my Aunt Irene. She stood with me at the Dean's office and gave him a piece of her mind, but she was very disappointed in me. It broke her heart. When she finally passed away, a part of me died too. I cried so hard at the funeral that her husband Leo accused me of overacting and told me to pipe down. I'll give her a last shout out when I go.

Scott had been in and out of trouble while I was matriculating. He came out just in time to join me on another spring break trip to Florida. I was currently carless and Scott never had one unless he stole it, so we hitchhiked out of GR and headed south. We thumbed our way into Ohio and hung out in Cincinnati for a while. We were busy chugging down Stroh's Bohemian beer at a downtown bar when we overheard something about a sin city across the Ohio River in Kentucky. Bam! We were there in a flash. Covington was the naughty place Pinocchio and his indolent friends went to and grew donkey ears. There were a dozen institutions of ill repute. Wanton women were everywhere and the drinking age was if you could crawl. We stayed for a few days. Scott had no money but got his for free, stud that he was. I declined. I was still a bit shy, especially with girls who had red, blue or gold color-coded permits of health certification.

Back on the road, we hitched a ride that came upon a railroad crossing with the barriers down for a slow-moving freight. Our car was first in line. We looked at each other and didn't have to say a word. I jumped out. Scott was right behind. We ran up to the train, got our bearings on its speed, jogged alongside until we were comfortable with our chances, looked for the first open sliding doors and finally dove face first into one of the freight cars. Off we went through a few hundred miles of Allegheny and Appalachian mountains. We gulped for oxygen at the breathtaking vistas. No stops. No food. No water. We were feverishly grasping for drips of dew falling from trees and rocks close to the tracks. The next morning, the train finally slowed down to a crawl, and we saw a big water tower with the iconic Lucky Strikes red bulls-eye. We were in North Carolina.

A few more hitches and we landed in Tampa. After commandeering a vacant yacht in a fancy marina, we set about scalding our skin with an obligatory Florida tan. In the weeks to come, we peeled 57 layers of skin and produced the impetus of a hundred future skin cancers. Then, to be even stupider, we got tattooed. In 1958, sailors and carneys and tattoo artists had tattoos. Not teenagers. But we went to the seedy tenderloin Barbary Coast of downtown Tampa and walked into the first parlor we saw. We had discussed this plan for hours on the freight train and had agreed to each get an eagle on our upper biceps. The tattoo artist came out from behind a dirty curtain and confronted us. Van Gogh managed artistry without his ear; this guy attempted his craft without fingers. He was missing all eight. Just stubs up to the knuckle were going to do this deed. Scott, the big tough guy, gulped loudly and said, "No way!" I had always been the Tonto to his Lone Ranger, the second banana to Phil Silvers and the Mortimer Snerd to Edgar Bergen. This was my moment to out-ballocks the master. I rolled up my sleeve and stuck out my arm, "An eagle please. Right here." In a few minutes I was permanently scarred with a pregnant mallard. Scott went across the street and got a professional eagle. I'd have been furious if I wasn't so preoccupied with the fourth-degree sunburn. The open ink-wound was an added shark bite, laced with lye. It would be months before I stopped peeling and 25 years before Daffy would be transfigured.

We had a hell of time getting home. Hitchhiking was in a slump. We kept ending up on deserted stretches of roads in the middle of nowhere, nowhere Alabama and nowhere Mississippi. We slept on country-church alters, scanned the highway shoulders for discarded cigarette butts and ate stolen pies cooling on window sills. And I dreamed of being home with the family—and getting back to college.

In the fall, I was readmitted to MSU. I had new curriculums, new majors and new dilemmas. I had changed majors so many times I should have known I was kidding myself. I eschewed the dorm and frat house and rented a small room off campus. By late October, my life was in a healthy routine. I was in the student union, minding my own business when out of the blue my long lost Margie Dormier dream girl sashayed by. She continued on to a nearby table and joined some girls but kept glancing over in my direction. I checked behind me and she laughed. Her come-hither looks were legitimate, beautiful, perilous looks. I mustered up the courage and walked over to her. She was all smiles and recalled our dances. I was terribly flattered. She touched me. I wanted her to pinch me. I couldn't believe this was really happening. By chance, there was a cool party that night so I got brave and asked if she'd like to go with me. Margie explained she was only in town for two more days and already had plans for tonight, a date with her ex-boyfriend. Like me, she had dropped out of school the previous year. Now she lived in Syracuse, NY, where her General Electric father had been transferred. And then she blew me away with her velour-coated purr, "What about tomorrow? It's my last night, Johnny. I'd love to spend it with you."

Shakespeare, Byron, Shelley, Keats and William Safire couldn't have put their heads together and found the words to convey how excited I was. This was unprecedented. How I managed to survive the intervening 24 hours I don't know. We had arranged a dinner rendezvous and another couple joined us. Afterwards, we went for a ride in his new '58 Chevy Impala convertible and stopped by a party. I was doing my best to satisfy the dream doll's expectations, but the pressure was so intense I almost wanted it to be over. She had a plane to catch in the morning and called for a cab back to the Jack Tar Hotel by the state capitol. We kissed goodbye, but then she extended our date by asking me to ride along in the cab. When we got to the Jack Tar, she dismissed the cab and invited me up for a night cap.

In her room, Margie put her arms around me and kissed me again. My knees where wobbling. We discussed possible future plans, and she gave me her Syracuse information just in case. We kissed goodbye again, but she stopped and said wait a minute as she dashed into the bathroom. She returned in delicate pajamas and pulled me onto her bed. Then the pajamas were gone. Now she was all blushing-pink naked with a tiny, wet bouquet of golden hair between her legs. Fragile inhibitions were tossed to a gentle breeze that was my gasp for sanity. I was in a state of apoplexy, frozen in seductive, stark terror. I'd only had sex once in my life, and that was first-time empirically clumsy. Now I was pressed against the most assured and alluring woman in the world. I was so scared my body closed down; it retreated into a tortoise shell. I literally went into shock, incapacitated and in need of resuscitation. Compassionate as a Red Cross nurse, she soothed me with her charity. I had always had a crush; now I was legitimately in love with Margie and nothing could stop me from pursuing her to the ends of the earth—or at least Syracuse. I stumbled out in a daze and fought my way home, thirty blocks at least. Screw the cab; I needed the air. The daze continued unabated; professors glowered, dogs growled and cafeteria servers grumbled. Mind blown, I was rattled, helpless and floundering in my morasses classes.

"Smith & Wesson" commiserated. Instead of writing term papers, I was composing love letters. She wrote back and gave me an A plus. The tone of her letter was pink and pretty as that night in her bed. That did it. I scoured the *Lansing Journal* want ads and bought a 1946 rusty, red Oldsmobile for $75. It burned a quart of oil every fifty miles. It had no heater. On a Friday afternoon after my last class, I drove off campus and headed for upper New York State: 500 miles, 9 projected hours and 10 quarts of oil. East Lansing to Port Huron and across the Blue Water Bridge into Ontario, Canada, to London and Hamilton and back into the USA at Buffalo and continuing on to Rochester and then Syracuse, and all in a blizzard with no heater.

I arrived unannounced at 4 a.m. Surprise! Her parents were bewildered. Margie had a sly gleam in her eye. Oh, and Margie was pregnant and the parents surmised I was the father. Surprise, me! Over the next few hours, I discovered she had been impregnated by her ex-boyfriend on that date she had the night before our date. The culprit was now long gone. Had I been man enough to perform sex on *our* date, she probably would have conceded fatherhood to me. How different the world would be. No Anthony. No RHCP band. No Blackie Dammett. No movie career. John Kiedis Jr., General Electric bourgeoisie. Mankind would have had an alternative scheme to deal with. I crashed on the couch and fell asleep.

The parents were gracious. Saturday night they took us out to dinner and Margie's foot was provocative under the table while her straight-laced father expounded on turbines and light bulbs. The Platters' "Smoke Gets in your Eyes" was playing in the background, and those soaring strings and falsetto harmonies still remind me of her. When we came home, they put me in the guest bedroom down the hall, and we all went to sleep. I was still exhausted from my drive across Canada. In the middle of the night, the bombshell snuck into my room and crawled under my covers to snuggle. Sunday afternoon, she drove us to a hotel, got a room and taught me how to make proper love. Lessons of love would define our relationship over the next year. Margie University graduated a magna cum laude stud. That night, I headed back, singing along with the The Skyliners' "Since I Don't Have You."

At State I was miserable. I quit school at the end of the term and returned to GR to help my dad at the Homburg. Mostly I was making a well-worn rut for myself on the road to Syracuse. After a couple more jaunts, the '46 Olds made one last trip and died on me. After that, I hitchhiked or took the bus. I became part of the Dormier family and would stay for a week at a time. That infamous upstate New York Snowbelt would pile up twenty, thirty feet of the white stuff. We literally had to dig a tunnel, not a path, from the front door to civilization. Snowed-in was a cozy situation for me, a roaring fireplace and all the Margie I could handle. Beyond a few pretences, we mostly went to hotels. By spring, the voracious vixen was starting to show her pregnancy, but she was still absolutely scrumptious. We were running out of hotels. Persnickety receptionists were becoming skeptical of our legitimacy. It was still the 50s and sex before marriage was illegal in many places. We checked into a new hotel and were just sitting on the bed discussing the future baby when the phone rang. It was the front desk; they wanted to know if we could show proof of marriage. A cloud strayed over our shenanigans, and soon I was back in Grand Rapids.

Spring turned into early summer. While the Dormiers went about with baby showers and appropriately decorating the spare room, I was running with my wild horses, Scott and Johnny Reaser and the rest of the Saint Hoods. We were getting too rowdy for our own good. At any given time, about a third of the herd was in one of the local detention centers; we were adults now and the long arm of the law was about to grab us by the scruff of our neck. Johnny and Scott and I rode out to Grand Haven in Reaser's old Dodge. There were plenty of sunbathers on their beach towels. We had come in street clothes but went back to the car and took off our pants. We figured our boxer shorts were close enough to a bathing suit. John and I meandered and Scott veered off. Unbeknownst to us, he scooped up an unattended wallet off a blanket when the victim was in the water. A good Samaritan observed the theft and alerted the beach. Suddenly, there was a chorus of vigilantes calling for our apprehension. John and I were caught in the middle, and as the angry mob formed, we ran away as fast as Scott did. "Stop those guys in their underwear!" There was no place to hide for the underwear gang. We split up. Scott went one way and John and I ran across the street up into the hills where all the cottages were. Word had spread like pigweed and we were soon captured, hiding under a dry dock boat. Scott managed to escape and worked his way back to town.

At the police station we explained our innocence. We ran out of fear. They replied we'd do big time in the slammer if we didn't give up the actual culprit, but we knew what Scott would do to us if we implicated him. They played good cop, bad cop. They played us against each other. They played cards while we mulled it over. We struck a deal. John wrote down Scott's first name in one room while I wrote St. John in another. Then the dirty rat coppers double crossed us with a mandated thirty days in jail. String 'em up; it's frontier justice. We went before a judge and were escorted to our unusual vacation. While the rest of the inmates were gnarly goons and itinerant beach-resort con men, we were clean-cut teenagers and became the immediate darlings of the female warden-jailer. There was one big cell with bunk bed cubicles and a bad guy count of about 20. John and I were elevated to trusties, with special privileges like Jailhouse Rock radio, working in the kitchen and piddling around in the front yard that faced the main drag. We'd wave at our astonished friends. It was embarrassing and yet kind of exciting. In fact, although it was not required, when I wrote my letters to Margie Dormier back in Syracuse, I intentionally handwrote Ottawa County Jail in the upper-left corner of the envelope as some misguided badge of honor.

The day of judgment finally arrived. John and I had to face the wrath of Scott St. John, handcuffed and shackled, on a prison bus from Grand Rapids, and for good measure and a totally different crime, Rich Klimavich. Our dimwit adventure might break out into a Jack-Warner-vendetta prison-movie. Scott and Rich were inducted and assigned a bunk cubicle next to ours. We parried, but our intellect prevailed over their thuggery. Rich's temper got him solitary confinement. We played cards like all good cons do and smoked cigarettes and swapped stories of our most heinous crimes. Then in a collision of coincidence, Jim Beard was also incarcerated. He was partial to tight leopard underwear and had no compunction about flaunting it. He was chasing me around the cell snapping me with a towel when our guardian angel warden heard the commotion and screamed, "Hey, you in the funny underpants, stop hurting Jack Kiedis!" For a while that was the cell anthem, sung with good-natured glee by the inmates and accompanied by the music of steel cups banging on the bars. It started with underwear and ended with underpants. John and I were given an early release and went back to normality—if such a stunt was possible.

I rushed to the bus depot and sprinted for Syracuse. I arrived in the most splendid disposition. I hadn't seen or heard from my girl for a long time. Unsuitably, I ran into her coming out of a neighbor's house. She hadn't been expecting me of course and was as startled as I was. She was irresistibly slim again, the Margie I had first seen strolling along the Red Cedar on campus and pouting provocatively in her flimsy pajamas at the Jack Tar Hotel. "What are you doing here?" she asked rather angrily. I told her I just got out of jail. "You better go right back," she emphatically informed me. My heart sank. She ran toward her house, and I hurried to catch up. It took all my persuasive talents to get my foot in the door. I told her I needed water or I'd faint, and I wasn't lying. Maybe her conservative parents were mortified by all the blatant county jail letters. Margie wouldn't explain. "Just go!" She pushed me out the front door with certitude. Desperate times required extraordinary measures. I might have committed suicide on a hamstrung Greyhound; I splurged and caught a rare airplane home.

I'd like to think it was all her parents' fault, and that Margie had pleaded my case with eloquence and love. And that for all the years that subsequently transpired she secretly thought of me, as I did of her. If there was a great pantheon of special girlfriends, Margie Dormier would surely be there in one of her fashionable Christian Dior outfits, flipping through the Yellow Pages for a new and exciting hotel for us to have sex in. But in truth, she probably just found another guy while I was doing time in Folsom Prison because Scott St. John stole a wallet with $13. The queen bee had given me my sex life and then banished me from the honey hive. She fucked me to death and left me to die.

8. Peccadilloes and Armadillos

In purgatory, I was a prisoner of my broken love, helpless as a crucified kitten. Sometime later I was at Johnny Reaser's house in his grandma's kitchen. Jim Beard was there too and trying to cheer me up. Beard was the squirreliest, creepiest, sneakiest and most untrustworthy guy you'd ever want to meet. So why, you might ask, did we hang out with him? Well, he had this impish-little-boy charming side too, and on this day he spoke as a prophet, "Don't worry, Jack," he said. "Someday, she'll turn on the TV and see you in a toothpaste commercial with your big white gleaming smile, and she'll be sorry." I'd like to think that was true.

John and I had dared to dream about breaking into the movies for years, and we grinned at each other with a knowing wink: our day would come. Hollywood was in our future, but first there had to be one more epic Scott St. John and Johnny Kiedis road trip. The dynamic duo bought a 1948 Pontiac for a hundred bucks and planned to recreate the great Route 66 trips our fathers took together in the 30s. We loaded up the trunk and back seat with just about everything we owned and provisions to last for months, if not forever.

Bobby Troup's 1946 "Get Your Kicks on Route 66:"

> Well if you ever plan to motor west,
> Travel my way, take the highway that's the best.
> Get your kicks on Route sixty-six.
> Well, it winds from Chicago to LA,
> More than two-thousand miles all the way.
> Get your kicks on Route sixty-six.
> Well, it goes through St. Louie,
> Joplin, Missouri.
> Oklahoma City looks oh so pretty.
> You'll see Amarillo, Gallup, New Mexico,
> Flagstaff, Arizona.
> Don't forget Winona,
> Kingman, Barstow, San Bernardino.
> Won't you get hip to this timely tip:
> When you make that California trip,
> Get your kicks on Route sixty-six.

I had traveled Route 66 with my dad from the time I was still in my mother's womb. I knew it like an atlas. The road revealed itself in all its glory one last time for me, but it was a bittersweet ride. It was its last hurrah. Route 66 had been one of the first U.S. highways, a major path of the migrants who went west. John Steinbeck called it "The Mother Road" in his novel *The Grapes of Wrath*. It enabled California to go from a desolate outpost on the Pacific to the most populous state in the Union. Now the Interstate Highway System created by President Eisenhower would change America forever and signal the beginning of the end for U.S. 66 in the late 50s. Within a few years, it would be transformed into superhighway Interstate 44 and 40. But on this day, it was all about the history as I knew and loved it.

We scraped up some cash and figured we'd work our way across the country. Secretly, I had taken my last $700 out of the bank and carefully folded the seven one-hundred-dollar bills into a small bindle and safety pinned it to my boxer shorts. Our final destination was open, but settling in the West was likely. It was a joy to see all the familiar spots. The old roadside tourist traps. The world's biggest ball of string and the alligator and armadillo emporiums were still there. So were the Navaho blankets and turquoise jewelry and the caves and meteors and oil derricks. The Stuckey's Pecan Candy Stores and Coors Beer, once you crossed into Oklahoma. Parched plains and purple mountains' majesty flaunted their grandeur. The radiator water bags tied to your grill for crossing the deserts and the signs that said "No gas for the next hundred miles." Apache, Hopi, Navaho, and Zuni pueblos dotted the landscape. The Grand Canyon and the Mojave were majestic. They lined up like postcards in a lazy trading post.

Hollywood was my destination and we did spend some time there, but Scott had his heart set on Mexico and we headed south. After a brief look-see in San Diego, we crossed into Tijuana. It definitely wasn't the crime infested, bloody drug cartel, turf war, ruthless kidnapping, car bombing, execution slaughter, doomsday city it is today. *Illegal alien* wasn't in the vernacular. There was a five minute wait to cross the border instead of the current five-mile-long lines. Today's Tijuana strangles in a cauldron of five million souls, the size of Philadelphia. In 1959, we entered a reasonably pleasant town of about 100,000 people, the size of Billings, Montana. It catered to college kids and even tried to promote a family-oriented destination. There was a colorful bull-fighting ring, dog racing and copious curio shops. The center of action was the *Avenida Revolucion*; a bustling street with several rowdy blocks of bars, nightclubs, strip clubs and if you knew the ropes, prostitution. The clubs were full of Hispanic women for varying degrees of sale, but there was a murky procedure we had no clue to. And yes, there were infamous donkey shows somewhere deep in the kinky, taboo underground. Yet there was a comical aspect to this Marx Brothers *Freedonia*. We were especially amused by the dysfunctional policemen who wore mismatched dissimilar uniforms. No uniform uniforms. We were after all, cognizant of law enforcement. The streets were full of American servicemen: sailors from San Diego and Marines from El Toro. The drinking age was much lower. To a couple of teenagers from West Michigan, this was nirvana.

We spent the first 48 hours just soaking up the flavors. We didn't sleep a wink. We liked this sinner's paradise so much we decided to make it our home and rented an apartment at the Linda Hotel, paying a month in advance. It was close to the Avenue Revolution and had parking. Occasionally, we ventured into the rest of the city, but mostly we lived on that Avenue. It was a colorful spectacle with vendors hawking their flowers, candies, ice cream treats and Mexican dog-meat tacos. Infants were pushing gum for a penny. Everywhere you looked, there were old blue-and-white Chevrolet taxis, with drivers beckoning tourists to come take a ride: 25 cents. It was plastered all over town. After a couple weeks, Scott got frustrated with the dancehall-dame game, so one festive evening we took up the cab proposition to see what all the fuss was about. We flagged down a four-door '52 Chevy and climbed into the back seat. A second man appeared out of nowhere and hopped into the passenger seat. It was two on two. There was a short dissertation, and as we had suspected it was all about sex. Fasten your seat belts; it's going to be a Bette Davis drive.

The Chevy staggered off and in minutes we were out of the city. They didn't speak much English, and it was impossible to know what the hell we were getting into. The paved road turned into a dirt road which turned into tire tracks through a seemingly never-ending field of bad dreams. Jounced and jostled, we eventually pulled into a mowed area around a rundown barracks. Los hombres motioned us toward the ramshackle structure. *Not in a million years* was my assessment, but Scott strode bravely toward the building. I just hung around, looking at my watch and feeling very uneasy. I still had that sacrosanct venture capital pinned to my underwear.

The driver wandered over and conveyed some bad news. It would cost us $10 apiece to be driven back to the city. It was futile to argue the original 25-cent contract. I was afraid they'd just keep jacking up the price, and we were obviously at their mercy. In fact, I had a much more ominous intuition. While the taxi dudes gabbed, I looked around for a defensive weapon, found a fist-size rock and surreptitiously slid it between the back seat cushions, just in case. Scott came out smiling and I explained the new deal. That turned his smile upside down, and he got into a shouting match with Heckle and Jeckle. I intervened and proposed a solution. Take us halfway back and we'll give you ten; when we get almost to town, we'll give you the other ten. We just don't want you to keep raising the price. They agreed.

As we had been positioned on the way out, I was behind the driver and Scott behind the co-pilot. We had only driven about a mile, and they asked for their first installment. We insisted that wasn't even close to halfway. A little angry farther on, they asked again and we just waved them on. The anxious co-pilot pulled out a knife and waved it around menacingly. Scott's tripwire temper hit Pancho so hard blood splattered on the dashboard. The astonished driver, still trying to navigate the bumpy field, reached around and wildly fired a small-caliber pistol into the backseat, without actually aiming at anything in particular. One shot. The gunpowder stung my eyes and nose. The sudden shock paralyzed me for a second. Scott yelled, "Bail!" And he promptly dove out his back door. He hit the heavy-grass cow-pasture trail and bounced a couple times like a cartoon character.

As I swiveled to follow his trajectory through the back window, I saw him rapidly diminish in size as we continued driving. But wait! The normally callous Scott St. John, realizing I was still in the Chevy and heading for disaster, jumped up and was running back toward the car. He was chasing the Chevy. As he had done, I yanked on my door handle, but it jammed and then actually fell off. To buy a moment so I could slide across to Scott's door, I blurted out a white lie: "He's got $700 on him." The driver hit the brakes and started to do a U-turn. I scrambled across the seat and jumped out just as Scott came running up. Bursting into the surrounding fields with the timely assist of adrenaline, we bound over barbed-wire fences and thorny thickets like cheetahs.

We finally reached the edge of town and saw the refuge of a well-lit liquor store where we figured to be safe. Huffing and puffing, we staggered in. Scott saw blood on my face, and there was a dime-size divot on the bridge of my nose. I had been nicked by the ricocheting bullet. As we were effusively celebrating our incredible luck, a battalion of mismatched policemen came running in with a raised menagerie of artillery and headed straight at us. "Hand's up!" Again we couldn't help but smirk at the preposterous Tijuana uniforms. But this time, we were confronted by a menacing mob of these Keystone Cops. I expected to see Charlie Chaplin saunter in and hear Mack Sennett yell "Cut!" Instead and in charge was a captain, wearing something like a Pakistani airline pilot. Second in command was an agitated drum major. One in blue could have been a theatre usher. Props to the Afrika Korps khaki-clad Rommel with a Pancho Villa mustache. Officer Krupke. An Eagle Scout. And finally, Sergeant Pepper. The Village People were back-up. On their starched shoulders were a symphony of epaulets, Teutonic brushes, a chip, dandruff and a talking parrot. The *Comisaria de Policia* must have procured their monkey suits at a film-studio wardrobe-fire-sale. The dipsy dingbats topped it off with an assortment of caps, hats, mats and a plutocrat. The two unscrupulous cab drivers were animatedly explaining their version of the events, and the constabulary was in agreement that we were abject criminals. As proof positive, they waved around the rock I had pushed behind the back seat. In the heat of battle I had forgotten all about it. I wouldn't forget the Tijuana Jail.

Curiously, one of the biggest hit songs of the year was a silly ditty *The Tijuana Jail* by folk-music sensations The Kingston Trio. For a while, everybody was humming the catchy melody and smiling at the lyrics. Folk was a big fad in the late 50s, and The Kingston Trio were the Beatles of the genre. At Michigan State, you couldn't escape their #1 hit *Tom Dooley*. Scott and I, however, were singing the blues. The Tijuana Jail was a medieval prison right out of Victor Hugo's *Les Miserables*. We were perfunctorily processed by sleepy guards and taken to an abysmal dungeon with stone walls and a dirt floor, sparsely covered with straw. No windows. No perspective. No toilets. You went on the floor. You slept on the floor. The menu was bread and water and primordial soup. There were dirty scummy rag-a-muffins that looked like they'd been in there for years. An American sailor cautioned us to take turns sleeping to protect each other from the other inmates. Neither of us dared to sleep.

The next morning a guard yanked us out of the dark ages. We were released without a lot of fanfare and told to leave Mexico immediately. Of course we didn't. I wanted to say goodbye to my favorite nightclub senorita, so we drank *cervezas* all day and waited for her night shift. Instead of going directly north into California, we headed east on a dusty Baja California road toward Mexicali, where we finally rejoined the States near Yuma. We had a loose plan to head for the Florida Keys and Cuba.

We hugged the Arizona border and drove east, migrated through a sliver of New Mexico, into Texas and finally back across the Mexican border into Ciudad Juarez. Scott got a second tattoo but no trouble. In fact, we didn't get arrested again until Miami, although Scott did break into a house in Albuquerque, and skipped out on an auto repair shop in Beaumont, while an angry mechanic waved our unpaid bill and chased the rehabilitated Pontiac down a lonesome Texas road. There was idle debauchery in New Orleans and a diligent donnybrook in the Florida panhandle. We made it out to Key West but discovered Fidel Castro had deposed Batista, and Cuba was now out of bounds.

We settled for Miami, which was relatively quiet and unassuming then. The North wasn't in dire straits, Miami Beach was. The future rust belt was blue steel then. Florida was just a vacation destination and a place to stash the elderly. There were no major-league sports teams. The only Disney Park was in California. The art deco hotels were in disrepair. The spectacular Fontainebleau was the lone jewel, and we hung around the lobby, winking at wealthy women but went home to our cheap motel in downtown Miami. Like Robin Hoods, we figured food was fair game and made off with some from a home in Miami Beach. The police pulled us over on the causeway and were suspicious our grocery bags weren't from Kroger. They took a look and found an open catsup bottle and a half eaten pot roast. We were toast. Justice was fast. It was the big main Miami jail with some pretty tough customers. Again we got off easy and left town. Next stop New York City.

Poetic justice held us up for our pound of flesh. In the Big Apple, we parked our Pontiac near Time Square to go sightseeing. When we returned, a window was broken and the contents gone. I had left Grand Rapids with a car full of my life's stuff. Now they had it. We had it too; it was time to go home.

In Campbell, Ohio, we were still hungry and raided another kitchen. While we were cooking, the front door opened and the owner arrived. We jumped out the sink window and waited until the coast was clear. Idiots, we had parked right next door. We tiptoed to our getaway car and were about to start it up when the stealthy four-man Campbell Police Department jumped out of the bushes and arrested us. That made three jails for the trip. This one was kind of cute actually, a row of six cells in a neat and tidy jailhouse. The jailor was a Don Knotts kind of guy who played checkers with us. For the entire time, we were the only prisoners. Our sentence was eight days, but the victim himself came to visit us and asked for our clemency. The city of Campbell released us.

Ohio to Michigan; in another six hours we were home. We had traveled over 8,000 miles, and my Holy Grail bindle was still intact. It was my nest egg for the next chapter of my life.

Connie & Alan at the Whisky 1971.

Chapter 9: Not for the Faint of Heart

Except for the three arrests, Scott got away with murder on our North American tour. He struck often and proficiently. But back in familiar territory, the Grand Rapids Police knew his modus operandi and had his fingerprints on file. Here, Scott had bungling burglar buddies to craft dopey capers. While I was looking for a job, he was looking for trouble and he found it. Ninety days in the county jail for a nighttime burglary of a machine shop business; dramatically, they came through a skylight.

With my pesky underwear financing, I rented a room on Cherry Street in the trendy area of Eastown. Suddenly I felt all grown up. My real mom came for dinner and provided the kitchenware. My domicile was one of two residences on the second floor above an antique store. They were both former business offices, and their front doors had large pebbled-glass windows. Two lesbians lived in the other flat, which was a rare curiosity in those days. I don't know if it was coincidental, but that area is now an openly proud lesbian neighborhood that may have had its very birth with those pioneering women.

Johnny Reaser helped christen my high-decibel party-pad when he wasn't at school in Ann Arbor. Not surprisingly, we got a few complaints from the lesbians across the hallway. Wrapped in only a towel, John wanted revenge and rattled their fragile door. He kept banging on it until they answered and were confronted by his masculinity. Not intimidated, the girls chased him back across the hall toward my door which I had shut either in fear for myself or as a joke on John. He was running for his life, couldn't stop in time and crashed right through my window. John was in stitches; the landlord wasn't laughing either.

On a particularly auspicious evening, I heard about a party at Shane Logie's in nearby East Grand Rapids, and drove over to check it out. It was crowded with high school and college kids, and I caught a glimpse of a petite cutie that flashed by and disappeared down a hallway. There was something special about her and I pursued. Little white moccasins and a wave of dark hair left a trail for my mind to follow as she glided into the next room and out of my vision. I struggled to thread my way through the crowd but she was gone. Up and disappeared. I went back to the scene of the crime and asked around. Shane Logie herself responded to the clues. "Peggy Noble. Goes to Central." Shane's kid brother John Logie would go on to become Mayor of Grand Rapids.

On further sleuthing, I discovered this Peggy girl's address was 143 Plymouth Avenue, near my childhood home on Fulton Street. I got slicked up and went to her house. It was average: white with red brick trim. I skipped up the stairs with apprehension and butterflies. My life was on the line. This could be it. I knocked and she came to the door, a bobby-sox school girl with big brown eyes and a swell smile. She had "Cutest Girl in Class" written all over her, and it was verified in the Central High School yearbook. (Peggy recently reminded me that my original response was, "Look who they had to choose from.") On her porch, I unload the charm. Brilliantly, I opened with, "Do you know who I am?"

to which she replied with a quizzical smile, "You're either Scott St. John or Jack Kiedis. I can't tell you two apart." And then she invited me in.

Once again the course of modern history was preserved. There was a certain cachet to being the last one married, the confident cocky bachelor. But now with Scott up the river and Reaser busy at Michigan, maybe I should settle down and be the first to marry. Peggy was a cachet of her own and too special to lose. However, there was one problem: Margaret Elizabeth was the most popular girl in school and had a gymnasium full of suitors, including Dennis Davis, the star basketball player at Central. No small obstacle for me; he was All-City, all cool, all handsome and all cloaked in a new political ideology of equality for all—he was black. Technically he was still colored; black as in *Black is Beautiful* was still a decade away.

Peggy turned out to be quite a rebel herself. She was into James Brown when the Godfather of Soul was still a fresh face new kid on the block. This was 1959. The landmark Civil Rights Act wasn't passed until 1964. Martin Luther King, Jr. wouldn't lead the March on Washington and deliver his "I Have a Dream" speech until 1963. In her own sweet way, Peggy was an early advocate for racial equality in America. I had always taken it for granted. My rock and blues had germinated in black cotton fields and big city ghettos. Royce Reynolds, the only Negro at Creston, had been a buddy. I confronted serious impediments to date the McGee sisters. Big John the carnival worker was my soulmate. I had always been color blind, but Peggy inspired a more tangible commitment. I was proud of her, and I was convinced this was the girl for me. Yet in order to win her, I'd have to defeat an adversary who was black.

Peg had a kooky family. She was the youngest and the only child still living at home. Her athletic father, William Noble, had worked at Michigan Bell Telephone for decades. He was a saint. Mom was on the cranky side and much more critical of Peggy's behavior, and of me. I wasn't exactly a big fan of hers either. The siblings, starting from the oldest, began with an astringent piano teacher named Polly, who had some of that cranky streak. Brother Bill was the black sheep, a ne'er do well trouble maker. Sweetheart sister Mickey was closest to Peg. She had all the qualities of their dad and was married to a terrific guy named Donald Dunkelberg. They were so cool I definitely wanted in. And finally there was her sister Katie, a hell raiser who'd married early and lived on the wild side with a bundle of babies. It was Katie who facilitated our secret fooling-around refuge in their laundry utility room.

Her side masterminded the wedding. They were Noble Catholics so I had to attend indoctrination classes with Monsignor O'Reilly for god's approval. Somehow, I slipped through the cracks of the confessional. Other than that, I didn't have much to do. I picked Scott as my best man. Dan Van Dyke and John Reaser were groomsmen. My sister Judy was one of the bridesmaids. We sent out invitations and rented their Catholic Church. We also rented our own apartment #4 at 536 Lyon St. NE in the Heritage Hill district, and transferred my Eastown gear and her bridal shower gifts into the makings of a cozy crib. We splurged on a high-end console TV, like every husband is entitled to. I was finagling for "just the right spot" to place it, got testy about a wrong spot, slammed my fist into the front door and broke my right hand.

Finally, on July 2, 1960, seventeen-year-old Margaret Elizabeth Noble and twenty-year-old John Michael Kiedis walked down the aisle and tied the Gordian knot. I guess it went all right. My right paw was in a bulky cast, so Scott helped me put the ring on her finger. My life passed before me like it does when you're dying. My Mollie Mom and my Eileen Mom and my dad and my family and friends and all of Peggy's near and dear got emotional. We cut the cake and got drunk and opened gifts. Dad managed to get into a bit of a ruckus with his long-time adversary Scott St. John, and even Marty Lipp and Johnny Reaser had to sidestep his glares. A family friend lent us their new top-down 1960 Ford convertible for our ceremonial drive off with the tin cans, old shoes and a "JUST MARRIED!" sign. Due to my handicap, Scott had to drive. Peg and I waved from the back seat like a couple politicians. For the honeymoon, we drove our own car to not-so-exotic South Haven on Lake Michigan. We had a doily-drenched tourist room at a bed and breakfast endorsed by the little-old-lady society. We had our first argument and left early.

Now it set in. Life. We were two unprepared youngsters playing house. I battled a smorgasbord of mundane jobs: golf-club factory, truck driver, accountant, used-car hawker, machine shop, salesman and astronaut. I truly felt sorry for Peggy; I wasn't prepared for this endeavor by a long shot. We struggled and went to a lot of movies. I took Peg to see Alfred Hitchcock's shocking *Psycho*. She was genuinely frightened, which surprised me. Our assumptions could no longer be taken for granted; my new partner had her own states of confusion. Misguided and a jerk, when we got back home I dug out an old scary Halloween mask, put it on and almost gave her a heart attack. She hated me for days. I felt the bitter cold shower of alienation. It wasn't easy being married.

Her parents missed her and probably wondered how this had all happened so fast. I think we all did. Peggy dearly loved her dad, and his health was declining. Less than two months after the wedding, he died. The funeral was traumatic, and I was already a confirmed funeral-hater. My fragile wife had to deal with macabre receptions and grieving lines of mourners. I took a break and walked around the block. I passed a sports-car dealership, and there on the floor was a shiny new metallic-blue Austin-Healey 3000 from England. I knew the car because Barb Folkersma and her now ex-husband Denny Shookman had a Healey 100, which I thought was the coolest car in town. Their marriage had been a well-chronicled train wreck, but they survived and actually thrived in divorce, which was encouraging. I took Peg to the showroom to cheer her up and a week later we bought it.

The Healey became our first baby: sleek, fast and only $91.79 each month in payment. We polished and pampered it. I raced it at Grattan Race Course against Triumphs, MG's, Alphas and Corvettes. Rich Klimavich was my pit crew. With all that muscle, I was drawn into street races too. A nightrider Chrysler 300 fatefully challenged me and lost. Vindictive, *she* turned off her headlights and T-boned me on a dead man's curve. The Healey flipped on its side but kept me secure. The sore loser's face was shattered by the arbitrating windshield. I visited her in the hospital but she was muzzled.

Time passed like molasses. I woke up to 10 below zero, a porous sports car encased in ice and a lobotomy job to go to. Breakfast was bleak, and the Miracles were singing "Shop Around" on the radio over our little kitchen table. The honey moon had set; moribund pushed aplomb out of bed. The cupboards were anorectic. Anxiety thrived in the medicine cabinet. Gradually, I was drawn back to my pre-wedding buddies. I returned to familiar bars and Snook's Billiards in the basement of the Cody Hotel, where pool shark Ace St. John could steal with legal skills for a change. Dynamically reunited, we ran around with the ex-factor Barb and Denny, and they introduced us to The Black and Tan nightclub where cool cats played jazz and smoked marijuana in the back parlor. Perilously, I mingled with the pungent scent of reefer madness. Peggy thought the whole thing stunk.

Barb Folkersma still had her infamous lair on Turner Avenue. Scott was dating Barb, and her attractive divorcee-best-friend Shirley Davis was frequently at the apartment. For better or worse, she was especially admired for her derriere. She was also scrumptiously intelligent and sincere. Since I was often with Scott, and he was often with Barb, by simple proximity I was often with Shirley Davis—too often for Peggy.

One night we were at the apartment having drinks and dancing around to Maurice Williams' new doo-wop hit, "Stay …just a little bit longer." Just a little too longer for Peggy. It was late and she decided to confirm her suspicions. Out with the girls earlier, she had the Healey that night and drove over to confront the four of us, as a couple of couples. The confrontation was brutal. She slandered my integrity, and dashed backed out. I chased her with apologetic excuses, but she beat me to the car and revved up for battle. Waving my white-flag arms, I stood my ground and dared her not to run me over. Peggy never hit the brakes. The collision threw me on the hood, then splat against the windshield, onto the roof and finally onto the street in a bloody pile of retribution. Peg just kept going. I got no sympathy and retracted my apology.

Scott and I continued to indulge at our playhouse, and within a month the unthinkable was thought. When we arrived one afternoon, Barb was in the kitchen whipping something up to eat, and Shirley was sleeping in Barb's opulent Felliniesque bedroom. I was told to go wake her up. Stretched out in a delicate wisp of sheer fabric, she rolled over and smiled. Seduced by a flick of her finger, she pulled me down. Her reputation was roundly in place. I was swallowed up and consumed. Shirley got pregnant and eventually went to Denver, not for an abortion but to have the baby, as was the custom of the day. She gave birth to a male, who was adopted by an unknown family. I have a murky memory of a hot summer night sometime after the birth and adoption. I don't think she ever realized how much I cared for her, but I was married and there was no exit. Shirley wasn't just an incredibly sexy girl; she was the mother of my child. It would be thirty years before I would find resolution and closure.

In 1960, a new show called *Route 66* debuted on CBS and rocked the ratings. Created by Academy Award winner Stirling Silliphant, it starred Martin Milner and George Maharis as two friends traveling around America in their Corvette sports car, finding a new adventure each week. There were 116 episodes, and I saw every one of them, except when I was on Route 66 imitating them. Nine months into our rocky marriage, I convinced my wife to let her brazen husband and Johnny Reaser to drive the Austin-Healey to Hollywood so we could crash the movies, get rich and famous and, along the way, have those same cool adventures. John had a crush on Annette Funicello, the star Mouseketeer on the *Mickey Mouse Club*, and he was determined to find her in LA. Recently, she had graduated to starring in the beach- blanket-bingo movies with Frankie Avalon.

Like the cool guys on *Route 66* with our Barracuda jackets, crew cuts and sports car, we headed for California via my favorite pipeline. It never got old for me, and I enjoyed introducing John to the Westward Ho experience. In LA, we rented an apartment on Hollywood Boulevard and Gower. They said Rock Hudson was discovered by talent scouts as he postured on the hood of his car. We tried that too. While we were at it, John kept his eye out for Annette Funicello. No luck with either, but we did bump into Frankie Avalon coming into PJ's, a famous nightclub on Santa Monica Boulevard, where Trini Lopez got his start. When I say bumped I mean literally, and Frankie wanted an apology. We had a little scuffle, and then his entourage separated us and off they went. That was as close as we got to stardom, although we did meet an agent who invited us up to his Hollywood Hills home, promising an audition. He plied us with liquor, sharp knives and a possible Cyrano de Bergerac festival. We woke up in the middle of the night to the smell of natural gas and his oven flame on. It was all too weird and we split. LA was more than we could handle, and we had another option. Barb's ex-hubby Denny now lived in San Diego.

We headed south. Denny lived at a seashell-laden beach pad in Ocean Beach, right on the Pacific. There were party-animal beach bums crashing everywhere, and we fell right into the wild vibe. Denny had his own folk music trio, and John had a pretty good voice so they offered him a spot in the band. Soon they were playing gigs, even performing at the world famous Hotel del Coronado. I wrote letters to Peggy but got no response. I think she had a mole in our beach house because she found out I was socially dating. Finally, a sliver of news arrived and it was shocking: Peggy was dating too. The nerve of her! The kicker was he had a pet monkey perched on his shoulder. I was indignant and hastily packed my stuff in the Healey and drove home by myself at an average speed of 100 MPH. I went from San Diego to Grand Rapids in less time than one of Reverend Bykema's sermons.

I had been gone for so long Peggy had moved to a new and unimproved apartment. It was dreary and inhospitable. And so was I. The monkey guy had been blown out of proportion according to Peggy. I suggested we move to California, where there were orange groves, warm beaches and cool people. Amazingly, she accepted, but just short of San Diego we broke up again. What would transpire next was a dizzying scenario of several moves back and forth between Michigan and California. Peggy stayed in Oceanside and I continued down to Ocean Beach. She rented a room, found a job and bought a mustard yellow 54 Plymouth with her mom's help. After too many his-and-her jealousies, we moved back home, driving the Healey and Plymouth in tandem.

The silliness continued in Michigan, and this time it was Peggy who took the Super Chief train to San Diego and moved into the folk music trio turned quartet. I rented a small bachelor apartment in GR and was back with Scott St. John. Having heard Peggy was hazardously close to Denny Shookman, I was angry, embarrassed and on a plane to California. I put on my best self-deprecating humility and managed to extricate her from his clutches. Peggy's take: "Again, you heard I was dating Denny and you flew to California to rescue me. We took the damn, freezing Greyhound bus all the way back to Michigan, arriving on February 3, 1962—the day I became pregnant with Tony boy."

It was a miserable ride. Not a great way to restart a romance. From the Grand Rapids bus depot, we dragged ourselves up to my pad in the Hill District. We dropped our suitcases and spontaneously made up for six months separation by fornicating all over the apartment. On the Murphy bed, off the Murphy bed, in the folded-up-in-the-wall Murphy bed, under the weather, over the rainbow, in the shower and kitchen sink and on the pile of luggage covered with Route 66 stickers, in an orgy of wild sex unique in all our union. We picked up the marriage sticks and got back on track. It was like the good old days again. I made up for lost time with my mother. Her husband got me a job at AMI, making jukeboxes. Mollie and Ted were drinking excessively, and there was a whiff of tragedy on the horizon. Peg worked as a legal secretary and brought in the premium bacon. My dad had mellowed with age. The gang was intact, and we still had the Healey.

Chapter 10: Anthony Kiedis Was Born Here

There was a new, lively bar scene on Bridge Street now, and it was anchored by Bob Sullivan's Shamrock Bar. This was our new spot. Hustlers made a living wage, working the pool tables. Out-of-town rock bands played on a tiny stage and drew a new pool of ladies. Although I had for the most part hung up my dukes, there was a night at the Shamrock that a timid, former high-school buddy approached me and said some bully was shaking him down. I felt like the Godfather. I was all spiffy in a pristine suit but went over and decked the offender anyway. He was out cold for ten minutes. Among the ringside viewers was an eighteen-year-old whippersnapper with fake ID named Dave Weaver. My lethal punch left an indelible impression on the young man, as he would on me in the years to come. Another interested viewer was the boss, Bob Sullivan, who tackled me and wrestled me outside into the snow banks. As he was the owner of my favorite nightclub, I stayed carefully on defense only. Bob was an outstanding athlete and at last we called a truce; I was 86'd for 30 days. The Shamrock threw a welcome back party when I finally returned. The GRPD busted me with an open beer in the parking lot, and I celebrated the night in jail.

Our home sweet home and the Shamrock were both in the path of new interstate freeways in GR, so we moved to a duplex on Franklin and Eastern. This was the no foolin' hood. With a little love and persistence, Peggy and I had accomplished detente, and soon enough we discovered she was pregnant. My dad had sold the Homburg and taken up real estate; he started looking for our own home. For now, we were copacetic with a local grocer, a gas station and a barber, right across the street.

Like most American men, I went almost every week to get my sides clipped around the ears. It was standard procedure. When I was a kid, I always had something daring like a flat top or a Mohawk or a ducktail, but now haircuts were routine and today I was due. I sat down to wait my turn and shuffled through the movie magazines. It suddenly dawned on me that celebrities didn't shave around *their* ears. Clipped may be practical, but why should main street look the fool? I'd prefer to escape the darkened theater and enter the spotlight. The robotic barber interrupted my train of thought: "NEXT." I said no thanks and walked out. I decided to stop cutting my hair. Jack Kerouac's "Beat Generation" and Herb Caen's "beatniks" were a tiny minority in 1962, and I was only vaguely aware of either. I wasn't being philosophical; my inspiration was vanity. I was one aspiring-step closer to chasing my actor's tail, and in the manhunt I would find yet another new me.

My dad found us a sweet-pie hunk of heaven in the suburb of Cascade: 825 Argo Street SE. We bought it on a land contract, which didn't require much of a down payment. The monthly costs were manageable. The baby was gestating, and we added a Norwegian elkhound named Panzer. What could possibly go wrong? Well, for one thing my old buddies seemed to be drifting away. Scott was illusive and Reaser had hooked up with Dave Nadowski, a dashing dentistry student we called Zeus. I was jealous and missed the action. On a rare night off from domestic bliss, I ran into my old friend Tom Smith from Michigan

State. Married now, he suffered the inevitable connubial issues. I admitted them too, and about that time I started to get eye-winking compliments on my long, slicked black hair. It was no coincidence that sexy sweethearts were asking for my phone number. I was no longer just Scott's sidekick. No longer just one half of the Dynamic Duo, I was...

An idiot! A month before the baby was due, Scott and I got in trouble. Who'd a thunk it?! I was a reluctant lookout with one eye on the wrong tomato. We were sentenced to a stint at the Kent County Jail. A few days into our incarceration, the Cuban Missile Crisis unfolded. The Soviet Union and the United States were on the brink of war. Nuclear annihilation was imminent. The sky was falling. Chicken Little and sitting ducks were all in a claustrophobic death row. Outside the wall, citizens were glued to TV and radio. In the desperate dark, we were deprived of current updates. We had nowhere to hide, nowhere to run. In the end Khrushchev and Kennedy and all the king's men put sanity back together, barely averting total obliteration.

I finally made it out of Sing Sing and back in time to do what every dad must do: run to the grocery store in the middle of the night for strawberry ice cream and pickles. Peggy was big and had anxieties to match. She had morning sickness and afternoon ill-temper and evening discontent. She had her own jealous support team. Girls' stuff. And I was the odd man out. I had always struggled to be a husband; I juggled the self-help textbooks but never make the grade. Now the kid who swore to never grow up was about to be a father. I missed my careless freedom. When it got unbearable, I went back to my rowdy pals for consolation. The treacherous conjugal transition to responsibility and commitment was always being derailed by my own heart of darkness.

It was close to crunch time, and Peg sent out a search and rescue. I was at a bowling-alley lounge, hunkered down with my own support team. Both contingents girded for the event and descended on St. Mary's hospital, but the wise guy baby wasn't cooperating. I know I left at least once. Zeus borrowed and then crashed the Healey, and I had to get it towed. Hours passed and attrition thinned the ranks. Back in the interminable waiting room, I paced and waged war with the clock. Eventually, I curled up on a couch and fell asleep. A nurse woke me at 4:30 a.m. on November 1, 1962, to announce the messiah had been wrapped in swaddling and was christened Anthony Kiedis. We had haggled incessantly over our boy's name. I wanted something cool like Clark Gable Kiedis or Courage Kiedis. Peggy wanted John Michael Kiedis Junior. In the end we compromised. I suggested Anthony after my father's father Anton Kiedis. It was a tribute to my Pa and an olive branch to my lifelong nemesis. Despite our endless warfare, I dearly loved my dad, and together we toasted euphoria. Peggy was amenable to Anthony, but again we couldn't agree on a middle name. I wanted Courage, she wanted John or Michael. We were at a nine-month stalemate. No middle name then.

I held my son, passed out cigars and watched the new mommy beam with pride. She was still a baby herself. Her joy was briefly interrupted when I pointed out the wrecked Healey in the parking lot across the street from her window. I was in the doghouse again, but the new pup was king. Whatever we did or did not do from that moment on was somehow beyond us, as though fate itself was Anthony's parent. There was a special destiny assigned to this child. Peggy and I would stumble along the way, especially me. But our little Tony survived and thrived.

Peggy called him Tone. We put to use his baby gear. Visitors came. Panzer acclimated. Snow fell. The bundle of jubilant bliss persisted for a time, but soon we smelled the baby breath of postpartum depression. I was depressed because she was depressed. At a time we should have been ecstatic we were melancholy. Even the Healey was down and out; it never really recovered from the smash up. It sat in the garage and never left, but Peggy and Tony did.

My father was moving to Florida: himself, Eileen, Cathy, Mary, Robbie, Tommy and Liz. Even Judy, a nurse at St. Mary's, would join them. The family had been going to Florida every winter for as long as I can remember. Now it was permanent. My parents were aware of Peggy's and my marital dysfunction, and they quietly asked Peggy if she wanted to go with them. She secretly agreed. Her own mother had already moved to California. The Kiedis clan left on New Year's Day. They left me with a problematic future.

Almost as if by cue, Thomas Creed Smith called me and relayed his own sad tale. His wife had been cheating on him. She left him and Tom was disconsolate. They had a nice home in Lansing, two cars, high-society memberships and the proverbial good life. Tom was so embarrassed he wanted to escape as far as possible. He came to my house to discuss a proposition. We sat down at my now empty kitchen table. He wanted me to join him on the adventure of a lifetime. Move to Paris, France. Get jobs and live happily ever after.

What? In 1963 average Joe's like me just didn't up and go to France, much less move there, but he had it all figured out. This was the era of the mighty RMS Queen Mary and her sister ship the RMS Queen Elizabeth, the SS United States, and the newest and most spectacular luxurious ship on the seas, the SS France. Its 1962 maiden voyage carried French film stars, aristocracy and even the Mona Lisa. And now, add to that illustrious manifest… us nomadic drifters.

I left our house to the wild, or to whoever held the land contract. I left my exhausted Austin-Healey asleep in the garage. We were dead serious about starting a new life in a faraway land. We purchased a two-person cabin passage on the next available voyage from New York to Le Havre, France. Tom's white-collar job at Ford arranged a car for our drive to Manhattan. We were going forever and packed accordingly: suitcases, books, golf clubs, typewriters—the works. Excitement was palpable as we charged up the gangway onto this magnificent ship, docked on the Hudson River. The SS France was the longest passenger ship ever built. It was the second-fastest. It was the most technological. It was as if we were boarding the Titanic.

For the pride of the French Line, everything had to be the finest; the palatial ballrooms and spectacular dining rooms and movie theaters and dance clubs and swimming pools and endless decks and miles of hallways and hundreds of cabins were only a mere taste of the experience. The mystique was thick as the cigar smoke in the men's club. There were 2,000 passengers and a crew of 1,300. Our sacred destination was Paris, and many of the passengers were à la française. Sophisticated, libertine ladies gallivanted about in haute couture and waved goodbye to their cowardly landlubbers.

At last the tugboats pulled the pride of Charles de Gaulle away from the dock, and we set off across the Atlantic Ocean. And right from the start, people were either liking or hating my long hair. Girls were smiling. Elders were outraged. There was one other young man who had long hair. He was English and very bohemian. Between the two us we ruled the ship like swashbuckling buccaneers.

It was a five day journey across the sea, and on the second day I met a beautiful French girl in her early twenties, who was married to a New Jersey policeman. She was going home to Paris on vacation to see her parents, without the husband. Being French, she was born sexy. She exuded sexy. Even her name Babette was sexy. We clicked and it was lovely lust at sight. In her cabin, she stripped down to reveal genuine French lingerie and my jaw dropped. I had never seen anything like her. I was dazed and amazed, and unlike the first time with Margie Dormier, I knew what to do. We spent most of the voyage together and made plans to meet in Paris at a park near her mother's house.

Tom worked on his poetry. He had been a gifted writer at State and now looked forward to a life on the Left Bank of the Seine. Tom was brilliant, but his sanity was fragile like that of any good artist. He had his foibles and conflicted insecurities. His temper was often violent, but nobody bolstered my intellect like Smitty. Not my most scholarly educators or the most acute political pundits taught me as well as the man with the common name and the uncommon talent to inspire.

The night before our arrival in South Hampton we were too excited to sleep. From the deck, we watched the fog disperse and the sandy hills of England's southern coast emerge in the early morning light. It was our first sight of another world. A few hours later our ship crossed the English Channel to Le Havre, where we caught a train to Paris. We rolled into the Gare du Nord and then taxied to La Rive Gauche. We were in the belly of the beast: Boulevard Saint-Germain and Boulevard Saint-Michel. We found a flat, smack dab in the middle of this caldron of art and poetry and amour. Our new home was at 19 Rue Monsieur Le Prince, right above the street, with a window that overlooked the Odeon Metro Plaza. We were a couple blocks from Notre Dame, the Seine, sidewalk artists and beatniks with long hair like me. I was in the City of Light, the town of Napoleon, Picasso, Kandinsky, Renoir, Matisse, Hemingway, Fitzgerald, the Hunchback, Louis XIV, Belmondo, Bardot, Godard, Camus, Sartre and Saint-Laurent. It easily lived up to its boast as the most beautiful city in the world.

My sexy French sweetheart Babette failed to meet me at the park. Hopeful, I returned to the rendezvous location again, but she never came. Still, it was romantic to be waiting for a lover in Paris who left me to cry. I was Charles Boyer or Jean Gabin, steely in the face of a broken heart, and anyway soon a new romance struck. She was running up the stairs of the Odeon Metro Station and continued across the busy streets in a big hurry. She was tall and lanky and very pretty—and very young. I chased her down and used my English to get her attention. She stopped, a bit amused by this American. I explained my story; she was fascinated. We went for a drink at a café. She was a high-school student and lived in a far southern suburb. She was affectionate so I took her to our flat. Tom was at the kitchen table, struggling with his poetry and chewing on a pencil. The seductive school girl and I went directly into the bedroom, which was quite nice. Within seconds she had undressed and we were having sex. Just like that. Just like we had been taught the French were. Our bathroom was out in a common hallway, so afterward the still naked beauty washed up out of a glass of water and then realized she had lost one of her fake eyelashes. She frantically tossed the sheets and covers about but couldn't find it which made her very angry, and she left in a huff. I was so smitten by her I twice took the train to her town south of Paris and hung around outside the school hoping to find her, but… Zut alors!

For a while Tom and I did little more than just explore. Unabridged, we crisscrossed the river Seine in search of adventure. We wandered the streets and discovered endless delights of architecture and culture. We went to battle with exotic cuisine. We watched French movies in française and James Bond's *Dr. No* in French sub-titles. We read the International Edition of the *New York Herald Tribune* in English. We discovered the American Embassy on the Champs-Elysees had cheeseburgers, and American Express on the Place de l'Opera could do financial business. Pope John XXIII died June 3, 1963, on our watch. He was the rock star Pope. On D-Day, the 6th of June, we went to the cinema and watched *The Longest Day*. The French still appreciated our efforts despite John Wayne's performance. The leaves changed colors and so did our temperament.

Sadly, our French Francs were dwindling, and we couldn't get a job. There wasn't much interest in a couple of inexperienced Americans who didn't speak the language. In the parks, I watched children play and wondered about my own son. I wrote post cards that had no destination. After a while, we caved in and went to the Embassy. There was an urban legend that a U.S. citizen who wanted to get home could, and the State Department would facilitate it. It turned out to be true to an extent. They were willing to arrange our passage back to the States on an Army troopship. Nowadays the military travels around the globe on transport airplanes, but in 1963 they still went by boat. Think: World War II movies with German submarines torpedoing our troopships, crossing the Atlantic. Twenty years later, they were still using the same old troopships. Ancient steel bathtubs. No frills. No amenities.

The base for transferring military personnel to and from Europe was in Bremerhaven, in the northern extreme of Germany on the North Sea. Our embassy provided us with official documents of passage to the USA and a few bucks to eat on, but getting there was our problem. It was a good 400 miles. We packed up our stuff and checked out of Dix-neuf Rue Monsieur Le Prince. At the Gare du Nord, we caught a train in the general direction of our destination and said goodbye to Paris. We had enough money to get as far as Luxembourg, and then we had to hitchhike or walk still another 250 miles. The cars in Europe were tiny. A guy could stow a lot of belongings in a Buick. Here they'd stop for us, but we couldn't jam our gear into a Fiat or Renault. We walked much of the way to the North Sea. Just two years earlier the Russian Army had built the Berlin Wall. The cement had barely solidified. There was a gloom over Germany.

Finally, we made it to Bremerhaven and the gigantic military base, replete with marching soldiers, tanks and anti-aircraft batteries. The dubious commandant accepted out papers, and we were temporarily inducted into the United States Army for the duration of the trip and treated like any other GI. We ate at the mess hall with the soldiers, slept in their barracks and drank beer at the canteen. But I can't say as they were too happy about it. They all had spit-and-polish shaved heads. By then, I was a full-fledged beatnik, with long hair and a whole new attitude. Tom had always been a crew-cut kind of guy so he was immune from the razzing, but I was the brunt of endless ridicule. They called me Jesus. "Hey, Jesus, when you gonna cut your hair!" I was tough enough to withstand their derision but not the North Atlantic.

We were loaded onto the relatively small USNS Upshur and packed in like proverbial sardines. There were 900 of us in a ship better suited for 300. Deep in the bowels, there was row after row of sleeping hammocks, stacked to the ceiling. The guy on top was nose-bleed high and had to crawl up a rope ladder to get there. The mess hall was so crowded we ate in shifts around the clock, but the real mess started once we got to sea. The North Atlantic was a tumultuous cold-water washing machine. Our ship rolled and tumbled and did the twist. Sea sickness was rampant and so was the regurgitation. There was nausea, gagging, vomit, throwing up, projecting, retching, hurling and spewing everywhere. The lines in the mess hall were suddenly empty. We were squeezed in so tight it was impossible to avoid being puked on. Stiff upper lip. We resigned ourselves to it. General William Tecumseh Sherman famously said, "War is hell." Jesus or not, I was a seasoned combatant by the time we got to the Brooklyn Navy Yard. Hallelujah! Home again. Tom and I came off the gang plank, flung ourselves on American soil and kissed the ground. The five-day cruise from NYC to Le Havre had been the best five days of my life. The return trip from hell was definitely the worst nine days of my life.

Having sworn we'd never return, slinking back to our home town wasn't an option. Our updated intention was to live in New York for a while at least. We took a subway from Brooklyn to Manhattan, and struggled up the steep stairs with that cumbersome baggage we'd dragged across two continents. As we emerged into the sunlight and stepped out onto the sidewalk, we bumped smack into vacationing Tom Gravengood and his wife, Sandy. Eight million people in New York, and we ran into a couple from Grand Rapids. Our cover was blown, but we asked them to keep our dirty little secret.

We rented a small apartment on the upper West Side, and I tended to some unfinished business. The beautiful SS France voyager Babette lived in New Jersey with her cop husband, but I remembered that she worked as a secretary at MacMillan Books just off Times Square, in a green art deco skyscraper. MacMillan was an elite publisher that had published Tennyson, Hardy, Kipling, Yeats, O'Casey, Jack London and Margaret Mitchell. I prepped myself with Wildroot Cream-Oil and went to find her. A bit before lunchtime, I took the elevator up to the main office, high over Manhattan, and walked in. And there she was with her mouth wide open in shock. She was rattled and cutely embarrassed as her fellow workers looked on. She asked me to please go. I said no, not until we talk. She agreed to have lunch and we went to a restaurant on 42nd Street. We talked for an hour. In the end, we embraced. She reiterated her husband had a legal gun and a bad temper. I knew. I just wanted to see her one last time. Tom and I didn't even stay for our full-month rent. We took a Greyhound home.

I missed Peggy, and there was a son of mine I had barely met. I asked her about getting back together—or at least coming down to visit. She was working for Honeywell in West Palm Beach, and lived over a liquor store. I bought a cheap-heap Ford convertible in awful condition and drove to Florida. I was so excited I could hardly contain myself. It took a couple trips, but we finally reunited. At last, I got to watch baby milestones pile up. While Peggy worked, cool dude Tony and I played on the beach and buzzed around in his stroller. Our family thrived with newfound love and, hopefully, my commitment. I got to spend time with my dad's crew too. Pleasantly settled in California, Peggy's mother was driving alone to Michigan on her vacation. Peggy was going up to visit her, and she was packed and ready to head north when we got the call. Her mom fell asleep at the wheel while crossing the Arizona desert and fatally hit the only tree for fifty miles. Soon we moved back to GR.

While I had been running wild, Johnny Reaser was at Grand Rapids Junior College, acquiring the requisite credits to get a law-school scholarship from Wayne State. He got straight A's, except for one B. So I figured why not me? Our newly retooled family was supportive and Peggy went to work for a law firm. I spent my free time taking care of Tony, and we bonded like super glue. He was walking, talking, reading *Playboy* and pretending to drink beer. And we had a new dog named Blackmale. Peg and I were content and optimistic. GRJC had a nice downtown campus with about 4,000 students. Unlike at Michigan State, I went at it with a vengeance this time. If John could get almost straight A's, I would get straight A's, period! I was possessed. I studied day and night. My family saw less of me than when I was in Paris. I maintained my perfect grade average for two years and was honored with several prestigious accolades: President's Scholar, Merit Scholar, Foster Foundation Scholar and the Delta Pi Alpha Honor Society. I sent applications to the Ivy League, Michigan, party-school Miami, and UCLA (after reading their film school booklet). Brown and Columbia both sent back letters of interest, but UCLA went for the jugular. They offered me free out-of-state tuition, books and supplies, and money for housing. I had been pointing at Hollywood all my life, and now the door had just swung open—wide as the Wild West. At the celebratory commencement, my hair was so long the graduation cap kept popping off the mop top. Tony napped through the ordeal. Peggy presented me with an indestructible Samsonite briefcase I still use today. I graduated Valedictorian. The beauty and the beast prevailed. I had finally found happiness in the bosom of family.

In the early summer of 1965, we bought a turbocharged Chevrolet Corvair Monza Spyder and hooked it to a U-Haul trailer full of our possessions, including my ever-growing library of books. Our little family headed west and to a memorable soundtrack that never seemed to stop playing on the radio, the Stones' "I Can't Get No Satisfaction." I was still just 24 and had already put on more cross-country miles than a gold-watch-retiree moving-van driver. When we crossed the border into California, the first town we came to in that vast wasteland of San Bernardino County was Needles. We pulled up to a McDonald's and went inside to eat. Everybody was staring at me. Someone yelled, "Get a haircut!" And then another. A chorus of disapproval and I was flattered. I was in the holy land where a couple years from now long-haired kids from around the country would be pouring in. I just got there first, giving them a sneak peek at one of the first hippies.

Tony, Peggy and Blackie.

Chapter 11: UCLA

The University of California at Los Angeles; there we were. We rented an upscale apartment at 10342 Wilshire Boulevard, between Beverly Glenn Boulevard and the Los Angeles Country Club, the most exclusive in town. It was the demarcation between Westwood and Beverly Hills. The Boulevard was lined with regal buildings and towering palm trees. The sun beat down and the place had a permanent glow.

Peggy went to work at a law firm in Beverly Hills. Tony had a nifty daycare center. My job was being scholarly, but fall term was weeks away. Since I was a Theater Arts film major, I got a head start and made a little film. I bought a Bell & Howell 8 mm camera, with a money-back guarantee. Two-year-old Tony was my actor who takes a hard fall off his tricycle, lands on a dollar and takes a Wilshire bus downtown. He's just a little tot out on his own, interacting with the colorful street people. He spends the magical dollar over and over on food, drinks, magazines, a family movie and an attempt to enter a burlesque theater. He weighs himself on a sidewalk scale and the needle goes up to 26 pounds. In the end, this adventurer wakes up back on the lawn where he began, still clutching that buck. Back to reality, he shakes out of his daydream, climbs on his tricycle and rides home. I was tickled vermillion with our guerrilla film and excited at the prospect of using Tony again once school started.

In the spirit of my curriculum, I spent time at movie theaters; LA was rich with them: mainstream, obscure, foreign, underground and 16 mm art. I also plied the darker side of cinema in the backwash of Western, Broadway and Main. On campus, I snared a job off a bulletin board; it was chauffeuring the elderly, diminutive and fussy Mrs. Rutherford around town in her old black Cadillac Fleetwood. She was a cross between Mrs. Magoo and Gloria Swanson in Billy Wilder's *Sunset Boulevard*. Her reality was every bit as interesting: she was the mother of former MGM actress Ann Rutherford, who played one of Scarlett O'Hara's sisters in *Gone with the Wind* and was Mickey Rooney's girlfriend in the Andy Hardy series. Now Ann was married to William Dozier, who created and produced the *Batman* TV series, a show so popular it played twice a week. Adam West was Batman and Burt Ward, right out of UCLA, was Robin. The show ran forever and made William and Ann Dozier very wealthy. They lived on Greenway Drive in Beverly Hills, next door to Debbie Reynolds. There were black-tie affairs and socials and garden parties and screenings at their own theater. It was my job to pick up Mrs. Rutherford and return her home. I was expected to stay at these functions and was often allowed to bring Peggy and Tony, especially to the movie screenings. We'd be snuggled in with Joan Collins, Jill St. John, Lucille Ball, Stephanie Powers, Robert Wagner and Cesar Romero, enjoying the films and the cocktails.

The elder Mrs. Rutherford lived in a grand old apartment building from the golden age on Wilshire Boulevard. I'd drive her to swanky stores like Saks, I. Magnin, Neiman Marcus and Bullocks-Wilshire. We'd have lunch at the Beverly Wilshire Hotel and shop some more on Rodeo Drive. She was at her best in the back seat, barking orders and admonishing me not to run into this or that! She was a real treasure.

School started in September and I couldn't have been more excited. A year ago, Reaser and I had been listening to the radio as my Michigan Woverines lost to UCLA in the NCAA Basketball Championship. Now I was part of the Bruin legacy that would lead to eleven national titles and an 88-game winning streak. Not surprisingly, the Wizard of Westwood, Coach John Wooden, had recruited Lew Alcindor, the highly touted freshman from New York City. I was scurrying through Macgowan Hall, came around a corner and banged into the seven-foot Alcindor. Our books went flying and we both apologized. It turned out he was in a class with me. He was soft spoken on campus but ferocious on the court. Later, he would change his name to Kareem Abdul-Jabbar and become the most prolific scorer in the history of the NBA. On this beautiful autumn day we were just a couple of insecure freshman.

I recognized Jim Morrison and Ray Manzarek on campus, both UCLA film students who dropped out to form The Doors in 1965. Morrison was cutting-edge slick and one day was wearing a colorful, beaded hippie necklace. I'd never seen anything like it on a man, but it opened my mind. I looked all over town for something similar but no luck. I ended up buying and wearing some silly pink plastic beads from the trinkets department at Newberry's dime store.

I was obligated to take an acting class and met a young man from Long Island, N.Y., named Larry Grobel, who would become a friend not only of mine, but of Peggy's and Tony's too. Only a freshman, Larry had already snared the editorship of the UCLA humor magazine, *The Satyr*. He went on to prodigious accomplishments, not the least of which was writing books on John Huston, Al Pacino, Truman Capote, Marlon Brando, James Michener and others. While neither Larry nor I took ourselves seriously as actors, we had fun and topped it off with earnest performances in Edward Albee's two-character one-act *The Zoo Story*. Larry Grobel introduced me to more than Albee, but that was a start.

Larry Bishop was another Larry-freshman in our acting class. His father was Joey Bishop, the comedian, late-night talk-show host and a member of Frank Sinatra's Rat Pack. Larry went on to act and direct in the film industry. A lot of biker flicks. He asked me to audition for a role in a play he and his Beverly Hills High School buddy were doing off campus. It was Max Shulman's *Rally Round the Flag, Boys!* I read for it, but Larry's friend wasn't convinced. Years later, I was talking to Bishop at Figaro's on Melrose, and the Max Shulman play came up. Larry was surprised I had missed an interesting element in the story and revealed that the teenager I had read for was Richard Dreyfuss. He of course went on to become an Academy Award winning actor, who performed in some of the biggest box-office films ever.

In a cinematography class I met two more characters who became friends of mine in school and eventual partners in show business. They were Jon Fizdale, an el grande person with a sense of humor to match, and his pal Greg Friedkin, a handsome and witty fellow himself, who lived in the heart of Beverly Hills. Greg's father, David Friedkin, was a Hollywood fixture. At this point, he and his partner, Mort Fine, had just developed the hit show *I Spy* that starred Robert Culp and a new comer named Bill Cosby, a young comic and the first African-American to star in a TV series. Friedkin and Fine produced, wrote, directed and even acted in the show. Its Executive Producer was the legendary Sheldon Leonard. They wrote the script for Sidney Lumet's *The Pawnbroker*, starring Rod Steiger in his Academy Award nominated performance. The Writer's Guild honored them with the Best Written Drama Award of 1965. As youngsters they wrote a syndicated radio series for Humphrey Bogart and worked on the epic western *Gunsmoke*. Greg, Fiz and I were always delighted to eavesdrop on the veteran luminaries and new cats like Cosby shooting the breeze. Another UCLA classmate of mine was Penelope Spherris, who went on to direct *Wayne's World*, *The Beverly Hillbillies*, *The Little Rascals*, *Suburbia* and *The Decline of Western Civilization* trilogy. Penny and I were lead actors in an advanced student-film directed by one of the department's star protégés. Halfway through the project, the young director was killed in a motorcycle accident on Wilshire and Beverly Glen, a half-block from our apartment.

After a semester of classes in film history, editing, cinematography and acting, each student made their own film. Classmates worked as the crew. Everybody had theirs in the can by spring, except for me. I hadn't come up with an adequate concept, and my instructor was concerned. I still planned to star Tony, but some of the competitive student directors had actually nabbed well-known Hollywood actors. I was taking a big chance on a just turned three–year-old rookie but felt secure in the gamble. I snuck him into my acting classes, and we worked on TV skits at home. Tony felt he had as much on the line as I did. We'd go down in flames or history together, father and son. We both felt the black magic. I ratcheted up the quest for a screenplay, and then it practically knocked me over. I was slumming on Venice Beach when I came across an eccentric, black derelict who was yelling bizarre witticisms at startled beachcombers. He was extremely tall and intimidating, Abe Lincoln style; a self-righteous rabble-rouser that still had the talent to evoke poignant pathos. Immediately, I had my concept but needed to convince the reluctant enigma. He bristled with contempt and refused me. Maybe Tony could turn him around; I rushed home and gathered up my leading boy. Could we find him again?

Tony and I swept the Venice dregs and eyeballed the low-life bars well into the night. Finally we spotted him in an alley. It was up to Tony to bring the volatile loose cannon into the fold, and sure enough they connected. Del Crawford Esquire received a stipend in advance with the promise of big dough and as much wine as he could drink while we did the shoot. Tony helped me scout locations, and we worked on dialogue. He was a fast learner and so was our new co-star. My life was riding on it and we went to work. Ultimately, we shot in Venice, Santa Monica and Long Beach. It was black and white with sound. We had Larry Grobel's assistance, a great crew and a swell of extras. We barely finished the film in time.

During the final week of school, all the projects were shown in our Quonset hut antiquated theater. Beginners presented their Project One films, upperclassmen their Projects Two and Three, the post-graduate projects were Advance Workshop and Thesis Films. A panel of celebrity judges picked the ten best to be shown at Royce Hall for the UCLA student body (by admission) the following fall, and then the body of *best films* went on a national tour. Virgin freshmen were terrified by the intense scrutiny. The upper-class critics tended to be brutal. The films were shown by random. A couple hours into the marathon, yet another scratchy film header unwound through the projector, passed against the lens and revealed the title card of my film, *The Hooligans.*

In a squalid tavern the down and out bum savors a draft beer at the bar. On the juke-box the Yardbirds play "Mister, You're a Better Man than I" with both Eric Clapton *and* Jeff Beck on guitars. The scraggly-bearded drifter finishes his brew and stumbles outside into the bright light. He staggers through the neighborhood, flops down on a pile of card-board in a vacant lot and passes out. A band of toddler juvenile delinquents come out of the woodwork like a pack of raccoons. Their leader is obviously Tony, who mugs like a young Brando. He sizes up the Gulliver giant and pokes him. Eerie jazz music sets an uncertain tone; the startled bum wakens and shakes his face to focus. "Are you OK, mister?" asks the catchy little voice. "I thought maybe you were hurt or something." Pipsqueak-and-a-half foot tall, Tony pulls the giant up and tugs him by his hand. First, they find a handy gas-station bathroom. Oops! It's the lady's room.

They've already bonded. Fast on his feet, Del sees the mistake and helps show Tony the proper gender toilet. Inside, Tony scrubs the bum with water from the sink. Next, Tony is pulling him into a fancy restaurant and sits him down. The waiter comes and Tony orders for Del. The waiter brings a sumptuous feast. Cut to Tony in the steamy kitchen washing dishes to pay for all this. Next, Tony is in a hotel lobby, checking out the ash trays until he finds a good cigar butt.

The satisfied bum is on a park bench, smoking the stubby stogie with glee. They walk around the park like best pals, while pedestrians ponder it all with shock and awe. They play on the swings and slider, hang from the rings and tangle in the monkey bars.

At an amusement park they ride a merry-go-round and bumper cars. Waltzing along the boardwalk, they come upon the "test your strength" bludgeon game. Ring the bell at the top and win a prize. Tony wants the stuffed animal and motions the bum to do it. The jazz music goes ominous. The bum shakes his head, no. Tony insists and there is anger in his expression. You better! The music ramps another notch. Now! The bum's lucky-break dream has turned into a nasty nightmare. Tony threatens with a wagging finger. Reluc-tantly, the bum takes the giant mallet and swings it back to strike. The music escalates. He whips the weapon overhead. There are rapid inter-cuts between the hammer descending and Tony's grip on a beer bottle, targeting the fitful noggin of the waking bum, back at the vacant lot.

Simultaneously, they hit the mark. The bottle breaks on the bum's head and knocks him out cold. Another rug rat goes through his pockets and comes up with 38 cents. Disappointed, Tony sighs, "Hardly worth the trouble!" The raccoons scamper away, and a valiant but scurrilous Tony gives one last smug look at the broken and bleeding man at his feet. He turns, and his little legs propel him off camera as the Yardbirds close it out, "Well, mister, you're a better man than I." The credits role: Starring Tony Kiedis and Del Crawford, Directed by John Kiedis, The End.

The auditorium exploded in one of the biggest reactions of the week-long screenings. It was an unequivocal hit. When they picked the 10-best films for Royce Hall, *The Hoo-ligans* was one of them. Months later at the auspicious premier, we walked the red carpet and blinked in the face of flash bulbs. My boy was a regular little movie star, and the film department had a new director to reckon with. Tony and I dreamed in Technicolor and schemed for the future.

For Peggy, hope was fading. I went to some silly UCLA hayride that a girl invited me to. I had no interest in her; it was just a campus event. Somebody took snap shots and gave me a print. I tucked it away and forgot about it. Peggy found it and didn't. We worked that one out, but our marital contract was running on empty. Our Wilshire Boulevard lease expired, and we moved to West LA. Peggy bought a brand-new red Austin-Healey we couldn't afford, but we were desperate. Tony and I took it on a road trip to Michigan. Peg had to work until her vacation but would fly out to join us. In Grand Rapids, I took Tony to John Ball Zoo and brought along a casual female I'd met at a party. Her brother was a priest. The poor girl was practically excommunicated. Peggy felt cheated; I felt repressed. For Catholic Margaret Elizabeth, my scandalous actions were unconscionable. The drive back to LA was a funeral procession. After the burial, I moved out to an apartment of my own. Our marriage was over. The contract was up. My candid confessions had only aggravated matters. Castigated, if not castrated, I was branded a scoundrel and a sociopath.

From my perspective I was nothing more than a humanist, faithful to reason and free of abstract theology. I was in lock step with the cosmos, in league with love, and amazed but unfazed by the possibilities. My life had always been linear, and suddenly it was assaulted by a confluence of new options. There were riots in Watts and earthquakes in the Valley. There was a Buckingham change at the sentinel guard to my mind. I had flirted with the asylum of celebrity and eaten from the forbidden fruit of California orange groves. The Jeannie was out of her bottle, and so were Jasmine, Jocelyn, and Juliet.

And then there was Jane. I picked up an old Peugeot to get me around the new west side of my life. On the corner of Pico and Sepulveda was a drive-in restaurant, not unlike the Homburg, so I stopped in one afternoon for the nostalgia of it. They had classic, roller-skating car hops and one in particular caught my attention. Jane caught my eye and a lot more. She wasn't gorgeous or drop dead; she was a typical teenager with braces and freckles and a sunny disposition. I asked her out on the spot.

That night, we went to the movies. I don't remember what film and doubt I did at the time either. I had met the parents earlier and they told me to have her back by nine because she had school tomorrow. We got home plenty early just to play it safe. She asked if I'd like to see her art studio in the backyard. Inside, she matter-of-factly asked me if I'd like to smoke some grass. She didn't wait for an answer, just rolled a joint, lit it and handed it to me. I had timidly flirted with reefer one time at the Black and Tan in 1961 with no reaction, but I took a drag and passed it back to her. If anything I was more concerned with her father, but she seemed totally comfortable. We smoked and she showed me her art and she giggled in a cute and endearing manner. In a few minutes I felt a tingle, followed by a cataclysmic buzz and then it really hit me. *It* was flashing iridescent rainbows, "Rock Around the Clock," the birth of my son, Christmas morning, Brando in *Streetcar*, Margie in bed, the white cliffs of Dover, Fatburgers and *Between the Buttons* tracks 1, 3 and 8—in a blender.

I spotted a leopard and mussed up my muse. The sinks were in sync, but there was no rest in the room. Jane was beyond beautiful now, and after a wayward while she gently nurtured me back to earth with soft puffs of her sweet and soothing oxygen. When I finally got steady she made me up a little doggie bag to go with a couple rolling papers on the side. I walked out to my car with a jaunty stride and a realigned psyche. I felt light years of enlightenment. I was a newly-ordained psychedelic warrior, ready to battle the forces of conventional mediocrity. I stepped into the kaleidoscope of a new age.

I still saw my boy, but now through rose-tinted granny-glasses and less often once Peggy moved to Culver City. At my hideaway, we'd sing and dance to the Beatles, Stones and Sonny and Cher. Ironically, they were all in our future. Peg kept the fire-engine red Austin-Healey and started dating a guy named Jon Martin. It was cool with me. She worked for lawyers and took care of the divorce. I never challenged anything; she never asked for anything. I would continue at UCLA, but my allegiance was all over the place, less to UC and more to LA. I took new classes and met new people. We'd go up to Berkeley and protest the status quo. I was grappling with decent scripts and there was still high expectation for a Project Two film. I maintained good grades and was a perennial on the dean's list, but I was erratic in attendance and short of course credits. I wouldn't get my UCLA degree for years. My film work at MGM would provide the deviate final credits. I graduated cum laude, and my diploma was signed by Governor Ronald Reagan.

My little stash from Jane ran out, and I didn't have a clue where to go for more. I didn't want to get my car hop in any trouble. I asked Larry Grobel and he gave me something better: Bob Dylan. He was determined to convert me to Robert Zimmerman and played me *Highway 61 Revisited* and *Blonde on Blonde*. The music for me was a changin'.

Around about this time, an old acquaintance from Grand Rapids arrived on the LA scene and looked me up. Fred Freel was a peripheral character from the Scott St. John era. A gawky guy, his personality wasn't so hot either. Nobody really liked him. He had served time in Ohio's Chillicothe Federal Penitentiary, a joint he shared with Charles Manson. Aside from his creepiness, Fred offered perks like writing for Peterson Publishing that promulgated everything from *Teen Magazine* and *Astrology*, *Guns & Ammo* and *Ray Bradbury* and *Hot Rod* and *Motor Trend.* Cars were right up his stove-pipe slacks, and he worked out of their prestigious building on the Sunset Strip. Fred was looking for a place to stay and found a vacancy in the building next to mine. GM, Ford, Chrysler and American Motors lent him new-model vehicles to test drive for his articles, so he always had a cool ride. He was also my only friend who knew anything about reefer, which pre-dated grass so you knew he was a veteran.

We hit the local bars and happened into a spot on Westwood Boulevard that had a pretty, blonde bartender I got friendly with. Sue Harris lived in Hermosa Beach and, before you knew it, we had a second front. Sue had a little girl, and I brought Tony in on the deal. He liked being my sidekick. There was a popular nightclub in Redondo headlining an Arkansas newcomer named Glen Campbell, who would go on to make a killing with Jimmy Webb's music "By the Time I Get to Phoenix," "Wichita Lineman" and "Galveston." We patronized the club while Glen was performing and hung out with him after hours. He liked to party and always had a big cowboy smile. Sue was my first post-marriage girlfriend, but the levee was about to flood.

Chapter 12: Lady Killer

With my reshuffled life and fresh energy, I started investigating Sunset Boulevard, the carotid artery of Los Angeles. The Sunset Strip was its heart, a metaphor whore of a boulevard, basking in tinsel and taboo. That celebrated hunk of road thrived with gambling and speakeasies during prohibition. Later, the nightclubs Mocambo, Ciro's and Trocadero were the destination of movie stars, gangsters and writers like F. Scott Fitzgerald, Raymond Chandler and Dashiell Hammett. I caught the tail of Ciro's, still hanging on to the last vestige of Bogie and Bacall. Up the block, Schwabs Drug Store was still there, along with the tale of endless Lana Turners. I delved into what was left of classic Hollywood: hallowed institutions like The Brown Derby, Musso & Frank's, the remnants of Earl Carroll's Theatre, and enough art deco architecture to find my way into the film-noir past of the Black and Blue Dahlias.

Even before the invasion of hysteria late in the 60s, there was already a current profusion of honky-tonks up and down the special two-mile stretch of Sunset called "the Strip." Elmer Valentine, an ex-cop from Chicago, operated the boulevard's flagship club, the Whisky a Go Go. Johnny Rivers played an extended engagement, and the original Go Go dancers were hung with care from the ceiling in cages. London Fog and the Galaxy were on that block too. Next door was Sneaky Pete's jazz lounge. I used to see Sinatra in there and Dino and Sammy. Dean Martin had his own club on the Strip near La Cienega. It was called Dino's Lounge, and I did drop by. The ubiquitous Doors were the Whisky house band for a while, and I saw them at London Fog and Bido Lido. Buffalo Springfield, Love and the Byrds played the Whisky too. By the turn of the decade, England came to the Whisky: Cream and The Who and even Led Zeppelin played the joint.

A tiny club called The Sea Witch had a nice niche on the Strip, and so did The Trip. The Velvet Underground played there. I should know: while they were in town our Art History prof got them to perform in our UCLA classroom. He also took us to *Happenings*. The Central was kitty corner from the Whisky at Sunset and Clark. Over the years, it got Filthy McNasty and then became Johnny Depp's Viper Room. At the top of the Strip where Crescent Heights and Sunset got cross with each other was Pandora's Box, a club on a traffic island in an awkward intersection. The tiny club looked like a doll house and was surrounded by a little yard with delicious cuties sitting in the grass. It had a well-deserved reputation for its naughty puerility. Vengeful, the law conspired to shut down the Sunset Strip scene in general, but focused first on Pandora's Box and in the cover of darkness condemned the property, tore the Box down and vaporized the island.

The LAPD had its own barnyard of bully Chiefs: William Parker, Tom Reddin, Ed Davis and Daryl Gates, all bound and determined to annihilate the 60s movement. But there was only one County Sheriff high-priest-and-executioner for the entire era, Peter J. Pitchess. As the Strip became a popular tourist attraction, it swelled with a burgeoning population of flower-power hippies, runaways, music aficionados, tourists, squares and enlightened West Hollywood natives. The police got nervous and speculated a revolution. They were right on. Their vile response was a full-on military assault. Bloody attacks precipitated the riots on the Sunset Strip. On weekends, the sheriffs would load up big, armored buses filled with cops, ready to unleash injustice. They would charge out like gangbusters, encircle terrified revelers, force them into the buses and cart them off to the downtown county jail. Doctors, lawyers, children, house wives from Dubuque, it didn't matter. If you were on the Strip, you were a target. They'd fingerprint us, harass us and then let us go. Of course, we were miles from our cars back in West Hollywood. We would walk back in excitable groups and often stop at Tommy's Burgers on Beverly Boulevard, which was on the way back to the Strip—deja vu! La lujuria y el lustro de Los Angeles.

Fred spread the word in Grand Rapids about all the fun we were having, and three of his friends came out to visit. One of them was David Allen Weaver, who knew a thing or two about me. He had been ringside when I knocked that guy out at the Shamrock, and he was best friends with Scott St. John's younger brother Pete. Evidently they emulated the Dynamic Duo and attempted to copy our moves. Dave was anxious to meet me and we hit it off. Looking for trouble was no trouble, and we found it all over town. There were illegal substances, angry husbands, bloody noses, warrants and reckless abandon. Weaver and his pals managed to escape before the National Guard was called out, but I knew he'd be back. I was looking forward to it.

Since I was barely going to class anymore, Fred and I moved from West LA to West Hollywood, where the action was. We rented an apartment on Fountain just off the Strip. Our place was surrounded by actors, models and a girl in the adjacent patio who sunbathed in the nude. She seemed to like flaunting her new breasts. I stepped from our patio into hers and then into her bedroom. My goodness gracious first experience with flagrant breast enhancement was a curiosity, but I came away unimpressed.

I was feeling invincible, meeting and dating girls so fast I couldn't keep track of them. No more monotonous monogamy for me. I had the pick of the titter. Double oh heaven license to thrill. I was cheeky to a fault and often stopped my car in the middle of the street to chase down girls for their phone number or just bring them home to my party. That crafty-commando move snared one of my favorite girlfriends of '67. Fred was driving down Sunset near Vine. I was the bombardier and spotted this exquisite blonde and her sister headed toward the Cinerama Theater. I told Fred to let me out, but he said the traffic was too hectic. Fearless, I opened the car door and parachuted out. A few bruises later, I had snared my prey. She was Linda and lived in the blue-collar suburb of Bell Gardens; for a while, so did I. She was in high school, but her family didn't seem to mind at all. In my dominion, we'd meet up at the Hullabaloo, a hip club on Sunset and Vine that featured some of the early psychedelic bands and the ubiquitous Doors. A club of many incarnations, it had been Earl Carroll's nightspot with its outdoor façade of movie-star autographs and the Moulin Rouge. A faded sign over the grand entrance read: *"Through these portals pass the most beautiful girls in the world."* It was still true when Linda sailed through that ghost of a glamorous lost era. In '68 it became the Kaleidoscope and rivaled Bill Graham's Fillmore and Winterland in San Francisco. The masquerade finally morphed into the Aquarius Theater where *Hair* played forever. I was at a few of those forevers.

Fred finally found a girlfriend, a little brunette named Denise. We were all sitting around the apartment high on acid feeling groovy and ruminating about the oppressed blacks in South Central LA. Playful hippies and guarded blacks had formed a bond of brotherhood, defiant of the Man. There was a fragile covenant between the Marxist Yippies and the Black Panthers; Jewish Abbie Hoffman and black Bobby Seale were blood brothers. Black bands like Time, Love, Sly & the Family Stone and Jimi Hendrix were into the same psychedelic beat. Sensitive to their plight, we conjured up a courtesy call, piled into Fred's white Rambler station wagon, on loan from *Motor Trend*, and headed for the ghetto to show our allegiance. We were high on good will.

I drove with Linda in the passenger seat; Fred and Denise were making out in the backseat. We swept through downtown and turned south onto Central Ave., the hood's main street. The Electric Prunes announced our arrival as we came upon a large gathering of brothers and sisters, milling about in a motel parking lot. We figured this might be a good place to share the love. I pulled in and stopped short of the crowd so I didn't run anybody over. The Rambler was still in gear with the engine idling; I kept my foot on the brake as my dad had taught me. Our hearts were in order.

Two bloods drifted over and were rather surprised to find four hapless honkies in the middle of their party. One attempted civil dialogue, but his pal whacked him alongside the head. Now I saw the whole mob was coming our way. The first arriving legion surrounded us, and some punk on Fred's side hit him square in the face through our open-for-business windows. Tenaciously, they started yanking on the door handles. The LSD trip wasn't helping. Our girls were screaming. An angry sister tore Linda's hair. They got my door open and Black Power salute-clenched fists were pummeling me. Fortunately, their overanxious haymakers nullified each other. Now they had my left arm and were pulling me out of the car. I was part-way to hell and only my right-hand grip on the steering wheel kept me from falling into the wood chipper. I had one shot. I knew the car was still in drive, and my toe made a desperate jab at the accelerator. It hit pay dirt. The car lurched forward, knocking a mob of bowling pins off their feet. I was still dangling half-out of the wagon as I plowed through the frenzy. Late-arriving stragglers threw beer bottles as I bounced over the curb and zig-zagged down Central Avenue. We took Fred to County General emergency; his jaw was broken. He got wired. All four of us had cuts, bruises and bummers. The *Motor Trend* Rambler made the cover.

I met a teenage beauty from Santa Barbara at a rock festival up there. Country Joe and the Fish, the Doors, the Airplane, Big Brother and the Holding Company played, and so did we. She was a bouncy brunette from a well-to-do family, a student at UC Santa Barbara, and quite a dish. She frequently drove all the way down just to see me. We listened to the first Pink Floyd album *The Piper at the Gates of Dawn* on acid when it came out. We smoked pot and dined and dashed. Like so many other times, I had this amazing girlfriend and threw it away.

I commonly went to supermarkets to meet girls, but this time I hadn't intended to. Santa Barbara was on her way down, and I zipped over to the Boys Supermarket on Santa Monica Blvd. to buy some quick wine. I was kicking ass with my longer-than-anybody-else's hair, Malibu tan, tight jeans with flaring bellbottoms and my favorite recycled tuxedo-shirt from Aardvark's second-hand goods on Melrose. Bearing down on the beer and wine, I turned a corner onto aisle—holy shit! There was a woman the likes of which I had never even dared to imagine. And we stood there, just staring at each other. She was tall, slender, sassy and classy: my first conscious exposure to a flaming redhead with alabaster-white skin and just the right sprinkling of freckles. She seemed as pleased to see me as I was to see her. I took a deep breath and made small but interesting talk. We threw risk to the wind and exchanged names. She accepted my phone number and we parted reluctantly. I was afraid I'd lose her. I knocked over part of a pyramid display of canned goods as I walked backward away from this cosmic creature named Katie Bramson. She laughed at my tangled predicament and returned for a moment to reassure me she wasn't a mirage. Katie gave me a hug and promised to call. I told her where I lived, just in case AT&T went out of business.

A few days later she showed up at my door, uninvited. Santa Barbara was there and I had to make a snap decision. I chose Katie. She invited me over for Sunday dinner with her three-year-old daughter, Gina. Katie had just divorced an ultra religious Jewish fellow who wasn't much fun, and the breakup had been ugly. Like me, she was excited about this new age exploding around us. *Time, Life, Look* and *Newsweek* all had cover stories about the seismic change in the psychedelic weather. Drugs were touted as a bold new way to look at life. Drugs were good for us. Like spinach. Timothy Leary and Marshall McLuhan espoused the benefits. The only acrimonious stigma came from the far right wing of society, the police and the *Joe Pyne Show* on KTTV.

She cooked up a lot more than dinner that Sunday on Sycamore. She was anxious to extricate herself from Mr. Bramson. Gina was a spoiled daddy's girl, but as soon as we tucked her into bed, Katie took my hand and led me to her bedroom. She had it tantalizingly seductive with candles, incense and sheer tapestries hanging from the ceiling. She undressed and revealed her beautiful white skin and pink areolas. Her pliant limbs reached out to me. I had never realized how special redheads were, and that single quintessential erotic moment influenced my sexual inclinations forever. We experimented with LSD, mushrooms, hash and grass. We danced and laughed and sang in the rain.

I got used to contending with the sheriffs. They saw hippies as communist rebels that must be destroyed at any cost. I was walking up to my Fountain apartment when a black and white pulled over and two cops jumped out and started asking me questions. When I took exception, they pushed me down into the underground parking garage and beat the hell out of me. Then they calmly walked back up the ramp and drove away. Another time, another sidewalk and another rogue cop. The fuzz jumped out and handcuffed me for wearing a blue denim shirt. Maybe I had escaped. Ridiculous! Everybody wore that army-navy-store gear. The lunatic got an emergency call and tossed me in the back seat. Racing toward the mishap, he explained how much he hated hippies and the delicious ways he would kill them, pulverize their faces and tear them apart. Take them out in the desert and shoot them. He got so worked up his face turned red and he spit all over his dashboard. He finally dropped me off at the sheriff's station and spared my life.

On weekends Katie and I went to the love-in at Griffith Park, where thousands of hippies cavorted in the nude, dropped dope and rode the carousel. There were kids galore, and we'd bring Gina and Tony. One Saturday love-in, we were singled out by a strange couple who handed us an invitation to a shindig the next day in the Wilshire district. Jimi Hendrix was on the West Coast and had come down to Los Angeles. In England he was a rising rock star, but here he was just starting to get attention. I only knew of him from his first local hit "Purple Haze," which was playing on selected radio stations and causing some excitement. The event turned out to be a good excuse for a party, and Jimi was there too.

It was held on an expansive lawn, surrounded by a large art deco apartment building. We walked into a garden soiree with the cream of the scene on display. Wild and crazy, fashionable insiders had us wide-eyed. At one point, Katie was off on her own when Jimi came up to me and asked if I wanted to toke on a joint. He was rolling it when Katie tracked me down—a bit upset with me for not bringing her along. We smoked the doobie, stayed a little longer and left the party. Jimi was so mellow about everything it wasn't much of a big deal at the time.

Hail, Cheetah, queen of the jungle. With all the mind-blowing events going on in this epochal year, nothing was more spectacular than the premiere of the Cheetah nightclub at the foot of the Venice Beach Pier. Opening night was the Jefferson Airplane, the Doors and the Peanut Butter Conspiracy. The line waiting to enter was *highly* excited from all the hype, but the hype couldn't even live up to the reality. The Cheetah was previously the old Aragon Ballroom, a big-band dance hall that probably featured Benny Goodman and Artie Shaw and Gene Krupa at some time. Later it was the ten-year home of *Lawrence Welk and his Big Band and Champagne Music.* As we made our way in, the future met us halfway.

The club had a huge circular dance floor that was surrounded with a retractable polished-steel curtain. Every time they unleashed the strobe lights, a flick of the switch would mechanically encase us in this gleaming silver-metal universe that magnified the explosive flashings a thousand times. There were psychedelic vendor booths, and a stage that could be wheeled out from a nether storage area. Sex and drugs found refuge in that nether land too. And to top it off, there was a sweet lounge restaurant enclosed in its own sound-proof bubble alongside the dance floor that was quiet enough to hear your date ask you for another Quaalude. And the banquette booths, chairs and bar stools were leopard skin.

Motor Trend gave Fred a loaded '67 Mustang convertible for his next report, so we took a road trip. We tripped all right! Friday night was always reserved for the Cheetah, but this time we left early because KLQ had promised to play the long-awaited new Beatles album just after midnight. As we tooled the Mustang through the streets of Venice, it started to play *Sgt. Pepper's Lonely Hearts Club Band.* Arguably the best album ever and I like to argue. June 1967. In a few weeks, we hit the road and played the 8-track all the way to Grand Rapids.

Peggy also went on a vacation to GR that summer, and by the time I arrived she had hooked up with... Scott St. John! We pulled up to her sister Katie's house, and Scott was standing there with his arm around my ex-wife. Totally bizarre, dude. But I felt no animosity. In fact I was happy for them. Scott was manager of a skid-row Tennessee Williams hotel on South Division. He had his own glorified room there too. Craig Betteridge was his new (but not quite as) dynamic-duo mate.

I touched base with Reaser and Klimavich, but it was Dave Weaver I really wanted to see. Recruiting him to California was my mission. I gave him a makeover, remodeled his image and renamed him David. In return, David resurrected my old nickname, Spider. My frisky sister Judy's boyfriend at the time was fearsome Tom Gravengood. He had come up with "Spider" years ago, something about the way I slid through a sorority or up a shining tower to find a damsel in need of distress. Fred and I brought along the gift of frankincense and myrrh and weed and serious pills and, the coup de grace, purple sunshine acid which none of these yokels had ever seen, much less dropped. They were LSD virgins. They offered me Valiums, and I exploded in laughter. Hey, I'm from LA, dude. I tossed down a couple of their funny blue prescription pills for harried housewives, and in 15 minutes I was passed out cold.

Marty Lipp was in Ann Arbor and I popped over. We double dated co-eds from Midland and went to the Schwaben Inn to see a red hot Detroit blues band called the Prime Movers that had a drummer named James Osterberg, who would come to be known as Iggy Pop. Later I'd get jiggy with Iggy in LA.

Fred Freel spent most of his time at his mom's on Guild St., and I crashed on various couches. I visited my own mother and spent a couple nights on her couch. She was drinking too much and always had that tipsy overly-loveable quality. She had fallen down an uncovered chute into the basement of a Robert Hall department store. The back injury had pained her for ages, and she was taking barbiturates. In Cali we called them reds and took them for fun. She still looked pretty but somehow empty and doomed. It would be the last time I'd ever see her. I love you, Mom.

Saugatuck is a lively Lake Michigan beach resort with nightclubs we had been going to for years, especially the Butler and Coral Gables. We swung out there for an evening: Weaver, St. John, Freel and a supporting cast. The bar scene went routinely, but somehow we ended up at a private party in Douglas, across the Kalamazoo River. It was the home of Ashley Pandel's parents, who were out of town. Ashley was the quiet introspective type, not terribly dynamic; but he was very generous with the family booze. And he was playing new hip music so I knew he was hiding something under that introverted veneer. I told Fred it was time to break out the ammunition. We had ten hits of acid with us and divvied it up. Scott St. John said no thanks. No way. My hero and mentor turned out to be chicken—or smarter than the rest of us. He did try to smoke weed but got all freaky and curled into a ball. Weaver was having a ball. He was beaming. The trips were pretty mellow and fun for the rest of us. I talked with Ashley and got a good feel for the guy. He said he was contemplating a move to the West Coast, and I gave him my address.

The girls in Michigan were rather lame, and I missed Katie. Fred and I drove back to LA. The good news was David's family had decided to move west too. His dad was an aspiring film producer with scripts and connections. Weaver would soon be joining my adventures. Peggy and Tony returned to California but not for long—they'd soon move back to the wolverine state.

Chapter 13: Rogers & Cowan
Vanity Affairs

In West Hollywood, I reunited with my scoop of strawberry-and-vanilla Katie. Financially, Fred was doing well as a writer, but I was not. My job was assimilating the Age of Aquarius. Fred always paid the rent, but he was getting tired of being the rube. To exacerbate matters, Ashley Pandel showed up from Michigan and he had a pal with him, an aspiring actor from New York City named Jock McNeill. Suddenly we had a boarding house. Ashley crashed on the couch. Jock slept on the floor. Fred had his small bedroom. And I enjoyed the master bedroom.

Jock was an entertainer, and boy was he funny. He'd mainly done commercials in New York but hoped to make it big in Hollywood. He had an admirable work ethic and got up early to pursue auditions. He also drank, smoked weed and popped acid. The comical side of Jock coerced us into Buddhist classes and had us doing the trendy *Nam Myoho Renge Kyo* chant.

Ashley was more practical and diligently looked for work in the music business. I slept till noon. Nobody had money but Fred; he finally bailed and got his own little place on Detroit Street. I moved in with Katie, who worked while I played housewife. It was destined to fail. A former boyfriend of hers came for a weekend, and I was exiled to Peggy's couch. I babysat Tony while Peg dated.

Katie and I still had a few good times though. One Sunday we ended up at Frank Zappa's log cabin in Laurel Canyon with a bizarre group of oddballs and a flock of kids including Katie's Gina. There was a bowling alley in the basement and bats in the belfry.

Peg and Tony moved back to Grand Rapids, but the Eric Weaver family arrived and set up shop. David would drive his dad's new Thunderbird over to Katie's and hop out in his gabardine sans-a-belt trousers. I'd admonish him for his Midwest style and worked on his wardrobe. My potential running mate needed fine-tuning. Katie was ready to tune out. I hadn't had a real job since chauffeuring Mrs. Rutherford's Fleetwood. I relented and started searching the want ads.

Fred Freel was approached by Lou Kimzey, a publisher who was starting a hip underground magazine he called *The Paper Bag*. Kimzey was a large flamboyant man in a small dull office with a bad view of the Los Angeles River. Fred took over several aspects of the magazine and employed me as a consultant. The first issue articles included Fred's "Student Power: A new Force and Killer Weed." Ashley Pandel authored "Hip Hobo Signs." The inimitable Paul Krassner penned "A Realist on LSD." Krassner was a key figure in the counterculture of the 1960s. He worked for the *Realist* and *Playboy*, wrote several books and was editor of Lenny Bruce's autobiography, *How to Talk Dirty and Influence People*. He was also a founding member of the Yippies.

Leon Russell was the music editor and wrote *Feed-Back Blow-Your-Mind Hip*. Leon was an integral part of the era's music, working with George Harrison, the Stones, Joe Cocker, the Beach Boys, Elton John and even Sinatra. It was quite a staff to work with.

The army of change was growing every day. There were similar publications all across the country now, *Berkeley Barb*, *Fifth Estate* from Detroit, *The Rag* in Austin, *The Paper* in East Lansing, and the *LA Free Press*.

The *Paper Bag* offices were close to the newly-located Weavers in Glendale. I had a family again. David's sociable father, Eric, loved to whip up gourmet meals, and I was always invited for birthday and holiday dinners. He made a seamless move into show business, and co-produced *Madron*, a western with Richard Boone and Leslie Caron. Disturbingly, David still wore wingtips and political philosophies stuck in Grand Rapids. He was a Nixon man and hated the Kennedys. My stand was at revolutionary odds with the right wing, but David Weaver was still a holdout. In June, 1968, Robert Kennedy was the Democratic frontrunner to challenge Tricky Dick. Witty satirist Pat Paulson from the Smothers Brothers was facetiously campaigning for president too. Like all the California primary candidates, he had a victory party planned on election night. Theatre of the Absurd, his was at the psychedelic Kaleidoscope. The runaway favorite and ultimate winner, RFK, had planned his victory party for the Ambassador Hotel on Wilshire Boulevard. The Ambassador was the swankiest hotel in Los Angeles and home of the world-famous Coconut Grove.

Weaver and I went to the Kaleidoscope that night. We probably would have gone anyway, but this was a special night. After Pat Paulson's fake defeat party, we went outside for a breather when word reached us that Robert Kennedy had been shot. People were abhorred, crying and screaming. Except Weaver, he was cheering. We came close to a fist fight, but instead we jumped into the Thunderbird and zoomed over to the Ambassador, where we joined thousands of vigilant people on the sidewalks around the hotel. We stayed all night until it was conceded RFK had in fact died. By dawn it even affected my restive Republican.

As the police continued to hassle our long hair and disturb our partying, David finally came around to the liberals. One of our nuttier monkey-shine escapades was a late-night episode on our diet of reds, yellows and Tuinals. I had been seeing a married girl and was anxious to get my mitts on her, despite the late hour. She lived with her husband on the third floor of an apartment building on Bronson. We could see the lights were out. The main entrance was locked so we shinnied up a drain pipe and worked our way to their window. We climbed in like it was normal. I tiptoed into her bedroom, with David right behind me. Except for the moonlight, it was quite dark. I knelt down next to her side of the bed and gently woke her up. She stifled a scream. Next to her, the snoring husband continued to sleep. Needless to say she was outraged and yet somewhat appreciative of our ingenuity. She carefully got out of bed and brought us into the kitchen. She kissed me goodbye and skedaddled us out of there.

While I was putzing around with *Paper Bag* and the possibility of working for Eric Weaver, I finally got a promising call from the California Employment Agency. They sent me to an interview on Canon Drive in Beverly Hills. The job was for a mailroom boy at Rogers & Cowan, the biggest entertainment PR outfit in the world. There were a dozen or more applicants applying, but I seemed to hit it off with the office manager. The mailroom job was traditionally a training school and stepping stone at movie studios, TV stations and talent agencies. It was perfect, and, considering I was broke, it paid pretty well. They hired me.

I was thrilled for Katie and rushed home to give her the good news. She barely feigned appreciation. She had a heart of cold now. There would be no growing old together. I desperately cared for her but knew our watch was running down. I truly loved Katie; she taught me the glory of soft pink femininity. It would plague me forever, and soon I would triplicate that redheaded curse in spades. We clung to last vestiges and the fury of Van Morrison's beautiful *Astral Weeks*.

I had to find a new place and hit the jackpot when I found a relatively inexpensive apartment behind a head shop on Clark and Sunset, the Times Square of the Sunset Strip. My new pad was set back off the busy intersection, and I had the second story all to myself. There was a cranky guy below me who always complained about my loud music and noisy bed springs. My phone was at the Sun-Bee Liquor Store; call Weaver, let it ring once and hang up. He'd show up in the T-Bird and we'd recruit new dames to our lair.

Grand Rapids tough guy Vern Carrier came to visit. The first thing we did with squares was pop a big joint in their mouth. After a few seconds Vern was bug-eyed, "Hey, how do you fight on this stuff?!" That's the point, knucklehead; we don't have to fight anymore. We get groovy on flower power.

I hitchhiked to get around. Thumbing was like carpooling. It was rapid transit. Soliciting hippies clogged the curbs on Sunset. I had my own westbound spot on the corner of Hilldale, one block west of Clark. Arthur Lee and Love had a song "Between Clark and Hilldale." It was *the* block on the strip and appropriately anchored by the Whisky. I was out there in front of the Hamburger Hamlet looking for a ride when a big white Rolls Royce stopped next to me. At first I thought it was just slow traffic on its way into Beverly Hills, but when I looked inside there was a young hip dude who said, "Come on; get in." Heck, yes! I'd never been in a Rolls before. He introduced himself as Dennis and then it hit me, Dennis Wilson of the Beach Boys. He was gregarious and bantered with me like I was an old friend. He lit a joint and ran down a plan; he was heading to his house farther out Sunset and asked me if I'd like to join him. There was swinging action at his place: music, a bunch of hippies--mostly girls, and I could catch a rehearsal. Dang; I was on my way to meet a girl of my own at Beverly Glen Park close to UCLA. She was sneaking out of her mother's house for a covert rendezvous. Reluctantly I declined Dennis's invitation, and he let me out at the park. The Charlie Manson gang was staying at the Beach Boy's house then and had I accepted his proposal who knows what might have happened to my life...or death. Dennis gave me a rain check and his address. I dropped by occasionally, but Manson had moved on.

As an apprentice Hollywood press agent, I'd go to a bakery in the morning and bring donuts and coffee back for the entire staff. The big bosses, Henry Rogers and Warren Cowan, had their grand offices at the far end of a long room; the rest was filled with publicist's cubicles. I would open the mail, sort and deliver it. Then the office manager would hand me my agenda for the day. It was like unwrapping a present. It could be a stop at any of the studios to pick up a script or deliver a talk-show host to his dentist appointment. Maybe to greet the Stones at LAX, or personally deliver flowers to the Shah of Iran at the Beverly Wilshire. Pick up a Jack Taylor suit for Cary Grant or jewels at Harry Winston's for an Academy Award nominated client. But most often, it was just relaxed visits to the homes of the biggest movie stars in the world, who lived almost in walking distance from each other in Beverly Hills and Bel Air. For instance, I would drive the company VW bug to Burt Lancaster's house and pick up Kirk Douglas's wallet that he'd left the night before when they were playing poker. At Kirk's home, I would sit in the kitchen and wait for him to finish his workout while the maid whipped me up a snack. Sometimes I would bump into Kirk's son Michael, home from college in Santa Barbara. And when I'd finally leave there'd be a big Russian bear hug from the man who was Ulysses and Spartacus and Van Gogh and Bix Beiderbecke and Doc Holliday and Dr. Jekyll and Mr. Hyde and the Champion.

I went to the home of legendary Edward G. Robinson, in his final years, and to the Tony Curtis house, flush from his role as *The Boston Strangler*. At Raquel Welch's, she'd make me lunch with a glass of milk, and I swear she was flirting with me, Mrs. Robinson. She was the undisputed sex symbol of the world then and she was giving me a milk refill.

Aaron Spelling had the biggest house I ever saw. Milton Berle always with the gags. Andy Williams always had a smile and a song. Gregory Peck was all class. Natalie Wood was in therapy. Even Warren Cowan's house on Maple was a treat; he was married to the lovely movie star Barbara Rush, who was high-society personified. Henry Rogers lived out off San Vicente Boulevard; he was a tall, handsome man with silver hair, dashing and elegant as any of his leading men. In Lucille Ball's gracious home just north of Sunset, I spent time with a lady who reminded me very much of my own mother. I even stopped by the home of "America's Sweetheart," Mary Pickford, the silent-screen superstar who was in her seventies. Rogers & Cowan represented many of the major-movie releases and the big TV shows, and the hottest show in the country was *Laugh In*. Inspired by their zany humor, Tony composed his first letter and sent some art:

Dear Dad, Thank you for the Laugh in gum and the shirts. 'sock it to me' Are you having a good time. Look at the back.

For weeks Katie and I had been hogtied by our perfunctory slow-death demise. She started chumming around with a burly pot dealer who lived next to the Alpha Beta, where he openly peddled his wares. Kate and I had always scrambled to find reefer, and this guy had kilos all over his house. She took me there a couple times; his stone-cold glare didn't kid around. He'd off me in a second to have Katie as his old lady. Finally she closed shop on Norton and moved in with the guy. In six months, he'd be in prison.

The tears for Katie had hardly dried when I first spotted Deborah Lee speeding down busy Little Santa Monica Boulevard in Beverly Hills. She was in a black MG convertible, and her curls were blowing in the wind. I was in the company VW, heading in the opposite direction on my way to a high-noon errand. I did an abrupt U-turn that endangered life, limb and the beetle, but caught up to her and shouted something clever enough that she pulled over in a no-parking zone. A cop pulled along too and told us to move. She bought some time by batting her mascara-laden eyelashes. While he blushed, I got her name and number.

Deborah Lee was a model with adorable and unashamedly prominent freckles. She had fighter-plane conical breasts and a Lake Placid smile. Like Katie, she was adorned with a brilliant cascade of flammable hair and had that same self-assured confidence to tell a guy "take a hike!" or "hike up my skirt." I was behind schedule when I got back to the grind but didn't care; Deborah had punched my E-ticket. The job was expendable. I called the number and it was the Sunset Marquis Hotel; I declined the connection to her room and decided to surprise her. After work I headed for the classic West Hollywood villa on Alta Loma. Her suite was on the second level, overlooking the pool. I rang the bell. She opened the door with a gasp. For one thing, she was wrapped in a towel and had left a trail of wet footprints from the bathroom. The second was more disconcerting. Her benefactor boyfriend that paid for the ritzy accommodations was due there any minute. The cuckold was Lee Lassiff, who with his partner had started White Whale Records, the label of The Turtles. White Whale was swimming with cash from the Turtles' 24 Billboard hits, including their signature blockbuster "Happy Together". Reason enough he could afford a new MG sports car for Debbie and lots more—clothes, vacations and a seat at the best clubs and restaurants. So why would she risk all this for a guy making 75 bucks a week? It blew my mind too.

We didn't exactly have sex standing there in her puddle of soapy water but darn close to it. She was naked and pressed so hard against my body those bullet-tits impaled me. Peeled apart, she promised to call when the stiff left. I said I'd wait in the lobby, even if it took all night. Later that evening we finished what we'd started. She also showed me the 45-magnum pistol he kept in the drawer next to the bed. The next day she took me to meet her family in the Valley Hills. Her dad gave me the third degree, and I felt all kinds of bad vibes. She showed me her little-girl photo albums and gave me a slew of her modeling photos. I still have them. On one of them she wrote "Will you marry me?"

Lee took her to Las Vegas that weekend, and I ached every moment. The first Led Zeppelin album came out while she was gone, and I spent the weekend agonizing over "Babe I'm Gonna Leave You" and "Your Time Is Gonna Come." When they returned she asked Lee to get her a regular apartment and he did on Waring, just north of Melrose. Now every day the VW bug made a special stop at Debbie's place right along with Danny Kaye, Joan Crawford, Fred Astaire and Ginger Rogers. The misspent VW time got me in hot water with the office manager and the publicists, but a burning geyser was on the horizon. Warren Cowan had me attend screenings and write him reviews. He appreciated the work and complimented me. It's what a mailroom protégé does, but other factions saw me less reliable. I must admit I was screwing Deborah Lee on company time, and occasionally I skipped across the street to the Beverly Canon Theatre for some Truffaut or Kurosawa, but I always got my work done. It was the gruff old curmudgeon of the staff, Bill Feeder, who faithfully supported me. He was my steadfast mentor and would come through in the storm.

David and I decided to get a bigger place for the both of us, and for twice the bread, we went for an upscale apartment in Brentwood called the Casa Granada. This was the quintessential sex-drenched young-moderns complex where hot babes in skimpy bikinis lounged around the Olympic-size pool and disseminated their phone and apartment numbers to swinger guys at the weekend barbeques. David and I were probably the only ones with long hair, but for the most part we fit right in with the wild, nonstop partying. I snatched the master bedroom and an Olds 98 for transportation. For a while, we fooled around with twin sisters from Georgia who lived right across the hall from us. We had a stereo on steroids and blasted our music at top volume, but most of the other tenants did too.

One of David's old associates had followed him to LA and got into the thriving drug business. Bomba stepped on some toes and emerged as Mr. Big. I never like him in GR and still avoided him whenever possible, but he came by sporadically to conspire with David. Fortunately I wasn't invited, but at the time I always wondered why. With his self-assured impunity, the 800-pound-gorilla boss and enforcer helped himself to whatever he wanted and cast a dark shadow on my parade. Bomba and Scott St. John had been both adversaries and allies; now my former dynamic duo and best man was engaged to marry my ex-wife.

I had my own mischief: a pretty school girl from Beverly Hills High School who wanted to date me. Her parents wouldn't have appreciated it. She knew Greg Friedkin's younger brother, so we staged a subterfuge date with him. I waited nearby in my camouflaged Olds 98; she jumped out of his and into mine and away we went, back to Casa Granada. The day before, I had purchased my first kilo of grass, a 2.2 pound brick of Mexican pot. A lid was one ounce and cost ten dollars. A decent quality kilo was about sixty bucks, so it was a substantial saving to buy in bulk. I broke it up on the kitchen table, and it expanded into a mountain-size pile. The more I loosened it, the bigger it got. It was flower-power art. I even took its picture. When we arrived, it was the first thing I showed her. Go ahead and Bogart that joint. I proudly presented our groovy décor, our record collection, my master bedroom, my library and my UCLA films in their canisters. I put Iron Butterfly's seventeen minute *In-A-Gadda-Da-Vida* album on the stereo and started dancing maniacally; she was entertained and laughing. We were flying close to heaven, and then the door bell rang. Weaver wasn't there, and he had a key of his own. I looked out the peephole. Nobody there. I opened the door and got hit by a big-rig truck. There were a dozen LAPD cops off to the sides, and they stormed in like troopers. Knocked me down and dove on top of me. Of course, the first thing they saw was the mountain.

There had been a recent burglary at Casa Granada, and a person with long hair was seen in the area. Someone piped up there were two guys with long hair living in the complex. Like there were only a million guys with long hair in LA by now. The pigs deduced we needed checking on. They handcuffed me and smacked me around, and scared the dickens out of the poor girl. The pot pile looked like more than it really was, so they thought they'd uncovered a major operation. Cops kept flooding in and tore the place apart, pulling feathers out of the pillows and stuffing out of the furniture. They desecrated the hippie décor with glee and were literally laughing at me as they stomped on my property.

And then they saw the UCLA film that had won national honors. They pulled the film out of the reels and ripped it apart, ranting that it was probably pornography. It was my only copy, and the first few minutes were lost forever. The LAPD dragged me out through the long and winding halls that led to the front door at Barrington so everybody could get a good leer at me. I felt like Jesus on his way to Calvary.

They released the girl; no charges. They booked me into the West LA precinct jail. Weaver went into hiding, so my one call went to Bill Feeder at Rogers & Cowan. How embarrassing was that? The loveable lug put up my bail and looked into lawyers. I tried to swing Masseurs Rogers & Cowan, but I was just too far behind the 8 ball. Casa Granada said adios and don't come back. I retained an exceptional lawyer in Harry Weiss, a renowned attorney who had won several high-profile show-business drug cases. The cops also found a couple of Weaver's barbiturates in the bathroom. At my pre-sentence, the prosecutor offered to drop the marijuana charge if I'd plead guilty to the Seconals. Weiss agreed; I was sentenced to one year probation, 90 days in county jail suspended, and to abstain from trouble. Trouble is exactly what I was in with Deborah Lee.

Screwed, I crashed at a Dan Tana waiter's desolate apartment while he was in Poland. I was at my lowest point ever, and it got even lower. Back in Michigan, it was Tony's 6th birthday. The Peg and Scott family were living on the west side. They had a small family birthday party that my mother and Ted attended. Afterwards she went home and took a lethal quantity of Seconal. I refused to go home for the funeral. I did not want to see that final image of my mother dead in a casket. I had never forgiven the funerals of my sister Jeannie or my Aunt Irene. My family hated me for it; I don't regret it. Tony wrote me.

Dear Dad, Thank you for the racing set. I had a nice birthday.
I miss you. Love Tony.

SKIN

Chapter 14: MGM

Greg Friedkin had pursued an acting career after UCLA. Now he was known as Gregory Enton. With his talent, positive personality and connections, he had already done roles in film and TV shows like *The Mod Squad* and *Hawaii Five-0*. Girls loved him. He was still pals with Jon Fizdale, his oversized standup-comedy buddy. The three of us got together at Greg's apartment. He retrieved his mail and opened up two residual checks. With a big smile, he said let's buy a bottle of Riesling to celebrate. The guy was born with good fortune and an agreeable manner. Jon was cracking jokes too, but they were often draped in pessimism. They came from two different places. On this evening in November, 1968, Greg invited us to one of those places, the beautiful home of his parents in Beverly Hills. It was an election night party for Hubert Humphrey in his battle with Richard Nixon. The place was full of show-business Democrats. Among them was James Komack, who had been a standup comic and an actor on Broadway, television and motion pictures; but he was better known for producing and directing the landmark television shows *Welcome Back, Kotter* and *Chico and the Man*, which launched the careers of John Travolta and Freddie Prinze. Komack had picked both of them from relative obscurity.

Greg, Jon and I spent the evening talking show biz with Jimmy and his vivacious wife, Cluny. Komack was especially interested in our UCLA films and scripts and future projects. Fizdale had long been pushing his idea of short zippy films to illustrate rock-and-roll songs and thus further promote them. Nobody paid any attention. Twelve years later, MTV radically changed music and television and made a fortune. But that wasn't up Komack's alley either. What was up, was hiring us to work on his new television project and give it a kick of youthful exuberance. He was hip to the change in modern culture and wanted to tap it. We made a handshake deal while the Electoral College gave Nixon a landslide victory and the Presidency on the television.

A week later, we showed up at the Metro Goldwyn Mayer main gate. It was the studio that exemplified Hollywood, even if it was in Culver City. The Lion's roar, Judy Garland and Mickey Rooney, *Gone with the Wind, The Wizard of Oz,* Greta Garbo, Jean Harlow, Clark Gable, Buster Keaton, Laurel and Hardy, Fred Astaire and Gene Kelly. While at UCLA, we had visited various studios. The instructors were movie people; they set up trips to observe the working process. Our cinematography class went to observe films that employed Vincent Price and a young Jack Nicholson. Now here we were actually employed at a studio, and a guard at the gate was saying, "Good morning, Mr. Kiedis."

Komack's new ABC-TV series was *The Courtship of Eddie's Father*, starring Bill Bixby and an ingratiating child actor, Brandon Cruz. The show produced 73 episodes, ran for three years and plays today in syndication. The show was unique with innovations. Harry Nilsson wrote the theme song and a soundtrack that seamlessly followed the action of the show with his vocals. Nilsson was a bloody genius. One of his Grammies was for the song "Everybody's Talkin'" from the movie *Midnight Cowboy* that won the Academy Award for Best Picture. He wrote and sang some of the most beautiful music ever, including "One" and "Without You." He worked with and learned from the best—Phil Spector, The Monkees, Randy Newman and The Beatles. John Lennon famously remarked that Harry Nilsson was his favorite singer *and* his favorite band. They became dear friends.

We came to MGM in the morning with the cast and crew and sat around the writer's table, throwing ideas for Komack and the head writer's approval. We went to casting calls, editing rooms and the soundstage itself. Fizdale and I concentrated on writing; Greg was always trying to nab an acting role in one of the movies shooting at MGM. As sanctioned writers, we joined the Writers Guild of America.

On spec, Fiz and I wrote an entire script for the show. It was based on a real experience of mine. When Tony was three years old, Peggy went to St. John's Hospital for a few days. I would visit her on the seventh floor, but rules prevented anyone under 12 from going up. Mom missed her boy so I devised a sinister plan. I got a big suitcase for Tony to hide in, and we drove to the hospital. I put him in the suitcase, closed it up, walked into the lobby, went up the elevator, down the hall, into her room, closed the door, opened the suitcase and Tony jumped out and shocked his happy mom. After a few minutes, we loaded him back in and went downstairs. That was our payoff in a script with Eddie in the suitcase and Bill Bixby in the hospital room. We handed it in with great expectations, but Jimmy Komack said it wasn't good enough. Sorry.

After bouncing around for a while, I moved in with Greg and his killer girlfriend Pamela at their new joint on Melrose Place. Pretty soon Jon moved in too. So did Helter Skelter and the Sharon Tate murders. The city was terrorized and paranoid. About the same time, we landed men on the moon. With my new earnings, I rented a compact executive apartment of my own. Deborah and I were moving stacks of my books from Greg's to the new pad, and the LAPD pulled me over with a phony story about a bookstore robbery. When they were done harassing my long hair, they did a body search and found a miniscule pea-size bud in my pocket. They arrested me with great fanfare and impounded my car. Deb was furious with me again. Greg bailed me out the next day, but the Deborah Lee affair aborted. I had given her the house key to watch my place while I was in the clink; she snooped around and found my little black address books, which were filled with hundreds of girls including a special section of *redheads*, twenty-one of them and one was her. On the following page, was a section of sixteen Barbaras. I had a Debbie section too, but she never got that far. She wrote "checked out" across her name and phone number. The confiscated pot was so miniscule the judge sentenced me to only one year probation and monthly probation-officer meetings. I received this letter.

Dear Dad, Im glad that you did not have to go to jail. you should be more careful. I am sorry that I did not write sooner. I miss you Love Tony. PS. I'm sending you some cookies I made.

The Courtship of Eddie's Father season debuted in the fall and there on TV was my script with a slight alteration, Eddie's hiding in a big cake instead of a big suitcase. I wanted to file a grievance with the WGA, but Fiz was afraid of being blackballed for taking on a big shot like Komack. I certainly appreciated all he had done for us, but he was ripe with hundreds of writing credits, and it would have meant a lot to a couple writers getting started. By then we had been promoted anyway; the studio itself wanted us to write a feature movie script for MGM.

Easy Rider and other hip films were the rage; stodgy old MGM wanted in on the action. Their au courant movie *The Strawberry Statement* was in production, but it would bomb. Greg, Jon and I met with studio head Herbert Solow in the same luxurious office where Louie B. Mayer, Samuel Goldwyn and Irving Thalberg once reigned like mogul kings. We signed a six-month contract with a seven-year option that escalated from $125 to $2000 a week. Translated into today's money, we would have been rich.

They set us up in a spacious suite with three big, mahogany desks in each of our dominions. We needed a megaphone once we started tossing out ideas. Every morning we'd stop at the liquor store across the street and buy a bottle of Grey Riesling. We had our own garden patio too, and smoked a little reefer. We zeroed in on the plot of a hippie simply named David who endeavored to transform our uptight society into the Age of Aquarius. Eventually he persevered and the world became a wondrous place not unlike a groovy acid trip. We met with Herb Solow and presented a 25-page treatment. He OK'd the project, and we were set to proceed with the full script. We were in sync with the heavens, but corporate America can be the devil. At the time, MGM was owned by Seagram's Edgar Bronfman Sr. and he wanted out. He sold the studio with its vast properties to Nevada millionaire Kirk Kerkorian, who wasn't all that interested in the studio but wanted the real estate and the glamorous MGM name for his Las Vegas Hotel. Like a change of administration at the White House, the new honcho fired the old cabinet and hired new. Overnight, studio head Herb Solow was out and Jim Aubrey in. Aubrey specialized in downsizing, takeovers and selling off properties. They cleaned house at MGM, and that included the writing team of Enton, Fizdale & Kiedis. We did get paid for our guaranteed six months. The script is collecting dust in a vault somewhere. There's an urban legend that the film *Xanadu* may have been influenced by our project.

I didn't give up on Debbie. She moved to a place on Fountain and found herself a new boyfriend with an antique Bentley. In the middle of the night, I'd wait on her back porch, where she parked her MG. She'd come flying in, and her headlights would illuminate me, hiding in the shadows. Therapeutically, she'd scream and punch me. Not a pretty picture. She let me stay with her when I was sick for a few days, but made me sleep on a shelf in her closet and taunted me by pressing her dauntless tits against my face, a cocktail of ecstasy and humiliation. I was caught in an untenable place, still beguiled by her angel face and poisonous grace.

Working with the Monkees.

Chapter 15: Topanga Canyon

After David and I were evicted from Casa Granada, he moved into Sal Mineo's house in Studio City, and about that time he met Caroline Pratt, nicknamed Phrogg. For better or worse, her sisters came with the package, four of them vacationing in Hollywood from the Detroit area. Weaver fell in love, and they moved into the garish Saharan Motor Hotel on Sunset Boulevard; an infamous place known for rock bands, hookers and drug dealers. Bigwig Bomba's secret headquarters was in Studio City, but he had a little stash house on Grace Street in Hollywood, where Weaver often slept to protect the goods. Eventually all the Pratt sisters moved to LA and became an integral part of our grand scheme. I dated the dippy youngest. Slightly prosperous, David and Phrogg up and moved to a house on the bluffs overlooking the Pacific Ocean in Portuguese Bend, just south of Rancho Palos Verdes.

Me, I was in a black hole. I'd lost two consecutive redheads and that many shots at show biz. I was a drifter, so I drifted down to Portuguese Bend. My boy was visiting from GR, and I took him to see his Uncle Weaver. We arrived to a full house of family and friends. Every day was party day at Weaver's, but Sunday had become an institution. His sudden transformation and success sprang from Bomba's industry. David was a solid soldier and appropriately compensated. Among other enterprises, they were cooking up batches of LSD, employing a sweatshop bevy of girls to pack it into capsules. Everybody would get high from ingesting the powder on their finger tips. There was never a shortage of volunteers. Kilos of grass were moving about the country, and Bomba Inc. had an even bigger empire in mind.

On this Sunday as the group was kicking around the inebriated kitchen, Ashley Pandel unexpectedly appeared at the front door. He hadn't been invited and Weaver's scowl was an unwelcome vibe. I'm not sure why, but everybody in this clique picked on Ashley. He was unjustifiably looked upon as some weird pariah. Weaver straight out told him to leave, which I thought was uncalled for. I took a giant step and for the first time ever physically challenged my best friend. I dearly loved David, but he was showing signs of megalomania. He playfully bristled when I took the master bedroom at the Casa Granada; now he was his own formidable kingpin. David gracefully relented and allowed Ashley to stay, but his bad boy side at its most frightening was what most intruders were confronted with. There was a darkness lurking behind David's twinkling eyes. He had always been flamboyant, and now he had blossomed like a rock star. After a while and of his volition, Ashley left. He had his own brand of courage. If Weaver was the lion, Ashley was the fox.

The first Newport Pop Festival was about to flower at the Orange County Fairgrounds not far from Portuguese Bend, and a week later we assembled at Weaver's for the big day. His loony family had partied all night *before* the concert; now they'd be interacting with a hundred thousand maniacs on a dust-choked plain for an entire day in the broiling southern sun. I arrived responsibly about 10 a.m., with a clear-rested mind. And then my mind took two blue wedges of pure LSD. The trip is still locked in my high. Before my magical eyes, friends morphed into grotesque monsters and fairytale aberrations, except for the transcendent David, who shone like a constellation. He was Moses with yards of flowing hair that swirled in the wind on the mount of psychedelics. A fair-skinned guy by trade, the sun turned him pink as his silly pink shirt with the long collars that could have flown him to Panama. By his own retrospective admission, the ensemble continued with spiffy, white bellbottom britches and hippie scarves tied to every limb. He did pass out at one point, but I came to the rescue and got his mojo going. On his second wind, he was twice as much fun. The bands bashed our senses into the night, and we managed to get backstage. Some of the acts we barely saw through our hallucinations were Jefferson Airplane, Quicksilver Messenger Service, Blue Cheer, The Animals, Iron Butterfly and The Dead.

Long-lost Fred Freel had shown up for the acid and the event. The early nucleus of 1966 had evolved, and Fred hadn't made the cut. Today he took too much hemlock. By late afternoon, Fred was screaming he found God, and the Beatles were in contact via alien telephone transmissions from Mars. He refused to share the phone number. For months he continued to negotiate with John, Paul, George and Ringo. A second member of our party overdosed and never did recover. We thought we were bulletproof, but in the end most of the gang took a permanent shot to the brain. The stars and the scars of the festival collided, but David and Spider survived unscathed. I went home with two Nordic blonde love-dolls who wanted to do a three-way at their home in Hollywood. It was my first and last. I was a sensitive lover and didn't appreciate two spoiled brats fighting over my penis.

The following year, Newport Festival moved to Devonshire Downs in Northridge, from Orange County all the way up to the San Fernando Valley. This was a three-day affair; Weaver and I went to all three. At the time, it was the largest pop festival ever—150,000 maniacs and 34 acts. We took acid the first day, mescaline the second and acid again the third. In addition to all the same groups we saw the year before, there was Joe Cocker, Creedence Clearwater, Love, Steppenwolf, Marvin Gaye, Taj Mahal, Jethro Tull, Booker T & the MGs, Chamber Brothers, Eric Burdon, Three Dog Night, Buffy Saint Marie, the Rascals, Johnny Winter, Albert King, Spirit, Poco and Hendrix. Jimi got me into the artist's area, and later I tripped to the entire Jimi Hendrix Experience flat on my back under the stage.

My incidents with Jimi extended right into a cozy estate overlooking the Strip, west of Laurel Canyon. Noel Redding, Mitch Michell and Ashley were there too. During those timeless experiences—or were they merely moments?—I continued to bump into Jimi and he was always cordial. In 2004, Red Hot Chili Peppers headlined the dedication of the (Jimi Hendrix) Experience Music Project and Science Fiction Museum and Hall of Fame in Seattle. In 2009, Jimi's sister Janie Hendrix, CEO of Experience Hendrix, visited Flea's philanthropic Conservatory of Music in Silverlake and donated Jimi Hendrix guitar tablatures, instructional DVD's and a catalogue of his recordings.

As my vigilantes cruised into the 70s, there was an ominous reality that our benign and enlightened drugs had turned problematic. Its power was malignant, and it killed like an epidemic. I don't know if it was Portuguese Bend cabin fever, or just that the outlaws had circled their wagons in a different western back lot, but my co-conspirator moved off the bluffs of Palos Verdes and nearer my comfort zone.

Topanga Canyon was tailor made for David Weaver and his big plans. The gorgeous gorge wiggled its way from the Pacific beach to the San Fernando Valley on a trail of craggy peaks, a silver stream and a parallel winding road, negotiated by hand-painted VW buses, rusty pick-ups, Harleys, dope-money Mercedes and sandal prints on the scorched-earth shoulders all tie-dyed together in a merry mosaic. Precedent vegetarian restaurants had bloomed early. There was a family grocery store and a Dodge City post office. A lonely gas station and auto repair was right out of Steinbeck. Girls wore flowers in their tangled hair and discarded their clothes on the flimsiest of whims. Mountain-men beards and bandito mustaches were fashion models for a reluctant America. The spirit of the West made its last stand in Topanga.

While Weaver and his ever-growing entourage rented an old farm house on Observation Drive in a secluded crook of the western Topanga hills, I returned to my senses in a homey duplex on Hilldale, a stoned throw from Sunset. I was back in my element, the last house on the left at the dead end. My duplex neighbor, Lenny, was a quiet well-mannered young man of Japanese descent, with a giant Great Dane named George. West Hollywood had always been the gay heart of LA, but in 1970 it wasn't so blatant. Lenny was one of my first gay friends. By now I was driving a sporty but ramshackle used Alpha Romeo.

David had distanced himself from Bomba and took on a new partner in Ronnie Desautels, who was newly arrived from Worcester, Massachusetts. So prevalent you'd think dealer partnerships were mandatory, like kayak or tennis tandems. Pisces & Spike Limited, Jasper & Son, The Rufus & Skippy Corporation of America. Ronnie was an exuberant and affable character, not terribly bright but sincere. Like everyone who knew Weaver's friend Spider from Hollyweird, Ronnie was aware I'd steal a man's wife if he went to the restroom. David's gang and the dark outsider were all assembled at a restaurant in Woodland Hills to celebrate Ronnie's birthday. He had with him a cute new girlfriend that was quite young but anxious to jump into the culture with big-blue-eyes wide open. At the head of the King Arthur table, Ronnie stood up and gave a pre-emptive speech. "Hello everybody. Thanks for coming to my party. This is my old lady, Deia. Spider, keep your hands off her!" He never let her out of his sight that night, and I don't remember how I managed, but the next day Deia and I were sleeping together.

The day after that, we went to the pound to get a dog. Just like that. We picked out a wonder mutt, and from that moment on, he rarely ever left my side. He was baptized Wolfer, a terrier mix with the moxie of a wild wolf and the wisdom of Doctor Who. Deia came and went, but doggy love was forever. Wolfer was my constant companion and partner for years. Spider & Wolfer Inc.

Weaver, competitive as usual and especially with me, got *two* dogs. Hubert and Dudley, a couple of droopy-eared Beagle hound dogs, who were like cousins to Wolfer. This kettle of canines was definitely unrefined. Whenever I went out of town, I'd leave Wolfer with them. At Weaver's, the dogs could run around in the rattlesnake gullies and scale the rocky formations. But like me, Wolfer was a Hollywood dog and just as savvy in the big city. I could take him downtown and leave him on a bustling sidewalk while I went up into a 20-story building. I'd come out a half hour later, and he'd be patiently laying there waiting for his master. If I said stay, he stuck.

There was always activity at the new Weaver house. Phrogg was the housemother and David's old lady. Attesting to David's party-boy status, the teeny Topanga groupies would flutter around and deliver homemade cookies and pies. And their mothers would try their own means of seduction. Free love was flourishing then.

David had new manly connections too, and the local mafia recognized a rising star in the firmament. One of Topanga's reigning head honchos was music producer David Briggs, who saw something special in Weaver. He put him under his wing and introduced him to the other luminaries. Neil Young was living with Briggs then, and along with Kendal Pacios they produced *After the Gold Rush* out of the basement studio. Kendal was another east-coast transplant who would become a critical component of our family. David's house was well off the beaten track and was surrounded with a lot of scruff-brush land where he could plant things. He raised a potent pot plant named Hector that grew to the size of a Rockefeller Center Christmas tree. There was always smoke emanating from Weaver's Vatican. With neither David nor I duly employed, we continued to fight our hirsute war full-throttle. Our hair was down to the 21st vertebrae. It wasn't just us; the movement calibrated stature by the length of your hair. It showed your commitment to the new culture that was just beginning for most of America. We didn't cut ours for years; and our competition, like our friendship, ended in a dead heat. David had a Baldwin brotherhood of brothers—Jeff, Scott, Chris and Eric, but our own brotherhood was sacrosanct.

Another fixture on Topanga's topography was The Corral, a rowdy, noisy, smoky, knee-slapping, drunken, dancing, brawling bar and nightclub, on the higher elevations of the main drag. The Corral cooked up as much action as any club in Hollywood, and it didn't have far to go for its acts. Topanga was full of musical entertainers who performed at the Corral: Canned Heat, just back from Woodstock: Neil Young, likewise with CSN&Y: Taj Mahal: Spirit: Etta James: Emmylou Harris: and a drifter with a harpsichord. Topanga had always been a lure to bohemian artists of all stripes. Residents past and present included Woody Guthrie, Joni Mitchell, Gram Parsons, Jim Morrison, Dennis Hopper, and Lynn Redgrave. William Randolph Hearst, Bertolt Brecht, Peter Lorre, Carole Lombard and Shirley Temple had homes in Lower Topanga, nearer the beach. The ubiquitous Charles Manson and his maniacs held up in the Spahn Ranch in nearby Chatsworth. His first-known murder victim, a week before the Sharon Tate murders, was Gary Hinman, a music teacher who lived and died in Topanga Canyon.

As a team, Weaver and I complimented each other's social life; he had clout at the Corral and I had some sway on the Strip. Once David became an established personality and financial force in Topanga, he extended his range and flourished in my neighborhood, thus stamping his star on both boulevards. He'd roll into the Whisky with his harem of stoned cult-cuties and take over the place, ordering one of everything and dropping generous gratuities. Soon he became a favorite of Mario Maglieri, who managed the club for Elmer Valentine. There was a prized booth in the shadows that was always held for rock royalty, reserved for whatever superstars were in town and out on the evening. But if Weaver and his entourage showed up, Mott the Hoople would be standing in a draft, and Billy Joel was hunting for a folding chair.

The Experience was a new club contender on Sunset. We knew the owner Marshall Brevits, and we were always more than welcome. The unique club attracted big bands that were in town for gigs at The Forum or The Shrine Auditorium. They specifically came to jam with other top musicians. Our friend Lenny Fagan, one of the top musicians and later a nightclub owner himself, jammed with Quicksilver and other cool acts. The Blues Magoos played there. Later, an early Alice Cooper Band got booed off the stage. Jimi Hendrix jammed at the Experience. Marshall Brevits, who was known to have burned a few associates, was tied up and shot to death in a field near San Bernardino a few years later. Weaver says he was the only guy Marshall never burned for cash. Me either, but then I never had enough cash to burn.

To top off the debauchery, Weaver and I always went to the International House of Pancakes on Sunset across from Hollywood High. None of that IHOP, KFC, DQ crap. This was when they made pancakes and waffles with a full name, like mom used to whip up on Sunday morning. Los Angeles was the Pancake House's hometown, born on 1958 in Toluca Lake. We had the reefer-fueled appetite to test the patience of late-night waitresses and we'd order several servings out of that magical mystery menu. For me, it was a quick trip to my West Hollywood abode, but for David it was a long and winding road to the baron's castle in the fiefdom of Weaver, The Pope of Topanga Canyon.

Dear Dad, If you would like to come and visit me we will pay your way. Here is a picture of me and Julie. If you come we can go to Grand Haven. Grandma Kiedis and your sisters and brothers are coming July 26, 1970. Please write soon. Love Tony

"Noon" by Terrence McNally.

Chapter 16: Costly Free Love

At some point, I would have to live up or down to that hyperbolic title Lord of the Sunset Strip, lurking in my future. I don't know which pundit ultimately coined me that, most likely the Rainbow's Tony Vescio, but I'm sure there were others more deserving. For now, we were both a twinkle in an apparition's black eye. On this splendid day in West Hollywood, I was still only a disciple, a choirboy in awe of my great fortune to live and love in this cornucopian megalopolis. The odds were a million to one against me, but I addressed the future and went surfing for serendipity. I applied for law school at UCLA and sat in on classes. I wrote some briefs and pestered professors. After a boring waste of time, I decided the law was a little too lawful for me. I was more comfortable in the artful arms of a woman.

California's '67 summer of love had given way to the 70s of lust. Free love became free trips to the free clinic. Swapping and group sex had supersized into temples of abomination. There was word on the street of a monster partner-swapping party every weekend at an ornate mansion up in the hills around St. Ives and Doheny Drive. It was only a short walk from my pad, and I was curiously tempted. The party was Caligula on hemorrhoids, a Cecil B. De Mille porn movie. There were concubine rooms teeming with entangled flesh and a hornet's nest of vitriol. In the extravagant main room with its towering ceiling, there were champagne and catered hors d'oeuvres for people having sex in food for thought because the smaller rooms were booked. Salacious teams vied for trophy wives and stud pokers. Hot nurses announced free sex and psychosis now available on the veranda. I stifled a gag and wandered home in a daze. Like the Newport three-way, the experience jolted my faith in sin. Love was a perplexing Rubik Goldberg Cube, and I was helplessly addicted. I was a criminal flirt in cheap's clothing. After all, I had been refining the art since kindergarten. I woke up every morning and plotted another sexual scheme. My job was to find at least one new love affair each day. I was a serial charmer and doubted there was a woman alive who could tame me.

There was a *Penthouse* centerfold in her future, but on that Friday all I saw was clickity-clack red high heels smacking the Sunset sidewalk on the corner of Sunset and Clark. She was raw, wanton teen woman, slender with important statements in and out of her swaying, sheer blouse. She wore lipstick so red it bled. I would have beaten my head against the bulletin-riddled telephone pole if she had given me the brush off, but instead she gave me a stiff proposition.

She lived above the Pool Room Bar at the top of Palm Avenue, with access from the alley. It was Hell's Kitchen. And it didn't help that she was a lousy housecleaner. Dirty clothes and make-up weren't made up; junk was everywhere, both kinds. Was it really worth it? She had a ditzy female roommate and hip music. Everything was pink and intoxicated. I opted on the sex-safe side for a change, but we remained close friends until she was immortalized by Bob Guccioni.

Years later, I ran into her in New York City at Danceteria, an eight-story joint with something different on every level. I was staying at the Iroquois on West 44th and was in this nightclub for the first time. She recognized me in the crowd and bought me a drink. She got bored and invited me back to her place above another bar on the lower east side. The bar was open till 5 a.m., and we kept going down for drinks and then walking back up to her 6th floor apartment, which hadn't gotten any cleaner than the one in LA. I had some toot; she did it all and got bored again. We had been sitting on her silk tapestry bed in the middle of the only room; she continued to disrobe incrementally. I steered the ship of procrastination. Now she was undressed and wanted sex. It was late and I was exhausted. She ordered sex. I said no. She demanded sex. I said no, I'm going back to the hotel. She winced and pouted and said goodbye. A few months later, a friend told me she had died from HIV/AIDS.

I was on Hollywood Boulevard and saw a tantalizing handful of allure. She was quite tall, graceful and wearing a mesh sweater with meshes that were few and far between. Her puffy, pink areolas poked through unencumbered. They begged me to trespass. We dashed for my Alpha Romeo and sped off for privacy. She wasn't about to wait and already had her hand down my pants. This was just too good to be true. I looked at that angelic face and long dark curls and I stopped to reciprocate. We pulled over on notorious Selma; I embraced her and thrust my own hand down into...him! It! Yelp! Help! Oh my god, wherefore art thou?! He-she apologized, kissed me gently on the cheek and sashayed off with conspicuous flair.

A prominent fixture those days was the infamous Hollywood Free Clinic on Third, but for West Hollywood residents it was the LA County Free Clinic on San Vicente and Melrose. It was like a club house. Coffee and candy bars and a small library. Serpentine lines weaved past contaminated communal tribes. A colorful revolving door of hippies flirted with other hippies who had just been dosed with penicillin. I only know about all this from secondhand accounts, of course. Or did I dream this, and what's this little band aid on my shoulder? I did leave the clinic with a girl once; mysophobic as I was, you can imagine just how hot this busty patient with cutoff jeans and no top must have been. Well, she was and more. She left me her 8 by 10 photo and a dose of retribution.

On Hollywood between Grauman's and La Brea was an old white colonial-style hotel. It had antebellum pillars, a long front porch and may have been a fine hostelry for D. W. Griffith's actors and crew on one of his silent movies. Now it was condemned and boarded up. In the future, some super structure would reside on its memories, but it had one last fling. For nomadic runaways, it turned out to be a godsend. No rent. No hassle. All parties all day and all night. Hollywood Boulevard was no stranger to me; I still loved to play on it. When Johnny Reaser and I trolled for movie roles in 1961, it was still a boulevard of glamour. Now it was hippie city, running the gamut from the purest of intentions to lost souls and infiltrating beggars and con men and killers. I happened upon the hotel's secret life quite by accident; from the street it appeared dead as a dormant. On this day, I befriended a lass skipping along the sidewalk of fame, and after we'd gotten to know each other, she invited me to her "occupied" home at this decrepit hotel. The secret entrance was through a broken steel door in the rear, and inside was a whole new secret world, a *Lord of the Flies* hotel with children running their own society. There were endless parties going on: drunk, stoned and crazy on psychedelics; a microcosm of the big outside. I was a citizen until the bulldozers destroyed our quixotic delusion.

Jon Fizdale had never been with a girl in his life as far as I knew. He was comical and earnest, but he'd rather eat than anything, or everything. At MGM, while Greg and I were selecting wines at the liquor store for our daily ritual, Jon would be piling donuts and corned-beef sandwiches into his shopping cart. When it was bedtime at Greg's apartment, Jon and I got tucked into twin couches in the living room. Jon would pop a few butterscotch candies in his mouth; I'd say, "Jon, you just brushed your teeth." "Yeah, but it tastes so good," he'd say.

Well, one day after a long absence, he called and said he'd met a girl and had a date! He was taking her to a well known romantic restaurant on Topanga Beach, overlooking the Ocean. He invited me to come because he was nervous, and I knew a thing or two about women. With both embarrassment and excitement, he added she had recently gone through breast augmentation and was very shy about it. At one point, I must have confided in him that silicone grapefruits had turned me off. I would have no trouble resisting this new friend of Fizdale's.

I arrived and met them at the table. The breakers were pounding and so was Fizdale's heart. He was sweating bullets. Being heavy he always sweat, but now he was constantly dabbing his face with a linen napkin. Normally facile and clever, this evening he was blushing and tongue-tied. I had to step in and save the day for Fiz. I put her at ease, and we made sparkling conversation. She was attractive and intelligent. Then like a well-orchestrated script, she removed a small jacket and revealed her secret weapons. Slender and willowy, she had done something I had only dreamed about: breasts as art. Her surgically-sculptured breasts were two precipitous torpedoes, torpedoes for libidos. They pointedly strained against the fabric of her blouse. I thought they'd poke through at any moment and give us a coronary. They threatened me. The way Degas and Matisse threatened Rodin. Now I was as nonplussed as Jon. I had to caress and fondle them. See them unencumbered by that nearly torn blouse. When Fiz went to the restroom for deodorant, I told her she was driving me to distraction. I needed to leave, but I wanted to see her as soon as possible. We exchanged phone numbers and I left. Tell Jon I didn't feel well.

But I felt just swell! We did hook up, maybe that night for all I know, and I did discover the holy communion of those breasts. As usual for me, it was a single event. Like Woody said, "The shark has to keep on moving or it dies." As for Jon, he was crushed, betrayed and again unloved. I was nothing more than a dastardly cad in need of therapy. Just what wouldn't I do for what I called love? Whatever it was I'd continue to do it; bless the torpedoes. Full speed ahead. It wasn't so much an addicted to sex as it was to beauty; I was a slut for the rapture of love. There were consequences to be paid, karmic vengeance. The Katies and Deborahs and others to come would extract revenge for my dreadful deeds. Secretly and repentantly, I was rooting for them.

David's best friend at Ottawa High in GR had been Alan Bashara, a clever fellow of Lebanese heritage. Weaver was always talking about Alan and extolling his class-clown sharp wit. Alan had been missing all this good LA fun because he was in Viet Nam. Fortunately, most of his fighting was with mosquitoes and MPs cracking down on smoking pot. Now at last, he was coming home and via Los Angeles. Appropriately, Weaver planned a welcome-home party and a thorough tour of our iniquitous paradise. He was hopeful of recruiting Bashara to locate in Southern California too. Alan had been through a war, but he wasn't prepared for a day in the life of Spider and the newly-improved Weaver.

I drove out to the Topanga party, a little apprehensive about this new guy Weaver called "the Rug." His nappy Lebanese hair resembled and felt like a Berber rug, especially when military-cut close. Was he going to steal my best friend? Would the three of us make a new dynamic trio? Would there be any really cool chicks at the party?

There were, and one especially; she was Alan's present. Phrogg found her, and she was Alan's blind date. I was the blindsided one. She reminded me of Deborah Lee. So smitten, I was willing to do anything: buy her, trade for her, go into servitude. I needed some leverage but didn't know what Alan's weaknesses were. Weaver had none. Was David going to freak on me for stealing the sacrificial love doll from the guest of honor who had served his country in the Viet Nam jungle for three years? I was concerned, but made my move anyway. With great relief, Alan relinquished her and everybody had a funny Spider-stole-my-girlfriend story to impart. It turned out Alan had his eyes on someone else anyway. The party got back to business, sidetracked with acid and mescaline and reefer. We all went to see Vanilla Fudge at the Shrine Auditorium, with opening acts Richie Havens and AB Skyy. Alan didn't know what hit him, but he loved it.

The blind date and I hit it off, and we both wanted more. A Beverly Hills girl, her parents also owned a retreat near Lake Arrowhead at high elevation where it snowed in January. She picked me up in her mom's Lincoln and drove Interstate 10 to San Bernardino, about 80 miles, and then up 20 miles of winding mountainous roads to their getaway chalet. It was a weekend party for just her friends, and it was dark by the time we arrived. I felt a bit awkward up in this wintery lodge a hundred miles from civilization with a bunch of college freshmen and high-school seniors that I didn't know. The girls were snobby and the dudes were crude. Blind-date girl was busy making drinks and laughing with her friends.

I plunked down on a sofa and tried to make Noel Coward conversation with a pretty blonde co-ed. I guess I got a little too cozy. I stepped over some imaginary line that females instinctively perceive, and men are blithely unaware of. There was a spat, and the next thing I knew the jockasses were tossing me out the front door into the snow. Blind date said have a nice walk home and slammed the massive door shut. It was freezing. It could only get worse. All I knew was I had to go down this winding road toward that metro Los Angeles carpet of lights spread out to the horizon.

I started walking and put out my thumb. The thumb got numb and never attracted a ride. I walked the entire way down the mountain, 20 miles in the stormy cold. On the valley floor in San Bernardino, I found a truck stop and begged my way home. I deserved every lousy minute of it, from stealing her in the first place to the pretty blonde co-ed all snuggly in the chalet. To be honest though and despite my frostbite, I was still thinking about that blonde. A few days later, Alan continued on to Michigan. He was ready to decompress after Nam. He got a publicity job at Eastbrook Mall, but that Manchurian Candidate bug had been planted; he was destined to return and add a new dimension to our psychedelic empire.

Happy Valentine's day, Daddy! Love Tony with lots of kisses, To my Favorite Dad.

Chapter 17: Tony Crashes the Party

While his pop was screwing up girls, jobs, cars and his life, Tony Kiedis was bopping around Grand Rapids with his virtuous mother and a new dad, who used to be his real dad's best friend. The not-so-best man at our wedding was now married to my ex, and his life wasn't going so well either. Although the bully fathered a sister Julie for Tony, he flunked matrimony and eventually Peg divorced him. Tony turned to his real dad and pleaded for me to come and visit. The cartel provided free airfare to their outlets, and, not surprisingly, the home town had one. I signed up and took the nebulous, mule-train flight to GRR.

Tony was no longer the malleable little novelty you couldn't help but squeeze and show off to your friends at a poker party. He was already a skilled technician in the art of life. And he loved me. I don't think anybody else did. Girls adored me. Friends were sincere. Family was inundated with prolific offspring. Only this little Anthony Kiedis bundle of electricity loved me unconditionally. I couldn't have found a more perfect devotion. AK in his book *Scar Tissue*: "My Dad would show up in six-inch silver platform snakeskin shoes with rainbows on them, bell bottom jeans with crazy velvet patch work all over them, giant belts covered with turquoise, skintight almost midriff T-shirts with some great emblem on them, and tight little velvet rocker jackets from London. Hair down to his waist and he had a bushy handlebar mustache and huge sideburns. I was just euphoric that he was there."

He had been coming to LA in the summers, and now I was returning the favor. He was gracious as the Plaza concierge. He gave up his bed and slept on the couch. He helped me carry my contraband Willy Loman suitcases down to the basement for safe keeping. He was my Biff. He challenged me to a race; even in my platform shoes I whipped his butt, but butt would kick mine in time. The day would come he'd leave me in the stardust, but I'd be cheering. Thankfully, he was just my kid now, and these were days to remember for a lifetime. We borrowed mom's car and went to see Woody Allen's *Sleeper*, a screwball comedy that had us rollicking in our popcorn. We emerged from the theater to find a new batch of ice and snow in the deserted parking lot and drove whirlies and loopty-loops all over the place. We couldn't stop laughing.

I had to get to work. My square dance was with a couple greenhorns out in the woods. We met in a horse barn like bad guys in one of my old cowboy movies at the Royal Theater. Mission easily accomplished. Next stop was the Putt Putt Bar on that pesky west side. Peripheral pal Vic Amato invited me to see his band at the spunky venue. As fate would have it, there was a killer female present. I wished she had been my present. The belle of the Putt Putt ball was Debbie Wauchope. She was fast and first class and girlfriend of the singing guitar player, local rock stud, Charlie Huhn. My work was cut out for me; I'd have to steal, but even Willie Sutton would have found it difficult. Not to test your patience, but she had breasts you could hang your winter coat on. Watch out: horizontal projectiles. I could look at a fully-clothed woman and know exactly what she was hiding. Like Superman's penetrating vision, I already knew the palette of her colors and the conical configuration beneath her sweater. My temperature had a rocket. I went to the bar and stuck my head in the ice sink. Despite my sly efforts, Debbie barely ratified the rat at the table. In the end, the rock band entourage left the Putt Putt intact, and disgustingly they were all in joyous spirits. I sat there alone in despair, down but determined. Mr. Dithers was anxious to see his suitcase full of dough. Dagwood had to go home. On my way to the airport, I conned Vic Amato into giving me Debbie's address so I could write her one of my compelling letters. One thing was for sure, I would sign up for another hitch on the Nebulous Express.

I got a slap on the back, and the bosses' assurance they'd be happy to use me again. In fact, I had a couple offers. Weaver had another pal who knew how to do his business. His name was Jimmy Lurie, and he lived in remote Los Flores Canyon, a couple canyons west of Topanga. Jimmy was a cool guy, sensitive, good-looking and a vegetarian who was always extolling the virtues there of. He was definitely a competing ladies' man.

The closest mountain man to Jimmy's homestead was a reclusive aspiring young actor named Nick Nolte. Nolte had the solitary disposition of Ted Kaczynski and scowled enough to keep the cougars and coyotes at bay. In the morning, Jimmy would wheel out fresh fruits and whip up delicious smoothies which he'd gladly offer you, along with the vegetarian ballyhoo. Whenever there was an exciting concert or party in Hollywood, David and Jimmy and I would be there in our Edwardian outfits, with pockets full of goodies. Both Weaver and Lurie had cut their skull and cross bones as lieutenants in Bomba's early business endeavors, but when the two of them finally consolidated for a period, their stock soared on Wall Street.

Debbie Wauchope was burning a hole in my heart. I had some cash and a plan to execute. My love letter was "A Short Story for a Tall Lady," an advance scenario of my next trip to Grand Rapids. Weaver sent me flying to the Furniture City, business and pleasure. But first, Alan had a huge truckload of pot to drop off in Rhode Island, and I was the muscle in case of trouble. On the way, Indiana troopers pulled us over for speeding, but I convinced the cops all those giant boxes were full of musical instruments. In Providence, we were outnumbered and out gunned in a nervous-trigger standoff, but they backed down and Alan left with the cash. He had screwed up his GR Eastbrook Mall job when he took an extended vacation skiing in Idaho. Now there was nothing to keep him from joining forces with Weaver in Topanga.

As my short story predicted, I slept in Tony's little bed, with my uncovered feet protruding beyond their confines. I heard the early morning charge of Apaches and an uproar coming from a silly Mickey Mouse alarm clock on a nightstand. A frosty window neon flashed *5 below zero - 7 a.m. - 5 below zero* on the frigid façade of a Fargo Financial. I was far from the usual warm Pacific breezes that rustle palm trees on their way to my gentle afternoon waking. Out of bed, I was into the swirl of heavy morning traffic. At breakfast, I sat between Brandy the three-legged dog and Julie Beth, the new kid. She asked for my credentials. "That's your brother's daddy from California," said Peggy. She was passing the eggs to Tony but looking straight at me. "I realize you've never seen him up this early, but that's him." Peg was still full of sarcasm but couldn't resist my offer of shoveling the snow in exchange for her car.

I sputtered up to Comstock Park High and parked. Runny-nose kids were shuffling their boots to stay warm. I asked where I could find Debbie Wauchope. Co-eds ran over the rugby team to show me her classroom. After an encounter with Mrs. Freitas, the muscular security cop who mistook me for the new Brazilian exchange student, I settled in and waited for the bell. She was the first one out the door and gave me a sweetheart kiss. We skipped school and started our happy ending. A brief affair, it lasted a lifetime of memories. Tony got to meet her too. Back in LA, I received his letter:

Dear Dad, how are you. Dad please work hard So I can go to California. My dog had puppies.
Tony Kiedis.

Time flew and Alan drove to California in his Camaro Z28. He met up with a bunch of us in Santa Cruz for a racketeer convention. Santa Cruz was more stoned than Topanga, if that was possible. We guzzled LSD, and one of our hosts died of a fatal heroin overdose.

The rest of us went to San Francisco. I drove Alan and my LA date in the Alpha Romeo. We were supposed to meet Weaver in front of Tower Records near the wharf, but Alan and I dropped more acid for the sixty-mile drive. When we got into the Oakland San Francisco Bay Bridge Berkeley cloverleaf we weren't so lucky. There was no Jean-Paul Sartre exit; no matter which direction we chose to follow it kept whipping us back into a bewildering labyrinth. A millennium late, we finally met up with Weaver and tripped the light fantastic at a Golden Gate Park love-in. After compulsory Haight Ashbury, we finished the trip at the Fillmore. We'd make many trips to SF over the years. I don't remember much about the most memorable. Wacked with substantial substances, Weaver and I went to Winterland for a Grateful Dead show. I was on the upper-level balcony, prowling around in my unstable high-heel platforms, looking out over the spectacle's edge and plummeted into the deadheads below. Fortunately, I landed on a packed house.

Alan Bashara moved in with Weaver up on Observation Drive and found his grove. Soon he'd become Big Al. The reunited twosome made for more hi-jinx, and not to be undone, Spider threw out the Hollywood welcome mat. Figaro's was at its zenith. Stoned stupid, I almost drowned in a movie-star daughter's hot-tub party full of naked girls in the Encino Hills. Alan ignored my plight and performed mouth-to-mouth resuscitation on the giggling girls.

Consummate hell raisers, we met with Larry Vallon, Alan's former foxhole partner in Viet Nam, just getting started at ABC. In his career he would boss the Universal Studios Amphitheater, House of Blues and AEG Live. He was already in cahoots with future show biz titans Tom Ross (CAA) and Jim Wiatt, who would become Chairman of the Board at William Morris and President of ICM. We shook them up at Wiatt's house in Benedict Canyon; they counted the silverware when we left. On our way back, Alan needed a pay phone. I swung by the Beverly Hills Hotel; it was a good place to show off movie stars and the Polo Club. We found a phone booth in the lobby, but a big dude was filling it up. We waited and waited. I got rather upset and banged on the door. He kept his back to us and ignored my protest. Finally, he hung up and squeezed out the door. Face to face, it was John Wayne. An ardent outspoken pro-war conservative who despised long-haired hippies, the Duke was glaring down at two of them. He grumbled some defamatory remarks and strode off into the proverbial sunset.

Soon enough, Alan discovered murder and mayhem flourished in Tombstone Topanga. There was blood on the cocaine. Hard drugs fought back. Debbie Lee and I were fooling each other around again and went out to visit David. He was snorting dope and knew I wouldn't, but shockingly Deb said yes. At this point I still hadn't used heroin, or coke, for that matter. I was the last holdout. I was intent on a career; they were all just content.

A few weeks later, I had third-row seats for the Rolling Stones at the Forum. I was taking Deb, and again we drove out to Weaver's for a preshow buzz. Day and night you could count on it like the bottle of wine on a Parisian dinner table. There was always something cooking on his kitchen table, a bowl of pre-rolled joints and piles of powders and pills. Deb got mired and didn't want to leave. Not even for the Stones' *Exile on Main Street* tour with Stevie Wonder opening. Disappointed, I left by myself. Alan gave me a bindle of coke in case I needed it; halfway to Inglewood I decided I'd give it a try. I took a little snort. Hmmm, that was nice. I remember thinking who needs Deborah Lee.

Although the Observation house was still secluded in the hills, the landlord knew exactly where his house was. Hector was a pot-plant beacon, and David's all-night parties ricocheted across those hills. For months the owner tried to evict them, and when that didn't work he actually set fire to the house. It was time to move. Tony came out for his annual visit that summer and helped. He was aghast to see me as a wrangler, battling a truck bed loaded sky high with Weaver's furniture. I was prostrated on a mattress at the top of the pile, grasping a rodeo rope as the bucking pickup made its way down steep and winding roads along Tuna Canyon. Weaver was driving, puffing on a joint and giving me playful grief with wild zigzags and fake-you-out quick stops.

They moved across the canyon closer to the social epicenter of Topanga Village, where a hippie festival flourished every Sunday. Their new house had a small corral, and they both bought horses. Weaver's brown-and-white pinto was Gypsy; Alan had a buckskin mare named Cinnamon. The house had a rugged feel of the Arizona Territory circa Wyatt Earp and Doc Holliday. Topanga was a badland; Weaver and Jimmy Lurie were Wyatt and the Dandy. Big Al was Yosemite Sam. Once he got that afro happening, his unique personality and clever repartee took the cake and the girl jumping out of it.

We ran across a band from Texas at a bar in the Valley. They were Slip of the Wrist, but the lead singer guitar wizard and driving force was Gary Myrick. Weaver convinced Myrick to give him a shot at managing them. Thus began a long and convoluted relationship. By then Weaver had connected with entrepreneurial manager Skip Taylor and was working for his band Canned Heat. They were a major-league band, but Weaver got them to perform at a small club called Boomers in Venice so he could put the new "Gary Myrick and the Figures" on the bill as the opening act. I brought Tony, and we put him up on stage with Canned Heat during their show. Comically, the elephantine lead-singer Bob Hite and pint-size Tony were dancing together around the mike stand. Over the years Gary Myrick cut a wide swath across the nightclub landscape, made some hit songs like "She Talks in Stereo" and "Havana 3am," and worked with artists like the Eagles, Bonnie Raitt, Jackson Browne, and played guitar on John Waite's #1 hit "Missing You." He would be an inspiration to high-school ninth-graders Flea and Anthony when I snuck them into his show at the Starwood, and, down the road, we tried to get an opening-act slot for the Peppers on a Gary Myrick show. He turned us down.

Chapter 18: In the Red

I met a young lady from Indianapolis at the Frolic Room on Hollywood and Vine. Deanna was a spirited cutie who was staying with friends in Beachwood Canyon. Although we dated for a while, I just wasn't that enamored and she asked why. I explained my persistent passion for foxy redheads. Rather than sulk, she gave me the prettiest red in all the land. They were old best friends, and she would introduce me. The prize was married though, so don't get my hopes up.

The redhead was Connie Kellman, formerly Connie Foreman. Katie, Debbie and now Connie; they made up my triumvirate of little red riding hoods, the genuine holy trinity. The new one was born and raised in Chicago, a Catholic school girl, conservative folks, sexually suppressed, and now married to Jack Kellman, the son of a wealthy auto-glass magnate. They had recently moved to Los Angeles and had settled in Topanga Canyon. It turned out Deanna herself was married and to a rugged Chicago carpenter named Ernie Lindberg, who also lived in Topanga. He had a Chi-town bro, Jerry, who lived there too. I guess she and Ernie were on a sabbatical. I kept pestering Deanna to introduce me with this angel-face friend of hers, who promised to be nothing but painful eye candy. Finally, she said OK and arranged it.

We drove up Fernwood all the way to the top near where the road ends at Rocky Ledge. From up there you could gaze across most of the canyon. We walked into a bedlam of big-city energy unusual in Topanga. Jack had just come home from work and was rattling on about his day with broad-shoulder hairy-back gusto. Connie had been shopping and was rationalizing expensive sexy outfits she held up for us to see. Ernie and Jerry were trying to get the Blackhawks on TV, and they were all wearing red–and-black Chicago hockey jerseys. It was utter cacophony, and they hardly paid any attention to either Deanna or me, especially me.

It was like I wasn't even there, so I took advantage and just fixated on her, thinking how it would be if I stayed there all night, unnoticed, watching her undress for bed. She fascinated me with a fury. Her moves were of a silky long-legged jungle-kitten. She had turbulent, wild red hair and skin as white as light. She was tall and almost skinny, with the breasts of a budding adolescent. But it was her face that ruled this aggregate temptress. She had a look. The look of a Catholic school girl deprived of males for all her young life and now determined to get revenge on her religion. She was capable of breaking every heart she encountered. Make them pay. I saw a hungry nymphet who wanted to feast on whoever had the balls to make up for all those virgin years she had endured. Eventually, our hosts threw us a few scraps of dialogue and offered a glass of wine. I certainly didn't leave satiated, but I knew I would be back. On the way down, Deanna made it clear these were not your average California hippie guys. They were bad boys from Chicago so don't even think about messing with them.

For a week, I fanaticized my assault on Connie while Jack Kellman and the Hardy Boys were at work. I could just picture her lounging around in some sheer madras blouse, surrounded with the scent of strawberry incense and Cat Stevens' "Tea for the Tillerman" or James Taylor's "Sweet Baby James." I had to be so audacious she would find me irresistible. I asked Weaver if he'd lend me his horse. I wanted to ride into her heart like Alan Ladd's *Shane*, or as Bashara described me, a young Lee Van Cleef. I got extra handsome in my black velvet coat with a flowing Victorian blouse and riding boots. It was an epic jaunt to Connie's house on the opposite mountain top; and I definitely wasn't an equestrian, but as I raced around those last winding curves and into sight of her ivory tower, I felt like prince charming. And just to make it perfect, she was outside lying on a boulder in her yard sipping a glass of wine and leafing through an erotic romance novella.

She was flattered, pleased and smitten. Her voluptuous pink lips were put into smile overdrive. We sat on the rocks and finished the conversation we never started the first time. We were in perfect sync. I think. Maybe we even fell in love. Inside, she made lunch and told me about her Chicago. She showed me her cool stuff. It wasn't what I had wanted to see, but I knew I would. Her delicate skin was blushing. A perfect sign and it turned out to be a perfect day. I played it cool and offered to leave early, well before anybody showed up. Now I was her crush. She hugged me hard when I left and wouldn't let go for a moment. I wanted to fly down that mountain, but it was slippery, steep and winding. Across the divide, I galloped into Weaver's spread as a conquering hero. The clan was excited that I had averted the disaster they had all predicted. What's next they wanted to know? She'd be at the Topanga festival on Sunday.

Sunday took forever, but finally the sunny day was upon us. I went looking for Connie at the festival. Weaver and Phrogg and Alan were there; they always teased me when I made an appearance at a Topanga event but were always glad to have me. Our two civilizations had an aberrant dichotomy. I parked and walked toward the crowd. It didn't take long before I saw Connie's radiant face smiling at me from across a sea of hippies. She started in my direction. I had to be shrewd. I was well aware of the inherent danger. She ran into my arms and we hugged like a Clairol commercial in a meadow. She felt so good I wanted to molest her, but right behind her came Jack Kellman and his merry men, Ernie and Jerry. Connie spoke up with the "Remember Deanna's friend from Hollywood." Yeah, they did. You could see the merriment. Weaver moved into position alongside me, and Phrogg intercepted Connie to relieve some pressure. They became good friends that day. Connie steered away from me after that, except for an occasional wink or an I-love-the-dickens-out-of-you smile. That dashing horseman episode was no mirage. We were for real.

I didn't see her for a while after that and didn't know what to do about it. Maybe Jack had laid down the law. Maybe he locked her up or killed her in a violent rage. One afternoon, Wolfer and I were at my Hilldale home, watching the little black-and-white TV in the bedroom. There was a knock at the door, and I scampered over to see who it was. I opened the door and there was Connie in a slight little blue-gingham summer frock. Her pulsating pink skin was on fire. She opened her pouty mouth and simply whispered, "Fuck me."

As a bachelor, I had to quick tidy up the bed before she could even sit down. She must have been in a big hurry; she was out of that little blue dress in no time. I wasn't wearing much to begin with so I caught up quickly. We were in the midst of wild passion that was tampering with the axis of the planet when the door bell rang again. Now a door-bell ring at my tucked away semi-secret location was rare, but two in five minutes was unprecedented. Connie flashed on Jack or the handymen. I was just pissed. I threw open the door and there was Scott St. John.

How he found me was a mystery. I hadn't seen him in a couple years, not since Weaver and I visited GR and went to Peggy's house. Scott came out of the kitchen, bouncing into the air like a Macy's Parade balloon. The old svelte Schuyler Ace St. John coolest-guy-in-town was a blimp, and David and I literally fell on the floor laughing. Now a hunted man, he was back at fighting weight. I told Scott to go back outside, and I'd talk to him in a few minutes. Connie and I put the finishing touches on our sexcapade, and she hurried right back into the blue dress. She said goodbye and left for home. Scott's eyes bugged out of his head when he saw her. Yes, Scott, you taught me well.

He had a ruffian partner. I wanted to divert him from my house so we went for some food and an explanation. Scott was parked in the driveway behind my car, so he had to drive; but first he opened the trunk and selected a new license plate, one of a dozen he had in there. He replaced Missouri with Arkansas and we left for Barney's Beanery, always good for laughs and indigestion. It turned out, Scott was on a running-from-the-law crime spree, after he had left Peggy and their marriage in Grand Rapids. On this felonious excursion, he would eventually be arrested in Oklahoma City, robbing a bank dressed as a priest. He went to prison for a long stretch. Finally, with a sigh of relief, I watched him head off to his dubious doom while I contemplated my next move with Connie.

Every now and then, I'd run into Ashley Pandel. I had been at the Cheetah the night creative band manager Shep Gordon first met Vince Furnier, the front man for an Arizona band called the Nazz. Before that they were the Beans. They opened for another band, but it was the Nazz that rocked and shocked me. The weak of heart evacuated. And later I was with Ashley at Shep's Laurel Canyon home when they decided to call both Vince and his band "Alice Cooper." Ashley had ingratiated himself with Shep and was doing roadie work as well as some cognitive thinking. Trying to nab a job with my Rogers & Cowan experience, I spent time at Shep's office on Wilshire and La Cienega. I did do a smidgen of consignment work, thanks to Ashley's recommendations.

Shamelessly, I was going to Connie's house during the day. We'd have wild sex on their wedded bed, and she would get so excited you'd think she was going to pop a blood vessel. She would spit and drool and scream and have explosive climaxes. I found it rather refreshingly curious that she had so much saliva to splatter me with. Fueled with fervor and bravery, I even invaded her boudoir when the guys were out for the evening.

The Alpha Romeo succumbed to a steady diet of reds and dinged fenders, so I picked up a '64 VW bug to continue servicing Connie. I put it to use and drove out on a Saturday night, expecting the coast to be clear, but the Chicago Bears were waiting in ambush. As I pulled in, they came running out; I fishtailed around and sped off down the mountainous roller coaster. They hopped in Ernie's pickup and the chase was on. Among other tactics, the fiends tried to force me off the narrow shoulders, and I seriously thought they were going to kill me. I made it down onto the main road and headed north toward the Corral where I hoped to hell Weaver would be. On a Saturday night that was practically a given. They pulled alongside me and brandished a gun. We played chicken with oncoming traffic. It was nip and tuck, or I was a dead duck. I slid into the Corral parking lot and ran for the entrance. I snatched David, blurted a quick explanation and dragged him outside for the showdown. Weaver dropped an innocent bystander in the hectic commotion, and then bounty hunter bouncers stopped the carnage.

We all became friends and Jack Kellman ended up back in Chicago. As it turned out, Connie had revelations for both Jack and me. She got jealous of my flirtatious behavior and vengefully admitted she had been having sex with Ernie during both our regimes. From then on, it turned into a marathon of mood swings. She was passively patrician or hurricane Connie. She violated Topanga's most handsome men, so I dated the foxiest Hollywood starlets I could get my hands on. Then we'd come together like colliding asteroids. We exchanged love sonnets and black eyes.

Wolfer was our mediator. Con started hitting the bottle. Prescription bottles of Quaaludes. "Ludes" were all the rage then; they made her happy and horny. Make that horn*ier*. She got strung out and moved in with a Quaalude dealer in the Valley. She missed me so I went over. The door opened and I saw a monster. Her face was a horrible mass of pimples and she looked twenty years older. Eventually, we weaned her off the boogieman. She stayed with her quintessentially quirky friend Adrienne Teeguarden for a time, and then she and Phrogg went on a vacation to England. They had eye-opening experiences and made friendships with David Geffen and his newly assembled American band, the Eagles, who were writing and working out the kinks in the UK. Connie was pleasantly enlightened and came home with a new positive attitude. She encouraged me to visit England and raved about Carnaby fashions, the Kings Road, the hipper hippies and the Mods and the Marquee club and the progressive music. I wasn't totally out of it and showed her my new British boots with outlandish colors and designs. Three great English boutiques had opened up in our West Hollywood.

I asked Alan about doing a run back East so I could pick up Tony boy and bring him to LA for summer vacation. Cash rich, Alan had recently purchased a big four-door Mercedes Benz and suggested instead of flying, driving. A load of cannabis bricks in a cavernous trunk made sense. To make it less conspicuous, we added Connie to the payroll as my prop wife. And thus a caper of considerable intrigue was born. This would be yet another cross-country drive, but doing it in the Mercedes, and doing it in the redhead was a great idea. So off we went, Wolfer too. Sexually-charged Connie was disbursing lascivious silliness as I tried to navigate the interstates. In Chicago, we stopped by and stayed with her parents in the far south suburb of Beverly. It reminded me of Margie Dormier in Syracuse, spending time with conservative parents while I had their nymphomaniac daughter in my pants.

We proceeded to Grand Rapids and an old Victorian house in Heritage Hill where Weaver's brothers were waiting for our delivery. We walked in and I fell flat on my face in funky love with a diminutive young hippie girl named Karla Dumbrowski. She was somebody's teenage old lady, but I was determined to spring her loose. The orgy pad was an ongoing love-in with all these young girls in skimpy summer duds frolicking about the place. Karla was gyrating on an overstuffed beanbag to the sensual sounds of Deep Purple. When she got up to go to the bathroom I followed her in, locked the door and got fresh. She teased with glee, but when I got serious with aerosol shaving crème she ran out. Her old man was pissed.

Connie was mortified and disappeared. I barely noticed and left the house without her; it was a small town compared to Chicago. Alan flew in that night to take possession of the loot but found Connie hiding in the bushes when he arrived. Connie ran to Hertz and asked for help. At a motel, Connie got revenge, and Big Al got Connie. Alan put her on a flight to Chicago, and she moved into a friend's apartment in the loop.

As planned, Alan flew back and Tony and I headed for LA in the Mercedes. We detoured through Chicago and launched pebbles at Connie's windows until she agreed to come with us. It was a long and cranky drive home. The battling Bogarts slugged it out. It was only in the middle rounds though, and I probably had one eye on the bikini-clad ring girl with the fifth-round placard. After we got home, Alan lost the Mercedes at the Tijuana border crossing when someone he hired to bring up some kilos was caught red-handed.

Freelandia was a hippie party airline run by rich kid Kenneth Moss, who gutted the traditional seats and turned his unique DC-8 into a flying love-in with water beds, oriental rugs, tapestries, organic cuisine, water pipes and interesting substances. After Tony returned to GR, I exercised my membership and flew to Hawaii on the jubilant missile. We caucused at the Honolulu Hilton Hotel and ran Johnny Carson out of his favorite resort. What a square. My neighbor Lenny took care of Wolfer while I was in Oahu, but shortly afterwards he moved two blocks south to Dicks Street, prized real estate! I helped him move some of his stuff, and once in a while I'd drop by just to say hi. He had kept our landing neat and clean and there were always flowers. And then there was George, his giant Great Dane, who had been little Wolfer's best friend. I was truly sorry to see him leave. A few months later, I came by and the landlord told me he had been shot to death in his bedroom by an intruder, or a disgruntled lover.

Wondering when I'd ever find an occupation other than replicating the exploits of Don Juan and Casanova, I tried my hand at standup comedy. A clever class clown as a kid, I was conversant with topical humor. Weaver was getting gigs for Gary Myrick and the Figures; with David's encouragement and Gary's begrudging reluctance, I opened some of their shows. These were often small bars and the crowd paid more attention to darts and drinks than whoever the band was. At least I got reactions. Nixon jokes: Boo! The Vietnam War: grumbles. The Lakers: Get off the stage! Bowling shirts: What'd he just say!? We were at a vacuous bar in Santa Monica; in vain I tried to catch a smile. The audience impeached me with insults and projectiles. Duck for cover! Shielded by his trusty guitar, Myrick snuck up behind me and whispered "You're bombing. You're fired." I retired. But I'd be back.

Univeral Studio's "Midnight Lace" subjects a San Francisco heiress and
newswoman, Cathy Preston (Mary Crosby) to a campaign of terror in a
rework of a 1960 chiller starring Doris Day.

Chapter 19: The Rainbow

Then a Vesuvius hit town and the world as we knew it changed forever. The Rainbow Bar and Grill opened up on Sunset Boulevard next to the Largo Strip Club, across from the 9000 Building, half a block from my house on Hilldale. In an earlier golden age, it was the glamorous Villa Nova, where Vincent Minnelli and Judy Garland, and Marilyn Monroe and Joe DiMaggio, and even Charlie Chaplin cozied up in front of the fireplace. Most recently it had been a stuffy restaurant with English-pudding cuisine, but now an edgy clientele was there to rock. Refurbished with a progressive attitude, it became the hot spot to party. I made it my headquarters and, in turn, it made me famous.

The Rainbow was another venture of Elmer and Mario; Weaver and I had an automatic lock. The heavyweights checked it out and made it a habit: the ever-present Jack Nicholson, Bill Cosby, Warren Beatty, Elvis, John Belushi, Led Zeppelin, Rod Stewart, Ringo, Neil Diamond, Ritchie Blackmore, Sonny and Cher and every band that blew into town, especially the British ones. Bill Gazzarri, who had his own club next door, was there. On the lower level was a king's ransom of plush red-leather banquette booths that had a certain pecking order. Lines would lengthen for those booths and only the elite got the good ones, or any ones. The upfront booth by the fireplace was especially prized, if you were pathologically extroverted. The yellow-brick aisles gave star gazers an opportunity to see and often touch the privileged.

Tucked away was a second nifty bar for the anonymous. Upstairs were the loos and a phone booth, which were no stranger to substances and consequences. From this bustling intermezzo was another stairway to the semi-private dance club known as Over the Rainbow. And even in that sardine-packed happy-land there was yet another level accessed by a ladder. It was called the Crow's Nest. It had a couple VIP tables and overlooked the steamy crowd below.

Tony Vescio had been Mario's right-hand man at the Whisky and became the natural choice for the Rainbow maitre d'. In no time, he achieved legendary status. He was as much a celebrity as anyone who ever sat at a prized booth. He was the ringleader of the circus: the sincere greeter, the lion tamer and the friendly uncle, the father confessor and your best friend, traffic cop and mediator, Solomon and Saint Peter, an Italian godfather, da Vinci and Fellini. His assistant Michael was a good man too. A crack crew of waitresses worked out of a little cubicle by the front door, where Tony paced around cajoling good cheer and putting out conniption fires. The Rainbow became your family. You'd eat your Easter and Christmas dinners there. Come there on your honeymoon or your wake. Meet your wife or divorce her. The Rainbow was a major character in my life.

Elmer would come early for dinner and always be with at least one very young beautiful girl, even though he was in his sixties. An ex Chicago cop, ex Mob and ex traordinary person, he was irascible to some but sweet as the crack of a Cub bat to his legion of friends and associates. He'd eat and leave early which opened another booth for the next rock star.

Elmer had his own busy booth back home in the Laurel Hills with his play-pal girls and his reefer smoking jacket.

Mario was the no-nonsense ruler who preferred the anonymity of the kitchen where he had his own little table. Weaver and I often ate in the kitchen with the boss, after picking something off the grill. Like Elmer, Mario was from Chicago and tough as Capone. Tough as Butkus, the south side and a Chicago winter. Occasionally, his young sons Mario Jr. and Michael came by the club, and they also made an exception for my 10-year-old Tony to frolic late into the evening. At this point, he was still only visiting from Grand Rapids in the summer, but I was already grooming him into the cast of characters. Everybody loved the pint-size celebrity. He was his own little Lord Fauntleroy of the Sunset Strip.

Nightly, our gang would swagger into the Rainbow with the old ladies in tow, take a great booth and raise holy hell with full impunity. I was kibitzing with Nicholson by the fireplace the first time he laid eyes on my girl Connie. He nudged me with his killer smile. Yeah, tell me about it, Jack. Our once immaculate affair was corrupt and imperfect by now and we were feuding more than fornicating, but it came out of Wrigley's left field when Connie suddenly moved back to Chicago. She rented a house on the Near North Side, got a job at the Playboy Building and was dating a wealthy guy who had a million-dollar condo at the top of a Magnificent Mile skyscraper. I fought depression and decided to rescue her if it killed me, which it almost did. It was December and the only heater my California VW had was our pup Wolfer. By the time we hit the high desert, it was freezing, and of course it was even worse in Chicago. Another of those worst-winters-ever they have every year.

Connie was appalled at my audacity. The Big Cheese was officially her mate. I was penniless; he was a tycoon. And yet, she let me stay at her house. Even gave me a key. I did what I could to help, and I remodeled the old house while she was at work. When Mr. Wonderful was off on business, we played platonically. She had an old school girlfriend who was happily married on the blue-collar west side. Theirs was a pleasant but rather mundane life. Maybe I was the lucky one after all. Con took me to her job at the magazine and to the Playboy mansion for parties. Free, I took advantage of the bunnies.

Connie even took me to Jet Setter's lavishly appointed condo when he was out of town. Nice bedroom. Eventually, she asked me to leave her house because the boyfriend that never came to her house came to her house and was shocked to find me there. He gave her an ultimatum, and she handed it to me like a hot potato. I packed up and set off for Christmas in Grand Rapids. Halfway there, a Michigan blizzard turned me back, but instead of bypassing Chicago and jamming for LA, I decided to give it one more try. I pulled up just as she was leaving in a cab for a Fleetwood Mac concert that Mr. Everything was co-promoting. "Can't talk. Meeting him back stage and I'm late. Bye!"

I found myself in the final act of *The Graduate*. I'd have been legal in the arena's side-stage handicap section but fought on with blind perseverance. I found the venue and VIP parking, whizzed past the bozo security and made my way backstage. Smack dab in front of Mick Fleetwood and a dozen.others, I confronted Mr. Whiplash and his iron grip on my slender redhead. He snapped his fingers and a brigade of bodyguards threw me to the floor, with the threat of a Houdini stranglehold. Surprisingly, Sir High Class turned out to be Mr. Not-So-Bad-After-All. He helped me up, brushed off my coat and handed me a ticket for the concert. I was trenchantly banned from coming backstage though. I passed on the show and drove home to LA with Wolfer.

I was petulant for the holidays, and the New Year was going to be a real bummer. I was inconsolable. There was a New Year's Eve extravaganza at the Whisky, and I was on the guest list so I went begrudgingly. At the same time in Connie's world, she and Mr. Perfect had flown to Cabo San Lucas for their version of the big night. Mr. Lucky was thinking a spicy Mexican wedding. I was at the Whisky, oblivious to the frivolous. South of the border, Connie thought about her lonely Spider. On impulse she bolted, took a cab to the airport and caught a flight to LAX. It was in the last hour of the year when she arrived. I was in a fog. She was in a taxi. She hit the Strip and saw the Whisky mob, "Let me out!" The devil doll dashed about and found me in the confetti just before midnight. We kissed at twelve strikes and swore our love for ever more. We ran up to the Rainbow to brag of our reconciliation and headed back to my love-bug cottage on Hilldale.

After our own *sleep-in for a piece,* Connie and I moved three blocks east into a bigger duplex at 937 Palm Avenue. It was a worn stucco house with a red tile roof. This would be the home Tony would grow up in from the sixth grade to UCLA. This would be the heartland of our father-and-son story, our battleground of immorality and redemption, of trust and misgiving and a bond that transcended heaven and hell.

Connie's avuncular godfather Elmer wasn't exactly pleased, but she assured him we were for real this time. An ex-cop, he knew the turf's high crime rate and warned her to be careful. Forebodingly, one day the next-door neighbor would look out his front-door peephole and get shot dead in the eye. Palm was peppered with a mix of quaint bungalows and apartment buildings. It ran three blocks from Sunset at the top, down to Santa Monica Boulevard in the flat. We were in the middle. We took a break from the world and furnished our honeymoon cottage with used furniture, spider plants and Connie's Topanga curtains. Eventually, a malevolent maelstrom would sweep just about every hot Hollywood girl into my art deco bedroom, but for a time it was our exclusive pandemonium. My infamous four-mattress bed was very high, like the occupants. We grew vegetables in the front yard and cultivated ivy to conceal Tony's little private apartment in the back.

We bred sophisticated comrades, and for a while everything was peachy. Connie's friend Karen Lamm moved to LA from Chicago and we indulged diligently. She had been married to Robert Lamm from the band *Chicago*, and later she would marry my old pal Beach Boy Dennis Wilson. Karen posed for *Playboy* and aspired to act. Eventually, she would steer me into Lee Strasberg and my own show business.

Ashley Pandel was grooming me for a lucrative spot in a Shep Gordon & Alice Cooper venture, but that too was still beyond the next heartbreak. Elmer got Connie a job. A new, private Beverly Hills club called Pips hired her to be their 1940s-style cigarette girl to walk around with a tray of smokes. Connie fit the bill perfectly and shocked the clientele in her glamorous gowns. She'd come home each night and tell me all about the international playboys who flirted with her. Fred Silverman, the powerful and influential head of CBS, was a prime example. Rock stars, movie stars, financiers and moguls were preying on my girl, but who could blame them. She would always say, "Sorry, I'm taken."

Snuggled in bed one ominous evening, Con relayed the night's activities which included a pleasant conversation she had with Sonny Bono. The dream team had been putting out number one songs like "I Got You Babe" since my UCLA days. Now they were the biggest act in show business and still cranking out the hits. Their *Sonny and Cher Show* on CBS Sunday night was televison's highest-rated program. They were the top act in Las Vegas, and they were America's sweethearts, the perfect couple. Make that triple, now they had Chastity, their darling little daughter, who was also an integral part of the show.

Sonny had invited Connie to an innocent lunch date, perfectly harmless. He was married to Cher, for god's sake. They were casual friends, out for food and conversation. I saw it as a great opportunity for both us. She took a cab to an upscale eatery at the Bel Air Hotel, and Sonny surprised her with a rather unusual lunch present. In the parking lot was a brand new green Fiat convertible to complement her red hair, and then the bombshell that he and Cher were breaking up but were keeping it secret to maintain the integrity of their act, which was worth a fortune. He was in love with my girl and prepared to put Connie up in an expensive Beverly Hills area house until the divorced was finalized. At the time, Sonny and Cher were living in one of the most beautiful and famous homes in Los Angeles, just off Sunset in posh Holmby Hills, neighboring Hefner's new *Playboy* mansion. It had been Tony Curtis and Janet Leigh's house in their heyday. Jayne Mansfield and Mickey Hartigay lived there when she painted the classic swimming pool pink.

Connie came home long enough to pack her bags and was gone. Well, it seemed like it. We agreed it was too good an opportunity to turn down. To tell you the truth, I was happy for her. This put her in the stratosphere where she belonged. I was a vampire and needed fresh blood anyway. Besides, I had a new roommate on the horizon. Tony gave his mom an ultimatum: let him move in with dad or he'd run away. Mom relented. He could move west when school finished in the spring. Although Tony had bedeviled the poor principal for years, in his final year at Brookside Elementary, he was voted class president. Within months, he'd be jockeying between my subterranean wonderland and Sonny and Connie's highlife.

I saw Cher at the Rainbow with her good friend David Geffen at one of the center booths. I slid in and suggested that, since Connie had stolen her husband, perhaps we should get together. Cher smiled, but a protective Geffen sternly advised me to leave the booth. By now the planet was in on the scandal, and gossip magazines splashed photos of Sonny and Connie on their covers.

Back in Topanga, Weaver & Bashara Ltd. asked me to do a reefer run to Michigan. Instead of suitcases, they experimented with an Anvil case, the classic red–and–silver trimmed metal case that musicians use to transport equipment. Alan loaded it up with kilos, and David drove me down to LAX. We went to check the baggage, but the agent classified it as industrial and sent us to the commercial area. I wheeled it over to the weigh-in. Weaver and an employee lifted it onto their big scale and we watched the arrow swing around to 102 pounds. "Too heavy," the guy says, "100 pound limit. Just take something out and put it your personal suitcase." I tried to sound casual, "No, we don't want to do that." The guy was way too accommodating. "It's no problem," he says and starts to unclip the metal snaps. Snap, crackle, pop. He's down to the last clip; once he lifts the lid, he'll be looking at 48 bricks of high-quality Michoacan. I'm sweating bullets and tugging at my collar. I looked around for my boss, but David is almost out of sight, running for the street. I was quick on my feet too. "Wait! Ah…that's Sonny Bono's music equipment in there," I declared, "and it's my first gig working with him. He's playing in Chicago tomorrow night, and he'll kill me if any of these sensitive microphones get damaged, moving them out of their foam rubber protectors." The guy was a fan, "Sonny Bono! All right, I'll let it slide. Next time weigh it in advance." It was the first time I had ever seen fear in the redoubtable David Weaver. A hundred and change could have gotten me a stretch in San Quentin.

While I was gone, Alan borrowed my VW. He visited one of my girls up in the Laurel Canyon hills and parked it perilously close to the edge of a cliff. While he was in her cabin shaking the bed and the landscape, my VW plummeted down the hill to oblivion in a grove of sturdy trees. He paid me $600 for screwing her, me and my car. I went without a vehicle for a couple weeks, but finally scraped up enough dough and bought a cherry, low-mileage Austin-Healey from a conscientious car lover out in the valley for only $1800. It was a classic.

During the 1973 Led Zeppelin tour stop at the Forum, Weaver called to meet him in Malibu, where the band was bivouacked at a private house on Pacific Coast Highway. We delivered the goods and Robert Plant provided the narrative, "The whole thing was just an absolute mixture of adrenaline, chemical, euphoria ... and there were no brakes." Weaver's friend Toby Roberts owned the house, and we piled into the bold spectacle of Jimmy Page, John Bonham, Robert Plant and John Paul Jones. Potent commodities were consumed, and after amusing ourselves we meandered outside for some moonlit air. Robert noticed my Austin-Healey and went over to check it out. He happened to love Healeys, and I let him drive it around the grounds much to his enjoyment. At the concert Weaver and I enjoyed backstage passes and all the privileges, but retribution was still on my tail. A car thief with good taste stole my Healey during the concert.

DEBORAH LEE

Deborah Lee asked to marry me on our first date.

Chapter 20: Alice Cooper

Shep Gordon, Alice Cooper, the band, and Ashley Pandel were living it up in New York City and Connecticut now. The band that scared the Cheetah out into a Venice street and was booed at the Experience had redeemed itself with mega-singles "I'm Eighteen" and "Schools Out" and top-selling albums *Love it to Death, Killer* and *Billion Dollar Babies*. Their reputation for outlandish and entertaining live performances was well established. They mixed Gothic torture, executions, boa constrictors, elephants, helicopters, decapitated babies and Alice's androgynous persona to create the world's most spectacular circus. Ashley had been a good foot soldier, working the road and then doing publicity, press and concept. Now with their fortune, Shep unveiled a new enterprise and handed the ball to Ashley:

NEW YORK--The Image Group, Inc., a new firm combining both publicity and promotional services, has announced its initial client roster of artists, management concerns and record labels, according to Ashley Pandel, President of the organization. The Image Group is currently retained by Alice Cooper; Alive Enterprises, the Cooper group's management company; Bearsville Records; Paul Butterfield's Better Days; Brownsville Station; Focus; Foghat; Lazarus; the New York Dolls; Queen; Lou Reed; Todd Rundgren; Sha Na Na; Three Dog Night; and the Peter Yarrow band. Several other accounts are currently in negotiation. Associated with Pandel in the new venture are Ron Ross, director of creative services; and Mandi Newall, director of press relations. Directing client services for the West Coast will be John Kiedis. A graduate of UCLA's film school, Kiedis has an extensive background in motion pictures and television, having been a screenwriter and production assistant at MGM, previous to which he was with Rogers, Cowan & Brenner public relations. The Image Group's office in New York is located at 75 East 55th Street, (212) 421-6432; in Los Angeles, the address is c/o John Kiedis, 937 N. Palm Avenue, West Hollywood, Calif. 90069 (213) 657-1801.

Suddenly, I was in the Stones' lyric, "Under Assistant West Coast Promotion Man." Bam! I'm jetting off to New York City and spending weekends with Ashley at his east side apartment, plotting strategy and partying with Alice and the boys, Glen Buxton, Michael Bruce, Dennis Dunaway and Neal Smith. They each had a Rolls Royce. I was winging around Broadway, the Village, Max's Kansas City and CBGB's. Ashley even had a piece of a restaurant on Park Ave. near Washington Square Park. And Ashley traveled west to Los Angeles. He took me to the Century Plaza for lunch with Keith Moon, where he had famously thrown the furniture out of his hotel window the day before. A few too many drinks later, the boisterous boy almost threw me out too, but before long the master of mayhem was actually babysitting Tony.

Ashley took me to the Roxy one afternoon to meet John Lennon. The Roxy was a new Elmer Valentine and Lou Adler club on the hallowed ground of the old Largo Strip Club, next door to the Rainbow. In the middle of the day, it was normally closed and empty, but today John Lennon was up in the private club all by his lonesome, playing Pong, the simplistic first-generation video game. We exchanged pleasantries, and John challenged me to a game. I had never even heard of Pong but was happy to go at it with the genius Beatle. We had a couple drinks at the bar and discussed my role as the West Coast man for The Image Group, which Lennon had agreed to affiliate with. John and his buddy Harry Nilsson were trying to put together an album. I had worked with Nilsson on the sunny side up of *Courtship of Eddie's Father* at MGM. This however was Lennon's self-proclaimed *Lost Weekend*, a reference to Billy Wilder's dark Oscar winning movie of rampant alcoholism. Yoko had booted Lennon out of the Dakota in New York, and he spent a miserable year wallowing in alcohol, drugs and despair in and out of LA and the UK.

I must admit he was the most arrogant person I'd ever met, but if he didn't deserve that honor who would. He was a cheeky Teddy Boy, but in a way more like an old friend we'd all grown up with.

Lennon and Nilsson had been kicked out of the Troubadour for an intoxicated heckling of Tommy Smothers' new comedy routine. The press overreacted, and the boys were back again. A messy aftermath propagated a loose rat pack of misfits and expatriates, raising hell for the weekend, a powwow of brilliant IQ and wild Indians on the rampage. Call Turner's Liquor. Alice Cooper had come to town, which made it a full deck: John Lennon, Keith Moon, Alice, Harry Nilsson, Ashley Pandel and me.

Tommy Smothers and Mickey Dolenz rotated, alternating comedians each night. Much of it happened at the Rainbow. There was rip snorting under the tables and in the ladies room. There was sex in and out of the controversial phone booth on the hard landing. There was Keith imbibing a reservoir of Courvoisier. There were chased skirts and ripped pants, and on to the quasi-private Over the Rainbow. Finally ensconced up in the privileged Crow's Nest, we looked down on vagrant kisses and incoming spitballs. Our pack was squeezed around two small tables pulled together on the tiny enclave. Keith Moon was bloody smashed and wandered down a short narrow path that led to a dead end in the rear of the Crow's Nest. None of us paid much attention. Somehow, he found room to squeeze into a crawl space between the interior and exterior walls and worked his way back to our approximate location. Suddenly the ersatz walnut panel wall behind my back exploded like a roadside bomb as prankster Keith bashed his way through. We were buried in Moon confetti and shattered ersatz.

The next night we were back in the Rainbow for more plundering. Word had come to us that Liza Minnelli was throwing a party for Frank Sinatra that was not far from our clubhouse. We got Nilsson's Volvo station wagon out of the parking lot and everybody crowded in. We drove up Clark and Devlin and into the Sunset Hills, found the address and trudged up to the door. John Lennon stood right up in front, with us Herman's Hermits supporting from behind. He rang the bell. Somebody opened the door, looked straight at John and said, "Sorry, but this is a private party". Say what? John Lennon. No trespassing.

We shook our heads and headed our shaken heads back into the Volvo. About a block down the hill, Keith yelled to stop, and insisted we turn the lorry around. This time he swore he was going to kick in the door, expletives deleted. So we went back and marched up to the front door again, but this time with steely conviction. The door was wide open, and no one paid any attention to us. We simply walked in and joined the party. Although anti-climatic, it was quite nice for me because after we circulated for a few minutes and staged a minor food fight, John Lennon pulled me over for a protracted chat.

We settled in on a comfortable bench next to a bank of windows that overlooked Los Angeles in her late evening lights. He was pensive and seemed to be in another world—most likely Manhattan. He was hitting the cocaine and whiskey pretty hard, but for whatever reason he chose to spend time talking with me about his life and my life and my position with the Image Group. He was genuinely concerned for a rookie like me up in the bigs. We discussed publicity Beatles-style and shared our mutual friendship of Elliot Mintz, who I knew from the LA scene. I confided my PR adventures with the biggest stars in Hollywood, working for Rogers & Cowan right out of UCLA. John frequently referenced Derek Taylor the Beatles' former press agent, and in his peculiar articulation implied I was a bit over my head as the West Coast rep for all these superstars, including his majesty. "You're no Derek Taylor," he asserted. I knew I was flying by the seat of my pants, but Ashley had confidence in me. I had given him shelter, protection and connections when he first moved to LA, and he never forgot it. John and I rejoined the party. Later that night when the bad boy mob dropped me off on Palm, John Lennon rubbed some final words of encouragement in my face and they drove off. Not a bad night.

Barely time to take a breath, I flew to New York for a special event. The New York Dolls were doing a whoop-ass coming out party at Max's Kansas City. As one of our clients, it gave me another opportunity to ply my craft on this star-studded stage. New York's Kennedy-esque Mayor John Lindsay attended and so did the usual celebs: Andy Warhol, Lou Reed, Deborah Harry, a handful of Ramones, Talking Heads, Richard Hell and Television. No doubt some Patti Smith and Basquiat. It was one of those nights, and I spent a piece of it with Johnny Thunders.

Back in LA, I went to work. Client Todd Rundgren asked me to lure the recently-deposed Spiro Agnew into doing an interview with Todd. Between us, we set up an elaborate exposé to bare the former Vice President's crimes. I went on tour with Sha Na Na and got a rubber-face seminary of Bowzer and his zany antics as the ringleader of their 50s rock-and-roll revival act. I had meetings at the *Los Angeles Times* with the esteemed dean of music critics Robert Hilburn, who graciously schooled me and did interviews with our clients. He was a particular fan of the Dolls, Lou Reed and Rundgren, and I advanced the agenda.

Peter Yarrow had been a member of Peter, Paul and Mary, one of the biggest folk-music acts of the sixties. Created and managed by Albert Grossman, they made high standards like "Puff the Magic Dragon" and "Leaving on a Jet Plane." He was on his own now, and I wanted to make an impression. I snuck into the NBC cafeteria from which it was easier to breach the security into the main building. I worked my way upstairs to the *Tonight Show* offices and introduced myself to the receptionist. She was dismayed I didn't have an appointment or a NBC pass and was about to call security. One of the bookers passed by and was intrigued by my initiative. We sat down in his office, and I gave him my sales pitch. In a snap, we sealed a deal for the Peter Yarrow Band to play the *Tonight Show* next week. At the 5 o'clock taping, I stood in the wings like a proud father, and when it was over the band surprised me with an unusual thank you gift. They piled me into their private plane, and we flew to Salt Lake City for their concert later that night.

I was on a no-holds-barred roll. The Sunset carotid artery was teeming with infamous and fascinating characters, like mayoral impresario Rodney Bingenheimer with his English Disco and KROQ radio show. Runaways founder Kim Fowley was a producer, songwriter, performer and preservationist. A big fellow, he was our benevolent, fatherly Sergeant O'Reilly. His larger-than-life figure on the beat gave us assurance and proof through the night that the rockets' red glare on Sunset would always be there. Wild Man Fischer was legendary on the rueful side of the rue: homeless, eccentric and volatile. He was the paranoid-schizophrenic godfather of outsider music, who would sing you a song for a dime in front of the cabarets.

A time was coming when the label-happy hucksters would make room for a new demagogue, one with balls and backbone, cohunes and chutzpah, flamboyant ubiquity, show business swagger, sartorial splendor, emerging clout and a way with the dames, draped all over his mischievous humility. The unruly arbitrators stuffed the gold key to the Boulevard in my Giorgio Armani pocket and dubbed me Lord of the Sunset Strip. I wore the crown uneasily, but I would grow into it and with the considerable help of my young Prince.

Chapter 21: Lords of the Sunset Strip

Connie's nomadic friend Bruce Riley was eggs and milquetoast, but a conscientious fellow. He was house sitting on Wonderland with Connie. Weaver, Alan and I had all partied there. Out of the blue, Bruce made me an outstanding proposition. He was about to road manage Love on a tour of the UK. The band went as "Arthur Lee and Love," after their charismatic black lead singer, who was idolized in England. Bruce asked me to accompany him and do publicity. In return, he'd pay for my plane and living expenses.

Connie had wanted me to see England, and now I would. Phrogg was actually living in London, and her British boyfriend Monte Wolpe rented me an apartment on Kings Road in Chelsea. I packed my bag, rolled a few joints, a little stash of coke, which I hid in my underwear, and flew off with the band for London Heathrow. I breezed through customs. My flat turned out to be quite spacious and right in the middle of everything. Kings Road was the equivalent of our Sunset Strip. *The Rocky Horror Picture Show* was in its very first theatrical incarnation a block from my place. Surprisingly, when I got back the same company opened at the Roxy Club on Sunset.

I walked the streets of London the way I had in Paris a decade before. My home was at 333 Kings Road on the corner of Beaufort. Bowie was god and stirring the mix with *Ziggy Stardust, Aladdin Sane* and *Diamond Dogs*. Pink Floyd was disseminating *The Dark Side of the Moon*. Zeppelin was at their brawniest. Punk was on the verge. London radio was a kaleidoscope of music we now revere on Mount Olympus. Kids were resplendent in hip outfits unimagined in the colonies. There was crackling electric energy everywhere. I saw Black Sabbath with Ozzie at the Hammersmith Odeon. Phrogg and Monte, who lived in classy Belgravia, drove me around in his Chevy Monte Carlo, which was quite unusual in England.

The original Hard Rock Café was in London near Hyde Park. Like the '63 embassy in Paris, I'd go to the Hard Rock for my cheeseburgers and malts. Connie had given me a list of places to look into, so I hit Speakeasy on Margaret Street and Granny Takes a Trip on Kings Road. Before long, there'd be one in West Hollywood too. The Marquee Club was mandatory and, of course, Carnaby Street. Connie gave me carte blanche access to several *Playboy* bunny tails she'd met. I picked up on young English birds in the Chelsea pubs near my Underground stop at Sloane Square. I met a girl at one of those clubs and later we took a train to her flat in north London. She wanted to shoot my coke. Nasty didn't have an outfit, so she fashioned the inner cylinder of a ballpoint pen as a syringe, and stabbed her arm. I didn't want to be a chicken, so pass the pen.

I had lunch with Lou Reed at swanky Blakes. Later that night I cavorted with double-take delicious "Melanie," who was doing tasteful modeling for Bobton's Agency 36 Kings Road. She sure looked a lot like Annette Walter-lax, but *The Who* cares. We took a cozy nap together. Her measurements were 33-24-35. I partied with Rod Stewart at Tramps and shared some lager. Love performed at several London venues, including the famous

Rainbow Theatre, where I also saw Pink Floyd. I was having so much fun in London I skipped the out-of-town road concerts. We also did a charity event at Harrods.

I flipped for London fashion, especially the snakeskin boots all the young dudes were prancing around in. Skin-tight and knee-high with wild platforms and towering high heels, they screamed British rock star. It was my duty to bring them home. I found that the best gear was on Kensington High Street and went to a popular bazaar with a renowned cobbler who made them to order. I asked the maestro what was the highest heel he'd ever built. He said eight inches. "Then make mine eight and a quarter!" I commissioned three pairs. Customs was stunned. Wrapped in the Union Jack, I finally returned to Los Angeles to welcome my new roommate and partner in crime, Tony Kiedis.

My son was moving into an increasingly complex and emotional cyclone I called home. My redesigned narrative was up for grabs. By now, Connie was living with Sonny in the Holmby Hills mansion, where Sunset rambled through royalty. She had always been a surrogate mom for Tony when he visited in the summer, and now she had him over there playing with Chastity and revelry. Sonny adored him and got paternal. Weaver and Bashara rushed over to celebrate. Topanga threw out the welcome afghan. My new girlfriends lined up to meet him. Alice Cooper and Tony watched cartoons on our little black-and-white television set. Keith Moon was his court jester. The Rainbow embraced him with muscular Italian open arms. It was Anthony in Wonderland.

Perhaps I was over compensating for Connie's disengagement, but I started dating with a vengeance. Like a fairytale, there was a family in Topanga that had three beautiful daughters. The youngest was Pamela Zinszer, who had recently been bestowed *Playboy's* Miss March. I finagled David into taking me to her house and we associated. She was the first of my bountiful *Playboy* centerfolds, certainly enough to fill a calendar. Pam was sexy in a pure and only slightly naughty way. Proliferating bunnies Patricia McClain, Cher Butler and Ursula Buchfeller are especially recalled, while the distinct memory of others has evaporated like the vapors over Hef's aquatic grottos.

The blitz continued with photogenic Judy from the beach and Beth, a USC co-ed at home with mommy and daddy in Hancock Park. We played golf at the Wilshire Country Club and in her bed. A Westwood rocket with red hair and a lot of pluck eloped with me to an escapade in San Francisco. Ricky Nelson's beautiful cousin Kathy Nelson, with her sleek black Irish hair, nursed me back to health when I was ill. I brushed up with a floozy named Busty. Brandy was just as busty but more responsible; I did have a kid now. Kitty Summerall was a sultry blonde actress singer songwriter. Guitar player Renee was in The B Girls, who played at the Whisky, Gazzarri, CBGB and my house. Shame was a *Hustler* cover girl. Leah Fulton was a stewardess. Kelly was Irish. Nan was a knockout. Sam was a young mother. There was a dipsy blonde that took the infamous photos of Tony smoking grass in the kitchen. *Mayhem* model Renee made artistic cards and my smile. Lovey from Haight Street had flowers in her hair. Kay was the demur *Playboy* bunny. Little devil Sunny lived up on Devlin. Roxanne was the fox in my Br'er bedroom. Victoria was victorious; best buddies, we often joined our friend Dodger manager Tommy Lasorda's son Tom Jr., who put us in great seats and into the locker room. Hail Victoria. We chased each other for years.

Religiously, Weaver and I did communion at the Rainbow, fueled with nitroglycerin Mexican coffees. Shaken or stirred or spilled on your lapel, it was a good slug of high-octane tequila, Kahlua, a big mug of coffee and a dash of cream. The club had security, but we took it upon ourselves to augment the firepower. Occasionally, we'd leave our booth for a quick dalliance upstairs with the disco dames. It was rare that David or I ever got on that dance floor unless we had dropped some reds or Tuinals, in which case we'd be crawling around on our hands and knees, recovering them. We were up in the Crow's Nest one night when a fight broke out below us. Without hesitation, we simultaneously jumped off our perch and down into the fray. We subdued the riff raff, wrapped them up in a package and hauled them down to security.

By 2:30 a.m., the club would be empty, but most of the patrons were still making yippee in the parking lot. Add in those who came from other clubs and there'd be hundreds of intoxicated oversexed and underdressed lunatics networking to bust a move at all night parties. A favorite destination was my 937 Palm. We'd make our final selection of lads and lucky ladies and head for my house. Invariably, there would be interlopers who felt the wrath of Weaver the enforcer. A loud lout who claimed to be John Wayne's nephew blundered in and made his self uncomfortable. David sent him packing with a broken nose.

If Tony wasn't with Connie in Holmby Hills, he'd be trying to sleep in his sweet suite in the back, or not. Sometimes he was up partying with us until some Mother Theresa in shredded nylons and smeared makeup on barbiturates would read him a goodnight story or sing him a lullaby. There were always unrelenting lollipops in varying degrees of undress and enough loud music to ensure a visit from the sheriffs. We'd scurry about collecting and hiding all the bad evidence. Tony would wake up to a sunny new day and survey the damage while I was still sleeping. He once famously remarked, "From the looks of all the blood on the walls, Weaver must have been here last night."

Pennies from heaven! Somewhere in that sweet asphalt jungle of mine I met an absolute dreamboat who took me on a royal rampage. I opened an account at the Bank of America on Wilshire and Rampart for the free toaster and left with a killer teller-crush. A week later I robbed the bank of her. Penny Lane became my getaway driver, and we went on a crime wave of whoopee. The clerical cutie turned out to be a beautiful bumpy love story with a tangled tapestry of infinite delights. She was a lissome tall order with blonde hair down to her willow waist and a leggy body of work that needed to play. Conveniently, Penny and her roommate Jane King lived on haunted Horn Avenue, only a couple blocks from us on Palm. Her partner was a moody beauty, and Penny called her Mona. Destiny called her doomed.

In the meantime, we took advantage of the proximity, and Penny frequently looked after Tony—often with Keith Moon's assistance. On our own, we managed to traumatize even our notorious Sunset precinct. We were ubiquitous at the Roxy, playing all the angles with everybody from the up and up Art Garfunkle to the *way up* Jack Nicholson, who pulled Penny into the men's room to offer some blow. Of course, I had to service and protect. There was Cheech and Chong mischief, Led Zeppelin at the Hyatt House, Jimmy Page in his house behind the hotel, and petulant John Lennon at the Troubadour and on the summer sand in Manhattan Beach.

Tony often tagged along, and one night we found ourselves at a party in the pandemonium of Mulholland and Coldwater Canyon. Maybe it was Richie Blackmore's, but the purpose was a Rod Steward send off: he was about to go on tour. In a spectacular welcoming, Rod greeted us at the door, swinging from a chandelier. He captured Penny right out of my pants and slammed the door on my face. All in good fun Penny's hand-slap integrity and the Gaelic prankster's change of heart let me in. There was naked frivolity in the swimming pool, and Tony jumped right in. We were introduced to Reginald Dwight, a rather nerdy piano player, recently arrived from England. He was proudly showing off his *Rorer 714* Quaalude T-shirt. Ironically, it was Penny's first night to experiment with the wonder drug. Now a Sir Elton John icon, for a long time he was just another character I kept running into, business and pleasure. The most egregious happening was undoubtedly when he played the Santa Monica Auditorium. I was part of the entourage backstage and well-lubricated with substances. During the performance, I was watching from the wings; first conspicuously peeking out around the curtains; and finally, completely out of my mind, I came all the way out to join him and attempted to take a seat at the piano. Security scrambled. I was tarred and feathered. Later, Elton borrowed the outfit.

In the high stakes of inspiring Cameron Crowe's groupie-with-a-heart-of-gold character played by Kate Hudson in *Almost Famous,* Penny had two beautiful legs up on the competition and a headlock on the honor. She coined the phrase "Riot House," inaugurated the Band Aides and racked up record band-tour bus-mileage credits. She treated me with glorious reverence, but in fact she was the rock star. Ultimately, Penny would grow up to be a big-time lawyer, but to this day she still recalls her friendship with a very young Anthony and how we both worked on his burgeoning lexicon. We were all at a party, and he met a lady friend of Penny's who had just graduated from law school. Tony was quite impressed with her mastery of vocabulary. A few days later, he brought a poem of his to show Penny. It was loaded with newly-inspired jargon.

LA based Three Dog Night joined the Image Group, and I got to deal with some new cards. Danny Hutton lived in Laurel Canyon just south of the Country Store. He was the most amiable and the closest friend. Chuck Negron lived on Outpost Drive with a beautiful woman in quite an impressive mansion. He was private and seemingly responsible, at least back then. Cory Wells was the least accessible but a nice guy. My first concert with the band was at the old Kaleidoscope, now known as the Aquarius Theatre, and their opening act was a weird new band called KISS. We shared the same big dressing room, and the overloaded upstarts were downright disrespectful of my headliners. It was a Three Dog Night show and the fans booed what's their name, oh yeah, KISS. Whatever happened to them?

I guess just to be brats, Weaver and I started going to Chasen's, the fanciest, most expensive restaurant in town. It was at Beverly and Doheny, straddling good taste on the edge of Beverly Hills. With a few exceptions, it personified the conservative right wing of Los Angeles and was hallowed ground for its constituency, although famous celebrities of all persuasions were drawn to its glamorous motif and delicious cuisine. Nixon and Reagan dined there regularly. Patrons past and present included John F. Kennedy, W. C. Fields, Jimmy Stewart, Cary Grant, Alfred Hitchcock, Groucho Marx, Marilyn Monroe, Clark Gable, Elizabeth Taylor and Richard Burton, Crosby and Hope, Bogey and Cagney, Howard Hughes, Prime Minister Margaret Thatcher and Queen Elizabeth, Frank Sinatra's Rat Pack, and Weaver, Bashara and Kiedis.

Our first time, we arrived in full hippie uniform, but they had a strict dress code, which required coat and tie. They had extra ones on hand for idiots like us. We looked pretty silly in our Brooks Brothers tweedy jackets and polka-dot ties. Rehabilitated, we were back tonight for Alan's birthday. Weaver was in charge of the evening. We had our English velvet coats and tie-dyed ties and our glamorous dates and some of Big Al's elite friends like Kendal, Wiatt and Vallon. At Chasen's, it seemed like each customer had their own waiter always circling the table like a benevolent vulture. There were at least a dozen of us, so our party needed a traffic cop. We ordered copious vinopious and extravagant meals that got rather rambunctious. Someone (Weaver!) brought out some celebratory cocaine and passed it down the table. One by one, the gutsiest of us flipped our salad plates over and snorted lines of blow off the fancy china. The waiters kept a stiff upper lip and Weaver left a hell of a tip.

We also patronized the Cock and Bull, another imperial joint on Sunset. Young Tony came to some of those and always ordered lobster. If we'd go to the Rainbow and I was short on cash, Tony still ordered lobster. I finally instituted the lobster rule; check with me first to see if we could afford it. All these years later when Anthony took me out to eat, I would ask if it was OK for me to order the lobster. He'd smile and say sure Pop, go ahead.

Dear Mom, I'm already having lots of fun. Were going to go to San Francisco as soon as my dad gets a car. I think I'm going to a Beaverly hills school. My new friends are Kurt, Kurk, BJ, Austin, Tracey, Sam and her kid, Kelly, Nan, Brandy, Dee, Tom and David and Alan and Connie. Me and my dad went to a great Mexican resteraunt last night. I like your long letters I just don't like to write them. xxx Love, Tony

I finally had a vehicle again, after picking up an old wreck of an Austin Healey for dirt cheap, which was its true value. The engine conked out on me before I got home. And if everything wasn't Barnum and Bailey enough already, an ex-lady friend with the lovely name of Collette contacted me for a favor. Her boyfriend had been busted for cocaine, and she needed money to hire a lawyer. She offered me his remaining stash for well below market price so I borrowed some money and bought the product as an investment. I hardly ever used coke, but everybody I knew did. It was rampant. Show business used it for rocket fuel, for currency, for power, for sex and forever. I turned it over and it was way too easy.

The Boss came up with a blockbuster project. He met a dude named Alex from Wisconsin, who was in LA, shopping for kilos. They asked me to do one last run and, because it was such a big load, it would go by train for a change. Momma Connie was jet-setting, so I had to take Tony with me on this prepaid vacation, and he agreed that would be good cover anyway. Wolfer went to stay with Weaver. Big Al drove us downtown to Union Station. On the train, we had our own private compartment with two little beds and six large suitcases. There was hardly room to move. The adrenaline was toxic, but I was accustomed. At age eleven, Tony was just as ice cool blue. I was playing Russian roulette, and Tony said deal me in. He thrived on the adventure and trusted in the cause. I fight back tears with the reminiscences but salute our fearless spunk. We were wildcat mercenaries sleeping on top of a Bulgarian train crypt full of explosive contraband. I drew the gypsy's *morte* card and spit it out; I read Mario Puzo's *The Godfather* instead. Punch-drunk giddy, Tony ran around from car to car.

I met a girl in the club car and spent myself. Tony met a girl too. We double dated. Scenic views streamed out of pleasure domes, and we ravaged three course meals in the dining car. We'd briefly disembark at lonely junction stops for a brush with the golden waves of grain. Three days later, we finally pulled into Chicago's Union Station, from where I once embarked to Milwaukee when I ran away as a kid. Now my kid and I were headed for the same neck of the woods.

In Kenosha, we holed up in Alex's amateur house while he tried to push the product. His people were disorganized, and we ended up sitting around for days. There was plenty of time to digest our caper. I broke down the worst scenario ramifications, but my co-pilot was undaunted. I smoked the goods; he drank the pop. His head was on straight. Mine was frustrated. Finally, they got Alex's shit together and we flew back to LA. Tony carried the money bags and kept going to the airplane lavatory to recount it.

When we got back, Scott Weaver picked us up at the airport and drove us to Topanga. Disturbingly, there was no sign of Wolfer, who I expected to be jumping into my arms the moment we drove up. They sat us down and informed us that Wolfer had been hit by a car while running the streets with Hubert and Dudley. They took us to the garage where Wolfer's body laid in state. Our hearts sank into hell. Tearfully, Tony and I drove him back to West Hollywood and buried the champ in our Palm Ave. back yard.

At Sonny's Christmas gala, curious Tony investigated the mansion's old fashion elevator, climbed in, pushed some buttons, lifted off and then got stuck between floors. Nobody could get it unlocked. Sonny averted a catastrophe by smashing through the wall with a fire ax to rescue the young adventurer. Tony's disarming smile and Sonny's good nature kept the mishap from ruining the party.

Sonny and Cher remained harmonious and preserved their act for a while. Sonny took Tony to their CBS tapings, to the Las Vegas shows and skiing in Tahoe. He treated him like a son. After the Cher divorce was resolved, Sonny bought a new mansion in Bel Air, and for Tony it became his second home. We used Sonny's address to get Tony into Emerson Junior High, a definite upgrade for what he would have had in Hollywood. When Tony got in trouble at school, Sonny and I would both show up at the principal's office to bail him out. Connie's reign as Bono's girl didn't last all that long, but Sonny never wavered with Tony. The next year, it was his new wife, Susie Coelho, who would meet me at the principal's office. When the dream team finally called it quits, Sonny went on to a variety of failed solo TV endeavors and later reinvented himself as a restaurateur, opening a classy joint on Melrose which was a popular destination. We went there for dinner when Anthony was in high school and they caught up on old times. Sonny moved to Palm Springs, became the mayor and then a Republican congressman from that district. In 1998, he died in a skiing accident on the same Tahoe slopes where he once taught Tony to ski.

Connie was a vagrant again. She stayed with Elmer, with Jack Nicholson and Roman Polanski, Adrienne Teeguarden and billionaire Bernie Cornfeld in his Grayhall mansion. Elmer sicked his dogs on me when I tried to scale his security fence, and Connie called the cops. Not to worry; there were plenty of damsels invading my lair.

At the top of the new heap was the sultry, oh my god, Liza Cruz. She enjoyed the company of father *and* son. She was one in a million, but with that many places to go. Lori Maddox was a pubescent nymphet and already an institution on the Sunset Strip. Legend said she lost her virginity to David and Angie Bowie, and her verified subsequent conquests were prodigious. Her partner in crime was Sable Starr, who made Lori look innocent. Sable was best known as Johnny Thunder's girl, but had also been with Keith Richards, Marc Boland, Bowie, Page, Iggy, Richard Hell and Stiv Bators and that was just for Lent. A horde of precocious nymphs spent most of their night life at Rodney's English Disco. I dropped by occasionally, but so did Elvis. The coterie was exemplary. Rodney's was a no-alcohol club, so girls of any age could come and go. There were clandestine drugs though and smuggled beers in the back alley. The place was perniciously packed with nubile teens and licentious rock stars, said the combustible kettle as I poked around.

So one day, Lori knocked on my door along with her highness Sable Starr and a young Mackenzie Phillips. Mac was the daughter of madman John Phillips, founder of the Mamas and the Papas, #1 with a bullet and several run-ins with drugs and the law. I was flattered to have the vivacious Lori Maddox looking me up, and I just liked looking. She was the tart of tarts, the queen of hearts. But I couldn't take my eyes off Mackenzie. At the age of 12, she had debuted as a saucy pick-up in *American Graffiti,* directed by George Lucas. As a teenager, she was about to capture American TV viewers as one of the leads in Norman Lear's new hit show *One Day at a Time.* She and Valerie Bertinelli would be sisters. Mackenzie was about to start cashing fifty-grand-a-week checks. Eventually, I discovered she had her father's predilections and addictions, but she was talented and a sweetheart. I bumped into her occasionally, most notably at a party that was playing early Fleetwood Mac's "Rattlesnake Shake" with Peter Green on guitar. High-velocity and absolutely dazzling!

I was good friends with John and Jason Mayall, who lived high in Laurel Canyon. They were a lot like Anthony and I; a cool father-son combo. In England, John had come to great prominence in the 60s with his band John Mayall and the Blues Breakers. Mick Fleetwood, John McVie and Peter Green had all been in the Blues Breakers before they started up Fleetwood Mac. Other alumni of the Blues Breakers included Eric Clapton, Jack Bruce, Mick Taylor of the Stones, and super drummer Aynsley Dunbar. I admit to smoking the herb with those Mayalls, and I never got tired of his *Blues from Laurel Canyon* or any of his other fifty-plus albums.

Another mad genius was Paul Fegen, a prominent Beverly Hills lawyer who enjoyed the company of beautiful women and started a society of the like-minded. Not surprisingly, I was an early convert and member. He called this bacchanalia *The Fig* and it was one sweet party, first at his home in the Beverly Hills, and, when that overflowed, he moved the orgasmic operation to the Century City Hotel ballroom. Paul was a Rainbow regular and drove a custom convertible, full of his own playmates. We became quite close, and he was my attorney for a time.

Speaking of madmen, wild and wooly Weaver got in a serious car accident and was hospitalized for quite a while. He had multiple broken bones in his legs and pelvis and was in a body cast from the waist down, with only a peephole to pee out of. Folks flocked to his Inglewood hospital, bringing the usual flowers, candy and stuffed animals. Not me, I brought a randy girl who was willing and able to give him a blow job through that peephole. When David added skydiving to his ventures, he racked up more broken bones than an archaeological dig.

Rodney's English Disco closed a few months later. The Lolitas had to grow up and move on. There was a final farewell and beautiful bedlam at the Palladium on Sunset and Vine; they called it "Death of Glitter." The New York Dolls, Iggy Pop and Silverhead played, and thousands of us crowded into that night of nights. My friend Michael Des Barres fronted Silverhead and later sang for Detective and Chequered Past and replaced Robert Palmer in Power Station. He also pursued an acting career, and for a long time was married to the beautiful Miss Pamela. Pamela Des Barres is renowned for her sinful past and insightful books *I'm With the Band, Take Another Little Piece of my Heart: A Groupie Grows Up,* and *Let's Spend the Night Together.*

With gusto, I encouraged my Tony Award to read, if not necessarily the works of Miss Pamela. And despite my merrymaking, I did facilitate his education. I minimized the parties and often drove him to school *before* I went to bed. I continued to teach him new words and made vocabulary a priority. A poet myself, I fed him creativity with an oversize ladle. His favorite game was trying to stump me with new words he'd learned at school. I'd always have the answer, but he kept trying. One momentous afternoon, he came home and threw *voracious* at me; pre-occupied I flashed on *vociferous* and gave him the incorrect answer. He bounced up with the biggest smile, "I gotcha, Dad; it means a great appetite." If I did one thing irrefutable, it was mandating the importance of reading and writing. Soon he would write for the world.

I arrived at the Rainbow one night and invited myself into an ace booth, beautifully occupied by an exotic French Romanian loaded with sophistication and hundred-dollar bills. She bought me drinks and then dinner. Intoxicated, I spent the evening there. She spread a carpet of C-notes on the table, rolled them into school-girl ribbons and stuck them into my tangled hair. She kept adding the Benjamins until there were six or seven hundred bucks in my mane. Crazed and extravagant, she was either a seductress or a serial killer. I pocketed my booty before she changed her mind and flirted with leaving. She pouted and put up a fuss because she liked all the attention we were getting. I stayed. Closing time snuck up, and she kidnapped me to her pretentious apartment for a nightcap. In a wink, she slipped into lingerie and vodka, but I told her my son had school in the morning and I needed to go. As a way out, I explained my kid's twelfth birthday was tomorrow and invited her to join us around eight at the Captain's Table, a popular seafood restaurant on La Cienega's restaurant row. Lobster for Tony.

The Captain's maitre d' took Tony and me to a small circular table with a big white tablecloth that hung almost to the floor. We ordered our lobsters, and I kept a wary eye on the door. We were almost finished with our food when the fille de joie showed up. She sat down and ordered a drink from our waiter. By the time he returned, she had crawled under the table and given Tony her own special birthday present. I never got a straight answer from either of them, but the nonplussed waiter summoned a purple-faced Captain, who summarily escorted us out the door. No charge for the dinner.

Tony and I ditched the strumpet and went to the Rainbow. We snuggled into the fireplace booth, where girls covered him in lipstick and good wishes. A month later on my birthday, the staff gave me my own kisses and a lifetime "Over the Rainbow" certificate with the membership number # 1.

Tony flew home to Michigan for Christmas. I missed him already. My amazing prodigy was a rising star. When he returned from the holidays it would be 1975. We had dumped the obsolete past for new lightning. I was slicked-back and double-breasted. A seamstress friend made a junior-size replica of my Yves Saint Laurent pinstripe suit for Tony. We'd sit at the fireplace booth like identical twins. We were a team like no other. Now we really ruled the Rainbow. We were as big an attraction at the Sunset Strip Mecca as ex-Beatles and old Stones.

Spider & Son

Our galaxy has its sun

Mr. Atilla a little hun

Brady's bunch bred some

Acme & Son

Kirk had Michael

Joe John Fitzgerald

Mao a Mao

A calf in a cow

A litter of chow

None from a nun

Son of a Gun

Abraham begat Isaac, who…

And that guy in the shoe

Whelped a few

In fact a slew

Dennis' dad

Had a menace

Jesus was an icon

Each god creates one

Caesar forged a Rubicon

Napoleon a Waterloo

And I have

You

Flea, Hillel and Anthony...very young.

Chapter 22: Lee Strasberg Method Actor

The Alice Cooper juggernaut slowed down a bit and so did the Image Group. I was in need of a cash flow and turned to my old friend Jimmy Lurie, who still lived in mountain-lion country up in the Agoura wilderness. He had an elderly friend who had been visiting Mexico for 60 years. He knew everybody at the border crossing and was just an old fogy who went there to fish. Or so they thought. I paid Jimmy a finder's fee, and the fogy starting coming around with an occasional delivery. I was discriminating and under the radar but started nibbling on the product.

At the time, I had a steady girl who lived in conservative Orange County with her parents. I met her at a club scene on the Queen Mary in Long Beach. She had a black-belt brother who taught Tony karate and nun-chucks. Slim had long limbs and religion. Inevitably, I pushed the conservative envelope, and one night she left our house in tears. I'm glad she got out when she could. Call me disingenuous, but I truly cared about my relationships, even if I didn't always remember their names.

We got a new dog though, a Westie terrier. Shark had a peculiar habit of biting anybody stupid on drugs. He kept them honest. A pretty, dizzy model was sitting on our floor, mumbling incoherently and Shark took a bite. The poser freaked out when she realized her lip was bloody, so Tony and I drove her to Cedars Sinai emergency. When I got the bill in the mail I thought it said $100, which I thought was a lot for two little stitches. I went to their accounting office to complain. The lady pointed out that the charge was not $100, but $1000. That hurt our cosmetic surgery budget.

I played in Alice Cooper's Celebrity Golf Tourney in the Valley, and brought Tony along. I thought he could caddy for me, but they had age restrictions. He decided to just hang around the clubhouse while I played golf. I left him my car keys in case he wanted to take a nap in the Healey. Instead, he took it for a ride. Seventh grade, stick shift with a stiff clutch, no license, no experience, no lessons, no damage! Of course, he didn't fess up for years, and he's still a daredevil.

Weaver came off the Canned Heat tour and whistled me over to the Whisky. A bunch of us piled into our favorite prized booth, wheeler-dealer Kurt and his gal Bunnie, an intriguing fresh-face named Gayle, Weaver with his date and Connie Foreman. It was a set up. Connie gave me seductive smiles, her new phone number and little love kicks under the table, but my restless eyes were on the fresh face and left with her. The next night during a thunderstorm, there was a knock at my back door. I pulled the little curtain aside and beheld a soaking-wet Connie. Drenched hair was splattered against her trembling body and makeup smeared her plaintive face. Like Pacino closing his mafia door on new wife Diane Keaton in the final scene of *The Godfather*, I closed the curtain on Connie and left her out in the rain.

If our six-year affair made Connie one of the most important females of my life, suddenly there was Kimberly Smith and a love story that was brief, but whose legend may outlive all the others. And no wonder; she was a wonder. Incredibly brilliant for a seventeen-year-old, she was delightfully independent and unlawfully angelic. She was the daughter of liberal parents who had recently moved to Oregon. Kimberly was in LA visiting her old posse of girlfriends when I met her in the Rainbow parking lot, as she was too young to be in the club itself. Beauty and brains, her big mouth spoke sophisticated wisdom. She was perfectly pure and yet tolerant of reprobates like me. She literally saw a world through rose-colored glasses. Her sensual eyes were declared illegally blind, and she preferred it that way. I was overly whelmed from our first meeting.

Both of us Kiedis kids fell in love with her. Tony and Kimberly cooked up a plan to snuggle, and I mean snuggle! Kimberly genuinely cherished the young brave, and they were off on a whirlwind happy rollercoaster. She was the perfect angel to entrust with his coming of age. For the record, Tony swears it was actually he who arranged the controversial deed.

Condemned, all three of us were designated pariahs by malcontents who mix their martini metaphors with spilt acrimony. The hippie lifestyle was practically a nudist colony. Free love was our sacred psalm. Children were free to be curious and encouraged to investigate life. Evolution depended on it. Eventually, Kimberly left for her home of the Ducks. Her father was a professor. A thousand miles was a tough-love struck commute, but the Healey gave it a whirl. Barry Manilow's "Mandy" played continuously on the radio. Its soaring ballad saved on fuel. I rented a motel in Eugene and she dug in too. I stayed for a few days and then dashed home. LA was my sovereign turf.

I was ambling down Hollywood Boulevard and bumped into Connie's friend Karen Lamm. I asked what's up. She had just left an acting class at the Lee Strasberg Institute, right there in front of my face. It was a nondescript three-story building with an iron gate and little evidence of the proprietor. Then she said something that clearly changed my life. "You'd be good at it; why don't you check it out?" And she was gone. Well, why not? I perused the directory and skipped up the stairs to the Institute on the second floor. It was simple and low key. Aspiring actors were coming and going. You could see into the various studios through the small circular windows on the yellow soundproof padded-doors. Acting classes, exercises, dance, voice, commercials; it felt good. Felt right. I went into the tiny office and sat down with the secretary. It was $90 for a class. There was a beginner course about to start in a few days. I signed up as Johnny McReckless.

My heart was pounding nails that first afternoon class. A dozen students were ready to go. The instructor laid out the rules and procedures. We started learning the Strasberg system of relaxation, and Lee's disciples burned it into our brains. The Ukrainian-born Lee Strasberg had been an early student himself of the Russian master Stanislavski. Strasberg was a pioneering member of the Group Theatre in New York with Clifford Odets, Elia Kazan and Lee's frequent adversary and fellow teacher, Stella Adler. Another founding member was John Garfield, the first of a new breed of actors like Montgomery Cliff, Marlon Brando and James Dean. Historically and unfortunately, Garfield never got the innovative respect he deserved. In the late-40s, Strasberg took over the Actors Studio in New York and revolutionized the craft. His influence on American acting can be seen in the work of Brando, Dean, DeNiro, Pacino, Marilyn Monroe, Geraldine Page, Steve McQueen, Paul Newman, Dustin Hoffman and a dazzling marquee of others. The master was also an accomplished actor in the theatre and finally did film work in *The Godfather II,* with a nomination for Best Supporting Actor. Now he had opened these acting sanctuaries in NY and LA, and here I was in one of them.

We got right into scene work. Pick a partner, learn it, and then do it for the class. I picked the cutest girl, of course, and we chose a scene from the movie *Come Blow Your Horn,* a Neil Simon screenplay, with Frank Sinatra as a swinger with a younger brother trying to learn the ropes. Played by Tony Bill in the film, I was the kid brother who masqueraded as his older playboy brother to put the make on an unsuspecting dame who got fooled. Jill St. John played her in the film, and my partner was every bit as sexy. I did the scene in nothing but my underwear and black socks with businessmen's calf-high garter belts. I was unloosed and set free. I felt explosive and unbeatable. The class and the instructor loved the performance. Nothing could stop me now, except for maybe women and trouble.

I was so excited I added a second class, and a couple months later, another acting opportunity smacked me aside the head. The new acting school, Sherwood Oaks Experimental College, opened a few blocks east on Hollywood Boulevard and it was wildly unconventional. The grand opening advertised a promotional party with free classes. Hundreds showed up and I brought Tony too. Master teachers got up in the large auditorium and doled out advice. A few celebrities lectured, and a young Robert De Niro gave a brief speech. He imparted this tidbit for the rookies, "People try to hide their emotions, not show them." Another speaker said, "Acting is doing. It's not speaking, it's behavior. It's something happening, even if you're only listening."

I had seen De Niro hanging around the newsstand on Las Palmas, reading the New York papers. Later, he would do a seminar at Sherwood Oaks. So would Phil Spector and Mel Brooks. There were also Orson Welles and Stanley Kubrick film seminars.

But on this opening day, everybody was anticipating the grand finale which had promised fireworks. One of the master teachers was Clu Gulager who had been a popular actor on *The Virginian* and in the movie *The Last Picture Show.* He was cut in that audacious method vein of Brando and Dean. He got up on a small portable stage surrounded by the anxious assembly and carefully surveyed us. He didn't say a word. We all waited for his message. He focused on the furniture which had seated the earlier speakers on the podium. Then without warning and with the agility, speed and strength of a furious wild beast, he proceeded to rip, crash, smash and break the furnishings into kindling, twisted metal and broken glass. Finally he took a deep breath, and said that's how he'd break us down and then rebuild us into new and better actors. The place went wild and scores signed up on the spot. I would have joined anyway, but I had an extra incentive from an astonishing blonde who sign up for Clu's class. I had been staring at her for hours. She was a tall model, oozing with class. She knew she was the bomb. Her name was Alana Collins Hamilton because she was married to actor George Hamilton. They divorced later that year, and subsequently she married Rod Stewart to become Alana Collins Hamilton Stewart.

Alana and I worked together in class and became friends. She had connections and set up an audition with a big-time agency in Beverly Hills. She asked me to do a scene with her for the agent, and we chose Philip Barry's *The Philadelphia Story,* which was one of my favorites. Originally written for Katherine Hepburn on Broadway, she went on to make the classic movie with Cary Grant and James Stewart's only Oscar. Our love scene was between Hepburn and Stewart; we practiced the piece for weeks and usually at her home in Beverly

Hills. We'd be working in the living room, and George Hamilton would come home with a "Hi, honey" and wander off into the kitchen.

The night before our audition, I was invited by a long-lost Connie Foreman to join her at a party with a rich brat society-boy. I bragged about my appointment, and the guests were excited for me. I had a couple drinks. Everybody was snorting lines of coke and some-one said, "Come on, one's not going to hurt." The millionaire suggested we rent the film, but it was too late. He called New York to get it flown out to us. He even suggested we all fly to New York to view it. That's how coked up he was. I finally extracted myself from the craziness and went home but was so high I couldn't sleep. I took a Quaalude to calm me down.

The next thing I knew, bright sunshine was blazing through the morning glories, and Alana was calling me from the agency, wondering where the hell I was. I was in a daze. I threw on disheveled clothes and downed a handful of aspirins. As I arrived, Alana came stalking out and fired off a corrosive barrage as our ships passed in the hall. She was furi-ous with me for life. I was the big loser. Fortunately, she recovered of course, and I like to think of her courageous friendship with Farrah Fawcett. I apologize every time someone reads this book.

I had a better record at Sherwood Oaks though. Clu, who was of Cherokee ancestry, made a film about an Oklahoma Indian lost in Hollywood. All the male students had to develop a transvestite character, while the girls had to play macho males. This was in preparation for us to do Hamlet with switched genders. I dolled up a buff transvestite char-acter with super-high platforms, tight cutoff jeans, mesh stockings and sexy garter belts. I projected plump avocados in my halter top for breasts. We shot the film on Hollywood Boulevard and pedestrians really thought we were hookers. In *Scar Tissue*, Anthony said I went overboard in preparation for the role to the point he thought I was turning into an actual trans-sexual. No, I was just dedicated to my new profession. I immersed myself in authentic preparation at the Queen Mary Club on Ventura. It was a notorious transvestite joint; I even took Tony to see the exterior.

Since I was acting, copycat Tony did too. He tagged along to Lee Strasberg and Sherwood Oaks. He also took some children classes. *Drama-Logue* listed casting calls for plays, student films, non-union films and extra work.

I auditioned for a USC film and got the lead role as Sam Spade, the 1940s private eye who was always mixed up with sultry dames. I got a screaming role in a low-budget Robert Vaughn film *The Lucifer Complex,* which we shot at LAX. I was in a plane full of passengers just before it crashed.

My best education and source of work was the theater. I attended as many plays as I could and auditioned others. I hung out at actor bars like Dan Tana, the Formosa Café and Boardners on Cherokee. I traveled east to see Ashley in New York, just to rub shoulders with other actors at Joe Allen's on 46th Street and Sardi's on 44th. At Elaine's on Second Avenue, I hoped to catch Woody on clarinet. I met a zinger of a girl at P.J. Clarke's on 3rd Ave., another great actor's hangout. She was vacationing from Florida, and I spent the night with her at the Waldorf Astoria. I made future plans to meet her in Miami. I embraced Broadway till she cried uncle. The box office and the boffo; I was in love. I saw *A Chorus Line* at the Shubert and *Kennedy's Children* with Shirley Knight's Tony Award winning performance. Tom Stoppard's *Travesties* at the Ethel Barrymore blew me out of the box. It won best-play awards from both the Tonys and NY Drama Critics' Circle. From that time on, I always used a brilliant piece of *Travesties'* dialogue whenever I needed a monologue audition. Acting had become my overwhelming drug of choice.

At home, I had to support 937 Palm. New rough-guy Ron was suddenly in my life and I wasn't so sure that was a good thing. This mug was a concrete-mixer amalgam of Rich Klimavich times the Hulk and Jake LaMotta. Ron was an avenging Jewish archangel, who called Mercedes "Nazi Cadillacs." He had off-kilter charisma that was intriguing but deadly, like having a poisonous snake for a pet. I think he started courting my favor because he had either killed or scared away his other friends. He was a real coke dealer; I was a novice with no intention of grandiose. He came over in his Cadillac and asked me to come with him on an errand. We drove up to a house on Sunset Plaza. He opened the glove compartment, pulled out a revolver and stuffed it in his belt. "Come on," he ordered. The target was some poor numbskull who owed him money; he got roughed up pretty bad. Ron brought me along for a taste of his ruthlessness and the consequences of crossing him. My old-fogy connection had dried up, and Ron wanted to be my new supplier—or else! On ludes, somehow I lost an ounce of his fronted product. It could have been curtains. Fortunately, he liked Tony or he might have rubbed me out. Ron was definitely into the funk and took Tony to a Parliament-Funkadelic concert. By the time Tony had grown up to be Anthony, he was one of P-Funk George Clinton's best friends, and Clinton produced RHCP's *Freaky Styley*.

Weaver's ex, Phrogg, was home from England and came by. She was headed for a Sunday afternoon party on Wilshire. Tony and I went along, but not before she and I dropped a couple Quaaludes. Phrogg's name wasn't on the guest list as promised, but Cher drove up and slid us right in the door. It was a lavish party with expensive champagne and a spectacular layout of food arranged on an elaborate centerpiece. The place was loaded with heavyweight star power. Right off the bat, I saw Paul McCartney standing there in animated discussion with Rod Stewart and Ronnie Wood. My first intoxicated thought was Tony's got to meet him. With infinite courage but little sense, I barged right up and interrupted them as if we were old friends. "Paul! I'd like you to meet my son, Tony." McCartney was compassionate, bent down to young Tony, shook his hand and made a little small talk. Then he returned to his pals and did the exaggerated aside, "Who the hell is that guy!?"

But I had only just started. I think the event was a birthday party for Tatum O'Neal, because she was all over the place. She was 12, one year younger than Tony, but already had an Academy Award for *Paper Moon*. Her father, Ryan, had raised his kids much as I had, in an environment that nurtured premature little adults. Tatum came up to us and introduced herself; I was blown away by her savoir faire. She was like a sexy woman in an adolescent's body. Fueled with Quaaludes, before I knew it I was trying to get her phone number and persistently chased her around the room. An angry Ryan O'Neal came at me; I stumbled backward and fell onto the extravagant table centerpiece. Lobster bisque, roast beef gravy and hors d'oeuvres splattered fresh, pretty party dresses and seersucker suits. I don't remember whether it was security, Mr. O'Neal or Tony who hustled me out of there.

Taxi Driver came out. Maybe there *was* a god, and he was definitely talkin' to me. Now I was more obsessed than ever. *Taxi Driver* was playing on Hollywood Boulevard at what is now the El Capitan Theatre, two blocks from the Lee Strasberg Institute. I saw it eleven times. A few years earlier, Weaver and I had seen *The Panic in Needle Park* in Westwood. That was Pacino's breakthrough, a stark film about heroin addiction. It had inspired David; now it inspired me to follow the gospel of Robert De Niro. I resurrected dormant ambitions and pledged to work even harder.

While Tony was on his annual summer vacation, I remodeled his funky little bedroom with new paint, stereo, bed and a big surprise—the neon sign from the Shamrock Bar in GR when they closed down for the new freeway. The fluorescent green neon was slick as anything in the LA Museum of Contemporary Art.

Work done, I still had time to catch up on monkey business, and it started with a young redheaded bang that lived in a motel next door to the Palomino Club. I found actresses Sara, Marcy and Tani at auditions. And then there was buxom dancer Shari Eubank, who I first met at the Classic Cat, appropriately on the Strip. We started dating about the time she got her 15 minutes of fame. She was in *Playboy* and then Russ Meyer cast her as the lead in his 1975 over-the-top movie, *Supervixens*. We playfully scoured *Variety* for acting jobs at her rented villa in the Sunset hills.

In an eerie castle on Helios off Beachwood, there lurked a strange blonde goddess calling herself Uranus. I'd seen her around town and had always been in awe of her statuesque black magic. Naturally, I managed to fall into her spider web bed. And finally I made a quick trip to Florida to see my family and the Waldorf Astoria girl I had met in NYC. I brought along Bruce Springsteen's new album *Born to Run* and played it for everybody who had a record player. It was one of the great albums of my life.

My second year at Strasberg I discovered that the grand guru himself came to the Hollywood studio for a semester course in the summer. I signed up and plunked down my $500. Comical extrovert Big Al Bashara decided to take a crack too. Soon we found ourselves in the same classroom with the old pro and some of the best young actors in town. Alan got a taste of relaxation and secret techniques, but now we also got Strasberg's tattered sermons, accrued over many years at the Actors Studio in New York. The same words he once uttered to Brando, Dean and Monroe. We did scenes as before, but now with precision critical review. Despite his age, he still got up on stage and showed us the right path to an effective choice for that moment.

The climactic final week of Strasberg's course allowed the press and the public to observe our progress. Lee would select a handful of the best actors, based on our earlier performances. It was the super bowl of scenes. During the semester, Alan and I had done a piece from *The Friends of Eddie Coyle*, a tough crime novel about gun runners. Nary a hitch, we nailed it. Regardless, the mentor's patented scathing critiques were de rigueur. A perfectionist, he really enjoyed chewing us out. Alan and I finished our scene and stood in front of the Strasberg firing squad. The students waited to hear him rip us apart. He took a long theatrical pause and then said "Get outta here! What do you need me for; you guys are ready to work. That was brilliant. The best I've seen all year." That of course got us into the final week showcase, and we set about to make an indelible statement.

We picked a scene from *Midnight Cowboy* with John Voight and Dustin Hoffman as gritty, down-in-the-dirt lost souls in New York City. I was the naïve fresh-out-of-Texas wannabe male hustler, Joe Buck (Voight). Alan was born to play the hopeless, dying street bum, Ratso Rizzo. We spent blood and tears and used unprecedented special effects, music and lighting. We would be in character and costume; Bashara as the gimpy and grimy degenerate and me as the wide-eyed buckaroo with a cowboy hat, snakeskin boots and a condescending attitude.

Alan was up to his old tricks dealing pot again and had a big-time connection named Otto in Ventura County. The night before our scene, Alan drove up to Santa Barbara to oversee a super-sized load. The police had a tipster and were waiting for him. He spent the night in jail and was lucky to get bailed out. Then he had to drive a hundred miles to LA, get his stuff together and be at the Institute by 11 a.m.

I was pacing around nervously, angry and upset. Relaxation is the key to acting, and I was a frenzied mess. The program had already begun by the time Alan arrived. We couldn't coordinate our sound or lighting, and there was no time for a last run through. Lee called our names and made a brief statement. The lights went down and came up again as I made my entrance from behind the audience. I forgot everything I'd ever learned. I exaggerated my Wild West walk. Alan entered at the wrong time from the wrong place. Our mojo was way off. We weren't Joe Buck and Ratso; we were a flustered actor and a man who was facing years in prison. We sat down in a booth at a rundown Times Square diner to do the majority of our dialogue. Alan had the first line, but he went blank. His blank-ity blank blanked me. Speechless, we sat there like stupid idiots for what seemed liked several minutes. We were convicted failures on our way to the gallows of hell's fury. Finally an embarrassed and angry Strasberg bellowed out, "Stop before it gets any worse!" He relaxed, adjusted and then meticulously analyzed our miscues and demonstrated how Strasberg-trained actors can learn from their mistakes. It was good press. We were ushered out and the next team came on. Instead of dwelling on *Midnight Cowboy*, Alan and I focused on *Friends of Eddie Coyle* and followed Lee's earlier advice to look for work in the industry. It was imperative we got ourselves agents and Screen Actors Guild cards. You can't work without them.

The Strasberg classes had done more for Tony than they had for me. I hired Martin, a well-known photographer on Sunset, to take my head shots. Tony came along and Martin threw in a few photos of him. One of them graces the back cover of his biography *Scar Tissue*. We put together resumes and photos and started distributing our most-wanted posters. Tony met Lance Kerwin, a young actor who was in the TV movie *James at 15*. They connected and the Toni Kellman Agency signed up my kid. Soon he was going on auditions for acting roles and commercials. One of Tony's first gigs was a Coca-Cola commercial. The televised Grammy Awards Show opened with the usual roster of famous stars' names that would be appearing on the program and then went directly to commercial. The very next image was Tony sitting on the stoop of a New York brownstone in his Coca-Cola commercial. It was so seamless it was as though he was also part of the Grammies.

I couldn't get an agency to take me; I had no credentials. I had however befriended Candy Clark, an actress with amazing credits; she was nominated best supporting actress for *American Graffiti*, played opposite Bowie in *The Man Who Fell to Earth*, worked in John Huston's *Fat City* and performed with Robert Mitchum in *The Big Sleep*. She had a younger brother Randy Clark with aspirations of being a theatrical agent, and he took me on. We were the blind leading the maimed, but we had fun and got it done.

Elvira, Mistress of the Dark...or as we know her...Cassandra Peterson. Our
Las Vegas showgirl, Bond girl, Elvis girl and Fellini girl.

Chapter 23: The Director's Cut

Tony went to Michigan for the summer. He had graduated from Emerson; I tried my best to enroll him in Beverly Hills High, but we were jurisdictionally screwed. Sonny's Bel Air address was for University High on the west side of the 405 and way too far from our house to be practical. That meant we'd have to go to Fairfax High on Melrose, a trendy Hollywood area in the colorful heartland of the Jewish community. Its neighborhood included Canter's Delicatessen, CBS Television City and the Farmer's Market. Fairfax's alumni were impressive: Carole Lombard, Ricardo Montalban, David Janssen, Timothy Hutton, Mickey Rooney, Herb Alpert, Al Franken, dancer Gower Champion, Phil Spector, presidential candidate and Buffalo Bills football star Jack Kemp, writer James Ellroy, Chanel Iman, Tito and Jackie Jackson, Warren Zevon and other wunderkinds. It also had crime and gang activity. I'd have been much more comfortable with Tony in 90210, but it did not work out. Whether I liked it or not, come September he would be a Fairfax Lion. Not worked out fine.

I met Exene Cervenka, who had recently arrived from Florida. She was semi-homeless, semi-disheveled and totally rampant with pent up anxieties. A frustrated poet, she was an enigma and I couldn't find her end game. We covered a lot of territory with incidents in both the Valley and Hollywood. Exene introduced me to her friend Fay Hart, who was also new from Florida. She made no secret of her affection and started coming to my house at will. Fay was attractive, outrageous, brilliant and also a poet. I made love to her on my big oak desk table. She never got over it. Now I was her little sex puppy. A year later, Exene joined with John Doe, Billy Zoom and D.J. Bonebrake to form X, one of the most critically acclaimed talents in music history. They took their rightful place alongside the great LA bands.

Alan connected with theatrical agent Billy Taylor. We went up to see him in the 9000 Building about representation. He had big clients and wasn't interested, but Alan and Billy did some blow. We didn't have our SAG cards anyway. It was classic catch-22; you need a card to work, but you can't get work without a card. Billy did give me a tip though; he was friends with wild-man director Jack Starrett, who might give me a shot at a small part in his upcoming flick. Billy set me up to meet him at his office at Paramount. There had been a series of *Walking Tall* movies, and Starrett was directing *Walking Tall -The Final Chapter*. The original had been a box-office smash for the studio. It was based on the true legend of Tennessee sheriff Bufford Pusser, who cleaned up crime with old school justice and a really big club.

Jack Starrett lived up to his billing. He was a big lug of a guy, gruff and grizzled with a scruffy white beard and a mischievous twinkle in his conniving blue eyes. He was an actor himself and understood the dilemma of getting started in the business. He had just played the irascible, blustering prospector Gabby Johnson in Mel Brooks' hit movie *Blazing Saddles*. As a courtesy, he was expecting a toot. It seemed everybody wanted a pick me up. I told him I wasn't up to speed with the currency. He liked me though and agreed to pass me off as a stunt man, get me on the payroll, and then throw me a line to speak on camera, which would qualify me for a SAG card. I'd be one of the henchmen for the evil boss of an illegal gambling club called the Three Deuces. The film would be shot on location in Jackson, 90 miles east of Memphis. I would be expected to get there on my own and don't forget the courtesy. I walked out of his office and wandered around the Paramount lot. Movie stars, bit players and extras in exotic costumes were bustling between stages. Writers, directors, editors and producers were plotting creatively. And I was too. I was part of this stark-raving-mad profession, going all the way back to Aeschylus, Sophocles and Euripides 2,500 years ago.

I needed a theatrical name. The production and Screen Actors Guild needed to know. Kiedis had been a pesky pronunciation problem my entire life. Everybody got it wrong. I wanted a crisp name like Rip Torn or Tab Hunter, but with the edginess of the times. It was the era of Johnny Rotten, Sid Vicious, Richard Hell and Stiv Bators. I wanted a piece of both. Although I had signed up as Johnny McReckless at Strasberg, I never really used the name; it sat in the office drawer with my application. I anguished. It was like naming your baby or a dog, but this one might end up in lights. I was shopping at the Safeway, and when I got back to the car there was a cuadrilla of Argentine gypsies hovering over my bleeding Healey. A few days earlier and slightly intoxicated, I had pulled out of Gazzari's parking lot and rolled into a Sunset Boulevard fender bender. Being a Friday night, the California Highway Patrol was right on the case, but inexplicably the CHP let me slide on the ticket and the Quaaludes in my system. It made up for all those times the law had chased me around over the last ten years.

The aggressive leader of the gypsies said they could fix my fender *and* paint it—all for $80. It sounded like a good deal to me. We all went to my house and into the back parking area. The gyps jumped to work and pounded it out with a ball peen hammer. Then they smeared clumpy brown Bondo on it and smoothed it over with a rougher. I could have done that myself and for a lot cheaper. It sucked and I let the boss know; and what about the paint job? He pulled out an aerosol can of blue paint and gave my fender a quick spray. No way. I snarled and I blustered. I put on my scariest look and said I'm not paying. In a calm voice, the gypsy leader replied, "Hey, no problem for us; but we'll come back in the middle of the night and burn your house down." I gave him the 80 bucks, but was determined to get my money's worth.

Suddenly, a cartoon light bulb flashed over my head. I appropriated the leader's fitting name, which was Blackie. My father's teenage nickname had been Blackie, long before I was born. It was all coming back to me. Clark Gable had played "Blackie" Gallagher in *Manhattan Melodrama,* the 1934 crime film I'd seen on the late late show at Peg's apartment, back when I was rescuing her from the monkey guy, 15 years ago.

I still needed a last name though. It was down to the panic deadline. I sat at my big oak desk, writing combinations. I happened to glance up, and my eyes hit a book lying sideways in my library. It was *Red Harvest* by Dashiell Hammett. The revelation worked in tandem, and I became Blackie Dammett. It was crisp as a shot of rye.

I battened down the hatches at 937 and flew to Las Vegas, where I spent the night watching roulette croupiers. In the morning, I boarded another plane for Memphis and was picked up by a raw recruit gofer from Atlanta. His name was Jay Brown, James Granville Brown IV. His father had some connection to Cox Broadcasting, who financed the film. A first for both of us, we became instant friends. A recent grad of Georgia, he knew the B-52s and other Athens bands in that critical stew that also produced R.E.M. Jay was never far from his camera. He was a renaissance man and one of the coolest guys I ever knew.

Jay dropped me off at the Jackson Holiday Inn. The first thing I did was phone Johnny Reaser in Detroit. Hey, I'm working as an actor in a real Hollywood movie! I had some catching up to do; by now he was a thriving lawyer with an office, high in the architecturally-venerated Penobscot Building.

Then I went to meet Jack Starrett. And boy was he glad to see me; you'd think I was Clint Eastwood or Burt Reynolds. I guess it had something to do with my favor. He had an office at the hotel and a private house near the local country club. Absolute royalty for the duration, Jack's entourage included his diminutive girlfriend Karen and a 6-pound Shitzu doggie named Studley, who rode shotgun on a stack of LA Yellow Page phone books in his black Rolls Royce.

For the first week, I just observed and drank in the educational opportunity. Jay and I took side trips to Nashville and Memphis on our days off. We broke into a Baptist Nurses College and let the cute ones free. We hit the country bars, the blues bars and the jazz bars. Being a Hollywood actor on location in rural Tennessee afforded me magnolia-antebellum hospitality from the local girls. Even the gnarly actors got southern fried love. Bo Svenson starred as Buford Pusser, patriarchal Forrest Tucker played Grandpa Pusser and Leif Garrett was a Lil' Pusser. Leif Garrett would grow into a *Tiger Beat* pop rock star.

Starrett had his own hired driver, a local teamster from Memphis. I kept the little stash in my possession since Jack would have wolfed it down like a lamb chop. A film shoot lasts forever, and I was there for the duration. Jack had an insatiable thirst for vodka, a lust for lovin', a hunger for chow and an obsession with blow. As the director, he had a million things to accomplish every day, and if anybody ever thrived on speed, it was him.

Late one night, Jack got drunk and broke his own rule. He sent his driver to my room to pick up a pick me up. Because the driver arrived unexpectedly, he got to see where I hid it. The next day I was on location, and when I returned the stash was gone. I freaked and called Jack; Jack freaked a bigger freak. His driver had not shown up for work that day; we knew who the culprit was. Jack relaxed and said he'd fly me back to LA for replenishment, but I was not about to let that Dixie delinquent get away with it. I borrowed a company car and armed with the driver's address in Memphis drove the 90 miles to hunt him down. His mother lived in a shanty town, south of the city not far from the Mississippi state line. I parked in their junk-riddled yard and started toward the front door when a Pontiac Firebird burst out of the back yard, kicking up gravel and roared off into the night. I jumped back in my vehicle and chased him down the road, following the cloud of dust in front of me. Then he cut off into cornfields and headed south through farmland and twisted back roads. I drove through a clothesline of long johns, got stuck in a creek and clipped a Magnolia tree. Eventually, I lost him somewhere in Mississippi, their state flowers stuck in my grill. Starrett sent me off to LA for refreshments; I took advantage and spent some liberty with the clever, talented and innovative Fay Hart, aka Fay Hard.

Back in Tennessee, I still had to do my scenes. The cast and crew were anxious to see the work of this mysterious stranger who was always taking notes. I was Jack Starrett's secret weapon. Finally it was my call, an exterior shot of the Three Deuces club going up in blazes. They had acquired a big old structure out in the middle of nowhere, ruthlessly abused it and then burned it down. Lots of fire trucks stood by just in case. I waited inside the death trap for the fire to rage; only when it was fully engulfed would I get the cue to drag my injured boss to safety. Once we got out the door, I gave my SAG card line, "She's gonna blow!" And did it! The explosives went off like the 4th of July, and flaming boards were flying all around us.

The next day, in reverse order, we did the Three Deuces interiors in a Jackson warehouse. The lively set was full of crusty thugs, gamblers, dance-hall gals, a full bar and me as the stickman at the featured craps table. I used my Vegas education to rattle off the lingo. As bait, we had Buford Pusser's fiancée tied upstairs, and Bo rushed in the front door with his five-foot-long club, scattering customers and bad guys. The roughneck lawman rushed up stairs to save his girl, and my boss nodded for me to take care of our nemesis once and for all. I grabbed a shotgun and went after him. At the top of the stairs, Buford was waiting around the corner with this club; as I got to the top, he stepped out and smashed me in the face like Babe Ruth hitting a slow curve ball. A special effects rubber club of course. Cut! Set up for the next shot.

The legendary stunt coordinator Paul Nuckles explained how he wanted me to fall back down the steep flight of stairs. It was my raison d'être; I was the alleged hired-gun stunt man. Astounded by the suicidal gravity of the stunt, I told Paul Nuckles there was no way I would survive a fall down two flights of merciless hardcore stairs! The place went silent and then exploded in cacophony. But the biggest voice was Nuckles who called out, "We need a stunt man for the stunt man!"

The next day, we heard those magic words, 'It's a wrap!' Starrett got some kidding from producer Charles Pratt, but then it was over. We all went back to LA. Even Jay Brown said he'd soon be moving to LA.

We barely got off the plane and Starrett started touting me as the next big thing. He called me the baddest bad guy in Hollywood. *Starsky and Hutch* hired Jack to direct their next show, and the episode would be a pilot for a Huggy Bear spinoff. I read for Joe Naar, the producer, and he dug it. Even executive producer Aaron Spelling, the white dark knight of 20th Century Fox, got on the bandwagon. I played Sugar, the candy-bar-chomping heavy, whose job it was to make life miserable for Antonio Fargas as Huggy Bear and his partner played by newcomer Dale Robinette from Georgia. Dale brought his Georgia girlfriend to the set, a lovely tomato and aspiring actress named Kim Basinger. We shot action all over town, The Bonaventure Hotel, Main Street, South Central, The Long Beach Pike, and the Fox lot. We wrapped, and on the way out they asked me if I'd do a *Charlie's Angels,* another Aaron Spelling show. I said check with my agent.

Suddenly, I was so busy I didn't have time for women—not even Fay Hart. She sent me endless, clever letters to Johnny Hollywood, Johnny Damn and Johnny Dunnitt, each with scintillating poetry. In Jackson, I had received a letter to the Holiday Inn with a photo-booth picture pasted on the back of the envelope. It was Fay in all her naked glory; pouty tits and all, with a fake return address as Fay Hard, St. John's Mental Health Care Hospital RM # 356. She was a sultry mad genius. In LA, she continued to flood my mailbox. She was Fay Hart, Fay Hard, Jane O'Kane and Farrah Faucette Minor. Eventually, she would settle into a serious relationship with Steve Nieve, the keyboardist for Elvis Costello and the Attractions.

The door wouldn't unlock - i knew it was you ringing in my empty house - i broke down the door - you stopped - the dull tone was just more torture from you - you always time it right - you just look and turn out the light on my lipstick - you unload your cinemagraphic parade - ride them over the rainbow - silver streamin' down your old boulevard - whore - you don't cut me like I want to feel - yours are just circus scars that never bleed on the night - you touched me once and the torture never left - missing your mouth with my bite - but only your holy words swear tears in my uncut eyes- your head's hung - hung like a mad dog on a rope of jealousy - you're hung indeed - in bed - in your own damn head - your lip stain on my cheap throat - your thoughts on my cashmere sweater - you're hung - like a Chinese cat - bad boy - i can't get the smell of your thought off my scarred mind and eyes. –fay

Jack Starrett was a name dropper. And the name was Blackie Dammett. He plastered it all over town. Even in lights. Jack was the locomotive that blasted my career from gray obscurity to shinning darkness. "Blackie's the dark horse," he boasted, "and I'm going to ride him in the Derby."

Anita Russell

While Warren Beatty and I fought over Anita Russell, young Tony Kiedis captured her. Several years later they did connect.

Chapter 24: Anita Russell

Tony was almost due, but I had a few days. I made a quick trip to New York. I wanted to bring Ashley up to speed and catch a Broadway play. I saw Peter Shaffer's *Equus* at the Plymouth Theatre, with Anthony Perkins and Tom Hulce. At each performance, they allowed a few customers to sit on stage in the middle of the action; action that included brain-busting dialogue, men as stampeding horses and gutsy Tom Hulce, totally naked. I was on the stage. The next night, we went to Ashley's restaurant on Fifth Avenue and the upstairs private club, fittingly called Ashley's. We had dinner and joined some friends of his. There were two unbelievably beautiful girls at the table, and I fell for both of them. A local hipster was bragging about his true love, Lisa Stolley, and eagerly whipped out his wallet to show me her snap shot and identification. She wasn't present at this dinner, but her name and address was now filed in my dark heart. In person and seated next to me for much of the evening was another bombshell, Anita Russell. She was a model if there ever was one: tall, blonde and of course gorgeous. We exchanged mailing addresses as she was interested in seeing LA.

I stayed at Ashley's that night and hardly slept, just thinking about Anita Russell. In the morning, I set out to find her. I took the Lexington subway up to the 86 St. Station, looked around the neighborhood and found her apartment building. I rang the bell but got no response. I sat down on the stoop and waited for hours. Late in the afternoon, she pulled up in a cab and wondered what I was doing, wet and shivering at her door. She would have shooed me away for my impertinence had I not shown such dedication. She took pity on me and invited us up to her boudoir for some hot tea. I spent the day and the night. I learned from her Zoli portfolio she wasn't just any model; she was a supermodel. She was on the current cover of *Esquire,* which back then was a bona fide authority on fashion and lifestyle. Brazenly provocative, the cover caption read, "The Sexiest Girl in America." She was in several other slick rags, including a ten-page spread, showcasing her uniquely different looks. She was also the face and body of the Rolling Stones' new album *Black and Blue,* which had her tied up, bloody and bruised. There was a giant billboard of her image on the Sunset Strip that taunted me for weeks.

In the morning, Anita wanted to play some more, but first I wanted to explore Lisa Stolley. It took courage to track down a complete stranger, but there I was in her East Village powder-puff apartment. Inexplicably, she let me in and drove me crazy with her lyrical slim body and cutie-pie mug. She gave me some of her modeling cards. I wanted to stay, but I had a plane to catch. She was flush. Her father was Richard Stolley, the original editor of *People Magazine.* I wonder what might have happened if I hadn't been in such a hurry.

Tony returns! He's 14 and he's in high school. I often drove him to Fairfax in the morning, but he usually walked home after school. I vividly recall the first time he brought his new best friend home to meet me. This Mike Balzary character looked mighty suspicious to me. He was midget-short, with a hint of wild madness. Not exactly what I was hoping for. *Damn it*, if only I could have gotten him into Beverly Hills. Of course, father doesn't always know best, and Michael would turn out to be a splendid friend for Tony…

and for me. More than a friend, he was like a son. This new kid they nicknamed "Flea" would join up with my son to form one of the most successful bands in the history of music.

Anita Russell made good on her promise to visit. She combined glamour-puss business with a stay at 937 Palm. We showed her our town. Of course, we had to share her with the LA elite, including Warren Beatty and his famous pad at the Beverly Wilshire Hotel. Tony and Anita dug each other, as I knew they would. We were invited to stay with her in NY whenever we wanted. Tony wanted. So did his dad.

My place was always a magnet for parties, so I shouldn't complain, but this time it was a doozy. Ronnie Caan was a Rolls Royce party boy and the younger brother of James Caan, who was no stranger to wild times himself. Ronnie was always dropping by with a variety of beautiful women and celebrities. One of our favorite escapades was when he pounded on my door, requesting an impromptu party for Oakland Raiders Kenny Stabler and sticky-fingers Fred Biletnikoff on the eve of the 1977 Super Bowl. I can tell you they didn't wear those pointed party hats. Evidently, the party didn't bother either of them either. The Vikings were vanquished. The Raiders won, and Biletnikoff was named Super Bowl MVP.

Aside from the monkey business, Ronnie was always supportive with acting opportunities for me. Ronnie was friends with famed director Sam Peckinpah, who was about to start his film *Convoy* with Kris Kristofferson and Ali McGraw. Ron set me up for a shot at a part. I met Mr. Peckinpah at his home, and we settled into his den full of lifelong achievements. It was just the two of us: the legend and the rookie. He had already cast *Convoy* but was gracious enough to advise me on the ways of our business from his unique perspective. We talked for an evening. He had achieved iconic status with *The Wild Bunch*, a film that crushed the parameters of film violence, but he also directed a variety of other classics including *Ride the High Country*; *Straw Dogs*; and two Steve McQueen films, *Junior Bonner* and *The Getaway*. Scorsese, Tarantino and John Woo acknowledged his influence on their work. James Caan had starred in his *The Killer Elite*. Sam Peckinpah was a hard-drinking, drug-snorting son of a gun, whose life mirrored the tragedy and broken taboos of his work.

Ronnie Caan also introduced me to his brother Jimmy who became a quasi-mentor. James Caan actually went to Michigan State at the same time as I did back in the late 50s. And he played on the Spartan football team. Jimmy and Ronnie got me an interview with Michael Mann when he was making *Thief,* a movie Jimmy starred in. Supposedly Jimmy read a script once and then never went back to it. I always had trouble remembering lines. Brando often had cards on the set. While Jimmy was married to Sheila they had a magnificent mansion on Sunset in Beverly Hills. It had a yard the size of a golf course. I went to a Sunday BBQ. Their son Scott was born in 1976, and I played with the little tyke. Now he's a potent can't-take-your-eyes-off-him, risk taking actor like his father.

I did my *Charlie's Angels*, "The Gardena-Vegas Connection" episode. We mostly shot at Fox. I was Freddy, the henchman assistant to Cass, top-billed Michael Callan, a suave and charming leading man. Farrah Fawcett-Majors had become an overnight super star, and her sexy best-selling poster was in every frat house, repair shop and many a young man's daydream. Fox had a studio tour that allowed visitors on the *Charlie's Angels* set while the primary actors weren't on stage. Giddy fans rushed in to caress Farrah's empty actor's chair with her name on the back. Later, they'd bring the memory home to last a lifetime. Jaclyn

Smith gave me what I perceived as provocative smiles and a wink; or maybe not. Kate Jackson shared her talent, and I paid close attention. Bosely was Bosely. We shot it just before Christmas, 1976. I met with Mel Brooks on the set of his current film *High Anxiety*.

I spent Christmas in New York with Anita. We went to Woody Allen's New Year's Eve party on Park Avenue. I hit on Shelley Duvall just because she was Shelley Duvall. Next time I brought Tony.

The sexiest girl in America took care of my boy while I saw *A Chorus Line* again. Anita Russell joined an impressive list of Tony's babysitters. I saw *Equus* again too, this time with Richard Burton. He hadn't quite memorized all of his daunting dialogue yet, and he was on stage most of the time. Powerfully expounding in the highly charged drama, he suddenly dropped his lines. Seamlessly, he moved into improvised pig Latin, non sequiturs and obscure grunts in such an innovative and transcendent manner that the audience stood up and cheered wildly. Everybody in the theatre had goose bumps. "Performances blaze with theatrical life...Broadway has found a triumph." Clive Barnes, *N.Y. Times*. It didn't take a genius to know my mojo needed a kick in the pants. The Image Group was in hiatus, but I still had my own client to promote. I doubled the effort and found notoriety on stage.

Candy and Tracii Guns. Candy and I were together forever. She is the
mother of my son James.

Chapter 25: Hollywood Actors Theater

With Broadway's inspiration, I hunted down theatrical operations that held open auditions and one was Hollywood Actors Theatre on Cahuenga, just north of Hollywood Boulevard. The first play I read for was *My Life* by Corinne Jacker; it was the West Coast premiere. The time-bending role was a deceased grandfather who kept coming back as a younger man to council his troubled grandson. He was a main character and I got the part. We had a low-budget minimalist set, but I ripped a few hundred slats of siding off a condemned house and built a funky woodsy cabin while everybody was sleeping. When the cast showed up for the next rehearsal, they discovered the new trouper's hammer, nails, saw and mettle.

So close to Hollywood Boulevard, the theatre always drew a good crowd, and opening night was a thrill for both Tony and I. The next morning, we rushed out to get the reviews and pulled the Healey over next to a *Herald-Examiner* newspaper box. Tony asked how many copies to take as he sought out the review while holding the lid up. "All of them," I said. After a quick read, Tony cautioned otherwise: "Ah, I don't think so Dad, it says you were weak." Weak! Fortunately, the Times and Drama-Logue gave me reasonable consideration, and Ron Bastone, the owner and general manager of the theatre, liked my performance and work ethic. He invited me to join his Hollywood Actors Theatre ensemble. Of course, none of this got in the way of my nightlife and skirting the edges of propriety, but I could hardly wait for the next production. Bastone picked a brand new play written by Bob Fraser and Bob Dames. It was *Frozen Stiff*, a mystery farce about a gangster, an innocent family and a dead body that kept getting moved from place to place.

> *Variety*: "For the record, Blackie Dammett was exceptional as the jewel-toting hood, for once an actor who lives up to the promise of his stage name."

> *Los Angeles Times*: "Blackie Dammett is very funny as a pomaded gangster named Russo—or is it the other way around?"

Perfect timing, the Carlos'n Charlie's chain debuted a spicy restaurant on Sunset. Her sister locations were in Cancun, Acapulco and Aruba. It was always packed and almost impossible to get a table, but I preferred table hopping anyway. I flitted to and from the largess of celebrities, hot babes, and even actual friends. Like an idiot, I punked Stevie Wonder by calling him over as though I was a personal friend. Above the restaurant, some heavy hitters including Shep Gordon opened a private club called El Privado. It was lush, hip and boss of the club scene for quite some time. The parking lot was flooded with Bentleys, Rolls, Aston Martins, Ferraris, luxury yachts and my beat up Healey. I paid five-hundred smackers for a membership, and Shep approved my pedigree for the board of snobs. Having dished out the cash, I made it a habit to frequent this Ritz and became a beloved regular, well known to the doormen, the waitresses, the manager and the chicks that adorned the velvet couches in the private enclaves—private enough for funny business. I usually came early to get a secluded booth I especially liked, but one night I got there too late and my crib was occupied by a dazzling brunette right off the cover of *Vogue*. She was a seductive charmer with class and poise and a bottomless reservoir of sexuality.

I-can't-believe-how-beautiful-you-are was accompanied by her only slightly less ravishing companion, *Keep-your-mitts-off-my-sister*.

They had played right into my mitts since everybody knew that booth was my spot. At the very least, I offered to share it with them. The sister showed me her muscles, but the doll face was conciliatory and even intrigued. "Audrey Maxwell at your service," she purred. Those eyes were basked in dusky black swaddling, her rip-your-heart-apart cosmetic trademark. And she wasn't kidding about the service. It was above and beyond. She was manna to my malevolent. Ours would be a clash of erotic sex and intellectual jousting. And there was a Tony in the wings who would finally have a new surrogate mom. The first time we dated, the sister came with us; why not mom and dad too? It was worth it; the whole Maxwell clan could have come as long as I did. And I did come. I was blindsided by her sparkle, curves and cunning. We went to fancy restaurants and wrong-side-of-the-track joints like the Frolic Bar and Pink's. Obscure films were de rigueur. We'd prowl the late night and dine at The Pantry, that all night steak place on Figueroa, where the waiters were ex-cons. She was a night owl and made a nest in my bed. No sister, just Audrey seared in my mind. She dug scratches so deep in my back I still have the branding. She loved my bedroom with its art deco wallpaper, the sleeping-beauty quadruple mattress bed, the music I played for her and the love I made to her. My nocturnal dream girl revealed a thousand naughty streaks under her flawless invisible pajamas.

I was rehearsing for another H.A.T. play, Woody Allen's *God and Death*. Because we worked for free and most of the actors had day jobs, we rehearsed at night and on weekends. I wasn't always able to watch my booth and protect my Maxwell. Not surprisingly, the Latino lovers and Hollywood wolves and New York gangsters took their best shot at my girl, Audrey. Fortunately for me, the sister was now a friendly colleague, but even her muscle couldn't hold back the mafia.

Audrey and I spoke on the phone, but it had been more than a week since my last appearance at El Privado. I'd make it up to her. Decked out in my best getup and slicked-back jaunty personality, I made my way through the club, showing respect to the staff and greeting the clientele. Suddenly, a character right out of *The Godfather* popped up in front of me with a strong stench of malice. He had a twisted double-cross Picasso-smile, dripping with rancor. Clad in a Cheez Whiz suit and white vinyl shoes, he talked like he had a mouth full of Brooklyn; and then he let me have it. "Dip shit! Stay away from Audrey, ya see. She's mine now and you're out on the street so run along before you get hurt." He held out his fist and dropped four bullets in the palm of my hand, evidently the universal language of goons. Apparently, I do as he says or he'll plug me. Perplexed, I looked around for my love bug, and there she was, seated at Scarface's boisterous table, right on the dance floor with a cartel of lugs and ladies. Bitterly stunned, I headed for the exit to get some air. On my way out, I asked the hatcheck gal who that mobster was. "Tony Sirico," she said. "Just moved here from New York." Twenty-five years later you could catch him every Sunday at nine on *The Sopranos* as Paulie Walnuts, the cold-blooded asshole. He took a circuitous route to that lofty role: reportedly as an associate of the Colombo crime family with more arrests than he could count, prison time, a dozen mob movies and as a cohort of Rudolph Giuliani.

Interestingly, a couple years later I would be in the same acting class with Tony "Junior" Sirico, as we both studied with the masterful Michael V. Gazzo. Another friend of mine was in that class too, Jock McNeil the actor who lived with us on Fountain in '67. Gazzo acted in classic films like Elia Kazan's *On the Waterfront* with Brando and *The Godfather II,* for which he was nominated as best supporting actor. He was also a member of the Actors Studio, but Michael V. Gazzo will always be best known for writing the Broadway hit play *A Hatful of Rain* about heroin addiction. Now he was writing a new play for our class that we rehearsed and presented to a public audience. Junior Sirico and I finally went at it on that West LA stage.

In *Scar Tissue*, Anthony wrote he inadvertently discovered heroin at a Malibu party with Connie Foreman. I always wondered what else he got into. Topanga's Kendall Pacios and I were out on the town one night, and he swung by a rustic house in Beverly Glen Canyon. Kendall had a serious addiction, and evidently this guy Ramone was one of his connections. Kendall was all pro smack; he did up a generous tablespoon full and let out a contented sigh. He fixed up a similar portion for me and poked the rig into my vein. His Kendall-size blast was way more than I could handle; I felt a lightning bolt and blacked out. Passing out is not uncommon, but Kendall recognized I was in trouble. My symptoms were potentially fatal, and immediately he began to slap my face, blast me with loud music, double dance my marionette body around the house, kick me in the britches and held me under a cold shower. Kendall kept it up all night until I was finally over the hump. He sacrificed his own high to save my life. Had I been with someone less experienced or more dispassionate, I would have surely died of the overdose. I got my own message, but many of my friends were seriously hooked, especially Bashara. Big Al was still looking for his acting breakthrough, and junk wasn't going to get him there.

In all fairness, Junior Sirico became a solid actor, even if he was always playing with himself. If David Chase cast him in the best television drama ever, you have to be impressed. By the way, wild side Audrey handed Sirico his own bullet-riddled walking papers soon enough. Our romance was never quite the same though. My Tony and I both adored her, and we remained frosty friends. One day we drove out to her family's house in the Valley. We arrived unexpectedly; plain Jane was terrified and refused to open the door. Without her patented makeup, she felt naked; with it she was the wickedly beautiful queen. We finally gave up and left. Audrey and I drifted apart like tectonic plates. Soon I was enchanted with Darcey, the El Privado cigarette girl. $20 a pack, but nobody was complaining; she only wore half a dress. We were platonic for a change and studied together with acting coach Alan Landers. Darcey and I are still friends.

Bang! The antithesis of Audrey popped into our life. Her name was Claire, and she was from England. The previous occupants above the garage had moved on. In place, we had spanking-new tenants in our back yard, a rock band with definite edges of the punk music that was surfacing. The core crew involved Detroit-tinged UXA, fronted by a blonde named De De Troit. There was a guitar boy with blue-black hair, the first I'd seen and soon dittoed.

Their friend Claire preferred our better equipped house below, and before we knew it, she had moved herself in. That English accent didn't hurt. She was spunky with lots of leather and torn stockings and frequent changes of hair colors. Tony and I were intrigued by this bird who was a fledgling junkie. Now she had worked her way into my bed, and I wasn't exactly denying her. One night, we had both taken a double dose of Quaaludes and were about to crash. Tony was sleeping in his annex. The last thing I remembered was Claire in bed, naked and smoking. Then I passed out. She did too. Her burning cigarette stayed up for a while and started a smoldering fire. I was deep in a downer hellhole, but miraculously bolted up in the middle of the night and realized the curtains and the bed were on fire. I yelled at Claire, but she was out cold. The smoke was dense, and I could hardly breathe. I left her and got Tony outside. Then I went back for Claire. Tony invoked the water hose, and I dragged the burning mattresses outside. About then the fire department arrived with multiple trucks and a load of bedlam. The house stunk for weeks. My four-mattress bed dwindled to two. Connie's Topanga curtains were toast. Claire skipped out, so I kept her leather jacket as a down payment on the damages. She snuck back and retrieved it.

Well, what's a little fire? Father and son were hot commodities. Tony was studying with the extraordinary Diane Hull and played the male lead in *The Proud Princess* at the Hollywood Children's Theater. He was cast in the film *To Catch a Tiger* and now had his SAG and AFTRA card. To keep everything in the family, we made his stage name Cole Dammett. Pa was right on Junior's heels; Jack Starrett cast me in the TV movie *Nowhere to Hide,* starring Lee Van Cleef. Oscar-winner Edward Anhalt supplied the screenplay, and we shot some of my scenes at the Point Mugu Naval Weapons Air Station in the Pacific Missile Test Center which was highly classified. I had my own high-security government laminate #09103 V.

Alan Bashara finally got his first role in the film, and also had a bit on Edward Bunker's *Straight Time.* I joined him on location and got to see a different side of Dustin Hoffman, gritty and menacing as a parolee. I had first met him back in 1970 during *Little Big Man* in his famous bathtub scene with Faye Dunaway. Director Arthur Penn was a friend of the Friedkins and allowed Greg, Fiz and me onto the closed set. Soap suds and brilliant comedy spilled all over.

La MaMa is an Off-Off Broadway theatre in the East Village with remarkable alumni including De Niro, Pacino, Billy Crystal, Nick Nolte, Sam Shepard, Patti Smith and Diane Lane. In the late 70s, they opened a La MaMa branch in Hollywood. Friedkin, now Enton, got in good company. He wrote, produced and directed the play *Five Flesh Flush.* It was zany as Greg's imagination, with characters like Labia, Everyman, Woody Woodpecker, a Poet and a Pirate. Greg asked me to audition for the Pirate. I became him. It was a small theater with a big buzz, thanks to the La MaMa tie in and the outrageousness of the production.

We packed it every night. The enterprising Greg Enton invited show business elite, and quite a few attended, including James Kennedy, who was a hustling director and writer of original plays. He was a member of the Los Angeles Actors' Theatre, one of the pre-eminent original-work gigs in town. There were three tiers of theaters: the 99-seat equity waivers, like Hollywood Actors Theatre; the big Broadway style palaces, like the Shubert and the Pantages; and mid-size theatres like LA Actors', the Westwood and the Henry Fonda.

James Kennedy was in pre-production for his own original play, *Hit and Run,* to open at LAAT. It was about a desperate mafia character who hijacked a men's room in Las Vegas. Kennedy was knocked out by my pirate performance in *Five Flesh Flush* and wanted me to play the lead. This was a big-time opportunity, but was I ready? The boss put together a sparkling cast and invited us to his house in Silver Lake for an initial reading of the script. Kennedy's long-time girlfriend Salome Jens actually owned the gracious home. She had been schooled at the Actors Studio in New York, but she is probably best known for her many *Star Trek* appearances. It was the first time I saw the *Hit and Run* script, and I hadn't ever done a cold reading. The pressure was hydraulic. When we finished I was rattled and drenched in sweat. The production already had an opening date, and we agreed it was too risky to proceed with a rookie lead. I had to settle for the role of Roman Bonnano.

Tony went to all my plays and I went to everything he did. We had rules and regulations to follow because he was a minor; there were permits, certificates and all kinds of red tape. He had his own teachers on the set. One of his early movies was *Jokes My Folks Never Told Me,* which was R-rated for nudity and rough language. His character Jimmy Doyle's dialogue was laced with sailor sexual jargon. The film was produced by Roger Corman's New World Pictures and the preview screened at MGM. Tony was way ahead of my curve; none of my film work had aired or screened yet.

While I'm in the neighborhood of the Westwood Theatre, I might move ahead a few years to an afternoon performance I was motivated to attend by a great review. The play I've long forgotten, but the volunteer usher I lingered with in the aisle was a young lady named Patricia Arquette, and after the show I waited for her like a stage-door Johnny. She called herself Psyche. She was born into show business and is well known now as an accomplished actor. *Stigmata, True Romance, Nightmare on Elm Street, Ed Wood, Flirting with Disaster* and her TV show, *Medium.* Her grandfather, Cliff Arquette, ran an improvisational acting school in a warehousey building in East Hollywood. He was a popular comedian on the *Tonight Show* and a beloved character on Hollywood Squares, as his alter ego Charlie Weaver. Patricia took me to his improv class where she was busy learning her craft. We sat on the bleachers and watched, but I couldn't get her on stage to perform for me. I had my own improv classes. But my home base was always the Hollywood Actors Theatre. I could be doing a play or a rehearsal and slip out the stage door into the alley for a quick stroll down to the main street of show business, catch a nearby bar, grab a quick drink with fellow actors and then rush back to make my cue. It was my comfort zone

The next play I did at H.A.T was *Harold Pinter's Review Sketches.* We did *Black and White, Request Stop, Last to Go, Applicant, That's Your Trouble* and my favorite, *Trouble in the Works.* Another bloody genius! My H.A.T is off to him, one of the greatest playwrights ever, the late Harold Pinter.

Francis Coppola's "The Cotton Club." I'm Weiss, your favorite hit man.

Chapter 26: The Newlywed Game

It was just another night out on the town. Westwood actually, which had a hot new club I was checking out. I was leaning on the crowded bar when a tall slender redhead nuzzled into the small slice of space I was already occupying. She was merrily extroverted, and so were her darling breasts, which couldn't seem to stay in their mirage of a dress. I had no objection. She bought me a drink; I bought her two. She laughed and went to buy three, but I said no; let's just go.

We spent the night in my rehabilitated taller-than-ever bed. I called her name, "Dot," a lot that night: Dot Lockart from Joshua Tree, out on the edge of the Mojave Desert. She had badland moves to share with her sweet touch of innocence. It made a nice combination. She was one saucy step ahead of the rapid punk infiltration and immediately adapted to our backyard garage band. She modeled occasionally and was the original cover girl and centerfold of a new punk magazine in Hollywood called *Slash*. She had all my friends saying, "Wow! You lucky bastard. How do you do it, Blackie?!" It seemed like I had struck gold.

Malcolm McLaren's Sex Pistols burst on the UK scene in mid-decade, but it wasn't until *Anarchy in the UK, God Save the Queen* and the addition of Sid Vicious that America caught up with the hysteria. Suddenly LA was unwashed with dirty new punk bands like The Germs, X, Fear, The Weirdos and The Mau-Mau's. Avant-guardians like Pleasant Gehmen, Keith Morris, Rick Wilder, Tomata du Plenty, Marc Rude, Mary Woronov, Pat Smear, Lorna Doom and Darby Crash forged a quirky vanguard. And in the fresh beginnings of 1977, there was a perfect place for them to go. Scotland's Brendan Mullen opened a punk club in the pungent basement of the Pussycat Theater, an X-rated porn pit on Hollywood Boulevard, between Las Palmas and Cherokee, with access entry in the alley behind. *The Masque* was the most raucous, wild and wonderful club you could imagine, if you liked blood and vomit and ankle-deep beer and ear-splitting punk rock music, which at the time we all did. The LAPD was there all the time, so they must have liked it too. Overnight, jalopies were moved out of their stalls, and garages were turned into punk clubs.

Even 937 ½ Palm had a running show. Punk sprang out in unlikely venues like the historic Roosevelt Hotel where the prestigious Academy Awards were once celebrated. Soon all the black sheep clubs were on the anti-band wagon, and they left a trail of shed blood, broken glass and shattered dreams. Before long, even the Whisky, Lingerie and Starwood were self-destructing. Every movement needed a quasi-intellectual mooring, and for us it was Greg Shaw's Bomp Records, out in the Valley. The retail outlet's walls were covered with Sex Pistols and the defaced Queen; the record racks were Clashing with Ramones and there were Stranglers and Screamers and Germs and Zeros and Stooges hot on the tail of the silly boys in Devo. The Damned did an in-store meet and beat. So did Blondie and The Dead Boys with their crazed leader Stiv Bators. Penelope Spherris captured the movement on film.

So Dot and I became an unlikely team, a punk rocker and a serious actor. And a young punk actor son makes three. All three of us had ambitions about the business of showing off. I had done quite a bit of film acting work but still nothing had aired yet. I craved exposure and had an idea. The Chuck Barris television hit *The Newlywed Game* was being revived. Pairs of newlyweds competed for the grand prize by divining your new mate's silly enigmas. Being newlywed, the chances were good that it would lead to hilarious bust ups. The popular host, Bob Eubanks, would rotate husbands and wives in the hot seat. The questions were purposely problematic to create havoc, and mortified reactions were the payoff.

I thought Dot was worth holding onto. Enough of this skirt chasing. She was pretty and fun and she was good with Tony. I asked my son what he thought about us getting married. He was delighted and anxious to have a full-time mom. Dot was ecstatic. I figured she had tabbed me from the start as a prospective husband who would take care of her and deliver a "happily ever after." We sat down at the famous kitchen table and laid out a plan. We go to Las Vegas, get married and then submit ourselves to *The Newlywed Game*. Most of the contestants were doofuses. There's no way they could refuse a darling dame like Dot and an up-and-coming actor. If we don't like marriage, we can always get an annulment after the show. Like Chuck Barris's other show *The Dating Game*, there was an emphasis on sexual innuendo, and they pushed the envelope with racy material, consistent with the recently loosened mores of the seventies. Dot had a pottie mouth, and I knew she'd be explosive. I would play the cool, calm and collected foil. We'd be George Burns and Gracie Allen, Lucy and Desi, Dot and Dammett. One of the perks for Dot was getting my name. As an irreverent punk she loved the idea of becoming Dot Dammett.

We went to Vegas. Encouraged by our wedding plans, wheeling and dealing Kurt and Bunnie came along with half a mind to tie the knot too. We checked into a hotel on the strip. First in order was the ceremony. We skipped the kitschy Elvis and other contrived chapels; we weren't exactly fresh with cash. Kurt picked up a lot of the tabs. It was, after all, a special occasion so we appropriately celebrated with plenty of Kurt's wedding gifts, coke, Quaaludes and even the bad stuff. We went to the Clark County Building and sealed the deal. Presiding Commissioner of Civil marriages was Loretta Bowman. Our witnesses were Cole Dammett and Kurt Siegel. Mr. Dammett, you may kiss the bride. Kurt and Bunnie wisely decided to kiss off their wedding.

Loaded to the gills, we went out on the town, Don Rickles at the Sands and Rich Little at the Riviera. Champagne and other alcohols on top of all those drugs had me upside down. At one point, I stole away and went to a pay phone. I called Anita Russell and told her what I'd just done. I called Audrey Maxwell and Connie. I don't know if I wanted sympathy or revenge. I ran out of quarters. They all said I was drunk and an idiot. I vaguely remember the rest of the night. We had a room with one bed for the three of us, although Tony slept on the floor. I know Dot and I did black market taboo and passed out.

Back in LA, Dot and I went to *The Newlywed Game* offices at KTTV studios in Hollywood. We breezed through the audition and were set up to do an upcoming show. They encouraged us to be controversial. We brought it back in spades. I wore a snazzy navy-blue double-breasted suit, much like the same slick gangster I brought to the movie set or the nightclubs. The other guys looked like they'd just come from the hardware store. Dot wore a sheer, flower-print dress with a plunging neckline, and I mean plunging! We scribbled our answers on low-tech cardboard signs. They encouraged us to get spunky so every time

I was incorrect, Dot would pummel me with her signboard. I was getting first aid from the nurses.

With all her animated flailing, Dot's perky pink tits kept popping out of her low-cut dress. Cut! They'd stop shooting and tuck her back into the dress, tape the neckline to her body and 30 seconds later those devils would pop out again. It was hilarious to the studio audience, but TV time is money. She'd fling the f-word with wild abandon. Cut! Re-do. Eubanks repeatedly came over to Dot and pleaded with her to relax, while all the time ogling her breasts that by now had become the star of the show. We finished second. The victorious couple was nice, and as the set swiveled to reveal the super winning prize, we burst out laughing at the rinky-dink record player. The contestants got a year's supply of products that sponsored the show. Listerine, Turtle Wax, Rice-a-Roni, and 4-gallon containers of linoleum glue I stored in my various garages over the next thirty years.

The show aired, and it was just as hilarious on TV as it had been in person. My *Starsky and Hutch* "Huggy Bear and the Turkey" episode finally aired too. And so did my *Charlie's Angels* in Vegas. Fox was good to me. I got a nice role in a World War II comedy pilot called *McNamara's Band,* but it got bombed. Producer Joe Naar signed me up for another *Starsky and Hutch* hitch, this time as a deranged Charlie Manson type killer in a mental hospital chasing Suzanne Somers with a knife through eerie corridors. She had just started *Three's Company.* The new episode was called "Murder Ward," and it was a lot like a horror movie. We shot it in the claustrophobic Veteran's Hospital complex in West LA. This time I got to know the co-stars; Paul Michael Glazer was an intellectual and David Soul had a refrigerator full of beer.

Cole Dammett knocked off some good work too, and I took him to the Luau restaurant in Beverly Hills. O.J. Simpson was dining a couple tables away. I knew it was rude to interrupt, but I took Tony over to meet him anyway. He was gracious and signed him an autograph.

Dot drifted a bit. I didn't mind. I got a 20th class reunion invitation in the mail and decided to do a quick visit with Grand Rapids. Dot stayed in LA with Tony, and I flew east. I hadn't been back in a while, and it was the first time since I'd taken up acting. I was never exactly acclaimed at Creston High, and now it was my turn for revenge. It was fun being a celebrity for the home folks. I did an interview with the *Grand Rapids Press,* and they turned it into a full page on the cover of the Sunday entertainment section. From that time on, editor David Nicholette kept the city apprised of my every move, every movie, every television program and every play.

I returned to discover Dot had been fooling around with Joe. Whoever Joe was? We talked and agreed our old plan B was still valid. Dot had gotten her Dammett and I had gotten my *Newlywed Game* exposure. We both got our annulment. She moved in with Joe up on Doheny at the same apartment complex where Big Al had been staying with Miggy. After the initial brief sting, Dot and I reaffirmed our friendship; we remained sister and brother and buddies to the end. Big Al's legal continuations over the Santa Barbara pot bust had run out of excuses, and he was required to turn himself in to an extended prison sentence. After a few years in the California penal system, he was released straight into the handcuffs of Michigan police who had dibs on him next. By the time he was released again, his California days would be over.

While Tony maintained his dark side Cole Dammett persona, he no longer liked being Tony. At school he was Anthony. At home he became Anthony. He was Cole the night we went to the Palladium for a Punk Rock and Fashion Show that drew 2,000 people. *The Los Angeles Times* even quoted him. The final paragraph of the Sept. 28, 1977 article reports: "Cole Dammett, 14, of Fairfax High School, summed it all up: 'There's not much punk at Fairfax right now. But it's inevitable that it will come. Older kids take anything that's a bit radical and they run with it. Kids my age are going to observe it all, and it'll rub off. Of course it's very gross. But gross is very different--and that's what everybody wants.'"

After the show we went to the Rainbow and then to the Tropicana Motel. The venerable motel was the destination of choice for hip out-of-town bands. We were tagging along to visit Deborah Harry and the rest of the Blondie band in their room. Deborah took an instant liking to the teen Jesus, Anthony, and they have been close friends ever since. Anthony was hip, thoughtful and mystical for his age. He had a fresh-faced maturity now; there was no turning back. He was also chalking up A's at Fairfax; A's in English, Geography, Algebra, History, Theater, Spanish and mischievous behavior.

Chapter 27: The Hillside Strangler

Alan was incarcerated. Weaver was on the road. Walking Tall Jay Brown had moved to LA and became one of my prime buddies. Over time he worked at Playboy Productions and Propaganda Films, on music videos and documentaries and several independent motion pictures. He also injected a new character into the landscape, his pal from Atlanta, Philip Stillman. Toni Kelman got Anthony a part on PBS's *Freestyle* in the episode *Good Signs* about deaf children. He gave a nuanced performance.

In the news there was yet another serial killer on the loose. More fodder for the media and blood curdling terror for the populous. We had already endured the Manson Family and the Zodiac Killer. Down the bleak road were the Garbage Bag Murderer and the Night Stalker. The current villain was the Hillside Strangler. Close to home, one of the early victims was Penny Lane's roommate Jane King, the doomed Mona. The press called her "a vibrant and attractive blonde with a figure like a model." She was abducted in front of the Scientology Building across from Lee Strasberg's on Hollywood Boulevard. One night she was there, and next day she was dead.

I was barely keeping up with expenses. We were paying for acting classes and portfolios and skimping on culinary flavors. We'd split a boiled Charlie Chaplin shoe for Sunday dinner. We cut down on brunettes. Our lives on the line; we hustled to workshops and auditions for those close calls. "I really like your work Blackie, maybe next time." I read for a TV bad guy and went up against Mickey Roarke. He was just getting started then. He got the role; I got the maybe next time. Hey, it's show business. 20th Century Fox came to the rescue. They called me back for a third *Starsky and Hutch*.

I was the heavy everybody liked to hate…or love. I played characters named Eddie Four Eyes, Lefty, Swifty, Weasel, Slick, Torch, Heavy, Sugar, Jazz, Slime, and Alby the Cruel. It was good to be somebody again. I had a couple weeks to work on my new body, a drug dealer. A repetitious cliché on crime shows by now, so how do I make him unique? I had quit trafficking, but I still had my own stash for lady and gentlemen friends. I was certainly conversant with the trade. I picked up a red hunting vest with rows of shotgun shell pockets and converted it to a traveling drug store. One of every drug in each pocket; it was Noah's vest. I wore it out on the town; it was real contraband and I truly felt the jeopardy. I was playing with fire. I wanted to do this role with burnt fingerprints.

I came home late and alone from the Rainbow, made a withdrawal from my stash closet and did a couple white lines at my kitchen table. The newly published alternative newspapers *LA Weekly* and *Los Angeles Reader* were loitering on the table. They were the new bibles of reality and amoral parables. I was religious for knowledge. These cutting-edge tabloids provided hard core political insight, the club scene, cool retail, L.A. DEE DA gossip and Matt Groening comics long before there was a family of Simpsons. These rags augmented their liquidity with a few pages in the back, featuring female entrepreneurs anxious to make your acquaintance. "Lovely minister's daughter seeks handsome intellectual male." "Call anytime and I'll be right over."

I had never indulged in any of these siren want ads; after all I had a library of my own little black encyclopedias. I wasn't paying any attention to the back pages this time either; I could have wrapped halibut in them or snorted coke off of them, which I did. I leaned over to take another one last line, when my eyes bounced off an ad that screamed, "Beautiful Swedish girl, 6 ft. tall, green eyes, 19 years old, needs affection." *That* got my attention. I called the number; she spoke divine Scandinavian. She was coming right over. I tidied up the house, put on some romantic music and shoveled some fresh snow on the mirror. I changed into a late show attire of Hef pajamas and a dashing black cape.

After a protracted and tantalizing anticipation, the doorbell finally announced good news. I swung open the door and was shocked to see a short swarthy heavy-set woman. I think her reaction to me was just as puzzled. "You called for me, yes?" the befuddled escort asked the befuddled handsome intellectual gentleman. I asked to the whereabouts of the missing Swedish goddess. She played dumb. I blocked the door and kept her on the porch. "Just a second," I said "I'll be right back." I returned with the mirror as a pittance for her trouble, but I had no intention of paying off her debts to society. She declined and left with offended umbrage.

The next few days I received phone calls from a mysterious woman who wanted to drop by and enjoy cocaine with me. I kept saying you must have the wrong number. There was an ominous weirdness about this, but it only shows what weirdos I was used to that I failed to make the connection. Anthony had just come home from school and we were sitting in the living room. Out my big picture window, I saw a mob of large scruffy men in bogus street gear marching up Palm Avenue from the direction of the Sheriff's Station a block away. This I calibrated in a millisecond, but it was not enough time to do much about it. The front door exploded off its frame and flew into the room. An assault team of heavily-armed agents burst into our worst nightmare. Simultaneously, the unlocked back door slammed open and a second battery of undercover sheriffs charged the beach of Normandy. They threw us down on the ground, and there were a porcupine of pistol barrels sticking into my head. My 15-year-old son Anthony was getting the identical treatment, hair-trigger guns pressed against his face.

Once the smoke cleared, the central-casting undercover cops worked off their initial adrenaline with some dorky cop humor, and we all got down to business. I'd been through this before at Casa Granada. The thugs started ripping the place apart on the testimony of the disgruntled impostor escort who had called the Sheriff's office after our encounter and reported that she had witnessed two lines of coke at 937 Palm, and that she had possibly uncovered the Hillside Strangler. In my dashing cape, she thought I was scary enough to be the feared killer. The *Starsky and Hutch* vest bomb full of miniature evidence was laying right there out in the open so they proceeded with the wrecking ball.

My infamous closet in the dining room was where my personal stash hid. Above the door on the inside was a ledge that extended farther than the normal 2 by 4 stud, and the stash was tucked way back into the wall. The first ten times they missed it. The rest of the house was relatively clean. They were frustrated and took it out on me: not so good cop, worse cop, lame jokes, cod liver oil, bible stories, Chinese torture and the Sheriff Academy Band anthem music ad infinitum. All right, I confess! They were about to settle for the underwhelming vest for which I had the TV script to substantiate a purpose. We had become tacit buddies. I was handcuffed and ready for minor shipping. Half of them were out the door already when one last dedicated officer took one last look in that closet and reached beyond the call of duty and into a fistful of felony contraband. Everybody got surly again, and within an hour I was booked into the downtown county jail, as big and bad as any state penitentiary and full of murderers, rapists, robbers, kidnappers, molesters, dope dealers and lobbyists.

Connie's carpentry boyfriend replaced the front door, and Anthony got busy raising my bail. Sprung, I went looking for a good lawyer. This was my third drug arrest, and the consensus was I'd do prison time. I was doomed to the big house. I retained Paul Fitzgerald, another defender of high-profile show business offenders. We delayed the trial as long as possible with continuations. I had to get a portfolio of success and show the court I was a working actor, and not a working drug dealer. As a first step to legitimacy, I took an old fashioned job at a furrier on Sunset, just a block up the hill from our house. It was menial and embarrassing. Every morning we'd roll out racks of fur coats and animal hides on the sidewalk where hundreds of pedestrians and thousands of cars would observe my indenture. Jeers and cheers from my new audience. The Lord of the Sunset Strip was practically wearing a sandwich board, cajoling customers to come check out our tawdry wares. I felt more like the Louse of the Sunset Strip. Hawking rabbit furs outside was bad enough, but my shifts down in the dank basement, where all the tanning hides and dirty work went on, were beyond torture. It was 100 degrees and smelled atrocious.

The owner, Wally Reid, was a wily master furrier, but he spent most of his time on the road, buying and selling. His son Tim pretty much ran the operation on Sunset. He was a tall husky specimen, but rather shy in other aspects. One day Audrey Maxwell was doing a photo shoot at Tower Records across Sunset and came over to browse. Tim was chatting to the marvelous beauty and couldn't resist bragging that he had a real live movie star working for them. When he mentioned Blackie Dammett, Audrey said she was an old friend and would like to say hi. So he dragged her down the treacherous staircase into the horrific dungeon. I happened to be cleaning the filthy dirty mess. She was wearing a fresh spring dress and was lovely as ever. She took one look at sweaty stinking me and ran back up the stairs screaming.

Anthony and Flea had one upped my tales of scaling tall building fire escapes in my youth. They snuck onto apartment roofs or balconies and dove into swimming pools. In addition to the height, they had to Evel Knievel over patios, lounge chairs and walkways. They kept pushing their limits. I had laid down the law; no more. I was at work and saw fire trucks and an ambulance turn off Sunset and dash down Palm. I felt it in my gut and chased the ominous parade. Paramedics were wheeling my son out of a three-story crime scene. His trajectory fell short of the pool, and he landed on the concrete veranda. We were both in shock, but I still managed to scold him like my dad would have. They rushed him to Cedar Sinai; diagnosis: broken back. I had visions of a paraplegic Anthony. Screw destiny. Would he ever even walk again? I was saddened and sympathetic but furious he had disobeyed me, a recurring conflict over the years. I had given him so much rope he had me hogtied in a lariat. On the bright side he proved to be the messiah I had predicted and walked away from the hospital in record time.

Dyan Cannon became an overnight success in the Columbia film *Bob & Carol & Ted & Alice* and was nominated for an Oscar. She got another Oscar nod for her performance in Warren Beatty's *Heaven Can Wait*. She had married the ultimate debonair actor Cary Grant when he was thirty-three years her senior. She wrote, produced, directed and acted in dozens of great films. More recently, you'd recognized her as a rabid LA Lakers fan on the sideline not far from Nicholson. In 1978, she was producing and starring in *Lady of the House,* a true story NBC Big Event movie about Sally Sanford, the Frisco madam turned mayor of Sausalito. Dyan cast me as a police detective who tried to bust her. It shot in Malibu and northern California. She was one of the nicest bosses I ever had the pleasure of working with. Ralph Nelson directed the film. His work included *Lilies of the Fields,* best actor Oscar for Sidney Poitier; and *Charly,* best actor Oscar for Cliff Robertson.

Anthony responded with a standout performance in the Busby Berkeley style musical stage production of *Dames at Sea* at Fairfax High. I had seen him in perfunctory children's plays, but this time they were cast as adults. He was singing, dancing and strutting around like a little James Cagney in *Yankee Doodle Dandy* as George M. Cohan. His mighty mojo gave me goose bumps. Cagney collected an Oscar as Cohan, and Anthony should have stolen a Tony for his performance.

I checkmated Anthony. *Starsky and Hutch* requested my services yet again. "Dandruff" was my fourth show and my best one yet. Ellis Moore (me) and my brother Dinty (New Yorker Madison Arnold) were two comedic bumbling gangsters who were inept in every aspect of crime. I had been in a fight at the Rainbow and had a big black eye which only contributed to my portrayal. Other guest stars were Rene Auberjonois and Audrey Meadows. I got good pay, prestigious billing and a great part to sink my actor's teeth in.

The next year, Anthony did Woody Allen's *Don't Drink the Water,* was inducted into the International Thespian Society and was elected Vice-President of the Fairfax Chapter. The kid was on a cyclone. He played a tough nut like his old man in an ABC *After School Special,* "It's a Mile from Here to Glory," and scored a plum role as Savage Boy in Aldous Huxley's *Brave New World* TV-movie at Universal.

Sylvester Stallone had just skyrocked to the top with *Rocky.* Ten Academy Award nods, best film and an Oscar director for Stallone made him a superstar. For his next film he chose *F.I.S.T.,* an epic labor union piece, co-written with Joe Eszterhas and directed by the brilliant Norman Jewison (*The Cincinnati Kid, In the Heat of the Night, Thomas Crown Affair, Fiddler on the Roof, Jesus Christ Superstar*). Anthony was cast as Stallone's son. Once the film started, we rushed to Sylvester's trailer to introduce his new son, but Stallone was surly. The pressure was on to repeat the massive success of *Rocky.* He booted us out of his delirium and never had a single friendly thing to say. The editors were just as bad; they cut out most of Anthony's big dinner scene with the family.

The role we really went after was in Art Linson's *American Hot Wax,* the story of Alan Freed and the early days of rock and roll. Anthony was up for the Buddy Holly fan club president and got call backs from casting director Don Phillips and then director Floyd Mutrux and finally producer Art Linson. It was a major role, a career maker. Eventually it got down to just two, Cole Dammett and Moosie Drier. We were called back so often, I started visiting other Paramount soundstages while Anthony was doing his thing. I snuck in on a *Happy Days* rehearsal and watched the taping of a brand new show called *Mork and*

Mindy with an unknown madman named Robin Williams. The series aired later that year and *everybody* went bananas.

Back at Art Linson's, the battle raged on and finally, and almost reluctantly, Art gave the part to Moosie. He said it was one of the most difficult casting decisions he ever made. After that, Anthony decided to concentrate on school; it was a difficult balance being an actor, slash student. Speaking of slashes, Saul Hudson a classmate of Anthony's struck a sweet note later on as Guns N' Roses' guitar virtuoso, Slash. Other fellow Fairfax alumni friends of Anthony are David Arquette and Demi Moore. And a couple guys named Hillel Slovack and Jack Irons.

Anthony went out in a blaze of glory as bad boy Vinnie on the new NBC series *Who's Watching the Kids* in the episode "Frankie's 16th Birthday." Scott Baio was Frankie, and Vinnie was the antagonist. The show was another production of the inestimable Garry Marshall (*Happy Days, Laverne & Shirley*). With that chapter over, Anthony hit the books, managed to keep up good grades and was hopeful of getting into UCLA. He was also into one catastrophe after another and had me visiting the principal so often I kept a cot in his office closet. Anthony was a carbon copy of his pa. Déjà vu. We went to the Rainbow one night and parked the Austin Healey on Doheny. When we came back it was gone, stolen like my last Healey. It was my final Healey. A dodgy Cutless was the replacement. Anthony said, "It's OK, dad."

Fairfax semesters melted together. Anthony grew up and bonded with peers. He was at that age when friends influence and parents are irrelevant. He came home late on school nights and was impervious to my protestations. My acting work was sporadic and the furrier was stingy. Food was in short supply but tempers weren't. Sometimes we got physical, and he was big enough to hold his own. My twelve-point rack and his new billy–goat-gruff horns were locked in stalemate. He was enjoying the feisty fruits of youth, and I smelled rotten tomatoes. On top of that, my apocalyptic criminal court day of reckoning had finally caught up with me.

In March, 1979, I went to trial before the Honorable Laurence J. Rittenband, the presiding Judge of the Superior Court in Santa Monica. All the famous Hollywood cases were adjudicated there, and Rittenband was the chief inquisitor. He enjoyed the show business spotlight and relished his notoriety. He had determined the fates of Elvis Presley, Cary Grant, Marlon Brando, Roman Polanski and now me. The prosecution set up their Kangaroo Court with rafts of specious evidence and misguided confidence, but my pen was mightier than the district attorney's sword. I wrote an impassioned twelve-page letter to Judge Rittenband. My spit-shine-polished-to-a-sheen letter was the UCLA Project 2 I never got around to, the MGM script we never finished, my eulogy for God and the love letter up my sleeve for when I meet the perfect woman. I had the goods and made the opposition look bad. They're lucky I didn't sentence them to repeat law school.

Even Anthony pressed his articulate thumb on the blind scales of Lady Justice. "My dad is probably the best all around guy in the world. Others in this league like Einstein, Lincoln and Shakespeare are all dead already. I personally will assure his good behavior in the future!" Signed Anthony Kiedis, student.

A rowdy mob of my influential friends wrote propitious letters to the court on my behalf. Although the prosecutor sought a term of 16 months in state prison, Judge

Rittenband sentenced me to only three years probation, time served and a fine. My debilitating nightmare was over.

Free at last, I hit the auditions and found immediate relief in Jack Starrett. I hadn't worked with him since *Nowhere to Hide*, but now he was preparing a grand scale Western on location in Mexico. It was the true story of Tom Horn, a legendary character of the Old West who was a Pinkerton agent and an army scout in the Indian Wars. Simultaneously, super star Steve McQueen was making his own competing *Tom Horn.* Suffering from cancer, McQueen underwent controversial medical treatments in Mexico while shooting his version and died shortly after the film wrapped. Meanwhile Warner Bros. and Jack Starrett continued with their own version titled *Mr. Horn.* David Carradine was our Tom Horn, and the cast included Richard Widmark, Karen Black and even Jack himself as General George Cook. Alan Bashara was going to play one of the rustlers, but his prison detour left a void that Jack filled with me now that my case was clear. I read for the producers and was given the green light. We set out for rural Mexico and a three-week shoot with a huge cast, including hundreds of Mexicans and Indians.

It was less than four star accommodations in the Wild Wild West. It was hell. Actors slept in bunk houses like real cowboys, and the Indians slept in wigwams. We were miles from civilization and Starrett cracked under the pressure. Normally he was General Patton on the battlefield, but this time he buckled under a series of disasters. We were scorched by extreme heat, and he had trouble managing the enormous army of actors. He was drinking vodka as usual but this time in lethal doses that had him half delirious. Early one morning, the entire cast of about 500 was assembled and ready for work. It was suppose to be a climactic battle between good and evil. It turned out to be a battle with Starrett's hangover. He would not wake up. Nobody could roust him. Finally, about noon, he careened out his trailer door and roared his impotent directions. We were behind schedule and in front of a fired-up squad of executives. My scenes were decimated by technical problems. Earlier delays piled up and plagued our agenda. They sent me back and said they'd do pickups at Warner Bros. I was extremely happy to get home.

Hollywood Actors Theatre was embarking on our own production: Pulitzer Prize winner Sidney Kingsley's final play *Night Life,* which opened on Broadway in 1962. I was cast as Sonny Drake, an outrageous entertainer patterned after Lenny Bruce; the plot bubbled with New York nightclub champagne. We had finished rehearsals and it was the day of opening night. There's nothing like the pomp and ceremony. The critics are mobilized. There's always a big after party. And then I get a call from my agent; they want to shoot the *Mr. Horn* pickups today. My old best friend Victoria was my opening-night date, and as a precaution I took her with me to Warners. The play started at eight but the cast call was 6:30. As the day went on, we ran into one difficulty after another on the set. I kept waiting for my part. Finally about six o'clock, it was my turn. I was shot by Indians and crawled across a corral. There were bloody special effects, difficult camera moves and an interchange of speaking lines; we just couldn't get a good take. Richard Masur was anxiously awaiting his own retakes and accused me of delaying the schedule. I wanted to punch him, but he was a major character and had more clout. Victoria bequeathed a curse on his career. We didn't finish until after seven. I had to turn in my costume and props, sign out, get to the parking lot and then drive from the Valley to Hollywood. I arrived just before the opening curtain.

REVIEW by Sigrid Macey. "It's the 1960s. The garish and glittering Key Club is the setting for Sidney Kingsley's 'Night Life', currently at the Hollywood Actors Theatre on Cahuenga Boulevard. Blackie Dammett gets frenetic as nightclub comic Sonny Drake, doing a very good job in a difficult role."

If they only knew!

Father and Son

Chapter 28: Manhattan

I turned forty in 1979, and yet here I was still dating teenagers and nothing beyond the roaring twenties. This to the constant chagrin of curmudgeons who wore their muddled morals on starched sleeves. I was comfortable with the fresh thinking maidens who weren't bogged down with incredible Jewish folklore passed down from the mountain tops. I had a Fontainebleau of youth and my righteous ravine continued to widen.

When a new Woody Allen film came out, I'd be there. It started with little tot Tony taking me to see *Sleeper* in Grand Rapids, and later I converted Weaver. The New York actors bar Joe Allen had opened a Los Angeles branch by the time *Annie Hall* swept the Oscars in 1977. I watched the awards at the hip gin mill, along with a full house of boisterous fans: best film Woody, best actress Diane Keaton, best director Woody and best screenplay Woody.

Manhattan opened two years later; David's entourage, Anthony and I went to see it in Westwood. The opening sequence with its grandiose tableaux of New York City set the scene. The music of George Gershwin faded gently into a microcosm of dinner, drinks and philosophy at intimate Elaine's. Woody's high school girlfriend is 17 and he is 44. As the film unravels, he vacillates between precocious Mariel Hemingway and the more mature Diane Keaton and in the end looses both. As in all of his films, there's humor, intellectualism, sexuality and pathos, but in *Manhattan* there's an unrelenting black-and-white poignancy to the conflict of age that mirrored my own drama. Woody had a pragmatic appreciation of pubescence and the assured right to share his charisma with the beauty and optimism of youth. Each of us is unique, and if our genetics and a sharp mind are desirable to another human, regardless of age, then that shall be *our* prerogative.

After extensive relationships with his leading ladies Louise Lasser, Diane Keaton and Mia Farrow, Woody controversially married Mia's adopted daughter Soon-Yi Previn from her earlier marriage to Andre Previn, the noted pianist. Although this Greek tragedy age disparity caused incrimination, hypocritical Mia Farrow at 21 had married 50-year-old Frank Sinatra. At 24 she stole a considerably older Andre Previn from his wife Dory. Not much different than Woody and Soon-Yi's 34-year difference. So zip it, jealous old at hearts. The greatest disparity between my age and a lover is over 50 years and counting. It will extend until I die, but not soon enough for the critics!

Jay Brown was shooting the Playboy Olympics on Hef's luxuriant lawn and invited me over. Hef and I weren't exactly bosom buddies, but we had a lot in common over the years; we both fought sexual bigotry back in the 1950s. Aside from all the centerfolds, I dated a hutch of bunnies too but preferred shy women, or at least ones who put on the pretense. That sweet dynamic was more gratifying than actual sex. I maintained a good look and was still carded at bars. My audacity never grew old either. There is an aphorism that if a man approached ten different women and asked if they would have sex with him, the odds were at least one would say yes. Ergo, any man with enough courage was always assured of sex whenever he wanted it. For me it was the reverse; if I asked ten women for sex I would get nine affirmatives and only one no. Darn it, I wanted the no's. I wanted the virgins who crossed their hearts and their legs and swore to say no.

While my *little* black book was flourishing, my up-and-down career was careening in the wrong direction. I worked in Jason Miller's *Circus Lady* at the Hollywood Actors Theatre and was in rehearsal for *Greeks 6-Trojans 5*. I read for James Caan's production of the *Ryen Duren Story* at Warner Bros. and for *Fantasy Island*. I swallowed my pride and worked as a featured extra on Steven Spielberg's blockbuster gone bust *1941*, a comedy about Los Angeles in the grasp of paranoia right after Pearl Harbor. Despite a massive all star cast, it failed to match his previous films like *Jaws* and *Close Encounters*. I did a blip with *Trouble in the Works* at the Megaw Theatre and had an interview at Paramount for *Are You Alone Tonight*. Randy Clark had sought another vocation or a long vacation; I was on my own and not getting any auditions. It came to my attention a new John Dillinger film, *The Lady in Red,* was going into production and they were casting extras downtown. I was so desperate for work I went. The film starred macho Robert Conrad, a TV Star in *The Wild Wild West* and *Baa Baa, Black Sheep*. Lewis Teague was directing, and the film was written by the acclaimed John Sayles. The lady in red was popular Pamela Sue Martin. Christopher Lloyd and Louise Fletcher were also in the cast.

The line was a long time coming, but I stuck it out. I had to fill out an employment form and listed my credits. An assistant sought me out and brought me to the production office. A speaking role actor had been injured, and they needed an immediate replacement because his scene was scheduled for that day. I read for it; they rushed me to wardrobe and threw me to the lions, a real Hollywood story. My scene was with Louise Fletcher, who four years earlier had won the Best Female Actor Oscar as Nurse Ratched in *One Flew Over the Cuckoo's Nest*.

Anthony was restless. He had been immersed in my history of rebellion since he was a kid. He knew by heart my escapades in and out of trouble on the wild side. Anthony and Flea were the reincarnation of my old dynamic duo. They stowed away on a Greyhound bus, went up to Mammoth Mountain, stole rental skis, hit the slopes and got busted. Eventually, we had to take a slow hound bus into the Sierra Mountains for his trial, where again I pled a case to an exonerating judge. The new "do or die duo" never relented though. Before long they were nude backpacking and cliff-jumping and smoking shitloads of pot. They went golfing on acid.

Anthony and I took Flea to his first Hollywood nightlife experience at the Rainbow. Told to dress fashionable, he wore a sky-blue polyester gold-buttoned, three-piece suit from his junior high graduation. He drank beer and vomited all over the place. They were 86'd. On a busy Saturday night, they climbed up on a billboard at the packed corner of Westwood and Wilshire and dangled their privates to the folks below. They climbed onto the Fairfax High School marquee and rearranged the letters to blasphemy a teacher they didn't like. They admitted to stealing and scamming their way into a well-deserved one-way ride to hell. They teamed up with the local thin man Hillel Slovak and started a gang called the Faces. Flea was Poco, Hillel was Flaco, and Anthony was Fuerte (aka Windman, Earthman, and Devilman).

Inadvertently, I had prepared him for his own flight from the nest. Since childhood I had plugged Anthony into music; now his best pals had started a band. It wouldn't take much aggravation for these components to combust. In his sophomore year, I had sent him home to Michigan when I couldn't control his behavior. He went to Lowell High School for one semester and was thrilled when I let him back after the brief ostracism. That strategy wouldn't work anymore. He was a senior now and ready to bolt. When he repeatedly came home late on school nights I gave him an ultimatum. He chose to leave. We both felt betrayed, but I was confident he would evolve with honors. He stayed with Flea's family at first. His mom still invited me to holiday dinners, and I met a living doll family-friend of theirs on Thanksgiving that I pursued diligently. Moving on, Anthony crashed with his friend Dondi and kicked around town. We still got along though, and he brought his girlfriend Haya Handel over to meet me. They had their own Romeo and Juliet scenario; Haya's father would only let her date Jewish boys. Haya, with her scholastic excellence, was accepted into UCLA, and I helped Anthony write the college application that got him accepted too. I was front and center for his Fairfax graduation at the Greek Theatre in the spring of 1980. So was Peggy, who traveled all the way from GR. His program blurb: "Anthony Kiedis. Play Production. Thespians VP. Career: Actor." Haya presided as class president. Anthony, Flea and Hillel embraced for photo posterity; a solidified force to reckon with.

After all the years together, our splitsville felt more like a heart-breaking divorce or a breach of the Geneva convention. It was painful for me and liberating for him. In 1999, the Red Hot Chili Peppers would release *Californication,* their most successful album. It sold 15 million and was highly honored. It produced timeless hits like "Scar Tissue," "Otherside" "Parallel Universe," the title song "Californication" and a personal song that took us both back to Palm Avenue and a congregation of spider plant pots. Anthony called it "Savior."

Dusting off your savior
Well, you were always my favorite
Always my man, all in a hand
To celebrate you is greater
Now that I can, always my man

Now you see what I came for
No one here is to blame for
Misunderstand, all in a hand
Just like you could, you make me
All that I am, all in a hand

A butterfly that flaps its wings
Affecting almost everything
he more I hear the orchestra
The more I have something to bring

And now I see you in a beautiful
And different light
He's just a man and any damage done

Will be all right
Call out my name, call and I came

Dusting off your savior
Forgiving any behavior
He's just a man, all in a hand
Your hero's destined to waver
Anyone can, always my man

I would never betray you
Look at me, who could raise you?
Face in the sand, safe in your hand
You were always my favorite
Always my man, all in a hand

We are the Red Hots
And we're loving lots the love me nots
The flowers in your flower pot
Are dancing on the table tops
And now I see you in a beautiful
And different light

I would be a prime witness to Anthony's successes and his failures. The eighties would be a difficult decade, but they also saw both of us reach heights we never could have dreamed of.

Chapter 29: Violet

Financially strapped as a dominatrix client in an S&M parlor on Western Avenue, I opted out of 937 Palm. Devoid of Anthony and my memories, I moved one block east to a small basement bachelor apartment at 940 Hancock Avenue. Mine was a phantom apartment, accessed through a secret wooden gate. I was immune from bill collectors, cops, old girlfriends and old girlfriends' boyfriends. And none of the old players could tempt me back into the white rabbit hole. My joint was a trip. It was one really big room with a miniature golf green carpet; my notorious bed was literally center stage, as it had always been figuratively. I still had my ponderous oak table that haunted Fay Hart. I still have it today. I had one of those new fangled VCR machines that had finally gotten affordable. I taped my TV and film parts in a reel for casting agents. With the help of insiders, I managed readings for *The Young and the Restless, Westworld, The Dukes of Hazzard* and *Who's Life is it Anyway?* with Richard Dreyfuss and John Cassevetes. I bellied up to the theatre and auditioned for The Mark Taper *Spin Drift* at the Cast Theatre, *Lady Chatterly's Lover* at the Fig Tree, and *Mr. Dracula* at the Alexander Rep Company. I also did the cover of an October issue of *SLAM* magazine as Dracula. It claimed to be "The World's Most Outrageous Humor Magazine." Finally! I beat out the mighty Bob Gallo for best actor at the Hollywood Actors Theatre yearly banquet. Anthony had won best actor at Fairfax High.

I still worked at Tim's furrier store on Sundays, but now they had moved to Beverly Hills. My Cutlass wheezed one last gasp and died a timely death. It had been an awful relationship. In the classified I saw what looked like a pretty sweet deal: A 1973 Cadillac Eldorado with low mileage, beautiful arm-chair leather seats, big music and a classy navy blue coat. Big Tim arranged a loan and I grabbed it. We had our own conservative set of bars like Dillon's on Melrose and the Jockey Club in Culver City. Hippie, disco and punk had faded. There came to be, of all things, a bar called Blackie's on La Brea that grabbed the scene for a while with rockabilly, cowpunk and new wave. They booked female bands that attracted a distaff cliental including members of the Bangles, Belinda Carlisle and Jane Wiedlin of The Go Go's. I had new buddies like the Kingbees, fronted by Jamie James, a Canadian who played with Steppenwolf and Bob Seger before he moved west. Jamie had seen my Gary Myrick stand up; we revived the infamous act and took it on the road. Anthony copied me and did a variation for Hillel and Flea's band Anthym. I got just as tight with The Textones: Carla Olson, David Provost, Mark Cuff on drums and guitarist Kathy Valentine, who eventually joined The Go Go's. Mark became my official photographer .

The Irish bar Molly Malone was an unlikely club. They had a special night of rockabilly that sold out every week. Its biggest attraction was the Rockats with Levi Dexter and Smutty Smith. The Havelinas and Plugs also played there. Downtown LA started rocking too. Al's Bar on the seedy east side was drawing upscale customers from the west side. In Chinatown, Madame Wong's drew big crowds and featured music from bands like the Motels with Martha Davis. I was practically in the Wong family, being there so often. Both Esther and her husband Harry would greet me with oriental reverence. Harry hung poster notices of my upcoming TV shows. A young Demi Moore was there then and kept us abreast of her theatrical progress. I remember the night she whooped it up after getting a role on the soap opera *General Hospital*. During the 80s, Madame Wong delivered Oingo Boingo, The Police, the Kats, Black Flag, X, The Knack, The Go Go's, The Ramones, Guns N' Roses and the Red Hot Chili Peppers. The Hong Kong Café next door followed suit and reinvented itself as a nightclub. I saw hard-core punk band Fear, with Flea on bass when he was in that band.

I auditioned against long odds for an important production of Joseph Heller's best-selling novel *Catch-22* at the Fifth Street Studio in the Wilshire District. After several call backs, I was hired to play two of the crucial characters. The World War II novel was the portrayal of an Army Air Forces B-25 bomber squadron stationed in Italy. Critics universally raved about *Catch-22's* frenetic pace and biting satire, its intellectualism, absurd humor and grisly realism. The 1970 film version was directed by Mike Nichols, with an all-star cast of Alan Arkin, Anthony Perkins, Martin Sheen, Jon Voight, Bob Newhart and Orson Welles. In our theatrical version production, I played the psychotic psychiatrist in one of a those frenetic scenes. I also played Colonel Korn, a major character. Buck Henry who wrote the movie screenplay had also played the role of Colonel Korn. Our play had a good run and was a huge success. I brought a different beautiful date to almost every performance. Most notable was Terri Nunn, the lead singer for the band Berlin. They were another of those new wave bands and one of the most successful. "Take My Breath Away" from Tom Cruise's *Top Gun* was one of their many hit songs.

Theatre Review: "Blackie Dammett's work as Colonel Korn was perfect - snide, conniving, simpering, and perfectly charming."

Los Angeles Times: "Blackie Dammett invests the production with a prevailing awareness of a theatrical event."

Los Angeles Herald Examiner: "Blackie Dammett, Steve Whittaker and Peter York evidence particularly inspired comic energies within the balanced, young ensemble."

After seeing my performance one night, wily Whitman McGowan recruited me to join his comedy ensemble that had a Theta Cable public access channel for a live hour show on Saturday afternoons in the LA market. They called it the *H.O. Comedy Show*, a kooky program with roots in Sid Caesar, Steve Allen and SNL. We had a good size group and I played my share of leads, a rockabilly singer, private detective, spaceman and a talk show host in Canada's Saskatoon, Saskatchewan. I brought in some friends of mine too. One was a struggling actor named Den Surles who maintained a day job. He worked in the office at a porn film company in the Valley, and he'd brought a bunch of videos home to watch. He dropped by my house with some buddies and asked if he could use my VCR. I was busy prepping for a date but told them they could watch until I was ready to leave. They settled in, hollering like sex-starved married men. By fate, I glanced up at the screen and saw a girl that caught my eye. I asked them to rewind a bit so I could see her again. She was one of the *Bad Girls*. I made a note of that.

A week later, I was at Al's Bar downtown. On weekends it was always packed, and I was lucky enough to get the high sign from the doormen. Most of the clubs let me slide past the lines. Inside it was dark and smoky. Bands played in one of the crazy maze back rooms. I was looking around for Jay Brown, who was now living downtown in a cool loft space. A girl squeezed past me; where do I know that face from? And then...what were the odds!? It was the bad girl from the porn video. Only now she was low key, no makeup, almost scruffy, seemingly in disguise. I tried to catch up, but it was so crowded I lost her in the labyrinth. I couldn't lose her twice. I kept navigating. Finally, I tracked her down in one of the quieter rooms and explained the story of how I met her. She was sweet, had a super smile and was from Brooklyn. She lived in Hollywood now, but had a boyfriend, and she had the beautiful name of Violet. I gave her my phone number just in case. She accepted and then immediately fled Al's Bar; incognito and on the run.

I'd see Anthony and his accomplices sneaking into clubs they were still too young for. He had a brisk case of street smarts and the craziest getups. His squad dressed anti-fashion and goofy as they could. I was cruising in my Eldorado sporting an elegant dame when I spotted my kid and Hillel striding down Argyle Avenue in polka-dots and stripes. I slammed on the fashion-cop brakes and pulled over. "Hey goofballs, it's the eighties; handsome is in." I hiked a thumb at my high fashion, and they gave me the "we know what we're doing" assurance. I laughed and drove off.

Anthony would drop by my new pad to see how I was doing but never stayed long. He had places to go. He was me in Grand Rapids with Scott St. John, full of mischief and looking for trouble. I often spotted him at the Atomic Café downtown. Anthony and I were already competing for celebrity and even for the same girls.

Violet called. She wanted to meet in a neutral place. We decided on the Source, a vegetarian restaurant on Sunset. She turned out to be clever, funny, smart, sexy, adorable and Violet Liquori. And best of all, she was pissed at her boyfriend who was screwing up with his cocaine addiction. She lived in a mausoleum apartment building on Cherokee, right in the middle of tinsel town. Her guy was the night manager. She wanted to lose him. She wanted to trade him in for a new model, like me maybe. She warned that he was a mean son-of-bitch and carried a gun because of his job. The patronage at her building was colorful but certainly on the unprincipled side of the law. After a second casual date, Violet made the decision to end it with him, but she was worried I'd get in over my head with this dude. I recruited Anthony to help deliver the verdict. The next night, we showed him a stiff push around his office and gave him his walking papers. The bloodless deed was done, and we left him with a bewildered look on his hard-luck face.

Violet's apartment was funky cool, a lot like her, earthy and natural. She worked in a billion-dollar business, but once the shift was over she was just an unpretentious Brooklyn kid. One of her best friends was fellow porn star Ron Jeremy, who was over there all the time. So were an assorted cast of knuckleheads, adult-film actresses and ubiquitous cockroaches. It was like a New York tenement. For as long as we were together, I only slept there once. It was always at my safe house. Sweet dreams. She rebuffed conventional sex because she was terrified of getting pregnant, but her mouth spoke for her. We tooled around town like royalty in my big Cadillac. She was used to being independent, but changed her ways for me. Her true love was photography, and she was determined to earn enough money to quit porn and start her own beaux arts studio. She had a master-photographer friend who let her use his studio and equipment. I helped out too.

Weaver and his latest gal would join us on double dates. By now he had finally found skydiving. David had always been a daredevil, and he immediately took to the sky. He spent half his life at the Perris Valley Airport near Lake Elsinore and in time met a Canadian skydiver named Tina. Before long they were a serious couple, and I hardly ever saw them anymore.

I received a letter from St. Petersburg, Florida: Fay Hart and Steve Nieve announced the birth of Mercedes Emma Hart on February 14, 1981. A bit earlier there had been a subtraction before this addition. X had advanced to acclaim and, after some explosive shows, were signed to a record deal with Slash Records. Ray Manzarek of The Doors produced their new EP, and they were doing an important coming-out performance at the Whisky. Manzarek, Exene and the band were getting ready for the sold-out audience. Fay and Steve and Exene's jubilant sister Mirielle drove up to the entrance. Mirielle stepped into traffic, was hit by a car and died. Bravely, Exene still did the concert honoring that old show business maxim, the gig must go on.

A casting director saw one of my plays and thought of me for a new late-night comedy show about to challenge NBC's *Saturday Night Live*. It was *Fridays*. Each week's show was rehearsed and performed at ABC studios in Hollywood, before a live audience. After a couple call backs, I joined a snappy group of supporting actors who would augment the main cast. We were an integral component of the ensemble, and we jostled for face space during the ritual ceremony ending. "Blackie, stop mugging!" Our controversial show was more perverted than SNL and boasted more sex and drugs. The cast was Melanie Chartoff, Mark Blankfield, John Roarke, Brandis Kemp, Larry David (*Curb Your Enthusiasm*), Bruce Mahler and Michael Richards, who went on to be Kramer on *Seinfeld*. Opening night we served up the audacious Diner of the Living Dead sketch that was so gruesome six ABC affiliates dropped the show. We had hosts like George Carlin and musical guests Tom Petty, The Pretenders, Beach Boys, and the Clash. I made sure Anthony came for the Clash. They made an impression on him, and eventually Anthony and Joe Strummer would become good friends.

Guest host Andy Kaufman helmed our most controversial show. He was a strange nut who loved to screw everything up for his own amusement. He'd ad-lib well rehearsed scenes and throw everybody off. We all knew this coming in, so Michael Richards asked me to watch his back. Sure enough we came to our Sword of Damocles. It was the climactic main course of the night, a restaurant skit with the entire cast. Friends at dinner kept taking turns going to the bathroom to smoke pot. Andy came back uber nonsensical, as though he really had gotten stoned. Who would put it past him! He was off on an unscripted tangent. I was sitting at the table next to Andy so I got caught in the crossfire. After a contentious exchange, Michael Richards grabbed the cue cards and tossed them at Kaufman. Andy threw water at Richards, but most of it went on the Melanie Chartoff and me. A fight broke out, and I gallantly tried to restore order. We were live so everybody was watching uncensored. The producers and crew jumped in, and it was one big brawl.

To this day, there's no consensus as to whether this was all staged and who were or weren't involved. The ones who weren't were throwing real punches. I can attest. One thing is for sure, ratings rocketed. Every newspaper and entertainment news show ran the story:

The New York Times: "How 'Fridays' Beat 'Saturday Night'."

The Los Angeles Times: "THANK GOD, IT'S FRIDAYS. How in the name of Saturday Night Live did these assorted nuts become the 'tasteless' sensations of late-night television?"

I was a nut.

Smile alert, I had two new ingénue actresses in my love story. One was Diane Sherry in the Valley hills. She was my prototype, slender and freckled with long red hair. She had done lots of film, including her character as teenage Lana Lang in Richard Donner's 1978 *Superman*, with Marlon Brando and Christopher Reeve. The other was Jennifer Mayo. I met her at the Santa Claus Parade, a big deal to Angelenos. Thousands of all ages come, and movie stars wave from convertibles. Crowds watch from building tops and the Walk of Fame. I was at a private party above Frederick's of Hollywood; Jennifer and her mother were there too. She was perilously young but so darn cute I couldn't help myself. We became friends so close it was downright scary. Jennifer's father, Garth Pillsbury, was an actor and photographer. I introduced her to some of my directors and casting agents, and she started getting work. Cute as she was, Jennifer became an actress.

A new actor's bar opened in Beverly Hills, called the Gingerman. It was an instant success with the show business crowd. One of its owners and the face of the place was Carroll O'Conner, the brilliant actor, best known as Archie Bunker in *All in the Family*. At the Gingerman, every worker was an actor, and one of them was my old buddy Jock O'Neil. Since our Fountain Avenue days, he'd chalked up several TV, film and stage roles. We started hanging again, and I went to see his baseball play *Rubbers-Yanks 3 Detroit 0*. Jock also invited me to his comedy improv class with Harvey Lembeck (*Mister Roberts, Stalag 17* and all the *Beach Party* films). It was a high-octane tightrope thrill just to watch, like a crash-car derby or a cock fight. Jock persuaded me to join, and I became a member of the notorious improvisational meat grinder that spat out the weak of heart. Because Harvey Lembeck was one of the top teachers in town, the class was full of sharp young talent. Jack Lemmon's kid Chris was in the class and most of the others were working the comedy clubs in town. On stage, Harvey threw out a situation and you had to deliver immediately. I was petrified every time I walked into that low-key brick building on the wrong side of the Beverly Hill tracks. I came up with a few strokes of genius and a few flat feats. The laughter and applause was priceless, but the groans and gripes were costly. One night I was juggling Jujubees, Sharks and the Jets and a cul-de-sac off the top of my head. I got so involved I forgot the backdrop covered a brick wall. I socked the vindictive vaudeville curtain and broke my hand. Jock had to drive me to Cedar Sinai. It was the biggest impression I ever made there.

I caught up with James Kennedy in his acclaimed production of *The Zoo Story* at the Hudson Theatre, where I met Chicago playwright Robert Reiser. He was prepping a new play called *American Piece* at the Orpheum on Sunset. It was an open call with lines up the street to take a shot at stardom in the elderly theater. I was cast in the major role of Wayne. We rehearsed for months and then retooled it all over again at the Hudson Theatre. Sal Landi, a friend and fine actor, ended up with the lead role of Melley. We did a couple dress rehearsals for invited guests, but Reiser kept tinkering with the production. Actors came and went and a new Olivia joined the cast. She was Rory Flynn, a very special lady indeed and the youngest daughter of Errol Flynn, the greatest ladies' man of them all. Tall and lanky as her beautiful father, she took me for a whirl and invited me to her home. Sometime later after stealing yet another girl on my rambunctious love roller coaster, an exasperated ex-boyfriend blasted me as a cross between Errol Flynn and a Doberman pinscher. Thank you!

SAG went on strike, and I joined thousands of guild actors that picketed Fox, Warners, Paramount, Columbia, Disney, MGM and Universal. My walking partner at Fox was Ed McMahon. I also brought Violet along to keep me company and then Jennifer Mayo. With TV and movies on the lam, I read for a slew of plays: Ira Levin's *Death Trap* at the Masonic Temple, Philip Barry's *Holiday* at the Music Center, Terrence McNally's *Sweet Eros* and *Witness* at the Lee Strasberg Theatre, Jean Giraudoux's *The Mad Woman of Chaillot* at the Megaw and William Inge's *The Last Pad* at the Zephyr. I took dialect classes at Los Angeles City College and volunteered with the American Film Institute, acting for their student films. One was *Even Cowgirls Get the Blues*, long before Gus Van Sant's feature movie. I even joined a group of actors who performed at senior citizen homes. Finally the SAG strike settled, and there were paying jobs again. I read for *Escape Artists* at Zoetrope and the ABC soap *Young Live*. I did a showcase at LAAT. I worked in *Arsenic and Old Lace* at the Fiesta Dinner Theatre. I was auditioning like crazy in the day and rehearsing at night. It was a wonder I could remember which lines went with which script.

Right in the middle of a couple plays, Jack Starrett cast me as Bat Paterson, a black-clad contemporary cowboy like my old hero the Durango Kid. The film went through a few different titles (*A Texas Legend* and *Summer Heat*) but ended up as *Kiss My Grits*. Anthony Quinn was the executive producer, and the great one spent time on the set. Bruce Davidson starred with Susan George, and the heavy was Anthony Francisosa. I was his enforcer. Bruno Kirby was in it too. They shot some of it in the Lone Star state; a Texan native, Starrett had a good feel for the genre. I managed to keep both plays during the film shoot, *Cocktails with Artaud* by Sam Birnkrant as Baudelaire and *The Adding Machine* at the Laurence Playhouse on South La Cienega.

> *Theatre Review*: "With stiletto-sharp skill and from a humanist viewpoint, Elmer Rice 60 years ago dealt lightly with assorted eternal verities for The Adding Machine. In their turn, director John Horn and actor Blackie Dammett deal zestfully with Rice's classic expressionistic comedy and devastating mockery."

Casting directors showed up for my performance in *The Adding Machine*; I had become a bit of a brand. The name Blackie Dammett meant something now. Violet's nom de porn wasn't working in the business much anymore; she was strictly modeling, earnestly pursuing photography and charming the pants off everybody who met her. I wasn't the only one who had been smitten by Violet's f-stop exposure. Fan mail from around the world went to the Valley offices. One day she came running to me with her big blooming smile. Cutie pants had mentioned a wealthy Saudi Arabian sheik friend of hers before. She'd always worn an expensive Cartier watch from him. Now he was offering her a state-of-the-art photography studio and clients to shoot if she would come spend six months in Riyadh. She had tears of joy all over her cheeks. I gave her my blessings, and she in turn gave me something she had never done before. Her trademark quip had always been, "You're in big trouble, little Mister." How prophetic she was.

I was still scouting for an agent. Dot Dammett called. She'd met a director named Ivan Nagy and asked if he had any work for me. It so happened he was in pre-production on a project. I don't know what nefarious gift she gave him on my behalf or vice versa, but sure enough the company called me to Universal Studios to read. The TV film was *Midnight Lace*, a remake of the 1960 Doris Day and Rex Harrison feature movie of the same name. The adaption starred Mary Crosby, the daughter of Bing Crosby. She was a regular on *Dallas,* the #1 show on television and notorious for shooting kingpin J.R. Ewing on the 1980 season ending cliffhanger episode. Also cast in our new *Midnight Lace* was Academy Award winner Celeste Holm, immortalized in *Gentlemen's Agreement* and the Bette Davis classic *All About Eve.* By the time I left the studio that day, I was set in the cast too. I played a stalker, Herman Laird, who was in love with Mary Crosby and making it tough on confused cops who were trying to solve the mystery of who was intent on killing her. I played it to the hilt. We shot some of the film at Universal but most of it on location in San Francisco. We stayed at the Fairmont Hotel on Nob Hill, and my scenes were at picture postcard locations. The comic Vegas headliner Shecky Greene played the cop who stalked me back. Mary Crosby wrote an introductory letter to her agency telling them I was, "A really fine actor, completely professional and a joy to work with." We kept in touch. The role paid well, and there was an extra benefit. Another agent saw the show on NBC and thought I was brilliant. He knew Ivan Nagy and invited me to his offices in Burbank. He signed me up. I had representation with John La Rocca & Associates. Now let the games begin.

Before long, I was a double busy body: auditions for *Gangster Chronicles* at Universal, *Taxi, and CHiPs;* more *Fridays,* a premier for the *Starsky and Hutch* episode "Dandruff" at MGM with limos; playing the horses with Bruce Reilly at Santa Anita, *Vice Squad,* call backs for a Biblical movie, a gay cab driver for AFI, Ron Koslow at Fox for *Lifeguard,* and a Uta Hagen class. A typical night was Dead Kennedys at the Whisky, George Carlin at the Improv, Gary Myrick at the Starwood and Adam Ant at Cathay de Grande after his stop at Tower records.

LA never stopped proffering new venues. New girls were always coming of age, replenishing the scene and craving the affection and attention of the opposite sex. Around town, I escorted Deirdre, Darcy, Jill Jacobson, Melissa, Skye Aubrey, Lisa Blount, Lehna from Sweden, Summer, Shannon, Veronica Blakely, Tallulah, Debbie Baker from Trashy Lingerie, Punky, Vickie, and Raven Cruel. Gumshoe sleuths will acknowledge that was but a fraction of them.

Furry Tim Reid dragged me kicking and screaming to a new erotic male-dancing club on Overland called Chippendales in the Palms district. It was the first of what would be a national and then worldwide phenomenon. Tim knew Steve Banjeree, the owner, and

Steve Merritt, the director of the male burlesque show. I just followed Tim. It was suppose to be for ladies only, but we masqueraded as consultants. Half-dressed men weren't our taste of course, but the packed house of screaming women driven sexually mad was rather interesting.

George Carlin was trying to put together a film called *The Illustrated George Carlin,* and La Rocca sent me over in a flash with a dossier of my Clu Gulager transvestite photos from Sherwood Oaks. The movie was typical Carlin, clever craziness with a funny transvestite character. Me and my pomegranate boobs drove to Carlin's temporary office in lower Beverly Hills. He kept laughing and I kept blushing. George and our band of merry makers putzed around with rehearsals for a time, but the film fell through for lack of funds. Devo was rehearsing next door. It was a notable experience for all of us. Seven dirty laughs.

I did a 3D western trailer for Europe. Read for Brecht's *Man Equals Man* paying $400 a week Equity, but evidently I wasn't man enough. I went up for ABC's *Open all Night* from Bernie Brillstein, met with Harold Ramis and Rodney Dangerfield at NBC and went to see Hillel and Flea's band Anthym play at Madame Wong's West in Santa Monica. Anthony was as interesting as the band, cavorting about on and off the stage. His UCLA days had been short lived despite his innovative college term papers: *Nueva Agua,* an appellation of New Wave Music, and *How to Roll a Quality Marijuana Cigarette.* Now he was working at a store. Obviously there was more in store.

I read for the film *Frances* at Zoetrope, courtesy of casting director Jennifer Shull. Fern Champion and Pamela Basker were another duo of casting directors who believed in me. Others were Al Onorato at Columbia, Marion Dougherty at Warners, Wally Nicita at MGM, Mike Hanks at CBS, Janet Hirshenson at Zoetrope, Mike Fenton at Fox, Joe D'Agosta at Raleigh Studio, Diane Crittenden, Don Phillips, and many more. Like hired guns, they'd move from studio to studio or go independent; they're an actor's best friend. Casting Director David Graham read me for the running role of Victor Casanova; a public defender, smooth with the ladies, defends the riff raff and swaps quips with the judge in a late night syndicated comedy *Night Court in Vegas.* It was a Viacom TV pilot. I thought I had the part, but they picked up a name, and I became "the man on a hook." Actually it was a funny role. We rehearsed for a week and then shot the pilot episode; we all crossed our fingers it would sell. It didn't get picked up, but the massive Saint Bernard that stole all the scenes was a hoot.

Mad Bomber, Strike Force, FBI, General Hospital, Beast Master and *Bosom Buddie*s, the Tom Hanks sitcom, were all in a day's audition work. The feature film *Maximillian* had my choice of Leopold or Arbuckle, but the project fizzled. I had a promising interview with John Hughes for his pilot *At Ease,* an army sitcom at Fox with Jimmy Walker. It was another Spelling project, but *At Ease* never got picked up. Barbara Clamen called me in to read for *Mafia Kingpin* at MGM. It was a 200-page script with 56 roles written by Sonny Gibson, starring Sonny Gibson about Sonny Gibson's life story in the mafia. Kathy Henderson had me back for the executives and Sonny Gibson. I got a good part as Mario Raffa, but after months of financial trouble the project died. Then it revived and was set to go at Laird Studios with British director Mike Anderson (*George Orwell's 1984, Logan's Run* and *Around the World in Eighty Days,* which garnered five Academy Awards). It turned out Sonny Gibson was a phony baloney and the film was dumped in the East River.

There was an elderly lady named Mildred Rand who lived above me on Hancock. She had been a leading actress in the golden era and loved to regale me with stories of her glorious career. In return I told her of my modern exploits. I felt a kinship with her and was happy to help bring up her groceries. Hollywood was full of elderly actors who didn't work anymore, rascally troupers who lived on their faded clippings and melancholy memories. I loved my profession despite the peril. It was a noble endeavor to sacrifice for the pleasure of others. Certainly there was comedic compensation, but for the most part ours was a difficult life, fraught with tragedy and travail, and when the fateful time arrives we are ultimately accorded a death with the heroic indignity of Lear.

"L.A. Bounty"

Chapter 30: Scott McClintock

After a year of unrequited work on Robert Reiser's play *American Piece,* I had finally dropped out because of rehearsal conflicts with plays that *did* reach the stage. Then one day I saw in *LA Weekly* that it was finally opening at the Show Room Theatre on Vermont. I marked it in my appointment book. Opening Night! Even vicariously there would be a rush in the air, and I would see some old friends. The lead actress, once played by Rory Flynn, was new to me and her name was Deborah Mullowney. The play was fine; I always enjoyed the theatre. After the final curtain, I went back stage to give the cast, director and especially the starlet my congratulations. She blushed and invited me to the cast party at her home in Benedict Canyon.

I drove out through Beverly Hills and into the affluent arroyo. It was an expensive home on valuable real estate, rather unusual for such a young lady. I rang the door bell and an exuberant young man graciously invited me in. Just to make sure I was aware, he announced that he was Deborah's husband, Scott. There was both pride and anxiety in his manner. He was talking a million miles an hour and soon enough he revealed the reason. He had a silver vial of blow and offered me some. I declined but he stuck close to me. He gave me a tour of his house and eventually we made our way to his wife, who was spectacularly beautiful and glowing in the spotlight of her opening night. The party went into the early morning and so did Scott's conversation and affinity. He was also an actor. They had recently moved from San Francisco, and his mother was Jessica McClintock, a wealthy blue blood of high society. Scott targeted me with multifaceted projects and one was to my liking; he wanted to produce Israel Horovitz's one act, two character play *Rats* and Terrence McNally's one act *Noon* as a duo. And it wasn't just the coke talking; the next day we got started on the project.

Scott was well-educated but most likely cruised through school more on his charm and reputation than his industry. In retrospect, I realize how similar he was to George W. Bush, from the influential family to a slight physical resemblance. A rich and powerful parent made it easy for him to advance through the phases of his life, but he was never quite prepared to meet challenges on his own when they arose. Don't get me wrong, he was handsome and charismatic, and, like me, he loved women. For the first time since Scott St. John, I had a pal who was capable of winning the battle for those women. He seemed to have a bottomless allowance from his mother and bought cars and changed houses with caprice and impunity.

Scott's only screen credit was a small part in the Frances Farmer film with Jessica Lange, an audition I failed. I introduced him to the H.O. Theater troupe and we worked on a few episodes. We put the *Noon* and *Rats* project together and got rolling. For a change, we were doing the casting. Scott was top billed in *Noon* and I was top dog in *Rats*. We had all kinds of cuties auditioning and chose Annie Wharton for the blonde bombshell. We hired a respected director in Michael Abrams and rented the Déjà Vu Coffee House in Silver Lake as our venue. The audience could eat, drink and watch in an intimate setting. Annie

Wharton and I spent most of jocular *Noon* in our underwear. *Rats* was an emotional and dramatic piece that gave me an opportunity to flex my muscular empathy. We had good crowds, and Anthony and Flea came to see it.

Reviews: "*Noon*, by Terrence McNally, could also be titled five characters in search of a perversion. Blackie Dammett (Asher) is on the right track. *Rats* is a 20 minute Israel Horovitz play about a pair of rodents and their day to day problems. Blackie Dammett played Jebbie with an up-against-it kind of scary desperation that seemed just right."

Scott and Deborah split up. She was taking acting classes at UCLA and fell in love with her teacher, actor James Farentino, who had a durable acting career and several marriages, including one with Michele Lee. Deborah married Farentino and changed her stage name to his. Her career is still viable (*Son of the Pink Panther, NYPD Blue, JAG, CSI Miami*). Scott played nonchalant but hurt inside, and I was genuinely compassionate. He started taking me to lunch just about every day, frequently at Barney's Beanery with *Bette Davis Eyes* on the jukebox.

He hit on almost every girl I dated and was occasionally successful. I was involved with a luscious lady with outrageous breasts who wasn't shy. There was a festive H.O. Theater going out of business party, and I asked her to be my date for the swan song. Scott had gotten to her first. I for once was the cuckold. I kept my cool though and she evaporated anyway.

Scott had another project, a screenplay somewhat like the concept of *The Treasure of the Sierra Madre* but with cocaine instead of gold. We worked on that for a while, but like a married couple we couldn't agree on any aspect of the script. We smoked a lot of pot, were going in circles and finally gave up on it. Scott invited me up to San Francisco. He had been reticent. He was intimidated by his mother, and I wasn't exactly high society.

Jessica McClintock *was* high society. Her fashion business was doing $75 million a year; in the early 80s that was big dough. She was an award-winning designer with a Doctorate of Humane Letters and a CEO of a major business with factories and showrooms around the country. Her Jessica McClintock Boutique on Sutter Street was a romantic marble Taj Mahal. Her opulent 16-room 19th-century mansion in Pacific Heights looked over the Golden Gate Bridge. They had purchased the home from Francis Ford Coppola and then spent millions to refurbish it. Chopin was in the air. Everything was priceless. Lavish parties were common. Her current neighbors include Senator Dianne Feinstein, Speaker of the House Nancy Pelosi, Gordon Getty, Danielle Steel, Lars Ulrich and former ones Werner Erhard (EST) and Nicholas Cage.

I was a black sheep with kaka on my hoofs and Jessica was never comfortable with me. Still, she loved her Scottie and Scott's only real friend was me, so she was conciliatory. He had the third floor all to himself. They had a large cupola on top of the house where Scott liked to sleep and smoke pot. We were way above the other Victorian homes with a breathtaking view of the city.

Scott took me to all the SF clubs, as I had done for him in LA. We went to a big party at a place called Club Nine. *People Magazine* happened to be there covering the affair. San

Francisco was well known for its debauchery and this club was one of the wildest. Scott wanted to make sure I saw the bizarre side of his city. There was an exotic young lady parading about in a wedding headdress and the wedding bottom of a wedding dress—but no top. She was naked from the waist to the ribbons in her hair. She had generous breasts and there was nothing Scott liked better than that. His eyes were popping out. I casually walked up to her, made my move and secured her for the evening. Her name was Miss Kitty Boudin. We took her back to the McClintock mansion. We slept with her upstairs and brought her down for breakfast, which had his mother in a state of seizure. Missy Kitty was in the morning newspaper next to our wheat toast and marmalade.

Back in LA, I fell into the ample lap of another exotic beauty. I was schmoozing at the intimate bar in Dan Tana's. The Italian restaurant was a celebrity favorite and another place Weaver and I liked to entertain friends. You couldn't move in there without rubbing elbows with the stars. Today it's Clooney and Seinfeld and Di Caprio. Back then it was old-school stars and seeing George Burns at 87 (who lived to be 100) snuggled up to a dazzling 17-year-old girlie with the biggest tits ever, whooping it up in a corner booth was captivating. I was so beguiled I went over by the ladies restroom to wait for her. The way they were going through the champagne I knew she'd eventually have to pee. And when she did, I had my speech prepared because I knew I'd only have a few seconds. I was pilfering from a legend. She thought I was daring and mysterious and gave me her name and number.

The name was Candye Hogan and she lived on eastside Nordyke Street. The first time I went to her mom's house and down into Candye's basement bedroom I was shocked to see dozens of oversize Sylvester Stallone posters plastered on the walls. That was a game killer and ushered in a more platonic relationship, but we dated casually for a while. She carried a crush for me and continued to write me sweet love letters. Soon she'd be known as Candye Kane. After our affair, she became an adult model, stripper and adult film star. She held the dubious record for being on the cover of over a hundred adult magazine covers over the next two years. She had a parallel career in music that defined her more appropriately as the talent she really was. She sang punk, rockabilly, country, swing, jazz, and blues; was an accomplished song writer and has been on just about every talk show. She's still touring and entertaining the troops.

John La Rocca kept the casting calls coming, but a pattern evolved: I'd be seeing the same old guys in the waiting room, the wise guys and the shy guys, the good bad guys and the scary bad guys. It was cut-throat camaraderie and high stakes; we all had car payments and SAG dues to pay.

Meg Leiberman had become one of my supporters and called me in for a film that would shoot briefly in LA but primarily in Berlin. The German project was *Comeback*, written and directed by Christel Buschmann, with music by Eric Burdon (of the Animals) who also starred. He portrayed a rock singer caught between art and commercialism. He gives up his family and the music business and returns to the streets of freedom. At the time, David Bowie was living in Berlin during his *Heroes* period. So was Iggy Pop. The film mimicked reality; Eric's character Rocco sought inspiration in the post-war city divided by reconstruction, politics and the Wall. In Berlin, he was caught up in intrigue, deception and betrayal. Nefarious double crossers hire a hit man to silence his song. That hit man killer was me.

A German crew came to California and shot the opening sequences in LA and the Mojave Desert. I worked for two days in the desert and tagged along on the rest of the two week shoot, even the sultry scenes between Eric and his lovely wife, played by actress Julie Carman.

Once we wrapped there, we flew to Berlin. The cast was predominately German except for Eric, Julie Carman, Michael Cavanaugh as Rocco's manager, another La Rocca client John Aprea as the lawyer, and me. The German star was Joerg Phenningwearth. We checked into the Hotel Palace, established in the year 500. That was Berlin, a city soaked with an incessant exhilaration in its history. The bustling Kurfurstendamm was a five-mile-long Times Square. I got up early every morning to explore the city before work.

West Berlin was divided into the American, French and English sectors; East Berlin was the Russian sector and surrounded by the infamous Berlin Wall. Berlin itself was surrounded by communist East Germany. The wall had been there for twenty years and would remain for another ten. Many successfully escaped to the western sectors, but there were 137 confirmed deaths. East Germans who attempted to scale the wall were often shot to death by the Volpos or *Volkspolizei*. As an American citizen, I was legally allowed to cross into East Berlin, but the Volpos were known to play by their own rules and sometime tourists just disappeared. On a day off, I crossed over at Check Point Charlie. It was dreadfully drab and Kafkaesque. Hunched citizenry shuffled about stoically. I bought a couple bleak souvenirs and got the hell outta there, but not before I encountered trouble at the border on the way back. You had to weave through a well guarded zig zag hallway that prevented the locals from bum rushing across. When I finally got to the end of the maze at the last check point, a burly Volpo flaunting his machine gun gave me static about my dress and behavior. One of the other Volpos meandered over with a big smile on his face. Starsky and Hutch, he said. Hey, Starsky and Hutch! They huddled around me and applied a hardy bear hug, followed by a booming slap on the back. Evidently they had been sneaking TV signals from West Berlin. The airwaves made a Maginot Line of the Wall.

The centerpiece of the film was the Metropol, a music venue with gravitas. Built in 1892 for operetta, it seated about 2,500 people and was one of Berlin's most famous variety theatres. It closed during the depression and was resurrected by the Nazi party during the thirties. The exteriors were severely damaged by Allied bombers in World War II and subsequently rebuilt, but the auditorium itself was still basically the same. Today it has been renovated as the opulent Komische Oper Berlin. It was our production headquarters, and naturally I watched the casting of extras. There was one who really stood out. She was sultry Ursela and was dressed in a man's suit. I struck up a conversation and a romance. Her English was flawed but my German was nonexistent. She lived with some anti-social fellows in a rundown section of Berlin and I went there with her. They seemed suspicious and I felt the tension, but I decided to spend the night with her. She tried to dissuade me but I was rigidly spellbound. In the middle of the night, she woke me and said we had to leave immediately so we went back to my hotel. She confessed her roommates were members of the Baader-Meinof Gang; a terrorist organization, socialist and anti-American. The most radical elements of the household actually considered killing me that night. A couple days later and in broad daylight, I went back to talk with them. The radicals would have nothing to do with me, but the moderates were willing to listen. I explained I was a Hollywood leftist hippie with no ties to American hegemony. I thought the very idea of *terroristes*, as they were called, was wildly exciting at the time. I cut a hunk of art from an article about the Red Faction and fashioned my own lapel pin that said TERRORISTES and wore it on my jacket. In a memorabilia shop, I found a black shoulder patch that said SAVAGE SKRULLS BERLIN and some Nazi memorabilia. I had no affinity for the *Nationalsozialist* party, but their military wore kickass fashionable uniforms.

I had finished all my scenes except for the Eric Burdon as Rocco in concert at the Metropol, a real show with 2,000 extras. My plan was to assassinate him on stage during the gig, but suspicious, he thwarted me. Not to be denied, I made adjustments during his final song; even as I lurked in the stairwell, I had to admit I was enjoying the performance. Rocco finished, exited the stage and ran up the sinister stairs toward his dressing room and fate. Face to face in the stairwell, I shot him dead as the crowd continued to roar for an encore.

We had a few days to wrap up. The German words were so long I never knew if I was walking into a funeral home or a gay bathhouse. The Berlin cabarets were wild and exotic. I entered a radical discotheque with a crowd of unruly dancers and a lady I was born to like. She had it all; I was enthralled. It was industrial-music noisy but I persisted. She refused me, but when I explained I was leaving tomorrow she did give me her phone number. At the Berlin airport, I called for her address and promised to write. When I got back to Hancock, I kept my promise. We started a long-distance writing affair that lasted for years. She was the beautiful and talented Karin Sommer. Genthiner Str. 6, Berlin 1000.

Variety: Around and about the Hollywood Filmex Festival 'Comeback' contingent including director Christine Buschmann and thesps Eric Burdon, who played Saturday night at The Roxy. Also along were Blackie Dammett, Julie Carman and Joerg Phenningwearth.

The film debuted at the 33rd International FILMFEST BERLIN. Its 1982 North America World Premiere was in Century City, with proper pomp and ceremony.

Lee Strasberg had died while I was in Berlin, but I attended the LA memorial. It had all started with him. Violet wrote from Saudi Arabia; she was enjoying her adventure, and then she discovered she was pregnant. It broke her heart, and I was to blame. She went home to her mother's on Long Island. Violet was Catholic, so abortion seemed out of the question. Whatever happened with the child she kept to herself, typical of the diminutive kitten with the fortitude of a Brooklyn Dodger. I sent her endless artistic postcards. I still have a list of them in a black leather-bound 1982 appointment book that Anthony gave me on my birthday. In it he wrote:

For a SLICK HIPSTER POP: TWICE AS MUCH FUN, TWICE AS MUCH SUCCESS and TWICE AS MUCH HAPPINESS in THE SECOND HALF OF YOUR LIFE. From a FINE LAD and SWELL SON, Anthony.

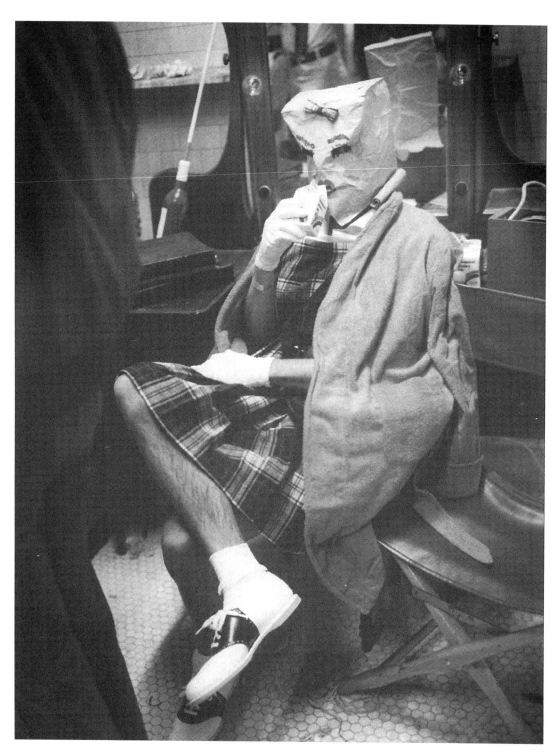

National Lampoon's "Class Reunion."

Chapter 31: National Lampoon's Class Reunion

The humor magazine *National Lampoon* was a 1970 spinoff of the *Harvard Lampoon*. It was irreverent and whimsically successful for a while but lost some of its best talent to NBC's *Saturday Night Live* when that debuted. Still, it was a major media player when it produced its first film *Animal House* in 1978. That became the reigning highest-grossing comedy film of all time. The world impatiently waited for the next edition. Lampoon contributor John Hughes wrote the anticipated script and called it *Class Reunion*. Hughes would go on to write and direct a litany of blockbusters: *National Lampoon's Vacation; Ferris Bueller's Day Off; The Breakfast Club; Sixteen Candles; Pretty in Pink; Planes, Trains and Automobiles, Mr. Mom, Weird Science* and *Home Alone*. Publisher Matty Simmons chose discredited Michael Miller to direct the film. In retrospect he could have had John Hughes' directorial debut sooner than later. La Rocca set me for an audition and I was speechless. *Animal House* was every red-blooded male's favorite movie, and we knelt to the ultimate anti-hero John Belushi. I'd need to regain my speech though.

I went to Karen Rae's West LA office near Fox and joined a mob of prospects for the major casting call. I had already read the script and it was funny, clever, and outrageous. It was a ten-year high school class reunion with typical Lampoon characters: a sanctimonious class president, the know-it-all busy bodies, a blind girl with a heart of gold and her foot stuck in a mop pail, jocks, stoners, weirdoes, dorks, cheerleaders, a beautiful homecoming queen, the nerdy go getter, and a mental patient, Walter Baylor, who finds his invitation tossed through the bars of his padded cell. He escapes from the asylum and exacts revenge against the smart asses that made high school so miserable he went crazy. I was auditioning for Walter Baylor the mental patient, who was the focal point of the film. The casting staff put us into teams of two, and mine was with Mrs. Tabazooski, the cafeteria rotten cook that my character dismembers with a chain saw. The actor was Anne Ramsey (Danny DeVito's mother in *Throw Momma from the Train* and Mama Fratelli in *The Goonies*). We had good chemistry and Karen Rae was entertained. Finished, I ran to a phone booth and called La Rocca. He already knew; they dialed him up as soon as I walked out the door and inquired about my upcoming schedule. I was definitely set for the final auditions with the big shot executives at ABC Motion Pictures.

I showed up a week later for the grand final competition at their movie-mogul skyscraper in Century City, on the top floor, overlooking their show business domain. I was up against a dozen well-known comic actors and Robert Englund, who would make his mark as Freddy on *Nightmare on Elm Street*. Once again I drew the inside rail for a partner. She was Shelley Smith, an elegant former model and a talented actress who had just completed an award-winning TV series in New York called *The Associates*. We plotted our scene and agreed to go wild, throw caution to the wind, do a high intensity improv and not worry about the exact dialogue. No script to worry about.

The scene they gave us was Walter Baylor trying to seduce Meredith Modess in my secret hiding place deep in the high school's basement. Our do or die stage was in ABC chairman Brandon Stoddard's penthouse suite, but on this occasion there were also several top executives from ABC and 20th Century Fox, director Michael Miller, Karen Rae and Matty Simmons himself. We walked into an exhilarating buzz that electrified the room; they were anticipating our performance and we didn't disappoint.

The jury was sitting behind a big conference table, and I threw Shelley right on the table in front of them. I tore my shirt off without decorum. The buttons flew around the room like exploding bullets. I dove on top of her, and she got so excited she ripped off her own blouse, filling the air with more flying buttons and the scent of her perfume. We rocked and writhed in the laps of startled executives. It was bravos and kudos and we walked out of there with all of Jagger's lost satisfaction. You should have seen the looks that half-naked Shelley got when we rejoined the other actors in the waiting room. Shelley and I were both cast in the film. Anne Ramsey was picked for Mrs. Tabazooski too, so I helped both my partners win their parts. La Rocca was ecstatic too; he pulled in ten percent of my $2500 per week for a minimum of eight weeks, by far my biggest paycheck to date. Still a rookie, I was the lowest-paid primary actor in the cast. Gerrit Graham was top billed and earned $60,000 a week. Matty Simmons pulled me aside and promised I'd get star billing too, even the boss was thrilled for me.

Except for a few exterior scenes, we shot the entire movie at an old gothic high school in Pasadena that was in the process of being converted into a College of Chiropractic Medicine. We worked in tandem with the renovation, and we pretty much had the run of the place. In the script, the school was also closed, deserted and almost haunted. It was our home for months, and we came together as a supportive ensemble with mutual respect. John Hughes was on the set every day, constantly rewriting. The head of the makeup department had done decades of great movies, including *The Wizard of Oz*. I had a variety of special effect disguises, body molds and my own Madame Trousseau space. I had a closet of costumes and a full rack of Catholic schoolgirl outfits that I wore in most of the scenes. My stunt man double stood in for the most dangerous situations, but I volunteered for many of the tough scenes myself. I did my own work high in the ceiling girders of the gymnasium, with a little safety wire and no net. I was routinely on the edge of disaster, whether it was smashing through break-away walls or being smashed over the head. I was attacked by the blind girl *and* her seeing-eye dog. A hapless villain, the whole class was chasing me around the school. I spent more time in the infirmary than the girl's bathroom. Between takes, I plotted my nefarious abduction of the leading lady and did interviews with the media.

Gerrit Graham was the leader, both on and off the set. Perfectly obnoxious, he was class president Bob Spinnaker and ostensibly invincible. You've already met Shelley Smith as Meredith Modess, Spinnaker's girlfriend in high school. At the reunion she's a successful model and my obsession. Fred McCarren as Gary Nash was the nerd nobody ever paid attention to in school or at the reunion. He would rise to the occasion and save the day. Miriam Flynn brought talent and experience as Bunny Packard the female ring leader.

Stephen Furst was the only carryover actor from *Animal House*. As Flounder the feckless pledge, he had been a pansy foil for Belushi. In our film as Hubert Downs, he was a cross between Belushi's Bluto and a playful gross-out trouble maker with a thick head. I loved him as a person and an actor. Misty Rowe was the sweetheart sex symbol as Cindy Shears, who flaunted her considerable wares and was one of my victims. Misty had been a pin-up cutie for years and well known from pulp fiction films and risqué layouts. Marya Smalls was Iris Augen, the blind girl determined to find somebody, anybody, to have sex with. Zane Buzby as Delores Salk had super powers and kicked my ass. Zane made a name for herself in Cheech and Chong's *Up in Smoke*. Jacklyn Zeman was a big star on *General Hospital*, who crossed the line to play snobbish but beautiful Jane Washburn. She was the one girl in the cast I had a crush on and the only girl I dated. Marla Pennington played the demur Mary Beth. Marla was fragile, sweet and lovely; I liked her very much. The stoners were Art Evans and Barry Diamond. Chuck Berry played Chuck Berry and rocked our class reunion before the party got nasty. Terrific character actor Michael Lerner played my alter ego Dr. Robert Young, who was actually Baylor in disguise. I also played my sister; boy was she unattractive!

In my early scenes, I did my terrorizing with a paper bag over my head. I had an assortment of them decorated with creepy lipstick smiles and a bow. My face had hardly been seen. We hadn't gotten to the meat of the film or the opening escape from the mental hospital. Now we were finally in the scenes without the paper bag, and Zane Buzby was using her magical powers to fling me high into the air and bash me against a wall. Special effects coordinator Paul Stewart had rigged up to an explosive catapult that launched me. His overcharged calculation was faulty, and I slammed into a support beam that split my breastbone. They rushed me to the hospital and put me back together, but the diagnosis was to take time off and recuperate. The production momentum was crucial and most of my already-edited coverage was incognito; the financial producers suggested replacing me. They could keep my early paper bag footage and let someone else finish the film. Whoa! There was no way I was giving up my part. I walked out of the hospital with my open–in–the-rear gown and returned to the set. Joyfully, my classmates welcomed me back and got us all out of character. I finished the film with all my scheduled daredevil stunts, fights and pratfalls, all with a painful separated breastbone. Along the way, I also crunched my elbow, had an eye injury and sprained my ankle. As it was, I worked 49 individual days, more than anybody in the cast.

A year later, Steven Spielberg produced *Twilight Zone: The Movie*, a three-part film directed by John Landis, Stephen Spielberg and Joe Dante. The lead actor in the Landis segment was Vic Morrow, father of Jennifer Jason Leigh. Morrow and two Vietnamese children were killed when a stunt went horribly wrong. A helicopter blade decapitated all three of them. The culprit was excessive SFX explosives that accidently blew off the helicopter's tail rotors. The special-effects explosives man was my *Class Reunion* SFX nemesis, Paul Stewart.

On my days off, I stayed busy reading for future parts. I zipped over to Universal for *Portrait of Lizzy Borden,* had a New York call for a tough guy, did Saturday volunteer work with Hollywood Park Acting, read for Garry Marshall's unique version of *The New Odd Couple* at Paramount with black actors Ron Glass and Desmond Wilson as Felix and Oscar, and I found time for a couple quick flings. My improv guru Harvey Lembeck died of a heart attack, and I went to the funeral. My son Anthony threw a party at his pad and was nice enough to invite me. We were still family; I did his taxes every year. I was also still on probation and had my monthly meetings with the officer on Vermont.

We finished off *Class Reunion* with a big everybody-lived-happily-ever-after ending (except for the ones I killed). My schoolmates forgave and embraced me, as I did them for their earlier transgressions. Musical crescendo, the dance of redemption and we segued right out of Pasadena. We had a big wrap party, did plenty of looping and went on *Entertainment Tonight* and *The Today Show*. To this day Walter Baylor has an international following, and I still get fan mail. The reviews were mixed.

San Francisco Examiner: Blackie Dammett is a certified psychopath.

New York Post: The fun is frantic, high spirited and quite accurately in the National Lampoon tradition.

Grand Rapids Press: National Lampoon horror is rotten comedy.

Los Angeles Times: This film is a howl if you don't mind parody that is crass, crude and irreverent. Director Michael Miller is totally askew, closed-in and dippy. It's totally obnoxious and totally hilarious. Blackie Dammett is perfection as the pathetic psychopath.

They erected one of those colossal Sunset Strip billboards to promote *Class Reunion*. It had a great spot right above Tower Records, with a picture of me swinging on a papier-mâché half-moon, ready to do my bloody business. They released a paperback book of the movie story with this blurb, "And then there's squirrelly little Walter Baylor, a butt of a ruthless practical joke back in high school. True he was a weenie then, but now he's killer weenie, and he's out for revenge." They put out a Walter Baylor comic book. The November 1982 issue of *Heavy Metal* magazine did an illustrated layout of my scary parts. There was even a Walter Baylor dance: "Everybody, do the Walter." In the final balance, *Class Reunion* may have been maligned by highbrow critics, but it has become a quirky cult film.

Chapter 32: Doctor Detroit

Bernie Brillstein and Robert Weiss had produced the box-office smash *The Blues Brothers,* directed by John Landis, with John Belushi and Dan Aykroyd. Now they were ramping up a new production, *Doctor Detroit*. The film featured Aykroyd, Howard Hesseman and James Brown, along with a cast of oodles. With *Class Reunion* on my resume, La Rocca was able to put me up for better roles in big budget movies. He called me on a Sunday and said Robert Weiss and director Michael Pressman wanted to see me. A Sunday audition was unusual, but I was more than willing. La Rocca filled me in on the story line and character. I would be reading for a big-time pimp, in fact the reigning *Pimp of the Year* at the annual Pimp's Ball in Chicago. On the lam from gangsters, Aykroyd was masquerading as a formidable pimp and running against me.

I dressed tacky, greased into my pimpmobile Cadillac and headed for Universal. Always cyclical, lately the cops had been somewhat lenient about hookers on the Strip, and recently I had noticed clusters of shady ladies working the street. I was driving east on Sunset by Fairfax when I saw four ladies of the afternoon in hot pants and push-up bras, waving at the cars. I slammed on the breaks and quickly explained my situation just in case the LAPD did happen by. Come on girls; we're going to Universal Studios. I had a drive-on pass and easily talked the gate guard into allowing the hussies to enter with me; it was a slow Sunday.

The meeting was at an active soundstage so I worked on my lines while they finished a shot. At the ring of "cut!" my entourage was taken to an ante room and finally into the producer's suite. Befitting a king of pimps, my seductive harem clung to me as we plopped down on the couch. Jaws dropped and eyes bugged out. I did my audition and Weiss went, "Yeah, that's fine, but tell us about these girls!" They hired me *and* the hookers.

I had an artistic friend named Pinky who made her own dazzling attire and brandished a big blonde bouffant and deadly white skin. Like every guy, I had a crush on her. Anthony did too. Once I got settled into the production, I brought Pinky to meet Weiss in her creative, long tight pink dress with contrasting black handprints on her ass and her breasts. They hired and featured her as a pricey courtesan.

After the early exterior footage shot in Chicago, we settled into our primary LA location, the grand old Biltmore Hotel on Pershing Square. That's where the Pimp's Ball was held with a legion of snazzy misfits and glittery dames caught up in plenty of skullduggery throughout the historic hotel's ornate suites, subterranean kitchens and a pompously prodigious ball room, with James Brown's explosive sweaty drop dead musical performance right out of a 1940s musical. Devo did a quirky opening act for The Godfather of Soul, both favorites of Aykroyd and Weiss. A Sex Machine myself, I danced my butt off in the big finale. Wardrobe had me in a metallic gold lamé suit that I was told Sonny Bono once wore in an earlier film. Lamé or lame, it's still the same.

Unfortunately, the production was shrouded in the aftermath of John Belushi's tragic death. Dan Aykroyd's best friend and blues brother had recently died of a drug overdose at the Chateau Marmont on the Sunset Strip. Grief-stricken, Aykroyd was forced to grapple with serious comedy. There was a Dan-dy Aykroyd brightside though. The four lead hookers were Fran Drescher, Lynn Whitfield, Donna Dixon and Lydia Lei. Donna Dixon was an absolute stunner; I couldn't take my eyes off her. She had a sleek Italian boyfriend on the set, but during the course of the film Donna and Dan fell in love. Ultimately they married and had children, but not before I took one last shot at charming her during the wrap party. I'm kidding, Violet. My campy character name was Eddie Four Eyes, and I had my own clique of pimps and hoes working the jive to retain my *Pimp of the Year* title. Actors Steven Williams, Cheryl Carter, Vincent J. Isaac and Diane Robin worked masterfully to create our plausible posse. They cut one of our scenes for time but sweetened the pot pie and beefed up our roles in the climactic blow-out.

John Belushi's overdose had impacted me too. I had an audition at the Chateau Marmont Hotel to read for *Once Upon a Time in America,* an epic film of organized crime that would be directed by the living-legend Italian director Sergio Leone (*A Fistful of Dollars; The Good, the Bad and the Ugly*). Robert De Niro, James Woods, Jennifer Connelly and Joe Pesci were among the star-studded cast that would work for over a year in Italy and New York. I got the script and auditioned for one of the gangster roles with casting director Cis Corman in one of the Chateau's bungalows. She raved about my reading and set me up to meet Sergio Leone and De Niro the next day; they were already at the hotel, meeting with various factions. "Sergio is going to love you!" she said. "His trademark is interesting faces." I went home with sky-high expectations. That night John Belushi partied at the Rainbow, returned to the Chateau and gorged himself on drugs. When they discovered his dead body the next morning, both Robert De Niro and Sergio Leone quickly skipped town. Leone finished his casting in New York and Italy. I never got my shot.

I bounced back and was called to a subtle office in West LA to discover I was reading for Brian DePalma, who was prepping a film called *Scarface* with Al Pacino. Producer Marty Bregman was there too. I read for the part of Sosa. Ultimately DePalma gave the Sosa role to Paul Shenar, who once portrayed Orson Welles. The very next day, I read for an equally impressive director, Bryan Forbes, for a *London Weekend* TV production of the *Phillip Marlow Project*. The character was described as: "Nasty smile, menacing soft voice, skinny pencil moustache, eye patch, hired killer, works for Mr. Big." I guess after working with Trevor Howard, Jack Hawkins, Richard Attenborough, Alan Bates, Kim Stanley, Laurence Harvey, Tom Courtenay and a King Rat era George Segal, Mr. Forbes wasn't duly impressed. I ended up with a beer commercial.

I still went to the Rainbow but often just for the parking-lot closing-time party. I usually parked in a loading zone across the street, picked up a quick late date or a party and scrammed out of there. Hustler magazine magnate Larry Flynt's wife Althea, portrayed by Courtney Love in *The People vs. Larry Flynt,* was a Rainbow regular and there that night. As usual, she was smashed out of her mind on pills and booze. I wasn't impressed by the booty-lot market and headed back to my car before I got a ticket. As I was about to climb in, I saw an out of control Rolls Royce backing out of the parking lot lickety-split and scattering pedestrians. It was taking dead aim at my car across the street. I dove for cover as the torpedo honed in. The noise of the metallic concussion wakened the zip code. The Roll's big rear end ruptured the driver's side of my Cadillac. Nonchalantly, Althea put the Rolls in forward and sped off west on Sunset toward their mansion in Bel Air. Notorious as she was, I had no trouble contacting her. I had a pitched battle with Neil Adelman at *Hustler's* legal department but finally got my car fixed. Althea started as a stripper and centerfold and then hustled herself all the way to co-publisher of *Hustler*; she died of an overdose and drowning a few years later.

Killing time, I hung out at Tony Roma's in Beverly Hills, a classy joint with a piano bar, show biz types and a sultry waitress I dated. It was my James Bond stage. Ellen Meyer put me up as a gay dress designer in *The Other Woman*. Sam Peckinpah kept the faith and brought me in for what would be his last film, *The Osterman Weekend*. I read for several of the major roles, but a typically competitive Peckinpah cast of Rutger Hauer, Burt Lancaster, John Hurt, Dennis Hopper, Craig T. Nelson and Chris Sarandon was tough to crack. Ivan Nagy popped up again, and I took a shot at his movie of the week, *Jane Doe* as yet another "crazy man killer." Laird Studios had me up for the role of a "homosexual Warhol type director." I was much more engaged by Bobby McGee's Mission Viejo Redheads International, 12 to 5 in Orange County; I think I made a day of it. And then bingo!

I went to the same Paramount office held responsible for the *Friday the 13th* movies, but this was a comedy summer-camp movie. Fern Champion had me up for *Meatballs II*. The character was a bus driver who hated kids, but the part eventually went to Paul Reubens (Pee-wee Herman). I became Paladin, a paramilitary Sergeant, whose boss was Lieutenant Foxglove (John Larroquette) a gay militant whose boss was firebrand Colonel Hershy (Hamilton Camp). Ours was a hawkish boot camp for kids. Richard Mulligan was top billed as Giddy, the guy in charge of the good camp on the good side of the lake. Misty Rowe from *Class Reunion* was Fanny the sexy camp counselor who did the jiggy with counselor Archie Hahn. Kim Richards and John Mengatti were star-crossed lovers. Unexplainably, there was an alien from outer space signed up for the good camp. The location was in Santa Barbara County at the same lake and cabins as the *Friday the 13th* movies. Ken Weiderhorn directed. We stayed at a cornball motel in Buellton, and I relied on Paul Reuben for entertainment. He was fairly fresh out of the Groundlings Theatre on Melrose where he conjured up Pee-wee. He'd done a few parts, a waiter in *The Blues Brothers*, a desk clerk in *Cheech & Chong's Next Movie* and *Mork & Mindy*. By the time our film was released, he was working on *Pee-wee's Big Adventure*, the blockbuster movie directed by Tim Burton. The rest is history. Some of it good and some of it controversial, but Paul remained a good friend to me over the years.

Frank Mancuso had just been made president of Paramount's motion picture division. Michael Eisner was President and chief operating officer Barry Diller was CEO and Jeffrey Katzenberg was chief of marketing. How's that for an executive dream team!

I spent Christmas Eve at Fox meeting with Terry Liebling and Mel Brooks for his next movie *To Be or Not to Be*. I read for Hitler. They liked my audition enough to entrust me with the complete script over the holidays. Not so festive, I grew a Hitler moustache and had to wear it on New Year's Eve. Mel Brooks decided to play Hitler himself.

I ran freely with Jay Brown and his actor friend Terry Kiser, the dead guy in *Weekend at Bernie's*. I also worked with an Olvera Street ensemble that gamboled to corral funds for a Hispanic charity.

I was growing a beard but quickly shaved when I was called to meet with Jim Wynorski, who was doing his first feature film, *The Lost Empire*. Wynorski went on to become famous for B-films like *Hard to Die, Chopping Mall, Deathstalker II, The Return of the Swamp Thing, Sorority House Massacre, The Wasp Woman*. Well, you get the idea. He also gained a reputation for busty babes and still has it. The *Lost Empire* was rampant with outrageous publicity: "A chamber of horrors, the secret island fortress of the mysterious Dr. Sin Do and the land of an undead wizard! A world filled with beautiful and sensuous women! A world threatened by sorcery and unstoppable evil forces!" Raven De La Croix was one of those beautiful women. Equally attractive was top billed Melanie Vincz as Angel Wolfe, an undercover cop. I was Prager, the bad cop. Veteran character actor Kenneth Tobey was my boss; he'd worked in the original *The Thing, Billy Jack* and *The Candidate* with Redford. In Chinatown my rookie partner was Tommy Rettig, who once played the little boy on the TV series *Lassie*.

We shot interiors at Roger Corman's Millennium studio in Venice, but mostly on location like the secret dungeon in Griffith Park's caves, embellished with caged and unclad women and a fake gorilla. It was late into night and everybody was exhausted. Now in my evil alter-ego black-clad getup, I was ravaging one of the blonde bimbo victims, played by rookie actress Linda Shayne who was struggling with her emotionless acting. Wynorski stopped her and said to put some life into it. On the next take, she came at me with an authentic knee to my groin; I writhed in horrific pain and was sent to the medic. Back at the studio, I finally confronted my arch enemy Angel Wolfe in the Dr. Sin Do laboratory for an epic battle to the death. I was beating the tar out of the beautiful blonde leading lady, but she rebounded and landed a few good punches. We were punishing each other with great satisfaction but inadvertently banged into a mounted laser gun that suddenly whipped around blowing up the evil hideaway. Zapping at will, the out-of-control hot pink ray blasted me right in the nuts. My genitalia couldn't catch a break. I disintegrated in flames.

Next up, Mary Ann Barton Casting sent me to Paramount for *Cracker Bros.*, a send up on the Marx Brothers from Sid and Marty Krofft (*H.R. Pufnstuf, Land of the Lost*). I don't think it ever happened. You'd be surprised how many costly projects never make it to the big or small screens. Sheila Manning had me up for a "tall dark thin outrageous Bowie - Jagger type" for a Pacific Telephone commercial. I got a call back but no schnitzel. Producer Mike Trikilis tried to do a *Gambler* sequel for me. Franz and Feldheimer talked to me about an NBC daytime project.

Violet and her clove cigarettes took me to Magic Mountain. Rhythm Lounge the next night. With Violet back in LA we were comfortably dating again.

No rest for the wicked, I read for Joel Schumacher, who wrote and directed *Capitol Cab* at Universal, with Jon Peters and Peter Guber as executive producers. It was later changed to *D.C. Cab* for legal reasons. I read for the Angel of Death no less, but did not capture the role. I auditioned for a film called *Surf II* which had no predecessor. Its quirky screenwriter was Randall Badat. They liked me enough to keep me involved with the project, and I even bleached my black hair blond to be a realistic surfer named Johnny. The project couldn't get much traction in the sand and seemed to slip away. A year later they did the film with Eddie Deezen and Eric Stoltz.

I took a spin at *T. J. Hooker* for Rick Husky at TBS as Ernie a little banty rooster, and I had a swing at *Lonely Guy,* a Steve Martin romantic comedy at Universal for Arthur Hiller. Casting director Caro Jones riled me up for a few minutes with the Martin Ritt project *Roadshow* that included Jack Nicholson and Timothy Hutten. Restless Scott McClintock had moved into a bulletproof downtown condo with a new old lady and the same old paranoia. My Jennifer Mayo turned 18 on May 1, 1983.

Cole Dammett age 14.

Chapter 33: The Joker of Clubs & Alison Queen of Hearts

Anthony continued to tag his name on the streets. The messiah wandered Hollyhood and broke bread with the underbellies. He robbed the sanctimonious and gave to the incorrigibles. Underground clubs were his beat. He crashed pads, shared an apartment on Formosa and another on Hudson. For a while, he stayed in an old office building on Hollywood Boulevard that rented out rooms to private eyes, scam artists and musicians. Tomata du Plenty threw a party there one Sunday afternoon and I came. Anthony was there too. And Alison, a very young girl we both seemed to like on first sight. I don't think either of us realized she was only 16. Alison Ridgway was a cultress for the Cure. Punk was passé and new wave wasn't. Robert Smith had been sworn in as the new boss. Alison and her Gothic advocates were devoted fans, and Siouxsie was their Queen. Alison had black hair, black make up and black glamour. I figured I had a shot. I chattered her up while Anthony glanced ominously from across the party-strewn floor. I had been cast in *Magnum P.I.*, the popular Tom Selleck show in Hawaii, and they had offered me either one first-class flight or two coach tickets to the Islands. I had just met Alison, but I asked her if she'd like to go with me to Hawaii. Her family had come from England, and her UK ties had opened a promising friendship with Robert Smith. Unfortunately, the Cure was coming to LA at the same conflicting time as my *Magnum P.I.* gig. Realistically, I didn't expect to subvert roly-poly Robert, but I asked that she consider it and gave her my number. Dot was at that party too but soon moved to Texas.

Although *Magnum P.I.* was a prestigious coup, I also came close to nailing a big role in 20th Century Fox's *Johnny Dangerously*. The script had been languishing for years but had new life and expectations now that Amy Heckerling had signed on. She was fresh off her remarkable debut with *Fast Times at Ridgemont High*, the movie that made Sean Penn a star. Michael Keaton was starring as a Cagneyesque gangster in a comedy spoof of the 30s genre. He had skyrocketed to stardom after his scene-stealing performances in *Night Shift*, at the expense of star billed Henry Winkler, and he'd also cleaned up with *Mr. Mom*. I had a promising private meeting with Amy for the part of Dutch, Johnny's boyhood sidekick, but it ultimately went to Mark Jantzen. As it turned out, it didn't thrill the critics.

Alison called and I invited her over to my Hancock apartment. She didn't have a license to drive so she brought a friend who did. We got in some trouble that night and dumped the overdosed friend off at a 24-hour medical clinic. We hid in the bushes until she was released. Alison's mainstream family lived in the Valley, but their dark daughter ran loose on this side of the hill, where almighty Goth godmother Julifer de Winter had a Hollywood dwelling for lost souls. She was intelligent, tall, slender, white as the page I'm writing on and a performance artist with a love of Oscar Wilde. I could marry somebody like that. The godmother didn't like me at all though, and she had her own ideas for Alison. She was a Siouxsie mother hen.

Alison agreed to go to Hawaii with me. I was pretty stoked about doing the show but even more excited about spending a week and change with Alison. *Magnum P.I.* spent five years in the top 20, and the CBS stalwart ran unbroken from 1980 to 88 with 162 episodes. It aired in 35 countries. Tom Selleck played a dashing and resourceful private eye who had a crew of heterogeneous helpers who worked out of a convenient millionaire's mansion. Magnum drove a Ferrari 308 GTS that was another revered character.

We flew out of LAX and landed in Honolulu. Staff picked us up at the airport and drove us straight to the set. The director brought us to Tom Selleck's office for an informal meeting. The night before, his 15-year-old son had driven Tom's jeep off the ledge of a parking ramp. Selleck was in the passenger seat and injured his hand and shoulder, which of course I did not know. I eagerly rushed up to him and vigorously shook his hand—his injured hand. That got us off to a shaky start. Later at lunch he gave me dirty looks, but I think it was more about young Alison than the hand jive.

An assistant drove Alison and lucky me to the Colony Surf Hotel, and we checked in. We got the super-duper royal treatment which had me perplexed. Who got what mixed up? The bell hop took us up the elevator, and it didn't stop until we ran out of room at the penthouse. He opened our door and it was a billionaire's lair. We had a 359 degree view of the ocean, Honolulu, Diamond Head and the beaches. The place was stocked with libations and expensive foods. There was a fruit basket the size of my old VW.

I was a top billed guest star and for once wasn't the scurrilous scruffy desperado. This time I was a wealthy and sophisticated crime boss with fine tastes, who lived in luxury. The script introduced me as: "William Skuler is an Ichabod Crane character; tall, lanky, praying-mantis like. He's dressed in silk pajamas, smoking jackets and kung-fu shoes…all black." The other top guest star was pint-size Cork Hubbert who played an ex-CIA midget who ultimately fought me in a climactic karate battle. "Waldo flies into action. He's a whirling-dervish of Oriental martial arts. There's only one person in the world more skilled than he. Unfortunately, it's William Skuler!" Stunt coordinators Bob Minor and Tom Lupo did their best to whip us into competency with a crash course in karate. We destroyed the set and our reputations. Aside from the unusual karate moves, I did well and back home I got an appreciative letter from the producer Doug Benton on a job well done.

As soon as I got back on the mainland, I scored another pay check as Joe, a Vietnam veteran in the MGM Television production *For Love and Honor* that had tones of Taylor Hackford's film *An Officer and a Gentleman*. Our cast featured Cliff Potts, Yaphet Kotto, Keenen Ivory Wayans, Kelly Preston, my *Class Reunion* target Shelley Smith and John Mengatti from *Meatballs II*. It aired on NBC.

As usual, my warped brain was searching out the latest hot spots and coolest clubs. LA was a wealth of endless pleasure. The tour starts in February '81. There was a gentle rouge-and-frilly-lace rebellion against the rude punk-couture. Guys and gals got dollied up with fine linen and hair high on gel and embraced new romantic and UK dance pop. The Veil was its first home, even if it was a bit rough itself. It started on Monday nights at the Cathay de Grande in the basement of a Chinese restaurant inspired by Steve Stange's Blitz club in London. In no time flat, it was full of flocking birds and dapper dudes. Early trendsetters Chris Trent, Dave Grave, Danny Shades and Reuben Blue paraded about on the sidewalk in front, unwary beacons that attracted new converts.

A big fellow named Dobbs and his partner Michael Brennan had been booking rock bands in that basement venue while the Chinese owner marveled at the spectacle, but now the cuisine had taken on a tasty new twist, at least on Monday nights. The Veil promoters and DJs were Henry Peck and Joseph Brookes from San Francisco; they had already shaken up Melrose with a new record store swinging the same sweet music. The store was Vinyl Fetish. Henry and Joseph ordered up the trendiest imported singles from England and a faction ready for something new to dance to. A raw young band with a penchant for bad spelling and behavior called Motley Crue did an in-store to promote their first independent album and bedlam ensued. Vinyl Fetish took its rightful place on Melrose's eclectic strip with other hip shops like Retail Slut, Aardvark and Let it Rock.

The Veil thrived and added another night on Friday, but like a stuck-up bitch she left her sweetheart deal for a better looking venue to strut her peacock feathers. Cathay de Grande went back to basics, and the Veil dropped in on Sunset Boulevard at the newly restored but still moribund venue formerly known as Soul'd Out. Owner Dave Kelsey coined it Club Lingerie. The Veil nights energized the new club, and when former Masque-eteer Brendan Mullen took over booking the Lingerie, it exploded. Now it staked out a big chunk of Hollywood's nightlife. With customers like Jagger, Dylan, Bowie, Springsteen, Depp, Sting, Prince, Bono, Waites, Cage and fast Eddy Murphy, it was a nice place to hang. The blast-off bar scene in *48 Hrs.* with Eddy Murphy was shot at the Lingerie.

Jay Brown and his girlfriend Sherry were frequent adventurers at Club Lingerie, and it was always on my schedule. Long lines persisted so I made friends with the door guys Dave and Jason; they'd get me around those lines and past door one. Then the gauntlet got tougher. The money collector was Melvis, a tall exotically attractive woman with muscles and a shock of blonde hair that had all the flamboyance of Billy Idol and Flock of Seagulls' Mike Score meets Alfalfa from *Our Gang*. I could afford the entries, but there was a certain prestige to getting in for free. I pretty much had it down at every club in town, and by now so did Anthony.

Another hip spot was The Fake Club on Cahuenga just north of the Hollywood Actors Theatre. Owned by Paul Fortune, it was a regular hangout for the Gang of Four *I love a Man in a Uniform* set and that included Jay and Blackie too. On a lucky night, we got cozy with Susan Sarandon and Kristy McNichol in one of the club's leatherette booths. Another night, I wandered into the rear lounge and found my underage son all by himself and reasonably well dressed, leaning on the bar. He had snuck in the back door. The kid had mastered the art of walking backward into movie theaters to avoid paying and used the same m.o. to get past ID checkers at clubs. He was swigging out of a Chivas Regal bottle he had hidden in his overcoat. He swiped it when the bartender wasn't looking. I missed my boy and was sentimental for the old days. There were places Anthony didn't have to sneak in; he had cultivated several club-owner friends. He was a player, and so was Scream.

Scream! The long and winding road of this resilient club started next door to the Lingerie in the Hollywood Athletic Club and was the brain child of DJs Mike Stewart and Bruce Purdue. Scream had an upscale opening in a lobby full of billiard tables, champagne and d'oeuvres; and I was there right from the start. But Scream wasn't comfortable dressed in argyle sweaters and soon found its rightful, disheveled hip clothing in the cavernous underground areas of the Embassy Hotel on 9th Street downtown. You could have hidden Cleveland in there and still have room for Louie Anderson. Bands like Jane's Addiction and RHCP would soon play there. In fact, that was the birth of a rivalry between those upstart

LA dueling bandfighters. As Scream evolved, they migrated to Park Plaza in an equally gigantic space of three different large auditoriums, two up and one down and a staircase to make Tara's look like a stepstool in a sleeping car on The Wabash Cannonball. The brass-and-glass lobby itself held revelers by the hundreds, content to stake out an overstuffed couch or a phone booth nook for nookie. The Park Plaza was originally one of those Moose Masonic Elks Club Grand Poo-Bah secret society joints. It was ultra ornate with marble floors and massive chandeliers. Whenever the cops showed up, they either got trampled or lost in the massive crowd and were never found. There were endless secret rooms to explore and find uses for. The lines to get in were endless, but I knew the right door dame Dayle Gloria, a sweetheart who was always accommodating. She adopted Anthony too. There was another roving club called Scream Parlour that set up fly by night speakeasy shops around town and in your nightmares. We could scream to our hearts delight.

Scream got competition from Power Tools, a new club that drew the same crowd and even the likes of Andy Warhol and David Bowie. Matt Dike and Jon Sidel started out in a warehouse on Washington Ave., miles from Hollywood in a fairly dark and sketchy area. Power Tools was one of the first clubs where Anthony and I would meet on equal footing; he knew Matt and Jon even better than I did. Colliding in the same club, we often found ourselves awkwardly un-reconciled. Like all the transient clubs, Tools eventually moved from squalor and its upset landlords to better nights and sweeter deals at the Park Plaza. In between honky-tonk permits, Matt Dike experimented with a more intimate club, the Nairobi Room in the residue of a former Caribbean motif. Opening night was pretty quiet; Matt thanked me for coming, sat me down and bought me a drink. Revved-up, he revealed the new record business he was putting together. It would become the Delicious Vinyl label, and his first success was Tone Loc's rap cover of "Wild Thing" which became a huge national hit. Another of his biggies was The Young MC hit "Busta Move" with Flea providing bass.

The Stardust was either an old ballroom or meteor void on Sunset and Western. Henry and Joseph did MIX there. Flippers opened a skating nightclub in an old roller derby on SM and La Cienega; Prince made his LA debut there in April '81. Henry did the glam Goth 'Fetish' club around town. The Brave Dog *was* downtown. Anthym played there in '81. Lhasa did the boogaloo too; Henry Rollins did his violent performance art there. The Dirt Box and Station also moved in the cover of night. When Adam Ant and his Ants played at the Cathay de Grande, the pre-Rollins punk band Black Flag spray painted over the Ant's posters: *Black Flag kills Ants.* Eventually though, the warriors of punk lost the ideological war to the genteel vampires of glam.

But it was the Zero that ruled the late night. Dark as Dante's Inferno. Mardi gras morals and flagrant fashion, it gave scandalous a good name. The infamous out-of-bounds dive was a creation of club maestro John Pochna, The Joker of Clubs. The Salvador Dali of nightlife. He was a dashing charismatic gentleman with the heart of a benevolent philanthropist. He was a Pied Piper and a galvanizer. By law, LA bars closed at 2 a.m. The contrarian Zero *opened* at 2 a.m. It was so verboten the foxy den was constantly on the run. Its first location was 1955 N. Cahuenga, hiding under the Hollywood freeway like a party in Hitler's bunker. It had been established in the year of our lore, August 1980, but avoided my attention at first. There was a hip quotient to finding these gems. I made my appearance in the second act and so did Anthony. It was another of the places we competed. It's where I first met the seductive Pinky Braightwate. She welcomed me into her campy operetta apartment, a swollen black-and-pink kiss from the Zero.

In March of '83, Pochna moved the Zero to the corner of Wilcox and Hollywood above Playmates, a sexy lingerie store that catered to strippers, hookers and some of my girlfriends. The police station was on Wilcox too, a couple blocks away, and we'd peer derisively through blacked-out windows at cop cars hustling back and forth in pursuit of justice. There were no age restrictions, so Anthony was downing cheap cans of beer with the rest of us. By now I was familiar with the door dudes and easily got past their muscled barbed-wire-barrier strategy to screen the good, the bad and the ugly. Reuben Blue was a gossip-rag Jimmy Olson snapping shots like it was the Stork Club. He stapled Xeroxed pages and called it *Scratch*. Eventually, he got high on tech, and *Scratch* evolved into a viable record of our antics and atrocities. The Zero was his beat, and he chronicled our nightlife.

I was dating a sweet young blonde with the political titular of Tori. I introduced her Wild West best friend Jennifer Bruce to Anthony as we cavorted on a landing of the stairway to the roof. He was 86'd for having sex with her on the roof. Cupid shot them up, and they became a fiery couple for a minor millennium. It was his first live-with alliance. Their first home together was a funny little bungalow on a runt of a trail called Banner off Vine Street, surrounded by fruit trees, weeds and litter that helped obscure it from reality. Together they wandered into drug addiction.

John Pochna's landlord pulled the rug out from over the Playmates. City hall had put pressure on the owner to close down the Wilcox Zero as Los Angeles prepared for the '84 Olympics. Ex-cop Mayor Bradley put the kibosh on punk porn rotten clubs to make Hollywood tolerable for the Olympic Committee and the expected throngs. Our boss was in a bind, the Zero fraternity was in need of a fix and the cops weren't getting enough overtime. Something had to happen. David Lee Roth happened. Van Halen was an LA institution and a powerful force for evil in town. When they returned from touring, Roth was dismayed to find his favorite late-night spot had been scrubbed off the map. He had always been a defiant night owl, and I used to run into him at all-night chuck wagons in the Valley and that 24 hour Norm's with the orange leather banquettes on Olympic and La Cienega. David Lee Roth helped John find and finance a new Zero on Vine and Fountain. We were whole again. Let the party begin again. The bare bones joint was irreverently raucous and sported underground noise like Wall of Voodoo, Killing Joke, T.S.O.L., The Mentors, Top Jimmy and the Rhythm Pigs, Tex and the Horseheads, Circle Jerks, Blasters, Tupelo Chain Sex and Taquila Mockingbird gigging at four in the morning. Theatre of the absurd performance artists like Joanna Went played to a packed nightmare. Reigning queens and nubile notables of the night prowled the double rooms, breaking hearts.

The come-and-go staff of Paul Dancer, Jason and Merrill Ward were stalwart celebs themselves, Solomonesque arbitrators of who got in at the bottom of the stairs. On the dark side, they had to endure combat, evade riot squads and take the heat when the shit hit the fan. The cocktail-chasing barmaids were just as vulnerable. One night we were having a rip roar when the code cracking LAPD arrived in a bevy of black and whites. The gateway guys locked the speakeasy door and ran upstairs. They turned off the lights and asked us to be quite as church mice. A couple hundred drunk and rowdy zeros hugged the floor and didn't make a peep, but finally the law busted in and arrested our leaders.

A block away a big Samoan dude, recently paroled from a murder rap, got into an argument with his 17-year-old sister and shot her dead. Neighbors called the police, but all the Hollywood cop cars were busy handcuffing the Zero. Remorseful, the killer waited for the keystone cops but finally got antsy and drove away. A couple days later, his conscience got the best of him and he turned himself in at the Eureka Police Station. The Zero bust and murder were linked for the life of the news story. Paul, Jason, Big Charlie, Marcie Malibu and Earache went to jail. Fortunately, Pochna had a good lawyer.

The Zero walls had always been splattered with avant-garde paintings long before their appreciation. John Pochna was a dedicated patron of the silent poetry of art. When there were raids, the police would confiscate the art as evidence of our debauchery. David Lee Roth brought MTV host Mark Goodman up to the Zero one night while he was in LA on assignment. He was thoroughly terrorized by the imminent torment and the smell of billy clubs. After a two year run on Vine, the Zero moved back to her base on the top floor of a Hollywood Boulevard building. The dowager was on its last run, and her clientele moved on to the next big thing. The masquerade had sobered up. It would lock the doors in '88. It had become more about artistry in the latter years, and John Pochna went on to build a thriving business in art galleries. Today his Zero One Gallery downtown is a major competitor. He's still at it, my friend the artful Jolly Roger dodger.

Zero extraordinaire Debbie Diamond was a beautiful blonde and one of the most desirable young ladies in Hollywood. She fronted a band and was covered with boyfriends. I met her at the pool hall on Western and Hollywood. We struck it off and dated for kicks. We were quite the image when we'd make our entrance into clubs and beds. After a nice while, we made our exit. I read for Stephen King's *Firestarter* at Universal with casting director Johanna Ray. She said it would shoot in August so I bought the book and started reading. It was going to be Drew Barrymore's first movie since *E.T.*

A new strip joint called the Kit Kat Club with occasional rock bands opened on Santa Monica Boulevard across the street from the Hudson Theatre. I perused the old Masonic Lodge to audition with the new Hollywood Center for the Performing Arts. They were offering repertories in theatre, dance and musical theatre. Now it's the ABC home of *Jimmy Kimmel Live*. I had a clean shot at the Jacqueline Bisset project *Get There*, but misfired. Scott McClintock broke up with his girl and downtown fortress after he was robbed at gunpoint. Joe Naar introduced me to Blake Edwards.

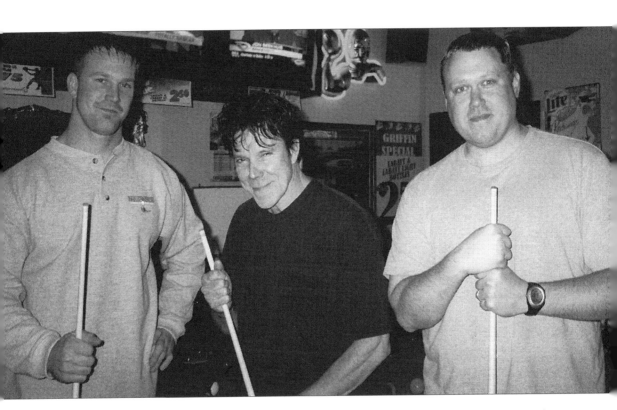

Brett Anderson and Scott Miller...Hearts as big as their muscles.

Taylor and James in Atlanta. James got the chicken pox and we were all in fear.

Foo Fighters at Slane in Ireland. Anthony, Taylor Hawkins and Dave Grohl.

Anthony Kiedis and Johnny Frusciante.

Guy Oseary and Anthony in London. And thanks to super photographer Tony Woolliscroft.

Chapter 34: Red Hot Chili Peppers

National Lampoon, Berlin, Dr. Detroit, Magnum, Meatballs, and *The Lost Empire;* I was *White Heat* on top of the world, Pa. But while I was working some minor movie magic, Anthony was laying the groundwork to re-engineer music. My revolutionary son was about to smash through the Sistine ceiling. While he had been mastering smoke and shadow skullduggery on the back lot of life and rope-a-doping an interim, he finally got down to dirty business and waxed poetic. Succeeding his ancestors, Anthony fostered a melodic Kiedis narrative in a new and furious form that defined him, maligned him and ultimately enshrined him. The tale is well told. At Fairfax High School, Israeli-born Hillel Slovack and homegrown Jack Irons flirt with music and fantasize creating a band not unlike their heroes, KISS. Hillel studies rudimentary guitar and Jack takes drum lessons. They add an accomplished musician, Chilean-born Alain Johannes, who can sing and play guitar. After an early bass player drops out, Australian-born Flea is groomed to play bass; they drop Chain Reaction and Anthem and become Anthym.

New influences like Queen, Zeppelin and Hendrix filter into their music. Flea injects a classical jazz twist from his stepfather. They play at school lunch periods and work their way to small venues. Anthony is the cheerleader rallying the troops to drop their peanut-butter-and-jelly sandwiches and listen. He does my Gary Myrick intro and then jumps off the stage and dances up a storm invigorating the audience to join in. He's the fifth Anthym.

Anthony never learned an instrument or sang especially well, or he would have certainly been more involved. Eventually Anthym opened for established bands at the Starwood and other Hollywood clubs. They appropriately changed names again to What is This. Flea had already busted off once to join punk band Fear and later flirted with Johnny Rotten's Public Image Limited. The direction of their music looked like a road map of roundabouts. Music *itself* was in turmoil with no dominating genre in control and newcomer hip-hop rap had captured an early niche. Flea and Anthony were quickly converted, especially by the likes of Defunkt, Grandmaster Flash and the Furious Five. Anthony had been writing poetry all along and had a repertoire. It was a combustible kismet at the right place and time. By a twister of fate, they mixed AK's rap poem lyrics with Hillel, Flea and Jack's guitar, bass and drums and came up with a one-night spin off, under the rock alias of "Tony Flow and the Miraculously Majestic Masters of Mayhem."

Of all the thousands of rag tag bars in LA, the slender hang out in a Hispanic neighborhood called the Grandia Room on Melrose just east of Vine was the last place you'd expect to find the manger. By day and most nights, it was just an unpretentious pub the size and proportion of a railroad car. One night a week, an entrepreneurial hustler took it over and turned it into the Rhythm Lounge, which booked cabaret artists and underground bands to perform on a tiny platform in the southwest corner. I was a fan of the Lounge and went quite often. The door stop and the barmen knew me well. I usually scored an ample dumpling, even if the acts were only mediocre. Cheap became priceless on that memorable Thursday night in February 1983 when the dynamics of music changed dramatically and altered the balance of the LA scene. Anthony's friend Gary Allen had been booked to do some arty curiosity and wanted a roguish opening act. He asked Anthony, who was known for his wild and crazy antics, to conceive an act of vaudeville and gave him free reign to put something together.

Put and together became history. Empowered by acid and adrenalin, the act attack was Anthony rapping his street poem *Out in L.A.* with Hillel, Jack and Flea playing new funky riffs. It snuck up and bit the audience like a cagey mosquito. It happened as fast as a mugging. One hot minute of frenzy that evaporated shots of cheap booze on the bar, and when it stopped so did everybody's heart. The city went into cardiac arrest until the next week when the newly-coined Red Hot Chili Peppers did a Rhythm Lounge encore with two songs! The city of angels breathed a sigh of relief and begged for more. *LA Weekly* and the underground buzz were all over the wild fire; suddenly my kid was the biggest thing in LA.

The third show was at Cathay de Grande on March 5, 1983. I brought Violet and we were both dressed in vogue, befitting the significance of the event. Anthony wore an orange baseball cap, a paisley suit coat, over a second suit coat and a contrasting paisley shirt. His girlfriend, Jennifer Bruce, was there in equal sartorial distress. Anthony was quietly confident and in good spirits, but as the large crowd continued to push in for a look at this miracle band, the more he was put on the spot. Expectations were exalted, and the band delivered. I was beside myself, and so were Violet and the guy who spilled beer on my Italian suit. Afterward, we hung out in the minuscule dressing room while noted LA photographer Gary Leonard captured the history.

The phenomenon had begun in earnest. They played 1 a.m. sets under the underground and knocked up makeshift anti-clubs. The encore was insomnia. Voracious mandates pistol whipped RHCP onto the menu at The Lingerie, Rhythm Lounge again, Cathay again, Green on Red, the Anti-Club and Wayzata's gigs. Jay Brown had gone to some of the shows with me and, like everybody else, was impressed. Jay introduced me to his friend Mark Richardson who knew a thing or two about band management. Three and he was sold. In April, Jay and Mark and I planned a meeting with the Chili Peppers at my house, but the band was a no show. After a capricious holding the bag pattern, we got our meeting, and Mark agreed to record some RHCP demos. With Hillel and Jack still concentrating on What Is This, the progress was often stifled, but on May 5th they went into Mark's studio and recorded the first ever RHCP vinyl demo. *Out in LA, Get Up and Jump, Green Heaven, Sex Rap and Baby Appeal.*

They played at the Plant, an important Valley venue on Ventura Boulevard, with headlining Minutemen, who were early influences on the young band. The Mutants were on the bill too. Two weeks later, they played the Fiesta House on East Olympic Boulevard, between the hilly tits of Boyle Heights and East LA. Multi-colors from their Hollywood base, the fresh sound oozed out in concentric rings across our cosmopolis. Fiesta House was a mixed culture club with a punk attitude, and I met a tall, raven haired beauty who put a strangle hold on my heart and kept me coming back to the barrio.

The China Club was a hip new restaurant on Third that I frequented for their cagey cuisine and lively bar. Business was booming, and there were long lines to get in on the action. They bought an adjoining building and added a second dining room. The inscrutable Chinese proprietors took advantage of the buzz and cleared out part of the new addition for eclectic musical acts ranging from classical to rock and now, the Red Hot Chili Peppers. As an entrenched China Club charter member, I was accustomed to snapping up impromptu liaisons, but for this special evening I brought the oriental delicacy of Violet. A succinct musical review on that May evening put it in a nut shell fortune cookie: "One of the wildest new ensembles to shake up the LA scene." One rattled waiter was all shook up enough to drop a platter of Chop Suey.

I was an ad hoc promoter and fanned the hype. The band's fresh success and my own cocksure repertoire had me pumped up as the child in me that once dared to imagine this payoff. I marshaled my forces and recruited fans. I flew Alan Bashara in from Grand Rapids to see the show at the Anti-Club on June 17. Dot was back from Texas and came in from the desert. The once-pale punk was tanned and wore turquoise. Jay brought VIPs. Weaver had my back. The Alley Cats headlined and "the disruptive, sexy, whiteboy psycho-funk" Red Hot Chili Peppers were second billed, but we had a fanatical following that made us headliners regardless of billing. Flea, Jack and Hillel came out first and warmed up the crowd. After a beat, Anthony came bounding out of the bed-sheet wings and infiltrated the medusa of amp cords. He was wearing a cut tuxedo and a bowler cap. As his fancy footwork snuck through the hazardous obstacles, he tripped but still managed to revamp the gaffe into a gymnastic flip onto the slightly lower stage. His bowler cap flew high into the air, and, as he landed perfectly on his feet, the cap came down right on his head. The kid was ordained.

More June tunes and they reprised Cathay de Grande. The Vex in East LA was next to get the treatment. "Shirtless, funky, sexy and chaotic, these crazed hypo-teens slam their instruments into James Brown overdrive while throwing their bodies around like Mexican jumping beans. Color them intense!" says the *LA Weekly's* Pleasant Gehman. They go back stage at *The Slam Dunk Junk Bunk Longest Night Fright Show* and do a cappella routines for their inspirational heroes, Grandmaster Flash and his Furious Five. Reportedly, the Flash was enthusiastic about the Chilis' spicy raps.

The third of July witnessed a controversial incident that burnished their bad boy image but diverted attention from the bright new music to an impromptu act of spectacle that gave negative ammunition to the mainstream critics. There was an open-minded sexuality to their music that wasn't surprising, considering my impassioned influences. It all exploded that night at the infamous Kit Kat Club. It was a place I was fluent with; I was dating two of the current dancers. The club booked bare-chested machismo rock bands to alternate with naked girls on the runways. They'd never seen the likes of the Peppers though, or their rabid fans. The opening band was Roid Rogers and the Whirling Butt Cherries. Finally, Red Hot Chili Peppers hit the stage and did their usual madcap show. Intrinsically provocative already, the band had their testosterone in a higher gear. They finished the set and scrambled to their tiny makeshift dressing room to await applause and their encore. Anthony felt slightly upstaged by the dancers' ability to draw wandering eyes from the band, and he convinced the guys to take it to another level. They got completely naked, pulled tube sox onto their cocks and balls and went on stage to perform the ribald encore. Flea's sock kept falling off, and the girls in the front row scrambled to pull Anthony's off. Once again, they were the talk of the town.

On July 18, just five months from the day they put this pepper patch together in Flea's living room, they opened for the mighty Washington D.C. band Bad Brains, whose hard-core punk and reggae had made them a national force. Unfortunately, the Lingerie was 21-and-over, which deprived RHCP of their contemporary commandos. A review raved about their hot, taut, James Brown-derived rift but wasn't keen on the adolescent horseplay. Back in their element, they headlined Jim Van Tyne's first anniversary of Theoretical, the ever-evolving music party that landed in the cozy confines of Al's Bar. This time they're "zany, volatile and disruptive punksters." Anthony's sexual Olympics at the Zero made it into the newspapers, and they headlined The Plant. The show turned into one of the club's busiest nights ever, with a generous helping of celebs. I went North with the band to open for Bad Brains at the Warwick Theatre in San Francisco.

I hardly ever missed a gig. After all the negative commotion about my fathering, I was finally vindicated, at least with the show-business faction. Of course, the damned-if-you-do contingent wanted my blood for unleashing this phenomenal new music maker and his gang of buster that pummeled it into our senses.

By now, they had settled into a busy circuit of clubs in LA, Orange and San Bernardino County. They were bona fide local rock stars. Anthony was running with East German punk chanteuse Nina Hagen, a legitimate superstar. She recorded a song Anthony wrote for her. Flea was still fiddling with Fear. What is This still was. Mark Richardson made a concerted effort to sign them, but the band leaned toward a more experienced manager, and Mark found them Lindy Goetz. I went with Anthony and Flea to meet him at his West Hollywood apartment; soon the word around town was the Peppers were on the verge of signing with a major label.

The big league venues were The Forum, Sports Arena, Greek Theater, Shrine Auditorium, Santa Monica Civic, Palladium, Hollywood Bowl and Universal Amphitheater. Anthony had become accustomed to his new fame, but he was still excited enough to drive over and tell me they were going to play the Universal Amphitheater. A world-famous venue, Frank Sinatra had played there the week before. Alan Bashara's Viet Nam partner Larry Vallon was the boss there now. They'd be opening for Danny Elfman's Oingo Boingo, an international band with a fervent following. A proud papa, I secretly bought two roundtrip airline tickets to London England for Flea and Anthony, a gift for all he had accomplished in just six amazing months. I would save the surprise until after the show.

I invited my agent. I hadn't forgotten Anthony's acting tour de force performance in *Dames at Seas*; maybe he'd be interested in repping him. While La Rocca was parking in my VIP spot below, Anthony was climbing onto the Amphitheater's roof and running amok high above Universal City. Staff security lured him down with some raw meat, and the police arrested him. The venue was so pissed off they cancelled our show, but Larry Vallon and Danny Elfman negotiated a salvaged set and guards kept them on a short leash. We did our opening act, but most of the crowd hadn't taken their seats yet. When they did arrive, the Oingo Boingo crowd booed us. According to Vallon, the lobby concessions applauded RHCP for driving people out of the auditorium and into their eateries. Nina Hagen went on stage to a big applause and sang a song with Anthony. When our set was over, I ran backstage and presented the tickets to London. The band had a few commitments, including another concert with Oingo Boingo in Pomona, but soon Anthony and Flea flew to

England where they made friends with a Brit named Gavin Bowden, who would marry Flea's sister and later direct the band's documentary *Funky Monks*. Anthony and Flea got innovative and squeezed in a quick visit to France. Like father like son.

EMI offered us a record deal. The time had finally come to decide who they were. Hillel and Jack chose to sign with MCA as What is This. Red Hot Chili Peppers signed with EMI. We hired drummer Cliff Martinez and a screwball guitar player named Jack Sherman. Flea officially quit Fear, and Anthony remained with his one and only band. Now bona fide recording artists, they went to work at EMI headquarters on Sunset across from Hollywood High.

Mel Gibson and Blackie Dammett are the lethal weapons.

Chapter 35: A Fall Guy for the Cotton Club

I went to Zoetrope Studios for a meeting about Francis Ford Coppala's *The Cotton Club*. They're looking for gangsters. I knock 'em dead. They set up an interview with Fred Roos in New York, but I had almost a month. Fernando Valenzuela kept us tuned into the Dodgers. Jay Brown was working on a television show called *Shake it Sexy* at Metromedia. Naturally, I dated one of the sexy shakers. I often went to auditions at BCI casting on Cahuenga and knew that layout well. I had a reading for the CBS Children's movie *Dirkham Detective Agency* as one of a couple crooks breaking into a veterinary; I was the dummy and my partner the brains. I find a little puppy and attempt to hide it from my evil twin. I brought Violet along and left her in the reception room with a real live puppy in her purse. At the prescribed time, she snuck over by the door to the audition room. On cue, I opened the door a crack and Violet slipped me the puppy. I turned to the director, cuddling the pup. I was part actor, part magician and partly skating on thin ice.

I read for the original *Police Academy* at the Ladd Company, auditioning as a borderline wacko security guard named Eugene Tackleberry, who had just been accepted into the academy and was on the last night of his old job. He hears a strange noise, kicks in a door and unloads his gun into a darkened office. Lights on, we discover he has blasted a surprise going-away party for him, a "Good Luck at the Police Academy" banner and a huge cake are shot all to pieces. His fellow workers crawl out from under cover. I liked to spice it up. I had Anthony waiting outside the casting room door with a prop cake full of bullet holes and a riddled banner. At the proper moment, Anthony entangled me in the frosting scenario and pushed me back into the room to do my shtick at the feet of a startled Hugh Wilson, who was directing. I had two call backs, but David Graf got the role of the recruit who couldn't stop shooting everything. He starred in all seven Police Academy films.

I did my most audacious audition at a twelve-story office building on Sunset. The opening sequence of the script and my audition piece was of a scuzzy killer, described as wearing a dirty white Beatle's suit, splattered with blood after a shoot-out. Most actors just come as they are. Anthony and I had gone to a Long Beach Flea Market a few weeks earlier, and he bought us both white double-breasted suits from a vendor who had a load of them. On the way home, we were laughing and wondering what had we been thinking! So for this audition I hauled out the suit and splashed it with bloody red dye. I had accumulated quite a set of movie prop guns and picked out a big caliber pistol and stuck it in my belt. I messed up my hair, tossed some dirt on my lapels, rubbed some blood and grime on my face and headed for the audition.

I parked a block away, walked into the lobby and over to the elevator. I pushed the button for the top floor. A lady came up behind me waiting for the same elevator. It arrived and we both stepped in, but as soon as she got a look at me, she quickly exited. I thought great; I look authentic. The elevator let me off at the top and I strode into the movie office. The receptionist at the counter got a kick out of my outfit, and I boasted how I had scared away a lady in the lobby. She said she could see why. They led me into the anteroom of the big wigs big office. The guy ahead of me reading for the same part did a double take. Inside, the director and producer were beaming and agreed it was the best moment of a long day. I had just started my reading when a secretary ran in and said there was a man with a gun loose in the building. LAPD declared a lockdown and they were doing a systematic floor-by-floor search. Next we heard a police helicopter circling the top of the building. Giggling employees surrounded me like mother hens and posted others at the elevator and stairway to explain it was an actor doing an audition. The cops poured in and the girls protected me until the situation could be explained. The SWAT team was miffed, but a few of the coppers got a good laugh and acknowledged my acting skills.

Not surprisingly, Scott McClintock moved again, this time to New York City. He'd stay at the McClintock Corporation's brownstone in Greenwich Village. Jessica kept a place there for herself when she was in New York. Scott would now have his own opulent apartment in the five-story building on Barrow Street. I spent considerable time packing and shipping all his stuff. Jay Brown celebrated a big birthday party. I put a wet towel on mine; I was twice as old as most of my friends and hoped those pesky birthdays would just fade away.

Auditions and grease paint I adored though, a *Sgt. Bilko* series, *Hear No Evil* for Rubin Canon at MGM and *Star Trek III* for Leonard Nimoy at Paramount. I had a power lunch with Art Metrano and writer-director Andy Sidaris for *Malibu Express*, a take-off on *Midnight Express,* the deadly-serious drug smuggling and imprisonment torture film that was shot in Turkey and shocked the world. The leering Sidaris cast featured Arlene, *redhead, sexually starved, provocative, and bitchy*; Lisa, *brunette, attractive, active and a smart-ass*; Contessa Foxe, *can't miss, kooky but she has it all*; June Khnockers, *beautiful voluptuous, blonde, race driver and sexually active*; Beverly, *slender, sexy, dark hair, moves like a panther, horny*; Maid Marian, *sexy, busty, not too bright*; Faye and Mae, *outrageous bodies, platinum blonde twins*. They may have started global warming. Incredibly, the comedy premiered in Islamic Turkey! Most of those girls came from La Rocca's Agency. He was known as the broker with the hottest super babes in town. His legitimate roster included Ken Barry, Bert Parks, Sonny Bono, Buster Crabbe, Victor Mature, Tony Curtis, Joseph Campanella, Robert F. Lyons, Frank Stallone, Perry King, Rip Taylor and Cassandra Peterson.

I flew to New York for my *Cotton Club* audition. Francis Ford Coppola was a mighty giant in the industry, and, like me, he was from Michigan and graduated from UCLA film school. When he was only 23, he made the classic chiller *Dementia 13*. He directed *Rumble Fish, The Conversation, Apocalypse Now, The Outsiders, The Godfather* and its sequels. He wrote *Patton*. He produced *American Graffiti* and all of this by 1983. Now he was directing Robert Evan's production of an expansive period piece, with an impressive cast of Richard Geer, Gregory Hines, Diane Lane, Lonette McKee, Laurence Fishburne, Bob Hoskins, Nicolas Cage, James Remar, Fred Gwynne, Gwen Verdon, Tom Waits, Mario Van Peebles and a young Sofia Coppola, who one day would win an Oscar for directing *Lost in Translation*. She was also Anthony's girlfriend for a time, and they collaborated on a film with Anthony and Debbie Harry as actors in *Sick*.

I went to a production office in Manhattan to meet Fred Roos, Coppola's long-time producer and right hand man. The script was a collaboration of Coppola, William Kennedy and Mario Puzo, who wrote *The Godfather*. The script was confidential, and I was going in blind. I had been sitting in the waiting room by myself for a while when another actor arrived and sat down on the couch across from me. He introduced himself as James Remar. Young, handsome and talented; James Remar had crashed into America's consciousness in *The Warriors* and a year later in *48 Hrs.* That was Nick Nolte's movie, but Eddie Murphy scorched the chemicals right off his celluloid debut. Remar left a powerful calling card too. In both roles he was exuberant, sexy and violent. Eddie Murphy became an instant superstar, and James Remar became one of those talented actors just below that threshold. He came up from the minors in TV with *Miami Vice* and *Hill Street Blues* and then films like *Drugstore Cowboy, The Phantom, Aliens, Blade, Sex and the City* and as Michael C. Hall's father in Showtime's *Dexter.* But today in this unpretentious office, the young man was waiting to confer with Fred Roos about Dutch Schultz, the antagonist in Coppola's gangster movie full of bad guys. I explained my blind mission and professed a fear of the dark. Remar, however, had a well-worn script full of earmarks and scribbles. "Here's my script, you can look at it if you want," he said and tossed it across the room to me. The secretary called him in, and I sped read for a flavor of the style or a moment of truth. When James came out, I returned his script; he gave me encouragement and left. The next time I'd see James Remar, I'd be shooting at him.

I had a chat with the amiable Mr. Roos. He shuffled through my resume and commented on my roles. He seemed to know my work. Coppola's nephew, Nicholas Cage, was getting one of his first shots at a major film role as a young hood with a few best friends who were his de facto mob mates. He'd done low budget flicks like *Valley Girl, Rumble Fish* and *Racing with the Moon,* but they hadn't been released yet. Cage had several good scenes in *The Cotton Club,* and they wanted me to play one of his cohorts. I couldn't have been more pleased and dedicated. La Rocca did the paper work, and they said I'd work in August. I'd have another month to prepare. I was free to go home, but first I wanted to visit Scott McClintock in the Village.

His classy brownstone was close to Bleecker Street and only a couple blocks to Washington Square Park. Scott was a prolific pot smoker and was always walking over to the park where it was easy to acquire. He did get mugged a couple times. Scott seemed conflicted and confused. He was always changing homes and cars and careers, and right now he wasn't sure which way to go. There was an altruistic sweetness to Scott, a graceful disposition that would never intentionally harm anyone. The world would be a better place with more Scotts. There was a small theatre playhouse you could see below us from his window, so I went to check out Sam Shepard's *True West* with Ed Harris as the older brother Lee, playing one of the great roles in the history of theatre. With all this positive karma, I was raring to get back to LA and more work.

It was practically waiting at my door. Casting director Cis Corman, who auditioned me for *Once Upon a Time in America,* wanted to see me in Culver City to read for Martin Scorsese and his next film *The Last Temptation of Christ*. I prayed knee deep in the Galilee for Johnny the Baptist...pending. Ray Davies from the Kinks had already been cast as Judas Iscariot. Sting got the part of Pontius Pilate and Aiden Quinn was Jesus Christ. Paramount was producing, but when the budget went awry and the religious protested vociferously, the film was cancelled. Three years later, Universal and Scorsese made the film with Willem

Dafoe as the Hebrew outlaw. A mere spectator now, I waited in long lines when it finally opened at the Century City Theater. Once again, there were large numbers of angry dissenters.

It was good to be home sweet from NYC and back in my realm. Gary Myrick played a prestigious gig at the Palace on Vine. It was one of those beautiful old theatres that had seen better days. Refurbished, the old bat emerged as a glamorous nightclub like the El Macambo or the Copacabana. Red Hot Chili Peppers and Black Flag played Cathay de Grande. Bob Greenberg gave me a shot at *Tales of the Midnight Demon.* Appointment books don't lie. Dates: Shirley, Pat, Monica, Dagmar, Elise, Karen, Kelly, Kristen, Karin, Kathy and 1492.

Far more attractive was a meeting with Rochelle Farberman at 20th Century Fox for the action-packed ABC series *The Fall Guy.* Lee Majors was the star of the show, and until recently he'd been the macho stud of the Farrah Fawcett marriage. That ten-year relationship had put them on the cover of show business. He was the golden boy and Farrah was one of the biggest stars in the galaxy. Lee's career had raced on a spectacular ride, first winning a coveted lead role in the ABC series *The Big Valley* with superstar Barbara Stanwyck, later joining the cast of *The Virginian,* and then co-starring in *Owen Marshall: Counselor at Law,* where he first met Farrah when she guest starred in an episode. All of which led to the starring role as Colonel Steve Austin in *The Six Million Dollar Man.* He became the pop-culture icon of the seventies. After a hundred episodes and 6 Bionic-man TV movies, he jumped to features and starred in six mediocre films. Producer Glen Larson recast him to star in *The Fall Guy* series as Colt Seavers, a Hollywood stuntman and part-time bounty hunter. Again he had a hit show.

I went to one of those sunny bungalows on the Fox lot to pick up my sides and size up the character that was described: "Joe Lustig is barrel-chested. A scar runs down his face from a wild eye. The result is the appearance of madness." My partner was "Ogden, a behemoth, 300 pounds of malevolence topped by a small head with pig eyes and a permanent snarl." It seemed I always had a funny partner or was one myself. Not only was director Russ Mayberry in the office, but executive producer Glen Larson, other producers and even Lee Majors. I soon discovered mine was a major role. I busted a cap on the audition, and they got on the phone with La Rocca to set a deal. Douglas Barr as Howie was the obligatory cute guy and Heather Thomas as Jody (who's practically another Farrah) were regulars. This episode's guest stars were Bo Svenson as Baker (the episode is called "Baker's Dozen"), Michael Macrae as Ferris, Blackie Dammett as Lustig, Dennis Burkley as Ogden and Carol Lynley as Ivy. Lovely Lynley had been a teen star in *Blue Denim, Return to Peyton Place, Under the Yum Yum Tree* opposite Jack Lemmon, and in *Harlow* as Jean Harlow.

I was paid three grand a week and had 49 scenes. I tore up the scenery and left a big mess. We shot in a van, on a truck, clinging to motorcycles, hanging from jeeps, in the woods, dunes and desert, a dude ranch, at Baker's army headquarters and barracks, a sheriff's office, the police department, in Joshua Tree, at the Motion Picture Home for the aged, car chases, drunk scenes, fight scenes, shooting scenes and even a helicopter. All great fun but I had a mitigating concern and that my upcoming *Cotton Club* job in New York was cutting it close.

La Rocca got me an audition for Tom Hank's *Bachelor Party*; that and *Splash* were his first two movies, both in 1983. No time for busy boy Blackie; we had to turn it down. I didn't care; I was having the time of my life on this show. Lee Majors and Bo Svenson were treating me as an equal and we bonded. Lee drank a lot of vodka; he still hadn't gotten over Farrah. Bo Svenson had been Buford Pusser, the star of *Walking Tall,* my first picture. He was god on that movie, and I was the skulking around stunt man who wasn't really a stunt man who wasn't even in SAG yet. When the "Baker's Dozen" episode aired, *TV Guide* had my billing over Bo Svenson. *TV Guide* liked my name.

We were days into the shoot and about ready to break for lunch. Alison had come to visit me on the set, and I was cavorting with flirty Heather Thomas, who had just signed her famous bikini poster with *Blackie, Thanks for helping me with our scene. Love & Laughs, Heather*. An AD came over and told me to call my agent; it's very important. The news was dreadful. Zoetrope had called and wanted me in New York the day after tomorrow. Coppola had gotten ahead of schedule and the Nic Cage stuff was ready to go. A conundrum like this was new to me, but it was explained that we had a contract with Fox for *The Fall Guy;* and we had to honor it, period. I was obliged to stay and finish the episode.

I was barely capable of performing, but there was a busy schedule of scenes to be done. Motion pictures trump television, but legalities trump Fox towers. The word got around fast, and soon everybody was consoling me. Lee Majors imparted a similar situation he had once. His *Big Valley* series was on its last legs, destined to die over the summer hiatus. Lee was offered the lead role in *Midnight Cowboy*, but Universal surprisingly renewed the faltering TV series for one last year, and he was legally obligated to stay. The role went to Jon Voight; *Midnight Cowboy* won the Academy Award for best picture, and Jon Voight was nominated best actor. Voight went on to win a best actor Oscar in *Coming Home*. Lee Majors never got another major film.

I couldn't sleep that night. *The Cotton Club* was playing hot jazz in my addled brain. The next day I was bitter. I used the anger in my part, but in my heart I was devastated. Lee and Bo took it upon themselves to save me with playful antics. Our scripts were essential and always close at hand, but mine kept mysteriously disappearing. When I was about to do a shot, my wardrobe cap or some requisite prop would be missing. The culprits were snickering like school kids. I had a short break between scenes and went to the restroom outside. While I was sitting on the toilet, they parked a car against the door so I couldn't get out. On the sound stage the AD was calling for me, "Blackie, on the set!" But I couldn't escape from the jokesters' trap. I pounded on the door until somebody heard me and moved the car. I rushed back on the set and gave a rattled performance while Bo and Lee were cracking up. The director let me do an extra take. Lee invited me to a barbeque at his Malibu house. Bo gave me a gift. Heather gave me hugs. In the end, *The Fall Guy* was one of my better performances, and the convoluted story alone was worth something. We finished our action desert scenes with somersaulting dune buggies. There were bazookas, grenades and explosions. A real stunt man playing a stunt man was injured and we scrambled to get aid out to our remote location.

The following Monday, I was back in the hunt. Meg Leiberman summoned me to MGM to audition for an NBC prospect *We've Got it Made* as "A trendy fashionable New Yorker.". Thanks for reminding me of where I should have been all along. One of my most reliable casting directors was Barbara Clamen at good old BCI casting on Cahuenga. She hauled me in for the *The XYZ Murders,* a slapstick horror comedy movie written by Ethan and Joel Coen and Sam Raimi. All they had done at this point was *The Evil Dead.* Now Sam Raimi has become his own industry with the *Spiderman* movies; and the Coen Brothers, well, *No Country for Old Men; Fargo; Raising Arizona; The Big Lebowski; Blood Simple; Miller's Crossing; Barton Fink; Bad Santa; The Hudsucker Proxy; O Brother, Where Art Thou; Burn After Reading; True Grit* and ten Oscars. On this day, they were struggling young men working on a quirky project that Embassy Pictures would totally screw up. I felt entitled; Raimi was born in Royal Oak, went to Michigan State and the film would be shot in Detroit. I was reading for Coddish, one of the two killer exterminators, and the part was easily the most interesting. The script wrote: "Criminal weasel like, kills rats for a living, has shocker device with bolts of electricity to kill humans (the evil corporation humans), lots of fun, runny nose, emaciated look of a conformed addict, nursery school education, incredible techno abilities, training rats to reason, rampant liar, gullible, slimy, sneaky and a bastard." My partner was Vic. They liked my reading, but when I boasted to Sam Raimi I had once played a funny killer in *Class Reunion* he flinched. The next day, they taped my audition for Embassy, but the studio wanted big names and even Bruce Campbell, Raimi's childhood pal and star of the *Evil Dead* films, was knocked out of the lead role.

My *Magnum P.I.* aired. Scott McClintock checked into the West Hollywood Tropicana. Liza Barton called me over to Zoetrope for a romantic comedy with the working title *Before You,* starring Richard Dreyfuss. A week later, *The XYZ Murders* called me back for a third time. I waited in vain but Brion James eventually got my part; his partner was Paul L. Smith. It was finally released as *Crimewave.*

I took Alison to her orthodontist. I'd take her anywhere. We took a limousine to Anaheim Stadium for David Bowie's Serious Moonlight Tour with a private suite and backstage passes. I sent her potent postcards when she was in England. One night I took her to dinner at La Scalla in Malibu. After a few glasses of wine, she established "The La Scalla Accords." It was my promise to always have Alison's favorite things in perpetuity.

Chapter 36: Painted into the Corner of Santa Monica & La Jolla

By October, 1983, I could afford a bigger place and moved from Hancock to 1004 N. La Jolla Avenue, a broken dream or two south of Santa Monica Boulevard. My eclectic new turf was alive with energy, guff and male bars with a penchant for names like Spike and Nail. The beacon on my corner was the 24-hour pink-and-white Circus Book pornaphernalia store. Sex had always been a current of commodity on S & M Boulevard., but it was also a lengthy trail of many colors.

The bastard orphan boulevard staggered west out of anonymity, an appendage of Sunset in Silver Lake. She crossed Vermont and made block-away eye contact with a blue collar education at City College, maligned but making the grade. She passed under the Hollywood Freeway and was crowned with the coveted emperor's new State Highway 2 designation. Go west, young mannequin. She was a thoroughfare not a thoroughbred. She snuck through the grey areas and collided with Olay! at Western Avenue, a Hispanic meeting of the grind. No largess on Van Ness. Cecil B. DeMille, Douglas Fairbanks, John Huston, Jayne Mansfield, Tyrone Power, Bugsy Siegel, Rudoph Valentino, Fay Wray and morbidly more at the Hollywood Memorial Park Cemetery on the left. Paramount Studios to the even lefter. Vine is fine; look to the right for the Hollywood sign. Now she was bland and busy, the under belly. Trendy Melrose to the south; to the north, sacred Sunset and hallowed Hollywood flank her and spank her. She was a workhorse with pugnacious pavement, while the flankers played in iridescent night lights. Out of the belly, next stop West Hollywood. At last some recognition: Samuel Goldwyn Studios and Technicolor. She purred Pussycat Theaters and enough naughty book stores to spread the gospel of porn. The Alpha-Beta at Fairfax, look left to the Jewish Ghetto and Anthony's High School, right to access Laurel Canyon and the Valley. Next stop Crescent Heights, Blackie's new neighborhood. It was still a long way to her swim at the Ocean. Keep your eye on the setting sun. Barney's Beanery, La Cienega, The Tropicana, Hancock, Palm, Larrabee, San Vicente; the heart of West Hollywood's village with her throbbing clubs, the Troubadour and show busy Dan Tana's. She's got better places to be, her coming out party. Across Doheny and she's Beverly Hills; mansions and millionaires and an endless park for Nick Nolte to bum around in. She has twins; the birth of a Little Santa Monica through the pricey shopping district and then the crossed swords of Wilshire and Santa Monica at the Hilton. Flow on through the aloof and silver towers of Century City and past the Masonic Temple. Westwood has Tony's Junior High on your right; UCLA on your righter; the 405 and West LA. She's at home in her own skin, the city of Santa Monica with her hues and rues of higher education; Berkeley, Stanford, Yale, Harvard, Princeton and then 26th Street, only 25 more blocks to the final stop, the Promenade terminus overlooking the Pacific. My tendril was dead center. Look both ways before crossing.

The 40s-era duplex had a small garage the Caddy couldn't fit in. In order, my blueprint was a living room, a kitchen, then my bedroom and a bath at the end of the hallway.

A final jog to the right went into one last bedroom and a back door to the yard. There was a plot of grass, a lot of sass and a self-perpetuating tangle of wild flowers at the fence that delineated our property. A stray black cat adopted the name Jet. Scott McClintock rented the back room when he was in town. I often received comedienne Elaine Boozler's mail; she lived at 1004 *South* La Jolla Avenue. Artful pal Jay Brown's loft was Polaroid-ized; he chronicled his life with instant images. I bought a Polaroid camera of my own and wallpapered my kitchen with girlfriends. Relentless, the images spread like a pretty plague. By the time I left, they covered every room of my life: megalomaniac or pie-eyed Pied Piper?

Fern Champion and Pamela Basker scared me into auditioning for *Friday the 13th The Final Chapter* as Axel. "He is a wild and weird morgue attendant at the hospital, a silly guy with a morbid sense of humor. He is titillated at the thought of having a quickie with Nurse Morgan, surrounded by corpses in the morgue." I got a call back with the producer. It was me or Bruce Mahler, my comrade from *Fridays*. Bruce got the Axel, and I got the axe. Moving on, I read for the lead role in *E. Nick Vanacuzzi Presents*. The dude was a bon vivant and slightly off center. Fit me to a tee, but the project didn't. Next was the biker flick *Leather Babies* from producer Albert Band at Universal. His forte was sci-fi and horror; he also made a spectacle of himself with sword-fighting warlords. Harry Dean Stanton was supposed to do the lead, but it faltered. Albert's son Charles Band was also a maven of the macabre who produced over 200 horror films, including the Puppet Master franchise. I must have read for him a dozen times up there in his penthouse office where the sun set on Beverly Hills. He was a sweet guy to have done all that horror.

Peggy came out to LA and celebrated Anthony's twenty-first birthday.

Casting angel Annette Benson beckoned me to the quaint but busy little Raleigh lot on Melrose, east of Paramount. It was for *Night of the Comet,* directed by Thom Eberhardt. A mean weird punk, it was me in a nutshell. I smiled; they requested I please come normal for a change. Zero rat Mary Woronov was in it. La Rocca said the part was too small.

Then suddenly a Jennie popped into my life and became my new mistress. We bum rushed the Zero, caught Scratch parties and double dated with Jay Brown and his gal. Jennifer Jean Cacavas was a UCLA co-ed who lived with her parents in Zeppo Marx's former house in Beverly Hills. She had a special room full of equestrian blue ribbons. She liked to party and did it with impunity at her alter-ego college dorm; I practically lived in her bed for a semester. Masque and Lingerie legend Brendan Mullen had a big crush on her and was upset that she had the audacity to choose me. I was oblivious and routinely expected to win those wars. He finally admitted this to me in 2010 when he came up to Portland and helped me with some nightclub references for this very book. Brendan was a loveable guy, more Santa than punk rocker now, and in retrospect I wish I had let him prevail in the Jennie Jean sweepstakes. With all my pipperoos, I could afford to be magnanimous. Brendan died unexpectedly at age 60, not long after he spent that week at my house. Hearts were broken, his and ours.

It was getting close to Christmas and an early present came my way: an interview for a film version of the *Dick Tracy* comic strip. Floyd Mutrux and Art Linson had secured the rights from United Artists when UA failed to reach a deal with Dick Tracy creator Chester Gould. Among my most influential Hollywood friends, they had produced and directed *American Hot Wax,* the movie Anthony came so close to. Over the last three years the *Dick*

Tracy project had struggled to find a heart. They took the film to Paramount and asked Steven Spielberg to direct; he declined. John Landis was hired, and they did a complete rewrite. Landis dropped out over the *Twilight Zone* movie fiasco that killed Vic Morrow, the same bungling stunt coordinator who split my breastbone on *Class Reunion*. Walter Hill took it on and set his sights on Warren Beatty as his Dick Tracy. Hill dropped out and Paramount opted for a lower budget version. They hired former actor Richard Benjamin who had just directed his first film a year earlier, *My Favorite Year* with Peter O'Toole. Warren Beatty was still the coveted Tracy. That's where I came in, the day in December 1983 when I read for Richard Benjamin. I auditioned for the major role of Big Boy at a warehouse in the Valley. I'll never know how close I came; the project collapsed again when Warren Beatty tried to take control of the film and Benjamin left. Over several years, I had five call backs with two different directors. Warren wanted a fortune to star and Universal dropped the whole tamale, but Beatty bought the rights to the film and spent the next six years putting it back together. It's been said over the ten years of the film's many incarnations just about every big name in the business was considered for *Dick Tracy*: Harrison Ford, Clint Eastwood, De Niro, Mel Gibson, Richard Gere and even Tom Selleck. Many of the best screenwriters in Hollywood took turns writing the scripts. There were six major directors and five studios. Disney ended up with the final film, and it was released in 1990. It won three of the seven Oscars it was nominated for. And who ended up playing my Big Boy role? Al Pacino. And he was nominated for best supporting actor.

I picked up Jennie at school, and we celebrated my birthday on this the 42nd anniversary of Pearl Harbor Day. Okay, I was 44! Anthony went to Michigan for Christmas as he always did. I spent Christmas Eve with Jennie at her party, and we had New Years Eve dinner at Sonny Bono's restaurant. "Jennie Jennie Jennie, won't you come along with me." The next day it was 1984.

In 1949 when I was only ten years old, George Orwell wrote his final masterpiece *Nineteen Eighty-Four.* Dying from tuberculosis, he gasped out one last warning that a totalitarian state of mind and a diminution of freedom would most likely poison our planet by 1984. Now with short memories and far from 1949, we were merrily skipping along on our blindsided journey through the late twentieth century, forgetful of his references *Big Brother, Thought Police* and *Doublethink*. Perhaps they were precognizant moles lurking in wait for the Bush Cheney era. For self-absorbed me, 1984 looked to be my best year ever, and I continued to attack with a positive vigor. I had a story to tell then, and I still do today. "If liberty means anything at all, it means the right to tell people what they don't want to hear." -- George Orwell.

Embassy Pictures finished a low budget "teen/cross country" film called *The Sure Thing* and held an afternoon screening at the Academy of Motion Picture Arts and Sciences on Wilshire. The film was directed by Rob Reiner and starred youngsters John Cusack and Daphne Zuniga. Just as young were Tim Robbins and Nicollette Sheridan (as The Sure Thing). Twenty-two year old John Cusack was on hand to greet people after the screening. It was his first starring role and only his fourth movie ever. He was certainly endearing, but on that day I didn't know him from Adophe Menjou. We filed out into the lobby and joined a long reception line to say hi and shake his hand. The crowd was ripe with afternoon women who had unspoken fantasies of this handsome young actor. The closer I got the more loquacious the gush got. It was a big praise-a-thon. Personally I'm uncomfortable with excessive praise, and I think most people are. The ladies ahead of me doted and moved on with a smile. And then there I was, face to face with the precious star attraction. I couldn't bring myself to more laudation. I shook my head, not his hand, and solemnly leveled an icy critique. Keep working and you'll get there I said with a straight face. For me it was a fine performance of my own. I walked quickly out of the lobby before the lynch mob attacked; to this day I wonder if he took me seriously.

As a youngster I admired Cagney, and what movie buff didn't bow to Brando and Dean. Along came jolting Jack Nicholson in *Easy Rider* and *Five Easy Pieces*. Forty years and more Oscar hardware than any male actor ever, he's still the standard. De Niro inspired me to learn the craft. Sean Penn was his heir apparent. I caught him at Club Lingerie, preparing a role. I tried to talk shop, but he stayed in character. I was lucky he didn't punch me. Gary Oldman's early *Sid and Nancy* and *Prick Up Your Ears* made him my next hero, until the ascendancy of Clooney and Depp, and the entire cast of *Wonder Boys*. Meryl Streep mailed her way into my heart with *Postcards from the Edge* and then just kept getting better until she was certified best. And yet, nobody's more cozy and comfortable to be with on the screen than the effortless John Cusack.

Violet was living in New York. Alan Bashara was in Grand Rapids. David Weaver was living in the sky, diving. He had given up the music business and had a straight job with a necktie. McClintock had a new home in San Francisco on 12th Avenue. I barely typed that line and he had moved again. Now he was on Spaulding in Beverly Hills. Jay Brown was on Le Brea and his Atlanta pal Philip Stillman moved into the other half of my duplex, or better put on the other side of the paper thin hallway wall. The elderly former tenant had left. Philip was acidic and confrontational. It had the makings of a sitcom noir.

I had a second read for Sandy Howard's *Underworld* (*Transmutations*) written and infected by Clive Barker, the man who gave us *Hellraiser*. I had two different Asian projects inquiring about my availability. One was *Snake* in the Philippines and the other was *Jungle* in Thailand, about heroin. Quite frankly, I wasn't crazy about snakes, jungles or heroin. Wendy, Carrie, Guinevere, Katherine and Michelle used my toothpaste on the following morning.

Am I available for *Prison Planet* in April? Are we interested in the teen comedy *All You Can Eat?* I sat in on Jim Wynorski's editing of *The Lost Empire*. I read as Gilbert, a gas station snitch for *T.J. Hooker* with William Shatner and Heather Locklear. Peanuts compared to what hit me the next day at Universal. Michael Mann was doing a mind-bending new action series that would make TV's timeline obsolete. NBC head Brandon Tartikoff had asked for a "MTV cops" show and Anthony Yerkovich (*Hill Street Blues*) delivered. It was *Miami Vice* and the pilot would be a two-hour premiere on NBC, with Don Johnson and Philip Michael Thomas as vice cops Sonny Crockett and Rico Tubbs. There was another team of vice cops in the same unit who were a lot less slick but involved in every episode, Stan Switek and Larry Zito. I auditioned for Zito in the penthouse office of Universal's president atop the infamous black tower that defines the studio. Michael Mann and all the Universal head honchos were there. NBC and the studio were sinking millions into the show, and it would shot on location in south Florida. The lengthy dead-pan executive desk demanded the goods. My scene was five pages long, and I definitely felt the Miami heat. I did admirably according to LaRocca, but I was up against every dude in Hollywood. Michael Talbott got the part of Switek. I knew him from Jock McNeil and odd couple Brian Dennehy and Morgan Fairchild. The little dude that got my part was John Diehl. He's got slick credits under his belt now and played G. Gordon Liddy in Oliver Stone's *Nixon*. *Miami Vice* was nominated for 31 Emmy and Golden Globe awards and won ten. The show had a tremendous impact on popular culture in the '80s, and it did wonders for Don Johnson's career. Don and I partied on and off over the years.

American Zoetrope called La Rocca; they'd found a different part for me in *The Cotton Club*. In two weeks I'd be back in New York and my scene would be with James Remar. I barely flinched; there was another juicy audition in Century City. The film is *American Ninja* and it shoots in the Philippines. The part is Alby the Cruel, a terrorist and one of the lead roles. It was a call back. I went to 1900 Avenue of the Stars and up to the 25ᵗʰ floor. It was a small office, and I sat across a low coffee table from the Indian producer Ashok Amritraj, the writer director Emmett Alston (*New Year's Evil*) and a few associates. The table was covered with hard work—scripts, sides, pens and papers, coffee cups, ashtrays full of cigarettes and the smell of lethargy. The corporate board was rubbing their weary eyes and looking at their watch for lunch.

The scene was a disappointed Alby confronted by terrible news in his secret underground jungle location. The script was opened on the table, but I planned more of an improv to wake up these non-believers. Prepared for a certain moment, I had an empty Bic lighter in my pocket. Angry and conflicted, I grabbed a cigarette off the table and flicked my defective Bic. It wouldn't light. The more I flicked, the more frustrated I got. I went into a rage, crumbled the unlit cigarette into a million tobacco shreds and smashed my fist down on the coffee table, sending Styrofoam coffee cups flying into everybody's lap. Their eyeballs were Steppin Fetchit and real terror raced across their faces. I cleaned the deck with a maniacal swipe of what was left on the table; ashtrays, cigar butts and a couple donuts sailed across the room. Miraculously, the Bic lighter was the only thing left on the table. It spun around for a second and stopped dead. I pocketed it, stood up and walked out. By afternoon La Rocca had made a deal and I was set for Manila in May.

Anthony got his own career boost. The band was booked on a new syndicated late night gig that competed head to head with Johnny Carson and Dick Cavett. The show was FOX-TV's first late night program of any kind, a spinoff of the *Alan Thicke Show* in Canada. The new kid on the slot was *Thicke of the Night,* hosted by the Canadian personality with his McMahonequin sidekick Richard Belzer. Arsenio Hall was the announcer. They taped it at Metromedia KTTV Channel 11. There was a small audience, and musical-guest family and friends like me sat on a tiny bleacher in front of the band's tiny stage. Thicke joked he got an earache at their rehearsal. Like the Rhythm Lounge, it was unchartered territory. They blasted a rousing rendition of *True Men Don't Kill Coyotes* from their new album, and the entire American citizenry finally got its first look at the Red Hot Chili Peppers. Half-naked Flea was wrapped in fluorescent duct tape; Anthony was a wild Indian with Jennifer's costuming. When they finished, a shocked Alan Thicke scampered over and blurted out, "What does it mean?! What did they say!? Where are they from? Do their mothers know where they are?!" Flea climbed on his back and Anthony roughed him up. Fox went to commercial; we converged on the stage and hoisted our conquering heroes. Years later when Arsenio Hall had his own FOX late night show, Anthony and Flea were frequent guests.

I was actually in New York when I watched the taped show a week later. Anita Russell, still looking scrumptious and now successfully wealthy, lived in Warwick about fifty miles west of Manhattan. Her horses had a separate phone number in the stables. We got together in the city where she kept a small apartment on the West Side. Good timing, St. Patrick's Day hit town, and I had a couple days to acclimate. I went to Studio 54 and The Limelight, a club in a former church on Sixth Avenue for their "Rights of Spring" party. I met a girl named Lisa; when I got home there'd be a postcard with her lipstick and gratitude.

I moved into the Chelsea Hotel. Talk about ghosts. Dylan Thomas, Mark Twain, Leonard Cohen, Tennessee Williams, Jack Kerouac, Jean-Paul Sarte, Thomas Wolfe, Sir Arthur C. Clarke, Bob Dylan, Janis Joplin, Jasper Johns, Willem De Kooning, Stanley Kubrick and we all slept in my bed. I checked in with *The Cotton Club* offices on W. 59th. They sent me to wardrobe for an appropriate gangster outfit. In makeup, they cut my hair short and shaved my skinny slit of a moustache which I had carefully nourished. Richard Gere already had the exact one. After five days of preparation, it was time to rub out some bodies.

The venerable Cotton Club in Harlem was the centerpiece of fascinating characters swirling in jazz, jealousy and blood. Richard Gere was a musician hired to entertain at a gangster party, where he met Diane Lane who was the girlfriend of extra evil Dutch Schultz played by James Remar. The friendly young man who lent me his script has been transformed into a vicious gangster that nobody in the script or on the set liked. Grouchy and creepy, everybody fears him. Lane prefers Gere, but that's dangerous. The whole town is dangerous. Gregory Hines gets a job at the Cotton Club as a dancer, meets untouchable Lonette McGee and falls in love. Nicolas Cage is Gere's little brother who is intent on being a mobster. Bigger mobsters get fed up with Dutch and hire a couple of hit men to rub him out. That's me and my partner, well-known New York actor Mark Margolis (*The Wrestler, Scarface, Hannibal*). I was Weiss and Margolis was Workman. All the characters in the film were based on real people. Richard Gere's Dixie Dwyer was based on jazz musician Bix Beiderbecke, but only Emanuel "Mendy" Weiss and Charles Workman kept their true names in the script. In his real life, my Weiss was an all-star hit man for Murder Inc. and died in the electric chair at Sing Sing.

Coppola had a unique way of directing. Rather than observe behind the camera operator, he stayed in a specially equipped silver-bullet trailer parked outside at the curb. Only in rehearsals was he on the set. He tested our competence with pistols and determined I was the most proficient. I became the quick-shot specialist, and crafty Margolis got the machine gun. Francis came in for a quick edit shot of a black cat crossing in front of us as we walk through the bar, and then he returned to his trailer. At last we heard the exciting command, "Action!" The targets were seated at a table; Dutch got up to piss. We entered silently and made our way to the dining area. I fired off several shots and wiped out his bodyguards; Margolis blew Dutch apart in the toilet with his machine gun. Coppola intercut our savagery with a sequence of Gregory Hines tap dancing back at the Cotton Club. His choreography dazzled its way as we did ours, slowly building to our own ultimate climaxes, alternating shots of thunderous applause and the cacophony of gunfire. It was quite beautiful. The next day *The New York Times* wrote: "Francis Coppola saved the violence for last. After seven months of production in New York, The Cotton Club is winding up with several brief, but important scenes, including the shooting of Dutch Schultz and his henchmen. The filming took place on Tuesday in a bar and grill on East 23rd Street, standing in for the Palace Chop House and Tavern in Newark, where the gangster was gunned down in 1935."

The Cotton Club is a stomach-churning bullet-riddled film, but it also tells a tender love story and features several show-stopping musical numbers, all set in a lavishly recreated period of Prohibition and racial conflict in the great depression. The film was nominated for best picture and best director at the Golden Globes and two Oscar nods.

I saw Ashley Pandel briefly in Manhattan, but, soon after, he moved back to the West Coast and started a nightclub in Palm Springs, about the same time Sonny Bono was elected mayor. It was a long drive from LA, about 250 miles roundtrip, but I'd stay at a motel that was part of the nightclub complex and make a few days of it. Anthony and I would bring double dates and enjoy the desert air. After a good run, Ashley moved on to Fort Lauderdale in Florida and bought a hotel and cabaret. Unfortunately, I've lost contact with him. I'll always love that guy. I owe him, and for that matter so does Anthony. I think our lives would have traveled a far different path without him. He pushed the Alice Cooper domino and the rest fell into an alignment with brilliant stars. I flew back to LA. It was time to do my thing again.

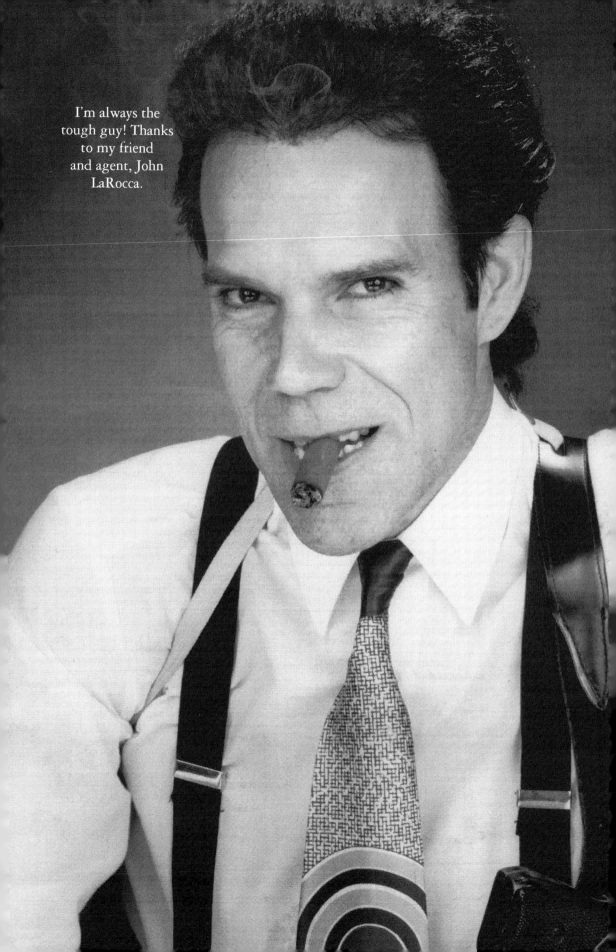

I'm always the
tough guy! Thanks
to my friend
and agent, John
LaRocca.

Chapter 37: The Thrilla in Manila,
9 Deaths of the Ninja

I checked in with La Rocca's cramped offices on Alameda in the morning shadows of Burbank Studios. The secretaries were all smiles, and even the boss was congenial. Now I was one of his busiest clients. We signed contracts for *American Ninja.* I had meetings with Emmett Alston and went through the script. We would be shooting deep in a real jungle. As always, I carefully plotted my character and delved into research. I went to the Philippine Tourist Bureau on Wilshire and checked out the lay of the land. I stocked up on Baader-Meinoff and met with dialect coach Robert Easton. I needed shots and medical exams and insurance assurances. It was like going to the moon.

Alison was on the phone. We went to see the English band 999 with outrageous lead man Nick Cash. I was also seeing Doreen and a girl from Grand Rapids who knew the Weavers. She was Karen Brush and I took kindly to her. She was staying at a little hotel on Wilcox and we had our little affair. My neighbor Philip was getting on my nerves, but his girlfriend Bliss was so sweet I tolerated him. Occasionally, she went back to New Mexico, and I enjoyed seeing him frustrated. My cat went missing after an argument; Jet never returned and I knew exactly who was responsible. I read for *St. Elsewhere,* a TV drama at Mary Tyler Moore Studios on Ventura. Across the street, I made a connection with a cutie in a mini-mall parking lot. It's funny how I remember certain ones. Shelly Staples was all over my appointment book and so was a showgirl from the Mud Club.

The over the title star was Sho Kosugi, a martial arts master and a huge movie star in the Orient. He played the lead in two of the genre's biggest movies, *Enter the Ninja* and *Revenge of the Ninja.* Brent Huff was our American male lead and a terrific guy. He's been on display in *Cold Case, JAG* and *The West Wing.* Emilia Lesniak was the female lead, a tall blonde with *Scarface, Star Trek* and a *Remington Steele* in her resume. Brent and Emilia were U.S. agents going after the terrorists. Regina Richardson had just come off Clint Eastwood's *Tightrope* in New Orleans. Regina was my right-hand bitch, Honey Hump; she was in charge of my rag tag army made up of beautiful, scantily dressed female soldiers. Vijay Amritraj the executive producer from India gave himself a role as a police bureaucrat. Lisa Friedman played the heroine tour guide with a bus load of VIP tourists and several children to protect after being captured by my bad guys. And then there was me, the psychotic drug tycoon and terrorist who demanded the release of a violent criminal (supposedly my lover). Filipino Sonny Erang as Rhaji was the prisoner. I coerced and blackmailed the authorities into releasing him. He was seven-feet tall, weighed a ton and had steel teeth. LaRocca wanted top three billing, we settled for "...and Blackie Dammett as Alby the Cruel."

In the waning days, I met Sherry, a six-foot, slender and very shy young lady who went to Hamilton High. Sherry and I had crushes on each other. I would definitely miss her. I started my regimen of malaria pills. A few last minute auditions, a *Sgt. Bilko* call back and *Gus Brown & Midnight Brewster* for NBC. The character is Killer Kenyon, forties, nervous and wiry. Good practice. *Ninja* wants me to do the film in a wheelchair. The layers were building. I have deranged images of a profusely sweating overweight Sidney Greenstreet, wearing a tropical white suit in one of those jungle movies like *Malaya* with Spencer Tracy and James Stewart. I taped fresh radio music off **KROQ**, Frankie Goes to Hollywood's *Relax* and others. Sherry brought me one of those darling little school photos to take along. A kiss goodbye and I was off to the other side of the world. It was a twenty-hour flight, but we stopped in Hawaii for gas and oil.

Manila was a bustling city of ten million people and there were at least that many jitneys, the peculiar open-air taxis colorfully decorated by their drivers. The authoritarian President Ferdinand Marcos had been reigning since the Paleoproterozoic age, or at least as long as Stalin or Franco. His wife was the implacable Imelda Marcos, notoriously well known in the West for her shopping sprees and most famously remembered as the "shoe lady" who had palaces just to house them all. Their reign was the oriental equivalent of Louis XVI and Marie Antoinette. His government was evil, corrupt, despotic, repressive, nepotistic, and sorely lacked human rights; not surprisingly, we found ourselves in the middle of a civil war between the pseudo-democratic regime and the proletarian New People's Army. The NPA was a Maoist guerrilla organization dedicated to bringing down the government and its puppeteer, the United States of America. Every shop in Manila, even a little curio shop, had an armed guard with a machinegun standing in the doorway. Welcome to the Philippines.

We stayed at the mammoth Hotel Inter-Continental in the safe zone. It was the nice part of town with expensive shops, movie theaters and restaurants. Across town was a red-light district with miles of bars and provocative ladies to entertain the American military stationed in the Philippines. The whole country was an armed camp. They processed extras in the hotel lobby, and one of the applicants caught my eye. She was Chantal Manz, an American who had been living and modeling in Manila for a couple years. The cost of living was dirt cheap; she had a beautiful home and even servants on her modest earnings. She was a stunning woman in any environment and especially here in Manila. She became one of my female soldiers in the movie. I basked in the sun at the Olympic-size pool and ran for the cabanas when the rain came. Every morning around eleven, the skies opened up and a deluge blotted out the universe. Just as suddenly, it would slam to a stop and the sun would dry it all off in a matter of minutes. Then the tropical drinks would resume, hand held high on trays carried by dark skinned waiters in starched white uniforms. Manila was a paradise for the rich and a rat hole for the poor. And we were about to enter that hole.

Like any location, the production shot in picturesque neighborhoods, but soon those of us in the jungle scenes boarded our early morning bus for the two-hour drive into the primeval forest. We'd have to drag lights, cameras and equipment into the dense jungle and drag it out at night, when it had grown even denser. The rains were torrential. The mosquitoes were vicious. The drinking water was malaria kool-aid. There were deadly chartreuse snakes and spiders the size of dinner plates. But that was the least of our worries; the NPA was everywhere once you got out of the cities. Our film crew had a regiment of Filipino Army soldiers to protect us from attack. We were exactly what the NPA liked: American tourists to kidnap and hold for ransom, just like in our script. Some days we were in claustrophobic caves with bats and exotic tarantulas. Others we'd be under water-falls or up on mountains. We filmed in obscure villages and would often spend the night in antiquated motels and drink the local brews at their idea of a pub. A bunch of us were exploring and got separated from the main group. Our car broke down and we tried hitch-hiking; locals who picked us up said it was too dangerous for us to be on the roads without police protection.

On my days off, I explored Manila. In a nearby department store, I saw the most adorable Filipino salesclerk behind the cosmetic counter. Her name was Flora. She was too shy to date me, and her father would never have allowed it; but I still came back, time after time, to see her. Eventually, she took a shine to me.

Chantal Manz, the model, showed me the night life. I even danced. She brought me to her alien home, and we spent the night…talking. A few goodnight kisses though, and it was daylight when I left.

And there was a third exotic woman in my Manila madness. Some of the cast went to the red-light district, an obligatory tourist stop. We wandered from bar to bar, and not surprisingly, I saw another amazing beauty. I was completely bewitched. I left with my friends but came back another night to find her. This time she came out and sat with me. Her name was Nimfa and I asked if we could date. She said tonight and I took her back to the Hotel Inter-Continental. In the morning, we went to the hotel restaurant for breakfast, but the patrons were glaring at us with furrowed brows. A tainted girl like her was not allowed. I stood our ground and defended her to the death.

Back in the jungle, I continued to rage war on the protagonists, but Brent and Sho had all the cards. They trapped me and my Rahji in our underground headquarters and blew us up in a fiery explosion that buried my empire under a mountain of molten rock. Or so you'd think. The next day we shot the final scene of the movie. The good guys were sitting around a veranda celebrating Alby the Cruel's demise. They even took a call from the President who was tickled pink. When all of a sudden Alby inexplicably arrived on the scene with a few of my henchmen, intact, and there was one last shootout. Losing the battle yet again, I attempted to escape on my new hopped-up motorized wheelchair, with big trouble on my tail. I scooted through the affluent neighborhood and headed onto a polo ground that had a match in progress. I was trying to get through the herd of horses and swinging mallets. From the sidelines, Sho shot an arrow into the back of my wheelchair and the attached hundred-foot rope flipped me over. Are you following this? To my horrifying screams of Nein! Nein!, the polo ponies trampled me to death in as grisly a demise as I suffered in *The Lost Empire*. Only this was much funnier. They threw my dummy under the horses, and arms and legs went in every direction; I was torn into a heap of angular body parts. Our movie was an action thriller, but for my peso it was strictly comedy. One critic wrote: "Incredibly inane tongue-in-cheek spoof, rating highly as a total campy riot."

The mayor of Manila and other luminaries threw a party for us at the Coconut Palace. First lady Imelda Marcos had commissioned this magnificent home for Pope John Paul II's visit in 1981. He refused to stay in such ostentatiousness, but we were pleased to kick back. I was told Imelda was there but don't recall meeting her. It was a spectacular place, but by contrast so much of the country was impoverished

I said goodbye to my three lovelies. Chantal Manz stayed in her adopted Manila but gave me six family phone numbers and their address in Redwood City, California. Nimfa Berol from the Zumi Inn Bar gave me sweet dreams. Shy Flora, Flordeliza Ochava, sent love letters to LA that pleaded for me to marry and bring her to America, and it was with the full approval of her parents. Crown International Pictures released our film with a new and improved title, *9 Deaths of the Ninja*. It was my most jeopardous movie experience.

Far from Hollywood, I was immune from replacement, and I chewed up salads of scenery. I had a tradition with my scripts, decorated them, had them autographed, covered them with call sheets and other memorabilia. There was so much carnage during *9 Deaths of the Ninja.* I saved the lurid headlines as chronicled by the Manila newspapers during my 24-day stay. Too much for my script cover by far, I created a life-size poster of my adventures in this beautiful, but traumatic, garden of evil:

36 Killed, 39 Hurt in 4 NPA Attacks, Violence hits Zamboanga, Negros, More Killings in Mindanao – Regional solon slain in ambush, 4-cock derby at San Pedro, Meet Force With Force Marcos Orders Military, 12 Soldiers arrested for Torture, 60 Killed in Election Violence, NPC Chairman, 6 others dead in ambush, NPA attack PC Unit; 4 troopers killed, 4 PC officers die in ambush, Sex Den Raided, 3 Girls Rescued, 8 NPAs Killed in Town Hall Raid, 32 entries in cock derby, 3 NPA chiefs, 7 aides killed in encounters, 5 rebels die in clash, Alcaneses orders arrest of hired goons, 65 Killed in poll Violence; 7 in Antique ambush, 2 killed in Cebu City, Locust swarm destroy crops in C. Mindanao, Cops Shot Dead, Armed Men Hi-Jack Jeep, Take Hogs, Ex-Rebel Chief Slain, Man Stabs 2 Children, Power Failure Obstructs Electoral Process, 3 NPA men killed; 1700 surrender, 11 die, 11 hurt in NPA ambush, 15 men killed in clashes, Stepped-up Gun Snatching by Rebels, Violence Continues 2 Mayors Killed; 2 survive attacks, Defiant Squatters fight off Police anti-riot squad, 24 Killed in NPA Raids, Ambush, Ex-Miss RP in Murder Rap, QC terror gang nabbed, PC Unit foils NPA Kills 9, 2 Slain 2 hurt in Bulacan clash, NPA ambush 8 slain, 2 hurt, 6 cock derbies at Tereas, Clarin 7 aides Killed, Cops kill 4 bank robbers, Chat, Cita, Eden, Tina – beauties all – in Gala Show.

And so I boarded another plane home from a mission accomplished. Back on La Jolla, I received a letter on Hotel Inter-Continental Hotel Manila stationary: "Blackie, Your performance reached beyond that which could normally be defined as acting. It had significant power and skillful balance. It could have easily become caricature, but you wove the fabric so delicately, I truly enjoyed observing you at work. You have my deepest respect!" Roy Wagner, Director of Photography.

Chapter 38: Night Court

No longer the private darlings of the underground, the Red Hots had become *maim* stream. The *Los Angeles Times* covered them with blue-blood ink. The band was booked to play the Olympic Auditorium with The Minutemen and Suicidal Tendencies, two of the biggest bands in town. The historic downtown venue was built for the 1932 Olympics. Parts of *Rocky* were filmed there; Jack Dempsey, Gorgeous George, Rudolph Valentino, Johnny Rotten and Bon Jovi all left their fitting mark there.

Detained in jail for warrants, Anthony was a no show for the big event, and the minimized Peppers had to recruit the Circle Jerks' Keith Morris to attempt an imitation. A week later, the full band of brothers topped the bill at the Lingerie with Fear and Circle Jerks, and then headlined a cavalcade of local talent at the Stardust Ballroom.

I was hunting down the next movie. Jay Brown was working with Tom Trikilis at Playboy Productions and got me in for *Trick of Trade,* a Ribald Classic as a 1900 magician, Larry Houdini. All I remember was meeting and befriending a bevy of playmates. The next one had my name all over it, the character was Spyder and the description was thin, cadaverous, crazy, articulate and a poet with a ghetto blaster. The film was *Savage Dawn*, a biker flick. The last time I was on a motorcycle I crashed Scott Weaver's bike into a wall of bushes at Casa Granada. Deb Rubenstein called me in for *Avenging Angel,* a Sandy Howard film. I had auditioned for his *Underworld*, earlier in the year. Sandy Howard got his start directing TV's *Howdy Doody* and *Captain Kangaroo*. Perhaps his biggest success was *A Man Called Horse* with Richard Harris, one of the first films to deal honestly with Native Americas. He also produced *The Island of Dr. Moreau* with Burt Lancaster. I read for the role of Ray, one of the bastards avenged by the beautiful Betsy Russell. I also tried out for Jessie a slick jewelry thief at MGM in *Rigged* with George Kennedy and as Steele in the film *Chase.*

Lisa with the pink lipstick postcard from New York came to visit me in LA. Tamla did a sit-in on my front porch. I stole Reuben Blue's girlfriend. She was unusually erotic with thick eyeglasses and padded clothing that still couldn't hide her quadruple awesome body. Throw in Cheryl, Fiona, Constance, Louise, Sara, Marcia, Anna, Elite model Liv and I was set for the whole week.

V was an alien invasion sci-fi TV series at Warner Bros. I was up for Episode Nine, "A Reflection in Terror" as Laird a deadly alien, thin, pale man whose intense eyes miss nothing. He has a reptilian smile. The reading was a bunch of mumbo jumbo about clones and laser guns. I was no fan of sci-fi but would have accepted the role; I didn't have to worry.

I got my first crack at *Night Court,* the popular show that ran for nine years on NBC. Comic Harry Anderson played it straight but charmingly as a night court judge in Manhattan. He had been a semi-regular on *SNL* and imbibed on *Cheers.* It was John Larroquette, though, who stole the show as Night Court's lecherous jester Dan Fielding, the narcissistic attorney. He won four straight Emmy Awards. Jeff Melman from Hollywood Actors Theatre was one of their producers now, and although I missed as sleazy guy Pina, I was told they'd use me soon.

The Red Hot Chili Peppers signed up for *The New Music Seminar* in New York City, an annual week-long gig for up–and-coming musicians. Anthony invited me to come along. MTV covered the event, televised musician forums and collected the best acts into a room for interviews. Sparks flew; Madonna and Anthony were tête-à-tête. Every time we got to our interview, some act with more prestige would cut in front of us with MTV's tacit approval. In the end we were the end! Anthony and Flea rapped their impromptu bit, and when MTV aired the show, Chili Peppers ruled. It was more potent publicity for the band, and from that time on RHCP was in like Flynn with MTV. The VJs loved the fresh kids from Hollywood and helped pave the way for their stardom.

We went to the Pyramid Club on Avenue A and played The Lone Star, a country bar in midtown Manhattan. Joe Ely was the headliner and the crowd wasn't pleased with our punk funk. They tried to yank us off the stage but the band fought on. Scott McClintock put me up in the brownstone, and I spent a few days in the Village with several forays into Washington Square Park for pot-pourri. Then it was back to LA.

I was at Scream in the marble lobby near closing time when I noticed an innocent young blonde who was as close to perfect as she could be. She was on the payphone, talking to her dad so I got in line behind her. She couldn't have been a day over purity. She watched me watch her and smiled. She said goodbye to daddy who was coming to get her, and then she confronted me. I was prepared to present myself, but she took the first shot and asked if I'd like her phone number. It was her first trip to the club and she obviously liked the feel of the place. She was all smiles and warmed me up nicely. I asked her out. She lived way south in Palos Verdes and looked like it. Well bred, well dressed, well mannered, well coiffed and well-rounded. Her face was flawless, clear and angelic. I managed to set up our date for the following Friday; she was still in school. Come next Friday, father dropped off the delicate doll on La Jolla, and I promised to bring her home later. We spent a corruptible hour getting to know each other, and as usual I took pictures for my wall of fame which by now boasted a flotilla of dreamboats.

The centerpiece of Sunset Strip's ritziest block was Le Dome, a hot spot French bar and restaurant for upscale folk, show biz luminaries and elegant women. Elton John was one of the owners and on any night you might bump into Carson, Minnelli, Taylor, Geffin, Ovitz, Sinatra, Lemmon or me. Tonight that *me* had a date that out shown all the starlets in the place. The bar was wall to wall with A-list revelers and tables were worth gold. Mingling in the crowd was better for us; she was underage. I bought our drinks from the bar and we drank incognito in the celebrity stew. I wasn't getting any soberer.

The next time I squeezed in at the bar to order more drinks I found myself next to a devil in a red dress that was so damn sexy I spent ten minutes measuring my chances of getting some of that too. She was one of those naughty beauties, sultry and pouty, and she had little red fingernails like a teen tart. Oops. I'd forgotten all about my date. By the time I found her in the crowd, she was almost in tears. I made up to her, but she was anxious to leave. I couldn't do that without the sultry tart's phone number. I had to make a choice. I was always making a choice, and they always paid me back for my insolence. The childlike adorable blonde princess called her dad to come get her. I offered to stick with her until he came. She weighed slapping my face or just turning away. She chose the classier. I deserved the worst. And I got it. By the time I made it back to the sexy doll with the short red nails, she was taken.

Clint Eastwood was doing a western out of his Malpaso Production Company, and I was sent to gun him down. The movie was *Pale Rider*, a respectful homage to George Stevens' classic gold standard *Shane*. I got cowboy scruffy and went to Warner Bros. Studios. I was escorted into the executive wing where all the life-size photos of Jack Warner's gods were hanging on the walls. The hall was alive with the ghosts of Edward G. Robinson, Cagney and Bogart, Al Jolson, George Arliss, Errol Flynn, Bugs Bunny, Joan Crawford and so many others, but none have done as much for WB's coffers as Clint Eastwood. I fondly remembered Clint as the young wrangler Rowdy Yates on *Rawhide*, a TV show from the late 50s. Today it was get down to *Pale Rider* business. First I met and read for a woman casting director, and then Clint came and gave me the look over. He was arrogantly dismissive like John Lennon had been. Superstars with super talents can get away with it. I took it like a man.

Sometime later I was at Paramount without a ride and decided to hitchhike home. I made my stand in front of the famously ornate Paramount gate. Clint came barreling out the lot and pulled up alongside of me in his pickup truck. I already had my thumb up but gave it an extra umph in hopes of lassoing the big guy. He looked straight in my eye with utter disdain, and that steely squint taunted me for a moment. Then his foot slammed on the accelerator, and he roared off without me. I smiled. No trash talk. No up yours! You have to love the guy; *Gran Torino, Unforgiven, Million Dollar Baby, Mystic River, Bird*, and the early roles: *Fistful of Dollars, Dirty Harry* and *Coogan's Bluff*. Keep up the good work, you son-of-a-gun.

Night Court gave me a call back, but there was something of more significance. I got an audition for a small but colorful part as Monroe Drake, a back-alley junkie with a gun for sale. He's a character with a lot of moxie. It's for Jackie Collins' mini-series blockbuster *Hollywood Wives*. I breezed through the first round audition on W. Pico and got a meeting with producer Howard Koch the following day at Paramount. It's like having a meet and greet with god. Howard Koch was all class. He produced John Frankenheimer's *The Manchurian Candidate* with Frank Sinatra and Laurence Harvey that was nominated best picture. Over his career, he produced Bob Hope, seven Sinatra films, eight Academy Awards Shows, Barbra Streisand's *On a Clear Day You Can See Forever* and several Neil Simon films, including *The Odd Couple, Plaza Suite, Last of the Red Hot Lovers*, and *Come Blow Your Horn*. We had a nice talk; he knew what he wanted and signed me up. He would have one more theatrical gem in him: *Ghost* with Patrick Swayze and Demi Moore. It was nominated for best picture and won two, including Whoopi Goldberg's best supporting actress Oscar.

Hollywood Wives was a three-part, six-hour adaption of the scandalous bestseller about spoiled rich brat Beverly Hills women having a field day with gullible and helplessly smitten men. British Jackie Collins, the younger sister of actress Joan Collins, was highly successful and knocked out 26 novels that made the *New York Times* bestseller list. *Hollywood Wives* was her most successful, selling over fifty million copies worldwide. The cast was packed with the biggest stars of the day: Candice Bergen, Angie Dickinson, Anthony Hopkins, Stephanie Powers, Suzanne Sommers (my *Starsky and Hutch*), Mary Crosby (my *Midnight Lace*), Roddy McDowall, Steve Forrest, Robert Stack, Rod Steiger and hotshot young heartthrob Andrew Stevens. The son of pin-up beauty actress Stella Stevens, Andrew burst on the scene with guest performances on all the popular TV shows and movies like *10 to Midnight* with Charles Bronson. My first scene with Andrew was on a stretch of busy Hollywood Boulevard. Later, I dragged him into my dumpster in a back alley off Cahuenga. After a contentious haggle, I sell him the gun he will use to spoil everybody's fun in the brutal climax on the final night. Aaron Spelling was the Executive Producer, my seventh job with the master. *Hollywood Wives* had astronomical ratings, and my reviews were satisfying. I really liked my work.

My Hamilton High Sherry had her 18ᵗʰ happy birthday. I took her to see RHCP in concert at the Greek Theatre opening for Sparks. The venue was similar to the Hollywood Bowl; other acts booked at the Greek that season were R.E.M., the Eurythmics, The Everly Brothers, Paul Anka, Psychedelic Furs and Liberace. Sparks were the brothers Ron and Russell Mael who played danceable synth-rock pabulum with a dose of quirky wit. The Peppers by contrast rocked solid, another milestone for them. We whooped it up back stage afterwards, even if the Sparky fans were left underwhelmed. *Variety*: "Openers RHCP, were clearly not what the young folk had in mind, and they made that clear on several occasions. While not really the proper billing for them, the group's performance continues to improve each time caught."

Billboard was pushing the album, "Antic West Coast quartet raps and rocks past pop clichés with a vengeance. Under the quirky lyrics and plucky attitude is skilled musicianship." New York based *CMJ Music Report* says JACKPOT! "Down and dirty LA boys combine hard rock and hard funk with gritty street feel. Kiedis' vocals are a cross between James Brown and Johnny Lydon."

MTV's *The Cutting Edge* was exactly that, a show that was hip, hot and happening. Restless Peter Zaremba hosted and interviewed Anthony and Flea in a rehearsal hall on Sunset. I was actually there at the time but couldn't recall the details so I asked my son, and he recently replied: "The *Cutting Edge* show was rad. Flea did his interview with a Saint Bernard and I was classically stone wise guy funk puppet from mars." I do remember they taped the mics to their bare chests because as usual they were half naked.

Another milestone was KROQ welcomes RHCP at the Roxy. Shoulder to shoulder with the Rainbow, it was where Anthony was first introduced to life on the Sunset Strip at the age of eleven. They were the only band on the bill; performance artists opened. The reviews were off the chart. The *Herald-Examiner* finally got on board with a screaming headline: HOT. "Judging from the Roxy show, the Chili Peppers' reputation as the Three Stooges of rock 'n' roll is both deserved and intact. They're taking this out on the road? The mind boggles! Unlike many punk or new wave acts whose influences are largely British, the Chili Peppers' roots are clearly local. Lead singer Anthony Kiedis' voice is reminiscent of such Sunset Strip favorites as John Kay, Love's Arthur Lee and Captain Beefheart--something between a growl and a bellow that is quite effective. These guys should go far. And, with any luck, they'll do it soon."

Hollywood Reporter: "Rambunctious punk funk, over-the-edge party atmosphere, Anthony Kiedis' spastic gymnastics and bass boy Flea's machine-gun barrage of low notes push the envelope. While the Red Hot Chili Peppers may not have the solid beat of the

Ramones, the social consciousness of the Sex Pistols or the lyrical poetry of X, you can't beat 'em for their zany shenanigans."

The LA Times gave the new video *Real Men Don't Kill Coyotes*, a Tune In. "For a low-cost performance video filmed on one delightfully garish set, this clip captures the Los Angeles funk-jazz-punk band's goofy wildness quite nicely."

I had a victorious audition for *Television Parts,* a show produced and masterminded by the innovative Monkee, Michael Nesmith. He had his own elaborate electronic stage 6 at the Hollywood Center Studios on Las Palmas. I played a pirate and got a nice letter from the director. "Dear Blackie, You're terrific! Your work on *Michael Nesmith in Television Parts* was a total pleasure for me and the piece will be sensational. Alan Myerson."

Keeping up with the Jones', I read for *Hunter,* the police drama with Fred Dryer as a homicide detective who breaks the rules. I was reading for a guy called the Hammer who was meaner than Mr. T. I wasn't quite that mean. Next day it was the feature film *Dead Wrong.* At MGM I read for Jeff Goldblum's *Transylvania 6-5000* for the role of Radu which ultimately went to John Byner, who had his own *Comedy Hour.*

Scott McClintock had come and gone and now was doing a modeling audition for his mom's Gunne-Sax clothing company. He asked me to help judge the beauty show at a studio in Burbank. We looked at 69 beautiful young ladies. One every 5 or 10 minutes from 10 a.m. to 4:30 a.m. Holy mother of god! We ranked them by the scale of one to ten, but I was generous with a few 11s and even a 12. I was in the wrong business. No wonder Scott was always smiling.

I was called back to *Night Court* for a new episode, the "Computer Kid." My judge was the show's creator Reinhold Weege and he sentenced me to play the derelict, Mr. Wainwright. Unlike a movie or TV show like *Magnum P.I.*, a live sitcom with an audience is more like putting on a play. A week of rehearsal, blocking, camera moves, dress rehearsals and finally the live show. In the opening prologue, John Larroquette as Dan Fielding is in the courthouse cafeteria complaining that his office phones are off, and he's missing out on the opportunity of scamming an old lady out of her fortune. He's being forced to rely on the public phone booths, a nightmare for him. As an enterprising derelict hanging around the public facility, I had been answering those phone booth calls for him while he was in court. I went on to be his "partner" and spent the episode delivering zingers. We wrapped and went out into the audience to soak up the feedback and adulation. I had a guest list of dates. Producer Jeff Melman invited me back.

Watch out! I'm into the frying pan for *Simon & Simon* with Gerald McRaney and Jameson Parker, private-eye brothers with contrasting temperaments. Extremely popular, it ran for eight years. I read for Mr. Lee, "Nefarious, ruthless, cold blooded professional killer, calculated, calm and efficient and always gets his man," except this time. It would have been a juicy role and the show was filmed in beautiful San Diego.

There was big news from Lindy Goetz: the Chili Peppers had booked a consequential tour. They would open at the revered St. Andrews Hall in Detroit on November 1st with Romeo Void, The Medusa in Chicago, Cleveland, Top of the Rock in Grand Rapids, Pittsburgh, Buffalo, The Ritz in New York City, Boston, Toronto, Milwaukee, Madison and Minneapolis.

The Grand Rapids show was promoted by Alan Bashara. Friends, fans and relatives poured into the Alpine Avenue club. Much had been made of Peggy being mother of the lead singer, and the local press was there en masse. It was a big day for young children and old grandparents. West Michigan's expectations soared. That was until the show began. Pumped with exuberance and a wicked bass beat, Flea dropped his pants and exposed himself. Uber pooper conservative hometown was put in a frenzy of condemnation. Fire and brimstone and the wrath of god came upon the virulent visage of our city. A stampede of embarrassment ran for the exits. *The Grand Rapids Press* critic said, "If it was my child I'd disown him." Peggy was backed up to the Wailing Wall. Alan went into hiding.

Booked to fly out for the Ritz gig in NYC, suddenly I had my own gigs. First was the action crime drama *Matt Houston* at WB for Aaron Spelling on ABC. Stud muffin Lee Horsley starred and the inimitable *Beverly Hillbilly* Buddy Epson was a regular. I gunned for "Tucker, a man you wouldn't buy a used car from."

I didn't get to be Tucker, but did get to be a dapper dancing musical gangster in a lavish video for Jermaine Jackson, brother of that other guy, Michael. The song is *"Do What You Do."* It peaked at #13 on the Billboard Hot 100, and spent three weeks at #1 on the adult contemporary chart. It was #6 on the UK charts. The video was a four-day shoot in a variety of locations, with a scintillating cast, including love interest Iman, the super-super model. We sang and danced and did our thing at Palette, the Manzio Mansion and other fancy exteriors around LA. With a definite *Godfather* guise, the plot was a tug-of-war between Jermaine, his date Trisha McFarlin and Iman, who was mysteriously connected to our gang of hoods. She actually tried to shoot him in his bedroom after they had a steamy love scene. I dragged her away with some help from my fellow mobsters, and we drove her off in a big old 30s gangster-mobile. Several of the Jacksons showed up to help and hinder the video, most notably a very young Janet Jackson who was frisky, feisty and funny.

The ever-loveable Alison peeked into my life again, along with two more auditions on the same day, *It's Your Move* an NBC sitcom and *Facts of Life,* both at Universal. The *Diff'rent Strokes* spin off ran nine seasons with a cast that included George Clooney and Molly Ringwald. We finally had a clean cut of *Ninja* and a screening at the ABC VIP room. I read for *Hunter* again; third time would be the charm.

I spent Thanksgiving dinner with my neighbor, Lorrie Levine who produced adult movies. Her pool was always wet with naked actresses. I had a mad crush on Traci Lords who Lorrie worked with and knew well. I offered to do a clothed cameo in one of Traci's films if I could have this billing: "Special Appearance by Blackie Dammett who did this film just to meet Traci Lords." Thankfully, Lorrie decided it wasn't such a good idea. Kim Kirby caught my attention though.

Chapter 39: My Dad

My father died in the waning days of Orwell's 1984. I was sound asleep in my La Jolla Avenue bed, by myself for a change, when the phone rang and a Floridian angel of death sucker punched me. The ultimate alarm rang. It was the annihilation of my own immortality, and it pushed the start button on the stop watch. Vulnerable would have been an upgrade. I was naked and cut from my creator. The impregnable reservoir of our 45-year bond had burst through the dam of invincibility and flooded me with a torrent of combative love retrospect. A bizarre love so powerful it had always threatened my very life with draconian paternity.

The environments of my life begin and end with him at the helm of our havens: Clancy, Livingston, Emerald, Fulton, Harrison Park, North Park, Plainfield, Leelanau and Honeysuckle. Even on my own, I felt the security of his safety-line grip that held me secure, no matter where I was. His muscular biceps were my compass. His sharp, handsome features cleared the path and pierced the fog of doubt. Was there ever a moment I wasn't aware and wary of his every thought, because they were so often of me? He was dedicated to creating in me what his generation was incapable of achieving, as I only lived to lay the groundwork for my son, and surely Anthony will do the same for his. The Kiedis electrolytic currency may have blown some fuses through rough times, but our tenacious dreams and destiny were inviolable.

Dad left a life of Michigan for Florida in 1963, but opened a door to the world. I rarely saw him after that: when I retook Peggy and Tony, when my sister Judy married, once when my Dad was ill and once when Eileen was. I was the family ex-patriot, the black sheep and the prodigal son, but so was my father when he was young. And so would Anthony be. We were dreamers and poets and entertainers. He was proud of what I had accomplished in the shark pool of Hollywood, as I was of his mature metamorphosis into an honest politician and devoted family man who raised a flock of devils and angels. He imbued me with faithless science. He taught me to reach for that which my peers were afraid to. He gave me life and the courage to live it on the edge.

We had finally begun to reconcile those dark memories from the painful past. Beatings today that are criminal were tough love then, and they didn't come any tougher than my Dad, nor I any more impertinent. Now we spoke coast to coast on the phone with genuine affection and clear consciences. He boldly critiqued my film performances, even as he boasted of them to his friends. He was proud of his son. What more could I want? We were finally complete, the circle of life. I revised the tales of his sordid reputation and found new praise to decorate the old soldier. He was still daredevil dapper, theatrical and always singing from daybreak to midnight. A clarion cross-country call in the wild I could hear in my heart. His death-defying spirit was unbreakable. How ironic at last I actually knew where he was and what he was doing. Now I was monitoring him the way he used to check on me: tucking me in with Hemingway bedtime stories, snapshots of my sprouting, swinging a sawed-off seven iron, tossing a pass through an old tire, tap dancing the balance of clutch and accelerator, keeping my shoulders back or get a whack, and always preaching the wonder of words.

Dad and Eileen had been up in Michigan visiting, his first return in eons. I tracked the adventure with a big smile but did not know he had fallen ill. They made the quick decision to drive back to Florida earlier than expected, even missing some long-anticipated reunions. In Georgia he gave out; a medevac aircraft flew him to West Palm Beach. Leukemia, pneumonia, a lifetime of hard work, seventy years, and then he died. I looked into Anthony's eyes and saw my reflection, father and son and the inevitability of grave implications. There was nowhere to hide. A Darwinist, my consolation was in the solemnity of evolution.

Both Palm Beach Garden newspapers ran banner headlines of his tragic parting. The Dixie Highway was lined with proud citizens, police officers and fire rescue for his procession. Fittingly, it was like a 4th of July parade; my Pop was born on the fourth. The current mayor, Mike Martino, spoke glowingly of the three-time mayor, three-time vice-mayor and 14-year city councilman. Proudly, he had been a member of the Professional Golfers Association since 1969 and was the pro at two luxury Palm Beach area courses. He designed, built and had a piece of two exclusive country clubs, Holiday and Frenchman's Creek. My sister Judy uncovered and sent me the memorabilia he had saved since I was born: my childhood drawings, my homesick letters to him from Camp Manitou-Lin and every report card from kindergarten to my graduation from high school. He still had my annual 8 by 10 photos taken at Herpolshimers Department Store on each and every December 7th birthday of mine. *The Grand Rapids Press* wrote a moving eulogy for my Pa. The large-point headline read "Actor's Dad Stricken."

Chapter 40: Shock

I started 1985 with a successful reading for CBS's *Trapper John M.D.* at Fox; my character's name was Slime. He was a misunderstood junkie hypochondriac suspected child kidnapper with a soft side.

The show was a spinoff of the 1970 satirical movie *MASH* (Mobile Army Surgical Hospital) directed by Robert Altman and written by Ring Lardner Jr., with Donald Sutherland as Hawkeye and Elliot Gould as Trapper John. Robert Duvall and Sally Kellerman ("Hot Lips" O'Houlihan) were also in the film. *M*A*S*H** the TV show with Alan Alda, Loretta Swit, and Jamie Farr ran from 1972 to 1983, and was one of the most successful television programs of all time. The final episode was the most watched TV show ever.

Our *Trapper John M.D.* ran for seven years, with Pernell Roberts as the lead character, years later working in a San Francisco Hospital. Pernell Roberts had been one of the *Bonanza* sons, along with Michael Landon and Dan Blocker. So I was Slime, perhaps the most interesting moniker of my career. Like *Midnight Lace*, Slime was a colorful red herring. I should have passed out bad guy business cards. Happily, I had guest star Ronee Blakely on the set. She was an Oscar nominee in Robert Altman's *Nashville*, recorded the duet "Hurricane" with Bob Dylan, toured on his Rolling Thunder Review and also recorded with Leonard Cohen. Another unusual guest actor working this episode was ex-Mouseketeer Paul Petersen, who achieved stardom as a teenage heartthrob on *The Donna Reed Show.*

Anthony and Jennifer came by my place to dye their hair pink and blue before we went to meet George Clinton about the Peppers' second album. Hillel Slovak had rejoined his brothers, and in May they started recording *Freaky Styley* at Clinton's studio in Michigan. When the band played their first Hollywood Palladium show for the album, the Good God of Funk joined Anthony on stage for butt-kicking vocals and audacious dancing to the delight of a thunderous crowd. Anthony always made sure I had tickets and backstage passes for his gigs. The new record was slightly more successful but remained well out of the mainstream. It did however produce the bizarre video *Catholic School Girls Rule*. Band buddy Dick Rude directed it, and it was universally censored for its excessive nudity, sex and sacrilege.

Speaking of indulgence, my current data base revealed record tryst tales. I was breast-stroking in compassionate currents. It was reciprocal of course, and I do believe they got their money's worth. Occasionally, those rascally ladies would get the last laugh though, retribution like the night I left Bar Deluxe and was walking home in a tipsy tumult. A lynch mob of pretty girls were across Sunset and I veered in their direction. They blew me kisses and wrapped me in luscious compliments. They whistled and feigned fainting. I waved them off and admitted I was tuckered out from a long night. Still, they embraced me and smeared their rainbow of lipsticks on my cheeks. They squealed and felt me up. I fancied myself as Clark Gable in his prime. "Ladies, please, I may be irresistible, but I have an audition at Cannon Films tomorrow; give a guy a break." I finally pulled away from their clutches and savored myself. My handsome devil was all smiles as I walked toward SM and

LaJolla. Back home, I went through the normal routine of unloading my pockets so I could hang up my trousers. That's when I realized the vixens had relieved me of my money clip and at least a hundred bucks.

Or the time on Quaaludes, I was leaving Lenny Fagen's Coconut Teaszer. Across the street of infamy was yet another siren beckoning me for attention. Tom Gravengood was visiting from Grand Rapids and warned me not to go. Instead, I staggered across the cobbled pavement toward the alluring prize and her phone number. I was lucky not to get run over, but did step in a pot hole and sprained my ankle. I was laid up for a while and spoiled Gravy's vacation. Fortunately, he ran out into the middle of busy Sunset Boulevard and carried me to safety. I did however insist that he carry me to the foxy far side so I could at least get some sympathy from the lady in red.

I hadn't been lying to the lynch-mob vixens about Cannon Films. I made a concerted effort for the role of a Russian named Nikko in the Chuck Norris film *Invasion USA*. I even spent a week with a dialect coach to master a Russian accent. Nyet! I did a photo shoot for Michael Nesmith with my new publicist, Harriet. *Love America Style* had been a TV hit in the seventies and like a fading marriage, Paramount tried to revive it circa '85. I did a few comedy sketches for Barbara Remsen, but like most lost loves, it didn't get off the ground. The next day, the next maybe, and it was Johnny Carson Productions in Burbank for an NBC Variety Special. They were looking for an ensemble to do improv comedy, something like *SCTV* or *Fridays*. I had a nice interview and got enough laughs to warrant a call back.

My racy nymph Jennifer Mayo invited me to a show of hers. Later we celebrated another of her birthdays, this time at Coconut Teaszer. She was still a kid. Jennifer continued to battle for roles and finally snagged a low-budget movie called *Scarred;* she played the lead, a teenage call girl trying to make in on the streets of Hollywood. The advertising hook was "Sometimes sixteen is anything but sweet." She may have been scarred, but to me she was sacred. There may have been enough girls in my life to populate Mumbai, but Jennifer was at the very top. Her sexy friendship is one of the highlights of my life.

Marcie Leroff called me into Paramount for John Hughes' *Pretty in Pink*. With *National Lampoon's Class Reunion* behind him, Hughes had achieved popular acclaim and could write his own ticket. Now he was producing his screenplay *Pretty in Pink* with Molly Ringwald, her third film with him. I was in the pink and feeling confident because Hughes had liked my work. Oops, Marcie said *Class Reunion* still gave him indigestion. Oh well, and I had always had a crush on Molly Ringwald. I had better luck doing live mysteries for *Capers,* under the direction of Lynn Chaplin. Superstation WTBS, now TBS, tested me for *Safe at Home.* Back in familiar territory at Raleigh Studios, I read for the appropriate *Booby Trap*. But *Capers* flourished, and I picked a new name for this endeavor, Blackstone Double Dammett IV.

Bar Deluxe had become one of my favorite haunts; I was minding everybody's business and sitting in one of the dandy leather banquettes when a peculiar leprechaun approached me. He was about five-foot tall, give or take a haircut, had a cute little round face, bleached-blonde locks and was dressed in leather doo-dads and a fake English accent. He was also literally up to his neck in bold, colorful tattoos. His name was Shock. I didn't have to tell him mine; he knew it and knew it well as he rattled off some of my credits. I hadn't trapped a bird yet, so I invited him to join me. He was the most effusively optimistic and good natured person I'd run into for a long time. He'd just arrived from England where he claimed to have been in GBH, the hardcore punk band with those memorable tunes "City Babies Attacked by Rats" and "Leather, Bristles, Studs and Acne." GBH was cop lingo for grievous bodily harm. Somehow I couldn't imagine Shock as very dangerous, but then I'd only known him for a few minutes. I enjoyed his company, but it was time for the opposite sex. He wouldn't take a hint, and I couldn't shake him. Indefatigable, he whipped out his charisma and went to work before my eyes. He lassoed half a dozen girls and presented them to my table. He was charming, cuddly, and he had that phony English accent. I was feeling intimidated. I was supposed to be the boss here. Gary Myrick and I had dueled for babes at Bar Deluxe, but this was ridiculous. He pestered me for acting advice and in return offered to share the secrets of his immaculate attraction. Little did I know I was selling myself to the devil.

I was currently working on *Lady in White,* an unusual film written, directed and produced by Frank LaLoggia. He had some financing but not nearly enough to make an entire film, so he was putting together an eleven-page twenty-minute movie. His plan was to show it around town and raise money to do it right. He had a union crew and 10 SAG actors, including the legit Katherine Helmond, matriarch Jessica Tate from *Soap* and currently in *Who's the Boss.* She had Emmy and Tony nominations. We were all promised a piece of the action when the big version came later. We sacrificed, took pay cuts and worked out butts off late into the night on locations that included Las Virgenes, out in the coyote and puma wilderness. It was an autobiographical story of a boy in a small New England town beset with portentous intrigue. Our low-budget schedule didn't afford us the luxury of waiting out cold and rainy weather. It was tough enough for the veterans, much less a child actor like Mark Goebel, who played the young LaLoggia. He was a valiant little trouper. We shot a total of 58 scenes, including 18 Blue Screen scenes at V.C.E. Studios on Highland. These were special effects of the lady in white and other ghosts, Frankie's imaginations, and me falling off a cliff and tumbling into the raging sea.

I brought Shock along for his first taste of movie magic. I also introduced him to Janet Cunningham, Hollywood's resident casting director for extras. Soon Shock was working on films and videos. At night we ran roughshod. We were two notorious serial lovers, and everybody in town knew we were a team of trouble; some may have even said predators. I burnished an orderly library of black books that housed a thousand darlings. My actor appointment books did double duty finding a spot for auditions; lipstick phone numbers blotted out the free space. Shock was volatile and in the moment. Every morning he made up a new list of his top 25 girls. They varied by his inclination. Once he made his list, he'd start calling them, beginning at the top. He crashed with hooligan friends he'd met on the streets. The apartment was on Hollywood east of Western Avenue in a shaky neighborhood. The pay phone on the sidewalk was his office. At the end of the day, he would crumple up his "list" and start a new one in the morning.

I got to know Shock's rotating girls, but there was a lofty name I had yet to meet, Katie Martin. Shock was reluctant to talk about her; she was his special love, an LA girl but currently living in San Francisco during her first year of college at SFSU. Having encountered my hot tamales, he couldn't resist showing her off to me. We drove up and surprised her at the dorm. She was thrilled to see Shock, and I was just shocked. Like all his girls, she was quite a bit taller than he, and when they embraced, his face met her breasts like two puzzle pieces. I wanted to play too. She was a dazzling golden-red retriever and had every right to join my triumvirate of Katie Bramson, Deborah Lee and Connie Foreman. On the drive back to LA, my perceptive little buddy seemed uncomfortable. At last he made his stand and told me in no uncertain terms that Katie was off-limits. It was pre-emptive, and it was futile.

We finished the *Lady in White* project with a big wrap party and glorious congratulations to all of us from Frank LaLoggia. Shock came with me and played the party like a Stradivarius. He was a born schmoozer and always had a little toot for those who were inclined. It would take a year, but ultimately LaLoggia raised his capital and did the film. Not surprisingly, he never kept his word about using the original cast. Katherine Helmond was the only actor to work in the big movie. Mark Goeble was replaced with Lucas Haas, who had just played the boy in Peter Weir's *Witness* with Harrison Ford, and my role went to Len Cariou, a brilliant stage actor with sixteen Broadway plays and a Tony for best actor in the musical *Sweeney Todd*.

Capers hit the jackpot, and we did a show at the Hollywood Bowl. And there were always new auditions: *One Hogan Place* for CBS, and another for David Lee Roth and his theatrical movie. Van Halen videos like *Panama* and *Hot for Teacher* had been all the rage. When Roth left Van Halen and went single with his *California Girls* video, his ego and his partner, Pete Angelus, set their sights on a feature movie of his antics. I knew Roth, so after my reading I took the opportunity of injecting Red Hot Chili Peppers in the context of, who knows, maybe an opening slot on one of his shows. He was lukewarm. The movie never happened. David Lee Roth went on with his rollercoaster career; I'd see him at Peanut's when it was the rage, inebriated at closing time and struggling to pick up girls. Unconscionable!

Suddenly there was a rush of work. First was a new ABC series of two New York families, one of cops and another of a New York crime syndicate family. The Godfather was one of Hollywood's great actors, Eli Wallach, and a young Michael Madsen was the hot-tempered son, much like James Caan's role in *The Godfather*. I got involved in the sordid conflict as a custom gunsmith, selling a special weapon to a hit man who in turn used the gun on me. I changed my voice and created a deep growl. I kept going outside the sound stage and screaming at the top of my lungs. Everybody on the MGM lot thought I was crazy. It was *Our Family Honor* and my role was Max Simonesky.

I succumbed to an affair that sincerely touched me. She was different than the others, not tall, slim and rangy like my other gals, but rather plump and conventional, like Joan from North Park grade school. Her name was Lisa Cloudy, and she resided in the mid-Wilshire area of Manhattan style apartments. She had a normal job. After a few dates, she invited me to see her own band, Partly Cloudy. On stage she was transformed into a chanteuse from the forties—lusty, mysterious and flamboyant. She dressed like the Black Dahlia and took me for a wild ride I'd never expected in a million years. Miss Cloudy, storm warning.

Who's the Boss was the boss; it was a top-10 sitcom for most of its eight seasons on ABC. So when I was asked to read for the show at Sunset Gower Studios (Columbia), I was psyched up and ready to go. The part was Torch, another of my funny bad guy names, a comical arsonist convict in prison with "The Prodigal Father-In-Law," played by Broadway institution James Coco. This was his first appearance in the series, but he went on to be a regular as the kids' grandpa. I ran away with the part and would report on Monday for a week of rehearsals and then the show before a live audience on Friday.

The troublesome team blitzed the clubs on Saturday, and I was prepared to take it easy on Sunday, but Shock talked me into going to a party at UCLA. Shock reminded me of Scott St. John; he was cool, nifty with the girls and never had a car. It was an afternoon affair at a fraternity house but much different than my old frat days at Michigan State. The frat had a swimming pool in the middle of a big patio surrounded by several small apartment units. Guests milled about and all the units were open. Each one had its own hospitality, food or beer or, in one case, a band that was about to perform. I had enough and was willing to go, but Shock wanted to see the band I had never heard of. We squeezed into a tiny space where the band had set up in the middle of the living room. It was like watching a band in a phone booth. The gyrating singer was wearing leather chaps and his exposed bare buttocks threatened the decorum of the front row. It was in my face and I didn't appreciate it. They finished just in time to save my hearing, and the fancy steppin' singer named Axl thanked us for coming. They were Guns N' Roses. In a couple years, they would emerge from this frat baby crib to become the biggest band in the world.

Shock and I went out and cooled off on a concrete bench alongside the pool. We were being mildly entertained by semi-nude swimmers cavorting below when a late-arriving super couple came through the front gate across the way from us. Shock and I both took one look at the mind-boggling female half of the couple, and we simultaneously fell backwards off our bench as though we had practiced the move with Busby Berkeley. The vivid vixen was the most perfect creature in the history of girls. She was punked out with fuchsia–and-blonde hair, camouflage shorts, combat boots and a revealing pink slip of a blouse adorned in hand-written anarchy. Her mate was a good match for this goddess with his glam-and-leather rock star swagger. I could only shake my head and wish I was so lucky. Shock informed me he was Tracii Guns, a former band mate of Axl's in Hollywood Rose, and now in his own band LA Guns.

I told Shock I needed to get back; tomorrow was my first day on *Who's the Boss*. Shock decided to stay and I started to leave, but halfway down the stairs I met up with Vandalyn. This slinky stunner was definitely on the edge and asked me for a ride to her home on the fringe of Culver City. I gladly obliged. Her family was not the least bit phased by this older man, even though she was still in high school. Cosmopolitan Vandalyn became my next bomb.

I spent the week rehearsing with Tony Danza, who played the hired-help maid. Judith Light was his boss. Danny Pintauro was the young son and teenage daughter Aylssa Milano would grow up to be a very sexy lady with quite an interesting career. And yes, I had a crush on her too. Katherine Helmond was the meddlesome mother-in law. I was an old sitcom pro now and hit all the right notes. My audience guests were Shock and Vandalyn. I had tasty bits with Tony Danza and Judith Light, but the big scene was my emotional testimony in a packed parole-board court, convincing authorities to pardon James Coco. We were apparent abominations but after my testimony of heartfelt adulation and appreciation for Coco's friendship in the joint, I broke down and shed pterodactyl tears.

"Thanks, Cupcake," I muttered with conviction. The blushing bad boys gave a wide-eyed Tony Danza and the assembled witnesses a new perspective. Order in the court!

Lisa Cloudy and the ever-popular Alison still peeped in and out of my life, but Queen Vandalyn ruled my heart for now. And further confusing myself, I was still rankled by the persistent memory of the gloriously confident girl with Tracii Guns at the frat party. It was the weekend, and Shock and I took to the streets in my Eldorado. He had his list and his toot and his pot. Like an ancient mariner, he navigated me to the propitious club, Cathay de Grande. There were local bands playing and one of them turned out to be LA Guns. We paraded in like champions but got little attention and had to readjust a notch or two. The place was full of glam-struck fans and glam-sham wannabes and a few of the real Mc Coy glam bands. But more pointedly, both of us were confronted by our special ladies. Katie Martin was home from college, and I caught another gaze at the pink-and-white wonder woman, who was once again squired by the guitar player of the headlining band. You just can't compete with that. Katie was with her friends and not paying much attention to Shock either. We left early and started from scratch. The evening's acquisitions were Sherry and Kim Jane.

I had an audition for the skateboarding movie, *Thrashin'*, courtesy of casting director Geno Havens, who was handicapped but drove his wheel chair with NASCAR daredevilry. We were working friends. I got a call back the next day with writer-producer Alan Sacks. My character was Sam Flood "the old timer," and I came back a third time before the part went to the popular actor Chuck McCann. I remember going to Venice and hanging with the skate dudes, even working on some rudimentary moves. Ironically, it was the Red Hot Chili Peppers that represented the Kiedis name in *Thrashin'*. The band, with the original lineup now intact, did a performance in the movie. Josh Brolin starred as the lead actor, beating out Johnny Depp.

I did a photo shoot with Vandalyn, Tara and Kim Jane. I read for a half-breed Indian in Peter Skerl's *Golden Spurs*; as an encyclopedia salesman on the ABC show *Growing Pains* with our old friend Alan Thicke; as a fastidious, no nonsense, stoic and serious character in *Warlock*; and yet another *Night Court*. And I met another new girlfriend named Nicole Noel from Des Moines, who crashed into Hollywood with all the energy and bright smiles of an Iowa electrical storm. Our encounter came in the land of encounters, The Rainbow. She was bound and determined to win me over, but there was more competition than the youngster could have ever handled. She made poster pictures of herself with captions like "Blackie belongs to me!" I did like her though, and we had some fun. Her mom came out West to visit, and I had to meet her too—at the Rainbow. I was spinning in cute circles with Vandalyn, Alison, Cloudy, Nicole, Kim, Susie, Sherry, Shauna, Carolyn, Lanelle, and Lorraine, even Liza Cruz resurfaced. And life was further complicated by Shock's untouchable Katie Martin, who I found myself falling in love with. Fortunately, I had all the others to hide behind and not arouse his suspicion. Shock and Katie did a music video with Ozzy Osbourne.

It was a relief to be working and avoiding women for moments at a time. Penelope Spheeris was coming up the ranks as a film director to be reckoned with. Her earlier documentary film *The Decline of Western Civilization* and *Suburbia*, the film Flea made his debut in, were both well received. Now she was directing a major studio film, *The Boys Next Door*, with one of Hollywood's hottest young actors, Maxwell Caulfield. For good measure, they cast another new actor with very little experience in his first starring role; he was the son of Martin Sheen and the brother of Emilo Estevez. He was Charlie Sheen. One of his last roles had been in a TV show as "Man Shaving." When I saw the news in *Variety,* I called Penelope and asked if there were any parts I could read for. She said not really but would write me a part. In the film, two ruthless buddies just out of school go on a trip to LA where they become progressively psychopathic. The Maxwell Caulfield character is a homophobic anti-social serial killer, and Penelope places him in a West Hollywood bar. The bad boys don't know it's a *gay* bar. I played the gay bartender who stokes Maxwell's anger with a protracted joke that doesn't set well with the young killer. The location was in an actual gay bar on the corner of Palm and Santa Monica in my old neighborhood. They had to rig the room with heavy, high-power lights for the cameras, and most of them were hung from the ceiling. While I was doing my scene and telling the vile joke, the whole lighting contraption broke loose and fell directly on top of me. Miraculously, one small opening in the rig is what came down around me—a little safe spot. I stood there in awe, completely surrounded with the busted metal gaff. Patti D'Arbanville, Christopher McDonald and Moon Unit Zappa were also in the film. It was reasonably well received, but Penelope's big successes were right around the corner with commercial hits *Wayne's World, The Beverly Hillbillies,* and *The Little Rascals.*

Shock and I branched out to clubs like Spatz in Huntington Beach and new LA joints Lip Stick Fixx, Seven Seas, Club Sandwich, and Lace. Shock was a tattoo, but he also did tattoos, and damn it, he went and tattooed Katie. I was really pissed but couldn't be too obvious about it. Little by little, Shock began to open up his dark secrets to me. The English punk rocker was actually a tough street kid from Cuba named Mario Cabrera.

La Rocca had me going up for just about every TV show on the air. I went to NBC for *Punky Brewster,* a cultural icon of the day, with her little girl pig tails. Rhonda Young called me in to read for *It's a Living,* with popular actress Ann Jillian who had been diagnosed with breast cancer. Her high profile brought attention to what had previously been a touchy subject. Eventually, Ann Jillian came back to the show and proved that women could overcome breast cancer. And the hits kept coming: I read for *Remington Steele,* with a baby-faced Pierce Brosnan in his first American acting job, long before his four *James Bond* movies. A week later, I was up for a feature film, Sylvester Stallone's *Cobra* at MGM. It was the opening scene and established Stallone as a stud who defused a nasty situation with an evil criminal, "Cho, sunken cheeks, dirty hair, mean, sadist, agile, Hispanic; in a 7-Eleven." I wasn't dirty or sadistic or Hispanic enough though. Sly's love interest in the film was Brigitte Nielsen, and they were briefly married at the time. Cobra grossed $160,000,000.

The next day, I was off to Burbank Studios for the action thriller *Kidnapped,* as Carl who abducts teenage Debbie for his boss Victor Nardi. My character: cold blooded, vicious, murderous, menacing, wicked, deceitful and physical. And the part goes to…Robert Dryer. At the audition, I met Pam who was reading for the Debbie part and added her to my book. I also added Devon. All hail the mighty Devon. She was actually a very petite young lady with long, black-as-night hair. She weighed about 98.6 and most of that was in her breasts. She was spectacular. We met at the Rainbow by the cigarette machine. She wasn't especially interested, but I persevered and walked off with a phone number I kept in my wallet for emergencies.

I saw that LA Guns was playing the Troubadour and thought about Tracii's bombshell. The Troubadour was the granddaddy of West Hollywood's music venues. It was small, unpretentious and Mecca. The front door opened into a small bar with a small bar and a few scattered tables. It was beyond the second door that history had been accumulating for thirty years and counting. That room was small too for a venue, and it had a small balcony of church pews. It had a decent-size stage but no backstage. There was a dressing room on the second floor, with room for three midgets, and a restroom that you'd find in a two-pump gas station. There was a safety-valve back door for when the temperatures reached in the hundreds. And yet it was heaven.

The owner, manager and friend was Doug Weston, a gangly guy who had started out with a beatnik coffee house in the 50s and built the Troubadour into an institution. There was a wall where you first entered that listed everybody significant who had ever played there, and there were hundreds of the greatest artists of all time. Lenny Bruce was arrested for obscenity in 1957. Pre-electric Bob Dylan jammed. By the evolving 60s, there were early Byrds, Buffalo Springfield, Joni Mitchell and Richard Pryor. Steve Martin was an unknown comic. Lou Adler discovered Cheech and Chong at a Monday Hoot Night. The Eagles' Don Henley and Glen Frey were regular customers. I was at Elton John's U.S. debut. Janis Joplin partied at the Troubadour and was found dead at the Landmark Hotel on Franklin of a heroin overdose the next morning. By the 70s we were enjoying the talents of Carly Simon, James Taylor, Billy Joel, Miles Davis, and Leonard Cohen. Bob Dylan and His Rolling thunder Revue dropped in for a surprise show. An unsigned The Knack headlined a show with special guests Springsteen, Tom Petty and Stephen Stills. John Lennon, Harry Nilsson and the Smothers Brothers were déjà vu.

I was often found high in Doug Weston's office overlooking the front bar commotion and our trail of evidence. The infamous list up to this October night in 1985 also included Arlo Guthrie, Neil Diamond, George Carlin, Sheryl Crow, Metallica, Motley Crue and a thousand more, including tonight's performer, Guns N' Roses.

Wait a minute! Guns N' Roses? And in their official live debut? They were last-minute filling in for the no-show LA Guns. It turns out Tracii Guns had jumped his own band and hooked up with guitar dish and ex-Runaway Lita Ford, who was performing in New York City and touring the East Coast. So I watched Axl, Slash, Izzy, Duff and Adler for the second time, and at least I could put some distance between me and Axl's butt. And as I had hoped, I came across Tracii's wet-dream doll. She was childlike this night, no glitter, no makeup, no pink hair, no pretense. She was wearing denim. She nodded with a friendly smile and introduced herself as Candy, but then turned to other friends, including RHCP's roady Nickey Beat, who happened to be the drummer for LA Guns. Not surprisingly, I already had a crush on Nickey's girlfriend too, and I had just been talking to her. I roamed around and finally went into the front bar. I spun my neck a quick swivel around the bar and was about to exit when I noticed Candy all alone in the far corner. I worked my way over and sat down next to her. She smiled again and my heart went boom. I learned she was Candy Lee Pearson, freshly 17, and drinking a beer. She lived with her mother and stepfather in West Covina, and Tracii usually lived with her too. Candy was born in Oklahoma, raised in Las Vegas and had moved to LA a couple years ago. Her Troubadour pals abruptly abducted her and they left. I drove up to the Rainbow for last call in the parking lot, but there she was again. We laughed at the odds and she accepted my phone number.

I got call backs from both *Kidnapped* and David Lee Roth, and some new directives from Johnny La Rocca. One was way downtown to Alameda and Flower for *Helltown* as a failed Hells Angel, and the second was at Warner Bros. for ABC's *Hollywood Beat* as Swifty. This was another Aaron Spelling cop-buddy show, and I wasn't the least bit surprised when I aced the audition and got the part. I had originally read for the pilot earlier in the year. I was more excited for Shock than I was for me. We worked on seedy underbelly locations and my scene was at a Hollywood Book and Poster shop on Las Palmas, where I made fake passports for criminals. There was plenty of action to entertain the likeable leprechaun. The cast featured Jack Scalia and his rookie partner Jay Acovone. In some very peculiar casting, former Oakland Raider football monster John Matuszak played an openly gay guy who was one of the local weirdo informants. As we left the shoot, Shock dropped a bomb; he was going to England for a few weeks on unspecified business but alluded to working with an unnamed band. Was it band or contraband?

James and Chanda on Secluded Lake, Rockford Michigan.

Chapter 41: Ingénues for Breakfast

It was one of those rare evenings at home, just lounging around and taking it easy. About eight the phone rang and it was Candy. A rush of adrenaline raised the hair on my neck. She asked me to come get her but wait outside so her parents wouldn't know. West Covina was about 35 miles from West Hollywood, due east through town and then out interstate 10 to the suburban burgs of squaresville. I cleaned up my act, jumped in the Caddy and started my epic voyage down Santa Monica to the Hollywood Freeway, which got me downtown to the five-level interchange and onto the San Bernardino Freeway. Then it was Boyle Heights, East LA, Monterey Park, Alhambra, San Gabriel, Rosemead, El Monte, Baldwin Park and finally West Covina. I exited south at the designated off ramp and found her house. Candy was supposed to be outside but wasn't.

After a good wait, I gave up and drove back home. It was a wasted 70-mile roundtrip, and I no sooner got home when she called again with a new story. Tracii had returned from NY a few days ago; they had been fighting and she was hiding in the bushes. She hadn't mentioned Tracii for fear I wouldn't come. We set new coordinates and tried again. Again, she was a no show. Now I was angry and drove home with a taste for her blood. All those "pretty pleases" and "I'll be wearing something really sexy" were only bitter kisses. I had logged 140 miles for this bonkers baby doll. If you think she had the audacity to call a third time, and that I'd actually make it 210 miles just to spend a couple hours in hell with Candy Lee…well, you're absolutely right.

She was plutonium. She was a heartbreak virus you can't survive, a burning obsession stoked in her heavenly blast furnace. I was as helpless as Mike Hammer in Mickey Spillane's *I, the Jury*, unable to resist the lure of a deadly woman who intends homicide. Candy was a wanton sex child who teased and tantalized and spit you out when she was bored. At the moment, she was far from bored and jumped into the Eldorado, with all the lively energy of a teenager dancing to the KROQ music on my car radio. It was hard to keep my eyes on the road she was so beautiful. She had a perfect goddess profile that belonged on a statue in the Louvre. She was bright and street smart but had quit school in the eighth grade. She told me about Las Vegas, where she had been dating rock stars since she was only thirteen. That her father was serving life in prison for killing a cop, and that her mom was a casino poker dealer who once played the dippy blonde assistant to a used-car salesman during those late-night movie commercials. Candy was not shy about her association with Hollywood rockers. She was intimate with all of them: Guns N' Roses, LA Guns, Poison, Rat, Skidrow, Warrant, Faster Pussycat and all the rest. She didn't think of herself as a groupie; the rockers were her groupies.

We pulled off the freeway and headed west on Sunset; she asked me to slow down as we passed the infamous 24 hour Denny's Restaurant that was a magnet for bizarre characters. After 2 a.m., all the Hollywood rug rats congregated. It was only midnight though, and she didn't see what she was looking for. She casually mentioned that Guns N' Roses lived nearby and often hung out at the liquor store there. Sure enough, there was the band's bass player Duff McKagan, and Candy screamed "Pull over!" They chatted briefly and surprisingly she came right back to my car. "OK," she said, "show me your house." She told me a fascinating history of boyfriends, adventures and aspirations. She raided my liquor stash and asked for drugs; I told her I had none. She pleased me with her one-two punch of sex kitten and girl next door, but she was setting me up for a knockout. Too soon it was time to get her home; a fourth trip would bring the total mileage to 280. It was a bargain. She was the real deal; the mostest girl I'd ever met. For a while I jumped every time I heard the phone ring, but it was always a mere mortal. I was on call for a dirty angel.

98.6 Devon hadn't responded to any of my calls. Totally irresistible, I wasn't surprised but finally caught her at home and she agreed to meet me for lunch. I bit my tongue for 48 hours, and, when the lunching hour was near, I drove up into North Hollywood. My arteries were pounding with excitement as I walked toward her apartment. I knocked. I knocked again. Finally she opened the door, yawning and covered with sleepy dust. Inadvertently perhaps, she was revealing her slender limbs and grownup girl breasts in nothing but a tiny T-shirt. How that frail body supported those jolting buttresses aimed at my heart I'll never know. It was a question for anatomical engineers. But there was more; right behind her was Candy Lee. They had been out partying the night before, and Candy spent the night. In retrospect, Candy's name had come up when I first met Devon at the Rainbow, but I never expected to find the daily double on my plate. Talk about torn. I was in love with each of them, and now they had me on the spot, but what a spot.

We went to a House of Pancakes, and I sat across from them in a booth. My vista was Devon on the left, provocative pancakes dripping with maple syrup and melting butter in the middle, and Candy on the right. And there were new profound revelations of Candy: she was wearing a man's sleeveless muscle T-shirt that clung to her own pointed promises. I was so close to heaven, demigod gave me unwittingly witty repartee with which to entertain our little world, and we laughed all through lunch. Before long I felt like the prey; they were batting more eyelashes than Ted Williams on a good day at Fenway. I wasn't sure which way to go, but by the time we left I was leaning toward Candy. I paid the tab and drove them back to Devon's. Too complicated to deal with both of them at once, I was content to just drop them off for now. They tattooed me with hugs and I headed for the car, but Candy came running after me and asked for a ride back across the Hollywood Hills. We made a beeline for my house and got started with stage two. When I finally took her home, I got the dubious nervous honor of meeting her attractive mother, Sue, and her husky stepfather, Fred, who was an ex-football wide receiver at Fresno State and a big fan of my TV and movies. Well, that was a relief. And last but not least, I met Candy's Tracii, who as it turned out was also a fan of mine. That was not so much a relief as a quandary. This was shaping up to be a complicated love story. When I left, I gave her boyfriend a ride into Hollywood.

Shock's bon voyage party had included an emphatic warning that he'd kill me if I hit on Katie while he was gone, but, because she was so vulnerable, young and adorable, he also wanted me to keep an eye on her. It was a dilemma for both of us. I had gotten to know Shock well enough to believe the threat. He had guns and knives and oriental weapons. I had seen the occasional mean side slip out. Behind that cuddly teddy bear with the perpetual smile was a grizzly-bear-size temper. I had my hands full already; I wasn't too concerned about adding Katie to my dilemma.

I got a call for a CBS pilot that the wacky side of Shock would have liked. It was *Tiny Time,* the brainchild of Bud Melman, an old friend of my work, who I had read for several times. Pee Wee Herman was going to be the master of ceremonies in a variety show with skits and music. Unique for an audition, it has held at the old Mayfair Theatre in Santa Monica, only a sailed straw hat from the beach. We worked on some vaudeville skits, but it never jelled.

Candy had made up with Tracii, and I hadn't heard from her. Devon happened and cheered me up. I had an audition for *Dynasty,* the new current top show on television, so I brought Devon along to Warner Bros. Studio in West Hollywood. If she'd put her mind to it, she could have written her own show business ticket. Afterwards, we went to the trendy new restaurant Ports across the street.

Shock had left in October, and by now it was already December. Katie lived with her parents in Manhattan Beach, but occasionally the All-American girl and her friend Megan would pop up to Hollywood. They'd often invite me along, and we were at a new club that wasn't exactly happening. Megan decided it was time to go home. Out of the alcoholic vapors, Katie said she'd rather stay a bit longer and asked if I would bring her home later. I agreed of course and as soon as Megan left we split for my house. Katie was upset with Shock and wanted affection. I wanted her. The next thing I knew, we were in bed and she was kneeling over me, unbuttoning her blouse. When it slipped away, I almost fainted at the beauty of her. We became more than just friends. With our high profile on the social scene, we dated discretely. I hoped Shock would stay in England indefinitely, but I also had a jones for Candy and all the others. Loving so many women was a full-time job.

I found relief in an unlikely place: Alfred Hitchcock. The master of the macabre had been dead for five years, but his spirit lived on in his films and the anthology television series of spooky stories. Hitchcock's career began in England in the twenties with films like *The Lodger* and *Blackmail.* In the thirties, he gained commercial and critical success with *The Man Who Knew Too Much* and then *The Lady Vanishes,* which was so entertainingly innovative that the New York Film Critics named him best director of the year. David O. Selznick persuaded him to cross the Atlantic and make movies in America. For these brilliant films we have to be thankful: *Rebecca, Suspicion, Saboteur, Shadow of a Doubt, Spellbound, Notorious, Strangers on a Train, Dial M for Murder, Rear Window, To Catch a Thief, Vertigo, North by Northwest, The Birds* and *Psycho.* Now, NBC debuted a compilation of original stories and remakes based on the old series, with colorized footage of Hitchcock introducing and closing each show. Even a vicarious job with Hitch was a special assignment. His wizardry shaped the art of cinema. My role had plenty of wry dialogue, and I worked with two very special actors. Robert Loggia was the episode lead. His career ranged from the early masterpieces of television to films like *Scarface* and the Academy Award winning *An Officer and a Gentleman* as Richard Gere's father. This year he was nominated for best supporting actor in *The Jagged Edge* with Glenn Close. On *our* set he received appropriate reverence. The other actor was in every one my scenes; he was Leaf Phoenix, brother of River and now known as Joaquin Phoenix. He was only eleven-years-old in this show, many years from his performances in *Gladiator, Signs* and his best actor Academy Award nominated role as Johnny Cash in *Walk the Line.*

Shock returned, but with a darker shade of pale. He thanked me for taking care of Katie. He moved in with her family at the beach and played the demanding Latino macho man. Katie would sneak calls to me, but he caught on and beat her up. He swore he'd kill me the next time we crossed paths, and if ever there was an arena for our donnybrook, the Ebony Showcase Annex in the ghetto hood was the perfect setting. At Washington and La Brea, it was halfway between her Manhattan Beach and my Hollywood. Ebony was a new incarnation of an old blues club that went glam; it was in and packed. I wasn't anxious to fight a bad-tempered weapon-carrying jilted lover, but it was the only way I could see Katie who was being kept under lock and key. I knew he would want to show her off, rub it in my face. I wouldn't mind.

I needed my own babe power and brought Candy. Shock had the hots for her as every guy did, even Anthony and Flea. I told her to dress extra half-naked. We arrived late, but to a lucky parking spot across the boulevard from the club. Inside, it wasn't long before we encountered the enemy. Shock growled and made funny faces. I accused him of kidnapping, but brainwashed Katie flaunted her love for Shock. He pulled back Katie's shirt to reveal a new tattoo spread across her arm and shoulder, embracing words of subjugation. He had desecrated her holy white flesh. We went at it. A flurry of tentative punches missed their mark and security intervened. The manager escorted the dandy combatants out of the club and onto the sidewalk, where reasonable patrons were catching some fresh air. Katie and Candy came tottering behind us in stiletto heels and a crowd formed. Shock marched to his nearby car and started back with a handful of chains, swinging them around like a Roman gladiator. It was improvisation time. I set a deliberate pace across Washington Boulevard toward my trusty Eldorado, a dueling gunfighter calmly measuring the count of ten with my back to the grifter. I relied on my ears to gauge his distance and bet my poker hand I could reach the saddlebag before he got to me. As I reached salvation, I could hear him right behind me screaming like an Apache. I carefully inserted my key, opened the trunk, reached in and turned to face the adversary with a tire jack in my grip. Shock slammed on the brakes. Katie threw herself in front of Shock, and Candy draped me with her soft curves. The blood bath was averted, but it would ferment for months. Candy and I drove back to West Hollywood and the Troubadour. I got in a scrimmage with Tracii, and while we were jawing at each other, Candy ran off with Slash.

Chapter 42: My Cheating Tart

Tracii and his Guns opened their own meat-market apartment in Hollywood, and Candy moved in with me. We ran frequent surveillance of his place so she could keep tabs on her ex. I bought her a cherry red motorcycle to get around town but was afraid for her safety. In the mean, I used it to practice for an old-fashion biker-movie Lorie Levine was trying to whip up called *The Harley Boys*. She threw a big picnic at Griffith Park with Hells Angel types, hotdog Harleys and a few celebs like Billy Idol and Chicago Bear Jim McMahon. With my infinite wardrobe and nifty tricks, I was able to arrive with the best-looking outfit at the clambake, a feast for the paparazzi. If only they knew my dark MC secrets. Anthony came by La Jolla and took the bike for a spin that left the boy and the bike with a few bruises. Always the hot rod, he had several motorcycle accidents to recover from.

Gifty, I bought Candy a 1973 Buick Riviera Rally Sport with the big 455 engine, but then decided that was dicey too. I kept her in an ivory tower. The next Fair Lady phase was with Janet Cunningham who was always after intriguing street people to exploit in mass media. A week later, Candy squeezed into a tiny bikini for a Wall of Voodoo music video. The song was The Beach Boys' *Do it Again,* and Brian Wilson actually appeared in the video too. I drove my girl to the shoot and dropped her off with the kinky band that was best known for their hit song "Mexican Radio."

I had an important meeting of my own: Shock had called and wanted a truce. He and Katie were fighting, and he apologized for the Ebony Showcase altercation. I already knew this because Katie had been calling me again. We shook hands and I helped find him an apartment. Shock and I drove back to the video stage and checked on Candy; she was contemptibly snuggled up with keyboard-and-bass player Bruce Moreland. That night, Candy dragged me to hell, or was it a Riki Rachtman party, to hang with more Moreland. I guess I shouldn't have been surprised. Candy made sure we drove her new guy friend home for last-call drinks and his GPS location. I liked his skulls motif on the mantle and set about finding my own; today I have a collection worthy of the Smithsonian. Thanks Bruce.

Tacitly, Shock and I were friends once more. With Candy already straying and Katie a free woman again, I felt no restrictions or obligations. Candy borrowed the Riviera to get cigarettes and came back the next day claiming she had fallen asleep in a busy intersection for 18 hours. I said goodbye, baby. Nice try. She moved in with Bruce Moreland and started using heroin.

While Candy nodded out in sweet dreams I played house with a new Darcy edition of slim blonde models. I read for an amusing character on a project called *Crazy from the Heat*. The ever-elusive Scott McClintock was living at the Mexican resort Club Med but came to spend a week at my place. We went to CBS. I was up for a pilot called *Downtown,* as Leroy Fester Baker who had just broken out of Soledad prison. I didn't get the part, but they would hire me for another episode later in the year. Three days later, I'd score an audition with one of the finest directors in film, John Frankenheimer.

New York casting director Lew Digiaimo hauled me into a meeting at Cannon. The film was *52 Pick-Up,* a screenplay by Elmore Leonard and a cast that starred Roy Scheider, Ann-Margret, psycho John Glover, Vanity, Clarence Williams III and super-sexy victim Kelly Preston. Captaining the ship of film noir was the inimitable John Frankenheimer, who made some of the best American films ever: *All Fall Down* with Warren Beatty and Eva Marie Saint and a script by William Inge; *Birdman of Alcatraz* with Burt Lancaster and four Oscar nominations; *The Manchurian Candidate* with Frank Sinatra, Laurence Harvey and Angela Lansbury and two Oscar nominations; *Seven Days in May,* written by Rod Serling, with Burt Lancaster, Kirk Douglas, Frederic March, Ava Gardner and Edmond O'Brien's brilliant award-winning performance, along with two more Oscar nominations; *The Train; Seconds* with Rock Hudson's only great acting performance and Salome Jens; *Grand Prix* in Cinerama; *The Fixer,* which garnered an Oscar nomination for Alan Bates; and later there was *Black Sunday* with its prophetic script of terrorism at a Super Bowl.

I read for the weak link of the three bad guys, a simpering, bald, overweight Jewish momma's boy wimp. For me to pull that off would have been an Academy Award performance but was perfect for an actor named Robert Trebor. Casting wanted to use me somewhere and sent me to powwow with Mr. Frankenheimer at his private office on the west side. I entered into the masculine den of a larger-than-life modern-day Hemingway. John Frankenheimer sat behind a massive desk with a titanic marlin mounted on the wall behind him. In his presence, I felt like one of Jonathan Swift's Lilliputians, but he was genuinely cordial, and we had a pleasant conversation. He marked me in for the heroin dealer who meets with John Glover and Ann-Margret on a bridge in San Pedro. She was on the set for the entire day, and I thoroughly enjoyed my prime time with her. She was extraordinary. Of the film, *The New York Times* said, "Fast-paced, lurid, exploitive and loaded with malevolent energy."

In that same territory of illegal substances and method acting, I had slowly slipped into affording certain friends of mine. The main conspirators were duplex Philip and his gangbusters, a few showbiz friends and Monte "the thug" Van Cleef, who once knocked me out in the Rainbow parking lot. Since I lived on the ground floor of an active big city, I beefed up with some primitive security. I nailed blocks of wood into the window sash to prevent them from opening more than a couple inches. I had a deadbolt lock on the back door and a shotgun in the front. I had purchased the fire power during one of the earlier Watts riots.

Katie Martin, sweetest little devil in the world, called and said she was ready to date again. She had paid her grieving ex-girlfriend dues. I wholeheartedly agreed; she drove up and we went out to dinner. On the way home, I picked up a fifth of gin and a bottle of red wine. We came in the front door and stopped to catch up on our missed kisses. In the kitchen, I fixed our gin and tonics. We talked for a while, and then I excused myself to the bathroom at the far end of the hallway, next to the back bedroom. I walked down the familiar path as I had a thousand times. I was thinking what a lucky guy I was; this might just be the best night of my life. Only one step from the bathroom as I passed by the alcove, I caught a something's-not-quite-right blur out of the corner of my eye, and as I instinctively turned to investigate I was confronted with a large hunting knife that was arcing from above toward my chest. The thrust was propelled at warp speed by a man I'd never seen before. He had hold of the advancing knife with both hands. All of this had happened in a micro-fraction of a second. By now, the speeding knife point was no more than inches from my startled heart. My adrenaline fueled hands flew up and caught the perpetrator's forearms just as the knife's tip punctured my shirt and epidermis. The same favorite white shirt with the cut off collar I had been wearing the day I first met the original redhead, Katie Bramson, in the Boy's Market. Within three minutes that shirt would be drenched in blood, but not mine.

We were in a dead man's stalemate. I had a strong grip on his arms and was 100% completely in control of my emotions as I contemplated my alternatives. His eyes were glassy, and he seemed almost in a trance as he attempted to push that knife into my chest. The action seemed to be going in slow motion, while my mind was whirling like a bank of industrial IBM computers. Katie laughed and inquired what I was mumbling about back there. I screamed don't come back here! Thinking he still had the upper hand, the assassin ordered me to coax her into the hallway. The last thing I wanted was this maniac getting that knife in her space. Now she heard his voice and realized something was really amiss.

A plan bounced out of my brain. "Grab that gin bottle," I yelled. With all my do-or-die adrenaline and my vise-lock hold on his wrists, I literally pulled him down the hallway and into the kitchen. "Hit him over the head," was my harsh command. In shock and instead, she picked up her drink and smashed it against his head. The glass broke and the damage was minimal, although he did begin to bleed and he bled on me.

"The wine bottle, Katie, hit him with the wine bottle!" She grabbed the still uncorked bottle and let him have it right across his forehead. He staggered and blood was spurting out of his face. It got so slippery I lost my footing and landed on my back, pulling him with me. I still had a hold of his forearms, and he still had a grip on the damn knife. Blood was raining on my grimace; the ripped-and-tattered white shirt was drenched.

"Katie, go next door and call 911, right now, fast." She ran into the living room and I heard the door open. I looked him straight in the eye from my prostrated position and told him the sheriffs would be there any minute. Santa Monica Boulevard is clogged with cop cars. "I'll let you run for it," I said. I had my own ulterior motive. When the police did come, they'd have detectives scouring my house for clues, and they'd find my contraband. In a bizarre code of dishonor, he helped me up. We faced each other for one last moment, and then he fled out the front door.

I ran to my closet and grabbed the stash. I went to the back and unlocked the dead-bolt that had trapped him in the first place. Obviously, he'd been looking for drugs and cash, and when he was cornered he had no choice but to kill his way out. I buried my stash in the ivy-covered fence area, ran back inside and relocked the deadbolt for the crime-scene detectives. By then, I could hear sirens and saw the flashing lights through my curtains.

I opened the front door and faced a curious panorama of neighbors, mobs of cops and a street full of patrol cars. The whole scene was pulsating in garish red lights. I stood on the front porch covered in blood and yelled for all to hear, "I'm the victim!" I wasn't taking any chances with those idiots. "I'm the victim! The robber has left the scene!" A phalanx of sheriffs and SWATs and even a few LAPDs rushed across the lawn and tackled me and clubbed me and kicked me and swore at me and handcuffed me. Katie tried to pull them off. The neighbors vouched for me, but the cops weren't taking any chances, despite their protective helmets and bulletproof vests and swinging billy clubs. The cops did more damage than the criminal. I only suffered the original puncture and a few cuts from the killer; the police cracked a rib and tenderized me with black-and-blue bruises. Considering the worse, Katie and I were fortunate to have survived. If I'd been drunk or high and oblivious, I'd have had seven inches of blue steel in my back.

The next day, detectives came and did a thorough investigation. The intruder had come through the kitchen window over the sink. My home-made security was no match for his brute strength and dope-crazed desperation. I selected a realistic prop pistol and wore it in my belt every time I opened the front door. I was convinced Thug Van Cleef was the brains behind the caper. He casually dropped by and was startled to see the gun. He never returned.

Katie and Blackie as a team were never the same either. She had scene of the crime nightmares and retreated to the South Bay. Soon again, I was fully embattled in life-and-death madness with Candy. I only saw Katie occasionally after that. The last time was before I left LA in 1990. We met up in her territory to say goodbye. She was successful and in a great relationship. That was good enough for me. I loved Katie Martin and always will.

Candy, on the other hand, was a beautiful ongoing disaster. She would disappear for days and come wandering back with her pretty, pouty mouth open for business. She dragged me to every hair-band concert in Southern California. We were made up in matching black eye-shadow and lipstick and dressed in black leather with chains and Sid Vicious swastikas. We were attacked by an umbrella and given a good lecture by an elderly Jewish lady at the Kentucky Fried Chicken on Sunset and Fairfax. Candy was the darling of clubs, and I'd have to watch her toy with the affections of tongue-tied bug-eyed boys with wet pants. She had unabashed affairs with guitar stars and sometimes with complete strangers. She'd come home from missing in action and claim she was abducted from a bus stop or raped in a motel room for days. She spent a night at the Guns N' Roses asylum, with their specially made bed with restraints that secured bimbos to the pleasure of one band member after another. Candy played the game and then called me in the middle of the night to pick her up at a payphone on Sunset Boulevard, across from their studio. There was a thunderstorm and it was pouring; her hair and makeup were streaked with rain and tears and her clothes were ripped. "I was raped over and over again," she said with a gleam in her eye.

Her addiction to heroin got out of control. Before long I was prowling back alleys in shady parts of town like St. Andrews Place and a certain graffiti-pocked block in the Valley. When those dried up we'd even poke around Main Street downtown or dabble in Boyle Heights and East LA. For a while, we had a reliable pusher in an art deco shooting gallery on Wadsworth; we went there nightly, like brushing your teeth before bed.

To placate her, I played along. When I refused, she would run off. She got caught up with an Iranian drug dealer and moved into his fortress somewhere in Korea town. After a few weeks, she got to a phone and said she was being held captive. Her stepdad Fred and I were planning a military commando raid to free her but she escaped, at least that's what she said. Free, she resurrected some of her hardcore gal relationships. I still have a framed front-page banner of the Los Angeles Times May 27, 1986, scribbled with her desperate cry for help, "Blackie your girl's goin' wacky." Off it, she was still hauntingly beautiful; on it, she was just haunted.

To keep her home and out of trouble, we'd sleep all day. Auditions were in word only, languishing in my appointment book and slurred at that. If I did venture out I couldn't concentrate or learn my lines. I had gone a month without an interview when suddenly there were two. *Modern Girls* was about tempting babes, hooked on the glamour and excitement of LA's rock-and-roll nightlife. So perfectly Candy, I hoped for a talent scout with the guts to cast her. I dragged her blood-stained sleeves along with me. I looked at the *Modern Girls*; even high, Candy was still more beautiful, but she refused to audition. I took a small role as "a waiter at the Gloom Club" for the rent money. The director threw around names like Bruce Willis, Dennis Quaid and Paul-Michael Glazer, but I never saw them. *NY Times*: "*Modern Girls* isn't notable for anything but its crassness."

The second audition was more productive. I drove to a nondescript warehouse called the GMT Studios in the industrial district of Culver City. There were a dozen actors up for the same role, mostly the same old comic types I'd see at most of my auditions. "Blackie Dammett!" Yup, that's me. I followed Peg Halligan into the building and met the creator, producer, writer and director, Tom Patchett. He explained this was a pilot for a TV show that NBC was interested in. It was *ALF* (Alien Life Form), the story of an extraterrestrial fuzzy creature that crashes into a garage and moves in with a sitcom family, where hilarity breaks out every 30 seconds. I was reading for the "Alien Task Force" character named Darnell Valentine, who was searching for the ALF. I got the part and a few days later showed up for work.

As usual, I brought Candy along, hoping the boss might be interested. Candy had hidden dope stashes everywhere; while I was working, she was secretly getting high in my dressing room. And then, ta-da, we had a surprise visitor show up on the set, Brandon Tartikoff, the wunderkind president of NBC entertainment. He was the youngest chief ever and had turned around NBC's dreadful ratings with programming like *The Cosby Show, Hill Street Blues, LA Law, Family Ties, Miami Vice, Cheers* and *Night Court*. He also kept Johnny Carson from fleeing to ABC, and he turned around a faltering *Saturday Night Live*. It was like royalty had popped in for tea. He was the ultimate star maker, and I ran back to get Candy; this could be her big break. She was higher than an *E.T.* bike, but this was a once in a lifetime opportunity. I pulled her into the reception line just as Tartikoff approached and shook my hand. With obvious indignation, he frowned as Candy rubbed her nose and nodded on the dope. I could see Tartikoff's demeanor grind gears.

After a few more politically correct good wishes, he left in a big limousine with his entourage. The cast and crew were on cloud nine. That he stopped by personally boded well for a possible pilot pick up. We finished the day's work, including the scene where I came to the front door looking for the alien, and the skeptical family made the choice to save Alf's butt. I got good response from Tom Patchett, the cast and crew, and even Alf, played by Paul Fusco. I might have a hit show; my life would be prosperous.

Later that summer, I was in my backyard getting an actor's tan with the *Herald-Examiner*. I opened up the entertainment page and saw the list of the new fall shows. *ALF* was ready to go on NBC. I was jumping around like crazy. I waited and waited for the big phone call, but all I ever got was a nice leather gym bag from Brandon Tartikoff at Christmas. I'll never know if Candy's behavior cost me the role, or if they just never dealt with the Alien Task Force once ALF got situated in his host home. The show aired in over fifty countries and is still in syndication today.

We captured an interesting photo shoot for Candy. Rueben Blue gathered the twelve hottest girls in LA for his *Scratch* magazine calendar called *Playmates of Hollywood,* and Candy certainly had every right to be one of them. Her classic pin-up ensemble was sheer negligee, sexy bra, high heels, garter belts and a leopard-skin pillbox hat. She was Miss February. Candy pants sparkled and showed what she could do if she only applied herself. Two days later she came close with *Slippery People,* a new project I was reading for. I was up for photo reporter Keith, but more importantly they were also looking for "a coke whore coat check girl who disappeared." We drove out to Ventura and Colfax and I read, but they wouldn't see Candy because she wasn't SAG. The movie shot in June in New York. Candy shot up in our candle-lit bathroom and shaved her vagina.

As Guns N' Roses acquired fame and a modicum of wealth, Axl moved into a high-rise penthouse pad in a ritzy apartment building on La Cienega, where Fountain Avenue dead ends. Candy spent time there, and I served mine too. Axl was the most contentious and Slash the least. I liked Izzy and got to know Duff along the way. On Candy's eighteenth birthday I took her to the Troubadour, and as usual the front bar was filled with local rock stars. Slash was passed out, and Candy played nursemaid, embracing him in her famous lap. I moved on, circulated the club and went upstairs to Doug Weston's office. I finally returned to get Candy; we had Rainbow reservation birthday-dinner plans, but she refused to leave Slash. I was upset. Candy had a tumultuous temper and slugged me. I admonished her and she hit me with a bottle; we were both 86'd. I've never hit a girl in my life so whenever Candy would start slam-bamming me with her fists (which was often) my only protection was clamping her arms until she got over the spat. Once, she said "uncle" and promised to be cool but then tossed my television through the window. It landed on the left-front fender of my Cadillac. Like a lot of girls, she craved sex after a fight.

Chapter 43: Lethal Weapon

The Candy Express continued to turn my once prosperous career into an oxcart on a muddy road to oblivion. The auditions were few and far between: *Dutch Treat* at Cannon, Mark Friedman's *Killing Hour* as Ryan the lead bad guy, the HBO project *Glory Days*, a drag queen role at Warners, another NBC pilot as Junior a hit man with a loped off ear, and back to Cannon again as a malevolent prisoner who controls the prisoners and the warden in *Penitentiary III*. All zilch!

I took Candy back to West Covina. The parents were anxious to straighten her out. My positive energy had been in isolation for months so I joined a health club and got back in shape. I pursued acting classes to get sharp and auditioned for plays. The prestigious Tiffany Theatre on Sunset was preparing a production of Sam Shepard's *Curse of the Starving Class,* and I gave it a shot. The actors were big-time talents; Craig T. Nelson and Carol Kane ended up in it. I didn't win a role but was exhilarated to compete. I even went to a school play at Grant High to see my old friend Collette's daughter. I ran a couple miles a day. Finally my fortune started to turn.

Helen Mossler, top-dog casting director at Paramount, called me to an important audition. The film was *The Untouchables,* a remake of the black-and-white TV show that debuted in 1959 and was based on the autobiography of Eliot Ness, a Prohibition Agent who fought the Chicago mafia and Al Capone in particular. Former movie-matinee star Robert Stack had played the role of Ness. Paramount's new feature film had already scored an extraordinary cast with Sean Connery as an incorruptible Irish street cop, Robert De Niro as Al Capone and up-and-coming young actor Kevin Costner as Eliot Ness. Costner had been playing extra parts as recently as 1982, bit parts in '83 and a role in *The Big Chill* that was entirely edited out. In 1985, he made a breakthrough performance as a rowdy cowboy in Lawrence Kasdan's *Silverado,* and now he had scored a career-making role in *The Untouchables.* The movie was directed by Brian De Palma, written by David Mamet and produced by my friend Art Linson. The part I was asked to read for was Frank Nitti, Al Capone's right-hand man. It was an important role that required an extremely vicious personality. I made the first cut and then went up against a strong field of villainous actors. I had a good run, but in the end was beaten out by Billy Drago, who ironically had also taken my Clint Eastwood *Pale Rider* role. Drago was ferocious in the part, and I came out a better actor. Costner and I would duke it out over *Dancing with Wolves* down the trail.

McClintock came and went. Next stop the Wyndam Hotel in New York and then to the Doral Park on 34th and Park. Shock was back in the saddle, and we spent our good fortune at Scream, which kept moving around town. We snacked on canaries at the just as illusive Cat House. Riki Rachtman, Nikki Sixx and Tommy Lee were always holding court in the far recesses of the club, surrounded by adoring young ladies. I helped myself to the overflow and plundered with the unabashed glee of a buccaneer. There was never a dull moment but always enough women. Shock found an agent, and we got involved in a low-budget Harmony Gold film in Venice, another of those projects where the wrap party was more memorable than the main event. We also wrote a comedy action thriller called *Sodomy Vigilantes* with right wing-nut religious zealots, killer robots, glam trash Nazis, fast-food grannies, and Little King Beer bottles. I wonder what we were smoking.

There were also legitimate projects to go for, as Joey on *Hunter* in a church lot, as Garth for *Sidekicks* in the Zorro Building at Disney, as Norman Blates in *Sledge Hammer!*, a satirical spoof of *Dirty Harry* at Laird Studios, and as Longo at CBS Studio Center for *Hill Street Blues*. I got competing call backs for Garth, Norman and Longo. There was no question which one I picked.

Hill Street Blues was one of the most decorated television shows in history. Its debut season won eight Emmys and, over its seven-year run, it was nominated for 98 Emmy Awards. It won Outstanding Drama four years in a row. It was the gold standard of the eighties. Steven Boscho, who created *Hill Street Blues,* became god for a while and went on to produce *L.A. Law* and *NYPD Blue*, both of which also won best-drama Emmys. The precinct interiors were done at Studio Center, but location shootings were all over the gritty sides of urban Los Angeles. Landscapes resembled a generic city like Chicago; there was no Hollywood sign or LA City Hall in the background. It had the feel of a grungy documentary. Lead cop Dennis Franz shook me down in a dive bar called the Sunset in the shadow of downtown. It was a fascinating script about a suitcase full of contraband that crashed with a plane and the circuitous travels it took. I was its owner for my time.

While I was working in a television classic, my kid was making his own notorious history out on the road. *The Miami Herald*: READY FOR BIG BREAK. "The funky foursome known as the Red Hot Chili Peppers will have their work cut out for them when they attempt to out-red and out-groove headliners Simply Red on Saturday."

A Tennessee newspaper: "They are insane you know. And they may be crazy. Occasionally they hurl themselves into the audience. Their words can make you grimace and chuckle at the same time. And they're scheduled to treat Nashville to their ribald power punk at Roosters." The headline: WILL THE RED HOT CHILI PEPPERS BURN NASHVILLE TO THE GROUND?

Another paper, another headline: THE RED HOT CHILI PEPPERS WILL POSE NUDE IN PUBLIC. And Anthony did just that with *Hustler* magazine in an article with photos of the *Sexiest Men in Rock*. He also got international and intellectual recognition when the *New York Times* did a sweet piece on George Clinton, *Pop Music's Precious Natural Resource*. The *Times* had a sexy photo of Anthony and referenced the Chili Peppers' *Freaky Styley*.

On my busy agenda was *Blood Games*, and a guy named Mino who was "extremely frightening, mean and vicious, a wasted Viet Nam war veteran with full battle gear and a big knife." These were good for my macho reputation but not my sensitive side. I sped from *Blood Games* to the police detective series *Downtown,* starring Michael Nouri. Other regulars included Robert Englund, familiar face David Paymer and Mariska Hargitay, best known now as Detective Olivia Benson on *Law & Order*. The episode was "Tracks of My Tears" and was set in a working dime-a-dance hall at 1024 South Grand. The place had been built by silent-film star Mary Pickford back when downtown Los Angeles was a place of magnificent movie theaters and famous nightclubs. *Downtown* was a contemporary cop show, but the club was eerie with history, and you could almost hear the music reverberating back from the past. Apropos to the nostalgia, I played an old fashioned barker, encouraging the disenfranchised to put down a pittance and snuggle up to a dance partner for a minute or two or until the dimes ran out. A mysterious and vulnerable woman played by Helene Udy, came looking for work; I felt empathy for her, watched over her and kept her out of trouble. It was the sensitive role I had been looking for.

I had gone up against Mickey Rourke in a TV cop show back in the Stone Age of my career and I auditioned for *The Pope of Greenwich Village,* which featured his brilliant performance. Now he was the lead in *Barfly* and I'd see him again as the commanding figure he'd become, this time playing Charles Bukowski in a film written by Bukowski and directed by Barbet Schroeder. I went to Barbet Schroeder's office on Wilshire and Rourke came by too. Schroeder had learned his craft in France, working with the likes of the ultimate master, Jean-Luc Godard. Schroeder's controversial first film, *More,* was about a young lady, Mimsy Farmer, dealing with heroin addiction. I had seen the film when I was in Berlin. Subsequent films included *Reversal of Fortune* winning an Oscar for Jeremy Irons as Claus von Bulow, and Bridget Fonda's *Single White Female.* I was auditioning for the mangy old geezer wife-beater Louie, who lived in the same hotel as Rourke and co-star Faye Dunaway. Schroeder enjoyed my reading but was looking for an older man: "Louie is a tall, thin man. His face is sallow and yellow, long thin hairs stick straight out from his face. His teeth are decaying and spotted with black." I chalked it up to experience and then found something totally different, *Heart of the City* at 20th Century Fox as Tux, a thirties British street-smart run-down Dickensesque character.

The poster said "Axel Foley is back. Back where he doesn't belong." Yes, the blockbuster of blockbusters, *Beverly Hills Cop,* was ready for its inevitable sequel. Eddie Murphy would be putting captain cops in the loony bin, crooks in the clink and the rest of us in stitches. That I was reading for Tony Scott in a Don Simpson and Jerry Bruckheimer production at Paramount in an office fit for a king was something I hadn't quite imagined when I was doing scene work at Strasberg. I read for the role of Joseph De Lessio, owner of a Detroit seafood joint, who was trying to pin a murder on Murphy. Neither of us succeeded. Then Tony Scott had me read for Vinnie which ultimately went to the much-respected and now deceased Robert Pastorelli. I'm certain the film would have done a lot better with me in it though. It only grossed $300,000,000. And if you're keeping track, Scott McClintock had just bought a new home in Olympic Valley near Lake Tahoe.

Night Court came to my rescue and changed my fortune, or at least my rent payment. I didn't even have to audition. They called La Rocca and asked me to play a significant cameo role that was crucial to the "Contempt of Courting" episode. It was nice to be back with one of the friendliest casts in town, and this would be my fourth time working with Larroquette. Afterwards, I ran out to see my Cutie Patootie. My bogus in-laws were still laughing and Candy managed a smile. I took her home that night, and not surprisingly she got exactly what she came for. We shaved all her translucent hair in the bath and spawned. There was no escape from her wiles. It was back to black tar and Cathouse and Scream and St. Andrews Place and downtown back alleys.

And UCLA. The Red Hot Chili Peppers played a Halloween night gig at Ackerman Hall, my old collegiate stomping grounds. The opening acts where the Dickies, Guns N' Roses and Thelonious Monster. I brought Candy who got three for the price of one; she was fondly imbedded with Axl, Slash, and *moi*. We spent most of our time in the Guns' camp of a few folding chairs. No dressing rooms or hot tubs. In seven months, they'd release *Appetite for Destruction*. On Monday, I went back to work and dragged her along to interviews for *Its a Living* at Sunset Gower and *Scarecrow and Mrs. King* at Warners. Actually, I had two interviews at Warner Bros. that Monday, and it was the second one that in many ways would define my career. It was *Lethal Weapon*.

Mel Gibson was the lead and a formidable one, with his resume of *Mad Max, Road Warrior, Beyond Thunderdome, Gallipoli, The River* and *The Bounty* as Christian Fletcher, a role he shared with Marlon Brando, Clark Gable and Errol Flynn. *Lethal Weapon* had Danny Glover as the buddy cop, a sharp young UCLA grad screenwriter in Shane Black and an action-packed director Richard Donner, who had just the right gusto for this project. After a solid career in television (Steve Mc Queen's *Wanted: Dead or Alive, The Fugitive, The Twilight Zone, The Streets of San Francisco, Gilligan's Island*!?), Donner had his big screen breakthroughs with *The Omen* and the original *Superman* movie with Christopher Reeve. That started the superhero movie franchises with Batman, Spiderman, The Hulk, etc. He'd also directed delightful films like *The Goonies* and Richard Pryor's *The Toy*.

Warner Bros. casting director Marion Dougherty asked me to hustle over for an important evening casting session. The film had already been shooting for months and was basically finished. A scene at the beginning established Mel Gibson's character Riggs as a suicidal loose-cannon LA cop, who didn't fear lethal consequences in the line of duty because his wife had died and he was shattered. It was at the beach under a pier with belligerent punks, a stray collie and Riggs.

Once the film was edited, they decided the important opening didn't have enough zing. Mel Gibson was a big fan of the Three Stooges and proposed a total rewrite that would incorporated some classic Stooges humor. *Lethal Weapon* was set during the holiday season anyway so they put the new scene in a Christmas tree lot, with undercover cop Riggs trying to make a cocaine buy from three hoodlums who used the tree lot as a front. Once the bad guys got wise to his undercover caper, they were about to unload hot lead. Riggs caught them off guard with a Stooges two finger poke in the eyes and a sweeping three faces at once slap.

Hopeful she wouldn't run off for dope, I left Candy in the waiting room, and I was led to Richard Donner's oversize office, befitting this oversize talent. He was energetic and happy to see me. "I've heard good things about you," he said as he took a seat behind his big desk. Everything in the room was big. So were my expectations. We batted some lines around and he smiled. "I think you'll be perfect for this scene." he said as he escorted me out. "Marion will set you up for wardrobe tomorrow and we shoot on Wednesday."

Candy and I celebrated that night, and she actually behaved herself. I had lines to learn and a character to create. Early the next morning, I waded into wardrobe, the first of the three coke dealers to arrive. I wanted first pick. A lady led me through the labyrinth to our dressing room, where she had a selection of drab grey, beige and boring outfits. We were surrounded with a million other getups, and over on another rack was a red-and-black plaid jacket that jumped out at me. Like a stop sign, it grabbed your attention. I pleaded; she concurred. Another part of my plan had been executed.

On Wednesday, I had a 6 a.m. call at the legitimate Christmas tree lot on the busy intersection of Victory Boulevard and Whitsett in North Hollywood. We spent the entire day doing this one big scene, five pages. Dick Donner was a total-coverage director, and he printed several takes of each setup. But first he had to work out our routine and dialogue. Jimmie Skaggs and Jason Ronard were the other two stooges, and we were all jockeying for the most screen time.

After an extended build up, thinking we were toying with a patsy, Riggs came back with a badge and his last-laugh comedy routine, which segued into a shootout that killed Skaggs and seriously wounded Ronard, which left me the last bad man standing. I ran into the Yuletide trees, and when Riggs came looking I got the drop on him. I had an arm lock around his neck and my gun pressed against his temple. By then, LAPD backup had arrived and had us surrounded. My intent was a hostage escape, but Riggs kept telling the cops to shoot us; he was willing to be sacrificed in a hail of bullets. The cops refused, and we had a stalemate until Riggs pulled a nifty move and gave me a head butt I'm still reeling from. Donner shot 14 takes of that dance in the pines. I racked up cuts and abrasions, a no-kidding headache and cracked ribs from arresting officers smacking me into their cop-car fender 14 times. Gibson was nicked up from my gun-barrel jabbing, and we both went to first aid for further bonding.

Unlike most big movie stars who spend their time off set in dressing room trailers, Mel hung with the actors and crew, drinking beer, telling ribald jokes and goofing around like a kid. A former *People* magazine "Sexiest Man Alive" in 1980, he personified the image of a legendary superstar, but in fact he came across as anything but arrogant. He was a cool dude. WB publicity took slick photos of Mel and me together brandishing our guns. Criminally, the noisy street traffic ruined some of the dialogue, and for the next week we all did looping at Burbank Studios, which was cool with me. I got an additional week's pay and more time with my pals. *Lethal Weapon* grossed over $100,000,000 and put Gibson on top of the Hollywood heap. Critics consider it one of the great buddy-films. Siskel and Ebert gave *Lethal Weapon* two thumbs way up! And there's never been a retrospective Mel Gibson compilation that doesn't feature our Three Stooges scene.

Shock and I waged war for our femme fatales.

Chapter 44: Blackstar the Evil Magician

I punched my clock and the actor assembly line knocked out another peculiar character. One minute I was a fast talking con man in the personal injury business for Al Onorato at Columbia, and then like a schizophrenic chameleon, I was Tony "Little Tuna" Bonatardi, a major mafia type for *Hard Knocks*. I was Don a sound tech for *Throb*. I was "the bastard" for Fred Roos, and then the confusing call backs all over again. Occasionally, something unique came along. As a child, I hated soap operas with a passion, those corny, afternoon melodramas with cheesy actors. Some of them had been going on for decades. *Guiding Life* had been around since 1937, every week day for seventy-two years by the time it was finally put to sleep. *As the World Turns, General Hospital, Days of Our Lives* and *All My Children* were all old enough to get a discount on the bus.

So I had to laugh when La Rocca's secretary told me to get over to ABC studio 11 to read for *Santa Barbara*. At least *Santa Barbara* was one of those flashy modern soaps with sex and spectacle and pretty girls. I never realized how difficult they were to do. An hour's worth of dialogue to memorize on the spur of the moment, marks and positions turning on a dime. Plots and characters, life and death, hate and jealousy, sex and religion tossed in a mix-master and shot out of a cannon on a slit second's notice. I was up for Weezil and wasn't going to weasel out. They gave me a script and I reported the next morning bright and early.

The tone of *Santa Barbara* was a bit like those William Powell and Myrna Loy *Thin Man* movies from the 30s and 40s with their light hearted repartee. As Weezil, I was hired to tap phone wires in a blackmail scheme involving a couple of the main stars. I was a tongue-in-cheek specialist with sight gags up my sleeve and a prank in my back pocket. After I fumbled the ball a few times and inadvertently ruined their nefarious intentions, I lost my credibility. Keith: "He came highly recommended. I had no way of knowing what he was like." Gina: "His name is Weezil. Did you expect a guy in a three-piece suit?" I worked for a week, until the plot moved onto a new melancholy story line. When I wasn't on the set acting, I was tailing the director, learning the machinations of the control room with all the hardware of NASA. I liked the whole experience and dated one of the regular actresses.

I bounced from the soaps back to prime time in Michael Mann's atypical *Crime Story*, an NBC drama based on real people. It had feuding crime-buster cop Dennis Farina and a mobster played by a criminally unknown actor named Anthony Denison. I played a cop at the casino. Although *Time Magazine* called it one of the best television programs of the 80s, it had a short and rocky two-year run. Michael Mann had hit pay dirt with *Miami Vice,* which preceded it on NBC Friday night, but the *Crime Story* ratings never clicked. I was in good company though; the high quality series featured guest stars like Julia Roberts, David Caruso, Kevin Spacey, Christian Slater, Deborah Harry and Gary Sinise. Del Shannon and my amigos Tod Rundgren and Al Kooper made music for the show, and it was shot entirely on location in Las Vegas. Because that was Candy's hometown, I spent a lot of quarters calling her from the Union Plaza Hotel, where we stayed.

After work one night, a bunch of us checked out a strip club in North Las Vegas, where I met a truly groovy dancer who actually lived in Inglewood. She was very pretty, very tall, very sexy and very anxious for me to hook up with her back in LA. When I returned, she invited me to come for Sunday dinner and meet her family from hell. I arrived in a semi-shabby secluded area and was introduced to her two burly brothers and a suspicious mother and father. I squirmed uncomfortably during dinner as all eyes were gunning for me. The big brothers were especially critical, but I tried my best to blend in with their card-carrying-right hot wings. I had downed a few too many of their Miller Lites and asked for directions to the bathroom. I excused myself and headed down the hallway. Curious, I took the liberty of peeking into one of their rooms to see what planet they were from. Bam! I was blindsided by Big Brother One, who threatened me with severe consequences for snooping. Big Brother Two picked me up by the scruff of my neck and lugged me to the exit. They wanted to bury me in the backyard, but the dancer decided that was overkill. Hoping a little humor might win her back, I asked if she'd make me up a dinner doggie bag to take home, but they slammed the door on me.

Scott McClintock had moved again; Candy and I flew up to San Francisco to visit. Scott had new digs at a predictably expensive apartment building on Clay Street. We were greeted sincerely and Scott got an eyeful of Candy. Scott had his own line of clothing and a men's cologne now. Over the weekend, we did a whirlwind tour of the city and visited his mother's palatial mansion. Just when I was happy to have my baby so fresh and bright, she pulled me aside and punctured my spleen. It was our last night, and I was already in my pj's when Candy gave me that look. She wanted to score. She grabbed her coat and threatened to go by herself. She owned me. She steered me like a NASCAR hot rod covered with heroin decals. We made up some lame excuse for the already–in-bed McClintocks and headed for the sex and rock clubs on Broadway. She scores, she shoots; she loses. We were moody on the flight home, and I drove her back to West Covina.

I secured a date with the low-budget action-slash-horror supernatural thriller film, *Moon in Scorpio,* with the Swedish bombshell Britt Ekland, who had been married to Peter Sellers, had an infamous liaison with Rod Stewart, and was immortalized as a Bond girl in *The Man with the Golden Gun.* In person, she was kind and sweet and still very pretty. She had done some classic films in her day: *The Wicker Man,* William Friedkin's *The Night They Raided Minsky's,* and the original kick-ass *Get Carter* with Michael Caine. The director was Gary Graver, who I had known for a long time, and we finally got to work together. The male leads were John Phillip Law and the formidable William Smith.

Stephen J. Cannell was a hands-on producer with a resume of work that included *Columbo, The Rockford Files, The A-Team* and *Jump Street.* After two earlier misses, I finally won a role on his popular NBC hit *Hunter,* another *Dirty Harry*-inspired rogue cop who was more concerned with justice than protocol. Ex-Los Angeles Rams defensive lineman Fred Dryer played the rule-breaking LAPD homicide cop. With a new lucrative contract and the opportunity to direct this episode, Dryer tore into "The Jade Woman," and I contributed. A bit doped, Candy came along and hung out with the LAPD officers that were always on location to handle traffic. We took a humorous photo of high her with a smiling cop.

Funny, I was playing a heroin dealer about to meet with a mafia boss. Fred wasn't in this scene so he was able to channel all his directorial energy. I had already convinced him to let me use my own costume, and now I offered a creative way to start the shot of me pacing on La Cienega for the limo to arrive. I suggested opening on a close-up of my crepe-sole leopard-skin rockabilly loafers as they anxiously danced back forth on the sidewalk. He bought it, used it and when the show aired, it looked great. My hair had gotten quite long in back, and I wore it as a pony tail of Shirley Temple ringlets. Fred got some hand held *cinéma-vérité* shots of me and my bouncing curls from behind as I awkwardly circled the limo, trying to decide which politically correct door I was suppose to climb in, again my idea.

"You and a guest are cordially invited to a special screening of *Lethal Weapon* starring Mel Gibson and Danny Glover on February 26, 1987 – 8:00 P.M. Wadsworth Theatre Building. Veterans Administration, Los Angeles. You must R.S.V.P to attend."

I called Candy and told her we had a hot date for a hot flick. We dressed up and headed for West LA. The large theatre was completely filled. I ran into Mel and his jocular buddies in the lobby; they all took a lingering look at my girl. Mel invited us to his private after party. The movie was awesome; I was digging my work and everything was perfect until Candy tugged at my elbow and said she had to leave. She wanted to get high, and she was persistent. The contiguous seats were shushing us. We left as soon as it was over. Like a tow truck, she pulled me out of the lobby as I looked over my shoulder at the ever-diminishing congratulatory ceremony and my lost opportunity. She stole an important piece of my life that night. I was down, and it took a while to recoup.

Mel Gibson went on to continued exemplary work and hit pay dirt with *Braveheart*, a film he produced, directed and starred in as the Scottish rebel William Wallace. It won five Oscars, including best picture and best director. He produced, directed and co-wrote *The Passion of the Christ,* one of the biggest-grossing films of all time. Lately, he's been vilified for drunk driving, religious rants, radical racism and trouble with his lovers, but who am I to judge. I'm no angel either.

I stumbled on to a couple of interesting projects good for a laugh or two. One was *Collision Course,* a movie that would be shot in my home territory of Detroit. The director was Lewis Teague, who I had worked with on *The Lady in Red.* Jay Leno had a starring role. Pat Morita, Chris Sarandon, and Ernie Hudson were in it too, but then they were actors. *Collision Course* was still making it into Jay Leno's monologues twenty years later.

The second film of interest was *The Blue Iguana.* My audition directions were to 8480 Beverly Boulevard, a familiar neighborhood near La Cienega. The three-story commercial building was next to the Rexall drug store on the corner. I was quite surprised, however, when I entered and found it intact but eerily deserted. There was hardly any furniture and even fewer people. After a bit of exploring, I came upon a secretary who explained it was soon to be demolished. She left and I nosed around in the weird situation; it was as though an epidemic had wiped out all the people and rendered the landscape barren. Finally, the secretary returned and showed me into the office of the writer-director John Lafia, and we had the normal chat. Dylan McDermott, Jessica Harper and James Russo were cast in major roles. He gave me a tour of the script, which was loaded with bounty hunters, crooked IRS agents, double crosses, laundered drug money, sexy women, murder, and all cooked up south of the border in a mysterious banana republic. Fury (later changed to Floyd), the character I was reading for was one of the more ornery cutthroat bastards in the script, and John Lafia seemed quite pleased with my performance. He also apologized for the unusual conditions and assured me they would soon be out of these temporary offices and moved onto the Paramount lot. I almost wondered if they weren't squatters on the property to save pre-production expenses.

Five days later, La Rocca notified me I had a call back at the same spooky location. As I did my usual preparation, I was searching for something really off the wall—or maybe to the walls. This guy Floyd is off his rocker and what a perfect place to go bananas, a building just about ready for the wrecking ball anyway. I arrived in an outfit that relied heavily on a tropical hat and a garish Hawaiian shirt. I hadn't shaved for the five days, and I greased up my skin to look sweaty. I was carrying weapons. In addition to Lafia, there were other executives this time. Fasten your seat belts. In the heat of the audition piece, I went ballistic and started tearing the room apart. I smashed the windows, tore the walls apart, beat the furniture to death and did a war dance on the carpet before I set it on fire. Some were enthralled and the others had fainted. I never heard back from *The Blue Iguana,* but ultimately I discovered that Flea, of all people, had won the role of Floyd.

I had no idea Flea was pursuing an acting career. I knew he'd been in the Penelope Spheeris films, *Suburbia* and *Dudes,* but pretty much as himself. And I knew about the band performances in *Tough Guys* and *Thrashin'.* After *The Blue Iguana,* Flea went on to a compilation of films like *Back to the Future II and III, My Own Private Idaho, The Big Lebowski, Fear and Loathing in Las Vegas, The Wild Thornberries* and *Rugrats.* Flea is one those rare masters of many talents, an everyman and a unique man. Even before *Blue Iguana,* Flea had finished a small part as an alien in a movie called *Stranded,* which starred Ione Skye, the beautiful breakthrough from *River's Edge,* a film with Keanu Reeves, Crispin Glover and Dennis Hopper.

Ione was the daughter of Scottish singer-songwriter Donovan, who provided a sound track for the 60s with hits like "Sunshine Superman," "Season of the Witch," "Mellow Yellow" and "Hurdy Gurdy Man." Flea raved about Ione and introduced her to Anthony who fell fast in love with the raven beauty. I had been unaware of all this while locked up in Candy's flawed addiction.

The band played the Palace again. I went backstage and down the steps to the Chili Pepper's dressing room. An ebullient Anthony introduced me to Ione as his new girlfriend. The 16-year-old cutie was applying his multi-color day-glo makeup, but Anthony was already glowing. It had been a long time since I saw him that happy. River Phoenix was there too, silly as a bashful show-off adolescent. He seemed so innocent, playfully swinging from a heavy-duty curtain rod in a stairwell. Watching the Anthony and Ione love birds, I reflected on my own endless relationships. I wondered if I would ever settle down with one woman. Was I capable, or just culpable?

I was forever faithful with the silver screen though, even when we stumbled. Soon enough, we found another lovely one-night stand. It was *The Bear,* an intellectual and prestigious project that had been floating around Hollywood for four years. Usually that's a bad sign, but this version had an extraordinary director at the helm. Jean-Jacques Annaud's first film *Black and White in Color* was awarded an Oscar for Best Foreign Language

Motion Picture. He followed that with *Quest for Fire* which won best film and director in the French Cesars. *Seven Years in Tibet* became notorious when the Chinese banned Jean-Jacques Annaud and actor Brad Pitt for life. My audition was a hypnotic dream. Annaud's approach was improvisational, and I ended up playing the Bear itself, even though I went in thinking I was the trapper. The film was not particularly successful in America but was acclaimed in the rest of the world. It won all the French Academy of Cinema awards. The experience was quite surreal.

The next stop to oblivion was a Showtime film, *Nightmare Alley,* which may have been a remake of the 1947 Tyrone Power and Joan Blondell film-noir. I was up for a rich avant-garde character in a nightclub, but that's about all I can recall. I was still under the caustic influence of the black widow's spell. There were large gaps in 1987 I'll never recover. After more unproductivity and contempt for myself, I took a cold shower and once again rethought my life. Disoriented, I stumbled into a mass open house audition for a major new play at a warehouse loft space on Santa Monica. The play was *The Minotaur* and the grit behind it was Los Angeles Arts Repertory Theatre and their Camelot Artists. It became my rehab, my detox and my recovery center. Some of their lofty tenets were to "enable artists to fulfill their individual and collective dreams, goals and purposes and to enable Artists to assume their rightful role of being leaders in their profession, community and country and thus assume responsibility for increasing the quality of life on the planet." The acclaimed acting teacher Milton Katselas was involved, and I learned my lesson.

The *Minotaur* auditions went on for weeks while John Megna, the director, and Joseph Scott Kierland, the writer, continued to search for the right actors. It was a boxing drama that reminded me of those old pugilist movies like *The Champion* with Kirk Douglas or *Body and Soul* with John Garfield. I didn't mind coming back for the auditions; every session presented me with new actresses laying their hearts on the line. It looked like I would be playing the role of Renzo Collucci who managed the Champ, promoted the bouts and worked the corner. Constant attrition kept us spinning our wheels though. Every time we found a suitable talent, another actor would get a movie and drop out. And soon enough it would happen to me.

My Traci Lords connection, Lori Levine, and her boss, Icek Tenebaum, who ran an adult video empire in the Valley were making a mainstream movie about the Magic Castle, an iconic Hollywood institution. It was a museum and also presented the world's finest magicians in a nightclub setting. Johnny Carson was a frequent guest. Icek's film would not be X rated or even R rated or PG —it would be G rated for children of all ages. *A Night at the Magic Castle* was a coming-of-age story about a seven-year-old boy named Max who is visited by the ghost of Harry Houdini and helps him in a life and bruised battle with a villainous adversary on Halloween in the shadowy confines of the Magic Castle. Arte Johnson, best known for *Rowan and Martin's Laugh In*, would play Houdini, the greatest magician of all time. The Magic Castle itself is the definitive repository of Houdini's legacy and even his spirit.

Lori wanted me to play Blackstar the Evil Magician, who was the arch enemy of Harry Houdini and a scintillating scoundrel who planned to transform young Max into his new evil protégé. Blackstar was a major starring role and easily the most dynamic character in the film. I was Snidely Whiplash with black-magic twinkle toes. I poured myself a double shot of Darth Vader with sparkling white teeth and a long dark shadow that made innocence cower. Some of my best assets came from our wardrobe that created my dashing ensemble of capes, prima donna skintight trousers, frilly camisoles and tottering black boots with stiletto heels. The makeup department added extensions to my already long hair, and the glossy ringlets often covered my face completely. I'd peek out from under my curls and scare the Dickens out of Longfellow. I added my own touches, a skinny moustache and a crisscross scar on my cheek. Before the shoot even started, Anthony, Candy and I went to the Magic Castle for one of their regular shows. Dressed to kill, I got a sensational reaction from the crowd and stole the show, something I hadn't done in ages when I was out with pop-star Anthony.

My credibility as a gruff, old boxing mentor with Shirley Temple curls and black fingernail polish was pushing it to the limit at *Minotaur* rehearsals. My persona got even more suspect when I was called to Universal to read for *Private Eye,* a 1950s-era crime drama with reverence to Sam Spade and Bogie. It was the brainstorm of Anthony Yerkovich (*Miami Vice, Hill Street Blues* and *Hart to Hart*). This authentic period piece starred Michael Woods and the young actor Josh Brolin. The Blue Movie episode unraveled the case of a missing young porn star that led them into the underbelly of Hollywood, a world of stag films, broken dreams and blackmail. I stole the part of Jerome and jumped into the depravity. Josh Brolin and I went head to head. I was a strip-club boss with a trunk full of eight-millimeter blue movies: *Slave Girls of Morocco, Savage Sisters, Jungle Drums*; you name it I got it, even the mysterious '*Exotica*' that would lead to a trail of murder. After the gun smoke cleared and I was set to leave, Yerkovich came over and said I embodied exactly the tone he was trying for on his show. The remarkable Benicio Del Toro was in the episode too; and Josh Brolin has become a true treasure with films like *No Country for Old Men,* Tarantino and Rodriguez's *Grindhouse* and *Planet Terror, American Gangster, W.,* and *Milk,* for which he was nominated best supporting actor. Jeannie Moore from the *Minotaur* had a party that night, and I brought one of the burlesque girls in all her fleshed out glory.

Scott McClintock bought a new house in Sausalito beyond the Golden Gate Bridge up in Marin County. David Weaver married and moved to Santa Clarita. Alan Bashara lived in a high-rise condo in Grand Rapids and was doing dog-and-pony shows at music concerts. Johnny Reaser was no longer practicing law and had become a restaurateur with his own supper club in Troy, just north of Detroit. Jay Brown was living in London working for Limelight Films. Candy was living with a lesbian drug addict. Crafty Shock had found a treasure chest of success. He worked as a tattoo artist on Melrose, had a band of sorts and still talked a good game. He was a born publicist, but I took some credit for showing him the ropes. His tattoo business was flourishing, and like me, he was still in the business of beautiful girls. We wore them as merit badges and snuck across enemy lines to steal them from each other.

I went to the Zero on Hollywood Boulevard during its final phase and found it nearly deserted. I checked all the rooms and felt a tinge of sadness as I realized this era was drawing to an end. I was heading for the exit when I bumped into a rangy brunette in long, black riding boots. She had an assured flair about her I just couldn't resist. I didn't have to contrive an introduction; we were both candidly lamenting the demise of the Zero. With that as a starting point, we segued into a passionate romance. She was the antithesis of

Candy. Educated and still getting more of it, she lived with her family in Santa Monica and was not the least bit tainted by Hollywood. She loved to play sexy but had a rock-solid foundation of standards and ethics. Cool fashion sense wrapped her in a big red ribbon. She always showed up at my door in another artful homemade outfit. As a couple we wowed everybody. She was quite liberated, preferred my bed but always drove the car. We were invited to a Lenny Fagan club opening, and she made her grand entrance in nothing more than tiny silk panties, barely a bra, black stockings, garter belts, and ankle-strap high heels. This new partner in love was a girl I could easily have married and lived happily ever after.

But like with so many others I managed to screw it up; and you had to know who the culprit was. Naked and naughty, Candy bashed back into my life, and I broke the good heart for the bad tart. My perfect relationship went up in smoke. I lost her. There was no second act. It was like she never happened. She sabotaged my memory and burned her identity. I throttle my mind for clues, but all I find are dead-end raw nerves. Her name remains a mystery. I honor her with anonymity. My heartbreak is your imagination.

There were more incriminating miscalculations. I went to a Sunday afternoon party with Anthony at Bob Forrest's pad on Fountain. There were two beautiful models there, and I was unable to make a choice so I went for the ditto. Surreptitiously, I managed to get both numbers. Laura Richmond was a girl-next-door sweetheart in blue jeans and unpretentiousness. We dated; I liked her a lot. I had plenty of competition though: Anthony gave her deliberation and Tracii Guns consorted with her. But I was just as intrigued by her acquaintance who was completely the opposite: glamorous and all dressed up like a 40s Heddy Lamar with her porcelain skin, black hair and classic features. I played tag with both of them; they fought with each other and then with me. In the end they made up, and I was the odd man out. Laura went on to a significant accomplishment. The 1987 film *Who Framed Roger Rabbit* featured a sultry cartoon nightclub lounge singer named Jessica Rabbit. She was universally acclaimed the sexiest cartoon woman of all time. *Playboy* exploited the palpable lust for Jessica Rabbit with a "Sex in Cinema" article that flaunted her across the cover in a slinky, low-cut dress and long gloves. The human model they chose to portray her was Miss Laura Richmond. "Cover Story: We've transformed our September Playmate, Laura Richmond, into Toontown's seductress Jessica Rabbit, torch-singing star of Who Framed Roger Rabbit. What an eyeful!" And you should have seen the centerfold.

So I blew it, and Candy worked her way right back into the rotation. I had a nice present for her too: *A Night at the Magic Castle* gave me my own well-appointed trailer to lounge and live in. I'd bring Candy to work with me at 6 a.m. and let her sleep while I went to makeup and blocking, and shooting, and eating lunch, and supper. And maybe by then, she'd wake up. Candy left her paraphernalia out; the assistant director came to get me, saw the gear and reported it to Lori and Icek. I was indispensible so they couldn't fire me, but it was embarrassing, and I stopped bringing the human orifice to work with me anymore.

Like *9 Deaths of the Ninja,* I had an outrageous role to die for; I could have gone stark-raving mad. I had an arsenal of medieval torture devices to scare my prey with, and having the power of invisibility, I could pop in and out of everything from boudoirs to confessionals; my, my, how the pretty girls scream with terror. Fortunately, our young Max was a tough kid, and I always got my comeuppance. In the tradition of slapstick silliness, I always ended up in a garbage can or on the lap of the fat lady or hung out to dry.

Blackstar and Houdini had titanic magical battles, but the odds were stacked. I plied the screenwriter with black magic, but alas I was thwarted again. I was destined to suffer an ignominious demise.

The film composer Michael Bishop and I had been casual buddies for ages, but now we started working the clubs together on a regular basis. Michael lived close to the Improv on Melrose, which became a regular hang out for us, more of a grownup club for a change, with fewer teenagers and more show-business types. Soon I was inundated with a new breed of fillies. I even dated my first girl past her twenties. She was thirty-year-old Rosemary who happened to be from Ireland, which certainly didn't hurt her chances. She would be the only serious thirty-plus relationship of my life. Of course, many grew into their thirties.

Michael and I also inhabited Joe Allen's, the actor's bar on Third in West Hollywood. The bar was filled with beautiful actresses and chances were they'd be interested. One of those chances was a model and aspiring actress from New York named Michele, 5'10, 34-24-34, excellent legs and hands. What the card hadn't mentioned was the way her smoldering eyes put me in hypnotic bondage. She was serving me a warrant for sex, drugs and pulsating music. She lived close by and had me out of there so fast I forgot to pay the check.

She pulled me into a living room bed and ripped open her blouse. That revelation alone was enough to launch me, and I couldn't have been more jacked up if…she cracked out her alkyl nitrite poppers and sent me into a cardiac arrest… for rape. Of me! She was throttling my oxygen and maximizing my delirium. I wasn't sure I'd survive the next few moments. We collapsed in the sweat-wet blankets, and I rolled out for some water. By the time I returned, she had cooked up some crack cocaine. I went no thanks. She went yes thanks. I placated her by tasting a stingy toke, and even that sent me reeling. This was all off my radar, and I thought this sex kitten was trying to kill me. On a bad cue, the door was knocked and a fistful of guy friends busted in with more crack and fear-laced adrenaline. The intruders were cranky with rabies. Michele realized I was worn out and useless, so she threw me under the bus, and the head pit bull was no Greyhound. I'd have loved to be shown the door, but they chose to show me the horror. I girded myself for a confrontation but saw an opening and bolted for freedom. They chased me out into the street but retreated when neighbors walking the sidewalk screamed with their own terror.

Karen Faye was another top model I got in over my head with. She was an awesome package of 5' 9, 110 lbs., Blonde and Hazel. She teased and taunted me. When I'd pick her up for a date she'd still be half-undressed and in need of help zipping up her back or checking her stocking seams. Back in her bedroom, she'd pour ice cold vodka and shock me with her cold white flesh. She would kiss me goodnight and make me go home in the morning. She signed a sexy photo of herself with the inscription, "To Blackie, See you tomorrow & tomorrow & tomorrow. Karen." I didn't realize she meant it literally. Three days, three dates, three tomorrows. That was it.

About halfway through *A Night at the Magic Castle,* we set an opening date for *The Minotau.* Now I was doing double duty: Monday through Friday on the movie and Friday, Saturday and Sunday at the Skylight Theatre on North Vermont. This was the biggest theatrical production I'd ever done. It was top class with stellar actors. Harold Sylvester as Jack Moore the black heavyweight champion had given up professional basketball and law school to pursue acting. At the time, he had already played leading roles in two important race films, *Sounder* and *The Autobiography of Miss Jane Pittman* and the pivotal role of Perryman in *An Officer and a Gentleman,* a film that won two Oscars. Queen Moore was played by Veronica Redd who trained at Interlochen and Juilliard, performed with the New York Shakespeare Festival and headlined at the Olympia in Paris. Locally, she had worked with the Black Ensemble Theatre. The rest of the cast was every bit as talented. Even the understudies were working Hollywood actors. My best pal was Jeff Weston, who played Danny Dunne the promising contender. He had an attractive mate, and we often double dated. Like all of us, he was working on his own projects: *Journey to the Center of the Earth* and Oscar nominated *The Player* with Tim Robbins.

A snippet of what the producer wrote in the program regarding me: "Blackie Dammett [Renzo Collucci] was conceived in Los Angeles and raised in pubs and pool halls and penal detention modules from Manila to Montauk. Eclectically educated at MSU, UCLA, MGM, CANDY and on the road with Alice Cooper, Jimi Hendrix, Led Zeppelin, John Lennon and the Red Hot Chili Peppers; Blackie studied acting with the late Lee Strasberg, the late Peggy Feury and the late Harvey Lembeck. Hmmmm..." Anthony came to the play, and with decent reviews we did good box office. There were always requests for tickets from show business celebrities. Flea and Loesha's house was nearby, and I spent time with his growing family as little Clara was blooming. Plays are the hardest to disengage from; it's no exaggeration to think of a theatrical cast as family. It hurt to end the run.

We also wrapped *A Night at the Magic Castle* after seven weeks of shooting. In interviews with *Variety* and *The Hollywood Reporter,* Lori Levine stated they spent $1.5 million on the film which is admittedly low budget, but in today's dollars that was still about $4.5 million. They took the film to Cannes and Milan to negotiate offshore sales, and it had a better success rate outside America. With those two critical projects finished, I flew to GR for my 30th Creston High class reunion.

I hadn't been there since the twentieth one. The old town threw out a welcome mat, and *The Grand Rapids Press* got dibs on an exclusive interview. Tom Gravengood offered to put me up in his Fisk Lake home with his lovely wife Sandy, who I used to court long ago. When their son Scott Gravy Jr. was young, I used to send him Hollywood dreams and RHCP gear. I was his unofficial godfather, and now he was graduating. The *American Pie* movies were modeled after his school, East Grand Rapids High, and the films were written by EGR grad Adam Herz. It was Scott's combative father who had tagged me as Spider when *we* were young. Gravy Sr. was a gangster aluminum siding salesman one week, and next it would be Nigerian oil futures or swamp land in Ocala. Sandy was a successful real estate agent. After an hour, my allegiance moved on to the party-savvy Gravy Jr. and I seldom saw much of Tom after that. Scott had grown up to be a tall, fair-skinned good-looking young man with his beautiful mother's looks and demeanor. He was Alan Ladd with length. He also had an edgy dark streak from his father.

Scott had two extra good friends, Tony Caprara and an enigmatic benefactor named John Wege, whose father Peter was an industrial scion and one of the city's indispensible philanthropists. The young Wege had his own mansion in EGR, another house in the northern resort area of Traverse City, and a rented party house straddling the border of EGR and Eastown for the singular purpose of giving Scott and Tony and their pals a place to raise hell. It was a 24 hour *Animal House* and the gang lived, loved and ruined their livers there. They were already on the funk and rap bandwagon after growing up on RHCP music. I brought along a different sound. Candy had thoroughly ingratiated me with Guns N' Roses as they built momentum toward the release of their first album, but they were still under the normal radar. The band gave me a preview cassette of *Appetite for Destruction,* and I played it all over Grand Rapids to the amazement of everybody on my frequency. I bequeathed the cassette to Scott before I left. *Appetite for Destruction* went on to sell an incredible 28 million albums.

Scott's EGR friends partied in fine estates while mommys and daddys were off in Aspen or Barbados. It was all quite remarkable. I slipped across the state and joined John Reaser at his nightclub Nicky's on Big Beaver Road. My long wild hair and black duster frightened his conservative customers, but he was cautiously happy to see me. John had a sweet home in a gated community and a Rolls Royce in the garage. I left Michigan with a spring in my step. I would definitely be back. As my plane approached LAX, I looked out over a thousand square miles of dark brown smog. I was home.

Chapter 45: Adolf

There was no drop off in the exquisitely high-class quality of the films I was reading for. *I WAS A TEENAGE SEX MUTANT* for instance. I read for the major role of Drax. I had 12 scenes tabbed on my script and made several call backs. Raymond O'Conner collared the part, and, cowardly, they re-titled it *Dr. Alien*. Next I read for *Moto Rama*, a black comedy as Gus. Then it was *Sunny Boy* as yet another Weasel, attired in a purple hairdo, hoop earring and stylish punk clothing. Jean Claude Van Damme's project was *Alamogordo*. Finally, it was the comedy TV show *Webster* and *Hide and Shriek,* which came with a disclaimer on the front page of the script that read "while this will be an erotic film, it will definitely NOT be X rated." No luck for this dead duck.

The Red Hot Chili Peppers were on the move though, off on their first big European tour. Their new album *The Uplift Mofo Party Plan* had just been released. Plenty of old-school fans consider it the best album of all, with songs like "Fight Like a Brave," "Me and My Friends," "The Love Trilogy" (with the line 'Then ask my Dad!') and "No Love Chump Sucker" about Hillel's awfully bad ex-girlfriend. *Mofo* would be Hillel's last album. He had moved into the historically significant Malaga Castle Apartment on Afton Place in Hollywood, and by some quirk of fate Violet lived across from his door. Violet was diligently doing her photography, and we set up a photo shoot with Candy. Violet provided the lensing and makeup; Candy provided the face. Since Violet had some experience with drug addiction, she took Candy under her motherly wing and tried to help. The one who needed it most was right across the hall.

Auditions and rehearsals kept me busy, but I still managed to get around and lately, more than ever with Mark Cuff. Mark's band the Textones had gone the way of fond memories and great standards. There was a new scene at the old Palomino on Lankershim in the industrial Valley sagebrush. Once a traditional country & western bar going back to the 50s, it had a lineage that would have pleased the Grand Ole Opry. Johnny Cash, Merle Haggard, Buck Owens, Patsy Cline, and Willie Nelson were just a few of the country icons that played there. In the 70s and 80s, rock reared its punch-drunk head and everything from The Bay City Rollers to full-throttle punk bands and George Harrison and Bob Dylan got on that well-worn stage. Emmylou Harris, Dwight Yoakam, Neil Young and Elvis Costello carved their initials on the dressing room walls. Canned Heat was playing the Palomino the night Bob Hite over dosed and died in the band van on their way home to Topanga, with David Weaver trying to revive him. Gary Myrick played the Palomino. So did a new wave of cow punk acts that adorned the ancient marquee. There were special nights though that still had an old time country feel, and they were packed with retro cowboys and comely cowgirls.

Mark and I went on that special night each week, and we both had our eyes on the belle of the ball, a young lady with a gift for flair. She had the biggest smile in Dodge City and always wore the best homemade country outfits, especially one in red that was low cut and unsafely risqué. It turned out her mom was protectively there; the boss knew the family, and they kept tabs on her. Coni Constantine was only sexteen but held up her end of the bar. So did her popular mom, Penny. We became part of their entourage, card-carrying characters at Penny's big table. When the cowgirl turned seventeen, mom allowed me to both date her and teach her how to drive. That must have been before the night we were pulled over for a suspected DUI, leaving the Palomino. A busy night and a lot of procrastinating. By the time they booked me, I was clean as a fresh quip. Coni had long black hair, snow white skin and always wore maximum red lipstick. She kept a job, went to school and helped her mom at home. My girl was sweet as country apple pie.

Another lady friend of mine was Cassandra Peterson, a drop-dead beautiful redhead with freckles and all that went with it. Occasionally, we playfully flirted and enjoyed it. I first met her at the Rainbow a few years earlier, completely unaware of her alter ego, Elvira, Mistress of the Dark. The two of her were as different as light and dark. Even back then, she never gave me any indication of her intriguing past life. She was a Vegas showgirl, James Bond girl, Elvis girl, Fellini girl and a member of the LA improv company The Groundlings, where the seeds of Elvira first sprung on Melrose Avenue. By now, superstar Elvira had become a cottage industry with infinite diversity. She was in movies, commanded the *Movie Macabre* television show and made frequent stops at Johnny Carson's desk. La Rocca represented her for a while. He had taken on new clients and moved from the small office near Burbank Studios to a new modern building closer to Universal.

There was another attempt to revive the downtown club scene when the ornate Stock Exchange closed down in the mid-80s. Optimistic entrepreneurs leased the building and transformed it from high finance to just getting high. It was vaguely cool for a minute. I was down there one night all by my lonesome, scouting the talent when I saw a vision of loveliness heading for the exit. I decided I'd had enough too, hurried my pace and caught up with her as she crossed Spring Street, heading for a parking lot. It was pretty creepy down there late at night so she was understandably defensive as she reached her car with me on her tail. I introduced myself, and she vaguely knew of me. She was Erin. She wasn't in a mood to talk, but I persisted. I couldn't help myself she was so pretty. The doll said she was Axl's girlfriend, as though that might shut me up. It didn't. Ah-ha! So she was Erin Everly, daughter of Don Everly of the immortal Everly Brothers. I was competitive and hypocritically alluded to Axl's heroin horseplay. She brushed me off and drove off. And that was that.

I'd forgotten all about it. I took Candy to another of the Chili Pepper shows at the Greek. I left her backstage while I flew around the arena, looking for more trouble. When I returned, Candy stopped me at the door and warned me that Axl was in the dressing room prepared to kick my ass. Okay. Surprisingly, Axl had become quite a RHCP fan and was talking shop with Anthony and Flea. He had also acquired a stack of their merchandise. But as much as anything, Axl was waiting for me to show up so he could settle the Erin Everly score. Cooler heads prevailed, but I think it would have made great theater to duke it out.

My agent kept me running on the Hollywood treadmill: *Frank's Place,* about a Boston professor; *Jake and the Fatman,* a crime drama with William Conrad; and *Sledgehammer!* still trying to make that work. And there were plenty more: *To Live and Drive in LA* at Fox as an over-the-hill hippie, to casting director Eddie Foy of the famous Foy vaudeville family for *Lauderdale Confidential* as a mortician who's a lot like Norman Bates, a German mini-series with the English title *All Inclusive,* and as Frankenstein in *General Hospital.* Whew! I took a big breath and went deep into *Subterranean* at Empire Studios. I tackled Roger Corman's film *Andy Colby's Incredible Adventure* in the role of Lord Chroma, and *Superstar* for Joe Hogan. And finally the one I was looking for in this list, *Elvira, Mistress of the Dark,* starring Cassandra Peterson and co-produced by her husband, Mark Pierson. I was up for Manny, a gold-chain laden fast-talking agent plugging Caesar's Palace, but Charles Woolf, born in 1926, got the role. No roles for me, decision by the husband perhaps, or thank god I just wasn't that old yet.

Candy was back with her mom in West Covina, and I dropped by to surprise her. I knocked and went in as I had a million times before. I was part of the family. Only this time Sue and Fred were ominously startled to see me. I asked where Candy was, and they motioned toward the bedroom. I opened the door and there was Candy in bed with some big bruiser of a guy. They were so nonchalant I dropped any idea of punching him in the nose. That and when he stood up he kept going to an unfurled six-and-a-half feet tall. He was John Forsyth and worked with Candy's parents as poker dealers in Gardena. Candy brushed it aside and pretended it was nothing. It was the beginning of a long goodbye.

Back when Candy and I were badass punks, she wanted to get a German Doberman pinscher and name it Adolf after the Fuhrer. We never found the right Doberman. That was ancient history now. Today, I was at the Beverly Shopping Center on a lunch date. Finished, I headed for the elevator, pressed the button and waited. I perused the window of the pet shop next door. Curled up in his little manger was a tiny bundle of brown-and-black fur about the size of my fist. I felt a curious connection. The elevator door opened and I found myself caught in mid-air. I let it ride and returned to the pet store. The clerk asked if I'd like to take "Peanut" into the puppy room. I was a kindergartener again, crawling around on my hands and knees with the spunky pup. We thoroughly exhausted each other, and the line waiting to use the puppy room had extended to the lizard patch. We just sat there face to face, smiling at each other and fell madly in love. On the spot, I named him Adolf. An Adolf Doberman would have been an obvious cliché, but this tiny Yorkshire terrier with the big bad name would cook up smiles across the entire Western world. I hustled out to show Candy, and she turned romantic on both of us. Adolf was a lady killer. As it turned out, pinscher in German meant terrier.

Producer Glen A. Larson was no stranger to me, I'd worked in both his *Magnum P.I.* and *The Fall Guy.* He'd also conceived and produced another forty hit shows and one of them was the fanciful *Knight Rider* with David Hasselhoff and a talking Pontiac Trans Am with artificial intelligence. Rebecca Holden as April Curtis was a regular and one of La Rocca's clients. Five years later, Larson upped the ante and created a similar action-adventure series called *The Highwayman* with another handsome broad-shouldered hero and another technological vehicle. The hero was Sam Jones who raised eyebrows and temperatures as comic strip character *Flash Gordon* in the 1980 Dino De Laurentiis flick. The Highwayman's Swiss Army knife vehicle was a large black truck, which opened up into a helicopter, or a futuristic sports car, or it could just be invisible, its "stealth mode." The Highwayman and his crew had super powers, super weapons and the support of F.L.A.G. (the Foundation of Law and Government). Now how's a bad guy supposed to survive in that environment? Glen Larson was looking for a bad man, and he put out an APB for Blackie Dammett.

La Rocca sent me to Universal for an unusual evening audition. I went to the office and discovered it was just Glen and me and one other actor. Even the secretaries had left. The other actor was Christopher McDonald (the bad husband of Geena Davis in *Thelma and Louise*, Shooter McGavin in *Happy Gilmore*), who like me frequently played the guy you loved to hate. *The Highwayman* series shot in Phoenix and they needed two major villains in a hurry. There were two parts to be cast and we had an audition-off. The synopsis of the "Billionaire Body Club" episode read something like this, "When a dead body drained of blood and missing organs is uncovered, Highway and Jetto are sent to investigate, and are soon on the trail of a blood-thirsty doctor trading in spare body parts for the rich and powerful." Glen Larson had written the script. The first parlor game was to pick the ruthless doctor, and Chris definitely had the respectable look of a doctor; conversely I was born to be Jazz, the crazy killer. We shook hands and went home to pack. Next stop Arizona.

Reality set in when I got home and saw Adolf waiting for me on the couch with a big smile on his mug. He still hadn't gotten any bigger, and he still hadn't barked yet. Not a ruff or a bow wow. Not a growl or a howl. He was so civilized, so urbane, so sophisticated and so human. I almost couldn't bear to leave him, but we needed the paycheck to buy kibble and veterinarian expenses. I called Candy and asked her if she'd like to stay at my house for a week and take care of Adolf while I went to Phoenix. She said "all rightie."

A limo snatched me at the Phoenix airport and dropped me into the *Highwayman* compound. It was surrounded with razor wire to protect the awesome arsenal and a modern film studio. The director of this episode was my old friend Ivan Nagy. I got my orders and went to work. We shot metro, mountains and even in a spooky cemetery with some lively models and a couple dead ones. One of the live ones caught my ever-wandering eye. She was JoAnne Wolf, and we almost got cozy on location and did keep in touch back in LA. The story revolved around these models at a beauty contest and a grand ball. My job was to tail their tail, and, when necessary, dispose of them. Jazz wore snazzy outfits, had a cool setup and his choice of beautiful women. Off the set in the evening, I was doing just about the same thing. Phoenix was an up-and-coming city in the waning days of 1987. I looked through the entertainment paper and discovered LA Guns were playing a local rock club. It was the *Sex Booze and Tattoos* tour. Tracii and I laughed over our experiences with the killer girlfriend. Other nights, I went out with cast and crew; we tested the night life and found it adequate.

I kept calling home to check on Adolf, but nobody was answering. I checked my messages and there were several with thick, Middle Eastern accents. The gibberish was decipherable heroin-dealer lingo, my worst nightmare. Who's watching the store? Is Adolf on a shish kebab? Is some doped-up dope going through my drawers? Am I screwed or what?! It was early evening and I convinced the motor pool to let me have a car for the night. This was eerily reminiscent of the *Walking Tall* chase to retrieve Jack Starrett's stash in Tennessee, except Jackson was only 90 miles to Memphis. From Phoenix to Los Angeles was almost 400 miles, and I had to work the next day. Fortunately, those desert roads were built for speed. It took me seven hours. Adolf was thrilled to see me. No sign of the naughty momma. There were syringes, balloons and all kinds of paraphernalia lying around. I was furious but kept my cool. I cleaned up the mess and packed up my dog. I locked the front door from the inside and dead-bolted the back on my way out. I'd deal with Candy when I got home.

So Adolf and I went on our first of many road trips. He was a brave little pup. He sat in the passenger seat and watched the scenery until he got tired and slept in my lap. In the morning, I went straight to the set with Adolf tucked into my jacket pocket. One of the assistant directors saw me holding Adolf and said I'd have to take him outside; no animals allowed. He explained the obvious: a bark during a take would ruin the sound track. I pleaded my unusual case: I had nowhere to put him, he'd freak without me, and he was a theatrical dog star who knows not to bark...ever. The AD said OK, you've been warned; if he barks and ruins a shot it's your career. Adolf never made a peep. Time for my scene, I poked Adolf under my shirt and climbed into the special-effects crash car. An exterior scene of my car really crashing off a real cliff would be another time; today we were doing my interior in a stationary car with a crew bouncing it around with two by fours. After a lot of jostling, I crashed off the cliff and acted the horror of plummeting toward death for the camera mounted on the hood. The second unit director, Gary Baxley, gave me the thumbs up, and they untangled me from my safety straps. I extracted Adolf and revealed the wonder dog. The crew was bewildered, and for the rest of the shoot Adolf was king. He was Rin Tin Tin, Lassie and Beethoven.

My spectacular final scene came a couple days later up on South Mountain, a landmark in the desert territory. Top-billed female guest star Cindy Morgan, who spiced up *Caddy Shack* for Chevy Chase, played Mink, an out-of-town cop looking for her missing model sister. I stalked her car along the winding road, perilously close to the edge and waiting for the right moment to nudge her car off the cliff. After Nagy got his coverage, Cindy and I got out, and stunt drivers took over the Highwayman's monster truck and Jazz's car. Good raced to her aid and bumped Evil over the cliff into a painful oblivion. That was a wrap for me, and I was anxious to get home. The next day I boarded the plane with Adolf hiding in my inside suit-coat pocket. Nobody knew. Even the man sitting next to me never realized a super pup was six inches from his shoulder. Pup sipped from a paper cup. He never peed; he never made a sound. The only sound at my seat by the window was the beat of my heart for the furry little mobster.

At home I tracked down the heroin dealers who were calling my number. One of them lived up on Fountain; I banged on his door and he turned out to be a wimpy, balding white guy. I rearranged his living room, and we never heard from him again. The Iranian dealers weren't so cooperative and reversed the charges with threats of their own over the phone. I was starting to feel a bit insecure on La Jolla. I had bounced back from the knife-wielding thief in the night, but insidious invisible Iranians were problematic. Adolf had grown a little and looked like a Beatles haircut, but he wasn't ready to defend me yet.

Four and a half mugs. Adolf, Blackie and best friend David Weaver.

Not sure who those guys are.

Chapter 46: The Bad Boys

1988. It had been twenty years since the halcyon glow of Portuguese Bend and Topanga. Ten since Anthony and I parted ways. LA had gone from the promise land to the lost empire. AIDS dominated the vernacular: death by sex. For a serial lover it was the kiss of death. Candy, it seemed, was irredeemable. My participation with her antics had cost me my reputation, if not my career. The Cubans had their hooks in me, another dead end. Yesterday, stardom was inevitable; now I questioned everything about myself. I needed a change or an antidote or a miracle. I tossed the dice and came up with another B movie.

Icek Tenebaum and Lori Levine were indefatigable. Although *A Night at the Magic Castle* hadn't been a huge success, the company had made enough money to reinvest in another project, and they asked me to play a part in *The American Scream,* a horror comedy movie that had its tongue firmly planted in a cankered cheek. I was the only actor they carried over. No audition, just the job. I was an enigmatic pastor of a small church high in the Sierra Mountains about 250 miles north of Los Angeles, the same general location as Humphrey Bogart's 1941 *High Sierra* with Hal B. Wallis' production, Raoul Walsh's direction, a screenplay by John Huston, and actors Ida Lupino, Cornel Wilde, Arthur Kennedy and Joan Leslie. So let's see how we sized up. Our screenwriter director Mitchell Linden had written *Friday the 13th Part V* and *Doin' Time* and edited *A Night at the Magic Castle,* Lori Levine produced, and for actors we had Jennifer Darling and Pons Maar as the leads and parents of a *Leave it to Beaver* family that are lured by a Wilson Creek tourist folder to spend a holiday in the Sierras. Darling worked on Broadway, had her own TV series and did a movie with Barbra Streisand. Pons was well-schooled in theatre, improvisation, mime, choreography and punk rock. His film work included Eddie Murphy's *Golden Child.* I was third billed and you already know my stuff, but this was my character's description in the Cannes Film Festival publicity booklet: "...as the man in the wide brimmed hat, a dagger-wielding, ominous figure who radiates evil while lurking in the shadows of a very strange town. His character will remind the viewer of a young Vincent Price, so chilling is his presence in the movie."

The kids and their dates were Kimberlee Kramer, Jeanne Sapienza, Kevin Kaye and Matt Borlenghi. Edy Williams the onetime bombastic bombshell did a stripper cameo. She was once married to Russ Meyer and came to parody sex with her roles in *Beyond the Valley of the Dolls* and other provocative films. She was also a *Playboy* centerfold and a regular at the Oscars and Cannes, famously wearing next to nothing. One of her movies was called *Nudity Required.* And finally there was Adolf, who muscled himself into the cast and crew and camera shots. The weather was quite cold up in the Sierras and often impassible from the snow and ice.

After a couple weeks of nothing but brawny mountain matrons and old geezers in long white beards, I started missing Candy. I had a three-day lull in my schedule so Adolf and I drove back to LA in my Caddy. We scooped up pooper doddle and brought her back up to the location. Of course she hated it. It was freezing and there was no dope. That left sex, and I refused to have it with her. If anybody had the potential of AIDS, she would. I had long since scaled down my sex life. I had a kiss-and-hug life. We were in my chalet late at night; she wasn't getting *anything* so she decided to walk back to LA in her skimpy pajamas. By the time I called her bluff, she was too far away to hear it. I spent the whole night ice fishing around in the wilderness and finally found her in the morning, half-frozen in an abandoned cabin. Our company trucks drove film to LA for processing every day, and I got Candy a ride back to civilization.

The company was invited to a wrap party in neighboring Springville, population a small number. It was held at the only bar in town with a knee-slapping country band, lots of free food and a well-stocked bartender. Romantically, I hadn't dialed in on anybody the whole time; the closest was Debra Lamb, who played the victim I attacked in a creepy *Psycho* motel shower. The schizophrenic film that was often quite funny wasn't afraid to get dark. So I perked up when I saw the young local girls on display at the party bar, and they were all anxious to meet the actors. There was a tall redhead named Missy turning double takes. Unlike the aggressive big-foot mares, she was sweet sixteen. She had an older sister named Patrice who was eighteen, and their mother wasn't shy at all. We exchanged phone numbers. In fact, I exchanged numbers with several hillbilly families that day. I was a victim of the Stockholm syndrome. A month later after several letters doused with cheap perfume, Missy and Patrice hopped a mountain bus to Hollywood and visited me. From shy to wild, I had to call their mother to take them home. Another Daisy Mae wrote me cute correspondences, with the approval of her grandmother. She even offered to bring her down to see me, but I declined. Sierra Springfield was for country cousins and goodness gracious, great balls of fire.

I came home to warm weather and a backlog of auditions; some had expired but others needed my attention. *I Married Scarface* was on the burner but wouldn't go until summer. John Frankenheimer's *Dead Bang* with Don Johnson was well worth a visit with Lynn Stalmaster, the dean of casting directors. There was a *Star Trek* at Paramount, *Flip Side* as a heavy at Universal, *Pit Bull Decker*, *Phantom of the Mall*, *Young Rebels*, *Busybodies*, *Something Out There* at NBC, an offbeat comedy *The Dark Backward* with Jud Nelson, *Night Wish*, *Blood Feast II*, and *Blood Diner II*. What the bloody hell!?

Nothing was copacetic, and it got worse when Candy overdosed on heroin and was discovered naked and unconscious in a downtown Los Angeles alley. She had been stripped of everything she was wearing and what was left of her dignity. In degrees, she had been ravished by bums, bag ladies, drug addicts and rats. When she got out of the hospital, her Granny took custody, and we put her in rehab.

By spring, I was anxious for another crack at all those sacrificial virgins in Grand Rapids. My timing was perfect; the long suffering NBA Detroit Pistons were in the play-offs. The perennial losers hadn't won a championship since they were the Fort Wayne Pistons and whipped the Sheboygan Redskins three games to two in 1945. That was back when the National Basketball League had teams like the Toledo Jim White Chevrolets, Akron Firestone Non-Skids and Chicago Studebaker Flyers, precursors of the NBA. Now with a rampage of publicity, the press had coined Detroit the *Bad Boys*. Basketball aficionado Alan Bashara, who played a wicked game himself, coaxed me to watch the Boston series at his pad. I made a fast break for Michigan. After a quick howdy with the Gravengoods,

I checked in with Alan and saw another side of my old town. He was promoting shows and wooing the ladies with charm and humor like he had back in Topanga. And he had a surprise for me. Our uptight hometown would be the last place on earth I'd expect to find burlesque. Churches, yes. In fact, the most churches per capita in the world and proud of it. Civic signs proclaimed it. Boosters boasted. The town shut down and businesses put up a closed sign on Sundays. Alan sat me down and told me he'd found a local strip club. LA was creaking from the weight of them. They provided transparency. You could see the package without taking them to dinner and a movie or meeting the parents. You wouldn't buy a pig in a poke, whatever that means, or a Stone Age religion slipped under the poker table. A bawdy strip club was like a cafeteria, something for everybody's taste.

Alan's find was on the Ottawa county line and was called Barnaby's. To be accurate, there was an old burlesque club on the west side called the Parkway Tropics which technically was such an establishment. It had endured since the 40s but only because it was grandfathered before the city's prohibition of nudity. In Grand Rapids, everybody kept their clothes on, even when they bathed. The Parkway, which I had never been in or dared to, was more like a haunted Hansel and Gretel house with creepy old witches. It was in a rough blue-collar district. Barnaby's was the real deal and jumping with lively young girls who were happy to meet me, so happy the manager asked them to get back to work. I gorged myself. Cheryl Brooks and Cricket still rattle around my sensory cortex. Both of them came out to see me in LA.

Alan had a cool condo set up with a constant stream of girls dropping by. He introduced me to twin models, and we flipped a coin. I had a platonic lunch with a now mature Debi Wauchope, the bullet busty girl I stole from the Putt Putt Bar band and the Comstock Park High School security cop twenty years ago. Her legacy was unassailable. Alan and his business partner, Jim Cornell, had taken over a large movie theatre and were converting it into a night spot called Club Eastbrook. He took me on a hard-hat tour. Excitement was suddenly brewing in Grand Rapids, and Club Eastbrook was at the top of the list.

We went up to the resort town of Charlevoix where Big Al had a recurring gig with an outdoor music venue called the Castle, a stone fortress with expansive grounds. The headliner that night was AC/DC. Brad Parsons the Toronto owner of the Castle had a beautiful young stepdaughter, Vanessa Chandler, who took me under her wing and gave me the royal tour. I helped count the stupendous piles of money they took in that night, hundreds of thousands of dollars. We had the Midas touch and made plans for the future which assured I'd return. At a bar in the harbor, we watched Detroit vanquish the Celtics to win the East. We lost in the finals to a Lakers team that sported Magic, Kareem and James Worthy, but the Pistons would be back next year. So would I.

I flew back. Johnny La Rocca and a black book of ladies needed me. My baggage included an appreciation for the tranquility of small town America. No busy deadlines or life on the line decisions. Michigan was green and blue and golden. LA was socked in pollution, traffic, gangs, pestilence, drug addicts and my stressful life as an actor. I loved Los Angeles, but a tiny fissure had crept into our relationship.

Even my prototype Hollywood doll was leaving LA. Candy and her parents moved to Colorado; Denver had legalized gambling. Migratory birds, Sue and Fred were off in search of a better life, especially for their drug-addicted daughter. Perhaps Candy acquiesced because they called Denver the Mile *High* City.

With Candy gone and my career in need of a tune up, it was time for another changing of the address, another cleansing of the late-night door-knocking patrons, another purging of the past. Or was it just another another. I rented an old Spanish Villa on Orange Drive, just north of Hancock Park. I was out of my beloved West Hollywood, exiled for the first time since digging in at Sunset and Clark in 1968. Anthony and Ione Skye lived just a block north on Orange Drive. Gary Myrick had a home between us; he was comfortably wealthy, painting and doing session work. It was handy being close to my son, and I could keep my eye on Ione when he was on tour. After I moved in, the band went on a European tour that included the influential Pink Pop Festival in Holland.

My rent was triple LaJolla's, so I was anxious to work. *Royal Pain* as Yugo a taxidermist for the Disney Channel and a call back. Lori Levine's latest project *The Harley Boys* was still trying to find traction. I read for *Horror Show* at Lions Gate. And then I clicked with Sybil Danning, the quintessential sex-symbol. Austrian born, she was a *Playboy* cover girl and a luscious beauty known for her action movies like *Chained Heat, Reform School Girls* and *Private Passions*. She also had entrepreneurial chops, and one of her projects snared me in her web. She co-wrote and produced the film *L.A. Bounty* and starred as an ex-cop turned bounty hunter who went after a crazed killer played by Wings Hauser. I read for bad guy Robert Maxwell who was targeted by Sybil Danning, still looking lovely in her producer's cap. Director Worth Keeter chimed in with an A-OK at their Noble Entertainment headquarters in WLA. They liked my work and hired me.

The band returned from Europe loaded up with more tattoos and escapades of Flea's latest bouts of nakedness. Pink Pop had been a success, and it seemed they were about to break big when the worst possible news hit the streets. Hillel Slovak overdosed on heroin and died in his Malaga Castle Apartment. Word spread like wildfire that a Chili Pepper had died and most thought it was Anthony, whose addiction was the most notorious. He almost did die of a broken heart. Anthony fled to Mexico. Grief stricken, he was inspired to write songs that would finally put them over the top. Hillel had started the band and would continue to influence it.

For a while though, it looked like the band wouldn't survive at all. Jack Irons quit. Anthony was a mess. Flea was shaken. Hillel was gone. They recruited one of George Clinton's guitarists, Blackbyrd McKnight, and former Dead Kennedys drummer D.H. Peligro to fill out the roster and put on a trial show at a small venue on Sunset. There were TV news cameras and the bristle of freshly sharpened pencils. Anthony was gaunt and the show was grim. I left with a queasy feeling for the band and, more importantly, for Anthony. The new lineup didn't jell, and eventually they auditioned new talent.

Matt Dike had opened another club called Enter the Dragon, and I was there working on a cold Corona. An old gal pal rushed up and said she wanted me to meet her new boyfriend. He was a young man with awkward charm, and he addressed me as Mr. Dammett. He went on to explain how excited he was about auditioning for the Chili Pepper guitar slot in a few days. I said good luck, kid. Young Johnny Frusciante shook my hand again and sauntered off with a big smile. About that time, the band also tapped St. Paul-born and

Michigan-bred Chad Smith to wallop the hell out of black-and-blue drums, and soon they were all working on a new album.

I still owned a piece of the night. My pretty parade felt comfortable with Candy del Mar from the Cramps, Paula Abdul's 650-9673, Kitty Leslie and a discreet manila envelope. The former gay club Probe on Highland was the new Scream with Dayle at the door again, smoothing my entrance with her gracious welcome. The place was always loaded with the coolest dudes and damsels. Close to fifty now, I was still competing with youth, but it was slippery on my way to the top of the food chain. One night, I stopped by at closing time and came upon a beautiful blonde named Jennifer, who was just a touch out of touch. She was brand new in town and didn't know a soul. She acclimated easily and slept in my bed that night. We went to clubs and made the rounds. We were doing fine and then I introduced her to Shock; she defected to the little prince. They broke up and back she came. I met a cranberry redhead doll face with a proclivity for polka dots and little white socks. She joined us in a party. Exhausted, the three of us went to bed and I slept in the middle to maintain order. Once Jennifer fell asleep, polka dots crawled on top of me and we tried to be quiet.

Barb Remsen, one of my friendly casting directors, thought I'd make a good fit for a new project at Raleigh Studios; it was *Instant Karma* and the baby of a team of young writer/producers named Bruce Taylor and Dale Rosenblum. They had already signed up a rather impressive cast for a first-time project that included actor, comedian, philosopher and New York City gadfly Orson Bean; comic, actor, entrepreneur and husband of Shirley Jones, Marty Ingels; David Cassidy, the former teen idol who had made fame and fortune with the Partridge Family, his good looks and pop star antics; William Smith, my co-worker in *Moon in Scorpio*; and finally, the immerging star of *Instant Karma,* the next big thing, Craig Sheffer. He would follow this film with Robert Redford's *A River Runs Through It* and have star billing over Brad Pitt. And add Blackie Dammett as the colorful Polish private dick, Ed Polinski. Roderick Taylor directed the unruly ship for MGM.

The catch line: "He has the hottest show on television, the coolest wheels in the parking lot, and the most beautiful girl in the cast. What could go wrong?" Of course it was everything, on and off the screen. For me, for a change, everything went right. Raised on the Polish west side of Grand Rapids, I knew a thing or two about playing a Polinski. Every grownup beer-drinking Polish fellow I ever knew had a big gut with his belt hiding somewhere below. Robert De Niro gained 60 pounds to portray the elder Jake La Motta in *Raging Bull* and won an Oscar. If it was good enough for the master, it was the least I could do to put on thirty pounds and get my own big gut.

I went up for Edgar Allan Poe's *The Pit and the Pendulum* from the creator of *Re-Animator,* Stuart Gordon. I read for a lead role, Mendoza, but lost it to Mark Margolis my assassin partner in *The Cotton Club.* I also read for the lead in *Manson: The Real Story* from Heritage Entertainment. Manson seemed to follow me around. A few weeks later, I had a crack at *Dusted* for Cathy Henderson in a Jean-Claude Van Damme film, first as Meyerso, an ugly runt with stringy hair and a runny nose who worked in the prison infirmary, and then as Konefke, a scruffy Hells Angel with numerous tattoos and a few other bad qualities. Two days later, it was a heroin dealer in a Century City office for *So Cool!* And I finished off the span as a demon in *Monsters*.

That summer, Alan Bashara bought a new Chevrolet pickup truck and drove west to visit his ever-diminishing circle of friends, including Weaver, Vallon, Wiatt and some of his old sweethearts. Attrition had decimated much of the old gang. We were definitely getting old. After the reunions were over, he talked me into driving back to GR with him. I had ulterior motives: cowgirl Coni Constantine and her mom had moved to Nashville, the home of country music. Alan agreed to swing by on the way. Adolf spent the trip perched between us, up on top of the bench seat like a pirate's parrot. Once again, I'd ride the old Route 66 trail. We stopped in Phoenix to see one of Big Al's past college sweethearts and then veered off to stay with Andrienne Teeguarden in Taos. Alan skied and I drank the hot toddies. Coni turned us loose on Music Row. Howdy! A few more truck stops and it was Club Eastbrook. Alan had a night of his own that he called Below Zero, after the former LA late-night spot. I was finding it rather boring when this Miss the mark but hit my heart appeared out of nowhere, all in black, with torn stockings and slender limbs. She moved in fluid drive. Thus began my first semi-serious relationship back in Michigan. I placed my exclusive attention on the tattered, torn and sultry Jennifer Jones. She was the toast of the town and the girlfriend of a local rock star, but she dropped all that baggage the second she saw me. It was reciprocally pivotal. She shared an apartment with other young kids with pink or green hair and wild delusions.

On one of the many pleasant evenings, I stepped outside of Alan's condo to revel in the brilliant stars that sparkled in the crystal-clear black skies of Michigan. In Los Angeles, the nights are grey and starless. The electric lights of twenty million people bounce and blur off the smoggy canopy. Pretend stars are painted on a backdrop at 20th Century Fox. Angelinos settle for a high-school trip to the Griffith Park Observatory. I sat on a verdant lawn under the full moon and marveled at the spectacle. It was peaceful, calm and welcoming. I thought of the rat race back in LA. For the first time in a quarter century, I thought seriously about moving home. From that moment on, I waged war with myself and it gave me a splitting dichotomy.

Home was where my mother had been born, lived her truncated life and tragically died. She was buried for eternity at Woodlawn Cemetery on Kalamazoo Avenue. My mother Mollie, rest her weary soul, had married a scoundrel named Elton Bosworth sometime after she divorced my dad when I was just a four-year-old tot. A marriage breaking son of a tugboat, Elton was a sailor himself. He had trouble acclimating to civilian life, and after the war he moved from job to job and tavern to tavern. He drank too much and had a chip on his shoulder. When Judy and I went to see our mom, I always hoped he'd be gone. The brooding husband was cocky and looked like he could hurt you. I know he hurt my mom. They had a baby and named him Rick. He was my stepbrother, whatever that meant to me at the time. Elton was killed in a car crash not long after that.

Rick looked up to me as his fantasy big brother, but I already had a raft of real Kiedis brothers and sisters. I never took him seriously. Our ties were tenuous. When I was around my mother, I wanted her undivided attention, not sharing it with Rick the interloper. As we got older I hardly ever saw him. Now he was grown up and working at P B Gast & Sons, and I went to visit him. His wife, Billie, happened to drop by, and I was amazed that he had married such a beautiful wife. I loved her name and maybe more. They were estranged, and there was something about the way she looked at me. When they invited me for dinner at her house, I gladly accepted. She fell for me, I fell for her and Rick just kept falling. They divorced and I continued to see her when I was in GR or when she came to LA. They had a daughter Mollie after my mom. Rick migrated to Los Angeles and tried to make a go of acting. He lives in China now. I was ready to head back. I also heard Candy and her methadone were home with Granny in El Monte.

Always the fearless actor.

Chapter 47: Nathan's Sheer Madness

The band released their fourth and final EMI album *Mother's Milk* and were about to do a video for "Knock Me Down" ('If you see me getting high, knock me down'), Anthony's personal, pulsating anti-drug anthem. He invited me down for the shoot. They were using friends to augment the cast. I couldn't go; I had a previous obligation to play a flamboyant drug kingpin lounging by a Bel Air pool, surrounded with beautiful women in Shock's video the same day. His band was called Homey Sapien, and the song was I don't remember. The featured babe massaging my bronzed back at the pool was Jennifer the Scream girl we had each taken turns with. She was Shock's again now, and I was more than content with Bethamie Heavenstone, a new girl from New York City I had met at the ever-generous Scream. She wore plunging necklines with a wire bodice device that supported her bodacious, protruding breasts as though they were confection on a shelf.

After all those years of anxiously checking Billboard to find a charting for RHCP, at last *Mothers Milk* delivered. The album peaked at # 53 and went gold and then platinum. The single "Knock Me Down" went to #6 and "Higher Ground" went to #11 on the Modern Rock charts. They had a song on the soundtrack of Julia Roberts' *Pretty Woman*. A new song later, I went to the Keystone Cop Stage in Silver Lake for the making of the "Taste the Pain" video directed by Alex Winter. Alex had been Keanu Reeves' nutcase buddy in *Bill & Ted's Excellent Adventure*. Alaine Dawn, the controversial nude cover girl for the album and poster, was at the video shoot too. After the tour, Ione and Anthony had broken up, although they remained friends. Anthony and I went to a picnic at Griffith Park for Ione and her new guy, Adam Horowitz. The Beastie Boys and the Red Hot Chili Peppers had a fascinating rivalry that matched East Coast versus West Coast: who was the first white rap band and who got Ione Skye.

Adam-12 was an NBC drama produced by Jack Webb (*Dragnet*), about a pair of Los Angeles police patrol officers played by Martin Milner (*Route 66*) and Kent McCord. Like *Dragnet,* its stories were taken from actual LAPD cases. It ran a successful seven seasons. Now they revived it as *The New Adam-12* and hired me for the "Witchcraft" episode, as the character Emerson Cooper, a funeral parlor director with a young flamboyant assistant named Dillingham, who I always referred to as Dilly. "Somebody has stolen our client, Mr. Valdez, didn't they Dilly?!" It was nice work and we shot the entire show on the Universal lot. I went directly from Universal to Culver Studios for a *Baywatch* reading with the notorious cast of bathing beauties, including another ex-girlfriend of mine, Alexandra Paul. And yes, there was a Pamela.

From the ridiculous to the sublime, I headed over to Raleigh Studios for what La Rocca explained to me as a western. It turned out to be Kevin Costner's *Dances With Wolves,* one of the most acclaimed films in cinema history. I read for the part of Spivey who was no slouch either, more shamed than acclaimed and despised with a vengeance. In the bitter climax, he stirred up enough enmity to scar for life, and in the end Spivey got what he deserved. I was excited about my call backs, and the casting director gave me reason to be optimistic. I'd see the boss bustling about the office, and his faithful Mustang muscle car was always waiting at the hitching post like a true stallion. Finally, I read for Costner and waited for news. The vital decision was killing me.

I swung my Caddy into the Chevron gas station on Beverly and Le Brea. While I was pumping, Costner rips in and starts to fill up his Mustang right next to me. He was probing his engine and checking it twice, testing the tires and polishing off bug spots. I just couldn't resist asking him how the casting was going, and he blew up on me. I had crossed a sensitive line approaching him beyond the studio walls and interrupting his personal Mustang time. The part of Spivey went to Tony Pierce. The film won seven Academy Awards, best picture, best director Kevin Costner, best writer, best editing, best cinematography, best sound, best original musical score and a best actor for Costner.

Business was bustling though, and I was right back at Universal for a shot at *The Munsters Today*, a remake of the *Munsters* from the 60s. I tried to be a sleazy attorney but didn't get the part. A couple days later, I was in the Billy Wilder Bldg. at Paramount for the *McGiver* episode "Halloween Knights" as Hank Greggs with the dubious qualities of edgy, adrenaline freak, crude lowlife, overconfident and on death row. I had just seconds to get out of there before the place blew up.

My idyllic Orange Drive hacienda blew up too. I had finished my one-year lease, after spending a small fortune in rent. I traded in for a six-story apartment building on Sierra Bonita, just off Sunset in a familiar old neighborhood that was home to the Guitar Center and Rodney's old English Disco. Rodney Bingenheimer was still living in the same neighborhood, and we re-invigorated our friendship. The building was relatively new, and I found a cool bachelor pad on the top floor with a loft. It didn't faze me at all when Scott McClintock leased an apartment there too. I didn't know it yet, but I was on a short lease.

Settled in, I went back to work at Dos Carlos Stages on East 6th Steet for some *Equal Justice,* starring George DeCinzo and Scott McClintock's ex-wife Debrah Farentino and a young Sarah Jessica Parker. I was up and down for sleazebag William Shapiro. Then a film called *Crazed* from International Film Group out of Houston fell in my lap. A friend of mine knew the writer, Rick Young, and set me up to meet the producers in Houston. I'd previously been involved with *Raiders of the Dark*, another script of his. I flew down and met the producers; one of their awesome daughters was going to be in it too. I was up for a good part and had pretty much set a deal. The shoot would be in Texas. Back in LA, I told my friend Jeff Weston from the *Minotaur* about the project; he contacted them too and then stole my part. That ended our relationship. I was pissed and took a lukewarm shot at *Speed, One Up and 4 Down* at Paramount.

The weather is unpredictable. *Santa Barbara* called me back for another run in the suds. This time I was a whole new character no one would ever mistake for Weezel. I was a maniacal derelict who hijacks and robs a community center. After six pages and a nasty standoff, Santa Barbara's top-billed star A Martinez as Cruz Castillo saved the day and disarmed me. A Martinez logged 438 *Santa Barbara* episodes! Another *Santa Barbara* regular, Robin Wright Penn, who was married to Sean Penn for many years, was in 359 episodes. Robin was the *Princess Bride* in Rob Reiner's Oscar-nominated film, Tom Hanks' sweetheart in *Forrest Gump* (six Oscars), the star of Nick Cassavetes' *She's So Lovely*, and the co-star with Sean Penn in David Rabe's *Hurlyburly*. Don't mess with the soaps.

I had been going to Powerhouse for a while. It was an old-school bar on Highland, just north of Hollywood Boulevard that had curried a hip new crowd. There were musicians (Chad was a regular), old timers, chrome bikers, assorted actors and upstart starlets. The music was jukebox, and the drinks were right off Elia Kazan's blue-collar *Waterfront*. Once in a while, there was a live band in the front window. I was used to seeing the melting pot of tinsel there, but I did a double take when I saw fourteen-year-old Drew Barrymore at the bar, drinking with the Bukowski crowd. She was adorable, spoke with a potty mouth and carried on as if she was in her twenties. I was straining to approach her but backed off. I'd been in enough trouble. The next time I looked she was gone. A couple nights later she reappeared and in the same spot at the middle of the bar, entertaining the bartender. I pulled the trigger this time, and whatever I had to say she bought. She ran with a small crowd, and I joined it for a time. The youngest of the Barrymore dynasty, her roots went back to Hollywood's first megastar, John Barrymore, who was her grandfather and the most acclaimed actor for a big hunk of the twentieth century. Her Uncle Lionel Barrymore and Aunt Ethel Barrymore were beyond brilliant, beyond adjectives. Drew had been acting since she was only a year old, and had done *Altered States*, *E.T.*, and *Firestarter* by the time she was six. I wasn't up to speed on her personal life at the time, but in fact she was reputedly pals with smokes at nine, alcohol at eleven, pot at twelve and coke at thirteen. She had been in and out of rehab a couple times by that night I met her. She took me around town to warm-and-welcoming private clubs I was unaware existed. And she was always drinking cocktails with impunity. We went to see the Chili Peppers at the Greek, and after the show I introduced her to Anthony. She made bad boy Anthony look like a choirboy and they became fast friends. Her never-ending story went through a few more bumps, but now she's a pillar of society. They're both successful poster kids, harnessing for good the positive energy of wild childhoods.

Jay Brown was working on one of those "We are the World" type videos to raise money for Native American Indian Children's Survival. The song was "All the Missing Children" and it was shot at a soundstage on Heliotrope. Robby Romero & Red Thunder, Robbie Nevil, Terri Nunn and Richard Marx were a few of the singers, along with about thirty other volunteer celebrities. Jay invited me to participate, and I brought Anthony too. We stood toe-to-toe, belting out the song until they finally got the footage they needed. It was the only time Anthony and I sang together, and it was a charitable blast.

La Rocca had a nifty gig for me if I could pull it off. He sent me to Sunset Gower Studios to audition for a coveted role on the *It's Garry Shandling's Show*, one of the most respected programs on television. Technically, it was a sitcom that featured Shandling as a comedian with his own TV show, the requisite screwball neighbors and a girlfriend. Yada. Yada. The three czars of this brain-trust enterprise were Garry Shandling, Bernie Brillstein and Brad Grey. The show broadcast on cable Showtime and then repeated on Fox. As an actor, Shandling had stolen his own anxious persona and created a comic character that was neurotic and paranoid, with a sharp undercoat of megalomania. A master of tentative timing, his oblique and esoteric wit was either refreshing or silly, depending on your sense of humor. For intellectuals, he was the mercurial small forward on our dream team of comedy. During the course of *It's Garry Shandling's Show*, he would often step out of the script and muse upon the progress of the show or the lack of it. Sometimes, he would solicit guidance from the audience, especially when he was up against a difficult dilemma which, in his befuddled life, was often.

I picked up my script in the morning and did a cold reading for Meg Liberman in the casting building. I passed first base with flying colors, and they scheduled me to read again for the elite team at 1:30, Building 13, 2nd floor. I had lunch at a nearby sloppy joe's and worked on my character. The episode in question was called "Nathan's Sheer Madness." I was going up for Nathan, a maven of horror not unlike Freddie Kruger in *Nightmare on Elm Street*. Nathan had his own darkly popular TV show that aired directly after Shandling's on the same fictitious network. My show was beating his in the ratings, and being contiguous it wasn't a good fit for a family sitcom like Garry's. There was bad blood between the two of them.

At 1:30 on the dot I showed up at Building 13 and hustled up the stairs to do my audition. Simultaneously, Garry Shandling came out of his office near the top of the stairs. He drew a bead on me and watched as I progressed toward him. I was already in character and wearing a ferocious countenance. As I hit the last step, he screamed bloody murder, and everybody on the busy second floor dove for cover. Garry feigned terror at the mere sight of me and retreated back into his office. "Get him out of here," he screamed. "I'm not coming out until he's gone." Meg Liberman grabbed me by the arm and quickly led me to a big conference room where a dozen writers and producers were sitting around a humungous table. We all sat there looking at our watches and waiting for him to have a change of heart. You could hear his fearful wolf calls across the entire movie lot. A studio cop came running up the stairs to check on us. One after another, the executives and the director and some of the regular actors went across the hall to coax Garry out of his sanctuary. When he finally did join us, he barricaded himself in the far corner of the conference room behind a couple burly office workers. The crafty small forward had buried a game-winning three-pointer and inspired me to pull off a victory. I was now officially Nathan, the most fearsome dude on television, and I'd scare the bejesus out of Garry every time we crossed paths for the next week.

Garry opens the show with a bit about hanging plants and how his girlfriend Phoebe (beauty pie Jessica Harper) likes everything well hung. When Phoebe has trouble reaching the ceiling, Garry tries to help but gets dizzy, which establishes his fear of heights. Neighbors drop by with news that their son is down in the dumps because his best friend tried to hack up his parents with a machete. It has something to do with "Nathan's Sheer Madness." Garry was unaware of this and they explain he's a crazy gardener who doesn't chop weeds, he chops people. They suggest Garry go to his network and file a complaint. Later, Garry agrees to watch the controversial show. The lights go low and "Nathan's Sheer Madness" begins. I'm dressed as a gardener walking through fog. I open my coat revealing knives and shears. "You know me; I live in your darkest fears. I am the evil inside us all. I am the embodiment of terror. I am…Nathan." I finish with a deep frightening laugh from hell. Garry says it's not a bad monologue, but he shouldn't laugh at his own material. A little boy named Joey won't eat his peas; his parents are insistent. I convince him to slaughter his parents so he doesn't have to eat those peas. I hand him one of my knives. The parents scream! The mother's bloody arm flies out of the TV and lands on Garry, who has a ballistic conniption. Oops, that's just Phoebe's arm. Garry agrees to support a neighborhood protest, a letter-writing campaign and to have a word with Mr. Stravely at the network.

Act two opens in the office of dithering Mr. Stravely, played with great glee by Richard Fancy. Outside his window, we see Phoebe and protesters waving placards up on the catwalk of a billboard. Stravely is bombarded by lunatic protestors on the phone too. He glares at Garry and maligns Phoebe. Now we see that the billboard has pictures of Garry and Nathan, but mine is bigger. The headline above us says "LOOK WHO'S AFTER GARRY SHANDLING." The representation of Garry is a basic head shot; mine has Nathan with opened gardening shears that intrude into Shandling's space and appear ready to clip off the top of his head.

Nathan enters Stravely's office dressed in an elegant suit, looking very dapper. Shandling is in sweats. I'm getting the chairman's undivided attention as I tell him I'm upset about the treatment I'm getting from these "lunatic protestors" and what they're doing to my family. On top of that, Garry's girlfriend is the leader. The boss leaves for a minute, but not before he bestows me with a boardroom hug and a promise of whatever I want. Once he leaves, I turn threatening and tell Garry I will make Phoebe pay. I pull out a small set of razor-sharp shears and terrorize him. When Stravely returns I seamlessly paste on my best civilized behavior.

In act three, Garry is totally paranoid and calling me a psycho. To the audience he bemoans this episode has turned into a Hitchcock movie. Phoebe leaves to run an errand; the neighbors discover she has spelled out HELP with dirty laundry on the sidewalk. A phone call from Nathan confirms the worst. She has been kidnapped. I give Shandling cat-and-mouse clues and lay it out with my maniacal laugh, "Hey Garry, me and your girlfriend are right under your nose. Why don't you come up and enjoy the view."

Production had built a full-size billboard with a steel ladder and catwalk in the soundstage, just like one of those towering Sunset Boulevard billboards. Aboard earlier were a dozen protestors, but in the climactic scene it was just me and my victim, high above the street below. I'm in my *Nathan's Sheer Madness* costume now, and I've dragged Phoebe all the way to the acrophobic top. Garry arrived but was faced with the soaring height. I taunted him and belittled his dizziness. Phoebe screamed and I enjoyed it. Garry inched up the ladder, trying not to look down. I mixed my own improvisation with the production's dialogue. "Let me tell you a little story," I belted out in the high winds "The story of the comedian's buttinski girlfriend. She came to protest. The wind blew. She tripped. She fell. She went to hell. It's not so much a story as a bad poem; top of the world, ma!" Garry finally reached the top. We were in a Douglas Fairbanks swashbuckle battle for the maiden. "Your girlfriend is about to do a half gainer onto Sunset Boulevard, Shandling! Say goodbye!" Garry the meek warns me, "Get away from her, Nathan!" Phoebe yells "Garry!" I yelled "Shandling!" Mr. Stravely has been working late in his high-rise office across the street. Startled by the commotion outside, he ponders the unlikely, "Shandling, Garry Shandling?" He opens the window and is shocked to see the network's meal ticket teetering on the slender catwalk high above the street. "NATHAN!!!!!!!!!"

Startled, I whip around; Stravely's eerie NATHANs echo, echo, echo as I lose my footing, plummet off the ledge and disappear. Garry yells out his thanks to Mr. Stravely, who tragically laments that he has just lost his number-one star. Garry peers down for confirmation; the camera angle now is on Nathan sprawled un-conscious or dead on the soundstage floor, with the crew scurrying to check on me. Shandling turns to the camera and deadpans, "Hey, there were suppose to be mats there. You know, to break the fall."

Chapter 48: Scrappy Badger

1989. On the first of December, I got a message to see casting director Vickie Huff on South Sepulveda for a TV movie of the week. It was *Summer Dreams: The Story of the Beach Boys (Heros and Villains)*. Once again, I was up for the part of Charlie Manson. On December 5th, I got a call back to Lorimar at MGM. It was nice to be back at my original studio. The memories were sweet, but the acrid taste of times lost and gone forever were a grim reminder of my waning. Komack's *Courtship of Eddie's Father* and the feature project with Fizdale and Friedkin in the 60s, Anthony's first film *Jokes My Folks Never Told Me* in the 70s, and my MGM readings and roles in the 80s were wistful reminders.

On December 7th, I had a third call back, and this time it was at the Judy Garland Building and into the office of my old friend Karen Lamm the co-producer. Karen Sullivan Lamm Wilson, the woman who steered me into Lee Strasberg's acting classes, cooked me up dinner parties with my best girl Connie Foreman and later married the pivotal Beach Boy who once befriended me. The fine actor Bruce Greenwood was set to play Dennis Wilson, the troubled phenom who had drowned in 1983 at the age of only 39. Karen and I had a long conversation and a short read; she liked me as Manson but was voted down by the other three producers, who picked Michael Reid MacKay. Linda Dona played Karen Lamm. I sauntered out of the defeated building and took a deep breathless. Whimsically, I danced some Gene Kelly moves across the historic Metro-Goldwyn-Mayer lot, savoring its strong scent of melancholy. I had turned fifty that 7th day of December. No longer the sleek panther, I was a scrappy badger who hated to shave and didn't care if I roughed up your soft pink cheek. I was seriously thinking it was time to go home and settle down on a hunk of west Michigan farmland.

Anthony and his new girlfriend, Carmen Hawk, took me out for a big five-0 birthday dinner at an Italian restaurant on Las Palmas. She was one my favorite of his girlfriends, but the relationship ended in a fast-moving wildfire. Anthony may not have been as bad as me, but he wasn't exactly monogamous. Carmen contested the breakup and fought it in the court of broken hearts. "Breaking the Girl" chronicled the emotional pathology and provided another classic lyric.

The band headed to Japan; they were certified international. In September, they had played their biggest LA show yet, headlining the Palladium before a sold-out crowd that accorded them a hero's welcome. An incredulous *Los Angeles Times* acknowledged they were now "the dean of the LA alternative rock scene," the local *quesos grandes*. It seemed like only yesterday they blew the lid off the Rhythm Lounge with just one song.

The day after my birthday, I was at Powerhouse and overheard giggling girls talking behind my back and throwing around the f-word; the fifty-word. I was dismayed that even strangers knew my birthday-candle count. I had always kept my age a secret. A few weeks ago, I was being squired around by a 14–year-old Drew Barrymore. My girlfriends were too young to ride the rollercoaster. My new main squeeze was a Valley girl named Allie. She was 18, with luscious golden-red hair and white skin and a face so beautiful that Scott

McClintock actually offered me a thousand dollars if I'd give her up to him. The three of us had a summit meeting at a trendy restaurant, and I turned him down.

There were Season's Greetings from a long list of ex's. My life was cluttered with ex's. I had Christmas dinner at the Rainbow for old time sakes and spent New Year's Eve with Allie in my Jacuzzi. Allie's dad collected skulls and liked to get high, a perfect father-in-law. On our first big date, I went all the way: I rented a Woody Allen movie. When I was serious about a seriously terrific girl, I would do the Woody litmus test and break the ice with *Annie Hall* or *Manhattan* or *Hannah and Her Sisters*, maybe even a *Sleeper*. But for a girl as cool as Allie, I'd bring out the big gun, *Broadway Danny Rose*. It was poignant, silly, witty and romantic; it always filled my heart with laughter, tears, hope and the innocence of love. Allie hadn't been up in my loft yet, and I planned the perfect evening. We swung by my favorite video store and *Broadway Danny Rose* was available. We got in line at the checkout, holding hands and exchanging little hugs. Finally it was our turn. I handed the cashier my membership card. She turned back from the computer with a devilish smirk and informed me in loud speaker volume for everybody in the line to hear, "You have a late fee for... let's see, *Traci Lords' The Sex Goddess* and, oh, another one, *Lust in the Fast Lane*." There was no place to hide. No escape from the embarrassment. No refuge in the Lord's fantasy. Allie smiled and gave me a reassuring kiss, "It's OK," she said. "Pay up and let's go."

Back at my apartment, we had some wine and climbed up into my lofty bed to watch *Broadway Danny Rose*. She got involved in the early plot and crawled down to the end of the bed, closer to the TV. I had seen it a hundred times but enjoyed it again, especially in her company. Obviously mesmerized, Allie was a good girl and didn't talk during the movie as though we were in a theater. I liked that. On the black-and-white screen, poor Woody endures bittersweet travail but in the end reconnects with Mia Farrow, and as always I had sentimental tears running down my cheeks. I was anxious for Allie's reaction. I asked but got none. I shook her foot that had been in my lap the whole time. She was sound asleep and had been since two minutes into the film. I can't say that was a game breaker, but obviously we didn't last forever.

Candy got permission to leave El Monte for a night: "come and get me, Blackie." Back in my apartment, she removed her winter coat to reveal a provocative low-cut dress and a flirty disposition. Off the dope, she had regained her curves and they were on display. She wanted to play and was irresistible. I hadn't had sex with her for over two years and couldn't have anticipated a resumption of our transgressions, but I hadn't seen Candy this beautiful since our early days together. She still had her quick wits and tactile tits. Irresistible, we had a few too many drinks and ended up in my loft for the night. We came close to reconciliation, but in the morning glare I regained my sensibilities.

La Rocca called me about the film *Hammer, Slammer & Slade* and sent me to 3961 Landmark in Culver City. It was the nerve center of an enterprise destined to nurture dynasties. It was the prodigious production office of Harlem-born Keenan Ivory Wayans, a black man who would rewire his business the way Martin Luther King changed conscientious morality and Obama changed change. I had first met Mr. Wayans on the TV show *For Love and Honor* when I was a guest star and he was a regular. Not unlike me, he had come up playing modest parts on TV in shows like *Cheers, CHiPs, Benson* and *Hill Street Blues*. He hadn't boxed himself in though and soon began stretching his skills. He produced the concert movie *Eddie Murphy Raw*. He created, produced, directed and starred in the 1988 classic *I'm Gonna Git You Sucka* and became a force to reckon with. That cast included Isaac Hayes (Hammer), Jim Brown (Slammer), Bernie Casey (Slade), Steve James and a couple of my old pals, Antonio Fargas and Clu Gulager. Later Mr. Wayans would produce everything from the relevant *Don't Be a Menace* to irrelevant fluff like *Scary Movie* and *White Chicks*.

His was a family operation with brothers Damon, Dwayne, Shawn and Marlon playing major roles, writing and performing in all the projects, along with another dozen relative Wayans. And most of them were buzzing around the operational headquarters on Landmark in Culver City the day I walked into the tornado. There was one big room in the center of the complex with all the action of *The New York Times* at deadline. The excitement was electric and it wasn't for my *Hammer, Slammer & Slade*. The Wayans were also working on a revolutionary Fox TV comedy called *In Living Color;* it was like *SNL, Fridays, The Marx Brothers, The Three Stooges* and the *Ed Sullivan Show* rolled into one madhouse of mirth. I was smack in the blinding mix of Jim Carrey, David Alan Grier, Rosie Perez and the Wayans zipping around in a frenzy of creativity. Jamie Foxx and Jennifer Lopez were on their way. Music was a big part of each episode with stellar acts like Public Enemy, Heavy D, En Vogue, and Tupac Shakur.

They pulled me into the shelter of Keenan's office, and I read for my part of a Catholic priest who was a former thug and convict working a parish in Los Angeles' south central hood. Thank goddess I didn't get the job right away; three days later I was able to enjoy the commotion again on my call back, but still no decision. Michael Shultz the director still needed to see me. On my third and final trip to the funny farm, I got the good news. I was Father McCarthy.

We did my scenes at Holy Cross Catholic Church and its parish playground at 47th and South Main Street. This was the epicenter of rough stuff. Gangs, crime and "big trouble little mister." The LAPD officers were protecting and serving the production, but in this case they had to call for backup more than once. Marauding teens would walk right into our shots or fire their own. They did rewrites and shouted out their own X-rated dialogue. They helped themselves to the craft service and our lunches. Weapons were pulled on both sides. It was exciting and so was working with this all-star cast. Bernie Casey, the ex-NFL star with the 49ers and Rams, was a fine actor, with films like *Guns of the Magnificent Seven, Cleopatra Jones, Brian's Song*, the James Bond *Never Say Never Again*, and Scorsese's *Boxcar Bertha*. Rock & Roll Hall of Famer Isaac Hayes had done it all: a Stax of Grammy and Oscar awards from standards like *Soul Man* and *Shaft*, an iconic TV character on *South Park* and a bona fide actor from early work like *Truck Turner* and *Escape From New York* to the current *Hustle & Flow*. The Sporting News declared Jim Brown the greatest professional football player of all time, and he was no slouch as an actor either, with powerful films like *The Dirty Dozen* and *Original Gangstas*. Between the Crips and the Bloods and accolades we managed to shoot a movie. It would be my final Hollywood hurrah.

There were still a few auditions, a wise guy detective in *Nameless*; a crack at *Brotherhood*, aka *Night of the Cyclone* with Kris Kristofferson; as Hurricane Sam on the TV show *Mother's Day;* and going global for *Task Force* an Asian TV movie. There were publicity confabs with Karen Best at the new MGM/UA glass-and-steel building for *Instant Karma*. This new MGM headquarters looked more like the Beverly Center than my revered old studio headquarters on the lot. It was one more sign of the times. I had trouble reading my daily newspapers; I needed glasses. What's next? Rheumatism, arthritis, a hip replacement? Moving into the Calabasas Motion Picture Home for retired actors?

Lori Levine had a party with all her porny babes and my dream girl Traci Lords. It wasn't enough. I capitulated. I took the Riviera out of mothballs, and turned it into a metallic blue suitcase. I packed it to the ceiling with just enough room for Adolf and drove across country for the 18th time. I was on a scouting mission to find a new home in the old world. My Hollywood lease was good until mid-summer; I had three months to resettle. In Grand Rapids, I put a down payment on an apartment in an old Victorian home in the Heritage Hill District. It was the historical Stickley Mansion, built over three years during the early 1900s. My third-story roost would be one-half of the top floor, with a view of downtown, and I christened it with a Brenda. I checked out the local theatre scene. The Civic Theatre was ideal for my needs and was rated the second-best in the country. I couldn't quit acting cold turkey.

I still had a Sierra Bonita lease to whittle away. La Rocca hoped to squeeze out every last ten per cent. String along my swan song. Bring on the footnotes. Box up my impact. I read for *The Adventures of Ford Fairlane* with Andrew Dice Clay, the Peddler in *Nightmare on the 13th Floor;* Mel Brooks' new project *Life Stinks;* Roger Corman's *Dark Obsession* as Sam, an off center leading man who stalks and kills; and finally, *Down and Dirty*. My heart wasn't in them. I had a different act to get together.

My friends were beyond belief that I was leaving. I had the perfect life: a movie career, a cast of a thousand beautiful starlets, a cool apartment and the Sunset Strip as my jurisdiction. Bland Rapids! Was I crazy? Candy wasn't going down without a fight. She called and said we were pregnant. I figured it was a ruse. How could she pinpoint a victim, considering her promiscuity? It was but a desperate ploy of the master manipulator. She hung up and put it on speed dial. John Forsyth accepted the responsibility, but I always wondered how many calls it took to find a buyer.

Moby Grape played Coconut Teaszer, and I made my last goodbyes to Lenny Fagan. New club scenes The Dresden and Small's whiled away my sentence. Mark Cuff and the shocking Mario Cabrera played the saddened disciples at our Last Supper. Weaver and I made our parting a family occasion at the Rainbow. I had a love off with my girls. I rented a Penske truck the size of those big rig road warriors I'd be competing with on the interstates. It was obliged to stop at the weighing stations. John Forsyth was so glad to get rid of me he volunteered the heavy lifting when we packed the truck. In return for his help, I gave him Candy's old red motorcycle. Tracii Guns came by and carried out a lamp or two. Anthony helped too. It took three days. My life was in a Penske. The Cadillac was too unwieldy to tow so I gave it to Anthony. In July of 1990, Adolf and I moved out of Los Angeles after 25 years. I left it in the capable hands of my son, and he would make an imprint that was indelible.

Chapter 49: The Gay 90s

The ex-patriot wolverine was nestled once again in the warm womb of Michigan. I was born again. I was young again. I was on top again, and it wasn't the missionary position. On top of a stubby town pedestal perhaps, but it was comfortable as a baby's pillow. I had traded capital crime for petty crime, drug addicts for smart alecks, and Sodom and Gomorrah for the holy city of virgins. With civic pride and enterprise, the bazaar vendors silkscreened the T-shirts: *Grand Rapids Home of God*. I wasn't so thrilled about sharing Grand Rapids with God, but I certainly appreciated the virgins. It was one of the reasons I had left Unholywood. Like the glorious decade of the 1890s that was coined the "Gay Nineties," once again it was a time for an emerging but equivocal high society. I had the high covered.

I had lunch with Civic Theatre CEO Paul Dreher and officially introduced myself. He was personally directing the first play of the season. *Inherit the Wind* was an account of the 1925 Scopes Monkey Trial, a contentious Tennessee law case over Charles Darwin's theory of evolution. It originally opened on Broadway in 1955, and there were several movie versions including Stanley Kramer's with Spencer Tracy, Fredric March and Gene Kelly as the H.L. Menken character I was auditioning for. Menken was a shrewd newspaper reporter for the *Baltimore Sun*, a novelist and friend of the great literary figures of the day: Theodore Dreiser, F. Scott Fitzgerald, Sinclair Lewis and Ayn Rand. I won the coveted role, and like Gene Kelly I was playing him as a sharp, dapper storyteller. With the principal and supporting actors cast, we began rehearsals and set our hearts on an opening in the fall. Many of the town folk extras were young actresses bent on show business which made me a popular commodity. Soon I had my own groupies. The little darlings rambled about in the capacious complex with its extraordinary resources. Their four historical buildings filled an entire block. Their wardrobe department rivaled a movie studio, and they stocked more props than Red Foxx's junkyard. Classic Otis elevators and secret stairways swept the unsuspecting into a scary attic on the higher floors that were home to a flock of bats which would circle around the golden, ornate ceiling of the main auditorium during performances. The batty sideshow was a tradition and an attraction. And then there was the Majestic Theatre itself, three tiers of balconies and a third one high in the ceiling, a holdover from segregation. There was an enormous stage and a *Phantom of the Opera* orchestra pit. It even had a good theatrical hangout, the Cottage Bar, across the park from the Civic and facing an ornate Gothic church. I felt more like a New York actor now, sitting around a pub with our internal characters, discussing Chekhov and Ibsen instead of Spielberg and Lucas.

The first Gulf War exploded in our faces during rehearsal and diverted us briefly. As the Clarence Darrow and William Jennings Bryan characters, our leads George Seibel and Fred Bogaert were local acting legends. Bogaert was elderly but witty and energetic. Seibel was more of a Cary Grant guy with smoking jackets and shiny Italian loafers. He threw gala parties at his affluent East Grand Rapids home. I was third billed, and fourth was Chip Laufer as the John Scopes teacher. Oddly, Chip had recently returned from Hollywood after a brief fling at acting. He was in his early twenties, but we became instant friends and terrorized the local ladies like two wild and crazy guys. Chip was another self-confessed womanizer, and we set the town on fire for a while.

Despite my fifty-year-old horse collar, I still had a lot of play in me. After barely skimming under the *Welcome to Michigan* sign at the border, my monster truck had gone straight for the seaside village of Holland to visit budding Brenda the Red. Now I was on the prowl again, and here I was heading to the Allegan County Fair for more than just the quilting, livestock and pie-eating contest. It was rural-weekend crowded, but I picked up a frequency across the midway. This marvel didn't fit in; she had short-cut blue-black hair, pure white skin and adventurous clothing for these woods. I made my way through the corn dogs and got a better look. I still wasn't quite sure how old she was, but the girl seemed to have a sophisticated soul and was fresh as the blue ribbon Allegan County produce. I didn't know what to do; she had a female companion who might deck me with that overstuffed carnival prize. What the heck. Just listen to me?! I was definitely blending with the territory. I introduced myself and she smiled with grace and style. Her big sister was tolerant, and I tagged along to the country music show headlined by Reba McEntire. It could have been Ernest Tubb for all I cared; I was there for the company of Pete. Her nickname was Pete, real name Christine and her sister was Sherrie. They gave me their phone number. I had enough info to leave, but they convinced me to stay for the opening act. We settled in the fifth row. Bring on the opening act. He was someone so anonymous I smirked out loud as he strode into the spot light, full of overbearing cheerfulness. He was a cowboy named Garth Brooks. It didn't register with me, but he stole the show and sent us scrambling to the nearest record store so I could buy and listen to *The Dance,* if only to remind me of Pete. Before his early retirement only a few years later, Garth Brooks would sell more albums than anybody but the Beatles.

Pete and I made an afternoon date, and I picked her up at Rogers High School in the suburbs. She took me to meet the parents, and her father, Gerald Fein, was a Grand Rapids police officer! Her mom, Frances, was cordial as a mint julep. I invited them to my play, and Pete brought me to see her school production of *West Side Story.* We became best friends in every sense. We went to her high-school football games, and I escorted her to the homecoming dance when her boyfriend bailed. Shocking responses didn't faze us. I was always invited for Christmas at the Fein's house, and I even brought Anthony. Pete was a devout girl with impeccable character and a heart of gold. In due time, she married a preacher from a Tennessee Divinity School, and they moved to a desolate small town in need of the gospel.

Anthony called; they'd broken their contract with EMI and signed with Warner Bros. after a great meeting with legendary Mo Ostin. With Anthony's upfront contract money, he bought a home on Hollyridge Drive under the Hollywood sign with views of the city and a wild canyon wilderness that was part of Griffith Park. Flea, John and Chad all bought similar million-dollar homes in various parts of the same Hollywood hills. Two weeks later, Anthony informed me they were rehearsing for the MTV Video Awards Show.

The closest thing to a nightclub in my burg was Sensations, a brand new strip club next to Club Eastbrook. It had been a comedy club the last time I was in town. GR politicians would rather give up their first born than allow a hint of nudity in God's town, but the suave owner Mark London pulled a wool cap over the despotic regime at city hall and came up with inalienable rights. This made three naughty places because the Parkway Tropics had emerged from its sleepy past and got wild and raw with a boisterous amateur night. Like always, I came for the take home. In no time, I was swinging with the entire Sensations lineup, and my new main squeeze became statuesque Amy Johnson.

Over my tenure, I dated dozens of sensational dancers, including one who was murdered by her jealous boyfriend. We had a stripper funeral accompanied by dancers from around the state as she lay in state. In the procession, there were a lot of fuzzy pink dice dangling from the rearview mirrors. Later, I dated her little sister who picked up the slack and danced at Sensations when she reached 18. Club Eastbrook was kind enough to offer a mini-skirt night, and of course there was Alan's Zero. I hit them all and left my mark like a randy terrier. I met a perfect stranger and she gave me her address. The next afternoon, I ventured uninvited to her secluded home in a rustic cul-de-sac. She wasn't there so I let myself in once I found an open window on the back porch. I made myself comfortable and waited. Would she arrest me or make love to me? She was startled but accommodating. Grand Rapids was a benign Disneyland without the Mickey, but definitely Goofy.

Bashara was working with the Great White band that was opening for White Snake at the Ionia Free Fair. Alan called from the fair and told me to get over there; he had a pass for me at the performer's gate. It was a 40-mile drive so I stopped in Lowell to get a pop. There was a cute as a button sweetheart sitting on the steps of the store, and I talked her into joining me on the adventure. But instead of directly continuing to Ionia, I doubled back to GR and we had a quick party; *then* we went to Ionia. She was hot. Too hot! I pulled her into the backstage area and showed her off. After hanging out with Great White, we moved up into White Snake territory, David Coverdale and Tawny Kitaen. Their guitar player got one look at my button and ripped her off. I was ready to rumble with the rocker, but there was Snake security, and I was out on my ear. Not only did my cutie stay with the ax man, by the time the show was over she joined the tour and rode off in the White Snake bus.

There was a heavy-metal joint called Palo's Lounge that featured touring second-tier rock bands and a good shot at a black eye or the clap. The place was rampant with mullets and trashy dames in faux leopard. Despite the rocky weekend we suffered in LA when she flew out, stripper Cheryl Brooks and I were still sort of pals. We banged into each other at Palo's, and she challenged me to shots of tequila and an aftermath. When we got to my pad we were both blacked out, and the next morning I found myself sleeping in the front yard with my pants around my knees. It took me awhile to find Cheryl; she was on the bathroom floor curled up around my toilet with a plunger for a pillow.

He that troubleth his own house shall inherit the wind; and the fool shall be servant to the wise of heart. Proverbs 11:29. It was opening night. It was frighteningly delicious. It was show time. We did our performance to 700 plus and were lavished with applause, handshakes and hugs in the lobby. Afterward we had our cast, crew and friends party; accompanied by the usual local luminaries. Excerpts from *The Grand Rapids Press*: "The 65th season opened for Civic Theater Thursday night with a distinguished production of the dramatic *Inherit the Wind*, the play based on fact by Jerome Lawrence and Robert E. Lee that seems to never lose its appeal…excellent performances by Lowell George Seible, Fred Bogaert and Blackie Dammett who enjoy personal triumphs in their characterizations. Performances are

Tuesday, Wednesday, Thursday, Friday and Saturday evenings and matinees on Sunday. The show will run for three weeks."

A star-struck fan was at many of those shows. On opening night she sat in the front row and threw me a bouquet. She sought me out in the lobby and again at the party. Joanna Polizzi was a high-school student who loved the theater and exciting actors. When she wasn't at the theater, she was often at my place. Infatuated, she watched my video tapes but was also a good-head-on-her-shoulders straight A student. She adored Adolf and became my sitter when I made what were to be frequent returns to LA. In the third week of the play, I flew the now fully pregnant Candy in to see *Inherit the Wind*. She was still my special girl and John Forsyth's punching bag. I bet she got some good shots in too. I joined war protesters at the Gerald R. Ford Federal Building and protested the demolition of Peck's Drug store where I loitered as a teenager. We saved the building, and it flourishes now with retail shops on the first floor and upscale condos on the second.

The *GR Press* was my unofficial promoter; it pumped up the box office and stimulated the bobby soxers. Erin Bourgoin was another smitten ingénue who followed me like a puppy dog. I found myself at her high-school parties with the rest of the Civic Theater kid clique. There was a slightly older teen in that group with the delightful name of Dawn Highhouse, who knocked me loopy, but she had a boyfriend who worked in the Civic crew. I bought up the store she worked at just to chat with her. Male or female, the showbiz kids found me refreshing from what they were normally exposed to in this isolated whistle-stop. In turn, I enjoyed their unspoiled qualities. My rough-water-rafting fountain of youth was the company of innocence. I was an alien Martian in Grand Rapids, their *My Favorite Martian*. If I could pull off outrageous in Hollywood, I could certainly fluster Conservative City.

Paul Dreher's wife, Maureen, ran an agency and got me work. I did a commercial for Amway and another for Spartan Stores. Alan Bashara was plugged in and introduced me to the dean of GR radio, Aris Hampers. He threw great parties but took a while to warm up to me; the establishment was threatened. There was, however, a DJ who was fearless; he invited me to WLAV for a ride on the radio waves. Robert Chase was a fan of the Red Hots and helped me promote them in West Michigan. Robert and I hit it off, and our run ran till cupid intervened.

Johnny La Rocca wanted me back. Casting directors were still looking for the Blackie Dammett type. One of the suitors wanted me for a remake of the sixties TV icon *The Fugitive,* with Alec Baldwin reprising David Janssen's lead role. They pictured me as the one-armed illusive antagonist. I had to decline. I was engaged to *Inherit the Wind*. John Douglas, *The Grand Rapids Press* movie critic, rang me up and we did lunch, not New York's Sardi's or Beverly Hills' Nate 'n' Al's, but Grand Rapids' Lakos on the Hill. We became intellectual curmudgeons in the pursuit and debate of cinematic excellence.

The junior Gravengood crew would often visit John Wege's vacation pad on the northwest gold coast. One night, we were bar hopping in Traverse City, and I met another of those passionately beautiful to- die-for redheads. She was Carman Rene Shay, a vocal stylist from Detroit, working an autumn gig at a resort hotel. The next night, I borrowed Wege's Lexus and drove over to the high-end hotel to see her show. She was a slinky torch singer. We set up relations, and she came to Grand Rapids for the holidays. She was so precious I wrapped her up and gave her to Anthony for Christmas. We all went out to his favorite Italian restaurant on Christmas Eve. Peggy had remarried and finally captured the flag, an outstanding attorney and a top-notch husband. After two bad apples, she deserved a good man like Steve Idema. By now, their daughter Jen was in junior high. Of course, Steve thought it unusual that an ex-husband from thirty years ago was still coming to their house for Sunday dinners, birthday parties and holidays, but Peg was like a mother to me.

A major motivation for my move to GR was Scott Gravengood and his merry mishaps. Bollocks to hell, my fetching stories of the West Coast inspired them to relocate there themselves. We had a brief interim though, and they introduced me to their legacy of debauchery. Eastown was ground zero with The Intersection and Mulligan's, the Anchor Bar held down the west side, and the drinks flowed at Bagby's and Flannigan's downtown. Interesting was an ancient bar in a ratty hotel called the Herkemer on the skid row stretch of South Division; it had a great jukebox that hadn't updated since the 1950s. They also dragged me into a nearby duo of high intensity gay dance clubs, the Carousel and Club 67. There were glittering moves, transvestite performers and all the razzmatazz of Gotham City.

About the same time I arrived, an adventurous young man from Chicago named Al Bregante popped into town and speculated on the night scene. Inspired by a punk rock club called the Exit in Chicago's Old Town, he plunked his dream down in that same rough stretch of South Division. He bought a broken-down tavern known as the Glass Bar, which had diminished into a bum spot for a cheap shot. Assisted by his mechanical engineer, Jeff Nodurft, Al fixed it up and marketed it as hip, hot and hostile to convention. They called it the Reptile. The underground swarmed to it, and overnight it was the place to go. The Reptile changed GR forever. It was the demarcation between the carcass of a lost civilization and a bright new city on the Grand. I seemed to have been either the lightning rod or the electrocutioner. The slick proprietor and his sidekick brought in cool bands and edgy sexuality. The women came to parade in scandalous attire. The lines to get in went around the block, and of course I cultivated the door guys. The Verve, Anthrax, Warren Zevon, Echo and the Bunnymen, Ian Astbury, Frank Black, Tool, Everclear, Mike Watt and Kid Rock were a few of the bands who willingly came to play in this bite-size joint. Smashing Pumpkins and Pearl Jam had both signed on but cancelled to join the Chili Peppers' Blood Sugar bandwagon tour the following year. When I brought Anthony to the Reptile at Christmas they rioted; the family encircled and protected him. Even the consummate LA chauvinist, Anthony got a kick out of the Reptile. I could walk to it from my house on Heritage Hill. I was king of the hill. My prude and profanity-challenged father always used to exclaim, "What the hill!" I was fifty, and I still missed my Dad.

Chapter 50: Blood Sugar Sex Magik

January 1991, the Grammy nominations came out with MC Hammer, Madonna, Sinead O'Conner and Phil Collins dominating, but in the Best Rock Group the startling nominations were Aerosmith, INXS, Midnight Oil, The Rolling Stones and Red Hot Chili Peppers! My son kept me apprised. They did David Letterman.

I did *Annie Get Your Gun*. The Civic did a bang-up musical every year, and ordinarily I'd have taken a wide berth on my way to the next intense drama. Taking a big chance for me, I tore into the exuberant story of Annie Oakley: songbird, sharpshooter and prototype feminist. I definitely wasn't a talented singer, but I plunged into the icy waters of mortification and went to the audition. I had done my research. Buffalo Bill was the larger-than-life star but a bit too old for me. Frank Butler was dashing and delightful as Annie's husband but would require a professional voice. The third best role was right up my alley cat screech. Charlie Davenport was the wily manager of the Wild West Show. He had snappy dialog and fewer songs than the other leads. He would however open the show with a boisterous musical sequence that set the tone and temper of the entire play. He also had a love interest which entailed a duet. I persevered in the auditions and put Charlie in my pocket.

The original 1946 Broadway production of *Annie Get Your Gun* came with the loftiest of pedigrees. Rogers and Hammerstein produced, Ethel Merman starred as Annie and Irving Berlin wrote the music, including ageless standards like "There's No Business Like Show Business," which Buffalo Bill, Frank Butler and I sang; "Doin' What Comes Natur'lly;" "Anything You Can Do" and "They Say It's Wonderful." The Broadway production ran for 1147 performances. We had to settle for our predetermined three-week engagement.

The sets were spectacular; our crew of artisans created a working railroad, campfires, log cabins, wigwams, a grand hotel, shooting galleries and the Wild West in all its glory. The large cast started at the top with Fred Bogaert as Col. William F. Cody aka Buffalo Bill. Our Annie was Lynne Brown, a double-barreled terrific vocalist and actress. Martin Zyla was Annie's duet Frank Butler and a song belter who delt out the chills. Eva Switeck was Dolly Tate my adversarial partner. I had to master a singing voice from scratch and drove the vocal coach and orchestra conductor to distraction. Humiliated time and time again, I was still determined to get it right. My fan club kept me upbeat and supported my fatuous falsetto with humor. By the end of rehearsals, I actually had the conductor smiling. Oh, that was the railroad conductor. Like *Inherit the Wind*, we garnered home team reviews.

Anthony called on Father's Day and spoke of his recent adventures with Gus Van Zant, Lorne Michaels, Milla Jovovich, Faye Dunaway, David Arquette, Rick Rubin, Ione and Adam and Christina Applegate, to name a few. In July, Anthony and Flea were going to Costa Rica with their friend River Phoenix to meet his family. Van Zant had directed River and Flea in *My Own Private Idaho*. Anthony's life was magical, and he invited me to come out and see for myself. There was more big news flying in from California too: Candy gave birth to a baby boy and named him James Dillon Forsyth. I told her she misspelled Dylan, assuming as in Bob Dylan or Dylan Thomas. She said, "No, I saw it on *Gunsmoke*, the TV show. You know, Marshall Dillon." I filled her in. "Oh well," she said, "it's too late now." I flew out to behold these wonders for myself. Anthony picked me up at the airport in his recently acquired 1966 RS Camaro muscle car convertible and proudly drove me around our new slant on Los Angeles. His house was sleek and modern, but he was funking it down. Bustling craftsmen were turning this crash pad into an old soul home with unique touches. He put me to work decorating a room with a collage of his memorabilia. It was a long-term effort which would fortunately require additional visits.

Second stop was Granny's house in El Monte. James was long and skinny and florescent pink and never stopped crying. Candy had a rough delivery, and the umbilical cord got twisted around his neck, which deprived him of oxygen for enough time that they feared he might be impaired. I was also concerned for James' other handicap, the drugs Candy used during the pregnancy. All we could do was hope for the best—and that he'd finally stop crying. I loaded James up with a bassinette, diapers, formula and a stroller. I felt a kinship to the kid and wanted to be part of his life. John Forsyth had already fled.

Anthony and I went out on the town with new friends like the outrageous artist Robert Williams. Anthony had already acquired some of his pieces, and he took me to a showing at the La Luz de Jesus Gallery on Melrose and then to Robert Williams' home in the Valley. We went to Rick Rubin's house on the Sunset Strip, blocked in by his mob of racy autos. Anthony hit the jackpot with new girlfriends too. I was thrilled for him and didn't mind the overflow that came my way. He took me to a Santa Monica nightclub where a lady friend of his was performing. She was Hope Sandoval, a fragile wisp with an eerily fascinating singing style and an erotic presence. Along with her partner David Roback, they were Mazzy Star. After the set, we conversed and then he ran off with her. "Grab a cab," he yelled as the throaty Camaro roared out into the night and left me waiting for Godot.

He took me to the scene-of-the-crime Harry Houdini mansion on Laurel Canyon where they had recently recorded their first Warner Bros. album. The place was haunted. David Bowie stayed in a home directly above them. Back at Anthony's pad, we played with high-tech toys and his growing collection of vinyl. Anthony had gone vegetarian and worked on my diet. An ever-ringing phone was practically welded to his ear. He was a busy man. The door would knock and a flock of angelic friends would float in. Fan struck girls camped on the road in front of his house. The Hollywood sign loomed above while we splashed in his pool and Jacuzzi. I came home on a blue sky cloud.

Back home, I looked up my eighth-grade sweetie Gerri DeVos, who was undoubtedly the most important girl of my life between birth and college. I had certainly progressed. Now she bossed Vandenburg Air Service, pretty as a picture with a green visor and her sleeves rolled up, ready for action behind a busy desk. Out the window, a crop duster and a biplane revved up for a tour of apple orchards and a flight plan to Mackinac Island. Over the years, she had followed my exploits in the newspapers. "I'm worn and weathered and married to an old codger," she said. "Remember me the way I was."

There were always new ones. I had a waitress at the Attic bar on Chicago Drive; a crush on the Kentwood librarian; a flirt with Melissa, the talented bartender at the Alpine Lounge, and a sweet deal with Dana, a Déjà Vu stripper from Kalamazoo, who had a child with Down syndrome. On the second team bench ready to go in were Tracy, Yvette, Paula, Vanessa, and Kisha.

Four months later, Candy and James came to visit. James was no longer a squiggly red crybaby; he was bright, bold and brash, and I fell head over heels in love with him. So did Peggy, who volunteered to babysit when I took Candy for a tour of my youth. All that was left of the old Mobil station was the concrete base where the gas pumps used to be. The house I helped build was barely still there, abandoned and lost in its past. The pine saplings Grandpa planted were only little squirts like me at the time. Now they towered sixty feet into the sky, frightening monuments to the elapsed time since my childhood. I dug up a photo of me at age four months lying on my back and took one of James in the same position. We were Minnesota Twins. Maybe James was my son. Whether he was or wasn't, I wanted him to be.

In September, the band released *Blood Sugar Sex Magik*. Songs like "Give it Away," "Under the Bridge," "Suck My Kiss" and "Breaking the Girl" gobbled up play lists of radio stations everywhere. The album went to #3 on the Billboard chart and #1 on hundreds of more thoughtful charts. In the end, it would sell over fifteen million records; producer Rick Rubin had built a masterpiece. One of the reviews spoke of Anthony's maturity: "Most impressive is Kiedis, who has grown both as a lyricist and a multidimensional front man who raps, growls and now croons with the best of them." Rick was culpable. The big guy with the big beard and the big mind had transformed Anthony, as he had everybody from Slayer, Jay-Z, Johnny Cash and Adele. Rick has remained a close confidant to Anthony for over twenty years now. The band did a clever commercial for Nike with Andre Agassi. They were courted by MTV and SNL and all the late night talk shows. A year ago, I had left LA to retire in a quiet town. Now my world had turned upside down again; I was drawn back into big-time excitement.

I got political. John Logie was running for mayor of Grand Rapids and Alan Bashara and I decided to help. For years, Alan had been lobbying for a new arena and a progressive downtown. I drove my jingomobile around town looking for some tall buildings but came up short. When I was born, Grand Rapids had about the same population as Nashville, Miami and Fort Worth. GR was bigger than Tampa, El Paso, Salt Lake City or Phoenix. After all these years of malaise, an atlas full of cities had passed us by. Here we still were, stuck the 1940s. We were a well-kept secret from the American consciousness, a phantom city hiding from reality and in denial of a future.

Most cities have sugar daddy philanthropists. At last some big guns weighed in and staked out a rebirth of our city. Back in 1959, Jay Van Andel and Richard DeVos started a door-to-door sales company, pushing vitamins and soap products. The company was Amway, and thirty years later they were a multi-billion dollar business. Forbes had both of them in the top six richest men in America. Now they were financing hospitals, museums, concert halls, institutes, towering hotels, convention centers and Bashara's Van Andel Arena. The Amway boys retooled and rebuilt Grand Rapids, but they received plenty of help from patrons like Fred Meijer, Peter Wege, former Ambassador to Italy Peter Secchia and a new young breed of dedication led by a man I had met earlier through Scott Gravengood. He was Sam Cummings, one of the Gerber Baby Food heirs from Fremont, just north of Grand Rapids. He was a dashing daredevil who liked fast cars and finance; he was Lance

Reventlow with an altruistic conscience. Sam inherited a pretty penny and his intellectual, broad shoulders built a dynasty of progressive enterprise that helped to turn Grand Rapids into a unique and special place.

We had the muscle; now we needed a visionary administrator. We needed to elect John Logie as mayor, and we did. Not without near life-and-death difficulty though, as I was sent to the front lines, canvassing for votes on the west side, home of our formidable incumbent. It was hostile territory and the mayor's committee chose me especially for this unnerving mission. I got pissed on and shooed off and yelled at, but I managed to change some hearts and minds. I persevered and so did the campaign. Logie brought a touch of JFK Camelot and the audacity of hope to our city. Next stop, Boom town!

Chapter 51: Racing Hearts

Dale Shumaker, a fledging local screenwriter, solicited me to work on a couple projects. *Fly-By-Night* didn't fly, but the second did. A local producer named Tom Beyer was looking for product and liked our script. We were in business. Press release: *"Racing Hearts* is the story of a blue-collar family on vacation at a small Lake Michigan resort, following the release of their oldest son from county jail. Surviving internal dissension, mom's cooking, first love, spectacular car crashes, rowdy rednecks, a saucy temptress and a titanic struggle to win the annual Sandstorm dune-buggy race, the family discovers its greatest strength lies not in the domineering father, compassionate mother, industrious brother, or precocious sister, but in the gutty integrity of the maligned rebel son in this action-packed romantic thriller. (Whew!) Locations will include Grand Rapids, Saugatuck, Pentwater, Mears and Silver Lake Dunes Park. Shooting projected for July and August 1992."

The location *was* the real star. Near the small town of Hart, Silver Lake was a glistening gem separated from Lake Michigan by an estuary and surrounded by mountainous sand dunes. There was an embedded dune-buggy culture with an army of adventurous vehicles powering around the landscape of what seemed like a distant planet. The sandy storm panorama embraced a state park, campgrounds, forest walks and water sports. Beyond were picturesque seaside villages and endless Eden's of asparagus, blueberries and cherries.

I registered our script with the Writer's Guild and convinced Tom Beyer to let me direct the film. We had open casting at my third-floor apartment, with a serpentine line of anxious applicants. After sixteen years of putting my life on the line, now I was the scary guy behind the audition desk. I tried to be benevolent. So up they traipsed, star struck and out of luck and others who were adequate and a few that were exemplary. We picked up some free agents to fill supporting roles but were hurting for our leading man when in walked Jandt Herweyer. He brought the requisites and added a healthy dose of humor, swagger and the potential to be my next co-conspirator. It took a casting jaunt to an agency in Detroit to find Jandt's leading lady, Ronnie Kowalski. Sacrificial, I personally road tested the maliciousness of "Daisy Mae" Angel Tubbs, our busty bombshell antagonist with the face of an angel.

Next I cast our main heavy, rugged beer-swilling hoodlum yahoo redneck, Roddy Pugsley, and found a lifetime friend in Brett Anderson. Brett was one of those invincible tough guys. He was a chiseled-out-of- granite champion wrestler at Rockford High School, with more ribbons than Becky Thatcher. He was a renegade prankster, a pride of lions and a stick of dynamite. He also had a sensitive side and a knack for business with a strong work ethic. His parents had a hundred-acre farm north of town, and Brett was always ready to roll up his sleeves and pitch hay or wrangle a bull. He was a ladies' man, a family man and a Good Samaritan. With Brett for a friend, you were covered for life.

Scouting locations around the Silver Lake area, Dale and I stopped by an outdoor music facility called Val-du-Lakes, built on rolling hills of Indian land. The culture was pervasive in that part of the state, with strong tribes of Chippewa, Ottawa and Potawatomi.

We hired Indian consultants and wrote their stories into our script. The venue itself had hosted acts like Alice Cooper, Aerosmith, Sheryl Crowe, Van Halen, Roy Orbison and Motley Cru. Built in a natural amphitheatre, the capacity was almost infinite. Even Lollapalooza played there. We were sizing it up for a potential scene when Paul Erickson introduced himself as one of the brass. His piece joined the puzzle.

Paul knew the area like nobody's business. He had connections and clout. He ran an auto body shop and was an avid dune-buggy and off-road racer himself. He took an Oldsmobile station wagon and cut out a hole in the roof with a blow torch so we'd have a camera vehicle for our racing footage. He bought a house trailer to take on location. He scrambled around like a Hollywood pro and was the glue that kept us high. Everything was hunky-dory until Tom Beyer's money dwindled away on pre-production. He got a substantial loan out of me and promised a guaranteed great return. On the first day of shooting, our buggy got stuck in a dune, and then wind blew sand in the camera, clogging up the mechanism. At lunch break, Tom Beyer said he was going for pizza; he never came back. And neither did my investment.

Paul Erickson took over as executive producer. He hired sharp cinematographer Peter Sensor and producer Michael Degutis who in turn got us a line producer from Chicago named Billy Higgins who already had legitimate credits on *Dr. Detroit; Ferris Bueller's Day Off* and *Planes, Trains and Automobiles*. He got Industrial Light & Magic involved, and they added a space ship that would descend on the Val-du-Lakes stage; the Red Hot Chili Peppers had agreed to emerge and perform a song. Industrial Light & Magic sent us their artwork layouts, blueprints and designs. They had a respectable resume: *Star Wars, Raiders of the Lost Art, E.T., Field of Dreams, Ghostbusters, Back to the Future, The Godfather* and a galaxy more. Today they're doing *Harry Potter, Iron Man 2* and *Pirates of the Caribbean*. With a bigger budget and promised funds, Michael Degutis and I flew out to Hollywood for two days of Hollywood casting at the Hollywood Holiday Inn on Highland and Hollywood. Hurray for Hollywood! While I was out there, La Rocca had me read for Jimmy Hoffa's attorney in the Jack Nicholson film *Hoffa*. Nicholas Pryor got the role.

Back in West Michigan, I continued to direct what essentially had become a short film to raise money for financing the big-budget production. On my days off, I kept scouting locations, and when I met a beauty named Joni who knew the lay of the badlands we packed up and did a day's ride through the backwoods. Adjoining Lake County was the poorest in Michigan and notorious for its hillbilly hamlets and Appalachian rusted cars and busted teeth. At one time, it had been known for its world famous Negro resort in Idlewild (just a couple miles from Nirvana) where every black entertainer from Louie Armstrong and Cab Calloway to Moms Mobley and Sammy Davis Jr. graced the stage. Idlewild entertained from 1912 to 1960 and was the real location of the 2006 Outkast movie erroneously set in Georgia.

Newago County was no slouch either. In nearby Bitely, where only liquored-up deer hunters and alpha wildcats dared to go, was a tucked away joint with a dilapidated sign that said Woody's Bar and Septic Tank Repair with a confederacy so frightening that Joni and I feared for our lives once we stumbled into the real live horror story honky-tonk saloon. Dressed as the city slicker dandies we were, the sallow living dead looked on us as lunch, and there was a hot tub size kettle boiling water on a medieval stove. Every bloodshot and missing eye was drilled right at us. The 400-pound owner, Woody, wondered what we were doing in his backwater bayou and stripped down to show us all the bullet holes that had failed to fatally penetrate his blubber during multiple attempted robberies. His not so tight, formerly white panties were even more frightening. Joni pleaded with me to exit this particular "location," but a couple yokels coerced us over to the game nook and showed us the fresh bloodstains where they'd killed an "uppity nigger" on the pool table the previous night, or so they claimed. Recoiled and revolted, we faked them out with a zig toward the unrestroom and a zag past Mt. Woody and fled into the daylight. The broken screen door and their laughter slammed behind us. We sped off and she kissed me hard with adrenalin. We finished off the color tour with a cherry ice cream soda at Johnny's Drive-in on US 10 near Scottville where my father was born, east of Ludington in Mason County.

Billy Higgins got pulled away to a real paying job, and Michael Degutis took sole control over the enterprise. We had speculative deals with bankers and investors in Taiwan, Singapore, Indonesia, India, Bulgaria, Amsterdam, London, Nigeria, and Salt Lake City. They always fell through. One by one, we lost crew and cast to other projects. Even I got fed up and started my own new script, *Vulnerable,* which I based on a young waif I'd met in the Parkway Tropics. I never tried to sell it, but I got a rush writing it. It's still registered with the WGA.

Dale asked me to join him again in a script about the Bath City murders, and we also considered a script about Rock & Roll Hall of Famer Del Shannon ("Runaway") who was born and raised in Grand Rapids and who had recently died. Del Shannon's mother spent some time with us, but eventually I got too involved with my own rock star.

The Amazing Wolfer in Topanga Canyon with Connie.

Chapter 52: Nirvana, Smashing Pumpkins & Pearl Jam

The band was set to tour their breakout album, and Anthony insisted the Lex Luther promoters make me a partner for the West Michigan concert. Detroit based Cellar Door and boss man Rick Franks had their hands full on the east side and gratefully let me earn my percentage by doing the nuts-and-bolts promotion on the west side. Grand Rapids was my obvious choice, but unfortunately the band had been ostracized after the infamous *Top of the Rock* fiasco, when Flea dropped his pants on stage. Trip Brown, the Chili Peppers LA booking agent, told me to forget GR and go with Wings Stadium in Kalamazoo, about forty miles to the south. The opening acts were Smashing Pumpkins from Chicago who I barely knew, and Pearl Jam, a grunge band I had never heard of. Until the very last minute, I wasn't even going to include their name on the posters.

The tour opened October 16, 1991, in Madison, Wisconsin. Six concerts and seven days later, they played Michigan State. Anthony's sister Julie was enrolled at MSU, so the family met at the apartment she shared with a dozen unruly co-eds and furniture fashioned from beer cases. She had Scott St. John's good looks and devilish ways, but would take advantage of her education, demonstrate solid skills and become a flawless mother of two. After the show, Anthony came out and sat on the edge of the stage to sign autographs. Later, we moved to the local bars across the street from the University. The Peppers mingled with the crowd and did an impromptu show at Dick's bar.

I continued to promote my concert, but it wasn't selling very well in reactionary West Michigan. I'd call the box office daily, and the lady would report two or three tickets sold. There were even days we'd sell none. I made leaflets and got my girlfriends to blanket the cities, towns, villages, hamlets and othellos. We canvassed colleges up and down the state and all the way to Notre Dame in Indiana. John Gonzalez at the *Press* gave me Sherwin-Williams coverage. *Music Review* gave us a cover story. Herm Baker at Vinyl Solution Records was an ally. I did interviews on radio stations across the state. KLQ's Aris Hampers got the rock out. Underground DJ maestro Steve Aldrich disseminated our gospel. Radio pundit Tony Gates applied some pressure. I even got a rap station in Muskegon to play the Red Hots.

Robert Chase dialed up Warner Bros. rep Darren Eggleston in Detroit to bounce some help my way. We came up with a good idea. The three of us flew to New York City for the week-long gig the band was doing at the historic Roseland Ballroom in the Broadway Theatre District. We stayed at the hip Paramount Hotel with its bizarre décor and Warholic inhabitants. I sent coded propaganda back home. In New York, I finally paid attention to our support bands and got addicted to Billy Corgan's chandelier exploding vocal stylings, but I still spent most of my time backstage with RHCP and the sudden cornucopia of celebrity guests and MTV veejays who had adopted our band with fervor. Smashing Pumpkins were second billed for the majority of the tour, but Nirvana was going to replaced them as our opener on the West Coast. Red Hot Chili Peppers, Nirvana, Smashing Pumpkins and Pearl Jam exploded simultaneously on the scene and will forever be linked.

Home but not alone in our diminutive cityscape, Robert and I hyped the gig locally and got serious with the skirts and sweaters. We had twin *Sensations* for a while, Cindy and Shelley. Blushingly, I recall borrowing Shelley's Michael Bolton CD. Ouch. As red-blooded bachelors, we occasionally patronized a big noisy college bar called Gipper's, and one life-changing evening we spotted an intoxicating waitress we were both willing to die for. We each gave it a shot. I proposed my Chili Pepper concert in Kalamazoo, and Robert Chase had a WLAV Smithereens show at the Welch Auditorium. She chose the Smithereens, or maybe it was just Robert's blue eyes. She was Stacey Koets, and before long she became Stacey Chase. I lost the battle and a partner, but the world got Mazzy, their amazing daughter who inspires in her battle with juvenile diabetes. She's a JDRF poster child.

I ventured out to the all-ages club Top of the Rock to check out the Red Hot infamy. It was dark and barely lit with black light, a lively mix of nymphets, gang bangers, pinball machines and a jiggy dance floor. And then I saw *her*. Natasha was too good to be true and too true to be good. She was from Canada, and she was beautiful beyond belief. She was wildly intellectual for her age, and we enjoyed each other from the start. I was blessed with her peculiar qualities and sparkling company, but her jealous peers wanted a bailout. When she came to my apartment, her dedicated bodyguards frisked my intentions. Ultimately, I proved they were honorable. Natasha vaulted to the top of my mountain.

The moguls in Detroit hadn't been able to jumpstart the ticket sales so they moved the concert from spacious Wings Stadium to the State Theatre in the heart of downtown Kalamazoo. They also lent me a one-man cavalry, a young protégé promoter named Don Dorshimer, who would bump musical chairs with me for years to come. The State Theatre was an intimate venue built in the vaudeville era. Alan Bashara produced a Metallica show there; I went. But tonight it was the Red Hot Chili Peppers, Smashing Pumpkins and Pearl Jam in a concert the State Theatre would never see the likes of again. In the end, we sold out the 1,440 seats. I brought along my new partner Natasha to help me with logistics. Anthony was wowed when he met her. Pearl Jam opened and Eddie Vedder set the bar higher than the ornate ceiling he climbed up into. He swung from both balconies and scaled the piled-high speakers that drowned out the small stage. In my flashy promoter cap, I was pulled in a million directions and added a delightful new one. In the lobby, I met a cheerful leader from nearby Mattawan High, who insisted on sticking close to me. I accepted the challenge and refused to leave her side. She was Amanda, and we would have our own little love story. Now I had both Natasha and Amanda helping me, and we saw the concert from every imaginable angle.

Smashing Pumpkins had feedbackitis, but RHCP made a bold statement about whose concert this really was. Anthony and Flea came out after the show and mingled with the crowd. There was a paraplegic man in the handicapped section who was valiantly trying to rock out. I brought Anthony out to meet him. He embraced the fellow and passed on words of support. The man had tears and so did I. Back stage, Rick Franks was on hand to pass out a big check to the band and a small fortune to me. After the celebration died down, we drove back to GR and prepared for the next two nights in Detroit.

The Motor City made my seventh and eighth shows already, and I felt like part of the team. Johnny Reaser's family was invited and afterwards I spent the night at his house in Bloomfield Hills. John and his wife Karen had divorced, and their daughters lived with mom. In time, mom would re-marry one of America's wealthiest men, William Davidson, chairman to one of the largest glass manufacturers in the world, and he didn't do it with mirrors. On the side, he owned the NBA Detroit Pistons, WNBA Detroit Shock and the Palace of Auburn Hills they played in, and the NHL Tampa Bay Lightning. He won three NBA championships, four WNBA championships, and one Stanley Cup. And he won John's wife. The combined family was a positive influence for the youngsters; John's daughter Elizabeth Reaser studied at Juilliard and became an accomplished actress with starring film roles in *The Family Stone, Puccini for Beginners, Twilight* and *New Moon*, and in *Grey's Anatomy* and other television shows, including *The Sopranos* and *Law & Order*.

Amanda came up from Mattawan for the holidays, and I took her to our Noble family Christmas dinner with Anthony at Aunt Mickey and Uncle Don's house. She was young enough to be seated at the card table with the little kids. Although the family was aware of my nervy iconoclasm, a few of the merry revelers weren't so merry. I was very merry. Natasha had the advantage of proximity, but Amanda bought a car and drove up as often as she could. Arguably the two most beautiful creatures on the planet simultaneously cared for me and gave me the gift of their affection. Not too long after that, Natasha died suddenly of a brain tumor in one of the cruelest quirks of fate imaginable. Her untimely death darkened faith and affected forever the lives of hundreds who adored her. She was only sixteen.

Anthony and I flew out of Gerald R. Ford Airport on a small commuter plane to Chicago, but at O'Hare we had a wardrobe malfunction, and they wouldn't allow Anthony on our LA bound first-class flight because he was wearing shorts. The fiasco was holding up the departure, and the crew and passengers were enraged. I got Blackie pants from my carryon luggage, and he changed in the restroom. Los Angeles here we come!

The concert at the Sports Arena was the first with Nirvana supporting, and there was excitement and a touch of tension in the highly charged air. Nirvana had signed up for this, but in the interim David Geffen released their second album *Nevermind,* and the single "Smells Like Teen Spirit" was a monster hit. For the Red Hots, it was a triumphant home coming and easily the biggest show of their lives, but the specter of Nirvana opening for us put a strange edge on the proceedings. In the afternoon, Anthony and I drove to the arena for sound check, and I caught up with my Eddie buddy Vedder. As a teenager, he had been a Chili Pepper fan and still was. In the Nirvana camp, I chatted with Krist Novoselic and the playful Dave Grohl, but Kurt Cobain was the brooding Brando, quiet and introspective. James was in the house too. Candy brought him to the arena so I could see the little tyke.

The concert exceeded the hype. Robert Hillburn dosed the praise out fairly. The morning papers were a love fest for all three bands. The show was packed with celebrities, and one of the most revered that evening was Perry Farrell whose Lollapalooza tour that summer had been a big surprise success story. The traveling music festival of Jane's Addiction, Nine Inch Nails, Siouxsie & the Banshees, Living Color, Ice-T, Butthole Surfers, Violent Femmes, Henry Rollins and Fishbone had crisscrossed America for six rollicking weeks. Everybody was speculating who Perry would put on the bill next summer. Perry,

Anthony and Flea were seen huddling backstage. Fully immersed in the rockin' moment, I brought a saucy groupie home, but she jumped ship in the middle of the night and woke up with Anthony.

The following day, we headed to San Diego for the next show. On the road again, next stop Arizona. More memorable was San Francisco and the New Years Eve show at the Cow Palace. The bands settled into the pastel Phoenix Motel that was the new hip place to be. *People* covered it and us. Kurt and a petite brunette were curled up by the pool. Cobain and Courtney married only two months later. I had known Courtney going back to Hollywood clubs, parties and performances of her band Hole. She worked for Brendan Mullen at the Lingerie, often as a booker where she would conveniently slip Hole into the lineup. Courtney Love had been a passion puss flexing her sexuality in the same major league I played.

Anthony and I went out to dinner with Bo Gardner, the band's accountant, who had come up for the show. All these years later, she's still at the helm and a dear family friend. Rick Rubin had come up too. Legendary Bill Graham of Fillmore fame promoted the show and gave us the royal treatment. Flea made his stage entrance thumping his bass upside down suspended from the ceiling and lowered by a cable. Later, the band unveiled their fire-spouting helmets and performed several songs with nothing but socks and an inferno. Afterwards, a limousine drove us around town to all the best clubs and New Year parties. I came up with beautiful backstage denizen Sarah and brought her along too. She was from Santa Barbara, and we ended up in a protracted rapport that lasted into several of my subsequent trips to Southern California. One of them was taking her to the MTV Rock 'n Jock Softball game at USC. A few of the all-star combatants on the field of dreams that day were Darryl Strawberry, Ken Griffey Jr., Barry Bonds, Dwight Gooden, Paul Molitor, Tommy Lasorda, Tommy Lee, Dave Mustaine, Lita Ford, Charlie Sheen, Tom Arnold and Roseanne Barr, Pauley Shore, Lori Petty, Richie Sambora and the biggest star of that time, MC Hammer. He showed up with a king-size entourage of sycophants and bodyguards. Anthony played first base, made some stops, got a couple hits and scored a run. I only got to third base.

The bands moved on to Oregon and Washington. Nirvana had an escape clause to avoid opening for us in their hometown of Seattle. I headed back to Hollywood to work on Anthony's memorabilia project before I returned to Grand Rapids. It was already late at night when I arrived, but I decided to hang a few pictures up near the vaulted ceiling. I was on an extension ladder and reaching toward oblivion. The next thing I knew I was falling in slow motion and watching the floor coming to greet me. I landed on my chest and heard the snap of dry twigs. I could hardly breathe. I crawled to the nearest 911 phone and they dispatched an ambulance, but then I realized the security gate was locked and so was the front door. I crawled down three flights of indoor stairs and then down another three flights of concrete steps to the locked gate. The ambulance and fire truck got there long before I did. I had five broken ribs and spent the night at Presbyterian Hospital. I had to stay another week before I could fly, and when I got home I had to sleep sitting up for months.

Rolling Stone named Nirvana artist of the year and Red Hot Chili Peppers were runners up. Pearl Jam was third. Perry Farrell announced the Chili Peppers would headline the second Lollapalooza tour in the summer with Ministry, Soundgarden, Ice Cube, Jesus and Mary Chain, Pearl Jam and Lush. Later that year, Nirvana and Red Hot Chili Peppers co-headlined a tour of South America.

Chapter 53: Lollapalooza

Candy, James and Granny moved to Deadwood, South Dakota, following the lure of freshly legalized gambling. Brian Hayes, an innocent young man from the cowboy state next door, came by to play a little poker. He drew an inside straight up Candy's flirtatious skirt. Pretty soon they were planning a wedding, and Candy asked me to take James for a while. I was happy to and caught a plane for Rapid City. Candy sent an Indian scout to pick me up. A carefully reserved James followed from a furlong. Once he warmed up to me, we made the local rounds and visited nearby Mount Rushmore. Just shy of two years old, he still hadn't ever spoken a word. In fact, he'd only just learned to walk. He was an extraordinary child. We wondered if he would ever talk, and if it was neurological. We made trips to the pediatric doctor who scratched his head and shrugged. They were always making tests.

We flew to GR, his first air flight. When he got scared, I comforted him. When he was bored, I entertained him. By the time we got to Heritage Hill we were dynamic soul mates. I put him in Everlast boxing trunks, hip hop caps, Mexican bandanas and leopard-skin cowboy boots. He flourished and came out of his shell but no words yet. We camped out at Toys R Us. We went everywhere together, much like I had with Anthony. It was my second chance to get it right. There was a defining moment that sealed the deal. I put him in my bedroom for his nap, and I went to work at my living room desk by the windows that over looked the elm branches and an occasional raccoon. I looked up and the little stinker was standing in the doorway. I took him by the hand and placed him back under the right-ful cozy blankets. I was stern this time and went back to the table. A few minutes later, he reappeared again, in the same spot with that same plaintive look on his face. I tucked him in again and was so tyrannical I was positive he'd stay put. But in less than a minute, he was back in that hallway opening, looking deep into my soul with his penetrating eyes. And then he slowly enunciated, "Blackie." Garbo speaks. I cried I was so happy. Needless to say we skipped nap time and celebrated his first word.

A few days later, we celebrated his second birthday with help from Peggy and Jen. They loved James too and volunteered to babysit anytime I wanted to check on things at the Reptile. I met a girl at a hair salon in Eastown who had a daughter the same age as James and we double dated. James and I worked on vocabulary and the once taciturn pip-squeak began using big words like *dog* and *cat* and *taciturn*. LA Guns blew into town and played a bowling alley nightclub. I snuck James in and introduced him to the tragically hip Tracii Guns.

According to plan, Candy and Brian were driving to Michigan and would retrieve James. He hadn't mentioned his mommy at all, and I was wondering how she'd ever get him to leave. I was anxious for them to hear him talking a baby step blue streak. Fickle as his own mother, when Candy came in the front door James jumped into her arms and never let go. They rolled around on the floor in ecstasy and laughed with true joy. He never paid another isotope of attention to me and wouldn't even say goodbye as they drove off.

A few weeks later, they sent me a video of the Wyoming wedding, sprinkled with guests right out of central casting for *Little House on the Prairie*. A DJ had set up on the town hall's stage, and he used his microphone to advance the ceremony. Brian lifted James up on the stage and encouraged him to say something into the microphone. He mumbled inexplicable babble, but when they cranked up some U2 James broke into song and wouldn't stop. The DJ repeatedly tried to get his mic back, but James refused to relinquish it. Long after Mr. and Mrs. Hayes had cut the wedding cake and performed the official dance and the custodian turned out the lights, James was still singing.

In warped time, Anthony kept me informed with his storybook life; tidbits of Sinead O'Conner tomfoolery; the intensity of Henry Rollins; dinner with Ric Ocasek and Pavlina Porizkova; breaking the sound barrier on the autobahn; skiing in the Italian Alps; sick in Liverpool; strip searched by gendarmes at the Paris airport; strip searched by French girls on the Champs Elysees; in the good company of Stevie, Prince, Madonna, Julio, and Michael; on MTV's *120 Minutes*; acting in *Point Break* with Patrick Swayze and Keanu Reeves; videos in the desert; MTV *Rockline*; Sophia Coppola and a Knicks game; Neil Young; Euro Festivals with Nirvana, The Pogues and B-52s; in England with the Beastie Boys; mixed-up monkeyshines with Mike Judge, Butt-Head and Beavis; and as always, sending his love.

In July, the 1992 Lollapalooza tour began in San Francisco; a week and half later it rolled into Detroit and set up shop at the outdoor Pine Knob Music Theater for a two-night stand. There would be no John Fruscinate; he had brashly quit the band in Japan which also canceled the Australian tour. A rushed audition for a new guitarist came up with Arik Marshall who was a sweet guy and an adequate player, but not the audacious ax man you liked to see in that slot. Lollapalooza however, was bursting with audacity. It was a unique and alternative music festival, a mad house carnival and a political road show with aggressive voter registration, propitious People for the Ethical Treatment of Animals and unmitigated conversion to the legalization of marijuana. There were tattooing and body piercing, exotic foods, virtual reality games, Shaolin monks and a sideshow with under-underground music and the self-mutilating freak antics of the Jim Rose Circus. The side stages offered alternative acts like Porno for Pyros, Perry Farrell's new band; Cypress Hill; Stone Temple Pilots; House of Pain; Rage Against the Machine and the Boo-Yaa T.R.I.B.E., a Samoan band of six brothers from a South Central LA Bloods gang. Anthony caught their show, and the Boo-Yaa hip-hops hoisted him up on their railroad-tie shoulders while they continued doing their act.

I took Jandt on one day and Robert Chase the other. With my backstage laminates, I managed to pull off a few personal meet and greets. The English girl band Lush opened the show. RHCP had encouraged Perry Farrell to put a girl band in the lineup and lobbied for L7 who formed the women's rights Rock for Choice. Pearl Jam played second, ostensibly because they wanted to finish early and watch the other acts according to Eddie Vedder. More likely they had coveted a better slot. That shifted the lineup, but made for an interesting billing; it pulled customers in to catch Pearl Jam's bright and early phenomenal performances which helped the other opening acts. They were at the top of their game with *Ten* and it's litany of hit singles "Alive," "Jeremy" and "Even Flow." Quirky The Jesus and Mary Chain (a big favorite of mine) were the oddballs out, both on and off stage. Founding brothers Jim and William Reid called Lollapalooza the worst ordeal of their lives. Serially uncomfortable, they kept to themselves and hunkered down against the cat calls, but Lush played nursemaid and banded with the Jesus Chain. Fortunately, the Scottish boys were always assured a specialized cadre of partisan fans at every stop along the way.

Next up was Seattle band Soundgarden, a standout band on the verge of glory. Chris Cornell was dynamic on stage and humble and generous off. He had a beautiful voice and a beautiful wife, Susan Silver, who managed the band. Ice Cube was third billed and had a special following in the Red Hot Chili Peppers who often watched their shows from the wings and frequently cavorted with them in the lavish RHCP backstage area. Tit for tat, I often ended up in the Ice Cube Band dressing room for Heinekens when Chad had polished off our allotment. Ministry was the runner-up act and a wilder front man I'd never met. Al Jourgensen always got his eight glasses of Jack Daniels a day. Their Industrial Metal music was a potent ingredient in our lineup and a great lead in for the Chili Peppers who did a ninety-minute set that featured fan favorites like their new single "Give it Away," Stevie Wonder's "Higher Ground" and Anthony's signature ballad "Under the Bridge" that always brought out the lighters in the darkened arena.

The Detroit shows were notorious for rowdy audiences that ripped up sod in the pastoral hills and pelted the stage with clods of dirt and grass. They started bonfires and they started a fad. Next day, the traveling musical freak show played Chicago, and I went along too. After that I took a break, but five weeks later I set my sights on Los Angeles for the grand Lollapalooza finale of three straight days and nights at Irvine Meadows in Orange County. During the interval, MTV announced the nominations for the 1992 MTV Video Music Awards. The Red Hot Chili Peppers had eight nominations, the most of anybody.

The whole family went. We had our own limousine and good seats at the awards in UCLA's Pauley Pavilion, with new host Dana Carvey. Howard Stern made a fake ass of himself. Nirvana, Guns N' Roses, Eric Clapton, The Black Crowes, Pearl Jam, En Vogue, Def Leppard, Elton John, Bobby Brown and the Red Hot Chili Peppers performed. We did "Give it Away" and the raucous performance had a stage full of best friends freaking out in a rowdy maelstrom while Ice-T served as our cop and kept things in relative order.

"Under the Bridge" won Viewer's Choice for best video picked by a nationwide vote. We also took Break Through Video for "Give it Away" (Anthony gave me his moonman) and Best Art Direction for "Give it Away" (this one to Peggy). We did media interviews and limoed on to several post parties, ending at the Warner Bros. gala in West Hollywood, where the label had a lot to celebrate: Van Halen and RHCP had dominated the awards, each winning three. I met Mo Ostin and a helping of heavy hitters, but by then I was totally exhausted. We had one day to recover; tomorrow began with three more days of Lollapalooza.

The crowds were crowded. The fairgrounds were fair game. The back stage was a rage. On Saturday night, Anthony, Chris Cornell, Eddie Vedder and I went to a screening at the Chinese Theatre and then on to Power Tools. Eddie Vedder was wearing camouflage and an army helmet and did he get wasted! He was singing to everybody and doing his acrobatics in the stratosphere. At one point, he peed in his helmet. On Sunday, Eddie performed with Soundgarden, and Al Jourgensen was supposed to sing with us. He got drunk, fell asleep and never made it.

Naturally, I had to find a new lady for the occasion. Weaver and I had scouted all day and were at our wits end, but suddenly, there on the cusp of the amphitheatre, high over the spectacle was the perfect her. Mount Everest tall, lanky long white legs cascading down from tiny mini shorts, teenage breasts so large she'd later have them reduced, freckled and sun-streaked and not the least bit interested in me. In fact, she was such a fan of U2, she made fun of my son's band for years. I had to summon up authentic charm before I could get the slightest reaction from this Caroline McBride. She was so reticent it took her best friend to convince the skeptical hot pants that I was worth taking a chance on. Honestly, I never got frisky with this puppy, only hugs and a case of terminal love sickness, but in the end I had myself a very good friend. Our last embrace was at a dinner with Anthony and Yohana at The Palms restaurant ten years later, circa *By the Way*. Happily, I'm still on her Christmas card list, and in last year's photo she was cranking up an ax with a Nicholson evil grin before a backdrop of evergreens that celebrated her cascading ruby red mane.

Lollapalooza was over, but I wanted to stick around LA for a while; there were so many friends to catch up with. Then I received a phone call from Paul Dreher at the Civic Theatre. Their opening play of the 67th season was the 1907 French farce *A Flea in Her Ear* (*La Puce a l'oreille*) by Georges Feydeau, and they were unable to come up with a suitable Don Carlos Homenides de Histangua, the flammable and flamboyant jealous husband who carried a gun and wasn't afraid to use it. They asked me to play the difficult role. The plot of course would thicken resulting in frantic complications of mistaken identity and the usual dashing in and out of rooms. I was the emergency actor who flew in to save the day. I grabbed a cab and headed for LAX.

While I tussled in the Grand Rapids jungle, replete with mounting debt, scary religious monsters and vengeful women, Anthony was tempted by fate and his tattooing Dutch friend Hank Schiffmacher to join in a hiking quest across the most unchartered and formidable country on earth. Dead on the equator, Borneo offered a difficult challenge even for the most experienced adventurer. From the western coast, they traveled by steamer until the river turned into a trickle and then, with the assistance of native guides, made their way with canoes and then on foot into the tropical jungles and unforgiving mountains. About three quarters across the immense island, Anthony contracted the deadly dengue fever. They were able to contact help and a helicopter took him to civilization in Australia. As soon as it was possible, he flew back to LA and Cedar-Sinai. Peggy and I were frantic; I rushed out on the first available plane. Weaver picked me up and zipped me straight to the hospital. The nurse led me to his bedside, and Anthony told me to get the hell out of his room. He was miserable and didn't want to see anybody. It hurt me like dengue fever. I bypassed a mob of friends Weaver had brought to see me and went right back to the airport.

My savings were dwindling and I needed a job. For the past 25 years I'd been employed in the business of show. Now what? I sucked in my gut and went looking. I soon realized the scope of desperation; nobody was hiring a 53-year-old actor with skills in shenanigans. I signed up as a door-to-door pipe dream financial scheme trainee but had so many doors slammed in my face the boss terminated me, thankfully. Running out of rent money, I tried the ultimate sales job, the traveling vacuum cleaner salesman. I went to suction school for three weeks, where we developed our spiel and presented it to the other trainees and the boss. It was like auditioning at MGM, except I was in the worn-collar business of shysters.

We hit the streets and conned our way into the demented homes of skeptical elderly ladies who certainly weren't interested; shades of 1948's movie *The Fuller Brush Man* with Red Skelton as a beleaguered door-to-door salesman. I thought of the classic routine of pouring dirt on the carpet to illustrate the vacuum's suction power only to learn the home had no electricity. Disparaged and disheartened, I turned in my loyal vacuum. I was long on tricks and short on treats until a double dose of better luck came my way.

Dale Shumaker and I Watuised into the rave dance-party scene and started a financial enterprise. Raves had been big in LA in the late 80s. Grand Rapids ate them up now, and we were doing five hundred people a night. The competitors got jealous and then belligerent. One night, they shot up a different rave party on the north side while Jandt and I were scoping it out. Bullets flew; we hit the deck and crawled for cover. Dale was already doing regular DJ gigs at established bars, and he decided to stick with them. Since he owned all the equipment, we quit raving.

Picking up the disparate pieces of 1992, the Red Hot Chili Peppers made the cover of *Rolling Stone*, naked of course and as a trio, since John Fruscante had left the band. They would make the *RS* cover nine times and counting. *Blood Sugar Sex Magik* finished as the number one album of the year in Australia and dozens of other perceptive countries.

Like taxes, I closed my little black books and did the final accounting. I had turned plenty of heads, but there were two that stood out. Scary, I practically moved in with Stacey and her roommate. The other wonder was deliriously seriously. I first met Tracee Bloemen in Lansing when she was going to MSU and dancing nude to pay her tuition. Ultimately, I got her a part in *Racing Hearts*. She became part of my family and helped me with James. She had a Boa Constrictor that kept me from getting too fresh. Still, no one had come close to deposing the impugnable princess Amanda, despite the fact that she lived in Mattawan fifty miles away and was still in high school. She still had the will, the deed and the safety-box.

I actually had diverse male friends too. Dave Deever owned the Intersection Bar in Eastown; before Dave came into the picture, I had dated his girlfriend Sarah, and then Anthony took her on when he came to town. Deever held a 20th anniversary party for his popular nightclub with a 70s fashion show and a $50 first prize for best recreation costume of that era. I stole the baby's candy.

Nate Neering was an eccentric artist who had a loft next to the Reptile; he gave me shelter and unlimited access to his quirky parties. Jim Starkey a photographer for the *GR Press* was a cool dude and an eclectic artist who threw great parties with the beautiful help of his girlfriend, Maria. Handsome Jandt was always reinventing his modeling career and spent six months in Spain. Robert Chase left GR for Chicago and was hired by the windy city's big alternative radio station Q101. Brett Anderson was a rock solid best pal despite his subscription to the Rich Limbaugh newsletter. He also had that danger-loving vibe that made things exciting. Adolf remained vigilant. Anthony anchored my world and gave me life. For the second Christmas in a row he gave me a $5,000 financial certificate in addition to the more traditional gifts. I was in the black. I had a Merry Christmas and solvency, and there was still more to come.

"Magnum, P.I." Top billing in Hawaii with Tom Selleck.

Chapter 54: Secluded Lake

I was sitting at my big old oak desk in the grasping shadows of those elms when the phone rang. It was Anthony and he simply stated he was going to buy me a house. When I first moved to GR and still had a nest egg, I tried to buy a little bungalow, but my credit wasn't established. Now he was offering to put me in my own home with a lifetime of security. Not a little bungalow; he wanted something special. Over the next few months, Anthony made several trips home, and together we looked at hundreds of homes from the shores of Lake Michigan to the chichi lakesides of East Grand Rapids and the Nuevo Riche suburbs of Ada and Cascade. We looked north, south, east and west. We wore out a dozen realtors.

In the end, we picked a ten-acre spread at 4400 Secluded Lake Drive on a quiet lake south of Rockford, not far from where I grew up. Our ten acres were surrounded by 600 contiguous acres of woodlands. There were endless fields of sunflowers and a school just up the road. We were in a private association of like-minded expensive homes all nestled around our little gem of a lake full of trout, bass and walleye and over flown with Blue Herons, hawks and even an occasional eagle. Mission accomplished. But wait! Anthony was having so much fun he couldn't stop. Addicted to the chase, he ran down a smaller house on a larger body of water, a place Indians once favored to settle around. It was Murray Lake and it was bursting with wildlife and surrounded by orchards. He bought that one too and turned it over to his sister Julie and her family. I remembered about Elvis buying his folks a car and then a modest house. By the time Anthony was done, he had taken care of his entire family. His generosity was unparalleled.

Winning an MTV Video Award was one thing; now they had a Grammy. In February, they beat out Guns N' Roses, Nirvana, Pearl Jam, Alice in Chains and Faith No More for the hard rock Grammy and drew headlines when they serenaded the press corps backstage with a heartfelt a cappella performance of the evening's big winner, Eric Clapton's "Tears in Heaven." Anthony and company were further immortalized when the band made an auspicious stop in Springfield to support a comeback for Krusty the Clown on *The Simpsons*. Joining in the celebration were Elizabeth Taylor, Johnny Carson, Bette Midler, Hugh Hefner and Barry White. Anthony followed that up with an appearance on Arsenio Hall's one-thousandth anniversary show at the Hollywood Bowl, doing a duet of "The Lady is a Tramp" with Madonna. They dressed in identical short black skirts, fishnet stockings with garter belts, devil caps and combat boots. Madonna threw herself at him; they tumbled down and she gave him a good humping. After the show, they had a quiet date at Canter's on Fairfax.

Anthony was a presenter at the 1993 MTV Movie Awards, hosted by Eddie Murphy who mangled the Kiedis pronunciation. Anthony gave him a stern reprimand. I had to laugh; I'd changed my name for that reason. Now thanks to Anthony, most of the whole world was getting it right. I wish my dad could have been there. Anthony and Marisa Tomei were co-presenters of the Best Kiss Award. In the irreverent spirit of the evening, they came out in the famous RHCP fire helmets, which for safety were turned off. After awarding the prize, they acceded to the audiences' plea for their own kiss. Now they secretly opened the gas jets and prepared to give the audience a *really* hot kiss. Marisa didn't activate her valve properly; the explosive gas built up and Anthony's flames ignited hers—ka-boom! They almost blew the beautiful face off the newly ordained best supporting actress Oscar winner for *My Cousin Vinnie*. Unfazed by the near catastrophe, she accepted Anthony's request to a picnic in the park.

Amanda turned 18 and graduated on June 4. At the time, she may have been the best girlfriend ever, in league with my Mt. Rushmore of pulchritude and the infamous triumvirate. As I got older, the quotient refused to depreciate; Blackie's beauties kept getting better and the best were yet to come. There was still a breathless Swedish beauty waiting to find me, but right now she was only six and lived on the other side of my world. At Christmas, Anthony had given me a 1920 girl's primer from a British publisher: "Messrs. BLACKIE & SON LTD., offices in London, Glasgow and Bombay." The title of the book was *Blackie's Girls' Annual*. The Christmas gift card read: "Pops— I saw this book in New Zealand and could not pass it up. I feel forever happy and lucky to be your son. Anthony."

The band was big-time now, but manager Lindy Goetz still worked out of a small office in Studio City. Shanon Chaiken was an industrious secretary who started a rudimentary fan club, and from 1990 to 1993 she distributed nine black-and-white newsletters. Anthony named it *Rockinfreakapotamus*. When Lindy fired Shanon for mismanagement, Peggy suggested me for the job. The band agreed. I accepted the challenge and became the liaison between the Red Hot Chili Peppers and their fans. Humbly, I chose the modest title of Head Honcho & Chief Potentate and went to business. I had the tongue in cheek for lunch. I flew out to LA and met with Shanon, who only had a hundred members to hand over. She left a financial mess to clean up but did give me some advice that was priceless: "Involve the fan club members." It would be the cornerstone of our *Rockinfreakapotamus*.

In West LA, Anthony and I met with Ken Kerslake while he was editing *Soul to Squeeze* footage for the new video. He had already directed five Nirvana videos. Our film was set in a traveling circus that reminded me of my days with the carnival. Ken used real clowns, contortionists and even a guy shot out of a cannon. Anthony stole scenes with a chimpanzee and wore a Medusa headdress with live snakes.

Close by, we made a quick stop at Scott McClintock's latest place, a new condo on the famous Venice boardwalk which had its own clowns, jugglers and mugglers. His place was ultra-deluxe, but there were scurvy activities at arm's length from his luxury porch overlooking all the madness. I hadn't seen him for a while. It had been over ten years since we bumped into our prince-and-the-pauper partnership. I gave him my love and asked him to be careful in his new environment. I lost track of him after that. In retrospect, it was hard to tell which of us was the prince and which was the pauper, and wasn't that the idea? On subsequent trips to LA, I'd always come back to that Venice Beach site like an anthropologist looking for clues as to his whereabouts.

I had fan club news to report: Arik Marshall was out and Jesse Tobias was in at guitar—for a minute. Dave Navarro hopped on board and we had a powerhouse lineup again. Dave let me into his life and I spent fascinating coffin nightmares at his house overlooking Sunset with his sweetie, Monet Mazur. Anthony got disparaging recognition when he made *People* magazine's Best & Worst Dressed '93 as one of the worst, along with fellow misfits Robert Downey Jr., Julia Roberts, Garth Brooks, Diane Keaton, Burt Reynolds and Whoopi Goldberg.

I flew out of LA with a briefcase full of magical fan-club seeds and planted a Garden of Eden. With acres of rolling hills, I decided Adolf needed company. I looked in the paper for a watchdog and found wolf hybrids. Hey, how cool was that? In Muskegon, I met my fortune, a four-week-old black wolf from a pure wolf female on loan from Minnesota and a mongrel wolf dog male by the name of Bud. He took a bite out of my macho image, but the congenial bear of an owner smiled and reassured me, "Oh, that's just Bud. Come on in." They were a couple of animal lovers who turned out to be the nicest people I'd ever met. They were James and Brenda Pearson, and they soon got seriously passionate about saving wolves. Within a year, they moved to a 20-acre compound in the wilderness, where they took in and cared for distressed wolves, raccoons, deer, badgers, prairie dogs, kinkajous, rabbits, opossums, stray cats and dogs, coyotes, bobcats, bears, foxes, sheep, goats, exotic birds, reptiles, a pasture of horses, an oversize steer and a donkey. Inside the home were a hundred and one dogs and two long-legged wild serval African jungle cats. Without a moment's contemplation, they would buckle into their unreliable vehicles and head off for California or Carolina or Maine or Minnesota to save an animal. They forsook any personal pleasures and spent their meager earnings on the injured and abused creatures. Jim worked the graveyard shift at a Muskegon factory and Brenda was an assistant to the principal at Ravenna High School. They were Mother Theresa and Saint Nicholas.

They said the black one was a biter; pick another one. I was stubborn and have the scars to prove it. We slept together with the lights on so I could quickly find and defend myself from his razor sharp teeth in the middle of the night. During the day, he trailed me like a shadow and loved to ride shotgun in the car. I named him Howlin' Wolf, after the Mississippi bluesman who transformed the sound of Chicago; my Wolf howled beautiful music too. Adolf kicked his ass for a while, but size mattered and pretty soon Adolf adopted a respectful behavior. Wolf grew up to weigh 160 pounds but was a gentlewolf who learned to like everybody, even cats and little children. These were the best of times.

And the worst of times. We lost River Phoenix that year, his life cut short by a drug overdose at Johnny Depp's Viper Room. River, Flea, River's girlfriend Samantha Mathis, Joaquin Phoenix and sister Rain were celebrating while Flea and Johnny Depp were jamming on stage. River slipped away, gambled on a fatal dose, stumbled out onto sacred Sunset and collapsed. Flea rode with River in the ambulance, but it was too late. Anthony observed his fifth year of sobriety.

I turned our house into the Rockinfreakapotamus Headquarters and went on a mission of enlarging the membership. I created a slick fan-club magazine with color covers and centerfold. A quarterly, it took a month to prepare, a month to layout and print and another month to zip-code sort and bag for bulk mail. I involved the fans; it belonged to them. I published their pen-pal letters and Chili Pepper art and posted member mug shots with contact info so they could network. In the early nineties, electronic devices were far from pervasive. Facebook, My Space and Twitter were only sprouts in the minds of mad genius.

"Dear Bon Vivant Discriminating Music Connoisseur & Crazed Maniac: From the rumbling thunder of their underground daze on a vagabond Hollywood circuit of Charles Bukowski bars and Fairfax bar mitzvah halls to the jagged peak of the rock n' roll heap, from the basement of depravity to the penthouse of notoriety, from Random Notes to the cover of *Rolling Stone*, from the bottom of the bill to the top of the chart, from the Kit Kat Club to Lollapalooza; the Red Hot Chili Peppers have always remained a band with a mission. No corporate bottom line. No media spin. No compromise. No surrender. Rockinfreakapotamus Peoplehood Inc. is your best bet to snuggle up to these knuckleheads. You'll get advance notice on tour dates, a crack at backstage passes and free concert tickets. You'll be subjected to the band's potent pontifications, anecdotes and humor. You'll have access to new merchandise, contests, prizes and home photos of the band. The best fans in the world deserve the best fan club. We guarantee it."

Rock and Roll heaven opened up and delivered a phenomenal kick in the pants that exploded our fan base. The band released *One Hot Minute*. The title was Flea's idea; it continued their winning streak and earned three and a half stars from *Rolling Stone*: "Ferociously eclectic, imaginative, thoughtful and spiritual." *Vox* said it was even better than *Blood Sugar Sex Magik*. It was #1 on the *Rolling Stone* Readers Top 20. It rolled out hit singles like the heavier than metal "Warped" and the lyrical "Aeroplane." The soulful "My Friends" personified the new band's camaraderie, and "Transcending" was a tribute to their lost friend River Phoenix. In the credits on the back of the CD, we gave the fan club address. The day after the CD was released all hell broke loose.

I had opened a post office box; Rockinfreakapotamus World Headquarters, Box 801, Rockford MI 49341, as the club's official address. The postal workers were swamped, but they'd get used to it. Andrew, Dave, Tim, Jan, Candy and a supporting cast became part of our family. Rockford was a small town, best known as the home of Hush Puppies; they'd been around since 1883. Now there was a new international enterprise with thousands of letters flowing into the quaint little post office on Courtland and Main. Box 801 turned cosmopolitan; it went from local to global and welcomed postmarks from Russia, Iran, South Korea, Mexico, Japan, Philippines, Cuba, Israel, Ethiopia, China, Ukraine, Somalia, Yugoslavia, Peru, Estonia, New Guinea, Lithuania, Latvia, Nepal, Brazil, Malta, France, Australia, Hungary, New Zealand, Colombia, Belgium, Norway, The Netherlands, Spain, Scotland, Denmark, England, Ghana, Slovenia, Thailand, Indonesia, Greece, Italy, Iceland, Guam, Chile, Croatia, Wales, Sweden, Lebanon, Singapore, Bulgaria, South Africa, Taiwan, Finland, Bolivia, Saudi Arabia, Germany, Poland, Argentina, Malaysia, Turkey and all fifty states and from military bases around the world.

News flashed on my ticker tape. Anthony and Chad played hard puck in a Celebrity Hockey Game at the LA Forum. Anthony fought a charity exhibition boxing match with WBO lightweight champion and pound-for-pound best fighter on the planet, Oscar de La Hoya. The event was a three-round bout to raise money for Oscar's old high school in East LA. Although he took a few good shots, Anthony was never knocked down and earned a standing ovation at the end. Anthony's corner man was former heavyweight champ George Foreman. Flea and Anthony had hefty roles in the Charlie Sheen comedy-adventure movie *The Chase*. And *Rolling Stone* did a cover story on Anthony. The cover photo of him was stark raving gorgeous and the title said it all: 'RED HOT CHILI PEPPER'S ANTHONY KIEDIS – CONFESSIONS OF SIR PSYCHO SEXY'. I flew out to LA again and participated in the interviews with Kim Neely who wrote the piece over a few days.

Excerpts of our rambling tale included: *Kiedis' dad, a handsome, outgoing actor and writer who goes by the stage name Blackie Dammett is visiting from Michigan. Moving through the house, they point out various treasures…an original Dali photograph; paintings by Robert Williams; a wrought-iron stair railing by a Hungarian blacksmith and a rather imposing stone fireplace crafted in the shape of a woman's body with purple glass nipples*

The two walk onto a terrace that offers a glorious, moonlit view of Griffith Park. Kiedis disappears to change his shirt for dinner, leaving his father to gaze out over the hills. "{U.S. Health and Human Services secretary} Donna Shalala saying he was a bad spokesperson for AIDS, she doesn't know him. He's a conscientious and altruistic person," Dammett says, eager as the next father to brag about his kids. "Do you know what he did on Thanksgiving? He brought meals to the homeless people downtown, 50 of them, with little place mats that he designed and signed"… Kiedis reappears, bringing the tattling session to an abrupt halt. It's interesting to watch the interplay between them; they seem more like siblings than father and son.

"That's the senior picture of my girlfriend Jaime Rishar," Anthony says, pointing out a high school graduation photo of a pretty blonde.

Stopping short, Kiedis looks like a hare caught in the headlights. What with all the time he spent yesterday deflecting questions about his Don Juan image, it won't do to blab to the journalist that his main squeeze is fresh out of high school. Trapped, Kiedis sneaks a glance at Dammett. Their eyes lock in a priceless display of hand-in-the-cookie-jar telepathy. The question hangs in the air a moment before Kiedis decides to bite the bullet and fess up. It's pretty recent," Kiedis admits a tad sheepishly, and then father and son burst out laughing.

The next day Kim Neely asked Anthony, *"Where do you think you'll be in 10 or 15 years? Could you see yourself doing this at 45?" "I could,"* Anthony responded, *"I think it would be cool to still be doing music at 45 with the Red Hot Chili Peppers."*

Well here he is in 2012, and he's doing just that.

Heidi Klum and Anthony Kiedis - hot couple in Las Vegas on New Years Eve.

Chapter 55: Woodstock

Back to the past, a rugby scrum of updates had Alan Bashara serving time in the Robert Kennedy Federal Compound in West Virginia for interstate trafficking and newly brazen James chillin' in Cheyenne, Wyoming. Sometimes I'd delivered fan club magazines in person to startled local members, like the Prize Patrol delivering *Publishers Clearing House* sweepstake checks. That's how I met a sturdy soldier for the band named Scott Miller. He had my back with a hockey stick and a generous heart. He was married and had little Nick, but we managed to get out occasionally. Jandt returned from modeling in Miami, but often stayed at his Aunt Minty's bordello north of Chicago.

There are hundreds of girls I can't fit into this memoir, but I am determined to squeeze in a few more, and Naomi deserves her place. Club Eastbrook sold out, had a make-over and immerged as a snazzy new joint called the Orbit. My concert business associate Don Dorsheimer took over. Jandt and I came upon two lovely ladies sitting at a table in the Orbit's refurbished lobby. We plunged right in and they took it like a woman. I can still feel the rustle of Naomi's silky blue blouse, but it was when she unleashed her lilting British accent I fell in love. She was perky, beautiful and an au pair, caring for the two children of a couple in suburban Jenison. Naomi became my next-big-thing affair. It was forty miles from me to her, but we made the trek like it was right next door—at first. She was adventurous and cosmopolitan. My home was her refuge, our playground was nightlife and we traveled around in my Buick Riviera like newlyweds. She painted and had an obsessive love of art. We were apt to drink, smoke and get lazy late into the evening; and sometimes I wasn't up to the long drive back to Jenison. Eventually her host family fired her, and she moved in with me.

Our rec room was the Reptile. Al Bregante adopted another popular Chicago club attraction, an inquisition torture rack with chains, hot wax and playful spanking. Kinky Naomi came dressed in black leather and garter belts and played it to the hilt. She also got chummy with one of the Reptile bartenders, and when the Don Juan invited her on a motorcycle run to Los Angeles she went for it. Naomi kept in touch over the years as she moved back and forth between London and The Storks, her family home in Ombersley. Of all places, she ended up with an abusive boyfriend in Detroit.

If there was a devilishly cool devil, his most imperfect creation was Woodstock, those three beautiful August days in 1969 that put Christmas, Easter and the 4th of July to shame. The convergence of a half million hippies, Viet Nam vets, war protestors, Black Militants, rednecks, politicos and advocates, newly-born babies and little old ladies, and almost as many bands was the event of the millennium. The thunder clap of thirty some odd indeed acts will never be matched. They cemented a revolution that changed the world forever. The ramifications were as cataclysmal as the Big Bang.

Three of the original four promoters decided to do a 25th anniversary Woodstock in 1994. What could be more gratifying than headlining one of the nights, and that's exactly what our rag-tag Fairfax High band would be doing in Saugerties New York. With a lineup nearly as powerful as the original, there were upstart acts like Cypress Hill, Rollins Band, The Cranberries, Primus, Salt-N-Pepa, Traffic, Arrested Development, Porno for Pyros, Green Day, Paul Rodgers, Neville Brothers, Jimmy Clift, Melissa Etheridge, Todd Rundgren, Blues Traveler and original Woodstock savvy holdovers like Santana, The Band, Joe Cocker, Allman Brothers Band and Crosby, Stills & Nash; but the evening headliners were the cream of the colossus. On Saturday night, it was Nine Inch Nails, Metallica and then Aerosmith. On Sunday to close out the event were Bob Dylan, Red Hot Chili Peppers and finally Peter Gabriel. Arguably, we had the best slot of all, the final show that everybody was still there for. When Peter Gabriel went on later that night, many of the mud-covered and tuckered-out 325,000 fans had already headed out to beat the mindboggling traffic jam.

And the band played on. The night *before* Woodstock, they played a charity event at the LA Palladium and then did a surprise show at the Lingerie before being whisked to New York. After Woodstock they played two gigs in Manhattan and then embarked on their Tour De La Sensitive. The band had called their *One Hot Minute* Hawaiian biker gang *The Sensitives* and actually made matching white suits just to be silly. On to Dalymont Stadium in Dublin, the Pukkel-Pop Festival in Belgium, the Reading England Festival, Las Ventos Bull Ring in Madrid, Roskilde in Denmark, the Go-Bang festival in Frankfort Germany, Caracas, Santiago, Buenos Aires, Mexico City, Australia and Japan. Anthony faithfully sent news back to the mother ship. In October, we did a show at the Rose Bowl with the Rolling Stones. It was their Voodoo Lounge tour and it grossed $320 million, which at the time was the biggest money maker ever. I flew in for that one and watched the show next to a jumpin' jack flash Nicholson who was having as much fun as I was. This was the next to the last time we would open for anyone ever again; a U2 gig was in the future.

Our ever-expanding Peoplehood Inc. fan-club membership wielded awesome support for good causes, and we were just getting started. Volunteers also poured in every time I had a new issue to zip code and deliver to the post office loading dock. We were growing into a benevolent empire. We had get-togethers with the band and eventually actual fan club conventions. The first was in Grand Rapids, the second in Toronto, and some of the others were in New York, Las Vegas, London, Paris and Los Angeles. Our fan club was family, never corporate. By the time I retired, we had thousands of cells propagating the message to millions of others, and we carried the band on our shoulders to victory. At the homestead, we beefed up on livestock. I acquired a sleek black female German shepherd to partner with Wolf. She was Sleeping Bear Dunes Defender, Bear for short, a dedicated protector who was affectionate and faithful. And cats; we had a Serengeti of cats. Not to forget families of raccoons, an opossum named Paddington and a passel of porcupines.

In early December, I answered the phone and a tiny succinct voice came over the line, "Blackie, come get me." It was the *James' 1994 Christmas Adventure 8200 Miles Traveled Between Us, 8 States, 29 Days, No Baby Sitters Tour.* Paul Erickson volunteered to co-pilot and provided the car; my Riviera was on its last wheels. I had always sent James cool stuff at Christmas, but this was *our* Christmas. Between me, Anthony and Santa, we really spoiled him. I didn't do so badly either. Anthony and Jaime drove my present across country, a brand new 1995 black Bronco SUV, just like O.J. Simpson's white one. James and I had a rousing New Year's Eve, and I brought him back to Wyoming on the train. On my way home, the locomotive whistle pierced the western sky with a lonesome reminder of the little guy I'd left behind. We needed each other, and it was James who made the move.

For a while, we were on auto-pilot. The band could do no wrong; another year, another *Rolling Stone* cover, another tour, and another healthy expansion of the fan club. Candy and Brian had two kids of their own now and the whole mob moved to Grand Rapids. Candy wanted James near me to ensure his good life. Their marriage was bleak and James told me of horrific fights. At least one time he had to physically defend his mother.

A guy at the Reptile asked if I was interested in a website for the band and I asked, what's a website? I was already looking for a magazine editor and now maybe even a website. Candy had already learned her way around town and turned me on to a few applicants. One was a paramour named Joe who lived on the west side and the Internet. He passed on the job, but his kids played with James, and Joe made himself a fixture on the night scene. He was on the ground floor of Internet dating and one of the first to advantage MySpace; more of him later. Another cyber spacehead was Jon Wade, a son of missionaries who traveled him around the world. Jon was hip and computer savvy; I hired him. We improved the magazine and created our first humble attempt at an RHCP website. He kept tweaking it, and in 1999 when MTV had their one-and-only Video Music Award for best rock website, we won beating out David Bowie, Jennifer Lopez, Sheryl Crow, Massive Attack, Smashing Pumpkins and Limp Bizkit.

Candy played Grand Rapids like a slot machine and Brian bailed; he took his own youngins' back to Wyoming. Candy moved in with west side Joe for a time and then with me; James got used to the comforts. I bought James a rescue Blue Tick hound named Scrappy. Candy messed around at the Reptile and got to know where the best trouble was. Eventually, she met a grease ball heroin addict named Dan, and they moved in with a local rockabilly band. The drummer gave James lessons. Candy was hooked again. Dan wore out his rockabilly welcome, and the calamitous couple found refuse in various drug dens and flop houses. James moved back in with me. Candy and Dan shuffled off to Denver, escaping the heat and settling into a faint memory. Before she left, I made Candy sign papers that put me in charge of James, and I went to court to make it official. James' Forsyth grandmother came all the way from Santa Cruz California to speak favorably for my custody at the Kent County Probate Court proceedings. The judge appointed me as his foster father.

Bonnie and Clyde got busted shoplifting in Denver and did time. The next time was big time; heroin and a protracted jail sentence. Suddenly I was a full-fledged dad with new responsibilities. James' life became my life. I toned down my obsession with females and concentrated on raising my new son. Anthony was a fan of young James and adopted him too. James had everything now but a decent mom. And it would be someone I'd already met when I first came to Grand Rapids five years ago.

FIVE FLESH FLUSH - La Mama Hollywood

Chapter 56: Chanda

The first time I saw Chanda was at Club Eastbrook, when she was fresh out of Podunk high school in bumpkin britches Morley (pop. 400) and forty miles north of Grand Rapids. The family had just moved down to my size and settled into a pleasant home in Ada. I was propped up *on* the bar counter like a spoiled brat, master of almost all I surveyed. The memory of her arrival into my life is as clear today as it was 20 years ago. She was angularly tall, stunning and strutting through the lobby, propelled at great speed and somewhat awkwardly by her endless skinny Olive Oyl legs and clunky black shoes. She was slender as my chances and full of spunk. She came and went through my space so quickly I barely had time to blurt out a misguided pickup line which she slammed right back at me like a Rocket Rod Laver serve. She was untouchable, and she had plans that most certainly transcended foolish me sitting on the bar, trolling for a lucky date. She was surprisingly generous with her condescending looks and future plans. She was headed for Michigan State in the fall and then either to med school or law school or both, and finally, she made perfectly clear that the possibility of me ever uttering another word to her was zero, nada, and none. And she disappeared into the crowd.

A couple calendars later, I was with Jandt on New Year's Eve at the Stadium, an old arena on the northwest side. It had been Atlantic Mills discount department store, the home of the CBA Grand Rapids basketball Tackers, a couple of defunct hockey franchises, the circus and the site of a boxing event with heavyweight champ Floyd Patterson that my dad took me to. And now, it had the second coming of Chanda. The New Year's party had a little of everything, including a rave with all the fizzle of tomorrow's leftover champagne. Unrecognizing her new mature embodiment, I tried to make some whoopee with the best-looking girl in the club, but she laughed in my face and reminded me of our first encounter. At least she remembered, even if I hadn't. The rambunctious giggling clique with her was one I'd get to know all too well. The snobs left united in distain for everybody there and especially me. Jandt and I hung around for another two seconds and went out to his car which was frozen and incapacitated, a bit like me. I couldn't stop thinking about Chanda and celebrated the strike of midnight with her imaginary presence.

In valiant vain, I looked around town for her, but eventually her case was classified cold. Unbeknown to me, Chanda and her gang bang had spent the next two years in Los Angeles, but now they were back. Chanda's family was close knit and never strayed for too long. It was Christmas again and Anthony was in town. Brett Anderson joined us for a bachelor's night out, and we were at J. Gardella's Tavern on Ionia in the now bustling downtown club district. Brett and Anthony were shooting pool. I was shooting bored looks at their game and was anxious to continue the bar tour. I gazed across the crowded tavern for anything worth…whoops! I stopped dead in my tracks at the sight of a supermodel at the bar, who obviously must be visiting from Manhattan or another planet. She was sitting on a bar stool with another attractive lady, but the special one was a *one* of a kind. I trembled with delight at the proposition. I straightened my state of mind and charged forward. I sidled up to the bar and turned to her with my mouth open about to put my foot into it when she calmly said, "Blackie, it's Chanda. Aren't you ever going to remember me?" They laughed and didn't run away so I stayed and we talked. The partner was her sister, Sherry, first lieutenant of her tribe. I wasn't making much progress of my own, so I asked Chanda if she'd like to meet my son. She said, "Sure, but I'm not going over there; if he wants to come here, fine." Women! I went to Anthony, made my pitch and pointed her out. He said, "Yes, she is beautiful, but I'm not going there; if she wants to meet me, let her come here." Rock stars! I had an impasse. I wanted to facilitate this opportunity, but they were intractable. The boys continued to chase the 8 ball and the girls went back to their own business. After a perfectly wasted hunk of time, Chanda and Sherry got up to leave and headed for the exit. As they passed within reach, I grabbed Chanda's arm with one of my audacious hands and Anthony with the other and thrust them together. Face to face. Anthony was about to blow his top, and Chanda was ready to punch me. Then they looked into each other's eyes and broke into pleasant conversation. They made a date for the next night at a funky fashion show and performance-art gig and I was included. I brought James and he stole her from both of us. Little James grabbed her lovely hand and wouldn't let go the entire evening.

Chanda had a maternal kindness about her, and she invited James to some of her family's holiday celebrations. Anthony and I were invited too, and we reciprocated by inviting her to Peggy's on Christmas. I had gone from anathema to a platonic friendship with the world's nicest beautiful woman. Every Christmas, Anthony and I had titanic battles over who could give the coolest presents to each other. Anthony could afford terrific stuff for me (and James) and we both relied on creativity. Anthony knew I was overwhelmed with the fan club, the Secluded Lake spread, the animals and now James too. He figured I needed a break. Chanda and Anthony wrapped a special present for me and the certificate said, "Seven 4-hour childcare services to be rendered by one loving Chanda Ulrich for one adorable hooligan, James Dammett." It turned out to be a godsend of a gift. I got a babysitter and seven times as much of Chanda as I'd never had before. By the time the lucky 7 were up, Chanda was so attached to James she continued to hang out with us. A tiny spark struggled for viability between Chanda and me. The Ulrich family was religious, and Chanda was darn right devout. Lutheran by tradition, the family had splintered in a mosaic of denominations—or demoninations. Her mother, Charlotte, was working with a rescue mission on South Division, passing out hot religion and scripture stew. Chanda was currently in the clutches of The Assembly of God, one of those arena churches with bible boy-band opening acts, fire and brimstone and Olympic-size bathtub baptisms. The multitude was interminable. The blessed evacuation after the service took an hour to exit the parking lot, and that seemed quick compared to the sermon. Every Sunday, Chanda took James to an assortment of churches, including the skid-row chapel. A good sport, I got religion. It was the ultimate sacrifice, but I actually went to church with them.

Chanda continued to drive me crazy, but a randy mob of cooperating females and my *Vulnerable* film-script inspiration Kathleen Kelly kept a smile on my face. And I was lured into international love with the first of several Australian girlfriends: Sarah Jane Forrest, a model with height, copper-color hair and green eyes. Warner Bros. threw a *One Hot Minute* party, and James and I flew out to the coast for the celebration. Sarah Jane flew in from the other direction and joined up with us. We took her to the shindig at a Moroccan mansion in the Sunset Hills and James had his coming out party, meeting and talking with respected musicians. He mesmerized Hal Negro and charmed Rick Rubin. Festive celebs joined us in the gala affair. Weaver and his new gal Molly and Anthony and Jaime came on motorcycles. We partied late into the night. Anthony's sister Julie and her hubby Steve were there too.

I took James to band rehearsals, Guy Oseary's Maverick Records and Madonna, Venice Beach, Universal Studios, NBC, Warner Bros., Flea's swimming pool and Clara, Melrose shopping, Alice Cooper, the Rainbow *and* they let him upstairs into the dance club; but mostly it was just great family fun with Jaime and Anthony and Sarah Jane and us two numskulls. After a glorious week, Sarah Jane returned to Australia, and we to our not-so-humble abode in Rockford.

Anthony slipped on a bindle peel and ended up in a Marina Del Rey drug rehab. Peggy and I flew to Los Angeles for some family meetings and Jaime came too. The staff bent the rules and let Anthony leave the facility for an hour so we could have a family supper at a nearby diner. The facility had seen substance-abuser celebrities come and go, but Anthony was in a particularly bright and difficult spotlight. Navarro, an ex-addict himself, visited and counseled his bandmate. The 12-step program became an integral part of Anthony's life, and it has sustained his recovery to this day. He still goes to meetings and is an exemplary example of what dedication and rocking responsibly can do. He's active in a number of causes that promote sobriety, including Musicares, which recently paid tribute to his long-standing efforts. Enough said.

MTV was RHCPTV. They did a RHCP *Rockumentary* and they had a RHCP Day. I was a quasi-correspondent feeding MTV tidbits for their ever-running documentaries. Veejay Kennedy was doing interviews with the band and camped in at Anthony's house. MTV's top 100 music videos of all time: 1. *Smells Like Teen Spirit* (Nirvana), 2. *Cryin'* (Aerosmith), 3. *Under the Bridge* (RHCP), 4. *Thriller* (Michael Jackson), 5. *Jeremy* (Pearl Jam), 6. *November Rain* (GNR). Allusions to the Chilies on *Beavis and Butt-head* were de rigueur. We covered Ohio Players' *Love Rollercoaster* as a single, in a video and as an integral part of *Beavis and Butt-head Do America* the movie.

Dave and Flea collaborated with Alanis Morrisette on her epic CD *Jagged Little Pill,* one of the biggest selling records of all time. The band did a track on *Working Class Hero: A Tribute to John Lennon.* Flea and Anthony hunkered down to work on new material in Taos after Flea returned from the Congo. And then the band was off to Europe again. A blitzkrieg of press coverage followed their every move. Salacious headlines heated the newsstands. *The Times of London,* no less: BAD-BOY HEROES OF SOCK 'N' ROLL NAKED and UNASHAMED! Others went beyond tea and crumpets civility: THEY'VE GOT A JACUZZI IN THEIR PANTS; MEN BEHAVING BADLY and THEY'RE FILTHY! THEY'RE FUNKY! AND THEY HAVE THE SEXIEST ALBUM OF THE YEAR. In Stockholm, AVKLADDA RED HOT CHILI PEPPERS VICTORIA PA NAKEN SUCCE-KONCERT translated as "Undressed RHCP and Sweden's Princess Victoria at Nude Successful Concert."

In February, 1996, the *One Hot Minute* tour landed in New York City and so did James and I. Not just any show: Madison Square Garden, the most famous arena in the world. We stayed at the Rihga Royal Hotel with the band. At sound check that afternoon, James was fooling with his harmonica and singing along with the band. Astonished by the whiz kid prodigy, they let him perform that night during intermission after Silver Chair's opening act. Five-year-old James walked out on stage in front of 16,000 people and played his harmonica to uproarious applause. During RHCP's set, James joined Rob Rule and Rain Phoenix singing backup vocals. He discarded his shirt to match the bare-chested Peppers. An MTV crew filmed the event and the first three songs were broadcasted live. Hundreds of fan club members were in the audience, and I brought some of them backstage to meet the band. Many of them became lifelong friends. It's impossible to implicate them all, those lusty New York nutcases, but Mikie Weed, Suzette Siegel, Katie de Rogatis and Keith Rothschild, who went to a Warner Bros. career, were a few who ended up in my heart and later my home. Sixteen–year-old Katie de Rogatis would be the first fan-club member to visit the Rockinfreakaheadquarters, accompanied by her baffled father. They came from Montville, New Jersey, and stayed for a week. Her poor dad was lost in Hicksville but kept a stiff upper lip; he hung a heavy Tiffany-style lamp over my big oak desk and fixed a broken toilet. Over my fourteen years as head honcho, fans from all over the world dropped by and stayed a while. Like the White House, 4400 Secluded Lake was the people's house. It belonged to the fans that propelled us to the top and kept us there during my tenure.

Anthony designed a new fan club T-shirt with a naked drawing of Madonna encircled with the words Red Hot Chili Peppers. The press had a field day when newlyweds Pamela Anderson and Tommy Lee, wearing that shirt, were refused at New York's Le Club for *improper attire. Rolling Stone* called it *an outrage!* They went to the Tunnel instead. Gabby Glaser, guitarist for the New York City female rock band Luscious Jackson, was quoted, "The Red Hot Chili Peppers are such penis people. When I picture the singer, all I see is this big hard penis. And that scares me." Courageous Johnny Cash wasn't deterred and welcomed Anthony backstage at his Carnegie Hall concert.

James and I went to England for the concert at Wembley Arena, the final stop on the yearlong tour: 64 shows in 21 countries; their first appearances in Eastern Europe, two tours of Western Europe, Canada, Australia, New Zealand, where AK bought a 169-acre hideaway with a priceless view of Kaipara Bay, two *David Lettermans, The Tonight Show* and three passes across the USA. Now there were rumors circulating that the band was about to break up. Ma Bell broke up, the Soviet Union, Prince Charles and Lady Di, even the Beatles, but the boys seemed in fine spirits as we arrived in London. James and I brought 60 UK fan-club members backstage to meet and greet before the concert. Chad smoked a big cigar and greeted everybody with the enthusiasm of a politician. Dave was sexy and several girls fainted. The fans knighted Flea, and an exhausted Anthony was endearing as always. It was at Wembly I first encountered computer phenom Terry Wells and his girlfriend Sarah. He would ultimately join our fan club administrative team. James had also sung backups in Detroit to more applause and was prepared to sing in London. He put together his own cool outfit and was practicing backstage when Anthony told us the band would prefer James not sing. He was a distraction. No Doubt opened, and Chad closed by smashing his drum set. Dave and Flea joined in and trashed their guitars. By then Flea was completely naked.

Anthony rented James and his pop an apartment on Hyde Park for two weeks. I rented a car at the airport but had my hands full, driving on the wrong side of the road. The damage done: scathed hubcaps from left-side curbs and banged-up bumper cars in the wild and wooly roundabouts. I parked it in the hotel garage for the duration. Anthony stayed at a nearby hotel with buddies Guy Oseary, Ben Stiller and Stephen Dorff, and we all went to after-hour clubs, including James who hung out deep into the night with British superstars. I found plenty of love in Lyn Hathaway, who took us shopping for a pirate flag I would unfurrow over Secluded Lake. I'd have purchased Lisa Plappert if she was more accessible. Emma Bates & her mates pirated my heart. The mates were two adorable young British school girls we met in Camden, Natalie and Lisa Martin from Essex. Their father dropped them off at our flat the next morning and let James and I have them for a day on the town. We carried on for months via the post. I had made plans to meet Alisha Prince in advance; we had exchanged sweet letters for several months. In London, we set up a meeting at Victoria Station. We were both going by photos, and I spotted her first. She'd gone from lithe to death, and I ducked down just before she scanned my position. I grabbed James' hand and we escaped. I'm terrible.

My bad back was at it again. Anthony, who once drove me on a harrowing hellfire drive to the chiropractor when he was 12, got the best doctor he could find on a Sunday. When I showed up at his typically British hybrid of home and office, he turned out to be the older brother of Duran Duran's Simon Le Bon. Feeling a bit better, the next day we went for a walk on Oxford Street. An angry Jaguar driven by an Arab with a bad temper almost ran James over when he blasted through an intersection. I kicked his fender as he sideswiped us. He seemed to have sped off, and James and I continued to walk along the famous shopping boulevard when all of a sudden the guy, who obviously had quickly parked and returned to the scene of the crime, came up behind me, grabbed my long hair, pulled me over onto the sidewalk and started punching me. Pedestrians that witnessed his first transgression took their own anger out on him and administered appropriate punishment.

James and I played in Hyde Park almost every day. Our favorite section of the park was right next door to Kensington Palace, the home of Diana, Princess of Wales, now divorced from Charles. We'd often see the big red helicopter bringing her in or out. One afternoon as Diana swooped over head, James got distracted, lost his balance on the monkey bars and fell quite hard. The nurse station called an ambulance and we roared off through an anxious crowd to the tune of the funny euro-siren. We spent several hours at hospital, but James was OK. The best friend we made in London was Victoria Hill, who was separated from her husband Barry Jepson, bass player for the original Cult, the Southern Death Cult, formed by Ian Astbury. Victoria and another friend, Denise Hughes, came to Michigan the next summer and stayed with us. We gave them the royal treatment. Both Paul Erickson and Jon Wade had sweet affairs with Victoria. Brett the loveable brute and dainty Denise made an interesting duo.

Myself, I found another lively redhead, full of monkeyshines and rumpled rural grammar. She was Nellie and she lived with her parents in Cedar Springs, north of Rockford. The burg was best known as the world's largest maker of red flannel pajamas with the old-fashion flap backdoor. Cedar Springs had more guns and broken noses than the Texas panhandle. Nellie was a checkout girl at K-Mart, and my blowtorch temperature set off the Blue Light special when I first saw her. We slipped each other numbers and started dating. She helped with the fan club and helped with my disposition. Nellie dominated for a while. She had a way of stretching her lengthy slim body out on the hood of my car or a broken-spring couch at her place. She modeled my new RHCP gear; sales and I spurted. I went to her high-school graduation, the sixth girlfriend graduation I'd attended since my homecoming.

James and I dropped by Brett's. His friends were watching videos and passing a hookah back and forth. James climbed on the couch in the middle of the pack and watched too. After a while James and I got up to leave and he seemed inordinately happy for a kid going to bed. On the way home, we drove past the McDonald's where James was a frequently flyer. He told me to pull over and get something to eat. It was kind of late, and I said no. He didn't back down. He was strangely adamant for a five-year-old, and I had to chuckle. I'd never seen him like this. I swung by the drive-thru and James ordered half the menu. Then it hit me. He had breathed in enough secondhand pot smoke to get the munchies. He ordered a couple happy meals with extra fries, two desserts and a super gulp. At home after he polished that off, he raided the refrigerator. Down the gullet, cereal, yogurt, cheese, even his vegetables. He was up all night eating. Fortunately, James had an aversion to drugs because Candy was always so dopey.

I heard Rich Klimavich lived in Harbor Springs, just south of the Upper Peninsula. I wanted to show James the Lake Michigan coast anyway, so we headed north. I hadn't seen Rich since we were a couple hazards to society. He was married now, an elderly couple that lived with doilies and knick-knacks. However I had to admit Rich was still a fearsome character who gave me the chills. They had a seventeen–year-old daughter, and you can bet your life I didn't flirt with her. I started to bring him up to speed, but they were already fans. Then Rich knocked me over with a proposition that made me laugh outrageously, which in turn made him angry and stifled my mirth. He was planning a heist and needed a getaway driver. Was I interested? Even James chuckled under his breath. I still see a reminder of Klimavich every time I look in the mirror, my 1950s battle scar from the rumble at the Tastee-Freeze.

Hold onto your hat and protect your belongings. Scott St. John showed up at my Secluded Lake door in a lime-green suit that was yearning to pop some buttons. Scott was more than just stocky. I was speechless and not exactly comfortable with the surprise visitor. From Peggy and Julie, I was aware Scott had been married for some time to Maria, a Colombian woman. They lived in Florida; this of course after most of his life in prisons. Macho man sunned on the Gulf beaches while his wife worked to support him. They had a daughter, Angel. Now the threesome had moved to Michigan, which was weird since equatorial Maria had never seen snow, much less a Michigan winter. I begged off when he invited himself to dinner, a few drinks and a loan. He finally left; I closed the door and exhaled a deep breath. James was my Geiger counter, and he got a bad reading.

Brett and I went to a Blimpie's and a cute teenager behind the counter asked if I was Blackie Dammett. I thought I was getting lucky, and in fact I had. She wasn't a flirt; she was Tom Smith's niece. I hadn't seen Tom Smith since the 70s and always wondered what happened to him. I had tried unsuccessfully to find his parents house when I first moved back to GR. Our days together at Michigan State and the adventurous trip to Paris were some of the most important times of my life. She told me he moved back to Paris over 20 years ago, was married to a French woman and had two grown French daughters. Suddenly, three of my old best friends had surfaced out of nowhere.

That summer the band went to the North Pole for the Molson Ice Polar Beach Party. The Molson brewery had done it the year before with Metallica. The band and 70 contest winners flew to the top of the world for a party on a Russian icebreaker. Freezing rain, horrible weather and thick Arctic ice forced organizers to move the concert from the ship to the tiny village of Resolute, a scientific research station and jumping-off point for explorations to the magnetic North Pole. More than 24,000 pounds of RHCP equipment and 60,000 watts of stage lighting dropped in on an Eskimo igloo with a population of 201, and that included the polar bears. Ironically the village didn't allow alcohol.

A month later Peggy's husband, Steve, died of a heart attack cutting deep-growth vegetation under a hot sun in their back pasture. He was a relatively young man for a heart attack, which made it all the more devastating. Peggy and Steve had been the perfect couple. Their kind and generous relationship was up front for all to see and admire. All these years later, Peggy still remains true to her guy.

After a rocky start at pre-school where James managed to turn field trips and holiday parties into exercise drills for the swat team and fire department, my little bundle of angst started kindergarten at Crestwood Elementary. It was *The Blackboard Jungle* without Glen Ford, but plenty of Principal Hoogerland. The tidy school was a Ben Hogan 2-iron from our house, and suddenly I was a soccer mom, baking cookies for class parties. I took James to an orthodontist for braces. We had a fight with a bully and the bully's dad on the school gridiron. PTA meetings were mandatory. James kept things interesting and turned out to be a mischievous handful who logged the most timeouts in Crestwood kindergarten history. I volunteered for the teacher's assistant plan to help supervise class and make up for his devilry. He improved slightly in the first grade but still got in fights and in one case the parents of a black-eyed son threatened to sue us. I tried to make up for his transgressions; I helped in the library, worked on the yearbook and captained the annual outdoor play-all-day activity party in the spring. It wasn't enough; Crestwood Elementary refused to pass him into the second grade, and the next year we had to take him to a special school for naughty boys. That brought the social workers out in force, and they determined he had chemical imbalances dating back to Candy's pregnancy. Another factor was that oxygen deprivation from the twisted umbilical cord. From that point on, the government monitored him constantly. Chanda and her family helped, and between us we strived to create a suitable environment for him.

Little League baseball didn't help his concentration; he'd sit on second base with his back to the batter and play in the sand. Bonk! Watch out for that grounder. Chanda came to all the games in all the sports. In the fall, we enrolled James in the special-needs school at North Oakview Elementary, within the gravitational pull of adjacent Northview High School, a colossus of academia, sports and cute cheerleaders. I drove him to and from every day for three years. I was involved with the class, monitored events and tutored. We got him into Rocket football; their home field was big-time Northview Wildcats Stadium. The coaches took a liking to him, and he played well in a league of tough farm kids from rural schools like Cedar Springs, Sparta, Ionia, Greenville and Caledonia. We also tangled with city slickers North Park, East Grand Rapids, and our arch rival Rockford. One year, I coached James' track team. For James, the best part of sports was the end of the season and the obligatory pizza party and trophies. He had a trophy case to rival his hero, Randy Moss.

Flea moved into a 1920s Hollywood Hill castle. Former occupants included Bob Dylan, Jim Morrison and Andy Warhol. Anthony was getting antsy too; fans were staking out his Hollyridge home. Odd-ball loonies themselves and no different than the day they met at Fairfax, Anthony and Flea were still a couple crazy kids. They scared the pants off Claudia Schiffer when the three of them were on stage at the 1996 MTV Video Awards, and Flea did an impromptu striptease. *Sassy* magazine put Anthony on the top list of flirts, along with Mark Walberg and George Clooney. He was also singled out as one of the sexiest vegetarians. *Bass Player* named Flea best in the world, again. *Goldmine* the collectors' record magazine, and writer Steve Roeser propitiously predicted they'd join the ranks of The Doors, Love, Byrds, Buffalo Springfield, and The Beach Boys and be inducted into the Rock & Roll Hall of Fame by 2010. And we hadn't even made *Californication, By The Way* or *Stadium Arcadium*. We wouldn't get enough votes in 2011, but here in the 90s the fan club was busting at the seams. We were the Palace Guard, the Red Army, the first line of defense, and I was the commander in chief.

Our sacrosanct family Christmas rolled around again. We had our traditional holiday dinner at Tuscan Express and Anthony dropped a hotplate bomb of pasta on me. He had spoken with the Miramax bros., Bob and Harvey Weinstein, who were fascinated by his tales of growing up with the "The Lord of the Sunset Strip." After being told I was a writer, they suggested I write them a screenplay of our era. At the time, Miramax had already produced *The Crying Game, The Piano, Pulp Fiction, The Crow, Reservoir Dogs, Trainspotting* and *The English Patient*. It was time to dust off the platform shoes, and the memories. I collected my wits and old appointment books and poked around a subject I knew a bit about. I was soon to learn it would be quite a task.

Chapter 57: Class of 1997

No doubt I was dating some of them. It had been forty years since my high school class of '57 and the remnants of our motley Creston crew put on a big class reunion. Weaver happened to be in town and we crashed the party at a country club on the west side. Old classmates thought Weaver was me, and that I was Anthony.

The real Anthony was on the other side of the world, traveling across the ancient and eclectic country of India, mingling with its one billion people and their languages, religions and philosophies. Traveling anonymously, he spent time at a tiger sanctuary, slept on beaches and house boats, took a 26-hour train ride north along the Bay of Bengal, volunteered in a poor tribal area and met with a Deity. The Dalai Lama grasped Anthony's hand and would not let go when they took a walk together. Anthony gave me a personal account of his trip for the fan club. I pieced together our phone calls and his notes and published it in our magazine. Personal as his journey was, he shared it with the fans.

In Los Angeles, Stephen Dorff threw Anthony a welcome home from India party. I flew out for the gala affair and the Miramax project. James and Paul Erickson came too and made friends with Jay Leno at the Big Boy and went to *The Tonight Show*. Anthony and I went to the party, well stacked with his rat-pack pals, Sex Pistol Steve Jones, Guy-O, Rick Rubin and Black Crowes producer George Drakoulias. Adam Sandler was there. Hillarious David Arquette was the life of the party. Ben Stiller, by comparison, was almost shy. I didn't have any trouble getting Traci Lords to open up. Interim RHCP manager Bo Gardner came; Lindy had retired. Video director Stephane Sednaoui of *Give it Away* fame showed up. Zoe Cassavettes and Lukas Haas were there. The next day, we joined Dorff and Lukas when Anthony, James and I went to visit the set of *Blade* with Wesley Snipe. Stephen Dorff had a lead role. We watched the controversial vampire nightclub scene that sprayed blood out of ceiling fire sprinklers and drenched the ecstatic dancers. It scared the living daylights out of James. Like the crew, we had to wear protective gear to keep from being splattered with blood.

While Weaver and I were brainstorming our best 70s memories for Miramax, James and Paul got the V.I.P treatment at *Dr. Quinn, Medicine Woman* at the Paramount Ranch and had lunch with Jane Seymour and guest star John Schneider. David and I hunkered down at a Mexican restaurant in Burbank and warmed up with a few Coronas. There were a half dozen of us, experts of our exploits. This was not uncommon; it was almost mandatory that every time we got together we reminisced about the good old days. The words started flying; we were on a roll, one hilarious or treacherous anecdote after another. This would be the quintessential account. We called on more fuel and ordered up Golden Cadillacs, the potent margaritas with Galliano. Now we were invincible; we were speed dialing ideas so Oscar worthy we had a hit movie before we even started. Our tales recalled, we closed out the daylong session with one minor regret. We had forgotten to bring a recorder, and the ideas had come too fast to write them down. The next day, we woke up to king-size hangovers and fuzzy blankety-blank recollections. I was so upset I dropped the whole project.

One Hot Minute finally caught up with its name as sales finally slumped. Concerts felt the heat when Chad crashed his Harley on Sunset and broke his shoulder. Then Anthony was injured in a motorcycle accident that shattered his right hand and wrist when an idiot pulled a U-turn in front of him on a side street, south of Melrose. Shows in Alaska, Hawaii and the Orient were rescheduled. The band did fulfill their obligation to headline the Fuji Rock Festival in Japan, but the concert was battered by a typhoon. Again there was speculation the band was breaking up. On top of Chad and Anthony's accidents, Dave wasn't the perfect fit we'd hoped for, and Flea had personal problems that kept him off the road. It was one of the darkest hours since Hillel had died.

Anthony came home that summer with his paw in a giant metal-and-foam rubber-cube contraption right out of Mel Brooks' *Young Frankenstein*. I had been working on a young lady who worked the drive-through window at my bank. Her name was Christine and she was the cat's meow. I had ingratiated myself with her family, and she had a brother the same age as James; they shot billiards in her basement. I couldn't resist introducing Anthony to her, and they went off into the romantic sunset. Out from behind the 8 ball, I went out and bought a full-size pool table for James, and he got even better. My six-year-old pool shark could beat most adults.

I had a repository of trim to fall back on and went to plan Juanita, aka Miss Curvacious, who sent erotic photos of herself. Her friend Edy, the sensitive one, sent me herbal healthy potions and photos of herself in the lab. They were from Australia and rather brilliant indeed. And in person, I found another fresh face named Alison. She was Jen Idema's best friend, which certainly complicated matters, and even more so when Anthony caught the same crush. Peggy, Jen, Alison, Anthony and I all went to Gipper's, the bar where Robert Chase beat me to his wife. Anthony and I were sitting next to each other across the table from Alison and both of our cupidities were working overtime. Anthony had a minor dalliance with Alison at Peggy's house, which caused a ruckus that disqualified him in the future. Plus I was the home team. There were no restraints on me, and I spent bountiful time wooing her. We had a relationship that bounced around Lowell from her dad's house to her mom's house to the bank she worked for and eventually to my house and her own apartment when she got older.

My webmaster Jon Wade and I were invited to Dragon*Con '97 in Atlanta to promote our new RHCP comic book. It was an annual convention of sci-fi, comics, art, crafts, seminars, live acts and parties. Our host was Jon Waterhouse, an avid fan-club member and music publisher. In addition to our Rockinfreakapotamus spot, I had a second booth in the autograph exhibit hall and signed photos for diehard fans of Walter Baylor, Eddie Four Eyes, Alby the Cruel, Torch, Sugar, Jazz, Swifty and Slime and all my Weasels. In the Grand Assembly, they held a major seminar. *Panelists discuss the important role that music has had on many different comic titles, especially Rock 'n' Roll Comics. From Blackie Dammett and the Red Hot Chili Peppers to Gwar and everything between, our panel of experts brings us up to date.* Of course, I got lathered up with sexy Slymestra Hymen from Gwar while I was at it. We polished off the week with a big party at the Hard Rock Café, where I gave a speech and donated Chili Peppers paraphernalia for their walls.

Back in the pack with the wolves, fan-club members were lining up to visit. Rachel Bayne was a vivacious hair's-on-fire from New York who talked her way over. Jonny Wade and I went to pick her up at the airport. Jon greeted her with a wolf whistle, but I reserved judgment. She was amorous, but as Head Honcho and Chief Potentate, I felt an obligation to be fan-club celibate. For ethical reasons, I never had sex with any members, but I curried friendships with Rockinfreaks from all over the world. With a name like Tami Trueblood, a perfect James-size daughter Timi and credible attributes, I almost succumbed. As it was, we did share love. She lived in Southern California, had her own business and a beautiful home. She was a well-educated knockout and built like a Lockheed F-22. She was an animal-rescue saint and a humanitarian. Timi was a little doll with big smarts for James' delight. They made several trips to see us, but I got sidetracked. Maybe it was Alison, or Nellie or Chanda. Or was it that I refused to fall into any serious relationship?

The wolves were a big attraction for everybody. They were stars in their own right and had their photos in the fan club magazine. They had inspired Tami Trueblood to save California wolves. Secure in their animal preserve, Jim and Brenda Pearson by now had fifty wolves and wolf hybrids. All rescues. On this special occasion though, Brenda bred pure wolves from Minnesota and offered me the pick of the litter. I couldn't decide so I bought three, the alpha male Handsome Devil, a buckskin brother Cowboy and a female sister Scarlet Fever. James and I bottle fed them every four hours and set an alarm for the middle of the night. We built a pen right in the kitchen for when they slept and for when they weren't wandering around the house getting into trouble. Anthony paid to construct a super-max pen on the Secluded Lake property as they outgrew the house. They were loveable and friendly as cocker spaniels, but their sharp claws and uncanny strength made them better suited for the great outdoors. Our elaborate enclosure had a ten-foot-high fence surrounding an acre of undulating terrain. I built a wolf cabin under a stand of trees, with steps to a treetop roof for them to take their "high ground." The enclosure even looked cool; the heavy-duty cyclone fence was clad in black vinyl. The preserve had four gates and one led directly into our downstairs. Howlin' Wolf still slept in my bedroom and spent his time lounging around the house or running free in the yard. Our menagerie continued with Adolf, Scrappy, Bear and our border collies Dixie, Buddy and Badge. Adolf celebrated his 10th birthday on September 13th.

In September, we had planned a fan-club convention in Las Vegas to coincide with the RHCP concert at the Aladdin Hotel Theatre. Like some of the *One Hot Minute* concert cancellations, the Aladdin literally bit the dust. The Aladdin closed down in November and the entire resort was imploded in April 1998. Most of the fans stayed home and got refunds, but a hardcore cadre of about 25 came anyway. James got kicked out of the casino for gambling. Brett went to strip clubs and the dancers lined up to get *his* number. Blackie's angels, Katie de Rogatis, Charlotte, Kathleen, Melanie and three lady fans from Japan converged on me. We would do a more successful Las Vegas convention at the Hard Rock Hotel when the band played on New Year's Eve in 2002. But right now things looked dire. Anthony wrote a letter to the fan club that began "THAT'S NOT ALL FOLKS" and continued:

"Some days you go ahead and get up a good head of steam, only to go off the rails a day later. Other days you can be feeling clearly tapped into the magic that we are all born with, only to end up losing your marbles in the middle of an invisible gorilla stampede. Change is the only thing that you really can count on. This is the story of life. It's also the story of my band, our band, everybody's band. When we started playing music together as the Red Hot Chili Peppers, almost 15 years ago, we were too new to have anything to look back at. Now that we have been around, I can look back at the pickleapotamus pattern we have lived through. Hell and heart attack. Low and behold cockamamie calamities abound. We cancel this and cancel that and fly around like a wounded bat. Round and round the Red Hots go, where we stop nobody knows. I can tell you this; music is infinite. So is love. Stay tuned for the next episode of love and music with the Red Hot Chili Peppers. I miss you all. Anthony."

The Aladdin and Navarro era weren't the only enterprises to implode. Al Bregante's fortune and fame dwindled away along the black tar brick road to drugs and disaster. He lost his piece of the Orbit and then his flagship, the HMS Reptile. The place was a wreck. Nobody came anymore. Not even the hardcore apples. In its glory days the Reptile had offered 25 brands of beer displayed on a long shelf behind the bar. The final night there were only two bottles on the shelf, a Budweiser and Bud Light and that wasn't just the brands left; those were the last two beers period. There was an inch of water on the floor and a rusty steel barrel on the dance floor, burning scrap wood to heat the place since the power had been shut off. I cried at the funeral.

After serving five of his nine-year sentence at the Federal Corrections Institute in West Virginia, Alan Bashara was released for good behavior and moved into a halfway house in Grand Rapids. I picked him up at the bus station and got him some civilian clothes at Montgomery Ward's before we presented him to the lockup. He'd be ensconced there for four months, but I could visit whenever I wanted. The Rug was back! About that time, Candy and Dan were finally released from the Denver jail, and they returned to Grand Rapids. They hunkered down in a low-rent apartment house on the west side. Every time we went to visit, Candy was asleep or staggering around in a daze. They professed to rehab and family-hab and blab-hab. I wasn't buying it and kept my eye on James.

Chapter 58: Kidnapped

Chanda's tall, tantalizing shadow put the other girls in an eon eclipse. The astronomer in me was well aware. I signed James up for swimming lessons at the Westside YMCA. He clung to the gutter and refused to delve into the deep. Sweetie that she was, Chanda volunteered to join me at the lessons and helped to coax him into the pool. We finally got him wet behind the ears but not without a lot of whining. Normally, she'd drop by for a few minutes and then leave for her own secret world I wished so much to be a part of. On a day we made excellent progress and James actually jumped into the deep water, I suggested a celebratory dinner and got up the courage to invite Chanda. She not only accepted but seemed quite anxious to join us.

We went to a nearby Mexican restaurant, had a good time and parted reluctantly. Was I imagining this or was Chanda empowering me? I was emboldened and asked her out again, and again. Her answers were always yes. She invited me to her tight-knit friend's parties. I got to know her peers, especially the guys who preened and wagged their bright red feathers to win her attention. I saw that didn't work so I played it cool. I decisively debated one of her young Republican suitors and caught her smile out of the corner of my eye. Perhaps Chanda's secret agenda was to convert me to her Christ. If so, I was willing to give it a try. That's how close I was to falling in love with her. I went dutifully, but still had to work at not falling asleep or hollering back at the minister's proselytizing. Not unlike my heathen behavior at Eileen's churches when I was a child. I argued for more diversity, and we started dropping in on black Baptist churches in the hood. We made a holy-water splash when we entered. The music was better and so was the vibe. Chanda began to spend more and more time at Secluded Lake. It was spring and romance was in the air. We were at the friendly hugging hello or goodbye stage, and one time I snuck in a little kiss on her neck. Sometime later, she admitted that she saw stars and lost her breath for a minute.

MTV had been successful with a Mother's Day show in May that featured rock star's mothers. Now it was almost Father's Day and they were about to tape a similar five-episode show called *Twelve Angry Fathers* to air over the course of a week. MTV invited me and eleven other father figures to the party. I asked Chanda if she'd take care of James while I was in New York and she agreed. I especially warned her to be careful with cagey Candy and demented Dan. Jon Wade said he'd drop by often to monitor my home and animals and assist Chanda and Sherry. MTV executive Joanna Bomberg arranged everything and I flew to NYC. A town car whisked me to the Sheraton Towers a few blocks from MTV's studios on Broadway. My call was at 8 a.m. The schedule was to do five episodes with wardrobe changes and hopefully, a wrap. The premise was judging a new batch of videos in the MTV rotation and some old favorites. And bring lots of baby pictures!

The twelve father figures were Big Daddy Kane; Brandy's father Willie Norwood; Pauley Shore's father, Catskills comedian Sammy Shore who entertained us non-stop; MTV gadfly Matt Pinfield's father George; Cherry Poppin' Daddies' Steve and Dustin; a few others I didn't recognize and a couple fathers they pulled out of the mosh pit in Times

Square; and Father John, a curmudgeon Catholic priest. The hostess of the show was popular MTV personality Ananda Lewis and her father, Stanley, was also on the panel. We spent the whole day reviewing videos, usually in relative consensus. Not surprising was the rancor over Rammstein's "Du hast;" James had loved the song, but the Sammy Shore lobby prevailed. Surprising was a singular bad reaction to Red Hot Chili Peppers' iconic "Give it Away." Father John had already made condescending comments on the smiling but blasphemes red devil T-shirt I wore for episode #3; but when he, and he alone, cast a big no for "Give it Away," the rest of us were up in Rammstein armbands. Father John said what the Chili Peppers were *giving away* was their "self-respect and dignity." We crucified him with sneers and cold shoulder isolation. Ananda Lewis tossed me a softball and asked if Anthony inherited his wild side from his father. Keeping it absurd, I replied that he got it from his mother who was in and out of mental institutions. It's a wrap! Just like the old days. They did a private interview with me after everybody left, and when we finished, the producer asked if I was going on to the big gig in Washington, D.C.

I hadn't planned to, but it so happened this weekend John Frusciante was rejoining the band. It had been six years already. Dave had fallen out of grace, or maybe we had. It had been an awkward year for the band. Our new reformed lineup did a couple unannounced warm-up shows at small venues in Hollywood. Now they were headed to D.C. for the annual Beastie Boys' Tibetan Freedom concert. We had donated our services to the previous ones, SF in '96 and NYC in '97. This year it was at Robert F. Kennedy Memorial Stadium, with a two-day lineup of the Beasties, Peppers, Radiohead, Beck, Pearl Jam, Dave Matthews, R.E.M. and scads more; plus human-rights advocates Xiao Qiang, Palden Gyatso and Wei Jingsheng speaking on behalf of the cause; 120,000 fans; and MTV covering the whole spectacle. The *Twelve Angry Fathers* producer told me I should definitely go too, and insisted they'd cover the expenses and arrange everything.

That night, NYC fan-club members threw me a party at the Hard Rock Café, arranged by the ever-popular Rachel Bayne. After the Hard Rock, we hit some other clubs, but I had an early flight. There were half a dozen female fans maneuvering to spend the night with me, but I was illusive. I tried to leave but they kept catching my coattails. Finally Rachel shooed them away and said she'd walk me to my hotel. She was the fox and the Sheraton was the hen house. In the lobby, I said bye bye, but she invented excuses and came up to use my hotel-room phone. Once in, she wouldn't leave and tried to crawl under the covers. My love was tough and I made her leave. The next day, I was in D.C. Anthony got me a room at the Ritz Carlton with the band. The vibe and John were back, but it was a delicate situation. He was fragile, on the edge and almost childlike. Anthony was seriously concerned. Be cool. Avoid any confrontation. In fact, just stay clear of John Frusciante.

The Beastie Boys Bonanza was Saturday and Sunday, but the band was doing one more warm up, a Friday night concert at the venerable 9:30 Club. Dylan, Petty, Ramones, Radiohead, The Go-Go's, Police and Fugazi were a few who had performed there. A crazed sold-out crowd packed the place. Everything was perfect. John was amiable. I ran into several Rockinfreaks on my run through the crowd. The band was tearing it up, and the mob was jubilant. A crew member nabbed me, and said I had an important phone call in the control room. It was Chanda. James had been kidnapped. I was stunned. It was so noisy I could hardly hear what Chanda was saying, but I got the gist. Candy and Dan asked if they could take James to a "church family rehab" session, and they never came back. I got the first plane available to GR, which was the next morning. I missed the Tibetan Freedom Festival and the monsoon rains and the lightning that killed one of the spectators. RHCP's Saturday slot came during the worst of the storm and was cancelled. Sunday, headlining Pearl Jam was rocking the stadium in the grand finale, and in a magnanimous gesture, Eddie Vedder cut their set short and allowed RHCP to finish off the concert.

I arrived at Secluded Lake to find a fleet of sheriff's cars in the driveway. According to the report, Dan had stolen his father's pickup truck and the three of them had vaporized into thin air. Bless-her-heart Chanda had thought it was a positive step for Candy to be seeking help. That was only part of it; the grifters had convinced her to cash a bad check for Candy at Chanda's bank, while Dan stayed at my house. He went through my papers, found a credit-card receipt and charged $800 on my card to the order of Dan Bowler via Western Union. Jon Wade had come by too and while he spoke with Dan, Candy rifled Jon's car and stole his checkbook. There was an All Points Bulletin out for the three of them. Guilt ridden, Chanda and I tracked down dead-end leads and got our hands dirty in some nasty neighborhoods. James was having the time of his life: Bonnie and Clyde and Jesse James Forsyth.

For two weeks, we canvassed for the stolen pickup. Finally, the police found it in an abandoned building near the Greyhound Station. Now it was a nationwide APB. They had taken the bus to Detroit, where Candy and Dan shunted about the desolate cityscape looking for drugs with their newfound cash, in and out of opium dens, James in tow. They held up in cheap motels and then caught another bus to Mississippi where Candy's mother and Granny lived now. Biloxi, like Deadwood and Denver, had legalized gambling. Private Black eye and the sheriff's department finally figured it out. The cops flew down, raided grannie's, arrested the James Gang and notified me I should come and get James. I thought they'd fly him back, but evidently it was my responsibility. I cranked up the Bronco for an 1,800 mile roundtrip.

Chanda was relieved to be off the hook now that James was safe. Well, maybe. He was in a hybrid childcare and juvenile delinquent facility which we'd later discover was closed down for excessive abuse. It was a baby Abu Ghraib. I asked Chanda if she'd like to drive down with me and she jumped at the opportunity. We took care of loose ends, packed light, grabbed Adolf and hit the road. Her father wasn't thrilled, but her mother Char gave us the OK. My heart was quite a flutter with Chanda in the co-pilot seat on such a long trip. We took turns driving and arrived in Biloxi the next day. I considered stopping by grandma's house, but from what I'd heard they all hated me now. I had legal custody of James, and Candy was a drug addict; I stood on my rights. We went to the naughty boy's facility. He came busting out of the cages full of Jimmy Cagney anger and shooting from the hip. "I'm a cop killer," he roared. "They're all dirty rats."

We packed him up and headed north. For the first couple hours, he was inconsolable. It took a stop at a Dairy Queen to get him to smile, and by the time we pulled over for the evening at a motel he was his old self again. It was hot and humid. We jumped into the pool and fought a welterweight water match, boys against the girl. We shared a room with two twin beds. James and I were in one and Chanda in the other. James couldn't sleep and asked Chanda to get in our bed too. I almost fell out of the bed when she agreed and crawled in with us. Everything I had ever dreamed of was coming true. I saw it in her smiles and green-eyed looks that made me blush. The rest of the trip became an enchanting adventure. We stopped at every Confederate roadside amusement, shopped at antique stores and fresh-fruit stands and bought funny hats and gilded gifts for the northerners back home. In Kentucky, we explored Mammoth Cave National park and descended deep into the cool caverns where hugs kept us warm. We were a family.

In Michigan, we put an exhausted James to bed, and Chanda and I collapsed on my bed. We snuggled up. We snuggled up for a year. Chanda virtually moved in with us. She gave up her law-school dreams and took a job as a high-school teacher; I made her breakfast and packed her lunch. James and I would drive across town to her school just to smudge a clean, cute note on her dirty car windows. Her dad provided their Lincoln. In the winter, I'd get up early, warm up the car, scrape the ice off the windshield and kiss her goodbye. She took acting lessons at the Civic and wowed us with her performance as Martha in *Who's Afraid of Virginia Woolf*. My stepmother Eileen came up for a Van Bree family reunion at a farm not far from Chanda's old stomping grounds in Morley, and the two titans of Jehovah bonded. I wrote a letter to Chanda's father that I was behaving myself, and I was. She'd bathe in our big tub and ask me to wash her back, but we played chaste. It was her religion and my affliction.

She bought a new video camera to capture James' milestones and was front and center at the parent teacher conferences, directing his birthday parties and taking him to church. We threw tickled-pink parties at Secluded Lake and entertained some bawdy Irish fans who came and stayed for a few days. We sent James to Camp Manitou-Lin and visited him when appropriate; he always wanted us to smuggle him out. While he was at camp, I stood in and accompanied Chanda to church at the god awful Assembly of What's His Name. The humungous arena was packed with lemmings being led to the slaughter. The minister was ranting about the power of the holy spirit, my old nemesis I'd backed into a corner as a 6th grader. The minister's sermon was reaching a crescendo; he had the place in a tizzy. Chanda was jumping around like the Fab Four had just stepped out from behind the Ed Sullivan Theatre curtain. The charlatan supplicated the cowered to feel the spirit and get their butt down to the pulpit for a meet and greet with the Holy Spirit. Chanda grabbed me by the arm and pulled me toward the aisle. She was certain I was feeling what she was. For a moment, I balanced the options; patronize her and live happily ever after, or be true. Truth transcends religion and even love. I couldn't lie; I told her no. She sprang out of the pew and ran toward the pulpit. When she returned she was flush with fresh pink blood under her white skin. She had her blissful revelation. I had denial. We had a paradox.

Candy and Dan were sentenced to a year in the Kent County Jail. They owed $3,000 in restitution but never repaid it. In jail, Candy met another criminal by the most-wanted-poster name of Dean Manos. His rough and tumble life had left him with an asymmetrical cubist face and a fierce temper. They got married as soon as they were released and moved in with his mother. For a while it flourished, but Candy's story followed the same old scenario of drugs, deceit and an added twist, armed robbery. And then she was back in the county jail.

Although Chanda was immaculate as a saint, her friends played the local scene and we went to a fashion show at the Orbit. Chanda had been a teen model and was still competitive. We dallied in the VIP area and when a skinny young model stepped out onto the runway I perked up and paid attention. Chanda and I knew the promoters and invited everybody back to our house. Chanda circulated the party as the reigning queen, but I kept watching the princess. Finally, I cornered her. She was Patty Kersjes and she was only in high school, but it was my high school, Creston. She had kittens that needed a home and asked me to take one. She laid on the charm and I would have agreed to anything. She gave me her address and phone number. After everybody left, Chanda called me out on young Patty. Her green eyes were jealous.

In LA, the revitalized band was writing their masterpiece, and Anthony had a new crush of his own. Flea took Clara to see The Spice Girls at the Forum and they brought Anthony along. He met Sporty Spice Mel C backstage and something akin to lust or love bloomed. MTV had a new black–and-white exploitive documentary series called *Biorhythm* that honed in on controversial personalities like Tupac Shakur; Madonna; Mike Tyson; Marilyn Manson; Jim Carrey; Steven Tyler; Martin Luther King, Jr.; Michael Jackson and Anthony Kiedis. It had no dialogue whatsoever, only visual images and a few staccato-typed transcripts at the bottom of the screen. In Anthony's episode, I was a silent conspicuous co-star, especially when they targeted his drug problems and my image was superimposed over the documentary like some omnipotent rogue with a bag of dirty tricks.

In the fresh Technicolor summer of Michigan, James and I kept our promise and took two Patty cats, Rat the Cat and Jet. Unfixed, that ultimately led to 18 more kittens. Patty directed the Creston senior play *Barefoot in the Park* and asked me to assist. Again I volunteered. Patty was outrageously pretty and always attached to a boyfriend. I bided my time and enjoyed our friendship.

Swinging like Sinatra

Chapter 59: Love Derailed and Heart Impaled

We didn't party like it was 1999. New Year's Eve was less than exhilarating as I sat at a table with Chanda and her girl clique in a tragically plastic nightclub. We had run out of conversation and I didn't dance. *The Sopranos* debuted. It was better than sex. Chanda's super-close sister Sherry and her friends rented an apartment on Lookout Hill, and it became the new party central. Sherry hadn't appreciated the way I monopolized her sister and welcomed her back into the Steel Magnolias. Chanda was unconditionally committed to James' life, but ours got flexible. Things opened up. I was chosen as a judge for a beauty pageant and exploited the opportunity. I had a summit meeting with Floyd Mayweather on the notoriety of Grand Rapids' favorite sons: Anthony versus Pretty Boy Floyd. Split decision.

My captain computer, Jon Wade, had connected in cyberspace with Terry Wells who I'd met at the UK Wembley concert two years earlier, and the webmaster wizards co-conspired on some fan-club projects. Jon had gone big time; he moved to Washington D.C. and created a half-dozen websites for the U.S. government-backed Fannie Mae and Freddie Mac corporations that owned or guaranteed half of America's multi-trillion dollar mortgage market. To what extent Jonny was responsible for the economy's meltdown ten years later, let's not get into that. With the band's approval, Terry became the new webmaster of redhotchilipeppers.com.

Chanda and Sherry went to Los Angeles for a while. Disparaged, I couldn't resist flirting with a wet-behind-the-vagina Lolita named Jessica Raymond, who smiled at me from behind the counter of an Arby's on Alpine. Her eyes were so blue I couldn't help but acknowledge them, despite the manager's insistence I mind my own business. I made it my business. She had a boyfriend which was no surprise, but I perfunctorily found myself in her home without much supervision from the pretty mother, Georgia. With Chanda out of town I hired Jessica to babysit James. And I babysat her.

On April 21, the day after the Columbine massacre, Marilyn Manson played Van Andel Arena. Eight-year-old anti-hero James requested tickets in advance and I obliged. In reaction to the Gothic killings, there was a nationwide groundswell against the queen of the macabre, Marilyn Manson his herself. We arrived downtown to find the arena surrounded by angry protestors, mostly religious zealots waving their bibles and hastily-created placards. They attempted to block our entry, shouted Christian obscenities like "go to heck" and "darn you" and threw fake blood at us, which was cool with me as I had shown up in full Manson gear. The concert was sold out and mildly interesting. Manson gave an impassioned speech about the massacre in Colorado. James had bragging rights at school the next day. Fortunately, Chanda was still in LA. My DJ friend Steve Aldridge had a band named Dry, and we arranged for James to sing with them at the Eastown Fair, an annual music festival that closed the streets and erected a big stage in front of the Intersection. The singer wasn't keen on it, but James rocked the street in his Ricky Ricardo red ruffled unbuttoned shirt while the really young girlies swooned.

MTV Networks turned to me again for their *VH1 Story Behind the Music: Red Hot Chili Peppers*. I dug out the photos, the history and the home movies. A month later, it was for the show *MTV's FANatic*. Ingrid Casares' Bar Room in Miami Beach was the hottest club since Studio 54; Anthony and his pals Ben Stiller and Chris Rock were dancing front and center in the media coverage, but Anthony's flowing locks were having their last fling. I had been to lunch with his crew at the Beverly Hills Saks, and Anthony asked when I was going to cut my now-long-again hair. Anthony hadn't cut his for twenty years and always whipped it into frenzy at every concert. It was his trademark. I told him I was thinking about it, and I did. Months later Anthony sent me photo coverage of his actual haircut, the locks themselves in a bag and a note. "Pappa San—in the late 60s, early 70s, it was long. In the mid and late-70s it went short. In the early 80s it began to grow. All through the late 80s and most of the 90s it was long, long, long. And now once again…like father like son. Love AK." His *Californication* tour was all in short bleached-blond hair.

Chicago called; Robert Chase's radio station was doing their annual music festival, Q101 JAMBOREE '99. We topped the bill, followed by Offspring, Hole, Blondie and a bunch more. Robert swung his weight and set me up royally. At the top of his game, he followed iconic DJ Mancow's morning show with his own midday show that throttled the ratings. Chanda and Sherry were returning from LA and stopped in Chicago for the concert. My girl was coolly aloof. I got more attention from Courtney Love. She traipsed out on the side stage to watch our set, snuggled up to me and purred, "You're the Dad!" "You're the Mom," I alluded, referring to her son with Kurt. After a pause, she tried again and asked if I had forgotten our partying days in Hollywood. Sorry, I was preoccupied by Chanda's newest revelation: she was about to vacation in Europe with Sherry.

Her former modeling agent set up interviews in Paris and Milan. Chanda wasn't interested but filed it away with the Alpine skiing, Greek Islands and Paris nightclubs. In Milan, she stopped by an agency, and they wouldn't let her go. Sherry came home, but Chanda stayed and became the next big thing on the runway. She worked Europe and led a charmed life. Chanda and I emailed true love letters for six months and then the inevitable. A communiqué notified me she would be there indefinitely. It wouldn't be fair to make me wait. Her manner was gentle and sincere, but it hurt like a broken heart. I wrote back. "I wanted to have your baby - Instead I have your maybe - The used to be - We'll never see - Afraid your endless Odyssey - Will be the end of me - The death of me – Gethsemane" I named my black kitten, Chanda's heart.

I flew to D.C. to meet with Jon Wade for the HFStival at Ravens Stadium. I met Anthony's new girlfriend Yohanna. Anthony gave me the unreleased *Californication* disc, and Jon and I went nuts. We had fan-club shindigs at the Baltimore Sheraton and on the stadium floor. The concert for 80,000 fans was supported by another sterling lineup. Jon and I needed a toke before the main event but security was tight. We found a sanctuary in Moby's green room. On stage, "Parallel Universe" propelled us into euphoria. Venetian blinds of Led Zeppelin. *Californication* would go on to sell 15 million worldwide and the tour would make a fortune. The press was on their hands and knees.

Woodstock '99. Ho-hum. Yawn. Headlining again. Two weeks later, the band played a free MTV special concert in Moscow's Red Square before a quarter-million crazed Russians. Soviet fan-club members emailed me that after the show rowdy crowds spent the night singing RHCP songs in the streets and subways. Anthony came home wearing a MOCKBA (Moscow) T-shirt and had one for me too.

Adolf departed horrifically when Scrappy mauled him in a deadly brawl. They'd been contentious forever. We had been together, inseparable since the pet-store window in West Hollywood. His love was unconditional. His valor was typically terrier. His pedigree always made me smile; Little Herbie, Sammy Wonderful, Little Girl Joy, Captain Tubbs, Spanky, Speck-O-Treasure, Tiny Midge Murphy and Sweet Pea. He was my partner for 12 years, my best dog friend ever. I buried him with honors under a boulder on the hill, overlooking the lake. I created an art-piece tribute of catholic crosses and barbed wire to mark his tangible legacy. The one in my heart will live forever. Adolf.

In the fall, James struggled in school but blossomed on the gridiron. Chanda visited frequently and went to his games. Everything was cool; we had always struggled with our bittersweet alliance, but somehow it persevered. We took James to Ken-O-Sha Center for psychiatric consultation. He was fearful of bullies and worried about his mom's drug addiction and her imminent death. He told the psychiatrist there had always been a destructive evil horror controlling his life, and there was nothing he could do about it. He described the destructive power as, "An old man who is very tall with sharp teeth and smoke coming out of his ears. He is so powerful that he can knock the President's home down." Was there a netherworld connection to John Forsyth who was tall and known to be violent? What about Candy's idiot boyfriends? James started visiting his Forsyth grandmother in Santa Cruz and eventually faced showdowns with his father in Reno. On our home turf, James and I had an epic chocolate-pudding fight; we were covered from head to toe. He wanted a Chihuahua and we got Dirt. He came from a tough Mexican hood and had a skinny pugnacious pedigree. "Dirt" was a tune on *Californication*. Billboard's Modern Rock chart had our first single "Scar Tissue" at #1 for 16 straight weeks, breaking the all-time record.

Millions had seen them this year, but now they were doing an intimate close up and personal K-ROCK radio station party for only 500 lucky ticket holders on the top floor of the World Trade Center. Snagging precious ducats was the talk of the metropolis. Riot squads were on high alert. I had so many east coast date proposals I went into seclusion with the wolves, but after considering the evidence I settled on a Pulitzer Nobel Powerball MVP Homecoming Queen. She was bursting with personality, had a N.J. State Police mother and was as drop-dead gorgeous as is legal in Jersey. She was Jessica Tabor. Mikie Weed arranged a fan-club party at Jeremy's restaurant close to the Twin Towers. He also provided room and board for Jonny Wade and James and I at his home in Amityville. His flag waved Family, Surfing and Computers Semper Fidelis. He once drove all the way to Michigan to install a computer for me.

Jessica's mother rented us a limousine for the weekend. I showed James the Dakota. We tread on St. Marks and loitered in Times Square. Anthony and Yohanna were staying at the Mercer Hotel in Soho and we dropped by. Anthony mentioned there was a Jean-Michel Basquiat art show at the Tony Shafrazi Gallery on Wooster and that John Frusciante was heading over there. I was interested in both so we went. There were a dozen of Basquiat's side-of-a-barn large paintings, and they were priced a million bucks and up. Spectacular waves of black and orange and lipstick red and Niagara blue washed over the breathless handful of patrons. As usual, I was chronicling for the fan club with personal photos. What could be better than a picture of John Frusciante, a painter himself, in front of a Basquiat masterpiece? The curator gave permission. John, still shy and barely speaking, waved his head with a firm negative. I had just shot Anthony and Yohanna half–naked, playing under their covers so this shouldn't be so difficult. With a scowl he relented and stood in front of the nearest painting. Click! Before the click had even resonated, John ran out of the gallery and disappeared into the colors of Soho.

You couldn't believe how substantial those Trade Center monoliths were until you got lost at the wrong building and on the wrong side. It was cold in late October, and it took an eon to circumnavigate just one of the buildings. Each had the girth of a Merchandise Mart but scraped stars with its pinnacle. My fan-club crew was following Wrong Way Blackie Corrigan, but eventually we got to the correct entrance, which was protected by extraordinary security. The Twin Towers had already been bombed once in 1993. I had an argument with the guards who tried to take my camera, and I ended up in the World Trade Center Police Station. Jessica and James tagged along. I persevered. The band played on a tiny stage the size of the Rhythm Lounge. A magnificent 107-stories high, I stood by a window and gazed all the way to Pennsylvania. After the show, Jessica drove back to N.J., and James and I went to Brooklyn with Katie De Rogatis and friends. By snowfall Jessica flew into GR.

Sam Cummings was the genuine article, the real Mc Coy and the cat's pajamas. He was an entrepreneurial preservationist, a financial wizard, city builder, crime buster, risk taker, record breaker and a booty shaker. He burnished that celebrity when he purchased the biggest and most expensive house in town, the Brookby estate, saving it from the wrecking ball or a condo conversion. The Gatsby-era mansion was a fiefdom that touted a gatekeeper's house, gardener's house, chauffeur's house and a twelve-stall garage perfect for Sam Cummings' collection of racing cars and luxury automobiles. It was on the National Register of Historic Places. With Scott Gravengood's old gang long gone, I'd lost touch with Sam over the years. Now he'd up and married one of Gravy's ex-girlfriends, a slightly dippy Barbie blonde from Grand Haven, Meagan Klempt. She had a sunny Judy Holliday disposition and a Republican elephant tattooed on her ankle. She served up parties and extravagant dinners that never stopped.

I was at a charity event in the Art Museum. Alan Bashara managed the band Nectar, which was performing, and the drinks were free. Belle of the ball Meagan Cummings came over, introduced us to each other and invited me into her sacred circle. I left with them that night and settled into an uneasy high life. These were the big shooters in GR: real estate magnates and pro-sports franchise owners, corporate CEOs with half-million-dollar Ferraris, armed bodyguards, uppity educations and just plain born blue blood. For a while, I spent almost every evening wining and dining at Brookby. There was a competitive display of glamorous dames on my arms, and that of course was my strength. Not always without peril, I brought a visiting young lady from Iowa to one of their parties and the tipsy floozy threw up all over the immaculate first floor. It was a long trek to everywhere in that house. I felt compelled to top myself each night. Certain members of the team looked forward to meeting each surprise package.

Ever since Chanda opted to stay in Italy, I had been binge dating. It would take a special gal to perk me up again, and not surprisingly she turned out to be very much like

Chanda. She was Sheila the temptress queen, slayer of skewered hearts. I first saw her in Eastown, but she wasn't returning looks. I only knew she was too elegant to be hanging around the Intersection and Mulligan's. She was tall, dark and handsome in the neon lighting that reflected off her long black tresses and graceful curves. I discovered she'd just broken up with a lover of her own. We were made for each other. I caught her when she was vulnerable and made a date, a date to Brookby. I picked her up at a cozy Cherry Street apartment that was artistic and well-stocked with libations and cool jazz. She was dressed to kill and glowed with confidence. I didn't want to leave her place but knew she'd make a jaw-dropping entrance at Sam and Meagan's. Meagan loved her; we were so in, we could have moved in. Sheila was sophisticated, intelligent and loyal. For the next six months, I hardly ever looked at another girl. In bed, I discovered a passionate, warm and voluptuous Gina Lollobrigida. Almost nothing could come between us. Except for Chanda, who kept coming home to visit and then there was a whirlpool of aggravation, mitigation, castration and litigation. The three of us took turns in tears.

On December 7, Anthony sent me 60 red roses and said he was prepared to send me 100, forty years from now. For me it was another millstone. I still felt like a kid. Sheila was close, but I still preserved my uncanny record of never trusting or dating anybody over thirty. Chanda came to our intimate Christmas Eve as she always had. Sheila was up in Traverse City with her family. On New Year's Eve, my son's band played for the truly grateful City of Angels at the Forum. I went to the Sam and Meagan Cummings' party and savored maddening mixed-up conflicting emotions at midnight. I love déjà vu, but which who?

JANDT

JANDT and I rumbled through Grand Rapids in the '90s.

Chapter 60: Lolita

I had taken a healthy 60-year bite out of the 20th century. How much of a nibble could I get out of the 21st? The fan club was healthy. *Californication* piled up sales, sold out concerts and gobbled up Grammys and Video Music Awards, including the lifetime achievement MTV Video Vanguard Award. Plugged directly into Box 801 and my personal email, Anthony, Flea, John and Chad were besieged with offers from females around the world. James and I got them too and took the beauties and the beast brunt. We were the firewall. We had our hands full of lingerie wrapped in seduction and held off the charge. They showed up in Rockford asking shopkeepers where we lived. The ingenious ones showed up at our door. The police were on alert. And when the devotees didn't come in person, they wore us down with the strangest of gifts in the mail that filled up room after room.

The *Californication* tour was wending our way, but we were impatient and got a preview in Columbus. Jonny Wade flew in from D.C. and Brett, James and I drove over. We met John Frusciante's new high-profile girlfriend Milla Jovovich, who was unrecognizable in her thrift shop duds. With Eminem on his ear phones, James wandered into our openers the Foo Fighters and joined up. I did a live radio feed back to GR. Once again, I would be co-promoter for the home-town concert. Scheduled for July 5, this time it would be at Van Andel Arena. I was all over the media and had conjured up creative press releases around the state. Everything was in order for a financial success and a blockbuster concert. Belkin Productions was bankrolling it, and I had a nice piece of the action.

Don Dorsheimer was running the show for the big cats in Detroit. It was me and Don. Our war room was his office at the Orbit. We met every morning to plot strategy. We had barely finished our coffee and donuts when the phone rang. Seconds later Don's face fell flat with a splat. His complexion turned grey and he hung up. He was about to hang himself up. What? What?! Rick Franks at Belkin had been given bad news that Q-Prime, the Chili Peppers New York management, was cancelling our date and giving it to Fort Wayne. Van Andel had played hardball and wanted too much for rental of the arena.

While Don looked around for a slipknot noose, I got tough and demanded he get Q-Prime on the phone for me. I'd straighten this out once and for all. My management liaison with the fan club was Gayle Fine and I talked to her often. She was four notches down from the top. Tony Dicioccio was next up, and the top-banana gambino bosses were legendary partners Burnstein and Mensch. They had handled Metallica and Def Leppard for years and at the time had Madonna and Smashing Pumpkins and several other top acts. The Peppers had gone from Lindy Goetz to The Ritz. And The Ritz had made them superstars. Cliff Burnstein was the gentle white-haired grandfatherly sweetheart who looked more like a hippie troubadour. He was the good cop. Peter Mensch was the stickball kid from Hell's Kitchen. He was a knuckle buster, a Bluto, a Darth Vadar and Edward G. Robinson in *Little Caesar*. He was the bad cop.

Don handed me the phone; it was Mensch. I cringed and started to explain what the concert meant to our city; the hometown boy returns after all these years... Bam! Peter

Mensch's straight arm interrupted time and laid out my obituary. He slapped me around for two minutes and then growled that they'd find my body in a block of cement under the East River if I didn't wise up. Business was business, and I was a pip-squeak twig to be snapped. With extreme trepidation, I crawled out from under Don's desk and politely told Mr. Mensch it was nice to have met him. The phone went dead—and I thought I might be too. I checked my pulse and looked for bullet holes. Don and I drove over to Van Andel and spoke with general manager Rich McKeigan. In the end, we lowered their cost and saved me from a calamitous concrete dunking. Official now, we put the tickets on sale. Unlike the Blood Sugar show I promoted in Kalamazoo that only sold a trickle of tickets a day, the Van Andel sold out in record time—minutes .

Sheila and I frolicked with the Meagan Cummings wives while the husbands made millions. We swam languid pools and sipped turbulent lemonades, stayed at seaside villas on the coast of Lake Michigan, went horseback riding at Connecticut flavored stables and cheered Sam on to victory at road races. Sheila wasn't particularly enamored with high society, and we secretly slummed at west side bowling alleys, Mexican eateries and funky bars. We had a lovely relationship, which of course was anathema for this serial lover. I had the urge to kill again. Jim Cornell, the original owner of Club Eastbrook and other hot spots in GR and Houston, was down to only On Broadway, an active club in Muskegon, where he lived now. He had youngish girlfriends, a yacht, thoroughbred racetrack gambling, blue-collar gravitas and a trio of cute kids, one of which was the notoriously sexy Melanie, who had been a naughty flirt since she was way too young. Now she was eighteen and living with her dad again, after a recent breakup. She usually slept all day, and looked good in bed. Jim had a son James' age and we started hanging out. I put the whole family on the guest list for Van Andel and the after-show party. I also put together the makings of an Old West gunfight, because Sheila was my date for the big night. The Cummings didn't need guest passes, their entourage owned the arena. Meagan talked Sam into letting us use Opus 1894, their private penthouse club, for our after-show party. Sam owned the building and the whole block.

On the day of the concert, I showed up early and went to work. Sheila was teaching that day; I would meet her at the employee's door at seven. I kept my eye out for Melanie and brought her back to my backstage office. Now I had the enviable task of watching her breasts bulging out of that little summer dress and at the clock for Sheila. I was distracted by lovers and torn by promoter logistics. It was dizzying, delightful and, in the end, disastrous.

The show however was a blast from the start. The band arrived from Louisville in mohawks and James got one too. Peggy and I had a hundred upfront seats for family and friends, and I worked a revolving excursion up to the side stage. On stage, Flea got emotional and told of his teen trips to GR, "I used to take the Greyhound bus from LA here to visit Anthony, and we'd climb up on the trestle over the Thornapple River, wait for the train to come and jump into the water at the last second." John Serba from the *Press* wrote this first paragraph of the event: "He's freshly mohawked. He has enough kinetic energy to fuel a third-world nation. He's one of the biggest rock stars in the world right now. And he's from Grand Rapids. Yes, that's Anthony Kiedis, lead singer for Red Hot Chili Peppers, a band that despite its front man's origins hasn't played in G.R. since 1984. Well, Kiedis' hometown has officially ended its Chili Pepper drought thanks to a sold-out concert Wednesday night in Van Andel Arena as his band continues to push the boundaries of rock'n' roll."

Al Green, another Grand Rapids native played the same night. *Press* reporter John Sinkevics opened his review: "Attention Grand Rapids: This is the Reverend Al Green's house. Anybody who doubts that couldn't have been in the audience Wednesday night at Welch Auditorium for Green's triumphant, soulful, spiritual, rock-the-rafters return to his hometown after an 18 year absence. Someone say 'Amen.'" Anthony acknowledged Al Green from the Van Andel stage and encouraged the 13,000 strong to send a shout out for Reverend Al, three blocks away. We got strong support from our Foo Fighters too. The *Press*: "Dave Grohl & Company absolutely wrecked the place!" Backstage, they certainly did. Food fights, smashed furniture and naked girls. The Cummings girls partied in their dressing room. That may have gotten Sam cranky, and it got worse. The private-club after-show party exploded into a riot when angry fans tried to storm the entrance and scale the three flights. Heart attacks plagued conservative dues-paying Opus 1894 members, who looked on in horror as their usual sedate decorum spiraled out of control. Not surprisingly, John Frusciante never came, but Anthony held court for his extended family. Flea was mildly amused and Chad was caught having sex in the girls' bathroom. The nitro madness of vacillating between Sheila and Melanie at the concert and the party cost me Sheila but got me a little piece of the kitten with a whip. In the long run, it was the worst trade since the Tigers shipped John Smoltz to Atlanta for Doyle Alexander.

A Cheyenne, Wyoming, fan-club friend Justine, who was always trying to finagle a trip to Secluded Lake, came up with a new proposal. She knew my weakness and acquired one, booked them both on a flight and waited for us to meet them at the airport. The prize was Davy: a cool name and an absolute knockout. Long luxurious golden-red hair, white skin, freckles, curves, length and she wanted to make a baby with me. Her plan was to get pregnant and marry into our family and spend the rest of her life in pajamas. She spent the entire week in my bed, and every time I walked past it on my way to the bathroom she'd reach out, grab me and pull me into the covers. Justine tried to join in but Davy kept her at bay. The two of them would dress up in the sexy outfits they'd purchased for the trip and parade around the house like pages of *Penthouse*. Davy wore me out, and I searched for excuses and hiding places. I was never happier than when she finally left.

Mired in all this hedonism and fed up with turmoil, I opened a letter that was brimming with sunshine. At the 9:30 Club concert in Washington D.C., when I was greeting fans just before I got the call James had been kidnapped, I had been confronted by a delicate and translucent young blonde named Alicia, who had come up from Roanoke in the mountains of western Virginia. She gave me a nice hug to pass on to Anthony, and I told her to join the fan club. In the meantime, she'd gone sidetracked over Darren Hayes from Savage Garden, Garbage, and her boyfriend Josh Bruton and his Texan band Blues Cats. In April, she had caught the *Californication* express in Roanoke, and it turned her world around. In her letter she claimed to be 19, when in fact she was only 16. We started writing and sent photos to each other. I had a decent friend who was pure as my 1950s.

Anthony's sister Julie was getting married and I invited Alicia to be my date, actually a three-way: Alicia, James and me. Three hundred guests was the limit and even close family were restricted to only plus one. I had to beg to get that third invitation. I paid for a rental car; Alicia, her older sister, Amanda, and their mother, Joni, drove up and stayed at our house. Like women do, they got lost and the men on each end fretted for two extra days. The wedding in Peggy's big backyard was grand. The absence of Steve Idema was rough, but Anthony stepped in and walked Julie down the flower-strewn walk to the altar, where Judge Steketee presided over the marriage. Twenty-five years earlier the Judge had married Peggy and Steve. I wore shades just in case he had an outdated subpoena floating around.

Nectar performed and Alan schmoozed. The party raged on all day and late into the night; after all it was Julie's wedding! James monopolized Alicia. They had a lot in common: James had struggled with an early education by Candy, and Alicia had been homeschooled by a hippie pot-smoking momma. Alicia was the sweetest girl in the world, innocent and incapable of deceit. She made a wonderful friend for James, and me. It was her seventeenth birthday that week. I spoiled her with presents, and Anthony and Yohanna played football in our backyard for her entertainment. Joni's friend Jeff drove up to drive them home. Alicia gave me a chill-up–my-spine hug goodbye, and we made plans to meet again soon.

Peggy and Jen traveled to Africa and spent 17 days in Kenya and Tanzania. That was wild, but so was a charity event in GR that asked me to perform at a celebrity fashion show that also featured Meagan and Sam Cummings, several local media personalities and Alan Bashara. There were also thirty professional models, including my ever-ongoing crush and the mother of my cats, Patty Kersjes. Although I hit on a few models, I made my primary move on Dee Morrison the blonde bombshell investigative reporter for our NBC affiliate WOOD-TV. She gave me the brush off, and I soon discovered she was engaged to the handsome normal man who walked around with an understandably big smile on his face.

Soon came and Alicia and her sister Amanda returned to Grand Rapids on a Greyhound bus. It was a major step for the little girl, the first time out on her own. The highlight was a Dan and Pam DeVos party. Dan was the son of Amway billionaire Rich DeVos, but found his own success as the owner of the Arena Football League Grand Rapids Rampage and the AHL hockey Griffins. He was vice chairman of the NBA Orlando Magic, the CEO of a dozen enterprises, and like his father he was a philanthropic civic treasure. Dan and Pam were part and party of the Sam Cummings crowd. Hillbilly Hills Alicia wasn't exactly the right fit, but she won everybody over with her implacable sincerity. And she was cute as double dickens. She was just as comfortable with my wrong-side-of-town friends and dealt them the same endearing charm. She embraced my other girlfriends with enthusiasm. One night, I went to visit leggy, exotic dancer Erin and her waitress sister Dana at Sensations, and Alicia came along, despite knowing she was too young to get in. We brought protective Badge, my oversize border collie, to growl away bad guys from within the Bronco. The sweet little girl was a thrill seeker. We watched the May-December movie *Guinevere*. Alicia was proud of her virginity and dedicated to maintaining it but also enjoyed playing the role of a Lolita. She was an actress at heart. Significantly, Alicia loved to help with the fan club. We both agreed there was a mutual advantage to this blossoming partnership. I kissed her goodbye when they left.

When Candy was briefly viable a couple years earlier, we had gone to a wedding dinner party and were seated next to a crimson redhead and her husband. I was in anguish the entire meal. Flash ahead to the Bucking Beaver Lounge and the very same still-pretty girl. She was Andrea and she recognized me. Unfortunately, she had tampered with her slender natural figure and had radically rebuilt her bust. I was appalled, but it was still a thrill to have found her again. She was single now and she wanted to date me. We had a fling, and a destination to exploit. *Sam and Meagan Cummings request the pleasure of your company at the Brookby Christmas Ball. Saturday the Twentieth of December Two Thousand. Half after eight o'clock. Black tie. Valet parking.*

I needed a spectacular date, and Andrea was truly spectacular. And aside from me, what man didn't love those big breasts in a low-cut evening gown for Christmas? The holiday dinner and party were most extravagant. Like the wiseacres in the Bible, titans and statesmen from around the world converged on the Brookby Bethlehem. Lavish would blush and apologize for the cornucopia. It was a David O. Selznick production, right down to the sweeping staircase and a Boys Town choir. Anthony and Yohanna played Mr. & Mrs. Saint Nick at our own private Christmas, and my boy gave me the Andy Warhol painting, *Skull #157*. Happy New Year.

Blackie in South Central on location with Jim Brown, Isaac Hayes, Bernie Casey, Steve James and (not pictured) Keenen Ivory Wayans. "Hammer and Slammer."

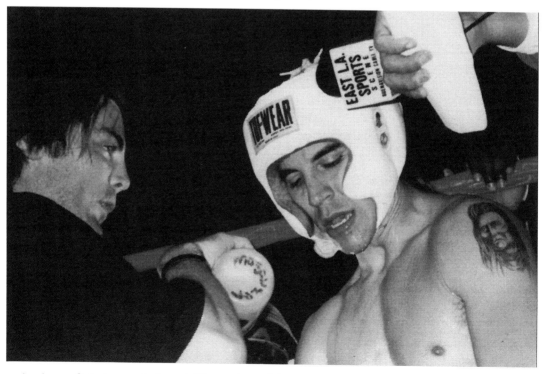

Anthony fighting undefeated Champion of the World, Oscar De La Hoya for a charity exhibition bout to raise money for Oscar's old high school in East LA.

Chapter 61: I Cried Wolves

Anthony and Yohanna had moved from their Mediterranean West Hollywood penthouse into an old house with lots of personality off Mulholland on a celestial cliff overlooking the clouds. Anthony set her up in business designing clothes, and she had a nifty office and workspace in the quaint home. A loyal boyfriend, he wore her *Teenage Millionaire* gear to perform in, and when they stepped out in style at *Vanity Fair*'s Oscar party, they matched sartorial splendor with the Julia Roberts, Donald Trumps and Angelina Jolies. The band racked up another *Rolling Stone* cover. The *Californication* awards kept piling up and my spitting-image son was named one of the Sexiest Artists in the World by VH1 and *Entertainment Magazine.*

On spring break, James and I drove down to see Alicia in the heart of the Confederacy at the foot of the Appalachians. Roanoke was much like Grand Rapids was in the 50s and quite picturesque, as was Alicia. They lived with Jeff the mechanic, who had driven them home from GR. His house was furnished with cardboard boxes, and he wasn't crazy about me stirring the pot he'd cooked up. The opportunistic Samaritan found the gals on the side of the road with a flat tire and took them in. Joni had a touch of Blanche du Bois. Alicia arranged a condo for us on Smith Mountain Lake and the females spent most of the time at our place. Alicia played early videos of her ballerina dancing, and they showed us photos of when their younger mom resembled Nicole Kidman. That set the bar pretty high, but they were right. Alicia took me to the place she dove naked into the lake to startle the fishermen. She wasn't shy. But her dialogue seldom strayed from this phantom ex-boyfriend, Josh Bruton. As previously planned, James and I headed up the Interstate to D.C. for some time with Jonny Wade. Washington was an education for James: we went to the Capitol Building, the White House and all the museums, monuments, memorials and strip clubs. Jon shot us up with fabulous photos for posterity.

That summer, Jon and James and I flew to England for the wedding of our webmaster Terry Wells. The skateboarding, Newcastle Brown Ale swigging, mad genius had proposed to his longtime girlfriend Sarah and invited us to the festivities. Brett and Scott Miller tended to the flocks while we were gone. We flew into London and were greeted by fans at the airport, who took us to our hotel near Kings Cross. After a little rest, we joined a full platoon of Rockinfreaks in the hotel bar for a fan-club party. That led to a few more bars and the beginning of a few romantic affairs. Zosia! The next day, a new contingent of fans joined our tour, and we visited the almighty Tate Modern Museum. Terry finally arrived by train from the north for his last-will-and-testament bachelor party. We put James to bed and ventured into our bender. Terry broke all the Guinness Book of drunken records and impartially mooned anything moving. Back at our hotel lobby with his pants down, I ran for cover before the Bobbies arrived. I learned the next morning he'd gone out again at 3 a.m. for more. We traveled north by train through Robin Hood of Nottingham territory and finally got off at a stop so small it didn't deserve one. It was the tiny village of Barnetby-le-Wold in North Lincolnshire amidst the donnybrooks of Brigg, Scawby, Cleethorpes and Scunthorpe.

The Americans were treated like royalty. We rode in the groom's limousine, ate from the wedding cake, swam in the champagne, puffed reefer in the car park, flirted with the cheeky teens and made nice with the Grandmas and Great Grandmas with their incredible wedding bonnets that put Savannah to shame. The reception was at Arties Mill in a ballroom under a realistic Dutch windmill. I was especially keen on lovely young Hayley Ramm, but I inclusively circulated with all the friends and relatives. I had Terry in tears when I read a clever limerick from Anthony wishing them well. James danced till dawn. After Terry and Sarah motored off to consummate their marriage, we helped clean up a bit and then Terry's 75-year-old father drove us back to Barnetby in his souped-up-on-wedding-whiskey '92 Toyota Corolla. It was a ride so wild it would have run Tarantino's *Death Proof* off the road.

Jon rushed back to Fannie Mae, but James and I carried on and set out for a side trip to Liverpool, where we paid our respects to the Beatles. We genuflected at the Cavern Club on Mathew Street and even snuck James in for a minute before they bounced us out. In deference to my brief friendship with John Lennon, I explored his Liverpool life, right down to visiting Oxford Street Maternity Hospital. John Lennon and John Kiedis were born only ten months apart. We pondered the River Mersey and the Memorial to the Titanic, as this was her home port. We had planned to take the ferry across the Irish Sea to Dublin, but James came up with the flu, and we hunkered down in our coffin-size hotel room on Mount Pleasant Street. Later we returned to London and stayed with fan club member Stacey and her kids: Louis, who became a good friend of James, Philip the sensitive prince and little Lottie. They were a creative hippie family with true values and good hearts. James and I did the obligatory photos at Abbey Road NW8. I reunited with Zosia, and we spent a romantic day holding hands in Camden. We finally had to part; James and I had one more adventure under our berets—Paris. I walked Zosia to the Underground and we delayed our goodbye for as long as possible. We had a memorable first and last kiss in the turnstile as the bustling Brits either whistled or wagged their accusatory fingers.

James and I zipped under the English Channel on the Eurostar train and swept across France into Paris at blitzkrieg speed. This was James' first trip to Paris and my first encounter with Tom Smith in decades. We stayed with Tom and his wife Francoise at their Rue Championnet complex, high in the sky. High, indeed; he had a nifty little vegetarian smoking balcony since his wife wouldn't allow the pot and pans inside. We shared the cannabiscuit and reminisced about our golden Parisian past and questioned our ever-diminishing futures. For now though, we made up new memories. Chanda, and Sherry who had been visiting her sister in Milan, came up to Paris and joined us. We climbed the Eiffel Tower, meandered along the Champs d'Elysee and found our old appartement at 19 Rue Monsieur Le Prince in Odeon. We enriched ourselves with gorgeous art from the Louvre to the sidewalk art stalls of Montmartre. Beneath the shadow of the Basilica of the Sacre Coeur, I felt the haunting artistry of Dali, Picasso, Monet, van Gogh, Modigliani and Thomas Creed Smith.

Sibel Borner, our European Rockinfreakacorrespondent, set up a fan-club meeting at the Lizard Lounge, a cheesy bar on rue du Bourg Tibourg in Le Marais. Elfi, from Munich Germany, fancied herself as my date but I was uncommitted. She was a friend through letters and her belly-dancing photos. She spent a night with us at Tom's. At the meet and greet however, I was introduced to an unimpeachable French pastry who came with her parents and little sister. She was Laetitia Brenugat, and I had never seen such a fresh and pretty young lady. Her hair was braided into a sinful concoction, and she had the most innocently sly smile since the Mona Lisa, who I'd just met the day before at the Louvre. Tom and Francois came too. As good as the food was, and beautiful as Paris and the women were, it was Smitty, cantankerous as ever, who made the trip so special. His gracious wife drove us to Charles de Gaulle Airport, and we headed home.

Back on the farm, I had a new Katie. Alicia dialed my number almost every day and talked for hours. But I was spending most of my time with Chanda, who seemed to always be flying home. She was still involved with James (and still is today), but now we had to share him with the Forsyth families in California and Nevada each summer. Chanda's friends and family had merged with ours to make one big happy family. And that included my wolves: Handsome Devil, the alpha from hell with a heart of black gold like his coat; Cowboy, the big lummox caught in the middle; and Scarlet Fever, the beautiful female who, like so many females, called the shots in the pack. Howlin' Wolf lounged in the living room like an uncle-in-law. By now, I was aware they were illegal in Kent County but always felt immune, tucked away in our own private estate surrounded by a wooded moat. I couldn't resist showing them off. Guests were wary, but once inside the enclosure playing with them, it was obvious these were the sweetest critters on the ark. Wolves howl; it's their smoke signal. Every time I heard a siren out on the main highway, I cringed because the wolves responded with a howl of their own, giving away our location. I'd rush to corral them into the house. But I wasn't always there, and now our once pristine township was developed with golf courses, expensive homes and housing tracts. Boulder Creek Country Club's par-5 seventh hole ran along our property. I came home from the post office and found a Sheriff of Nottingham proclamation nailed to my front door: "OFFICIAL NOTICE OF COMPLAINT Kent County Animal Control. You are required to respond to this notice of VIOLATION Sec.904. We have received a call that you currently have wolves in your possession. Wolves and wolf hybrids are illegal in Kent County. Officer #54."

Toody and Muldoon, *Car 54. Where are you?* Joe E. Ross, Fred Gwynne, Al Lewis, Nipsey Russell, Ossie Davis and all the king's men couldn't put this mess together again. I didn't panic. I called Jim and Brenda in Muskegon and told them of the emergency. They borrowed a van and rushed over. It was a 45-mile ride. The only time the wolves had been in a car was when I brought them home four years ago. Now they were massive and wild, and unlike Howlin' Wolf they had no travel etiquette. It was a nightmare getting them into the vehicle, but the trip itself was an adventurous calamity. They freaked the entire way and ripped apart the upholstery, the seat belts, the floors, the walls and even the ceiling. The shit hit the fantastic and me as I tried to console them in the back of the van. The damage was incalculable. In Muskegon, we put them into temporary housing and rushed to build a new preserve. Scott Miller helped us with the rugged work. There were many preserves, but ours became the Taj Mahal. I visited them often, and every time I drove into the compound they'd recognize my car and go into their dance-of-daddy's-here celebration.

I don't know where I got all the energy, but James and I flew out to LAX, where Anthony had a sleek black Lincoln rental waiting for us. Anthony was with Yohanna, so he booked us into the hip hot Standard Hotel on Sunset. Originally, Arby tarty Jessica

Raymond and momma Georgia were going to accompany us but chickened out and missed a wild time. The Standard had a nightclub that was packed on weekends and scandalous with drinks, breasts and cocaine spilling out into the pool area. Up on Mulholland, I finally met Anthony's Rhodesian Ridgeback Buster, who he proudly put through the paces. Anthony's Porsche and my hot rod Lincoln had a bloodthirsty race from Mulholland to Sunset and Gardner on way to a dinner at Toi with Flea and Clara. Anthony still gets high on competition. James and I sat in at rehearsals for their next album, *By the Way,* at a studio in Hollywood. James played basketball with Flea and the crew at break time. We spent a day in Malibu at Rick Rubin's and got neighborly with David Arquette and Courtney Cox next door. James joined Arquette and his poker pals in a game of five-card stud. Time to go, but before my flight, I put James on a plane to Reno and his Forsyth dad. When he would return, I'd have a couple Boston Terriers for him. Lulu became his muse, and Bubba muscled his way into my top cop.

That summer we held a rip snortin' once-in-a-lifetime exclusive-to-members-only fan-club convention in Grand Rapids. A lot of familiar friends showed up and along came a spider, a new contender for my heart. She was a southern belle from Georgia and she was perfectly fit for her name, Desiree. I kept her in my sight and eventually in my site. We cooked up a lighthearted spoof of those fraternal conventions like the Benevolent Order of Elks or Loyal Order of Moose, with their funny hats and requisite binge drinking at hotel bars. We caravanned to see the wolves, spent a couple days at the Rockinfreak house fishing, boating, swimming and playing RHCP trivia games with super prizes, and finally there was the 11-stop tour of historically significant places in Anthony's life.

The headline in the *Press* was RED HOT PILGRIMAGE. As they reported, this was anything but your typical bus tour. "Aboard the luxury tour bus of black clad patrons the energetic tour guide bounced frenetically from one monologue to the next in a blur of history and rock 'n' roll. No, you couldn't find any fanny packs on these tourists who embarked on a journey through the old haunts of Red Hot Chili Peppers' lead singer Anthony Kiedis. Nor could you expect to be swiftly guided from one location to the next, not with Kiedis' infamously zany father, Blackie Dammett, at the helm of a group made up of people who had trekked from as far away as England, Germany and Japan. Dammett made travel arrangements, borrowed a private bus from longtime friend Brett Anderson, laminated tour passes for everybody and showed the group around town at no cost. He made sure it was OK with his son. If Kiedis had seen his father and the fans on tour, he probably would have been amused indeed. As the 30-foot tour bus pulled off to visit ordinary-looking neighborhoods, Dammett hopped out and pounded makeshift historical markers into private lawns signifying a birthplace, or the place where Anthony lived when he went to elementary school. Cameras clicked while Dammett bounded up sidewalks in an attempt to greet some of the current home owners." Peggy served cookies and lemonade at her house, and we went to Julie's Murray Lake cottage. We pounded the gavel and picked Toronto for next year. Desiree stayed on after the others; her sunny personality was the very last to leave. Our tender bond matured over the years, and she is still one of my favorite sweethearts.

In the fall, Alan and I cooked up our own one-night-a-week honky-tonk club in Eastown. The Rabideau Brothers, who owned a dozen bars around town including Mulligan's across the street, had purchased and rehabilitated a bar they now called Billy's. We convinced the bosses and manager Lyndi Charles to let us have our night. It was casually hip with eclectic music. We hauled in sofas and overstuffed chairs and hired hot-as-hell waitresses. Brett took over front-door security and valet parked vehicles in his carwash, right down the street. We called it Bar Deluxe, after my old haunt on Sunset. I was the DJ and Alan the gracious greeter. We put Thursdays on the calendar. We promoted it skillfully and opened to raves.

Adequately rehabilitated, James rejoined Crestwood Elementary. Next year he would be going to East Rockford Middle School, and we all agreed it would be helpful if he reunited with his peers. He had a conscientious young 5th grade teacher, Mrs. De Witt, who gave him much love and attention. We were optimistic for a while, but weren't helped by a clique of snotty girls who made things miserable for James: they were ruthless and relentless bullies. So of course there were still plenty of visits to the principal, and I had an appointment to see Mr. Hoogerland on the morning of September 11. While I waited in the outer office, a small TV above the secretary's desk showed CNN coverage of smoke damage after a stray plane had hit one of the World Trade Center towers. I casually mentioned James and I had recently been to the top of it. Then a second plane crashed into the other tower and it was suddenly crystal clear. The world had just changed forever.

Two days later on our Thursday was Bar Deluxe night, but the city was hiding under the bed. The following Thursday was the night George Bush gave his important 9/11 address to the nation and everybody stayed home to watch it on television. The Rabideau brothers didn't like our luck. Al-Qaeda blew up our Bar Deluxe too. On the brighter side of 2001, the Grand Rapids Rampage won Arena Bowl XV, trouncing the Nashville Kats 64 to 42.

I had my own Late Night Show in Saskatoon Canada.

Chapter 62: Vampires Anonymous

In March, Jon Waterhouse from Atlanta called; he'd written a script called *Vampires Anonymous* and was ready to roll on location in Georgia. The guy had always been probing me about my MGM writing ventures. For the lead, they had cast Dian Bacher who co-starred with South Park creators Trey Parker and Matt Stone in *Orgazmo* and *BASEketball*. Another solid actor was Bill Nunn; his resume included Spike Lee roles in *School Daze*, *Do the Right Thing*, *Mo' Better Blues* and *He Got Game*. He would also go on to the *Spiderman* trilogy. Professional wrestling legends Larry Zbyszko and The Iron Sheik provided some bulk. Jon had a juicy cameo he wanted me to play, a badass vampire who gets everybody bloody in a scary dark alley. I told him I'd have to bring James. He said he'd write him into the script as a pint-size vampire extra. He could earn a little cash toward college and meet the Waterhouse's adopted five-year-old Russian kid, Levi. Zap! Light bulb! Alicia was the queen of Anne Rice vampire novels and always had one in her purse or under her nose. I didn't even bother to ask Jon. I knew they'd flip to add the curvaceous blonde bombshell to their cast of extras. I also knew Alicia would jump at the opportunity.

We swung by Roanoke, scooped her up and set out for Atlanta. We stayed at the Waterhouse and went to work every day, even when we weren't on call. It was a community effort and everybody rolled up their sleeves. We had one bed for the three of us, but James preferred the floor. Alicia was still a tease, if an inadvertent one, but for me it was painful no matter how you spun it. Alicia loved to play but stayed clear of harm's way. Bill Nunn had to excuse himself for a bigger role, maybe *Spiderman;* it was 2002. Conversely, our director Chris Mills had turned down *The Blair Witch Project.* Jon asked me to take over Bill Nunn's part as moderator of the Vampire Anonymous meetings. The scene was poignant and clever; Alicia and James were both in it. Alicia sparkled in the super-sexy gown we bought her in Atlanta, and James arm wrestled The Iron Sheik.

The revolving bedroom had a motorcycle gang booked next. With fancy footwork, we hit the road to Michigan; we had an LA invite for the ESPN Extreme Sports & Music Awards. This time RHCP were being inducted into a hall of fame for their contribution to skateboarding. Home for a moment, Alicia and I confronted her virginity. Her *when I turn 18* date had expired. She had carefully monitored my playboy reputation. I'd been good for five minutes. She dragged me to the scary condom counter at the local Rite-Aid. I'll pull an opaque curtain over the rest of this paragraph, but her critique was, "a wild ride and the most exhilarating moment of my life." Moment? Busted!

We brought Scott Miller to LA for the weekend; he was always taking care of my house and animals while I flung myself around. His wife, Christie, took care of James while we were gone. We stayed at the Hotel Sofitel. French style and Hollywood glamour was their tag. It was the first time in California for both of them. We'd barely unpacked our bags when Anthony told us to get on over; he was taking us to dinner at the dressy grand opening of Jennifer Lopez's Cuban restaurant Madre's in South Pasadena. Alicia slid into a sexy, sheer summer dress of pastel yellow and blue hues. We caught up with AK at Guy

Oseary's Mulholland home. Anthony and his friend Natasha got in his Porsche. Guy and his lady got in his Porsche. We got in our Lincoln. The armada roared off in a race to the finish. The Porsches were doing a ninety on the Ventura Freeway, and I had no choice but to join in or get left behind. With better suspensions, they came close to losing me on a skid across eight lanes to catch a last second interchange. Finally, we wheeled into a closed off street with cops galore and a barricaded mob of fans who all screamed "Anthony!" as we exited our overheated engines. Jennifer Lopez, her father and her husband, Cris Judd, met us at the door and welcomed us into her party.

Inside was a brash clash of celebrities, which is exactly what I was hoping for. Alicia was a star-struck kid from Roanoke and this fulfilled her wildest dreams. Right off the bat, a sweep of the floor: Johnny Depp, Winona Ryder, Jay Leno, married Dave Navarro and Carmen Electra, Brooke Shields, Donovan, Moby and Kobe. Old pal Christian Slater gave me a big hug and a handful of wisecracks, all the while flirting up a storm with Alicia and asking if she'd like to get out of there and go some place with him. She declined. In fact, she held her own in that star-studded arena and got plenty of attention from most of the men and some of the women. We were seated at a table with Anthony and Guy's entourage that was getting a lot of traffic. And then Alicia spotted Nicole Kidman, who was sharing a small table with Ben Affleck. Alicia went giddy. I restrained her and explained we play it cool in LA: we don't run over and ask for autographs. We.... Where'd she go? Oh shit. Alicia was already standing at her table chatting, and then Nicole invited her to sit down. Ben seemed a bit miffed, but Nicole was totally pleasant, and I'm sure she was getting the "my mom looks just like you" treatment. After a few minutes, I went to retrieve her. Nicole complimented Anthony and asked us to join her, and later she did come over to say hi. It only got crazier as Alicia had a few more glasses of fine wine. By the time we left, she had crème de la Cuban cuisine stains on her bodice and a flirtatious swagger as we walked to the car. It was also the night Ben Affleck had a personal and romantic bouquet of flowers delivered to Jennifer Lopez during the party; it was the unofficial start of "Benniffer."

The next day, I took Alicia to meet Shock, still doing tattoos on Melrose. I did an interview with VH1 for their *Ultimate Albums* show about *Blood Sugar Sex Magik*. From out of the past, I was asked to contribute my favorite memories for Chris Poggiali's biography of the late Jack Starrett, late for those early calls and late for his own funeral. He had died in March 1989 of larger-than-life complications, and we threw a rip-roaring wake for the loveable lug at Warner Bros.

That evening a limo took us to the Universal Amphitheater for the ESPN event. Alice slapped Vernon (Mini-Me) Troyer; his wandering little hands made a surprise visit to her thigh. We also had a spat with a row of drunken Extreme bad Sports. I schmoozed with Larry Vallon and met with publicist Christie Love, collaborating to secure a star on the Hollywood Walk of Fame for the band. The boys didn't seem enthused for some reason. RHCP closed the ESPN Extreme night with their new title track "By the Way." The whole shebang was just 48 hours from GR to GR.

The band wandered the planet like irrepressible troubadours: Ellis Island, Korea, Japan, Hawaii, South America, Singapore, Australia—freeze frame on Australia. Anthony meets Heidi Klum, the audacious and outspoken reigning top model in the world, and they fall in love despite her marriage with faltering Ric Pipino. Goodbye Pipino; hello the germane German, the Teutonic wonderbra woman, the *Sports Illustrated* swimsuit cover girl, and the mouth that roared and kissed my son. Welcome to our family.

Anthony spent a rather frenzied Christmas that year but still managed to put the biggest Christmas gift ever under my tree, a brand new 2003 black on black Cadillac STS. The year before, he'd given his mom a Lexus. The next day, he hopped a sleigh and extended the Yule festivities with the Klum family in Germany. Almost lost in the chaos were RHCP "Best Live Act" and "Best Hard Rock Act" prizes at the MTV Europe Music Awards in Barcelona, and their gig at the Winter Olympics in Utah, which NBC aired nationally.

The band polished off 2002 by playing New Year's Eve at the Hard Rock Café Hotel and Casino in Las Vegas, where I finally met Heidi. Boy was she a handful. But boy was she beautiful. She bossed us around and I didn't mind a bit. She grabbed my camera at dinner and shot photos of me and my boy. Then I shot them; Christmas presents for the fan club. Heidi may have been Victoria's Sweetheart, but she was connected like Bugsy Siegel. When she wanted lions and tigers for Anthony and couldn't dig up Siegfried and Roy, she arranged a Vegas safari with the Tropicana Hotel wild-animal-act guy so we could play with his white tiger cub. On the way back to the hotel, we stopped at a party store, and she bought half the stock of New Year's Eve toys. She was a little kid and a dominatrix. We had a massive Rockinfreak contingent at the show, and I got plenty of love. UK Zosia, who was visiting friends in LA, showed up in the middle of the night; I wouldn't open my Hard Rock door. I was exhausted.

Chapter 63: Slane

2003 may have been the busiest year of my life; *By the Way* was prevalent and profitable. I started the year with a touch of humor. My Three Stooges bit with Mel Gibson in *Lethal Weapon* was included in the NBC 75th Anniversary Show of the loveable numbskulls Curly, Moe and Larry. The fourth stooge, James, was in middle school and hot water. It wasn't funny. He had cultivated the worst possible meathead friends and was in constant trouble, not only with the principal, but at this level, the school cop. I helped him with his payoff creative projects, incorporating our travels and the lessons he'd learned along the way. They managed to keep his grade-point average above water. Creativity was one thing he was good at, like secretly pawning my most expensive possessions for a happy meal or a 64 oz. bottle of Mountain Dew. I discovered the fan-club funds were gone, and I didn't need Sherlock Holmes. It was stashed away in his bunk bed. His crime wave washed out junior high too. After consultations with Chanda, the school police and reeling counselors, he was expelled and moved in with John Forsyth for some tough love. James enrolled in an ornery Reno Nevada Junior High and rumbled with the junior Mexican mafia.

I went to work and put out my press release for the upcoming tour stop in GR. "Fresh from their sold out critically acclaimed tour of Europe, Asia, South America and the South Pacific, this year's Band of the Year will invade Grand Rapids on May 10, 2003, packing an arsenal of new hits from their latest release which has already sold over 6 million records in only nine months. *By the Way* has astonished the critics. *Rolling Stone*: "Soulful vocals, electric ladyland melodies and Flea's Bootsy-fied bass. All pimp juice and suntan lotion. The best argument for quitting drugs in rock history. Unspeakable bliss most often found in the work of Brian Wilson and the Beatles". England's *Q Magazine*: "RHCP are the first truly great LA rock band since the Beach Boys hit their stride. John Frusciante is a revelation. He was always capable of being a special guitarist. Now, he's surely the best of his generation. *By the Way* is a work of a band that, after 20 turbulent years, as late as their 8th album, is at the top of their game. They are also at the peak of everyone else's game. A fantastic record, full of wonder." *LA Weekly*: "The Chili Peppers' latest release is one of the most interesting and creative new records around and arguably belongs in the pantheon of greatest Los Angeles albums with the works of the Doors and the Beach Boys." *Classic Rock Magazine*: "*By the* Way has the hallmark of a classic work. I'm hearing latter-day Beatles and the Beach Boys."

It was a slam-dunk sold-out show. Peggy and I split 128 seats for our closest allies, and Anthony dedicated "Don't Forget Me" to me. He had written the poignant ballad for his now ex-lover Yohanna, but I loved the song, identified with it and he knew it. We had another dramatic after-show party, this time at Louis Benton's on Monroe Avenue. A monsoon rain soaked us on the brief walk over. Bedlam prevailed and hordes of fans tried to bust into the private area. Anthony's date was a Russian waitress he'd met at the Amway Grand Plaza where the band was staying. When they left, he skipped a taxi or limo and walked her back to the hotel in the romantic rain. Along the way, they talked with startled fans still mingling downtown after the concert.

As usual, I jumped on the traveling circus tour and the next stop for me was West Palm Beach, home of the Kiedis dynasty. I figured it was time to introduce Alicia to the family. Brother Tom's son, Paul Kiedis, was graduating from King's Academy and everybody came from far and even farther for the commencement. Alicia was a big splash for a little girl and everybody adored her, especially my mother Eileen. Nineteen and ninety and sitting next to each other like little chipmunks. We spent most of our time with my sister Judy, her daughter, Melanie, and my hippie smokin' sister, Cathy. In an emotional confrontation, I went to my father's grave for the very first time, almost twenty years after his death. He was buried in a simple green area next to my Aunt Marie. I knelt down and a sudden force of reconciliation body-slammed me onto the bronze marker with my same name. Prostrated, I cried uncontrollably; the grave was soaked with my tears. Don't forget me.

At the family reunion party, Tommy showed slides of our lives growing up, originally captured by my father over the past sixty years. Sweet poignancy for some, but others like Judy still felt bitter animosity. And then the whole damn Kiedis clan went to the RHCP concert at the Coral Sky Amphitheatre. John Frusciante's Florida family was there too, including some very elderly grandparents. I finally got to meet John Frusciante Sr., who I had been in contact with over the years. He was a judge who dealt with abused children. Our John Jr. guitar maestro had been born in New York City and was raised on Beethoven and Bach and the Juliet School of Music. Eventually, he and his mother, Gail, moved to the San Fernando Valley, and he went to high school in Woodland Hills. *Rolling Stone* had recently placed him #18 on the best 100 guitar players of all time.

Rolling Stone was in Florida too, covering the concert "On the Road" with photos by Anton Corbijn. The cover-story photo was arm in hammer Anthony and Blackie. The title text: "Red Hot Papa Pepper." Anthony Kiedis: "This here is a picture of my pops and me backstage after a show in front of the largest Kiedis colony on earth. I have a lot of family in the West Palm Beach area—aunts, uncles, cousins." Angelina Jolie *Hot & Single* (after the Billy Bob breakup) was the yummy cover that helped sell a few extra million copies of that issue—in addition to all the ones I bought. Reversal of fortune, James came to spend his summer vacation with me. We hit the tour stop in Denver. By then Snoop Dog was opening, much to James' delight. My lady host was Ashley, and Justine came down from Wyoming.

With James back in Reno, I continued my *By the Way* tour overseas. Nikki Carr, one of my favorite fan-club members from the UK, convinced me to carjack an impulsive concert ride of the V (for Virgin) 2003 Festivals, Slane in Ireland and the Big Day Out in Glasgow, Scotland. Nikki made arrangements for our hotels and airlines. Terry Wells drove over from Lincoln, and we rolled into the West Midlands where the Staffordshire Sentinel headline already read: 12 ARRESTS AT V FESTIVAL. The Virgin sacrifice hadn't even started yet!

Coldplay headlined one night and RHCP the other. The backstage campground was atmospheric with artists PJ Harvey, Queens of the Stone Age, The Hives, David Grey, The Cardigans, old pal Foo Fighters and newcomers Distillers and Amy Winehouse, all fused up in a hippie love-in. Evan Dando from the Lemon Heads banged into me as we exchanged places in the loo. Zosia showed up and so did another 80,000. After the show, Terry and I spent a rowdy middle of the night with Tony Woolliscroft and his loony mates in nearby Hanley. Woolliscroft worked for the influential British rock magazine *Kerrang* and was the unofficial UK photographer of the Chilis. Later, he would publish his own RHCP book. I skipped the Chelmsford V 2003 near London, and Terry drove us to Barnetby-le-Wold so I could say hello to Sarah and meet their baby boy, Arik.

I resurfaced with Nikki and flew into Dublin where I fell madly in love with the dynamic Temple Bar district. I stayed at the Clarence, overlooking the Liffey River. The classic hotel was the place to be and it was owned by U2. Dublin was everything I expected and more. It has to be the coolest place on earth. Friendly, vibrant, steeped in tradition and culture and demographically young, it was paradise. I had plenty of time to explore and popped into the Abbey Theatre one afternoon. The curator gave me a tour of his domain and the ghosts of William Butler Yeats, J.M. Synge, Sean O'Casey, George Bernard Shaw, Brendan Behan and Samuel Beckett. The Abby had recently closed Arthur Miller's *All My Sons*. I once hitched a ride across the USA just to see Arthur Miller's *Death of a Salesman* on Broadway, with Dustin Hoffman as Willie Loman and John Malkovich as Biff.

Dublin was also home to Oscar Wilde, Jonathan Swift, Bram Stoker and arguably the greatest writer ever, James Joyce. As they had, I spent my nightshifts swashbuckling taverns where rosy-cheeked folk broke into Irish songs and big smiles. Nikki and I went on a tour of the main Guinness Brewery. In the courtyard, I got in a scuffle with an old geezer by his picturesque horse-drawn wagon when he wouldn't let me take his picture without compensation. I quick took a shot and ran into the brewery. An hour later, on the way out, he was waiting and chased me down the cobblestone road with a gnarly staff.

The band stayed in a cloistered hotel away from the main area. We had dinner one night to unravel anecdotal mysteries of "Under the Bridge," a song worthy of a future episode on the VH1 show *True Spin*. I had been asked to appear on the show to elucidate its origins and needed the low down. It was revealed that the song's lyrics were psychologically created out of John and Anthony's sudden alienation at the time. I ended up shooting the VH1 piece at Secluded Lake later that summer.

Built by Norman conquerors, Slane Castle was an estate so large you could hold a party for a hundred thousand guests in Lord Henry Mount Charles' front garden and still have room for a massive stage; spacious artists area; picnic grounds; 4 star restaurants; vendor booths; parking for cars, tour buses and helicopters and workers to service the crowd with food and merriment. And it was only accessible by a scrawny path out in the middle of nowhere. That aspect was a bloody logistic nightmare, but they'd been dealing with it since 1981. Unlike most festivals, Slane was a canonizing. It seemed to acknowledge that a great band had reached iconic status. The opening acts were court jesters and the courtyard hundred thousand were witnesses. Previous acts to headline the hallowed ground were Bob Dylan, Queen, Rolling Stones, Bowie, Springsteen, U2, Guns N' Roses, Neil Young, R.E.M. and Robbie Williams. In 2001, U2 headlined for a second time, an honor they shared with the Stones. Red Hot Chili Peppers had been U2's lead-in act. Two years later we were picked to headline this christening in County Meath, about 25 miles north of Dublin. A limo picked me and my Nikki up at the Clarence and we sped through the beautiful Irish landscape toward Slane, dodging the throngs of spectators walking along the road. The band arrived by helicopter but wouldn't be able to fly out due to darkness. It set up a dicey exit to beat 100,000 people out of that clogged artery that meandered for miles.

I was spread thin. I had the band. I had Nikki. I had backstage activities. I had hundreds of fan-club friends who wanted to meet up, and I had Mr. and Mrs. Gerry Mullen from the nearby town of Drogheda with their five-year-old son Nicholas, one of the fan club's youngest members, who wanted to meet Anthony. I arranged it and got him back into the compound for a brief visit with his idol. In tomorrow's *Drogheda Leader* newspaper the Red Hot Chili Peppers would have to share the spotlight; the headline read "Nicholas (5) was the envy of 100,000. Drogheda boy met his Chilli heroes backstage at Slane." It was a two-page layout with four photos of Anthony and Nicholas at their summit meeting in my son's private suite.

I pulled another Irish fan backstage, the prettiest girl in the multitude. She was from Belfast in Northern Ireland, and we watched the show from close enough to touch them. I could have joined her later camping out with friends that night on the Slane grounds, but I preferred the Clarence. We emailed and exchanged photos for quite a time. She was awfully awesome, but we never met again.

As the RHCP set got close to the end, tour manager Louis Mathieu warned us all to be ready for a quick escape. Once the concert ended, the onslaught would attack that little road. It would take all night to get them out. The plan was to have our fleet of vehicles warmed up and ready to go right off the back of the stage. Everybody but the band had to be in seatbelts once the last song started. On the final encore note, they ran down the stairs and dove into their lead SUV as our caravan roared off with an escort of a dozen police motorcycles. By the time we made our way out of the backstage area, staggering drunken fans were converging on the pathway. And yet we blasted down the center line with screaming sirens and flashing red lights, dangerously close to knocking them off like bowling pins. We had to keep up with the cavalcade no matter what. Nikki's friend threw up it was so scary. The next morning, one Dublin newspaper wrote: "Basically last night at Slane Castle the Red Hot Chili Peppers were better than sex." Venue spokesperson Justin Green gushed, "This is one of the best Slanes ever." Tickets for the sold-out concert had gone for $500.

It was with profound sorrow I left Dublin, but we still had the final stop of our tour in Glasgow. We flew across the Irish Sea and along the rugged coast of Scotland. From the sky, it was just stunning. Super-fan Euan Ross met us, and the girls got a small hotel near his place. I stayed with the band at One Devonshire Gardens across town. It was very old and stuffy. The band always registers under an alias; Flea's was Paddy McGooglepuss. I quite enjoyed Glasgow. We partied at Euan's apartment and partied backstage at the Big Day Out @ The Green. It was another sold-out show in yet another beautiful park, this time with beautiful freckled Scottish faces. There was an adorable doll and her boyfriend getting crushed against the bulwark fence; I rescued them and provided a spot on the side stage. I moved over on the other side, away from the guests. The 16-day party was coming to an end, and I was feeling sentimental. I was mesmerized as I watched my boy command and orchestrate this love fest, the object of unabashed adoration from thousands of complete strangers. I stood there as I had so many times before at the biggest venues ever played and in tiny corner bars. I was suddenly overtaken by a wave of objectivity, as though I was just another spectator. I mused how humane, generous and charismatic he was, this man so dedicated to the power of equality and mixing it up until there were no pedigrees. Tears of unmitigated joy started to roll down my cheeks as I thought back over the years of his growing and learning and surpassing my wildest imagination. For those legions who have denigrated my upbringing of Anthony, I point to the finished product, this magnificent prototype of what humanity could and should be. Back in 1992, *Esquire* magazine ran a portentous cover with the young mugging faces of Flea, Anthony and then drummer Cliff Martinez under the ominous banner AMERICAN MEET YOUR FUTURE. Well America, the future was here and the future never looked better.

I spent the last of summer in Michigan. James had stolen his Reno dad's tools and precious old coin collection to buy protection from the Chicano teen mafia. For weeks, James and a slacker buddy spent every day in a vacant house instead of going to summer school. His dad beat the tar out of him. James begged to come home, and I said I would give him another chance. Chanda, Alicia, James, big Al Bashara and I spent a week on Mackinac Island in the Upper Peninsula. Lots of bicycling, touch football, miniature golf and Mackinac's famous fudge. It was our Martha's Vineyard. Alicia, James and I drove even farther north to Sault-Ste-Marie and into Canada. The interrogating border guard asked what my profession was and I told him actor. "What films?" he asked. *Lethal Weapon* I told him. Still suspicious, he asked what I played. "Drug dealer," I said reluctantly with a disingenuous smile. "You just played one though, right?" he asked. They searched the car. I bought Alicia a cat tag with my phone number to wear around her neck.

An alley off Melrose Avenue.

Chapter 64: The Biggest Band in the World

No, not the USC marching band or the Mormon Tabernacle. Our guys. In 2004, following the spectacular success of last year's triumphs, the band returned to Ireland and England for an unprecedented series of events. In Dublin ,they played to 110,000 at Phoenix Park. Newspapers used terms like "legendary," "the best band in the world," and quoted Kurt Cobain as listing them as a main reason for the existence of Nirvana. U2 took our band to dinner the night before. Bono and The Edge came to the Phoenix Park concert with their kids. The Edge's critique: "Tonight they were just amazing. The songs are getting better, they're getting better and they're sort of defying gravity and everything else, so it's great to see. Just blew me away, really, really good." RHCP had now played to 300,000 Irish fans in just three concerts. Only six days later and 206 miles away in London, they played a three-night stand for another 300,000 in Hyde Park, which grossed over 17 million dollars. The concert also spawned the bestselling *Live in Hyde Park* CD.

The band was voted Best Live Band in the World by MTV viewers, Best Live Act by *Hot Press* readers, Best International Band at the Brit Awards and Best International Live Band at the Meteor Ireland Music Awards. The three pre-eminent music magazines in Britain concurred on cover story headlines. *Kerrang*: "The World's Greatest Band." *NME*: "The World's Biggest Band Invade the UK." *Mojo*: "The World's Biggest Band." The *London Daily News-Telegraph*: "After seeing these four extravagantly tattooed, tough-but-tender Californians on this brief UK tour, I'd have to say that they are currently the best rock group in the world. Most extraordinary of all is the fact that they have been together for 20 years, a career point that for most bands would be the signal for some kind of revival/ reunion tour; for the Red Hot Chili Peppers, it's a new peak." The BBC conducted a vote for the best fantasy rock band of all time and announced on drums, Keith Moon; on bass, the one and only Flea; guitar, Jimi Hendrix of course; and your front man, Bono. Anthony did a cover for *Italian Vogue* and was writing his memoirs, but like me was restless for love.

He had ducked out on Heidi Klum a while back and went through a void of relevant women. In an email he added, "...there had, until yesterday been a new girl in my life, but it seems that her flight home to NYC is most likely a one way ride. She was 20 and divine but not ready for the prime time Kiedis connection cruise. I need a girl that can help my cause to build some family action. We had fun and now the world turns. Sorry to hear you're having a spell of loneliness. Always know that you are most certainly loved by me. AK." At this stage of his life, starting a family and having a child was foremost for Anthony.

After all the excitement, I was dawn-to-dark back catching up with my alpha roles to James, the fan club and the animals. Scott Miller and I were out at a bar on Alpine. On the bulletin board, Scott spotted a notice for a movie audition that Saturday at Grand Valley State. It asked for cool teens and twenties, but I went anyway. After all, I was still 19. It was a local production with an out of town producer, John Cluff from Utah, who had done SPX on Will Smith's *Independence Day*. The low-budget sexy comedy was called *Busty the Vampire Slayer,* which promised lots of flesh, blood and a token of talent. The crew was pumped to see me when I walked into the audition. Some weren't shy about asking for an autograph. The script was a parody of the current *Buffy*-mania, and they were looking for an equivalent professor of the *Buffy* movie's Donald Sutherland or the TV series' Anthony Stewart Head. I sealed the deal with one reading. The crew was talented, the acting was serviceable and then there was Cassie and the Devil Dolls—fire-eating organized mayhem in lingerie. A national legitimate blood and guts production company called Shock-O-Rama was financing us. The success of the film depended on a Busty, but we were having a hell of a time finding her. The crew sacrificed to spend tough endless hours at strip clubs, searching for that perfect candidate.

Chanda broke up with her Italian boyfriend, Robbie, and moved to Chicago. For Christmas, she bought *Phantom of the Opera* tickets for herself, Sherry and a pair for me. Alicia was who Chanda expected me to bring, but she couldn't get out of Roanoke. Creston model citizen Patty Kersjes was also living in Chicago now, and she became my Phantom. Alicia missed the Phantom but moved heaven and hell to get up here for Busty auditions. I created a part for my gal and named her Lily Whitetail.

In March, James became a teenager. In December, I became a senior citizen. I was eligible for Social Security and Medicare but still acting like a teenager. Anthony wrote, "James at 13. Why must I be a teenager in love? Why not! It's time to enter the incredible world of teenage superflight, time to take a bite out of time, time to dance like you've never danced before, time to toss those troublesome 12s out the window and go high steppin' thru the door. 13 is the great underground number of good luck and good times. Happy birthday James; I hope this will be the happiest year of your young and beautiful life. Love from the west coast bro, Anthony." Is it any wonder I chose to enjoy the company of youth? I couldn't see myself playing gin rummy or shuffleboard at a doddery retirement home.

We rehearsed *The Vampire Slayer* every night and became a fairly-well-oiled ensemble for a bunch of amateur hambones. The company threw a wild party, populated with outrageous Grand Rapidians who perfectly matched the walls splattered with horror, sci-fi posters and movie photos. Rick Reed was a terrific comic actor and one of the madmen tenants. Ryan Lieske was another. He had just finished his own film *Fiction*; he was also in a band called Tentacle that was doing the music for the film. There were beer-keg drinking games, pot smoking rooms, loud music and even louder pretentious conversation. They were the local intelligentsia, and they all had a project in some state of completion. A flirtatious actress with shocking pink hair circled us androgynously. Guys were falling all over Alicia, with failing grade pick-up lines. The dress code was wacky frat house, but Alicia and I had arrived dressed to the nines. It was also crowded and drunken so we opted to leave for a civilized club. As we were exiting, another couple every bit as glamorous as ourselves was entering. Our shoulders brushed. The perfume lingered. They were Gable and Lombard. He was dark and handsome; she was blonde and beautiful. She devastated me. I lamented having already committed to leaving, but inertia swept me out the door. For days I wondered who she was.

Our director, Scott Carr, encouraged us to support this Tentacle band, and they were scheduled to perform at Ten Bells. Dutifully, we went. The Devil Dolls opened, and there on the sideline mingling with the roadies and all the other film folk was the handsome couple from the party. The headlining Tentacle band turned out to be a trio. Ryan Lieske handled guitar and vocals. Eric Stanek was a mad scientist strangled in a spider web of cords and a cocktail of Kurzweil, Korg and Roland electronic keyboards, mixers, and groove boxes that punched out more music than the Philharmonic. And then there was the drop-dead torch singer, the chanteuse, the heart breaking Sue Stanek. Alicia and I both stood there with our mouths open. She was golden in the stage light and sang like a frightened angel. Eric and Sue, it turned out, were an institution. Not only were they married, they'd been together since grade school. They were one of the great love stories of our time, and I was sick about it.

Doing my civic duty, I continued to support Tentacle. One Sunday afternoon, James and I dropped by their sound check at the all-ages Liquid Room. The band and their sycophants were in a back alley having a smoke. I mugged my way into the stream of consciousness and employing a weak subterfuge introduced James to Sue. She was underwhelmed and moved on to more scintillating conversation. A couple weeks later, I had better luck at the Radio Tavern where they were playing. Alicia and I alternated conversation with Sue and Eric, and the next thing I knew we were friends. Sue was as much an artist and writer as a singer and showed us her wares. James and I were about to leave for LA on business, and Alicia was staying at the house to take care of the cats and dogs. Sue agreed to help her.

In a pleasant reprieve from Busty mania, James and I headed west to ringmaster the biggest and best of all our fan-club conventions. Again the Rockinfreaks came from around the world, and the main events were a tour bus visit of all the RHCP historical locations: a Dodger game that was preceded by a celebrity baseball game that Anthony played in, an intimate Josh Klinghoffer and John Frusciante concert at the Knitting Factory on Hollywood Boulevard that Anthony and Flea attended, the ESPN X Games, Pink's chili dogs, Melrose Avenue, Universal City, a picnic at Venice Beach and a dinner party with Anthony at the House of Blues on Sunset, with special guest stars Flea's mom, Pat, and Frusciante's mom, Gail. A quick Dutch salvo to the Essers and the roll off your tongue Tiny and Tony Tati, and from Chile with love, I acknowledge my dear friend Ursula Becker. After several hours at the House of Blues, most of us went to the Rainbow Bar and Grill where everybody met Tony and Mario—and Weaver.

Anthony procured us a suite in a trendy Beverly Hills boutique hotel. James skateboarded all over Rodeo Drive and had a compatriot in fan-club member Cassie Fenkle from New Jersey. They had a cute budding romance. By now, Anthony had moved into his own Beverly Hills Spanish villa, a former residence of the Hilton Family. He had a new girlfriend too, a teenage model named Heather from Simi Valley. His live-in housekeeper/secretary Michelle Dupont was in a relationship with Academy Award winning actor Adrien Brody, who was a frequent visitor and a cool guy. He was preparing for a trip to New Zealand to shoot *King Kong* for Peter Jackson. Buster was still king of the jungle on the woodsy estate overlooking paradise. Girding for the election, Anthony was wearing his Re-defeat Bush T-shirt. In the neighborhood, a block away on Cielo Drive was the old Roman Polanski and Sharon Tate home site with Manson's bloody legacy. In happier days, Henry Fonda, Cary Grant and my former boss Dyan Cannon had lived there. In the 90s, Anthony's Nine Inch Nails friend Trent Resnor lived and recorded in the house, and AK was part of the retinue.

That, my friends, will officially be the final Manson reference, as many of them as there were of my Route 66 trips across America.

By the time I got home, Alicia and Sue were blood sisters. They swam nude in lily-pad ponds and explored the floral woodlands surrounding the Stanek home in the far south village of Caledonia. Sue did a large portrait painting of Alicia that was sheer as fine linen and delicate as a flower. She was brilliant. We became the Mertz and the Ricardos. I loved Sue like everybody else did, but I respected their truly cool marriage. Even Ryan, their guitarist and lifelong friend, was blatantly vocal about his steamy feelings for her. Eric was used to it, a confident guy indeed. We became friends and spent a good deal of our lives searching for the best stout and ales, which turned out to be at Fenian's Irish Pub in Conklin, a folksy hangout that featured volunteer Irish music every Sunday.

James went into the 7th grade, and we wrapped up *Busty the Vampire Slayer*. Alicia returned to Virginia, and I got a new roommate. Anthony's autobiography *Scar Tissue* was in full throttle, and his collaborator Larry "Ratso" Sloman was interviewing the important characters in his life. Ratso had coauthored Howard Stern's *Private Parts* and wrote books on Bob Dylan, the New York Rangers, Abbie Hoffman, David Blaine and Harry Houdini. The original concept was Anthony's life as he recalled it, intercut with insight from his colleagues. Ratso's mission was to get their stories, and he came to Secluded Lake to get mine. He stayed with me for eight days. Like literary explorers, we rummaged my memories and the secrets buried in the dark shadows of Anthony's home town. We went through the attic archives of Brookside Elementary, tracked down Scott St. John at his taxi-job depot, and dug deep into the underbelly of young Tony's sordid adolescence. Eventually, the publisher decided against that concept, and all our ruminations were rerouted through Anthony.

In October, *Scar Tissue* went on sale and sold like cosmetic surgery. It got as high as Fred Freel, or numerically at #15 on the *New York Times* bestsellers. It was one notch behind Bill Clinton's *My Life*. Hyperion Press threw a snazzy party in NYC, and I was invited. I grabbed Patty Kersjes by her hand and brought her with me. We took a room at the Washington Square Hotel in Greenwich Village. The party was at The Cutting Room on 24th Street, and we were in the gun sights of paparazzi and back-slappers. I had a fawning conversation with Anthony's friend Edward Norton who I much admired. We met literary agent David Vigliano and other notables. Natasha Lewin the editor of *High Times* invited Patty and Blackie to their offices on Park Avenue, trouble in the works. Later, Anthony took us to dinner at trendy NOBU, where a constant stream of celebrities kept dropping by.

The next day Patty and I went to Q-Prime on 7th Ave. so I could arm wrestle with Peter Mensch, but he was hiding in the executive wash room…or maybe he was just on the phone with client Jimmy Page. We were talking with Gayle Fine in her office when alarms went off, and we all had to abandon the burning building! Times Square was full of NYFD ladder trucks at the foot of Q-Prime. In the evening, we walked over to the *Scar Tissue* book signing at Barnes & Noble in the East Village. Hundreds waited for hours in lines poking the Battery, and they all left with big smiles. Anthony did the media book promotion with Conan O'Brien, Regis and Kelly and Howard Stern's radio show. After reading the book, Stern said he'd have disowned his father. Later, Howard Stern accepted the hypocrite of the year award. While Patty and I spent a day with Ratso and his wife Christy, Anthony did interviews with *People Magazine*, MTV, Xtra, FUSE and the papers.

The fan club ran "Frusciante for President '04" and circulated the bumper stickers, but Bush kept stealing the election like *Groundhog Day* the movie. At least Christmas was nigh. And then catastrophic news! For the first time since Herod barely missed Christmas, Anthony was not coming home for the holidays. He was going to the Guatemala border to surf and sun with Heather and some British surfing buddies. In Michigan we all accepted it, even thought of it as our gift to him. In the past, he always came home, and *then* dashed off to exotic paradises with Rick Rubin or Johnny Cash and his wife, June Carter, or Jessica Stam or Heidi Klum. This year would be a big break from tradition, and we were all resigned to a low key holiday. No Christmas dinner with Anthony at the head of the table, no big night out on the town, no assurance from Anthony that it would snow on Christmas day.

And then like a Christmas carol or a Jimmy Stewart movie, he showed up at the last moment with Heather and surprised us. We had our Christmas dinner at mom's and went to Christmas parties. We had our night out on the town. We opened presents; one of mine was an all-expenses-paid trip to the Grammy Awards in Los Angeles. We frolicked with the wolves, and Anthony had the guts to climb into the new black bear's domain. Anthony had financed his salvation, and Brenda named the beast after his benefactor. And *then* they left for LA and their rendezvous in Mexico. At Christmas, Anthony had also delivered my proverbial "gold watch" from the band, as I had recently announced my retirement after 13 years of running Rockinfreakapotamus and redhotchilipeppers.com. Under my tutelage we'd done pretty well. My gold watch was, in fact, a check for fifty grand.

Chapter 65: Chaste

I had the fan-club transition to deal with and fans were wary of the corporate takeover. My head honcho signature on Rockinfreak communiqués would be sorely missed. So would my partner's tag, "Sexy blonde assistant Alicia." She'd been a fan-club fixture for years and was coming to the end of her era too. My promise to continue answering fan club email in perpetuity proved impossible; there were just too many. Incrementally, I drew back from my extended family around the planet. The Ann Lewis family came all the way from England just to say goodbye in person. I also retreated from my patented lifestyle. After five controversial decades, I had finally mellowed out. The drunken sailor pursuit of women was thrown in the brig. The destroyer dry docked. The libido took a sabbatical. Alicia chafed at my chastity, but I was adamant. We downgraded to platonic. I was just shy of immaculate. I still felt desire. I still felt lust. I still had a bent imagination. I was just ready for celibacy. I hadn't kept count of all my conquests, but it would have challenged integral calculus.

For years, computer Joe had been raving about his MySpace chicks, and every time I saw him out on the town he was with another girl he'd met online. The computer was always pulsating at his house, and he monitored it like a Wall Street ticker tape. Boastfully, he'd drag me on a tour of his MySpace friends. Cyber maidens might be just what I was looking for. Petticoats I didn't have to actually deal with in person. I signed on. I may have been a late starter, but in no time I was inundated with pretty girls, hundreds of them. Certainly I might even find the perfect one in that intergalactic haystack. The one I'd been chasing all my life, the odyssey that began with Brenda when I was four years old. I tried to sign up as Blackie Dammett but found that name was already taken! Turned out a Red Hot Chili Peppers tribute band in Florida had named themselves *Blackie Dammett*.

First in line online in my line was Britt, a wise teenager from the Philadelphia area. She was a working model, smart and sassy, tall and lanky and way too sharp to ever be victimized. She had a New York agent and frequent flyer mileage to and from Europe and Japan. We became real friends on top of cyber friends. Her parents were cool with me taking the family to the RHCP concert in Philly, and they invited me for dinner to their suburban home. It was all set, and then like a stereotypical teen flick, she was caught passing a note in class and its subject was pot, not American history. Pop grounded her and our meeting was postponed.

Marike was another skyscraper. She lived in Holland, although she could throw a fit across her fence that straddled the line with Germany. There was an exquisite woman in New York City, who was tall, blonde, intelligent and in love with a song-and-dance man. She still took the time to make friends with me. There was a Turkish girl who lived in the Netherlands who tried to commit suicide when I didn't reciprocate her feelings. There was Hélène an eighteen-year-old girl from Burgandy, France, who paid her own way around the world to meet me, and nineteen–year-old Vanessa from Tuscany, Italy, who did the same. Everyday there were new sexy, beautiful girls who wanted to play. The predator was now the prey. But I felt safe; it was mostly make-believe, and most were in far-flung lands. To be honest, there were stalkers, but I was skilled in illusive maneuvers. Unlike Joe who catered to locals for sex, my scope was worldwide and nutritiously unadulterated. We could tease and project and fantasize, but my celibacy was reasonably secure.

And then I met Kelly. Her show-business parents had moved into the Malibu house and gave her the big white Spanish Beverly Hills house. Kelly ran with a clique of spoiled 90210 brats. She traveled the globe, was an educated siren, extremely pretty and, for some reason, had a big crush on me. It got serious; she inundated me with her risqué images and called me every time she got in her car. I warned her of the peril, but she just laughed and kept on calling and driving. At Christmas, she went to Florida to see her grandmother who had a stroke and was in a coma. In Sarasota, Kelly spent every day at the hospital, but on the drive to and from she kept calling me. She was speed dialing to me on her way home from the hospital when an errant car crossed the line and smashed into hers. She was crushed, punctured and almost died. She was in her own coma for weeks. Anthony visited her in the hospital when the band swung by Tampa. Ironically, it was my recorded daily cell phone calls from Rockford they played for Kelly that finally woke her. I hope she's getting better all the time.

From LA, Anthony wrote, "Blackschtein, it's been too long padre. I hope that you are singing, dancing, laughing, loving, inventing, and representing. I heard you got some spring snow that is threatening the young gardens of the great fertile mitten. Though I imagine you enjoyed the unseasonal atmospheric ambiance, I hope your flower beds didn't take a beating. The record's going very well but nowhere near finished. I've got heaps of work to do but am able to see the potential for this to be some of our best work we've ever done. …love, AK."

Yes, the Lord of the Sunset Strip had been relegated to gardening. Of course, I actually liked gardening. Secluded Lake was an oasis of floral pulchritude, and I had the shovel scars, bee bites and poison ivy to prove it. We repainted the house a glorious triple-sharp shade and reconfigured the interior to match my new life. I had begun to dabble in painting with the support of Sue Stanek. The fan-club area became the art studio. As I packed up the remnants of my past, I came across a collection of postcards from my son. Chestnuts like: "Pops, where would I be without you.* To the greatest Dad I ever had. One day I too will be a Dad like you. * No better Dad was ever had. I'll love you for all time. * Dad, am I glad you were born. You are a very amazing man. I love you * To the blackest dad a son ever had. From the Son * To Pa, From the Young in', The Grateful Dead can have their Deadheads; You and I, we'll take the Redheads * Dad, long may your love be strong and your heart be smiling, your number one son."

Father's Day rolled around again and a new piece of his heart arrived. He wrote: "Dia de los Padres. Well…twould seem it's that time of year again when Hallmark reigns and Black & Decker sees its profit margin jump a percentage point or two. When Applebee's fills a few more tables, Batman sells a few more tickets and CBS golf ratings get a mild boost. It is also a day when I can think back and appreciate the meaningful things you did for me along the way and the interesting times we shared. Thanks for taking me to see Deep Purple, Iggy Pop, The Tubes, Bruce Springsteen, David Bowie and Tower of Power. Thanks for introducing me to Ernest Hemingway, Woody Allen and Jim Dine, and for teaching me that the arts were the way to go. Through hell and high water we have trekked and tread. I am grateful for all of it. Enjoy your day, Pa....love, AK."

Anthony and Heather arrived for our annual cottage on the big Lake. We did the usual explorations, including a five-mile hike through giant pines and rugged landscapes of circuitous paths to the beach where a mountain of a dune challenged us. Neither Heather, Alicia or Sue could climb it, but Anthony did and I got to within twenty feet of the summit. It was so steep at the peak a step forward slid you back five. Retracing our five-mile route to the car park, I was so dehydrated that Anthony ran ahead to get me water. I was feeling my age. The highlight of the week was listening to the new-but-still-rough songs the band was working on. We took turns on the headphones and smiles erupted.

Sir Bob Geldof sent me a letter in the mail that incited a healthy double take. He wanted my help getting Anthony involved in a Mama's and Papa's project with the BBC. Yes, Siree Bob. And Anthony Sir-tainly did. In August, Las Vegas celebrated its centennial with a party 100 years in the making. The city gave a free Red Hot Chili Peppers concert, and the 50,000 tickets were scooped up in minutes. The *Las Vegas Sun* wailed "Electrifying Show!" The band teased the audience with some of the new music. Happy birthday, Las Vegas.

Scott Miller's wife had an affair and was divorcing him. I felt vicariously guilty; how many hundreds of marriages had I seduced? Another reason I had cooled my jets. Scott and I did infidelity surveillance. One night we went to a Rockford bar to catch the bitch in heat, but instead I ran into a long-lost friend of sorts. Badass Creston golf-team partner Denny Simmons' daughter Laurie had grown up and was married to a warbler who took his turn when the karaoke girl hollered, Todd! He restored Mopar Chargers, Barracudas and order. The bar was the Rouge River Tavern, and it became my swan-song hangout. The place filled up with guys and dolls and I had a few affairs, but no sex. I was refreshingly sainted. Retired, I traveled a lot; Todd and Laurie were dependable and loving stewards of my animals when I was gone. Denny Simmons, once a stalwart on my list of toughest dudes in town, now showed up in the Secluded Lake woods with a Little Red Riding Hood basket to pick mushrooms. We were ravaged of our ferocity and one step from the assisted-living facility.

By now I had a new boss in the dog house. Howlin' Wolf had passed on after a good long run and was buried in the raspberry bushes on a hill overlooking my front yard. Dirt, the wily Chihuahua, had been roughed up one too many times by the Boston Terriers and had succumbed, sadly. He was buried next to Wolf for protection. The Border Collies, Dixie, Badge, Buddy and Clowy ran off with impunity, a breed of vagabonds on a quest for sheep. Surrounded in this unholy canine conundrum, Alicia, James and his cockeyed white-supremacist pal Cody and I were visiting the wolves in Muskegon. Brenda talked us into a rescue Pit bull puppy recently cast out of a gangster ride in crack-happy Muskegon Heights, where Candy resided. Blackjack became my right paw and my right to party. Blackjack was a female with more gumption than a ring full of pay-for-view mixed-martial monkeys. She was a gleaming black panther and an old man's best friend.

I spent time with Sue too, a most unusual anti-relationship. The verboten divide between us created an interesting dynamic that was not unlike oxygen deprivation to increase sensuality. The sign said "Do not touch," and the anticipation or expectation never fatigued because it could not happen. It was the best of both worlds. All my life, I had relationships that reached a point of no return and imploded. With no conjunction, we stayed fresh, relaxed and secure. Sue was my perfect friend. She was a contagious inspiration. I started painting like a mad genius. It was cerebral excitement and more thrilling than drugs or sex. Within a year, I'd done fifty oversized paintings. Sue had several art shows during that time and like all her friends, I was there supporting her. Eventually, we did shows together, and I started selling my paintings. Sue and I did one at Studio 71 on dicey South Division, a block from the old Reptile. By then the neighborhood had become a mongrel mix of galleries, trendy shops and artists' lofts with a disingenuous mix of old bums and soup kitchens. When our month long show closed, Alicia and I packed my remaining paintings in a van we had parked across the side street. It took several trips to load, and I set some of the paintings against an iron railing while I tried to fit them all in. Eventually, we finished and went home. Once we unloaded the art, Alica noticed something was amiss and screamed.

"Where's *Scream?*!" *Scream* was a film noir murderous painting and one of my favorite works of art. I had put a $5,000 price tag on it to dissuade anybody from buying it. It was hung for show, but I wasn't ready to part with it. Now I remembered I had set it against that railing. It had already been an hour. With great trepidation, I called the curator, Jamison Dick, and asked if by any chance it might still be there across the street. It was. Even the bums hadn't taken it, much less the connoisseurs. At Christmas, Anthony and Heather gave me positive and thoughtful reviews of my art and an unlimited lifetime of free art supplies with the hope I'd live long enough to break their bank.

Anthony's generosity never flagged. On my 66th birthday he gave me three strapping peach trees, a crabapple tree, a cherry tree and a partridge to put in them. The accompanying fax: "Blacktacular Dammetticus! Like trees, heyday memories, leather jackets, attitudes, jeans, tax breaks, friendships and my father…. You only get better with age. Here's to good health, big love and many more years of sharing this earthly experience. Love, AK." It was December, so the 7-foot tall trees with roots incased in big burlap bags of dirt went into the furnace room until spring, which made it a bit difficult to navigate through that area. Soon I would need that space.

In January, Brenda sent me an email with a picture of the most beautiful black-and-white wolf pup you can imagine. She was a pure Northern Michigan wolf found wandering on an Upper Peninsula highway. She needed a home. Brenda had a connection that could get it to us. The wolf's name was Sheba. Would I be interested? Yes! I had a new plan for this one: I'd shelter her and keep it a secret. No more showing off. I'd hide her like Anne Frank. I brought her home and built a wolf retreat *in* my house. It was winter and the thick snow storms made it easy to conceal her when she was in the big outdoor enclosure. I stopped plowing the road to the enclosure so cars couldn't stumble onto her lair. She started out relatively small, like a midsize dog, but before I knew it she'd sprouted up to be a thundering, beautiful wolf with spirit and a friendly disposition. Tidy she wasn't. Sheba romped around in my art studio while I painted, and twice she knocked over gallon paint cans—one pink and another yellow. Not only all over the carpet but all over herself. She ate a big push broom when Brett was babysitting. Alicia and I went to the movies and came home to find she'd unlocked her indoor pen and ripped up 14-years worth of accumulated good stuff in the basement, turning my history into a six-foot-tall pile of junk. Had it been a double feature, our house would have been blown away by her chiny chin chin. Sheba was a wild tempest. She shredded a cyclone fence like it was pasta. She picked the lock on the main gate of the enclosure and was gone for several days. We scoured the county and finally found her miles away at a suburban Humane Society. The volunteers said she looked like a wolf, but I insisted she was a Shepherd Akita mix. They were more merciful than the Kent County dog pound that banished my other wolves.

I had another runaway, one who ran on Mountain Dew and two legs. The Sheriff's found James and another knucklehead sleeping on the shoulder of a busy country road on the way to *their* Jack Kerouac adventures. Three generations. James was on a first name basis with the Rockford police and was a homicide suspect when a local girl disappeared from the annual Summer Days Carnival. She turned out to be a runaway herself. After barely graduating middle school, he started Rockford High School with some optimism, but a week into classes he just plain refused to attend school. He kept stealing. He was so anti-social I finally sent him to his Great Grandma Maxine in Oklahoma. He came back for another go but was just as belligerent; his venomous friend Cody was cruel and criminal. He ended up in prison, and James seemed destined to follow. John Forsythe wanted nothing to do with him. Like his mom, James never went further than the eighth grade. I finally went to probate court and Maxine took official custody of James. She was one of those no-nonsense tough-love grandmas. Apart we got along better, and he often came to visit. He had the Greyhound schedule down pat. He also stayed with Chanda's parents for a while but defiled their trust too. Eventually James, Candy, Grandma and Great Granny congealed in South Florida. Candy kicked her drug habits and got married. She even went back to school. James worked as a stable groom at a horseracing track and flirted with joining the Marines. A current update is less affirming, but we can be hopeful. Candy has a good heart. Her unlucky black-cat son has been in and out of rehab, after a stab at the streets of Portland. Chanda and I are still optimistic as always.

Well, we finally had a sound track to all this madness. The double album *Stadium Arcadium* was released to rousing reviews and worldwide smiles. FedEx dropped off a couple early release CDs while Alicia was visiting, and we exchanged our garden tools for headphones. Don't step on that rake. Hallelujah, it was like the first time I listened to *Sgt. Pepper* or the *White Album*. It was an LSD trip in my ear. I played it for everybody the way I did when *Born to Run* came out in the 70s.

"The *Q Magazine* 2006 Essentials: The must have albums. The must see bands. All you need to know for the New Year. #1 Red Hot Chili Peppers. The biggest album of 2006 and the most ambitious. Eighteen months after the Chili Peppers' three shows at London's Hyde Park confirmed their position in rock's big league, they're returning with a double album, *Stadium Arcadium*. #2 Radiohead. #3 the Killers." *The Sun* newspaper: "*Dani California* was single of the week: Hazy, hypnotic funk from one of the biggest bands on the planet." *Mirror Ticket*: "*Stadium Arcadium* 4 stars. The Chili Peppers' front man Anthony Kiedis recently unburdened his gory wild-child upbringing, along with the drug and sex overload of adulthood, in his bio *Scar Tissue*. On this sprawling double album those experiences provide fuel for several of the 28 songs. Four years since the monster-selling *By the Way*, the Chilis risked accusations of self-indulgence by putting out a 28 track CD.

Remarkably they've produced an album that consigns such criticism to the dumper!" Even the mainstream Dick Clark *American Music Awards* handed out the hardware, Favorite Pop/Rock Band and Favorite Alternate Artist. Q-Prime on radio ratings: "We remain at #1 at Rock, #1 at Adult Alternative, #1 at Active Rock and #1 at Modern Rock. We have achieved the Grand Slam of radio formats."

We passed U2 for the most #1 Modern Rock songs in history as we had previously knocked off R.E.M. When the Grammys rolled around the following February, *Stadium Arcadium* would win six Grammys, including Best Rock Album, Best Rock Song and Best Rock Performance. The single "Dani California" won four. In a dead heat, we barely lost Album of the Year to the Dixie Chicks' *Taking the Long Way*, which featured the anti-Bush single "Not Ready to Make Nice." Rick Rubin produced both of the albums, and Chad played drums on both albums. The Red Hot Chili Peppers provided the Grammys' grand finale with a spectacular rendition of "Snow." I co-promoted the West Michigan concert for the fourth time. I helped the new fan club, UltraStar, and kept a presence on their website. Maria Costa was my liaison at the Brooklyn-based corporation and UltraStar wasn't short on clients; aside from RHCP, they represented Madonna, The Police, Usher, Kenny Chesney, Rolling Stones, Mariah Carey, Slayer, AC/DC, Garbage, Bowie, John Mayer, Blue Man, Barbra Streisand and Elvis Presley.

Wanderlust had struck again. I pulled out the stops and invited the intimate cast of my life to the concert. Among the guests on the best seats in the house were Sue and Eric, my doctors and dentist, Alicia and her father Vernon, Todd and Laurie and Denny Simmons, Brett, Jandt, Alan Bashara, James up from Tulsa and with Cassie Fenkle and her dad from NJ, my next door neighbors the Richardsons and even the Joker of Clubs, John Pochna from the Zero in LA. A row of my allotted seats went to chasteful one-last-fling females: Jenny, a waitress from Mill Creek; Heather, a statuesque beauty from the Rogue River restaurant Reds; Laetitia from Paris, who in the end couldn't find passage; a trio of cuties from Connecticut; Stephanie from Florida; and Desiree from Georgia, who once again stayed the longest. I serenaded her with Lucinda Williams, and she still to this day embraces a decided distinction. Although I respectfully gave her the best seat, Alicia was there as my best friend, not my lover. I'd been telling her that for ages, but she was always in denial. It broke my heart to break her heart. There was no after-party that night, but I brought a hundred friends backstage after the show. What all of these close friends weren't aware of is that this night was my going away gift. After almost twenty years in Grand Rapids, the Black cavalcade was about to hit the road again.

Chapter 66: Throw the Lions to the Christians

My conflicted city embodied everything I despised about religion. The sanctimonious big three were equally intolerant of the other, and that dogma won't hunt. It's ancient witchery. Beheading or believing, they're both incomprehensible. I was already an outcast in most of the precincts, adored by some for my integrity and despised by others who saw a disruptive force in the community. It came to a head when a citizen used the f-word in public, and a respected news columnist implied the nasty reaction was more egregious than the word itself. Somebody swore; it wasn't a calamity. Local vigilantes attacked. *The Press*'s editorial letters were always filled with missionary vitriol which I in turn felt compelled to expose. I defended the piquant word from defamation.

In a letter to the <u>Public</u> <u>Pulse</u> I wrote: "How utterly nonsensical is this f-word phobia championed by Jeff Carter in his Feb. 21 letter to the Press. The f-word, innocently, succinctly and without pretense, indicates the single most basic, honest and necessary act in life—procreation. Sexual intercourse (the f-word) is programmed into every living creature. It is more important than science, literature, art, sports, and most certainly, religion. Without the f-word, life on this planet would cease. Bird calls, wolf howls, the roar of insects in the night—they're all using the f-word. Jeff Carter wouldn't be here without the f-word. There is a more repugnant word than the f-word, and it is intolerance. Ironically they are both basic human instincts. In society there is no final arbitrator of philosophical differences—just perpetual social and sexual intercourse."

The chess match public debate continued. They tried to run me out of town with pitchforks. Personally, I enjoyed getting the controversial *word* out; it was good to see it bantered around on the <u>Public</u> <u>Pulse</u> like some miscreant badminton shuttlecock.

Crazy MySpace Joe was a wise guy after all. I continued to meet interesting people on the Internet. Sly revelations emerged; we were suddenly all in the same small world with no borders or nationalities. We *were* the world. Age was irrelevant regardless of the old guard. Affection wasn't wrong. Toronto came knocking in the form of a slender business woman with refined tastes, beauty and intellect. And she was married. Caution to the wind, global warming taboos were melting on the Internet. Playing in her pile of musical maple leaves, I discovered Feist and Chantal Kreviazuk. That alone made the Canadian propinquity invaluable, but Miranda Smith had so much more to give and take. I was a certified virgin now; I had no problem with a rational affirmative action affair, even with a married woman. We wanted to meet and looked for an excusable opportunity.

The *Stadium Arcadium* tour headed to Chicago, and I teamed up with three of my favorite women for a weekend not out of the Loop. Ashley flew in from Denver. She hid from me when we first met, but wanted to rewrite history. It couldn't be undone, but I liked her dearly. A Colorado State co-ed, she was one of my first online girlfriends. Patty Kersjes came up to Grand Rapids for a quick visit with her mom, our cats and to drive us both back down. She offered me her Chicago home, but I stayed with the band at the

Park Hyatt. Miranda Smith flew in from Toronto and stayed at the same hotel. Scandalous! Scott Miller came for the concert too and would drive me back to Grand Rapids. Miranda loved John Frusciante almost as much as she did Vincent Gallo, but got uncharacteristically bashful when I introduced her to our guitar hero. We ate a post-show dinner with the band, and she failed another opportunity to speak with him. Miranda and I rode back to the hotel in Anthony's tour bus. On the elevator, we ducked out on her floor, which raised my son's eyebrows. I only wanted to tuck her in. She flew out the next morning, but it wasn't long before she was flying into GR. We had a weekend on Secluded Lake, but in the end I fought off both Miranda and temptation. I painted her a work of art and named it *Miranda*. She also has my *English Garden Path*. A while later she and Conor divorced; he moved to Hong Kong. She's a ballerina financial investor with a terrific doggie named Mr. Scamper. Her own words, "Surely I didn't make it into your memoirs! I was but a blip and a temporary muse in your revolving door of lovelies." Au contraire, she was a quite a blip. More like an 8.8 blipquake.

In July, I was back in Chicago. We were headlining Lollapalooza again, 15 of my years later. Donnie Dorshimer gave me a lift on his way to the Sturgis Bike Week festival in South Dakota and dropped me off at the Peninsula Hotel on Michigan Avenue next to Saks. I fell under the spell of a torch singer in the cabaret lounge and helped her out of her costume. At the venue, I caught up with the incredibly busy impresario, my old friend Perry Farrell, the Lolla-extravaganza lion tamer. I met the incomparable Patti Smith, and Perry introduced the Red Hot Chili Peppers as the biggest band in the world. Our old Jane's Addiction rival for supremacy had acknowledged the inevitable. We all had a great time, but my time was fading like the purple sunset over Grant Park. The show was over. I drove Peggy home in her Lexus. We passed through familiar well-traveled territory along the Lake Michigan coast, not to mention South Haven where we spent our ill-fated honeymoon, forty-seven of my years later. How much later can I get? I skipped my 50th class reunion, had to skedaddle. By then I was already packed and ready to flee in the cover of darkness. The United Moving Van was idling and the GPS was raring to go.

Anthony and I had conspired to find a new location for my final years, a place with liberal sensibilities with freedom and justice for all. We sought a sanctuary friendly to wolves where civilization hadn't encroached. Brett and Alicia helped me pack a pickled pack of my life, but I gave them much of it to keep sake. Jim and Brenda took several wagonloads of my George Carlin *Stuff*. They were starting a secondhand store to help finance their animal kingdom. The moving van and my goods and my bads and my Caddy and Blackjack and I were about to set out for an outpost on the West Coast.

The final indignity and my parting shots were predictably over nudity, free and unencumbered as their god had made them. Mark London had been a long-time friend, who at one point took me in as a partner in his industrial nightclub The Works in Eastown. But he was best known as the guy who took on Tammany Hall and started up the first legitimate strip club, Sensations, way back when I first hit town. It was located on the edge of suburbia and paid its taxes like the Joneses. It had always behaved itself. By other city standards, it was practically puritanical. Now he had spent a small fortune building a palatial undressed club called Lady Godiva in an industrial area south of downtown, within the current laws and specifically to satisfy the out-of-town convention trade which GR had fought so hard to attract. The city had spent 220 million dollars to erect a massive convention center and built another skyscraper hotel. With much fanfare, the pricey publicists had created the town's new slogan "Cool City." But along came the religious right, which already had over 300 churches but couldn't accommodate a single strip club downtown, its rightful and logical place to be. Mark London took it to court. Guess who prevailed. Guess who had something to say about it. I got back up on my soapbox and emailed *The Grand Rapids Press* editorial page's <u>Public</u> <u>Pulse</u> (if it hadn't been banned also):

"Welcome to Taliban City the Oligarchy of Grand Rapids (re: Judge Robert Bell rules against the human body) where the mayor is a minister and religious zealots make policy and adjudicate it; where a four thousand year old book of Jewish folklore dictates our behavior. Where there's advocacy for extremists but none for those who find the human body beautiful, and that religious wars raging around the world are ugly, shameful and senseless. Goodbye lucrative conventions, goodbye hip natives, goodbye 'cool city', hello women wearing burkas, hello Jay Leno jokes, hello the inquisition, hello the dark ages. At this rate the real axis of evil will end up being Grand Rapids, Cincinnati, Salt Lake City and the state of Confusion."

Grand Rapids gave me melancholia, but I took two aspirins and marveled in something miraculous, something that eclipsed the open road and new real estate and religious outrage and painting and packing and Lollapalooza. That something was an anonymous incognito mosquito we'll call Revia, and she knocked me off my ergonomic computer chair. A friend of hers was infatuated with Anthony and had shared photos in which I also appeared. Twenty-one-year-old Revia wasn't the least bit interested in my son but fell in love with me. Timorous as a blush, she joined MySpace and then Facebook just to meet me. How fortunate I was. She was six-foot-one or even two. Her legs prolongated from heaven to hell. She was beyond slender, a green-eyed cat and flawlessly white; her ancestors were Laz, a Black Sea mix of Turkish, Georgian and Ukrainian. She exhilarated me like I'd never been, and yet she calmed me with her Eastern philosophy. The anonymous Revia was a legitimate super-model, Islamic, virgin and deadly determined to remain so. She was not fond of the West but tolerated it. She had modeled in just about every country on earth. She was cultured, wealthy, intelligent and adorably shy. She spoke perfect English. She lived on the other side of the world but uprooted herself and came to America to find me. Most of the rest I shall leave private for her sake.

What's so remarkable is that I was ancient by comparison, and here I was with one of the most perfectly beautiful women in the world. The ultimate countdown was subject to her propensity for self-destruction. Skittish as a fawn, she found hostility behind every shadow. The East West conflict was tainted with Byzantine acrimony and that old bugaboo, religion. She even faked her own funeral. I slipped away. After a tempestuous four-year whirl, we finally broke up. The crafty fox returned to her country and eye to mine. From her basket to the casket – cradle to the hospital table – broken appendages and bloody bandages – true to the color of her crescent flag – true to the blue of her mountain hue – pure as the cure of a smitten kitten – a phoenix who out slicks - the pundits – and always comes back to black…or maybe not.

WANTED
ANTHONY KIEDIS
For Advocating FREAKY STYLEY

ALIASES: Swan, Swa, Mymain, Swana-licious, Lowdown Dirty Dawg, The De- Man.

DATES OF BIRTH: After your mother and before your little sister.

HEIGHT: Shorter than Cliff and taller tha his manager.

WEIGHT: Fluctuating.

HAIR: Brown into blond.

EYES: Closed

COMPLEXION: Reptilian

BUILD: Sex-God

NATIONALITY: Lithuanian Hairless

RACE: In the mix.

SCARS OR MARKS: Circumcision scar that spirals up to his neck, a scar on his elbow from a sali infection, a bulbous wart on a confidential part of his body next to his Willie Nelson tattoo.

CAN USUALLY BE SEEN WEARING: Nothing or a sock on his cock.

CAN USUALLY BE FOUND: In Church or wallowing in his own juices, or in warm, wet environment

OCCUPATION: Spazzrapper, part-time philanthropist, part-time dirty dawg, part-time rapscallior Rock Star.

CRIMINAL RECORD: Has committed many U-turns and other traffic related offenses. Sodomy in public places with a pre-school watermelon.

M.O.: Putting the excellerator to the floor and singing Mongo Santa Maria songs in watermelor patches.

CURRENT VIOLATION: Cutting up and devouring a five year old melon, recording FREAKY STYLEY and covering his tracks.

IF DANGEROUS: He should be approached from the rear . . . with caution.

IF SIGHTED, CONTACT: EMI, a Rabbi, a lawyer.

Suspect's Signature

OFFICIAL USE ONLY

Chapter 67: Obituary

Was I raconteur or racketeer, icon'd or just conned, on the loose or on a noose, appropriated or fabricated, bona fide or cockeyed, Pooh-Bah or bourgeois? I knew this: I was a wiseguy mentor to an impressionable kid who grew to be Olympian. My blood nourished, skilled and sharpened him. I showed him the ropes and the dopes. I brandished a warrior and banished doubt. The more formidable he became, the more fallible I was allowed to fall. He was my greatest strength and my weakest excuse. Over the years, he affirmed his influences and heroes, and I was always prominent, good and bad.

AK's confessionals: "My dad was my hero and idol when I was a teenager; I wanted to be just like him." Asked who influenced him other than musicians he responded, "My father, and standing in front of thirteen-foot-tall Salvador Dali paintings." In a magazine, he wrote an article called *My Heroes*. "My first hero was my father. He was very significant in my mind. I looked at him as a superhuman person because the love was so concentrated. He was incredibly enthusiastic about fatherhood and teaching me a condensed, boiled down super-intense version of everything that he had learned in his life. So I would get these high-concentration lessons of culture and love and would walk away just reeling and rocking. I remember saying to myself, *that guy is deep*. Even as a toddler I had that sensation that he was different. He was my dad, my hero. That lasted for a very long time. Different events stick out in my mind. I'd get these packages in the mail from my dad, love beads, posters of Bob Dylan, psychedelic memorabilia, shirts from London—and I thought wow, this guy is tapped into another planet. I felt like I was opening a world of magic. He was so cavalier toward convention that it blew me away. I was surrounded by all these regular people who were so concerned with fitting within the borders of what was perceived as acceptable, and he walked in with a handlebar moustache and hair down to his ass, eight-inch platform snakeskin shoes and rainbow-colored suits, never feeling out of place. That kept elevating him as a hero to me. That he was so bold. The dictionary refers to a hero as bold as well. There was just the sheer size of your father when you're a kid—he's the fastest man on the planet, the strongest, no one will ever beat him in a fight, he's obviously the smartest man—it gave me a trust and a bond with him that opened up my senses. He was the one who planted the seed of creativity that has lasted throughout my life. He taught me that it was OK to think and be and act and invent differently. In high school, I started to challenge my hero on a daily basis—just who was the boss, that whole power struggle. It wasn't a bursting of my illusion bubble; I became more information-bound. I started to realize that other people had great concepts as well. And there was just a need to say "fuck you" as well. I was going to do to him what he had done to his dad. It was time to rebel and find new heroes."

Well, at least I was able to provide him with my male XY chromosomes, and he certainly took advantage. Our family has a masterpiece; we have Everly. The irrepressible young man they call Bear will one day carry the Kiedis banner into his own battles and hopefully a healthy dash of peace. I expect he will find appropriate heroes too, and his dad will certainly be at the top. Anthony has already proven himself a stellar father, and it is reflected in the magical child himself. Deep in constant scrutiny, Everly's smiling eyes reflect my Mother's ocean-blue eyewitness. Your Grand Daddy-O loves you.

My leading role was father, but the resume is convoluted—actor, writer, artist, desperado, good scout, bad dancer, party crasher, hippie, hot shot, half-wit, advocate for social justice and Lord of the Sunset Strip. I tasted the sweet love of a thousand paramours and the poison flavor of as many broken hearts. I saw the world and the movie version. I worked often in that blue moon when there were only three channels before the hyper-electronic age. I juggled a cumbersome handful of credible kudos in the spectrum of arts. I challenged the puritanical phobia of sexagenarians in harmony with youth. A palaver problem the Jesus Crisis couldn't solve. I never forced myself on anyone, never had to. Never broke the rules, only hearts. If there's been a richness of raping, it's on the street of greed in lower Manhattan. Mr. Gorbachov, tear down this Wall Street. Perversion is imbedded in the mental institutions of fat cat partisan politics, bloated business, lobotomy lobbyists, war mongering militaries, merchants of death and the biggest sinner of all—salvation. In god we lust. Someday, hopefully, eventually, logic will prevail. Blackie's beauties will not dance atop any testaments of granite. It will be the specter of Anthony Kiedis that will forever define me.

The BBC came halfway around the world to interview me for a television special that delved into the deep dark secrets of the most notorious rock stars, as revealed from their parent's perspective. I was in pretty good bad company, Amy Winehouse, Courtney Love, infamous lead singer Suggs of the British band Madness and nasty UK rapper Asher D. A female reporter and a video crew spent an entire day poking me with tongs and terror. I'm a Sagittarian remember and am honest as Abe. They set me up and shot me down. West Hollywood sheriffs were more cordial. The interviewer tore emotions out of my heart with a rusty scalpel and swept the bloody entrails into my garbage pail. They got what they wanted—my confessions and my tears and good ratings. My friends and fans found it heartfelt, candid and compelling. The sheltered and the squeamish did not. For some, the program shocked England with all the sensational dirty laundry of the Profumo scandal with Christine Keeler and Mandy Rice-Davies. *The Guardian's* exposé reporter Sam Wollaston kept his cheeky humor appropriately depraved:

"Forget Doctor Spock and all that lot. I give you a brand new parenting guru: Blackie Dammett, father of Red Hot Chili Peppers frontman Anthony Kiedis and star of **ONE life: Help! My Kid's a Rock Star** (BBC1). Frankly, after all that go-and-stand-on-the-naughty-step nonsense, Blackie's approach is a breath of fresh air. Touching, too. 'We were best friends,' he says about his son. 'We were the perfect couple, and very much in love with each other.' See? Blackie led by example, exposing his young son to all the things he valued highly himself. There was always a party round at Blackie's house, with movie stars, rock stars, sports stars, and they'd all be taking drugs, because in those days people weren't embarrassed to be doing so. Young Anthony was naturally curious; he wanted to play, too. 'It wasn't so unusual that I let him take a little bit of acid, or a little bit of marijuana,' remembers Blackie. Then there were girls. Blackie himself had grown up in the 1950s, dark days when girls wouldn't have sex with you. He obviously didn't want Anthony to have to go through that same nightmare. So he helped out a bit."

"And it was easy, because Blackie had loads of lovely girlfriends, some of whom weren't that much older than Anthony. So this Kimberly from the Rainbow Bar and Grill, certainly the type of girl it would be nice to have sex with for the first time, agreed; and she and Anthony had sex. 'I knew I wanted him to be the first guy in his class, instead of the last, like I was,' says Blackie. 'And that did make him a big hit at school - it was like, Whoa, you had sex! I'm not going to have sex for like' - Blackie looks at his watch - 'six more years, you lucky guy!' It's hard not to think of your own upbringing when watching a programme like this. It was pretty much the same in my family. My own father was hanging around with some hot chicks from the bars and grills of the Colchester area, and on my 12th or 13th birthday, I forget which, he arranged for this one girl to have sex with me. Oh, actually, no he didn't. Sorry, my mistake - he got me a fishing rod. Damn him. I actually thought I had a reasonably liberal upbringing. Now I'm beginning to realize how Victorian it was."

"And look, the Blackie Dammett approach works. A fishing rod gets you a poxy TV critic for a son; drugs and sex gets you the frontman of one of the biggest rock 'n' roll bands in the world! OK, so there have been a few problems: Anthony's former drug addictions, the massive binges, the times he's come as close to death. But at least he's not an insurance salesman, living in the Midwest, says Blackie. That would have been truly tragic. Or a TV critic. And look at the positives. 'He's bought me two houses now,' says Blackie. 'Big, beautiful houses, not little ol' houses. And cars for Christmas, Andy Warhol paintings - he's been very generous to all of us.' If I were a publisher, I'd be on the phone to his people right now, signing him up to do Hell Raising: Bringing Up Kids the Blackie Dammett Way. There were other parents on this amusing show. Suggs's mum is strangely obsessed by the inaccuracies in the lyrics to Madness's *Our House* that wasn't in the middle of the street apparently, more towards one end. Amy Winehouse's dad, who's just like Terry Venables, is worried, as you would be if you were Amy Winehouse's dad. Proud, too, though. English rap artist Asher D's mum is the same: dead proud the first time she saw her boy on Top of the Pops, a bit concerned when he got locked up for having a loaded firearm. And Courtney Love's dad says his daughter hates him. Why? 'I'm fat, I've got a barn, a bunch of horses; they go poo poo.' All good reasons. They're all good value, mad, amusing - but totally overshadowed by Blackie Dammett, I'm afraid. Only Blackie gets the book deal."

Sailing into an uneasy future, I look back on a sweet stormy journey down the river of life, bountiful with aesthetic sojourns along the way. I was born on the Grand, baptized on Huck Finn's big muddy, educated along the Red Cedar and trained on the hobo tracks of the Rio Grande. I washed up on the LA River and traveled the River Thames and Seine. I splash in the Willamette and Malibu now, an Ol' Man River myself. Around the bend beguiles a River Styx and a crack at damnation. Dementia is nipping at the big silence, and a long-lost Faye Hart love letter written in blood stands by for a kinky eulogy:

Johnny, charge you, attempted neglect, we wrecked, you saved the scar, put it on my heart, banged me in my coffin, banged me on the stairs, banged me, who cares.

Torn from a wanted poster someone did care. Out of the dark a golden phoenix breathed new life into this abstract painter and alpha to a pack of wolves. A precious gem, her sleek and sexable name was Stevie, and she *was* an All American. Born blue and blonde in Sweden, Connecticut-bred, California surfer, Berkeley grad, daredevil, delicate, and sublime. She was 27 years old and inexplicably ready to take me on. Stevie was peerless and fearless. She gave up her inheritance to be with me, shades of The Duke of Windsor and Wallis Simpson. In the end, the family embraced me as I wrapped my love around the slender sliver of Stevie. The ocean of devotion tacked comfortably close to her beloved Pacific and our pack of navy canines and felines. Nine lives were not enough for our crazy love adventure. Twin peaks, a distaff Dawkins, entrepreneur, peaceful at last; she inspired me to live forever.

And there was even more to be thankful for. The band blasted to the top of the charts once again with their new album *I'm With You* and new guitarist Josh Klinghoffer. And the long-awaited news finally kicked the door off the hinges of the Rock & Roll Hall of Fame with the announcement of the 2012 performer inductees: Guns N' Roses, Red Hot Chili Peppers, Beastie Boys, Donovan, Laura Nyro, The Small Faces with Rod Stewart. The explosive ceremony went far into the night, and there I was with my son and his mother, surrounded by the ghosts and legends of rock n' roll warriors Alan Freed, Elvis, Beatles and Stones, Zeppelin, U2, Dylan, Jimi, Bowie, Springsteen, Chuck Berry and Little Richard, Aretha, James Brown, Beach Boys, Doors, Stevie Wonder, Michael Jackson, Johnny Cash and Hank Williams, Billie Holliday, Jeff Beck and Eric Clapton, The Ramones and The Clash, and now Red Hot Chili Peppers. Cris Rock introduced us; the other inductees got the business from Chuck D, Smokey Robinson, Green Day, Bette Midler, Carol King, John Mellencamp, Robbie Robertson, Stevie Van Zandt, Kid Rock and the ZZ Top guys. My old friend Alice Cooper was there too, an inductee the year before. The obligatory rip-roaring finale with Ronnie Wood, Slash, Billie Joe Armstrong, Tre Cool, George Clinton, Chad, Josh and Flea rocked the Hall as unrelenting maestro Anthony Kiedis enflamed the beasts and belted out his inimitable rendition of "Higher Ground" to close the night.

13112434R00222

Made in the USA
San Bernardino, CA
12 December 2018